OUR GRIEF IS NOT A CRY FOR WAR

OUR GRIEF IS NOT A CRY FOR WAR

The Movement to Stop the War on Terror

JEREMY VARON

THE UNIVERSITY OF CHICAGO PRESS
Chicago and London

The University of Chicago Press, Chicago 60637
The University of Chicago Press, Ltd., London
© 2025 by Jeremy Varon
All rights reserved. No part of this book may be used or reproduced in any manner whatsoever without written permission, except in the case of brief quotations in critical articles and reviews. For more information, contact the University of Chicago Press, 1427 E. 60th St., Chicago, IL 60637.
Published 2025
Printed in the United States of America

34 33 32 31 30 29 28 27 26 25   1 2 3 4 5

ISBN-13: 978-0-226-82768-1 (cloth)
ISBN-13: 978-0-226-82769-8 (ebook)
DOI: https://doi.org/10.7208/chicago/9780226827698.001.0001

Library of Congress Cataloging-in-Publication Data

Names: Varon, Jeremy, 1969–, author
Title: Our grief is not a cry for war : the movement to stop the war on terror / Jeremy Varon.
Description: Chicago : The University of Chicago Press, 2025. | Includes bibliographical references and index.
Identifiers: LCCN 2025008179 | ISBN 9780226827681 cloth | ISBN 9780226827698 ebook
Subjects: LCSH: Iraq War, 2003-2011—Protest movements | Afghan War, 2001-2021—Protest movements | War on Terrorism, 2001-2009—Protest movements | Peace movements—United States—History—21st century | Anti-war demonstrations—United States—History—21st century | BISAC: HISTORY / United States / 21st Century | SOCIAL SCIENCE / Activism & Social Justice
Classification: LCC DS79.767.P76 V37 2025 | DDC 956.7044/31—dc23/eng/20250326
LC record available at https://lccn.loc.gov/2025008179

♾ This paper meets the requirements of ANSI/NISO Z39.48-1992 (Permanence of Paper).

Authorized Representative for EU General Product Safety Regulation (GPSR) queries: **Easy Access System Europe**—Mustamäe tee 50, 10621 Tallinn, Estonia, gpsr.requests@easproject.com
Any other queries: https://press.uchicago.edu/press/contact.html

CONTENTS

List of Abbreviations vii

Introduction 1

1. "Reconciliation, Not Revenge": The Antiwar Response to 9/11 7

2. "The Way to Prevent More Deaths Is Not to Kill More People": Arguing the War in Afghanistan 31

3. "The Dominant Frame Is War": The Birth of the Antiwar Movement 50

4. "Not in Our Name": From the War in Afghanistan to the War in Iraq 74

5. Uniting for Peace and Justice 108

6. "The World Says No to War": A Day of Global Protest 138

7. "To Bomb This Site Would Be a War Crime": From "Stop the War" to Shock and Awe 171

8. "Are We Protesting the War or the Occupation?": The US War in Iraq 203

9. From "Bring 'Em On" to "Bring Them Home":
The Unraveling of the Iraq War 227

10. "Sorry, Everybody, We Tried": The Antiwar Movement
and the Reelection of George W. Bush 254

11. "REAL Support for the Troops": The Antiwar Movement
and Military Dissent 280

12. "Fervent Calls for Peace": The Turning of the Iraq War 311

13. "The End of an Error" and Endless War 341

Conclusion 361

*Acknowledgments 369   Abbreviations Used in the Notes 375
Notes 377   Index 443*

ABBREVIATIONS

AFSC: American Friends Service Committee
ANSWER: Act Now to Stop War and End Racism
AUMF: Authorization for Use of Military Force
AWOL: absent without leave
BFP: Brooklyn for Peace
CAIR: Council on American-Islamic Relations
CARECEN: Central American Resource Center
CCR: Center for Constitutional Rights
CIVIC: Civilian Innocent Victims in Conflict
CPA: Coalition Provisional Authority
CPT: Christian Peacemaker Teams
DASW: Direct Action to Stop the War
DNC: Democratic National Convention
EITs: enhanced interrogation techniques
FTAA: Free Trades Agreement of the Americas
GSFP: Gold Star Families for Peace
IED: improvised explosive device
IGC: Iraqi Governing Council
IMF: International Monetary Fund
IPS: Institute for Policy Studies
IPT: Iraq Peace Team
ISG: Iraq Study Group
ISI: Inter-Services Intelligence
ISIL: Islamic State of Iraq and the Levant

ISIS: Islamic State in Iraq and Syria
IRA: Irish Republican Army
IVAW: Iraq Veterans Against the War
MAB: Muslim Association of Britain
MFSO: Military Families Speak Out
MGJ: Mobilization for Global Justice
MPM: military peace movement
NAACP: National Association for the Advancement of Colored People
NATO: North Atlantic Treaty Organization
NION: Not in Our Name
NGO: nongovernmental organization
NLG: National Lawyers Guild
NYCLAW: New York City Labor Against War
NYPD: New York Police Department
PTSD: post-traumatic stress disorder
RCP: Revolutionary Communist Party
RNC: Republican National Convention
SBVT: Swift Boat Veterans for Truth
STORM: Standing Together to Organize a Revolutionary Movement
StWC: Stop War Coalition
VFP: Veterans for Peace
VVAW: Vietnam Veterans Against the War
WCW: World Can't Wait
WMD: weapons of mass destruction
WTC: World Trade Center
WWP: Workers World Party

INTRODUCTION

On September 14, 2001, President George W. Bush mounted the rubble where the World Trade Center had stood. Flanked by firefighters, he spoke through a bullhorn. Three days earlier, nineteen members of al-Qaeda had seized control of four commercial aircraft. They flew one into the World Trade Center's North Tower shortly before 9 a.m. Another struck the South Tower minutes later. A third hit the Pentagon. Passengers subdued the hijackers of the final plane, likely headed for the US Capitol. It crashed in the Pennsylvania countryside. Nearly three thousand people from more than one hundred countries were killed in the attacks, though early estimates were much higher.

Surrounded by shouts of fury, Bush said, "America today is on bended knee, in prayer for the people whose lives were lost here, for the workers who work here, for the families who mourn." "I can hear you!" he told the seething crowd. "The rest of the world hears you! And the people—and the people who knocked these buildings down will hear all of us soon!"[1]

With these words, Bush called the War on Terror into being.[2] It claimed, at its heart, to avenge the 9/11 victims and their families. In other speeches, Bush vowed to defend "our way of life" against "evil" terrorists and their accomplices.[3] The War on Terror would also be a global battle, fought for civilization itself and the security of all decent nations. Within weeks, the United States began bombing

Afghanistan, whose Taliban government had harbored al-Qaeda and its leader, the Saudi national Osama bin Laden.

Proponents of the War on Terror cast it in intimate terms: *anyone, anywhere* could be a victim. This made Americans feel personally invested in its success. At the same time, Bush described the war as the high-minded defense of American values, like freedom and tolerance, that the 9/11 attackers were said to disdain. This gave the conflict a deeply moral purpose as well.

The same day as Bush's bullhorn speech, Phyllis and Orlando Rodriguez shared words of warning and protest. Their son Greg was in the World Trade Center on 9/11 and now presumed dead. "Our government is heading in the direction of violent revenge," they wrote, "with the prospect of sons, daughters, parents, friends in distant lands dying, suffering, and nursing further grievances against us." "It will not avenge our son's death. Not in our son's name. . . . Let us not as a nation add to the inhumanity of our times."[4]

Soon, other families of the 9/11 dead spoke out to reject war as an answer to their loss. They were joined, as the war in Afghanistan erupted, by small numbers of intellectuals, pundits, students, and peace groups pleading for a response to 9/11 rooted in international justice, not military action. As talk of war with Iraq ratcheted up, the antiwar ranks became a mass movement.

The opposition also saw the War on Terror in personal terms. Originating in New York City, the slogans "Not in Our Name" and "Our Grief Is Not a Cry for War" were claimed by countless Americans who doubted that the War on Terror served their safety, global security, or justice. Protesting the war, for many, meant rejecting an entire politics based in fear and aggression.

The War on Terror overwhelmed its times with an inhumanity few could at first imagine. It became a vast military-political project that defined the new century in the United States and large parts of the world. US forces committed atrocities, from prisoner abuse to civilian massacres, in Afghanistan and then Iraq. The hunt for terror suspects gave rise to a global torture program. The United States conducted drone strikes and special operations across the Middle East and in Africa. To defeat the Islamic State, forming in post-invasion Iraq, it pummeled Iraqi and Syrian cities with bombs. US forces left Afghanistan only in 2021, with the Taliban returning to power. In scattered countries, US military operations under the banner of the War on Terror continue to this day.

The human cost has been staggering. More than 7,000 US military personnel and 8,000 US contractors have died, with tens of thousands wounded.[5] More than 200,000 national military and police in Afghanistan, Iraq, and elsewhere were killed, along with 300,000 opposition fighters. Civilian casualties now exceed 430,000. All told, nearly one million people have died as a *direct* result of the War on Terror. Indirect deaths from hunger, disease, and ruined infrastructure approach four million. Thirty-eight million people have been displaced. The US price tag has also been enormous—$8 trillion and counting, as costs for the treatment of veterans and the service of war debt mount.

・・・

This book is about the people in the United States who protested the War on Terror in its first, most pivotal years. It is also about their collective efforts to try to prevent, and then end, Bush's wars. It is a history of the War on Terror through the lens of opposition to it, and a history of America's early twenty-first century through the domestic strife the war spawned. This "war at home" has left a largely unexamined legacy. Were the monumental costs of the War on Terror remotely worth it? Would the world have been better off had US leaders heeded the war's opponents?

The key policies of War on Terror were formed within weeks or even days of the 9/11 attacks. A brief window existed when other options were available. With great conviction—and often chilling foresight—antiwar voices warned that armed conflict would lead to "endless war," with America corrupted by the fight. The War on Terror was neither destiny, nor a case of blinding rage or fear driving rash action. It was an emphatic choice, steamrolling past thoughtful words of caution. With hindsight, these warnings take on a special power.

Far and away, the Iraq War was the most consequential aspect of War on Terror, defining the conflict as a whole. The greatest number of US military dead were in Iraq, as were most civilian casualties. Like nothing else, it damaged the United States' standing in the world and Americans' trust in their government.

The Iraq war also inspired the greatest protest, whose story makes up the bulk of this book. Throughout, I seek a fair-minded picture of the antiwar movement's strengths and weaknesses, what it could and could not achieve, within the circumstances it faced. The challenges were immense.

Many Americans were spooked by the Bush administration's talk of Iraq's destructive capabilities and intent. A credulous media rarely questioned its claims. Bush was popular, riding apparent success in Afghanistan. Iraq's Saddam Hussein was a brutal dictator, with no defenders in the United States.

The US peace movement, long focused on nuclear arms and US proxy wars, had been greatly diminished in the post–Cold War era. The left was riven by internal conflicts. Prior to 9/11, the most dynamic activism had been the youthful global justice movement. It fought economic inequality and environmental ruin, not US militarism. When that movement collapsed, it never fully shifted its energies into antiwar protest. Few Americans had personal connections to Iraq, limiting a politics of solidarity.

Pushing past these barriers, the antiwar movement quickly reached stunning heights. In February 2003, it organized the largest, coordinated protests in human history, *before* the threatened invasion had begun. Up to thirty million people demonstrated in hundreds of cities worldwide. A journalist declared the existence of "two superpowers on planet: the United States and world public opinion."[6] Eventually, millions of Americans participated in thousands of acts of protest, from mass demonstrations, to vigils, to peace encampments, to civil disobedience.

The movement's very success at mobilizing also signaled the limits to its power. The enormous public outcry in early 2003 did not prevent the US invasion. Thereafter, the movement worked to make opposition to the war fully a part of public debate, with the ability to shape policy.

The antiwar movement had only an episodic presence in the public consciousness. To many Americans, it was largely in the shadows. They may have been aware of major protests, or the statements of antiwar celebrities, or the 2005 stand of "peace mom" Cindy Sheehan at Bush's Texas ranch. But they likely had no idea that there were 9/11 families against the war, or American peace activists in Iraq, or Iraq War veterans fighting to end the conflict.

The antiwar movement's limited place in the political landscape at the time is reflected in its even smaller place in the national memory.[7] Popular histories of the Iraq War barely mention the antiwar movement. When they do, they mostly dismiss it as naive, gauzy-eyed, and ineffective.[8] A leading scholar of the anti-Vietnam War movement declared in 2010 that "there was no anti–Iraq War movement that periodically brought hundreds of thousands into the street."[9] Widely shared, this impression flies in the face of the facts.

I seek to bring the post-2001 movement into clearer light, capturing the intensity and persistence of antiwar dissent. Activists displayed enormous commitment, creativity, and even courage. The protest of 9/11 families and the military community stands out, as do the humanitarian efforts of Americans inside Iraq. Dissent came in great varieties, often born of personal tragedy. Protest was also profoundly global. Antiwar publics and many politicians condemned the War on Terror itself as a great threat to world peace

So much antiwar protest was driven by what I call a "politics of truth." Antiwar forces relentlessly worked to expose the war's deceitful origins and disastrous course. From the invasion on, they combated Bush's false claims about swift victory and then halting progress. They also fought a mainstream press that underreported the extent of US harm in Iraq.

Behind these efforts lay a basic civic faith: that as the gap between Bush's false image of the Iraq War and its grim reality was revealed, the country would turn decisively against the conflict. Popular opposition would then "trickle up" into the political establishment.

This was, in part, how things played out. But the Bush administration was expert at imagecraft, at times reveling in its ability to promote a warped vision of reality. A post-truth politics, beyond the distortions of conventional propaganda, had set in.

Still, the antiwar movement was vindicated in its core positions and finally embraced, in its wish to stop the war, by the mainstream. Ending the US occupation took Iraq becoming an unmanageable maelstrom of chaos and death. Even then, "endless war" persisted in other theaters, like Afghanistan. Much of the moral rot of the War on Terror, like the US prison at Guantánamo, survived as well.

All along, the movement's main strength was the power of its insights, predictions, and hard-won knowledge. Its greatest success was being proved right. Its story shows how a mobilized citizenry, speaking truth to power, can make a difference. In the process, it created powerful communities of resistance. Uniting people in their common humanity and wish for peace was its ultimate rebuke of the War on Terror.

And yet, the War on Terror also offers a lesson in the terrible price that may be paid when genuine, democratic deliberation is shut down and informed, conscientious voices are ignored. Mountains of the dead, wounded, and abused are the enduring monument of the War on Terror.

CHAPTER 1

"RECONCILIATION, NOT REVENGE"

The Antiwar Response to 9/11

Within minutes of the collapse of the second World Trade Center tower, journalist Laura Flanders posted to a blog surely the first public statement in the United States on the 9/11 attacks from the political left. Just blocks from the impact zone, she observed, "There's been a tragedy."[1] She pleaded, "May all of us in the media not add to it," noting that the 1995 bombing of the Federal Building in Oklahoma City had been at first widely attributed to Middle Eastern terrorists. Two hours later Flanders took stock of the ruin: "I think of Baghdad, Belgrade"—scenes of devastation from US bombs she had covered as a reporter.

In its offices blocks north, the War Resisters League, a decades-old peace organization, crafted its response. Posted by early evening, it expressed great sympathy for the victims. But it noted that American militarism had caused "millions of deaths," from Vietnam to Iraq.[2] US "support for armed resistance" to the Soviets in Afghanistan, it said, had "resulted in the victory of the Taliban and the creation of Osama bin Laden." The group urged that the United States seek "alternatives to violence" in a spirit of "reconciliation, not revenge."

By nightfall in Washington, DC, President George W. Bush addressed the wounded nation on television. He declared, "Our way of life, our very freedom came under attack" in "evil, despicable acts of terror."[3] "We will make no distinction between the terrorists who committed these acts and those who harbor them," Bush also warned. "None of us will ever forget this day, yet we go forward to defend freedom and all that is good and just in our world."

With these words Bush sketched the entire political, military, and moral template for the American response to 9/11: to wage a global war, in defense of absolute virtue, against evil enemies and their enablers. 9/11 was to forever remain the war's beating heart.

"In Manhattan we aren't in a state of war," Flanders continued the following day. "We're in a state of mourning."[4] To the idea of war, she countered: "Violence against an innocent civilian is a crime; against a group it's an act of terror. Nations governed by the rule of law investigate crimes, arrest criminals, hold trials. . . . They don't strike out at a nation or a people because they share the race, the region, the nationality, or the religion of a person or people who are alleged to have committed a crime."[5]

Others on the left quickly weighed in, publishing pieces on September 12. Rahul Mahajan wrote in *Common Dreams* that "the war that the United States has been waging against the nonwhite peoples of the world for over half a century came home yesterday."[6] In the same venue, University of Texas professor Robert Jensen declared the 9/11 attacks "no more despicable [than] the massive acts of terrorism" committed by the United States during his lifetime.[7] Middle East studies professor Stephen Zunes added in *The Baltimore Sun*, "It is no coincidence that terrorist groups have arisen in an area where the world's one remaining superpower puts far more emphasis on weapons shipments and air strikes than on international law or human rights."[8]

In the British daily *Guardian*, Saskia Sassen described the attacks as a "language of last resort" of "the oppressed and persecuted," shattering a deceptive "peace and prosperity."[9] The Canadian writer Naomi Klein wrote, "Did the United States deserve to be attacked? Of course not." But another question loomed for her: "Did U.S. foreign policy create the conditions in which such twisted logic could flourish, a war not so much on U.S. imperialism but on perceived U.S. imperviousness?"[10]

Then there was Noam Chomsky, the celebrated American intellectual. Overwhelmed with journalistic queries, he issued on September 12 "A Quick Reaction." It began, "The September 11 attacks were major atrocities. In terms of number of victims they do not reach the level of many others, for example, Clinton's bombing of the Sudan with no credible pretext, destroying half its pharmaceutical supplies and probably killing tens of thousands."[11] The United States now faced a stark choice: to lash out in "justified horror" or "to understand what may have led to the crimes."

Within days of 9/11, the main contours of an antiwar position also came into view: that the destruction Americans felt was commonly felt elsewhere in the world; that US policies fed the rage of the 9/11 perpetrators and must be reexamined; and that the attacks were criminal acts of terror demanding a rule-of-law response based in justice, not vengeance.

In the next weeks, progressive pundits, academics, activists, and authors elaborated these views. They commonly wrote in left-wing forums like *The Nation* magazine or online platforms like *Common Dreams*. Reposted on American websites, critical writings flourished in the foreign press. And sometimes, as if fulfilling a tiny quota, mainstream US media published critical perspectives. Such commentary ran against the tide of presidential pronouncements and public sentiment, attracting charges of disloyalty. In the pushback against this censure, the defense of dissent itself became a key part of antiwar opinion.

The War on Terror unfolded with such ferocious speed that it seemed inexorable. President Bush was intent on swift, decisive action, and Congress obliged. On September 14, it passed with just one "no" vote the Authorization for Use of Military Force. It gave the president sweeping power to direct operations against the alleged perpetrators of 9/11 and those aiding them. A week later in a speech to Congress, President Bush put Afghanistan's Taliban in America's gunsights.

On September 16 Vice President Dick Cheney said on national television that the United States might have to work "on the dark side," foreshadowing the CIA's torture program.[12] A day later Bush issued a secret memorandum authorizing the CIA to capture and interrogate alleged terrorists, setting that program into motion.[13] By

September 26 CIA officers were secretly on the ground in Afghanistan to support the Northern Alliance, the Taliban's main rival.[14] On October 7, the US bombing began.

Back at home, the FBI launched a massive investigation, PENTTBOMB, into the 9/11 attacks. Starting on September 11, the FBI and other law enforcement apprehended Arab, Muslim, and South Asian people, mostly in the New York metropolitan area. In the weeks following, more than twelve hundred were detained on the basis of alleged immigration violations and other infractions.[15] Some were subject to grave mistreatment while in custody. From the outset, the violation of civil liberties, as well as punitive profiling, was part of the War on Terror.

Despite this rapid chain of events, for a brief period following 9/11, the US response was unsettled. Other options were, in principle, available. The first war America fought after 9/11 was a war of ideas seeking to make sense of the destruction. Why was America attacked? Did fair-minded consideration of the perpetrators' motives justify abhorrent acts? Were the assaults acts of terror requiring police action or acts of war demanding a full-blown military response? How far did culpability extend? What were the roots of terrorism, and how could the United States best address them?

So much depended on the answers to these questions and whether they were even subject to genuine debate. The historian Gerda Lerner wrote on October 1: "The decisions made by politicians in the next few weeks and months may affect the lives and resources of the American people for years to come."[16] The consequences were greatest for the nations and peoples primed for a US attack.

The contest of ideas proved terribly one-sided. Prowar voices dominated public discussion. Historically weak, the American left now struggled against a surging patriotism. Dissidents were largely confined to media and communities already skeptical of war, where they made arguments against the path the Bush administration chose. However faint, the public expressions of their views were some of the first acts of a budding antiwar movement.

9/11 posed enormous challenges for traditional opponents of

US power. American civilians, as well as new immigrants and foreign visitors, suffered horrific violence. But critics did not judge the United States a guiltless victim. Did the country have the track record—or even the moral authority—to pursue genuine justice, in accord with global laws and norms? Skeptics invited the criticism of knee-jerk anti-Americanism. Those on the left open to war appeared to suspend critical insight into US militarism and place questionable trust in war-hungry leaders seemingly bent on vengeance or even conquest. All positions grappled with profound judgments on the nation's history, identity, and place in the world.

"HONEST TRUTHS FROM WRONGFUL DEATHS"

For a swath of dissenting opinion, the 9/11 attacks were a prompt to think also about American violence. Their relation was the key to understanding 9/11 and how the United States might best respond. The uneven effort spanned whole orders of analysis, from geopolitics to philosophy. It yielded penetrating insights but also tenuously severe judgments.

For some on the political left, 9/11 delivered a blow to an illusory American innocence, rooted in the county's myth of exceptionalism. That myth holds that America was established through its voluntary separation from a European world burdened by sectarian strife, persecution, and the dead weight of tradition. In that separation the country enjoyed the blessings of both safety and unequaled virtue, serving as a beacon to the world. (As the myth evolved, taints like slavery could be redeemed through episodes of moral regeneration within a steady arc of progress.) In more modern times, Pearl Harbor, participation in another world war, Cold War entanglements, and the schisms of the 1960s challenged American innocence. But it was substantially reborn in a post–Cold War world in which US security and supremacy, enhanced by a globally expanding capitalism, went largely unchallenged.

September 11 changed all that. *Harper's Magazine* publisher John MacArthur wrote that "'the City Upon The Hill'" imagined by the Puritans was "supposed to be an impregnable citadel of Christian morality, once protected by God and now by the atomic bomb. Thousands of innocent people died on Tuesday in part because of a naive belief in that moral impregnability." "Our Puritan citadel," he concluded, is "badly cracked. I hope our false belief in our own essential goodness has cracked as well."[17] The British novelist and essayist Martin Amis saw the message of September 11 as this: "America, it is time you learned how implacably you are hated. United Airlines Flight 175 was an Intercontinental Ballistic Missile aimed at her innocence."[18]

Both commentaries suggest that 9/11 should have led to a redemptive American reckoning. The country now knew something of the devastation felt in much of the world. Its conceit of virtue had suffered too in an act of payback for the military and economic domination underwriting its prestige. The evil that America must now fight was not only that of an alien enemy but also its own.

Others turned to contemporary metaphors. Naomi Klein felt that 9/11 should "mark the end of the shameful era of the video game war."[19] By that she meant the bloodless sport of watching footage of American bombs vaporizing hapless targets, as debuted in the 1991 Gulf War. The spectacle was lightened by the knowledge that few Americans would die in the conflict. The fiction of the "safe war" is, of course, believable only if the pain caused by one's violence is invisible. Largely ignored by the US media, that devastation is surely known to the victims. Klein therefore saw 9/11 as the eruption of a "blinding rage" at the "asymmetry of suffering." As "twisted revenge-seekers," its perpetrators, she said, "make no other demand than that US citizens share in their pain."

Such views these were hardly confined to non-Americans and the foreign press. Novelist Barbara Kingsolver wrote in the *Los Angeles Times*, "There are a hundred ways to be a good citizen, and one of them is to look finally at the things we don't want to see.... Some people believe our country needed to learn how to hurt in this new way. This is such a large lesson, so hatefully, wrongfully taught, but many people before us have learned honest truths from wrongful deaths."[20] Margaret Chrome urged in a Wisconsin newspaper that America move past the "denial" phase of grief and acknowledge that the country is "viewed as the enemy by millions around the globe."[21]

The most probing meditation on innocence came from the Slovenian intellectual Slavoj Žižek. Within a week of 9/11 he penned his reflections, which circulated widely on the web. His starting point is the common perception that the 9/11 attacks were a bolt from the blue, unimaginable and somehow unreal. Distant and near witnesses felt like they were watching—or were themselves inside—a movie. But America, Žižek points out, was familiar with the image of apocalyptic destruction. "The shots we saw of the collapsing towers could not but remind us of the most breathtaking scenes" in disaster films.[22] Like a movie indeed.

For Žižek, another genre of American film provides the deepest clues about 9/11. Typified by *The Truman Show* (1998) and *The Matrix* (1999), it stages the anxiety that life in "late capitalist consumerist society" has the quality of a "staged fake," or even a dematerialized, virtual reality. Behind this worry lies the sense that there lurks somewhere an earthy wasteland upon which the bubble of prosperity depends. Borrowing from *The Matrix*, Žižek terms this space—imagined in cinematic scenes of desolation—the "desert of the real." The 9/11 attacks, then, were the invasion of the "digitized First World," represented by the World Trade Center as the center of global finance, by the "Third World 'Desert of the Real.'" The intrusion was engineered by a distant, evil Other—Osama bin Laden, foreshadowed by scores of shadowy movie villains. Žižek concludes:

> It is the awareness that we live in an insulated artificial universe which generates the notion that some ominous agent is threatening. . . . In this pure Outside, we should recognize the distilled version of our own essence. For the last five centuries, the (relative) prosperity and peace of the "civilized" West was bought by the export of ruthless violence and destruction into the "barbarian" Outside: the long story from the conquest of America to the slaughter in Congo. . . . The US just got the taste of what goes on around the world on a daily basis. . . . Therein resides the true lesson of the

bombings: the only way to ensure that it will not happen HERE again is to prevent it going on ANYWHERE ELSE.

Žižek all but says that al-Qaeda hijacked a disturbing American fantasy to bring to life its deepest fears. In his own moral fantasy, 9/11 issues a near-cosmic mandate: that the United States not merely right particular policy wrongs but also work to rid the whole world of its ills—to banish all "deserts of the real" and the madmen they spawn.

In *The Guardian,* the Indian intellectual Arundhati Roy brought a sharper edge to similar points. "Could it be," she asked, "that the stygian anger that led to the attacks has its taproot not in American freedom and democracy, but in the US government's record of commitment and support to exactly the opposite things . . . ? It must be hard for ordinary Americans, so recently bereaved, to look up at the world with their eyes full of tears and encounter what might appear to them to be indifference." Rather than indifference, it was "the tired wisdom of knowing that what goes around eventually comes around."[23]

Ward Churchill, a radical Native American scholar and University of Colorado professor, took a giant step further than other critics. In a September 12 essay, he *fully justified* the 9/11 attacks as payback for US aggression.[24] Those killed in the Pentagon, he believed, were fair game as military targets. Those in the World Trade Center were scarcely less guilty, given their alleged complicity in murderous economic policies. He caustically asked, "If there was a better, more effective, or in fact any other way of visiting some penalty befitting their participation upon the little Eichmanns inhabiting the sterile sanctuary of the twin towers, I'd really be interested in hearing about it." Here Churchill likens today's finance professionals to the "desk killers" who, in Hannah Arendt's famous phrase, did the bureaucratic work of the Holocaust.

Published on an obscure anarchist website, Churchill's incendiary essay had negligible public impact at the time. It caused a firestorm only years later, when it was dug up prior to his giving a public lecture. Its gross insensitivity to the 9/11 dead and extreme claim of collective guilt were well beyond what other critics of US foreign policy would conceive or utter.

Together, this critical commentary answered an influential take on 9/11 by the conservative pundit George F. Will. On September 12 in *The Washington Post*, Will wrote that 9/11 ended the United States' "holiday from history."[25] Since the end of the Cold War the country had largely withdrawn from global leadership. But if it felt done with the world, the world was not done with it. In the Twin Towers and the Pentagon, al-Qaeda hit targets representing the "vigor of American civilization" and its "ability to project and defend democratic values." Americans' "proper anger," Will felt, "should be alloyed with pride," as the country rejoins the global fight for its values.

With Will, Žižek and other critics share the premise that 9/11 ended America's deceptive separation from the world. But there the similarities end. To the critics, the myth of exceptional virtue collapsed with the towers, revealing the likeness between America's violence and that of its enemies. However stinging, their point was not to proclaim the moral equivalence of tit-for-tat violence. Instead, it was to present existing global conflicts as the essential context for 9/11 and to recommend humility—not martial pride—as the response.

"THE CLASH OF CIVILIZATIONS WILL DOMINATE GLOBAL POLITICS"

The United States made no conventional declaration of war, even as it prepared launch what President Bush called on September 16 a "War on Terrorism."[26] Such a declaration would have seemed unnecessary to many Americans. The country already appeared to be in a war declared by its enemies. A progressive columnist confessed supporting a "real" American war because "someone is waging a real war against us."[27]

Small teams in the national security apparatus had long been aware of the threat al-Qaeda posed. Most others in government now scrambled to connect dots back to the 1993 World Trade Center bombing, reassess al-Qaeda's prior attacks, and take stock of bin Laden's chilling 1998 fatwa "Jihad Against Jews and Crusaders." It called on Muslims to "kill the Americans and their allies."[28] Politicians, pundits, and all manner of experts rushed to put the now-seething conflict into a larger framework. "Clash of civilizations" became the master frame.

The idea originated in a 1993 article written by political scientist Samuel P. Huntington.[29] In it, Huntington predicts the persistence of violence in a seeming era of newfound peace. The essay shared many of the premises of the famous "End of History" (1989) argument of Huntington's former student Francis Fukuyama.[30] The age of conflict over territory, both men believed, was over. So too, the Cold War's ideological battles had been settled, with Western-style capitalist democracy victorious. Yet it was too early, Huntington warned, to declare the end or even the decline of geopolitical conflict. "The clash of civilizations," he boldly stated, "will dominate global politics. The fault lines between civilizations will be the battle lines of the future."[31]

Huntington defined civilizations as clusters of humanity bound by cultural affinities like language, custom, and religion. And civilizations, especially as the nation-state declined in importance, were prone to clash. "As people define their identity in ethnic and religious terms, they are likely to see an 'us' versus 'them' relation existing between themselves and people of different ethnicity and religion."[32] Huntington predicted growing resistance to the further spread of Western practices and values. He saw special danger in the resentment of the West by the Arab world, which took on a strongly religious cast. In the face of this, the West should defend without apology its values and interests, while steeling itself for armed conflict.

First known to academics and foreign policy professionals, Huntington's view gained broad resonance after 9/11. The attacks, within this frame, were eruptions of a "clash" well underway from an enemy that saw its struggle in strongly civilizational terms. As its flip side, the essay encouraged that the United States wage a war to defend the West. In both aspects, Huntington's thinking underwrote the War on Terror.

Even before 9/11, Huntington's ideas met criticisms from the left: that "civilizations" are always mixes of many cultures and lack the strong identities on whose bases they could clash; that Huntington divides the world into "the West versus the rest," seeing conflict between them as inevitable; that it caricatures the Muslim world based on stereotypes; and that Western influence, far from a vague cultural threat to non-Western peoples, often entails economic, political, and military domination.[33] After 9/11, the essay appeared most troubling as a new justification for US aggression.

The clash of civilizations frame also pointed to the complicated place of Islam—and Muslims—in early visions of the War on Terror. Though absent overt prejudice, Huntington's ideas fed a sense of indelible differences among cultures and the inferiority of Arab and Muslim peoples. Arab-Muslim "civilization," it implied, was not terribly civilized, given its alleged rejection of liberal Western values. Scholars like Princeton University's British-born Bernard Lewis burst into public view to argue that the Arab world had failed to achieve a proper modernity and the progress that comes with it. Instead, many in that world blamed the West for the failures of their own societies, giving rise to fundamentalist groups like al-Qaeda.

These historical theses aligned with the belief of some Americans that Islam, unique among the world's major faiths, has both an extremism and a violence problem: that Arabs and Muslims *anywhere in the world* might have "civilizational" loyalties at odds with modern values and seek to harm the West.

President Bush formally rejected these views. Just after 9/11, he participated in interfaith events that included imams and stressed the peace-loving values common among religions. Directly addressing the world's Muslims, he said in a September 20 speech: "We respect your faith. It's practiced freely by many millions of Americans, and by millions more in countries that America counts as friends. Its teachings are good and peaceful, and those who commit evil in the name of Allah blaspheme the name of Allah. The terrorists are traitors to their own faith, trying, in effect, to hijack Islam itself. The enemy of America is not our many Muslim friends."[34] Bush narrowed the adversary to a tiny subset of Muslims who had betrayed their faith. His defense of Islam was also a tribute to religious tolerance as a key part of the American creed. To embrace Muslims within a commitment to pluralism was to reject the intolerance of an extremist enemy.

Much of the nation took Bush's message to heart, or already shared its spirit. In public polling, favorable views of Islam hit historic peaks *just after* 9/11.[35] Unfavorable views declined. More than anything else, according to researcher Joseph Margulies, "the bipartisan effort by cultural elites to shame expressions of anti-Islamic bigotry" accounts for this trend. "Interfaith demonstrations of religious unity became a fixture on the national landscape." Diverse communities rallied in solidarity with their Muslim neighbors. The media ran tender profiles of patriotic Muslims and Arab Americans, whether a Girl Scout wearing a hijab or a devout Muslim in the US military. The point was to say that "they" are just like "us" as normal, loyal citizens, bearing no responsibility for 9/11.

This sentiment was far from universal. 9/11 sparked a fierce backlash against Muslims and Arabs, drawing on their long-standing association with terrorism in the minds of some Americans. Hate crimes spiked. These included, Human Rights Watch reported, "murder, beatings, arson, attacks on mosques, shootings, vehicular assaults and verbal threats."[36] At least three people were killed by self-professed vigilante-patriots in the weeks after 9/11. "I did it to retaliate against those who retaliated against us," said the murderer of an Indian convenience store owner in Texas, thought to be Muslim.[37]

The bigotry was as crude as it was severe. Ignorant Americans lumped Muslims, Arabs (most of whom in the United States are Christian), and South Asian peoples into a faceless, internal enemy. Some targets merely "looked Muslim." One murder victim was a Sikh in Arizona, attacked on account of his skin color and headdress. Whole labor sectors—like taxi drivers in New York City, hailing mostly from South Asian countries—felt under threat. Terrified, the targeted populations might respond by staying out of public view or concealing their culture and faith. New York cabbies put American flags on their vehicles in hopes of winning some safety.

Bush's defense of tolerance—echoed by community leaders, other politicians, and much of the press—was partly a reaction to this backlash. Congress passed a resolution on September 15 condemning prejudice and acts of hate against Muslims and Arabs. The defense of Islam against al-Qaeda extremists and the virtues of tolerance remained a staple in Bush's early speeches. But government conduct also belied this goodwill.

The PENTTBOMB detentions disappeared Muslims, Arabs, and South Asians from their workplaces and homes.[38] None of those rounded up were guilty of involvement with terrorism. Immigration law was weaponized to hold people in de facto indefinite detention while investigations proceeded. Their confinement in federal, state, and local lockups often entailed gross physical abuse and punishing isolation, anticipating the torture of terror suspects apprehended overseas. Access to attorneys was denied altogether or severely limited. When released, many were deported, tearing families apart. Their detention and handling were challenged in lawsuits and later investigated at the highest levels of the federal government.

The Justice Department and other law enforcement created new security measures—like invasive surveillance, "no-fly lists," and the compulsory registration of foreign nationals from Muslim-majority nations—that trafficked in indiscriminate suspicion and religious-racial profiling. The deportation of Muslims soared. Cultural stigmas were hurtful as well. By a common prejudice, many Americans saw Muslim women either as victims, in need of rescue from their faith's patriarchy, or as threats, harboring secret esteem for terrorist groups.

Muslim and Arab communities hardly felt soothed by Bush's appeals to tolerance or convinced that the United States had in no way made them and their faith an enemy. A near-requirement for Muslim and Arab American advocacy organizations was to first proclaim their disdain for the terrorists and their loyalty to the United States, as if these were already in question. Waging foreign wars as part of a "clash of civilizations" fueled both popular hostility and domestic measures against groups seen as threats to the nation.

"FOR THE FIRST TIME THE GUNS HAVE BEEN TURNED THE OTHER WAY"

The left had its own sense that America was already locked in war, though not between "civilizations." Far from being sucker-punched on 9/11, the United States was a willful, longtime combatant, with Arab nations and beyond. The country "believed itself not just at peace," Naomi Klein charged, "but war-proof, a self-perception that would come as quite a surprise to most Iraqis, Palestinians and Colombians. Like an amnesiac, the U.S. has awakened in the middle of a war, only to find out it has been going on for years."[39] Critics spun this idea of persisting war, even as they implored the US government to treat the attacks only as acts of terrorism. But what kind of war was it? And against whom or what?

Answers varied in their scope and provocation. Rahul Mahajan used a blunt racial lens in declaring 9/11 a counterstrike at historic US hostility toward "nonwhite peoples."[40] Arundhati Roy viewed the attacks as "a monstrous calling card from a world gone horribly wrong. The message may have been written by Bin Laden . . . but it could well have been signed by the ghosts of the victims of America's old wars."[41] Here she performs something of the "stygian anger" deeply felt in the Global South. The risk in such rhetoric is the elevation of mass murder to the settling of the world's score with the United States. Nothing at the time suggested that bin Laden felt any special solidarity toward America's victims outside of the Middle East or nonwhite peoples as a whole.

Susan Sontag, the American essayist, added her own bite. Where in public discourse, she asked in the September 24 issue of *The New Yorker*, "is the acknowledgment that this was not a 'cowardly' attack on 'civilization' or 'liberty' or 'humanity' or 'the free world' but an attack on the world's self-proclaimed superpower, undertaken as a consequence of specific American alliances and actions? How many citizens are aware of the ongoing American bombing of Iraq? And if the word 'cowardly' is to be used, it might be more aptly applied to those who kill from beyond the range of retaliation, high in the sky, than to those willing to die themselves in order to kill others."[42] For Sontag, the means of US war-making were as distasteful as its ends.

Tariq Ali, the famous Pakistani English intellectual, stressed in *The Nation* the need for evenhanded compassion with respect to all victims of violent conflict. The 9/11 dead deserve "deep sympathy." "But to accept that somehow an American life is worth more than that of a Rwandan, a Yugoslav, a Vietnamese, a Korean, a Japanese, a Palestinian . . . is unacceptable."[43] To acknowledge shared suffering, he felt, is also to recognize shared guilt, which might spur efforts to quell the world's many wars.

Chomsky also addressed the colonial legacy to make sense of 9/11. He first shared his views in interviews with the foreign press. By mid-October these were published in the United States as the slender volume *9-11*, which served as a lodestar for the antiwar left. "The horrifying atrocities of September 11," Chomsky told an Italian newspaper, "are something quite new in world affairs, not in their scale and character, but in the target."[44] They were, he noted, the first time US national territory had been attacked since 1812. (Hawai'i, at the time of Pearl Harbor, was not yet a state.) The United States, by contrast, had long committed mass, extraterritorial violence in places like Mexico and the Philippines. European colonialism was rife with violence, though the independence movements fighting it did not, with rare exception, attack the homelands of the colonial powers. Chomsky says of 9/11, "for the first time the guns have been turned the other way."

It is remarkable commentary. Chomsky folds 9/11 into the long arc of Western imperialism and resistance to it. By seeing the target as its shocking aspect, he excludes other grounds for 9/11's terrible novelty: Al-Qaeda's pursuit of wanton slaughter over political goals; the morbid ingenuity of the attacks, designed for global witness; and the deliberate mass murder of civilians, which terrorists mostly avoid.

Chomsky's core view is that the United States is an empire, maintained by coercion and violence: sanctions regimes, covert actions, insurgencies and counterinsurgencies, air and ground wars, and support for state terror. Conveyed with a matter-of-fact moralism, his account of US misdeeds undercuts any faith in American benevolence in world affairs. To charges that he presents a caricature of the United States as an imperialist monster, Chomsky typically replies that his judgments are grounded in the observable record and continues his plodding work.

Chomsky's sense of persisting war grounds his key claims, filling out the arguments of the antiwar camp. One was to see 9/11 as a terrible case of the "blowback" of US policy. The CIA supported the bin Laden network when it fought in the 1980s to expel the Soviets from Afghanistan. "The attacks are not 'consequences' of U.S. policies in any direct sense," Chomsky noted. "But indirectly, of course they are consequences." "The U.S.," he added, "was happy to support [bin Laden's] hatred and violence when it was directed against U.S. enemies."

September 11 was a chessboard move to escalate war with the United States. Echoing the British journalist Robert Fisk, who had interviewed the al-Qaeda leader, Chomsky cautioned that "a massive assault on a Muslim population would be the answer to the prayers of bin Laden and his associates, and would lead the U.S. and its allies into a 'diabolical trap.'"[45] (Peter Bergen, based on exhaustive research following the capture of bin Laden, found no evidence that he specifically sought on 9/11 to bait the United States into invading Afghanistan.)[46]

For Chomsky, the brutal assaults were unjustifiable expressions of justified outrage. "The likely perpetrators," he explained, "draw support from a reservoir of bitterness and anger over U.S. policies in the region, extending those of earlier European masters."[47] Chomsky referenced hostility to America's support for authoritarian Arab regimes like that of Saudi Arabia, its ongoing assaults on Iraq, and its siding with Israel over the Palestinians. These grievances, expressed by bin Laden, were also felt throughout Arab societies.

Here lay a great challenge for critics, which colored the antiwar response. To them, the relevance of US policies to 9/11 was obvious. Chalmers Johnson, an ex-military foreign policy analyst, coolly asserted that, "the terrorism of Sept. 11 was not directed against

America but against American foreign policy."[48] To Middle East expert Sandy Tolan, religious fanaticism and "evil" were poor explanations for 9/11. The larger context was the "flammable mix of rage and despair" in the region, rooted in chronic humiliation of Palestinians and the staggering Iraqi death toll from sanctions.[49] "Do Americans know about this suffering?" he asked. "Do they care?"

Edward Said, the Palestinian scholar and Columbia University professor, explained: "There is a dialectic between specific US actions on the one hand and consequent attitudes towards America on the other hand that has literally very little to do with jealousy or hatred of America's prosperity, freedom, and all-round success in the world. On the contrary, every Arab or Muslim that I have ever spoken to expressed mystification as to why so extraordinarily rich and admirable a place as America (and so likable a group of individuals as Americans) has behaved internationally with such callous obliviousness of lesser peoples."[50] And yet, to suggest any link between US policy and 9/11 was to invite vicious backlash.

Outrage abounded. When the *Houston Chronicle* republished his essay comparing 9/11 and US "terrorism," Robert Jensen faced calls that he be fired.[51] "I wanted to walk barefoot on broken glass across the Brooklyn Bridge up to that despicable woman's apartment," wrote a *New York Post* columnist in response to Sontag, "drag her down to ground zero and force her to say that to the firefighters."[52] Andrew Sullivan, in the once-liberal *New Republic*, called Sontag "an ally of evil."[53] *Newsweek* opinion columnist Jonathan Alter complained that "the same people urging us not to blame the victim in rape cases are now saying that Uncle Sam wore a short skirt and asked for it."[54]

A letter to the *Los Angeles Times* called Barbara Kingsolver a "little horror of a human being."[55] Even perceived slights at Bush's presidential toughness stirred anger. Two local journalists were fired for criticizing Bush, on a presidential visit to a Florida school, for remaining far from the danger on 9/11. *Nation* columnist Katha Pollitt confessed her ambivalence at her daughter's wish to fly the American flag outside the family window. To her, the flag connoted "jingoism and vengeance."[56] To her daughter, it meant, "standing together and honoring the dead." Pollitt's compromise was to permit the daughter to fly the flag from her own bedroom. Pollitt was told to "Shut Up!" by a *Chicago Tribune* columnist and treated by Sullivan to the rape victim analogy.[57]

Said complained of the stifling atmosphere, in which anti-Muslim prejudice swirled: "Any attempt to place the horrors of what occurred on 11 September in a context that includes US actions and rhetoric is either attacked or dismissed as somehow condoning the terrorist bombardment."[58] Chomsky stood by his convictions while choosing his words carefully. He repeatedly used the image of al-Qaeda drawing "from a reservoir of anger" over US policies to frame his sense of America's guilt.[59]

"THE AYATOLLAH OF ANTI-AMERICAN HATE"

Whatever his caution, Chomsky drew fire from across the political spectrum. On the political right, David Horowitz played attack dog. A prominent 1960s radical, Horowitz loudly converted to conservatism in the late 1980s. He became a zealous cultural warrior whose specialty was to condemn "tenured radicals" for poisoning America's youth with contempt for their country.

In the usually liberal *Salon*, Horowitz published in late September an essay that began, "Without question, the most treacherous intellect in America belongs to MIT professor Noam Chomsky."[60] "In Chomsky's demented universe," he charged, "America is responsible not only for its own bad deeds, but for the bad deeds of others." Horowitz dubbed Chomsky "the ayatollah of anti-American hate."

Professor Jeffrey Isaac, writing from a liberal perspective, took Chomsky to task with a message aimed at the US left. Though conceding that Chomsky does not "condone" terrorism, Isaac accuses him of plenty: insisting on "the equivalence" of 9/11 and "U.S. policy"; describing with pointless monotony the "evil" of American imperialism; and failing to present any realistic way of reeling in American power. Uninterested in genuine remedies, Chomsky's voice, Isaac says, is one of "cynicism," not "courageous dissent."[61]

The most stinging criticism of Chomsky came from a past ally,

Christopher Hitchens. Adding to the drama, the quarrel was partly carried out in the hallowed left-wing publication *The Nation*. Their conflict underscores the passions 9/11 inspired, the ways in which thoughtful people disagreed, and the deep fractures facing the antiwar opposition.

Hitchens was a prodigy of the 1960s British student left, becoming a journalist in England and the United States. He relished the role of provocateur, captive to no ideology. In the 1980s he identified with his countryman George Orwell and took up the anticommunist cause. The September 11 attacks, and the views of figures like Chomsky, prompted Hitchens to break finally with the left. With other intellectuals, he joined the flock of "liberal hawks" who loudly supported much of the War on Terror.

In a battery of articles, Hitchens addressed Chomsky's statements about 9/11. He blasted what bothered many others: Chomsky's immediate mention of the Clinton administration's 1999 bombing of a pharmaceutical plant in Sudan.[62] The death toll from the lack of medicine, Chomsky stressed, likely dwarfed that on September 11. So scandalous was this remark that he spent long parts of interviews defending it. Unmoved by his critics, Chomsky judged morally irrelevant whether the United States *intended* to kill Sudanese civilians and condemned how cheaply it must view the lives of poor Africans.

Hitchens was having none of it. He rejected the premise that the 9/11 assaults were a referendum on US policies. What the attackers "abominate about 'the West,'" he declared, "is not what Western liberals don't like and can't defend about their own system, but what they do like about it and must defend: its emancipated women, its scientific inquiry, its separation of religion from the state."[63] Hitchens also dismissed the idea that changing policies would appease al-Qaeda. "Only a moral cretin" would "suppose that an Israeli withdrawal from Gaza would have forestalled the slaughter in Manhattan." Al-Qaeda represented "fascism with an Islamic face." Its intent was "to subjugate, not liberate, fellow Muslims, while massacring infidels."

To the charge that the United States aided the ascent of the Taliban, Hitchens responded that it therefore has a special responsibility to eliminate the contemptible, theocratic regime. He pleaded that Americans summon the "self-respect" to "say that we have met an enemy and that he is not us, but someone else."[64] Judging the coexistence of "us" and "them" as impossible, Hitchens saw war as the only option.

Hitchens's diatribe exposed the fault lines over which opinion, including within the left, divided. Was America attacked because of its commitment to its ideals or their violation, the best or the worst of what it represents? Did 9/11 reveal a troubling likeness between the Unites States and its enemies, or confirm its superiority?

Behind conflicting answers lay very different understandings of terrorism. In one view, terrorism is a "weapon of the weak" used to wage "asymmetrical warfare."[65] Lacking proper armies, the combatants deploy fear as a force multiplier in the coercive pursuit of political goals. However grisly, terrorism may be diminished by addressing the conflicts at its core. Those seeing US policies as a cause of 9/11 clearly favored this understanding, even when recognizing al-Qaeda's cruelty.

In a second model, terrorism is a form of "cosmic war." Conceived as an epic contest of good against evil, cosmic war seeks the restoration of moral order—often in defense of collective identities perceived as under threat—through divinely sanctioned violence. This-worldly political goals, while also present, are secondary to a larger, life-and-death struggle.[66] Figures like Hitchens, who saw in al-Qaeda apocalyptic fantasies and a fascistic will to power, echoed this view.

Yet a danger in seeing terrorism as cosmic war is that the struggle against it may also take on a cosmic cast. The common result of a shared, cosmic frame is the intense, mutual demonization of the enemy; extreme violence justified in moral terms; and a politics of annihilation that dismisses opportunities for compromise. Though nowhere endorsing all this, Hitchens suggests a sacred frame to the war he embraces. Above all, the battle against "Islamic fascism" is profoundly just, recapturing the glory of past antifascist campaigns. It may be redemptive as well, in senses relevant to both Hitchens's evolution and the make-up of the "liberal hawks." First, it permits

America to atone for past sins, such as its support for Islamic extremism. Second, it promises to sweep away the self-hating rationalizations by which the left debases itself.

A sense of personal atonement may also be present in Hitchens's conversion. Hitchens praises by name the two Flight 93 passengers thought most responsible for subduing the plane's hijackers. "One iota of [their] innate fortitude," he declares, "is worth all the writings of Noam Chomsky."[67] It is a striking insult from one intellectual about another, all but accused here of effete cowardice. Hitchens contrasts manly, self-sacrificing physical courage to the whole vocation of criticism that he shares. An enthusiastic conscript in the War on Terror, he spent the next years soldiering against intellectual naysayers to war.

The literal debate *The Nation* staged between Hitchens and Chomsky was a disappointment. Chomsky largely refused to attend the duel. He insisted that Hitchens says things about his positions that he knows are not true and cannot, therefore, be taken seriously. Hitchens saw this as damning evasion.[68] The debate ended quickly with each of them, once mutual admirers, declaring the other sadly irrelevant. "It no longer matters," Hitchens bluntly concluded, what Chomsky and his America-hating colleagues "think."[69] The left's near-unity in opposing US military action was another casualty of 9/11.

"THIS IS CIVILIZATION'S FIGHT"

To the opponents of looming war, the views that mattered most were those of George W. Bush and the American people. Bush's first major statement on the War on Terror came in his September 20 address to Congress, watched by millions. In it he fleshed out the purpose, scope, and means of a military campaign already secretly underway.

"On September the eleventh," Bush stated, "enemies of freedom committed an act of war against our country."[70] This line had enormous significance. It placed the country in a state of war, led by the military and not law enforcement. It also painted the attackers as threats to America's essence. Bush insisted that they "hate our freedoms—our freedom of religion, our freedom of speech, our freedom to vote and assemble and disagree with each other." ... This is civilization's fight." The speech aligned the battle with America's greatest triumphs on the world stage, while ensuring final victory. The attackers "follow in the path of fascism, and Nazism, and totalitarianism. And they will follow that path all the way, to where it ends: in history's unmarked grave of discarded lies."

Bush pledged the defeat of "*every* terrorist group of global reach." The threat extended also to nation-states. "By aiding and abetting murder, the Taliban regime is committing murder. They will hand over the terrorists, or they will share in their fate." So too, "any nation that continues to harbor or support terrorism will be regarded by the United States as a hostile regime," subject to removal by US guns. To the world Bush thundered, "Either you are with us, or you are with the terrorists."

Bush's words had a grandiose simplicity to them. In his view, 9/11 was an act of evil, committed by evildoers, supported by nations later named an "axis of evil." The way to defeat terrorism was to capture and kill the terrorists and their accomplices. Days before his speech to Congress, Bush announced that America's "responsibility to history is already clear: to answer these attacks and rid the world of evil."[71]

It was a compelling vision that wrapped the War on Terror in extraordinary virtue. And it was a vision often repeated in Bush's speeches and public statements. The Pentagon first named its post-9/11 campaign "Operation Infinite Justice." The conceit was inescapable. After Muslim scholars objected that only God can deliver infinite justice, the Pentagon chose instead "Operation Enduring Freedom."[72]

Bush's worldview was profoundly at odds with opponents of war. He offered no admission of America's history of devastating civilian populations and supporting authoritarian regimes. Nor was there any suggestion that the United States had anything to apologize for, or critically examine in itself, save complacency in a dangerous world. Antiwar critics struggled to have their voices heard in a climate of shock, fear, and anger, in which the American people looked to their government and president as their protectors. They were also running into the headwinds of full-blown, militaristic nationalism based in a revitalized exceptionalist ideology.

Žižek wrote in his mid-September essay, "It is as if we dwell in the unique time between a traumatic event and its symbolic impact, like in those brief moments after we are deeply cut, and before the full extent of the pain strikes us—it is open how the events will be symbolized [and] what acts they will be evoked to justify."[73] More than he realized, the national will was already cauterizing around war. Roy warned that "war is looming large" so "whatever remains to be said must be said fast."[74] "Patriotism seems to be falling to whoever claims it loudest," worried Kingsolver.[75] "It is infuriated by thoughtful hesitation, constructive criticism of our leaders, and pleas for peace."

The American people seemed little swayed by such pleas. By the evening of September 11, major media already began surveying Americans' reaction to the attacks. Ninety-two percent said they would "support military action," including outright "war" if the United States could "identify the groups or nations" responsible.[76] Eighty-four percent also favored military action against "countries that assist or shelter terrorists" uninvolved in the attacks.

Bush's promise to deliver swift "justice" met instant acclaim. On September 13, 91 percent of respondents approved of his response to 9/11, with 77 percent supporting military action even "if it meant innocent civilians in other countries might be hurt or killed"; 69 percent would back a "long war with large numbers of U.S. troops killed"; and 85 percent supported going to war against Afghanistan if it did not turn over bin Laden.[77]

Other surveys confirmed a hawkish public. A September 19 Pew Research Center poll showed 82 percent favoring "robust military action, including ground troops."[78] Just 9 percent opposed such a war. Bush got high marks for his September 20 speech, leaving eight in ten viewers "more confidant" in the government's ability to deal with terrorism.[79] A majority of respondents thought a potential war would last "several years," with more than a third anticipating sizable US military casualties.

Americans largely saw the War on Terror, whose first target would surely be Afghanistan, as a "good war." In its official framing and public perception, it sought to punish those behind horrifying crimes and rid the world of terrorism. Opponents of the war faced a daunting challenge.

CHAPTER 2

"THE WAY TO PREVENT MORE DEATHS IS NOT TO KILL MORE PEOPLE"

Arguing the War in Afghanistan

The belief that US policies were among the root causes of 9/11 yielded the highly general plea that the United States empathetically engage the world. America had met "the sharp limits of the security that can come from the boot on the neck," one critic explained, and must try "the open hand."[1] However poetic or wise, this sentiment did little to directly address what many feared was the coming onslaught. Specific arguments were needed to stop a war before it started or, if begun, to limit its damage.

President Bush made clear that a US attack on someone, somewhere, was a question of when and not if. As to its scale, the famed nuclear weapons critic Jonathan Schell shared his worry: 9/11 appeared to call for a "response commensurate to the horror."[2] Yet there were likely only "a few score directly involved in the attacks," backed by "a few hundred co-conspirators." The Bush administration was therefore searching for "larger targets," like the whole fledging state of Afghanistan, or even Iraq. By this effort, a visceral politics of overkill was built into the War on Terror.

Adding to the risk, the US military designed a war in Afghanistan for the capabilities it had: aerial bombardments and conflict by proxies followed by quick land operations to destroy the army of a nation-state. It had little capacity for the targeted capture of terror suspects, or for nation building, or for counterinsurgency operations.

The official outbreak of war on October 7 was met with great enthusiasm by the American public. The overwhelming majority—94 percent according to a *Washington Post* poll—supported the first air strikes on Afghanistan.[3] Four weeks out, 90 percent backed the campaign, with only 9 percent registering opposition and 3 percent "strong opposition."[4]

Support for the assault hovered between 86 and 92 percent from mid-October through the end of November. By that latter date, 90 percent of Americans favored the deployment of ground troops in what they thought would be a "long war."[5] More than three-quarters also favored the forcible removal of Saddam Hussein from power in Iraq. Americans differed over whether the main purpose of the Afghanistan campaign should be to disrupt terrorism, capture or kill bin Laden, or take out the Taliban.[6] Judgments of whether America was winning at points wavered. Yet these doubts, along with the deaths of civilians, had little effect on attitudes toward the war. Opposition barely topped 5 percent.[7]

The war's relative ease and swift, apparent conclusion sealed its popularity. The first US combat casualty, a CIA paramilitary officer named Michael Spann, occurred only on November 25. By early December, the Taliban were driven from power. On December 20, the United Nations Security Council unanimously passed a resolution establishing a multinational security force to bolster the new interim government.[8] Not until January 2002 did the first US soldier die by hostile fire. By that point, the war appeared in its mop-up phases, with the key challenges now political.

Antiwar voices struggled for a foothold. They stressed the hell of war in general, the danger of this war in particular, and the value of alternatives to armed action. Added to the opinions of professional critics were appeals for peace from families grief-stricken by the 9/11 attacks. A lone member of Congress dissented as well.

Calls for peace may have appeared to many Americans a naive or even noxious cry in the wilderness: passive in the face of peril; callous toward the suffering on 9/11; and irrelevant to the fast-turning gears of policy, best left to trusted leaders. Some normally in the peace camp hedged, arguing that a military campaign could be both beneficial and just. Others were firm in their dissent. Their challenge was to find the right message and emotion for the moment, while weathering the backlash against their views.

That moment quickly passed, as military success in Afghanistan seemed to sweep away antiwar concerns. Yet their importance did not vanish. Together, they were an index of worry and warnings against which the war in Afghanistan, and the War on Terror more broadly, could one day be judged.

"TERRORISM AND WAR BECOME EQUALLY UNPARDONABLE"

A small antiwar chorus voiced profound caution over US military action. The most basic concern was that it would kill civilians. Inevitable in any war, civilian losses had particular significance in this conflict. The essential wrong of 9/11, after all, was the cruel wasting of civilian lives. Just after 9/11, Detroit journalist Michael Betzold asked, "If we are willing to accept 'collateral damage'" in armed strikes, "what makes us any different from the terrorists?"[9] When a colleague told him, "Children will have to die," he protested, "The way to prevent more deaths is not to kill more people."

A more combustible encounter played out on national television. On September 13, the Fox News host Bill O'Reilly interviewed Sam Husseini—a Palestinian Jordanian media activist and former spokesperson for the American-Arab Anti-Discrimination Committee.[10] "What sickened me" about 9/11, Husseini explained, was the death of innocents. "But now I hear a drumbeat of having our soldiers kill women and children."

"That hasn't happened," shot back O'Reilly, who insisted that the United States would not engage in "indiscriminate bombing." Husseini countered that the country had a long history of harm to civilians. "If you're gonna justify [9/11] with past atrocities, I'm gonna pull [the] plug on you," O'Reilly threatened. "I'm saying all atrocities are bad," protested Husseini, nearly in tears. O'Reilly cut his microphone.

Religious figures were especially attuned to the moral hazards of war. Anthony B. Robinson, a popular theologian, wrote in a Seattle newspaper that "violence cannot be redeemed by violence."[11] Condemning the premises of cosmic war, he rejected the idea that "the only way to restore order is to beat down and destroy all that represents chaos in the world."[12]

The famous peace minister William Sloane Coffin held a sermon on the Christian view of war. "It may be impossible for the Taliban," he preached, "and hard for some Americans to believe, but there is no special Providence for some nations at the expense of others."[13] The godly response to 9/11 was to say, "We will not seek to avenge the death of innocent Americans by the death of innocent victims elsewhere, lest we become what we abhor."[14]

One day after the attacks, Reverend Jim Wallis drafted a statement that denounced the "utterly evil acts" of 9/11 and offered houses of worship for prayer, reflection, and healing.[15] It also pleaded that the United States not "retaliate in ways that bring on even more loss of innocent life." Only "by refusing to submit to a world created in [the terrorists'] image" could America "deny them their victory." The statement gained thousands of signatures from diverse faith leaders and laypersons. Religious eminences offered their own counsel. "I believe violence will only increase the cycle of violence," wrote the Dalai Lama in a letter to George W. Bush.[16]

Military veterans spoke out as well. Just after 9/11 Greg Nees, a former marine with Veterans for Peace, wrote Bush urging that he not "widen the spiral of violence" with rash military action. A Japanese peace group donated tens of thousands of dollars to have Nees's remarks run as a full-page ad in *The New York Times*.[17]

Howard Zinn, the legendary peace activist, explained how terrorism and war take on a fateful likeness:

> I can see an immediate objection to this equation: They (the terrorists) deliberately kill innocent people; we (the war makers) aim at "military" targets, and civilians are killed by accident. . . . Even if you grant that the intention is not to kill civilians, if they nevertheless become victims, again and again and again, can that be called an accident? . . . The absurdity of claiming innocence in such cases

becomes apparent when the death tolls from "collateral damage" reach figures far greater than the lists of the dead from even the most awful act of terrorism.[18]

"When children die," he added, "terrorism and war become equally unpardonable."

Even cautious supporters of military action echoed this point. "We must respond with force," wrote the anarchist philosopher Crispin Sartwell. "But we had better try as hard as we know how to kill the people responsible and not cities full of noncombatants. Otherwise, you can call what we're doing infinite justice or shoo-fly pie, but it's still murder."[19] A war of virtue could not mirror the very violence it claimed to oppose.

This was far from a rhetorical point or hypothetical possibility. Dick Cheney openly urged the country's passage to "the dark side" to defeat terrorism. With respect to interrogation operations, that meant the likely commission of war crimes. When the bombing started, Marion Winik shared her horror in *The Philadelphia Inquirer*: "I hate the Taliban, I hate Osama bin Laden. . . . If punishment were what I felt was most important, perhaps I could share in the grim patriotic fervor of this moment. But I care about keeping people safe . . . Somewhere still, there are people running and debris flying and children crying. It was New York; now it's another place full of innocent strangers."[20]

By December of 2001, according to researcher Marc Herold, the civilian death toll from US operations in Afghanistan likely exceeded the three thousand or so killed on September 11.[21] Lower estimates still put casualties at a thousand or more.[22] Among the dead were children.

"THE WILL TO SPEAK OUT"

The objection to answering civilian deaths with more civilian deaths took on singular power when expressed by those closest to the suffering: the family members of people killed on September 11.

Consumed with sorrow, some also felt profoundly uncomfortable with the war path set by President Bush and the invocation of their loved ones to justify it.

They went public with their opposition to war, in some cases just days after 9/11. Their voices percolated in the print media, if mostly at its edges. Their statements circulated more widely on the web, allowing them to find one another.

The country and much of the world expressed enormous sympathy for the 9/11 victims. In New York City, emblems of grief and solidarity appeared at hospitals, churches and fire stations, turning the city into a maze of open-air memorials. Local politicians and community leaders extolled the victims with great eloquence. Throughout the country, Americans showed their solidarity: in official remembrances and volunteer vigils; in the cards written by schoolchildren for firefighters and police; and in the spontaneous creation of memorials, replete with flowers and menageries of stuffed animals as might adorn the site of a traffic fatality. In October, *The New York Times* began running profiles, titled "Portraits of Grief," of each victim in New York, Pennsylvania, and Northern Virginia.

The 9/11 victims were powerfully implicated in the national response. On the morning of September 14, President Bush came to New York City to give his "bullhorn address" at Ground Zero—the instant name for the impact site, taken from the atomic blast in Hiroshima. His condolences for the families of the 9/11 dead quickly turned to threats against the perpetrators. They would, he vowed, "hear all of us soon."

With his words and very presence, Bush claimed Ground Zero the political and spiritual center of the entire War on Terror. The victims and their kin were its moral heart. In his address, their voices are transformed through sympathy into a mortal threat to the perpetrators. This link of suffering, solidarity, and war through the figure of the 9/11 victim became a staple in Bush's speeches.

The families pushing back were deeply aware of the importance of the 9/11 victims in the government's response. David Potorti, whose brother died in New York City, said of family members like himself: "To be touched so closely by violence and death was, for them, to demand an end to the possibility that others would suffer the same fire. And because the killing was being undertaken in the names of their loved ones and their families, they felt something else: ownership. This war would be *their* war, fought in *their* names. This gave them the will to speak out."[23] Phyllis and Orlando Rodriguez were the first to do so. On September 14, they penned an open letter titled "Not in Our Son's Name," which friends help them spread online. Military action, they wrote, "will not avenge our son's death."[24]

For Rita Lasar, it was Bush's public mention of her brother's death that caused her to speak out. On the twenty-seventh floor of the North Tower, Abe Zelmanowitz delayed evacuating in order to be with his wheelchair-bound friend until the firefighters came. He died when the building collapsed. The evening of September 14, Bush directly referenced his sacrifice in his speech for the National Day of Prayer and Remembrance at Washington's National Cathedral.

Bush's address was also a call to arms. "This nation is peaceful," he said, "but fierce when stirred to anger. This conflict was begun on the timing and terms of others; it will end in a way and at an hour of our choosing."[25] Hearing this, Lasar had the grim thought that "my country is going to use my brother's heroism as justification to kill innocent people." On September 18 she published a short letter in *The New York Times*. Its last line read, "It is in my brother's name and mine that I pray that we, this country that has been so deeply hurt, not do something that will unleash forces that we will not have the power to bring back."[26]

Amber Amundson lost her twenty-eight-year-old husband, Craig Scott Amundson, at the Pentagon. She deliberately chose the *Chicago Tribune*—a mainstream Midwestern newspaper—to express her grief and anger. In a September 19 letter, she described her husband as a "patriotic American and citizen of the world." He saw his work with the US military as way to "prevent violence and war." Addressing the nation's leaders directly, she insisted, "My family and I take no comfort in your words of rage. . . . Craig would not have wanted a violent response to avenge his death."[27]

Interviewed at his daughter's memorial service in California on September 21, Derrill Bodley told the *San Francisco Chronicle*, "We must not retaliate in kind as if our cause allows us to." Operation Infinite Justice, as the military campaign had been named, "frightens me more than the terrorists' attacks. I shudder to think they chose it because they think God is on our side. That is what the terrorists think."[28] Only in vain could God or his daughter's name be taken as a justification for war.

The National Cathedral service that had so angered Lasar stirred another opponent of war, Congresswoman Barbara Lee (D-CA). The morning of 9/11, members of Congress were evacuated from the Capitol for fear of additional attacks. By nightfall, they sang "God Bless America" on its lawn. This unity was a prelude to passage of the Authorization for Use of Military Force (AUMF), signed into law on September 18. Two days later, Senate leaders Trent Lott (R-MS) and Tom Daschle (D-SD) proudly declared, "There is no opposition party."[29] There was, at least, the opposition of one.

Lee held the congressional seat in Oakland-Berkeley that had once been occupied by the famed Black antiwar activist Ron Dellums. Lee, also Black, had her own peace pedigree. She was the sole representative to vote against the continuing bombing of Iraq following the Gulf War and one of just five House members to oppose the 1999 military campaign in Kosovo.[30] Breaking even with the Congressional Black Caucus and progressive leaders like Bernie Sanders, Lee was the *only* legislator to vote against the AUMF.

Lee felt the tragedy of 9/11 deeply, as one of her staff members had lost a relative in one of the planes. As the vote neared, she attended the National Cathedral memorial to pray on her decision. "As we act, let us not become the evil that we deplore," Reverend Nathan Baxter said at the gathering. "At that moment," Lee reports, "I knew what the right vote was."[31] Trusted colleagues urged her not go out on a limb by opposing the AUMF. Even so, she was shocked to learn that hers was the only dissenting vote. It was both an "awesome" and "lonely feeling."[32]

On the floor of Congress, Lee said of her vote, "I am convinced that military action will not prevent further acts of international terrorism against the United States."[33] The immediate wake of massive trauma, she also felt, was no time to make decisions of grave consequence. "Let's step back for a moment," she cautioned, "and think through the implications of our action today so that it does not spiral out of control."

Lee had, in her antiwar stance, few institutional allies in Washington. One was the Institute for Policy Studies (IPS), a left-wing think tank that had opposed US wars going back to Vietnam. Its downtown office was periodically evacuated in the days after 9/11, when fears of new attacks abounded. Sitting on the sidewalk during one scare, IPS cofounder Marcus Raskin and its Middle East expert Phyllis Bennis made edits to Lee's floor speech just before she delivered it. As a jeep roared by with "ninja soldiers," Bennis remarked, "There could be a military coup." "There might have already been one," Raskin replied, "and we wouldn't know it."[34] Congress would soon make such a plot unnecessary. With the AUMF, it gave the commander in chief nearly limitless powers to wage war, including in secret.

Lee became a lightning rod, with 20,000 emails flooding her office. Some called her a "traitor, a coward, a communist, all the awful stuff," while a special security detail saw to her safety.[35] She also heard words of appreciation from her liberal district and other supporters. "Her voice is being joined by tens of thousands of activists," trumpeted *The Nation*, "who say—as posters in the San Francisco Bay Area declare—'Barbara Lee Voted for Me.'"[36]

Just after the AUMF vote, IPS published the statement "Justice, Not Vengeance." Developed with Harry Belafonte and Danny Glover, it was endorsed by progressive icons like Rosa Parks, Ossie Davis, Ruby Dee, Grace Boggs, Helen Caldicott, Barbara Ehrenreich, and Ben Cohen of Ben & Jerry's ice cream fame. Insisting that a military response to 9/11 would "spark a cycle of escalating violence, the loss of innocent lives, and new acts of terrorism," the statement closely mirrored Lee's own words.[37] However lonely, Lee and other opponents of war were not alone.

"A MASSIVE CAMPAIGN OF LAW ENFORCEMENT"

Peace advocates also argued that war was both counterproductive and unnecessary, and that better options existed for safeguarding the United States. The main pragmatic objection to military action was that it would lead to more violence and fail to stanch the terrorist threat. After the bombing of Afghanistan began, Arundhati Roy explained, "For every 'terrorist' or his 'supporter' that is killed, hundreds of innocent people are being killed too. And for every hundred innocent people killed, there is a good chance that several future terrorists will be created."[38]

Robert Scheer, the gadfly journalist, worried about the "morning after" apparent victory. "The Taliban," he predicted, "will retreat to its caves, ready to fight an endless war of attrition."[39] Forecasting years of futility, he asked, "Is it possible to install any Afghan government with a popular base and sufficient integrity to rule? Can this new leadership keep the battle-hardened Taliban in check militarily?" Roy prophesied, "Once war begins, it will develop a momentum, a logic and a justification of its own, and we'll lose sight of why it's being fought in the first place."[40]

Rare in public conversation, an Afghan American lent intimate despair to warnings about war. Amin Ansary, a longtime US resident, remained connected to his homeland. After 9/11 he sent an email to friends that circulated widely on the internet. He spoke "as one who hates the Taliban and Bin Laden," likening them to Nazis. Yet he shuddered at the thought that their main victims—Afghan commoners—would likely bear the brunt of a US assault.[41] "We come now to the question of bombing Afghanistan back to the Stone Age. Trouble is, that's been done. The Soviets took care of it already. Make the Afghans suffer? They're already suffering." Crushing bin Laden and his protectors would require a ground assault and occupation. This was, he wrote, sure to inflame Muslim peoples and tempt a wider war.

Avoiding war meant seeing the 9/11 attacks as criminal acts and mobilizing global bodies to mete out justice within the framework of the law. This position incensed the 9/11 hawks, who believed the exact opposite. "This is not crime. This is war," insisted *Washington Post* columnist Charles Krauthammer. "You bring criminals to justice; you rain destruction on combatants."[42] A *New York Post* pundit advocated a response "as simple as it is swift—kill the bastards. . . . I don't mean hunt them, arrest them, extradite and prosecute them in a court of law. I mean . . . blow them to smithereens."[43]

There was scarcely time, before a US attack, for peace advocates to develop a detailed vision of legal action as a substitute for war. They mostly argued the benefits of a legal approach and sketched its broad contours. Author James Carroll, a former Catholic priest and longtime *Boston Globe* columnist, contrasted the "rule of law" with the "rule of war": "In war the ends justify the means. In law enforcement, the end remains embodied in the means. . . . In the death-ground of combat violence, self-criticism can seem like fatal self-doubt, so the savage momentum of war is rarely recognized until too late. . . . Law enforcement, on the other hand, with its system of checks and balances between police and courts, is inevitably self-critical. The moral link between act and consequence is far more likely to be protected."[44] Carroll pleaded for "an unprecedented, swift, sure, and massive campaign of law enforcement."

Kevin Danaher was a cofounder of the San Francisco–based Global Exchange. It played a leading role in global justice protests, while working on high-profile campaigns like fair trade. Drawing on this cachet, Danaher wrote in *The Washington Post*, "If we define [the violence of 9/11] as war, it couches the issues in nationalist sentiment and separates us from the people of other nations. If we define it as a crime against humanity, it holds the potential for uniting humankind against the scourge of terrorism."[45] He called for the United States to create an "effective international criminal court," while allowing its traditional virtues, like democracy and the freedom of worship, to ground its credibility.

Closer to the mainstream was David Cortright. A military veteran of the Vietnam War, he became an outspoken critic of that conflict and later led the nuclear disarmament group SANE. To him, a rule-of-law response required an international police force to capture the perpetrators, authorization by the United Nations of a special court, and diplomatic and economic measures to secure support for it, especially among Arab nations.[46]

Noam Chomsky noted that time-tested mechanisms existed to channel national grievances away from war. The British government, for example, responded to Irish Republican Army (IRA) terrorism by prosecuting the assailants, not by bombing Belfast or Boston, full of IRA backers. Nicaragua, when illegally assaulted by the United States in the 1980s, took its complaints to the United Nations and the World Court. It did not attack Washington, DC. "That is the course if the intention is to reduce the probability of further atrocities."[47] In the weeks after 9/11, Chomsky remained oddly hopeful that the United States might choose this path.[48] "An aroused public," he maintained, "can direct policies towards a more humane and honorable course."[49]

Yet Chomsky's own analysis suggested the utter improbability of a US response based in international law. The great deterrent, he felt, to the United States appealing to international courts was that they might one day find the United States itself, or US leaders and soldiers, guilty of crimes. At times, Chomsky's near-obsessive mention of tiny Nicaragua appeared less to mark a path of true justice than to signal the absurdity of mighty America pleading its case before some global court.[50] A futility hovered over his arguments, capturing the difficulties of the antiwar response to 9/11. It urged that 9/11 serve as a great awakening, at last propelling the United States to do the right thing in world affairs. But US perfidy and double standards, taken as a given in antiwar circles, all but ruled out options other than war.

"THE HATE THAT PRODUCES THE HATE"

"September 11, and the Bush administration's reaction to it," wrote the Bay Area's Bob Wing and Max Elbaum, ushered in "a new and dangerous period in international politics. Washington's agenda is to entrench the national security state and a new level of international dominance on the basis of a permanent war on terrorism."[51] The War on Terror, they felt, would in truth be "a war on whomever

Washington considers an enemy." Like the Cold War, it would reach into "every aspect of economic, social, political and cultural life." A broad-based antiwar coalition was needed to resist this juggernaut, certain to wage racist wars against Arab and Central Asian peoples in a new era of US imperialism.

Wing and Elbaum's analysis first circulated online on October 5, two days before the bombing of Afghanistan began. Predicting overreach, it warned that the War on Terror could spin "totally out of control," leading to "human disaster" on a vast scale. History showed that when "imperialism goes to war" in a major way, as in Vietnam, it is stopped only by "undisguisable failure." Their urgent hope was to forestall this terrible outcome.

Wing and Elbaum were activist-intellectuals on the Marxist left, not progressive pundits at the edges of mainstream debate. Their key insight was to see the nascent War on Terror as a comprehensive project that would define American society for years or decades to come. If absent from editorial pages, their views were deeply resonant among activists quickly mobilizing against war in Afghanistan and girding for the longer haul.

Their efforts also underscore the importance of Bay Area radicalism, rooted in 1960s protest, within the larger antiwar landscape. An Asian America, Wing had been a student at UC Berkeley, active in anti–Vietnam War protest and contentious efforts to establish ethnic studies programs.[52] Elbaum became a self-described revolutionary while a student at the University of Wisconsin in Madison, later moving to the West Coast. Both men affiliated with internationalist strains of Marxism-Leninism, becoming intellectual leaders within a strongly leftist milieu. Elbaum was editor of key publications in that world. Wing wrote prodigiously about capitalism, race, and racism, founding *ColorLines* magazine. Years of activism and analytic work equipped them to see the broad structures and trajectories of US power.

In the early '00s, the two were key voices within a still vibrant network of Bay Area Marxist organizations, attractive to youth of color and other young radicals. Among these was STORM (Standing Together to Organize a Revolutionary Movement), whose roots lay in protest of the 1991 Gulf War.[53] Van Jones, soon a rising star in national progressive circles, was a STORM organizer.

In the early morning of September 11, Elbaum was planning to go for a run with a friend. After learning that the second tower had been struck, they went for their run nonetheless, powerless to affect the unfolding tragedy. Put off by spectacles of suffering, Elbaum did not see footage of the Twin Towers being hit until years later.

By evening, Elbaum was in a meeting organized by STORM to formulate a response to the day's events and their likely aftermath. Within days, the group organized antiwar vigils, developed a platform, and founded a local antiwar coalition. Coming to sensible views took some struggle. At the initial meeting, one participant referred to the 9/11 perpetrators as "freedom fighters."[54] The attacks were "a crime against humanity," Elbaum countered. The current task was to oppose both terrorism and the state terror sure to follow. Elbaum's view prevailed.

Later in September, an "old comrades" meeting brought together veterans of diverse causes. It organized forums to discuss 9/11 and its implications, guided by Wing and Elbaum's statement. Part of the purpose was to convince hard-line leftists—long enamored with armed, anti-imperialist movements in the Global South—to see the value of peace politics, including to the socialist cause. Awful on its own, war impacted every worthy social struggle. Wing and Elbaum also urged that "oppressed sectors" of US society like Blacks and the working class, disproportionately hurt by war, anchor antiwar opposition.[55]

By late November, this circle proposed the idea of a national print publication, written in plainspoken English and Spanish, about at the War on Terror. Titled *War Times*, it captured what the post-9/11 era quickly became. The publication would serve as an unofficial mouthpiece of a major antiwar coalition, grounded in both an anti-imperialist framework and efforts to influence the American mainstream.

Back East, another antiwar initiative was taking shape. On October 16, Damu Smith convened Black organizers, academics, activists, and Christian and Muslim leaders at Howard University in

Washington, DC, to reflect on the 9/11 attacks and US government's response.[56] From the gathering was born Black Voices for Peace (BVP), with Smith as its co-director. Its mission was to rally the Black community to "organize, resist, and speak out against war."

Raised in public housing in St. Louis, Smith was a longtime resident of Washington, DC, where he became a powerful activist leader. He led protests against apartheid in South Africa (including frequent arrests at its US embassy), organized against the 1991 Gulf War, and advocated for the Palestinian cause. With Greenpeace, he also did pioneering work fighting environmental racism.[57]

Black Voices for Peace was important in both its message and its messengers. Vulnerable to backlash, it went out of its way to condemn the 9/11 attacks and any effort to rationalize them. At the same time, the group squarely saw US conduct—chiefly its historic support for "state-sponsored terrorism" in the Middle East, Latin America, and elsewhere—as part of the "root causes" of terrorism. "It is the hate that produces the hate," Smith declared, "that we must come to grips with." Only a "U.S. foreign policy that is forged in peace and respect for human rights" could deliver long-term security.

Reverend Graylan Hagler, also a Washingtonian and BVP member, cast this point in religious terms at a November forum on 9/11 and civil liberties. True prayer, he said, requires the confession of one's sins before God and the pledge of changed action. But Bush and so many in the country now sought God's blessings—including in war—without this self-critical step. The role of clergy was to tap into Christianity's prophetic tradition, speak the word of God, and force the nation to confront uncomfortable truths about its conduct. Both Smith and Hagler rooted BVP in the legacy of Martin Luther King Jr., who assumed this prophetic stance when denouncing the Vietnam War.

The group also sought to promote Black voices within antiwar politics. Historically, Black Americans have been more critical of US foreign policy than whites, as well as more sympathetic to global grievances with the United States. At least as far back as the Vietnam War, Blacks have been among the least supportive of US military action.[58] This pattern held, as polling showed, for the War on Terror.

Dr. King and Black Power leaders helped build a rich tradition of Black resistance to war and empire, attuned to the racial dimensions of colonial and neocolonial violence. For groups like the Student Nonviolent Coordinating Committee, the struggles for racial justice and against war were one and the same. Both challenged a white power structure that pulled resources from home, so important for the poor and communities of color, to subjugate foreign peoples.

Black Voices for Peace sought to grow antiwar sentiment in the Black community and translate it into action. To that end, it held antiwar forums and workshops based in the assessments and concerns of Blacks. It also sought to communicate that analysis to larger antiwar forces, shape national antiwar discourse, and secure a place within emerging antiwar coalitions. September 11 and the Bush administration's response was a call for dissident voices to speak up.

"THE VIGILANCE OF AN ACTIVE CITIZENRY"

There was another, far different option for longtime critics of the American state: to endorse a limited war. In Richard Falk it found a distinguished spokesperson. Falk had for decades taught international law and criticized what he saw as America's often lawless exercise of power. He later became the Special Rapporteur on Palestine at the United Nations, courting controversy for his pro-Palestinian views. Yet he wrote in *The Nation* on October 11 that "the war in Afghanistan qualifies in my understanding as the first truly just [US] war since World War II."[59]

In articles published before and after the US invasion, Falk demonstrated how even a strong advocate of international law could give war a chance. Much more than *The Nation's* anodyne editorials urging restraint, his thinking framed the view of 9/11 in the left-wing publication.

Al-Qaeda, Falk wrote on September 20, had authored "the greatest display of grotesque cunning in human history."[60] "Reconciliation" was out of the question, given its "genocidal intent" toward

Americans and Jews. Military force was "essential to diminish the threat of repetition, to inflict punishment and to restore a sense of security."[61]

Falk stressed the need for constraints on a prospective war. These included UN authorization, narrow war aims, safeguards for civilians, and the protection of civil liberties at home, for Arabs and Muslims especially. The "pacifist" view rejecting war, he charged, "overlooks the nature of the threat and is thus irrelevant." Though conceding the role of US policies in fomenting hate, he felt that addressing the root causes of terrorism was a fruitless endeavor while its danger remained clear and present. Public criticism remained vital, if only to promote a kinder, gentler war. "The vigilance of an active citizenry" would ensure that the US assault would obey limits, making "true victory" possible.

Most striking was Falk's dismissal of an international law approach. His objections were many: that prosecution of bin Laden would be a "legal martyrdom"; that evidence for a conviction might not be available; and that the United States would be loath to consent to a court unwilling to exact the death penalty. It "strains the imagination," he said, to believe that the Bush administration would cede either security or justice to weak global institutions like the United Nations.

Falk found an unlikely comrade in Katha Pollitt, who had angered the prowar crowd. After attending a peace rally, Pollitt lit into the protesters for presenting no credible alternative to war. "Osama bin Laden," she scoffed, "is not likely to mail himself to the International Criminal Court."[62] Even the "peaceful" option of a police response would likely require armed action to apprehend terror suspects, complicating what it meant to be "antiwar." "Say for the sake of argument," she added, "that the 'chickens of American foreign policy are coming home to roost': You can see why many would answer, Well, so what? Why not just kill the chickens?"

Incredulous *Nation* readers took Falk to task: for giving up on international justice so easily; for bending to US unilateralism; and, as Howard Zinn remarked, for confusing "a just cause with a just war."[63] As the war in Afghanistan unfolded, Falk at first waivered.

The carpet bombings by B-52s deeply troubled him. "With each passing day," he wrote in early November, "the United States is waging an unjust war."[64] But a month later he judged the "overall undertaking" to be "reasonable." With the Taliban gone and al-Qaeda in disarray, the Bush administration deserved "credit for reaching its preliminary international goals."[65] This success "permits, even mandates, a provisional endorsement of recourse to war."

Falk's thinking is a powerful window into why opposition to the Afghanistan war was at first so small. Prior to 9/11, a great range of Americans were primed to oppose US wars. Among them were veterans of the anti–Vietnam War movement; people active in antinuclear weapons and Central American solidarity campaigns in the 1980s; and staunch pacifists, leftists, libertarians, and isolationists. Yet only a fraction of these groups spoke out against—or even privately opposed—the assault on Afghanistan. Likely sharing some of Falk's views, countless war skeptics found a way make peace with war.

Yet there were weaknesses in Falk's positions, threatening his prowar stance. Believing that war can be bound by limits overlooked the tendency of war to intensify and to spread. Casting this faith as "utopian," one reader objected that Falk "invites the very excesses he warns against."[66] What constitutes "excess" was a perilous judgment call. Only by hard-hearted calculations could one see the killing of thousands of civilians as "reasonable" in the pursuit of US objectives.

A "limited war" stance also meant placing enormous trust in leaders seething with militaristic ambition. Their war aims were expansive, not narrow. Nor, for the Bush administration, did the diabolical nature of al-Qaeda's terrorism strengthen the need for US adherence to international law. To the contrary, it believed that this new kind of conflict made international law mostly irrelevant. Nor, finally, did the administration appear open to criticism. Its constant tack was righteous conviction and disdain at any effort to check its power. "No one at higher levels of government is willing to listen" to dissent, protested a *Nation* reader, making true "vigilance" impossible.

Most fragile was Falk's verdict—and the country's praise—of a job well done in Afghanistan. At his peak concern, Falk feared that the US bombing had, "created a sense of revulsion and distrust, as if the lessons of Vietnam had not been learned and we here in America would be in for a long and savage military campaign that would inflict great suffering on the Afghan people." Here he echoed the dire forecasts of the peace advocates he otherwise dismissed. Time would tell how warranted their pessimism was.

CHAPTER 3

"THE DOMINANT FRAME IS WAR"

The Birth of the Antiwar Movement

Washington, DC, in September 2001 was set to be the scene of the next great protest against global inequality. Instead, following 9/11, it became host to the first stirrings of a national antiwar movement.

Months earlier, activists had put out a call for demonstrations at the annual fall meetings of the World Bank and the International Monetary Fund (IMF). The weeklong gathering was to bring to the city foreign dignitaries and thousands of staff. The protests, known as the Mobilization for Global Justice (MGJ) and organized by a coalition of the same name, promised to attract many more. Fearful of the demonstrations, the World Bank/IMF moved their meetings to more secure locations and shortened them to just two days, September 29-30.[1]

The mobilization came on the heels of major demonstrations that were the hallmark of the "global justice movement." (Activists and the media also often called it the "antiglobalization movement.") The first was two years prior at the meeting of the World Trade Organization (WTO) in Seattle, Washington. Environmentalists, trade unionists, students, and antipoverty advocates came in the tens of thousands to protest. A militant faction shut down the WTO meetings with street blockades. Riot police turned downtown Seattle into an armed camp, attacking demonstrators in scenes reminiscent of the 1960s. Dubbed "The Battle of Seattle," the protest appeared to herald a new era in global politics.

As activists celebrated, the world's media, political and corporate leaders, and law enforcement sized up a movement that had seemed to appear overnight. In truth, it built on protests in the developing world against austerity policies dictated by wealthy nations and the institutions they commanded. After Seattle, the movement staged raucous demonstrations at World Bank/IMF meetings in Washington, DC, and in Prague; at a summit to negotiate the Free Trade Agreement of the Americas (FTAA) in Quebec City; and at a meeting of the G-8 in Genoa. Law enforcement escalated its response, turning the protests into combustible affairs. The S30 (September 30) convergence in Washington, as activists named it, promised to be no different.

"The maturing anti-globalization movement," organizers wrote on September 8, "is poised to make history."[2] They trumpeted the unprecedented involvement of organized labor and mainstream environmental groups. Some protesters planned elaborate disruptions, while police sought to erect miles of fencing to protect both the meetings and the White House. The whole spectacle would draw intense media attention and further spike debates about global inequality. "This opportunity," the organizers declared, "may not repeat itself."

Like so much else, 9/11 changed all that. After learning of the attacks, the MGJ canceled an afternoon press conference. A day later, the Ruckus Society suspended its Global Justice Action Camp in nearby Virginia out of "respect for the victims of this tragedy, their families, and this country."[3] On September 16, the MGJ canceled its mobilization.[4] The following day, the World Bank and IMF announced the postponement of their meetings.[5]

The halt to S30 actions did not mean the end of all protests that weekend. The vastly smaller mobilization split into three main efforts. Anarchists pressed on with a September 29 "anticapitalist" march, now with antiwar themes. It joined an antiwar rally organized by the newly formed Act Now to Stop War and End Racism, or ANSWER, with roots in the communist left. The next day saw a smaller march of traditional peace groups.

9/11 forced a turning point for the left, reversing a rare ascent. The chance to protest global inequality on such a scale did not come again. "Part of the devastation of 9/11," an organizer lamented, "was how quickly that whole movement collapsed."[6] At the same time, the retooled protests marked the birth of a national antiwar movement when it was unclear whether one would emerge. After the Washington rally, antiwar energies were unleashed in a new way.

The September demonstrations also signaled what the antiwar movement would become. Global justice forces went into retreat. ANSWER was the first major antiwar group out of the gate, holding large demonstrations within a hard-left politics. Its emergence revived long-standing tensions on the left. Leery of ANSWER, other antiwar forces organized rival groups and protests. Unity was the watchword. Division was the reality.

ANOTHER WORLD IS POSSIBLE

Covering the WTO demonstrations in Seattle as a journalist, L. A. Kauffman was drawn to the protest scene she saw there. After Seattle, she immersed herself in global justice work, later joining the September 2001 mobilization. "People were talking about capitalism in a way that they simply had not," while "finding fresh ways to communicate about structures of power."[7] From its confrontational tactics to its "carnival exuberance," the movement also had an "audacity" that broke with the "tired language" of a "socialist left" that had grown "stodgy."

Kauffman was a bridge between eras and movements. Born in 1964, she came of age in a Wisconsin cradle of the Reagan Revolution. "The shadow of the '60s," with the storied radicalism of nearby Madison, draped her adolescence. She became "the kind of geek" who obsessively read the 1970 feminist anthology *Sisterhood Is Powerful*. Without telling her Republican parents, she testified before the Wisconsin legislature against antiabortion laws.

Moving to New York City in the late 1980s, Kauffman found a new political home. ACT UP confronted the HIV/AIDS crisis with a life-and-death urgency and a bold aesthetic. Local struggles, from the push for community gardens to support for low-wage workers, addressed inequities in a city whose affluent enjoyed a new Gilded Age. The global justice movement projected that critical spirit to world affairs.

A touch older than Kauffman, Nadine Bloch came to the movement through antinuclear and environmental activism. She protested nuclear-equipped Trident submarines, joined encampments near a Nevada nuclear test site, and, in 1987, went on a "peace walk" from Moscow to Leningrad. A lover of the ocean, she also worked with Greenpeace—best known for its daring confrontations at sea with offending governments and corporations.

With Greenpeace, Bloch helped train a new generation in direct action. When the group pulled away from its grassroots, she and other Greenpeace veterans formed the Ruckus Society. It became a key player in Seattle, offering its skill in protest tactics and democratic group process. Bloch jumped "whole hog" into global justice work, getting arrested in Seattle and landing a major role in the 2001 MGJ.

The movement sought, above all, to address the global wealth gap. Much of the world's poorer regions, dubbed the Global South, suffered staggering poverty. Wealthy countries prospered as never before. This was, protesters charged, the world's key divide, long concealed by a Cold War conflict framed in the West as a battle between freedom and tyranny. Activists assailed trade agreements disadvantaging vulnerable economies and multinational corporations competing to find the cheapest work force. Through their "structural adjustment" loans, the World Bank and IMF often worsened the poverty they claimed to alleviate, trapping poor countries in debt. The movement's great promise was to create a more just global order, captured in its slogan "Another World Is Possible."

The movement featured new coalitions and actors. The WTO protests drew together US workers and environmentalists—the fabled alliance of "Teamsters and turtles." NGOs brought expertise, resources, credibility, and paths to institutional reform. Religious groups and celebrities like U2's Bono championed debt relief. San Francisco's Global Exchange sponsored foreign travel, partnering with Global South organizations. The World Social Forum, founded in Brazil in January 2001, brought global justice forces together to share ideas and plan actions.

A new, youthful breed of activists drove the movement at its grassroots. In the United States, the way in for many had been the campus-based No Sweat campaign. It sought to expose the dismal conditions in the distant sweatshop factories of manufacturers of university gear, like Nike. Students Transforming and Resisting Corporations formed chapters on campuses nationwide to carry out global justice work. Naomi Klein's *No Logo* became an iconic text. It guided a Kulturkampf, swirling with anticorporate memes and hacks, against the great merchants of brand capitalism. Indymedia collectives formed to cover the movement, carried in zines, broadsides, and websites.

Global justice work bore the strong imprint of punk: anticorporate, antiauthoritarian, and DIY. This spirit informed everything from the handcrafted props at protests to bottom-up organizing. Loosely networked, the movement aspired to be leaderless, nonhierarchical, and radically democratic, with key decisions made by consensus in representative bodies known as "spokes councils." As the sum of all this, the movement embraced a "prefigurative politics" embodying the values of the liberated society to come.

It was also drawn to direct action. That meant confronting systems of power with creative, and often risky, protests. Direct action was a deliberate break with the passive demonstrations of recent years that gather people in public space in hope that the media would take notice. Disrupting the meetings of major institutions forced the media and authorities to reckon with protest. Direct-action tactics included blockades, occupations, banner drops, and, at the edges, property destruction.

Those joining the Black Bloc were the movement's militants. In a Black Bloc, dozens or even hundreds of people marched in thick formation, clad in combat boots and bandannas covering their faces. This gave them anonymity, some protection from police, and the ability to wreak mild havoc. To detractors, the Black Bloc was the menacing face of anarchism, bent on destruction. To participants, it was an exhilarating show of force, able to intimidate even police.

The movement also broke with an American protest culture that could be both depressing and shrill. Its protests had a festival atmosphere, with wild costumes, puppets, and drum circles. Seriousness and satire mixed, often to chide law enforcement for its heavy-handed response to nonviolent protest. In Quebec City, activists built a wooden medieval-style catapult to lob stuffed animals into the police perimeter garrisoning parts of the city.

With diversity came tension. Street confrontation elevated public interest. But too much militancy could alienate mainstream partners, turn off fellow activists, and discredit the larger protest effort. The challenge was to balance the respectable and the radical, popular appeal and provocation.

Nadine Bloch saw in global justice activism a power that the peace movement lacked. Peace protests, in her experience, were mostly small and inconsequential. But "when we do something that is actually threatening to capitalism," then people "really turn out," including the police.[8] Lisa Fithian, a fellow S30 organizer and direct action powerhouse, agreed. In the 1980s, she organized against US intervention in Latin America, led dramatic protests at the Pentagon, and later served as coordinator of the Washington Peace Center. Following work on successful labor campaigns, she embraced the global justice movement. "The state," after Vietnam, "learned to manage the playing field of war."[9] But it "had not learned yet how to deal with a movement going after its heart, which is capitalism."

The global justice movement harkened to past dissent, whether militant protests against the Vietnam War or the prefigurative politics of the antinuclear encampments of the 1970s. Reinvigorating those traditions for new times, it seemed to turn history's page. Today's protesters, Bloch joked, "were no longer vaguely reminiscent of the Sixties. We were now vaguely reminiscent of Seattle!"[10]

For the first time in years, the left drove major public debates. The World Bank and IMF were on the defensive, while key institutions echoed the movement's concerns. In 2000 the United Nations announced its Millennium Development Goals, meant to guide improvements in global health, education, and material well-being.

As it pushed toward a new peak with S30, the movement was also showing signs of strain. Protests at international summits risked becoming ends in themselves, reserved for activists able to trot the globe. The essay "Where Was the Color in Seattle?," first published in *ColorLines*, became an instant classic in the US movement, pointing to its uncomfortable domination by white people and poor attention to domestic issues of great interest to people of color.

The law enforcement response grew more sophisticated and severe. At the April 2000 protests of World Bank/IMF meetings, official attendees were secretly brought into the security perimeter before the proceedings began, thwarting plans to disrupt them. Police still made hundreds of arrests. At subsequent gatherings, protesters met fully militarized police forces, illegal arrests, and physical abuse. In Genoa, a protester was killed by police in a street confrontation.

A shift to domestic issues hardly eased the crackdown. In August 2000, global justice and antiracist activists joined forces in Philadelphia to protest the Republican National Convention, set to nominate George W. Bush for president. (The "prison-industrial-complex" and its underlying racism were chosen as major themes for the protests.) Infiltrated by law enforcement, the protesters were subject to mass, "preemptive" arrests, trumped-up charges, astronomical bail, and abusive treatment while in custody.

Despite all this, hopes for S30 ran high. The plan was for ten days of "activist training, large spokescouncil decision-making, educational and networking activities, a prayer vigil, and numerous legal and illegal demonstrations."[11] Twenty-nine organizations, including high-profile groups like Friends of the Earth and Public Citizen, sponsored parts of the program. Many more were informally involved. An elaborate structure coordinated the activities of organizations, working groups, and direct-action cells.

A major partner, the AFL-CIO, planned a two-day Protest Blitz in mid-September. It was to send organizers to union households to educate them about global issues and encourage attendance at the mobilization's main event: a massive, legal rally at the White House on September 30, followed by a march to the World Bank/IMF offices. Direct-action groups planned that same day to shut down the World Bank/IMF meetings by blockading parts of the city. Word also spread of an uncommonly large Black Bloc with rumored plans to take over an abandoned hospital.

MGJ leaders hoped to push the "rhetorical revolution" at the World Bank/IMF meetings stressing poverty reduction toward "meaningful change." More broadly, the protests sought to make inequality a newly urgent problem for the world's governments and leading institutions to address. To Kauffman's veteran eye, the mobilization's promise lay in the strong involvement of organized labor, extensive community outreach, and the tolerance of direct action by more mainstream groups.[12] By Bloch's guess, many thousands of protesters—far more than in Seattle—were willing to be arrested in likely the biggest civil-resistance action in US history.[13] The stage was set.

"ANOTHER WORLD IS NOT ONLY POSSIBLE, BUT MORE NECESSARY THAN EVER"

The 9/11 attacks came as a special shock to S30 organizers. The sense of horror was universal. The question also loomed: What to do with a mobilization months in the making, sure to attract controversy even in normal times?

Claire Bayard had spent weeks in Washington organizing with the MGJ. Also part of the Anti-Capitalist Convergence, she served as a bridge between the groups. "Will there be a crackdown today?" she and others worried, as "tanks and jets" descended on the city.[14] Her household of fellow activists was multiracial, though it contained no Arab Americans. Their immediate fear was being victim to a "second wave" of repression, given "who gets targeted most intensely" by law enforcement. Discussions soon turned to the fate of the mobilization.

Born in 1976, Bayard was part of a new generation of activists. Her father had served in the Vietnam War, emerging with "great disdain for the government." Both her parents were involved in Philadelphia's Quaker-influenced Movement for a Free Society. The Riot Grrrl subculture was big in Bayard's youth, pushing her toward "feminism and queer liberation." Her radicalization came after college during a long stay in Greece. There, she befriended a Palestinian woman who mentored her in world affairs.

Settling in the Bay Area, Bayard worked with Food Not Bombs—an anarchist group fighting militarism and poverty. The US bombing of Kosovo in 1999 hit her hard, given what she had learned about the Balkans while in Greece. In response, she did educational work about the conflict. To the WTO protests and then S30, Bayard brought experience organizing against local and global power structures.

The dilemma faced by S30 organizers was immense. Tens of thousands had planned to come, with some geared for major disruptions. Yet the nation's capital in the wake of 9/11 was a forbidding place for *any* protest. Those in Washington consulted with distant organizers over what to do, though the input was spotty. Small groups would have to make decisions for many others.

Geography played a major role in activists' views. Those in New York City were most shaken by 9/11. Their voices carried special weight. L. A. Kauffman remembers the "palpable" sense in the city that the attacks had been "a break in time." "Nothing was remotely back to normal."[15] In Washington, Bayard reports, "people weren't seeing the towers burning." Yet the city remained on edge, fearful of another attack. "You have no fucking clue what it feels like in New York and DC right now," she told California activists, still gung-ho on the protests.[16]

The MGJ coalition in Washington decided on the overall mobilization. Immediately, the coalition began to fracture. The AFL-CIO was the first to drop out.[17] Nearly 650 of its members, it feared, had died on 9/11. Its Protest Blitz became humanitarian relief, taking donations of blood and money. More coalition partners followed suit. Others waited for a major MGJ meeting before deciding.

On September 15, approximately 150 people attended a marathon meeting at a Washington church. Their decision was to cancel nearly all planned events. What remained was a People's Summit featuring educational work and an Interfaith Service for Justice and Restoration. The MGJ press statement cited "respect for the victims" of 9/11 as the main reason for its choice."[18] It closed by adapting the movement's slogan to newly perilous times: "We believe that another world is not only possible, but more necessary than ever."

Other concerns drove the decision: that the protests' message would be badly distorted; that law enforcement and the media would see them as a terrorist threat; and that attention to economic issues would distract from organizing against war. Post-9/11 travel restrictions threatened turnout. And people might still feel too stung by 9/11 to have any enthusiasm for risky street protest.

Political standing was a major consideration. Mainstream organizations like the AFL-CIO "withdrew to preserve their credibility with the general public."[19] To Bloch, they were "scared shitless" of being "perceived as un-American" and bleeding membership.[20] Their message at the meeting was "We'll let the peace movement take over" whatever could be salvaged of the protests. Bloch saw this stance as a "total fabrication" to mask their own loss of nerve. "I am of, by, and for the peace, movement," she fumed, "and we are nothing! You are selling us out!" Caution also gripped many younger activists. They were "in front of TVs, 24–7," absorbing messages about the need for national unity. Canceling the mobilization, Bloch and others argued, would deflate the movement at a moment of great promise and abandon issues no less important after 9/11. People had to "toughen up" and take "real risks," given what the Global South endures.

The Anti-Capitalist Convergence (ACC) mulled its portion of the protests. "Someone is going to get killed," many feared, if they went ahead with the intended disruptions.[21] After an emergency meeting, the ACC issued a new call to action.[22] It still welcomed protesters, but for a very different protest. The centerpiece was now an un-permitted Anti-Capitalist March Against Hate, Capitalism, and War on September 29. Confrontational actions were called off. They "would have been met with a much harsher police response," recalls an ACC organizer. And "no one would here [sic] anything other than 'These terrorists (the anarchists) are trying to weaken

America.'"[23] Even the new plan was too much for some, who stayed home. Other activists were "very angry at DC" for what seemed to them a weak-willed compromise.[24]

Back in New York City, Kauffman had designed a "masquerade project" for S30. Its goal was to deliver a thousand gas masks, decorated with glitter and rhinestones, to the protesters. The idea came to Kauffman as she watched police firing tear gas canisters at FTAA demonstrators, thrown back by "Black Bloc types." "How would it change the whole tableau if the front lines of resistance were dressed in pink ball gowns" and playful masks, "if we didn't replicate the aesthetic of militarism in our response to the militarized assaults on us?"[25]

Kauffman canceled a cheeky fashion show, scheduled for September 12, to debut the decorated gear. City officials soon put out a request for respiratory devices for use at Ground Zero. Kauffman spent hours tearing the sequins off the masks, which she took to Ground Zero to give to police (she doubts any were used). About S30, her circle agreed: "We were going to be staging a major confrontation with our government in the nation's capital, and self-evidently the timing was wrong."

Certain that 9/11 would be used "as a pretext" for a wide-ranging war, Kauffman began attending peace vigils. "No part of me," Bayard echoed, "felt dropping bombs on Afghanistan was either morally acceptable or strategically useful."[26] She learned of the war's start at a Midwest diner, while breaking from the long drive back to California.

"NOW THE DOMINANT FRAME IS WAR"

While the Mobilization for Global Justice was deciding its fate, the planning for another demonstration was underway: the National Student Day of Action for Peaceful Justice on September 20. One hundred and fifty or so campuses participated, making it the first nationwide peace protest since 9/11. Antiwar feeling was intergenerational, hardly confined to graying veterans of past campaigns.

The protests also showed the early influence of the global justice movement on antiwar activism.

The idea for the protests originated with students at Connecticut's Wesleyan University. Junior Sarah Noor was primed to play a leading role. Raised in Berkeley, California, her big leap into activism came in college, where she worked on local labor issues. In her first year, Global Exchange's Kevin Danaher barnstormed the campus, inviting students to "make history" at the WTO meetings in Seattle. The protests were "completely life-changing" for Noor. She felt the power of the massive crowd, a spirit of international solidarity, and the blinding sting of pepper spray fired by police. She began the new semester mobilizing students for S30.[27]

The 9/11 attacks stunned the Wesleyan campus, like campuses everywhere. Students, many with family in New York City, were in tears. Some at the strongly liberal school also expressed fear over the US response. At a campus vigil, a professor read Mark Twain's poem "The War Prayer." In it, a Christlike figure interrupts a prowar sermon to describe the grim reality of war. On September 14, Wesleyan's president told students, parents, and alumni, "In this time of crisis, we have an unusual opportunity to see past stereotypes, identify and diminish our own prejudices, and experience a complex world through the sensitivities of others."[28]

Noor "knew right away that there was a potential for highly destructive reactions" to 9/11.[29] Hurried meetings of like-minded classmates led to a national call to action and outreach to activists on other campuses. One was Hampshire College's Kai Newkirk in Amherst Massachusetts, who joined the organizing effort.

Newkirk was born in West Virginia to "back-to-the-land hippies."[30] He developed a strong "ecological consciousness," growing passionate about forest defense in the Pacific Northwest. Before college, he was part of a Volunteers for Peace program in Ghana, where he came to question traditional approaches to development. Also recruited to the WTO protests, he experienced in Seattle his "baptism into the power of mass nonviolent action." When back at Hampshire, he helped found the Western Mass Global Action

Coalition and became a local leader in Students Transforming and Resisting Corporations (STARC).

The rapid organizing for the antiwar protests drew on the networks of existing student groups, like STARC and Student Peace Action. They and others formed the National Student and Youth Peace Coalition (NSYPC). The protest call asked demonstrators "to mourn the devastating loss of life, to speak out against attacks now occurring because of ethnic and religious identity, and to raise our collective voices for peace."[31] Word of the protests spread on email through activist circles, with Noor fielding queries from domestic and global media.

The campus gatherings added to antiwar actions across the country. On Sunday, September 16, twelve hundred people rallied in Portland, Oregon.[32] That same day, a peace vigil in New York City drew several thousand, while smaller vigils dotted American cities and towns. In Wethersfield, Connecticut, Judy Keane, whose husband died in the World Trade Center, warned against military retaliation at a five-thousand-person prayer vigil near her home.[33]

The student actions on September 20 ranged from a few dozen protesters in places like Eastern Michigan University, to thousands at Boston-area colleges, to two thousand at UC Berkeley alone.[34] At Oberlin College, a student warned that "war created people like Osama bin Laden, and more war will create more people like him." An MIT professor told the campus rally that "the best way to begin a war on terrorism might be to look in the mirror."[35] The Wesleyan protest turned out 750 demonstrators in the college's small host city. Public views had not yet so deeply hardened. Even the Sicilian-Americans in the pizza shop where Noor worked cheered on the students. Inspired by the protests, Noor dedicated herself full time to antiwar work, becoming a NSYPC spokesperson.[36]

Media coverage of the protests captured core messages like "Justice Not Revenge," expressed on signs bearing Gandhi's slogan "An Eye for an Eye Will Leave the Whole World Blind." The press also reported on students' fears of a military draft, as well as prowar feelings on campus and some university administrators' disapproval of protest. The campus climate was toughest for Arab students, who feared backlash. Dozens suspended their studies, leaving for the safety of their home countries.[37]

Nine days later in Washington, DC, the crackdown was well underway. "Even though I've seen all this shit before," reported a participant in the September 29 march, "it was different today."[38] The swarming militants the Anti-Capitalist Convergence (ACC) once expected were now just a thousand or so demonstrators. Their march was to pass near the White House and then the World Bank Group headquarters, before joining an antiwar protest at Freedom Plaza. Hundreds of police in riot gear lined the marchers.

Things turned "extremely chaotic."[39] As protesters tried to run or push past police lines, they were met with water cannons and pepper spray. Street medics treated hundreds for exposure to the chemical. When the marchers reached the World Bank/IMF buildings, police surrounded them. For more than an hour, protesters, journalists, and even bewildered residents were penned in. The detention ended only after attorneys got an emergency injunction for their release. Police then escorted them to Freedom Plaza. "This is a peaceful, patriotic march and we're being treated like criminals," complained one demonstrator.[40] A dozen or so people were arrested, alleging police provocation.

Media coverage of the ACC march and larger fate of the S30 mobilization was scant. The progressive radio, internet, and cable TV program *Democracy Now!* captured the passion in streets but also how radicals strained to bring 9/11 into their protest. The march's lead banner read "Anti-Capitalists Against War Racism Terrorism Property" in a clunky chain of targets. Some marchers insisted that the War on Terror was only about "oil and power," not any concern with the country's safety.[41] Among mainstream media, *The Boston Globe* alone explored how 9/11 had impacted the global justice movement. 9/11, it concluded, left the movement in "tatters," evident in a frayed coalition and the sudden retreat from militant protest.[42]

Many in the movement agreed. Walden Bello, one of its intellectual leaders, likened 9/11 to a "deus ex machina" that "that swings a destiny in the balance in favour of one of the protagonists."[43] Eddie Yeun, who edited a book about the Battle of Seattle, was more blunt:

"The radical political space which had been opened up by the anti-globalization movement was instantly pulverized."[44] At the book's release party in March 2002, speakers called for solidarity with immigrants detained after 9/11. "Barely concealed in these pleas," reports activist Ben Shepard, "was a frustration that no one knew how to do much more than scream."[45] Global justice protests did not cease altogether. The following fall, demonstrations resumed at the World Bank/IMF meetings, with some fanfare and hundreds of arrests. "After months of 9/11 backlash," Shepard declared, "opposition is alive and well."[46] But 9/11 was a lasting setback.

How much transformative power the global justice movement had cannot be known. Domestically, it had begun to organize a new coalition to address America's growing wealth gap. With real success, it advanced a positive globalism promoting the exchange of culture and ideas and coordinated action against economic and environmental harm. By a great irony, its mission was to lessen the very inequalities and injustices seen by left-wing critics as terrorism's deepest roots. 9/11, and the climate it spawned, shut down this work.

In the short term, 9/11 all but knocked militant confrontation out of activism. "The anarchist movement," a Black Bloc member conceded, "took a big kick in the stomach."[47] Militants now had to contend with enhanced state security measures, breeding both paranoia and caution. They also faced the challenge of distinguishing their "actions from those of terrorists" in the public mind.[48] Direct action, for reasons of risk and optics, was scarcely a part of early antiwar protest.

Most broadly, 9/11 caused major shifts in perspective and energy. The global justice movement had declared the gap between the haves and have-nots as humanity's great divide. Powerful actors like the United Nations agreed. Following 9/11, Bush declared support or opposition to America's War on Terror as the world's great choice. Activists from myriad causes were now thrust toward antiwar protest. Russ Davis, head of a group active in the MGJ, described the entire, rapid evolution: "A growing frame in people's consciousness was global inequality, the global economy, corporate globalization. And within that frame we were gaining on them." 9/11 "just wrenched that frame, pulled the rug out from under the movement, and now the dominant frame is war."[49]

WAR IS NOT THE ANSWER

At noon on September 29, ANSWER's Larry Holmes kicked off the Rally Against War and Racism at Freedom Plaza. To a crowd of thousands, he intoned, "We reject the unimaginable act of terror that took so many lives on September 11. We nonetheless will not follow President Bush into a mad war against the people of Afghanistan [and] the Middle East. . . . We say no to more innocent victims . . . no to the racial profiling against our Arab sisters and brothers. . . . If there was ever a time when we need the right to come out and demonstrate and say 'No, no, no, do not kill people in our name,' we need it now!"[50]

Two dozen speakers followed, representing causes as diverse as immigrants' rights, Palestinian liberation, and health care reform. They included clergy, human rights attorneys, community organizers, students, an EMT who had been at Ground Zero, and professional revolutionaries. Ninety minutes in, exhausted marchers from the ACC demonstration arrived. After the speeches, the protesters marched to the US Capitol chanting "1-2-3-4, our grief is not a cry for war!"

The demonstration was like countless others before it: long speeches addressing a central issue from many points of view. But the protest was far from normal. It was remarkable that it was happening at all—in Washington, DC, so soon after 9/11, and before US retaliation had even begun. C-SPAN, the public affairs network, broadcast it live, boosting the demonstration's reputation as the first major antiwar protest.

C-SPAN's panning shots show a young, mostly white crowd. A survey by a social-movement scholar detailed just who showed up. All respondents were involved, whether as "activists" or "sympathizers," in one or more existing movements, like women's rights or the environment.[51] Many "were extremely educated," placing them "overwhelmingly towards the left pole of the political spectrum." They saw the protest "as part of a general struggle for justice." Its purpose, one protester declared, was to show "world media that many citizens oppose the manufactured war hysteria, blank check to the Pentagon, . . . [and] the savaging of social services and civil liberties at home." The first to take the unpopular stand of opposition to the War on Terror were already critics of the American state.

The speakers repeatedly praised those attending. "There are millions of people in this country who are guarding a secret," Holmes said. "They are opposed to a war, but they have been made to feel that they are all alone. . . . If they could see you, they would say, 'Oh my goodness, I'm not crazy!'"[52] The protest, another organizer felt, "gave a lot of confidence to people [to] step up and fight back."[53]

The rally also framed positions for a national movement that had so far appeared only in scattered commentary and small peace actions. Many speakers made the fiery charge that the United States was itself a sponsor of terrorism, backing authoritarian governments and brutal insurgencies throughout the world. While condemning the 9/11 attacks, the Palestinian activist Amer Jubran saw them as "a direct result of [US] policies in our region."

Speakers championed oppressed peoples everywhere. Reverend Graylan Hagler declared, "We stand with the people of the world who yearn for justice and peace and dignity and self-determination." Afghan women predicted that civilians "will be the main victims" in an "all-out war," and pleaded that the Afghan people have a say in their future. The antipoverty activist Cheri Honkala condemned the "economic terrorism" waged on the poor. "Let us bomb the world with food, housing, and employment," she implored. Everyone rallied around the message that "war is not the answer" to the threats America faced.

ANSWER touted the protest as a great success, claiming attendance of 20–25,000 people. (Police estimated 7,000.)[54] Media reports were hardly as enthusiastic. *The New York Times* ran a tiny story on the September 29 demonstrations, badly distorting the day's events.

Titled "Protesters in Washington Urge Peace with Terrorists," the article quoted former President Bill Clinton saying that al-Qaeda would not permit the right to protest enjoyed in America.[55]

The most damning stories came from other progressives. The left-leaning *Guardian* reported that "confusion, rather than fear, stalked the streets of Washington." "Whatever happens in this crisis, there will still be a hard core of indomitable peaceniks in the most improbable places."[56] In the *Los Angeles Times*, Marc Cooper declared the rally a "missed opportunity" at a "time when America needs an effective and mature political left."[57] The gathering seemed to him a "robotic rent-a-demonstration," with speakers suggesting that "America somehow invited" 9/11. "Demagogy," he warned, "can only render the left irrelevant."

Leftists, he felt, should accept the futility of "nonviolent moral suasion" as a response to al-Qaeda and instead support "limited military action." Like Richard Falk, Cooper was no trifling critic. He had served in Chile as translator for the socialist president Salvador Allende, whom the United States helped depose on September 11, 1973. (The coup has since been described as "the other 9/11," with the United States as its culprit.) Todd Gitlin, a 1960s student radical like Cooper, blasted the discomfort of some with patriotic symbols like the flag. So troubling was antiwar rhetoric that "many on the left—myself included—feel varying degrees of queasiness with this war, but still forswear anti-war rallies."[58]

Liza Featherstone, the youthful journalist covering protest for *The Nation*, was skeptical as well. Opponents of war "did their best to avoid the thorny question of how to fight terrorism without bombs."[59] To worries of widespread casualties, she glibly responded: "George Bush is not presently proposing to take any military action against innocent Afghan civilians." Featherstone also warned of the takeover of a budding movement by the far left. ANSWER, in her telling, was a "front group assembled by the International Action Center (IAC), in turn a front for . . . the Workers World Party, which is justly reviled for supporting [Serbia's] Slobodan Milošević, among other gruesome dictators."

"THE RACE IS ON"

Born on September 14, 2001, ANSWER was at once brand-new and deeply familiar. It advanced an anti-imperialist position long held by an energetic wing of the American left. Its rapid rise, and the resistance it met, show both the great passion and chronic conflicts coursing through left-wing politics.

ANSWER's name came directly from 9/11. Cofounder Brian Becker was in New York City that day, with friends in the Twin Towers. At a Union Square vigil days later, people were singing, "War is not the answer." Becker and others "turned that very soft mild chant, which is almost like a pacifist slogan, certainly not an anti-imperialist slogan" into an acronym: Act Now to Stop War and Racism, or ANSWER. Becker instantly knew that they had the message and the moniker.[60] He and a dozen or so left-wing groups began holding conference calls to plan an antiwar rally.

ANSWER's first goal was "to transform the September 29th demonstration into an antiwar demonstration," with or without the larger MGJ coalition.[61] "The only way to dispel war hysteria," he felt, "is to go against it." Already anticipating war beyond Afghanistan, ANSWER also sought to build a durable antiwar movement.

ANSWER quickly made its mark. The Washington protest featured professionally manufactured signs with its name and website, broadcast on TV. Most speakers were long-standing allies. Organizers drew on a network of IAC chapters to establish ANSWER groups nationwide. In many communities, ANSWER was the first organized face of the antiwar movement.

True to Featherstone's description, ANSWER was largely a new version of the IAC, connected to the Worker's World Party (WWP). The IAC's roots lay in opposition to the US invasion of Panama in 1989, which took out the Panamanian strongmen (and occasional CIA asset) Manuel Noriega. In this work, American radicals formed an improbable alliance with former US Attorney General Ramsey Clark.

Clark was the son of Tom C. Clark, himself an attorney general and then Supreme Court justice. While in the Justice Department, Ramsey helped draft the Civil Rights and Voting Rights Acts. He was appointed attorney general in 1967 under President Lyndon Johnson, just as anti–Vietnam War protest was escalating. After leaving government in 1968, he turned publicly against the war and embraced left-wing causes, like Palestinian liberation and opposition to the death penalty.

Clark traveled to North Vietnam in 1972 with the International Commission of Inquiry into US Crimes in Indochina. There began his signature activism: fact-finding missions in countries at war with the United States. "I believe in the goodness of the American people," he said in North Vietnam. When "they fully understand the truth, they will be grieved to the bottom of hearts" and never support "the bombing of innocent people again."[62]

In 1989, Clark visited Panama to investigate the impact of the US invasion. Becker and other WWP members approached him with the offer of research help.[63] Clark welcomed their assistance, no matter their communist beliefs, and invited them to work in his Manhattan law office. In August 1990, Iraq invaded Kuwait, just as they prepared to publish their findings on Panama. The Gulf War soon followed, deepening their relationship.

Soon after Iraq's invasion, the WWP formed the National Coalition to Stop US Intervention in the Middle East, run out of Clark's office. Prior to the US assault in January 1991, Clark met with Saddam Hussein in hopes of winning the release of Western hostages and averting war. Becker lead a second delegation, joined by Muhammad Ali. (As attorney general, Clark had prosecuted Ali for defying the military draft. The two later became friends.) Attracting international attention and the ire of the Bush administration, the trip brought back fifteen American hostages.[64]

Two weeks into the US bombing, nearly all Western journalists had fled Iraq. Undaunted, Clark toured the country. He witnessed civilian suffering and the destruction of industrial and religious sites, documented in his book *The Fire This Time: U.S. War Crimes in the Gulf*.[65] Drawing on Clark's work, the National Coalition held a war crimes tribunal in New York City, complete with eyewitness testimony. It symbolically convicted senior members of the Bush administration, including General Colin Powell.

Clark and WWP activists next joined forces to oppose the UN's economic sanctions against Iraq. Through the 1990s, Clark and other US activists made trips to Iraq to bring in medicine and other restricted supplies. "He was the most well-known American, besides Muhammad Ali, in the Middle East," Becker reports. "Wherever you went with Ramsey, people said, 'Ramsey Clark!' because he was considered pro-Arab."[66]

The IAC formed in 1993, with Clark as its president and Becker its first codirector. In the lean protest years of the 1990s, it gained a reputation for its strong anti-imperialist politics and controversial positions. Like much of the left, it opposed NATO's bombing of Yugoslavia. But it also backed the Serbian president, Slobodan Milošević, widely seen as a war criminal. Even so, the IAC's affiliation with Clark (who defended Milošević in international courts) and willingness to take physical and legal risks earned it a certain credibility within the broader left.

The WWP was the not-so-hidden hand behind the IAC, continuing a striking feature of the American left: the outsized influence of socialist and communist groups on national politics. Founded in 1919, the Communist Party USA was always a small, minority party, reviled by much of the country. What it lacked in size it made up for in its members' dedication, knowledge of world affairs, organizing skill, and commitment to both racial equality and civil liberties. Communists and socialists helped shape the New Deal, the trade union movement, the left-wing culture of the McCarthy era, First Amendment law, and the 1960s civil rights movement. In the decades since, groups of the "sectarian" left have been fixtures at protests—at the fringes selling newspapers, but also often as lead organizers.

Founded in 1959 from a split within the Socialist Workers Party, the WWP was for years pro-Soviet—a stance rejected by much of the US left. In the 1960s it gained greater appeal through its youth wing, Youth Against War and Fascism (YAWF). YAWF embraced Black Power struggles and was among the first US groups to strongly oppose Israel's treatment of the Palestinians. Though doctrinaire in its core beliefs, the WWP was open through its front groups to new political currents and strategic alliances with liberals and progressives. The IAC and ANSWER carried on that tradition.

Brian Becker embodies the remarkable journey to prominence of the radical left. Becker was born into a middle-class family in Rochester, New York. When he was eleven, Black rebellion rocked the city. Employed at Eastman Kodak, his father supported the integration of its workforce. The company "demonized" him as a result. Attending multiracial political meetings was part of Becker's youth.

Becker was suspended from high school for supporting Muhammad Ali's fight against the draft, and he quit school at age sixteen. He next worked in an Episcopal youth ministry seeking to integrate white working-class neighborhoods. He also protested the Vietnam War. His older brother Richard, later a WWP member, played him Phil Ochs's "Love Me, I'm a Liberal," which skewered liberals' weak commitment to their professed ideals. Becker broke further left.

During the 1971 Attica Prison uprising, Becker connected with YAWF, helping to bring inmates' families to vigils at the prison. He was with them when the police and military retook Attica, massacring prisoners. That sealed Becker's involvement with the WWP, beginning his rise in the organization and leadership within an influential pocket of the American left.

The IAC was an exception to the sectarian left's distance from the global justice movement. In it, the group saw "the possible reemergence of a militant, grassroots, radical movement."[67] In 2000, the IAC was part of the World Bank/IMF demonstrations in Washington, with Becker organizing a march on their first day. Police broke up the procession, holding protesters for hours on buses. They were released with the offer of a small fine. Becker, his teenaged son, and a handful of others insisted on proper arrests, subject to legal challenge. They were "hog-tied," wrist to ankle, and sent for rough nights in jail. Their lawsuit was settled a decade later, with $13 million going to seven hundred or so arrestees for their wrongful detention.[68]

The IAC helped anchor the S30 mobilization, mounting challenges to the proposed security fence and getting permits. Yet it had doubts about global justice organizing. Among the movement's "fatal flaws," Becker felt, was its consensus decision-making within officially leaderless structures. Some people remained in charge but "camouflaged" their power behind democratic principles.[69] In political terms, the IAC favored "a class-based approach" focused on how globalization drives down wages over the anarchist view that "evil institutions are creating a new form of world government."

Becker agreed that "9/11 was a turning point" for the US left. "The antiglobalization movement had to become an antiwar movement." Not all S30 organizers felt that way, at least when it came to backing ANSWER's rally. A major protest, some feared, would look like they were "demonstrating over the bodies" of the 9/11 dead. Even some in the IAC were hesitant. "Better to bend with the trees," they reasoned, "than to be broken by the wind." Becker disagreed. "Do you buck under the pressure, or are you a genuine opposition?"

Some organizers objected less to an antiwar protest than to who was leading it. Many MGJ partners thought that the IAC was "too undemocratic in its decision making and too controversial in its goals" to support the protest.[70] Hostility ran deep. "They had been toxic my entire political life," recalls L. A. Kauffman. "I remember the shrill rhetoric and the bad typography and the terrible politics."[71] The IAC, in Nadine Bloch's experience, had long bedeviled activism in Washington. "They didn't play well with others" and "usurped people's work" by claiming it as their own.

The MGJ struck a compromise. It would not endorse any antiwar action but encourage individuals to attend whichever event they wished. The great majority of the MGJ coalition stayed away from the ANSWER protest. Very few labor activists, in particular, attended. Other individuals, who had planned to go to the World Bank/IMF demonstrations, did participate.[72] From the start, global justice and antiwar protest meshed, despite the rifts among organizers.

Alternatives quickly emerged. The Washington Peace Center and American Friends Service Committee sponsored a rally and march, "Peace and Justice, Not War," on September 30. Bloch found it "incredibly beautiful and heartfelt," as thousands traveled "all over the city and into neighborhoods." The folk duo Emma's Revolution made the Washington debut of "Peace, Salaam, Shalom." Written in New York City just after 9/11, it became a staple at antiwar protests.

All over the country, opposition to war was building. On September 29, thousands rallied in San Francisco. Organizers were mindful of the nation's grief, anger, and frayed nerves. "None of that is going to fly now," said Reverend Cecil Williams of the "stopping traffic, flag-burning, love-ins" of past protests.[73] "There is no one who will talk about how the other side is 'good,'" reported Medea Benjamin of Global Exchange. The *San Francisco Chronicle* described the protest as "passionate but upbeat," with Aztec dances and "high-pitched Arab ululation" coming from the stage.[74] Speakers linked the current anti-Arab climate to the persecution of Japanese Americans following Pearl Harbor.

Dozens of peace actions took place on the last weekend in September.[75] In cities like Los Angeles and Denver, they were large events, with sponsors from major churches and human rights organizations. Smaller cities and towns—like Helena, Montana, Hudson, New York, and Medford, Oregon—held modest vigils and peace walks. Fremont/Hayward, California, home to the country's largest Afghan community, hosted "Women United for Peace." Organized by Global Exchange and the Afghan Women's Association International, it celebrated "our common humanity, through music, song, and poetry."[76]

The far-flung protests coalesced around core messages. Saint Louis organizers used the slogans "Our Grief Is Not a Cry for War" and "Let Us Not Commit the Evil We Deplore." Those in Durham, North Carolina, offered "War Is Not the Answer—Don't Kill More Innocent People" and "End US Policy That Breeds Terror" to frame their protest.[77] A shared movement language, facilitated by the rapidly growing internet, was taking shape. But the message was just the start. "The movement," wrote Seattle columnist Geov Parrish, "has to grow up, fast, pull together a wide variety of ideologies and perspectives, and figure out how it can have an impact in policymaking—all before the U.S. commits itself to a tremendous, irreversible mistake. The race is on."[78]

CHAPTER 4

"NOT IN OUR NAME"

From the War in Afghanistan to the War in Iraq

"The mementos of death are everywhere," wrote a journalist surveying New York City's Union Square just after 9/11. "But in this park," adorned with photographs and flowers, "mourning for the dead and missing mingles with yet another, more unusual sentiment: a call for peace."[1] The call started with simple signs bearing slogans like "Pray for Peace" and "Islam Is Not the Enemy" left at the park's main statue. Daily peace vigils soon blossomed. These made Union Square the first unofficial site for antiwar protest in the city. Blocks south in Washington Square Park, pro- and antiwar messages appeared on "democracy walls," forming elaborate citizen dialogues.[2]

A week after 9/11, one hundred or so people, clad in black and wearing respiratory masks, stood silent in Union Square. Each held a large printed placard reading "Our Grief Is Not a Cry for War." The slogan had been coined by Dred Scott at a meeting of fellow artists. With the vigil, they sought to call out national leaders for exploiting the city's sorrows.[3] An Associated Press photo of the protest zipped around the web, bringing the park's spirit to the world.

Much of the national response to 9/11 was framed as solidarity with the city and its residents. Some surely favored strong retaliation. Yet New Yorkers on the whole were among the most leery of military action. This stance owed in part to the city's robust peace community and progressive bent. (In the 2000 presidential elec-

Silent antiwar demonstration at New York City's Union Square, just days after the 9/11 attacks. Library of Congress, Prints & Photographs Division, Exit Art's "Reactions" Exhibition Collection LC-DIG-ppmsca-01701. Photograph by Jim Contanzo.

tion, Democrat Al Gore carried some boroughs by margins of eight to one.)[4] Pacifist groups like the War Resisters League and the Catholic Worker had their headquarters in Manhattan, as did prominent human rights organizations.

The city's trade unions had a long tradition of opposing US wars. Global institutions like the United Nations were part of the city's fabric, challenging narrowly nationalistic feelings. The roundup of Muslims and Arabs was felt as a blow to the city's proud diversity, prompting protests. Most important, the city's suffering led many New Yorkers to question what would be gained by making more victims half a world away. "It wasn't fucking true what [Bush] was saying," Dred Scott insisted, about "what literally millions of people in New York felt."[5]

The day the bombing of Afghanistan began, more than ten thousand people gathered in Union Square for a preplanned protest titled "New York: Not in Our Name." The speakers included three Nobel Peace Prize recipients; Daniel Berrigan, the radical Catholic priest and peace movement legend; Rita Lasar and Ruben Schaffer, who had lost family on 9/11; a City Council member; and advocates from the Arab American community.[6]

This city's first mass demonstration against the war in Afghanistan would be its last. Major combat quickly wound down, with the Bush administration claiming victory. The next large peace protest was in Central Park one year later. Thousands came to speak out against domestic repression, murky foreign detentions, and, above all, escalating threats against Iraq.

Mixing politics and public ritual, the crowd recited a "Pledge of Resistance." It ran:

> We believe that as people living
> In the United States it is our
> Responsibility to resist the injustices
> Done by our government in our names
> Not in our name
> Will you wage endless war . . .
> Will you invade countries
> Bomb civilians, kill more children . . .
> Not by our mouths
> Will we let fear silence us
> Not by our hearts
> Will we allow whole peoples
> Or countries to be deemed evil . . .
> We pledge to make common cause
> With the people of the world
> To bring about justice, freedom, and peace.
> Another world is possible and we pledge to make it real.[7]

The protest was organized by the Not in Our Name Project (NION), led by the NYC-based Revolutionary Communist Party. Dozens of other cities held Pledge actions, making NION an early force in the antiwar movement. The group also helped seal "Not in Our Name" as the era's defining antiwar slogan.

The October-to-October rallies were emblematic of antiwar protest in the first year after 9/11. It quickly came together, fell off in winter and spring, and rose to new heights in the fall of 2002. A progressive pundit, little aware of prior protest, praised in September "an anti-war movement that [has] seemingly materialized from thin air."[8] The race to stop the invasion of Afghanistan was all but lost before it began. The race to stop a war with Iraq was now on.

"RETALIATION WOULD MAKE SENSE"

The war in Afghanistan was difficult for Americans to follow, adding to the burden of its opponents. The desperately poor, combat-ravaged country had no US embassy and little Western presence. US bombs hit far-flung cities, largely out of range of press reports in real time. The United States armed and directed the Northern Alliance—a Taliban rival unknown to the American public, operating in a confusing terrain of ethnic, tribal, and religious rivalries. The fast-paced plotline consisted mostly of the capture of cities with exotic-sounding names, ending with the Taliban's fall in December 2001.

A major story was the capture of the twenty-year-old American John Walker Lindh. Lindh converted to Islam as a teenager in the Bay Area. He later traveled to Afghanistan, crossing paths with al-Qaeda. Lindh was pulled, badly wounded, from the rubble of Qala-i-jangi prison, where US bombers put down an uprising of Taliban captives. Branded "the American Taliban," Lindh became a turncoat villain, a perfect object for the country's wrath.

In Hamid Karzai, the war got its protagonist. Karzai was the Pashtun leader favored by the West to head a new Afghan government. He was embraced by Americans for his impeccable English, elegant native dress, and support for US policies. A view of the good guys defeating the bad was Americans' main image of the war.

Still, dissent persisted. Critics highlighted the hardship of refugees fleeing violence, allegations of Northern Alliance atrocities, and civilian casualties at US hands.[9] "The bombs must stop falling," pleaded an Afghan women's group at a Chicago event, or the country "will take generations to recover."[10] In late October, mainstream US Muslim organizations ended their cautious support of the war, calling on Bush to cease military action. "The senseless starvation of women and children," feared as winter approached, "will fuel hate and extremism."[11]

Antiwar voices were rare in the print media and almost nonexistent on television. *The New York Times*'s TV critic opined, "Most viewers, still aching over the attacks of Sept. 11 are in no mood to listen to views they dismiss as either loopy or treasonous."[12] "If you get on the wrong side of public opinion," CNN's president said, "you are going to get into trouble." MSNBC's head stated that "there was not enough dissent to warrant coverage."[13] Such claims worked as self-fulfilling prophecy. They discouraged the war's opponents from taking public action, reinforcing the illusion of a prowar consensus.

When the media did cover protests, it often stressed their "muddled message" and awkward use of Vietnam War–era slogans.[14] Congress was even more one-sided. Weeks into the Afghanistan campaign, a reporter observed, "There is virtually no criticism on Capitol Hill of the American war effort."[15]

Protest could be suspect and even dangerous. A Maryland peace vigil was nearly hit with gunfire.[16] In a Washington, DC–area high school, an Iranian American student was tormented for writing an antiwar piece in the school newspaper. A West Virginia teen was suspended for wearing a shirt that read, "When I saw the dead and dying Afghan children on TV, I felt a newly recovered sense of national security. God Bless America." Filing a lawsuit in protest, she received death threats and transferred from the school.[17]

National figures got into the act. In November 2002 Lynne Cheney, the wife of Vice President Dick Cheney and herself a conservative leader, issued a report titled "Defending Civilization." It declared, "College and university faculty have been the weakest link in America's response" to 9/11.[18] The report documented 117 instances of allegedly anti-American speech on campuses.

Some of the cherry-picked quotes were harsh. "The ultimate responsibility [for 9/11] lies with the rulers of this country," said a New York City professor.[19] "Anyone who can blow up the Pentagon gets my vote," said University of New Mexico classics professor Richard Berthold, who later apologized for the remark. But the great majority of offending comments simply argued the virtue of peace. "We offer this teach-in as an alternative to the cries of war and as an end to the cycle of continued global violence," said a North Carolina professor, earning a place on Cheney's list. Even the slogan "Our Grief Is Not a Cry for War," appearing on a poster in a New York City college, was flagged as anti-American.

For those in its crosshairs, the report was no small matter. Tim McCarthy was a graduate student tutor at Harvard, beloved for his passionate teaching. At a September rally he asked where Bush's war rhetoric might lead, making him number 32 on Cheney's list.[20] The morning it was published, he was flooded with interview requests from both conservative and left-wing media. McCarthy thought, "Oh fuck, I'm going to be fired." His spirits were lifted by a supportive phone message from Noam Chomsky, also on the list, and assurances from Harvard faculty that they had his back.

The rapid demise of the Taliban further muffled antiwar concern, even among progressives. Recording feel-good scenes of "men shaving unwanted beards" and "women casting off the tent-like burqas," Jonathan Schell concluded that "many people hated the Taliban far more than they hated the bombing."[21] Liza Featherstone praised the perseverance of antiwar students, while doubting their sense in opposing a war that liberated Afghan commoners.[22]

Among those persevering were students at Hampshire College. Shortly after the nationwide protests on September 20, Kai Newkirk began organizing Students for a Peaceful Response, spanning five schools in Massachusetts' Pioneer Valley.[23] Its platform opposed US military action and denounced anti-Arab and anti-Muslim violence in the United States. An ambitious idea took hold: to have Hampshire College cast an All-Community Vote on an antiwar resolution. The student-drafted resolution condemned the civilian deaths in Afghanistan, poor humanitarian relief, invasive security measures at home, and "racial, ethnic, and religious scapegoating." "We have no choice," it declared, "but to condemn the current 'War on Terror,' and demand that it not be expanded to Iraq or any other countries."[24]

On December 5, students, faculty, and staff passed the resolution in a landslide, making Hampshire the first college to officially oppose the country's new war. Newkirk called the vote a victory of "conscience and conviction."[25] A *New York Post* headline ran, "Kooky College Condemns War," while Fox News pundits demanded, "Bomb Hampshire College."[26]

Around the same time, progressive forces within New York City's trade unions weighed in. "September 11 has brought indescribable suffering" to "working people," began the founding statement of NYC Labor Against War (NYCLAW).[27] By its estimate, one thousand union members of "all colors, nationalities, and religions" died in the attacks. Yet it believed that "Bush's war is not the answer" to the threats America faced. The statement—signed at first by a half dozen presidents of union locals and more than 150 other union officers and rank-and-file members—hewed to the "justice, not vengeance" message of the antiwar movement. It also stressed the "heavy toll" of war borne by the working classes, who disproportionately served in the military and were most hurt by the diversion of resources from health care, education, and other investments in domestic needs. Ideologically challenging war, NYCLAW also challenged the whole image—promoted by the media and politicians alike—of the city's first responders and a larger "hardhat America" as the patriotic base of the War on Terror.

To Brian Becker, the myth of the just cause bedeviled opponents of the Afghanistan war. "Retaliation would make sense to the average person. 'They just killed thousands of Americans. We need to defend our country.' That's the argument of the War on Terror."[28] Convincing Americans that the war was served a "predatory imperial agenda"— indeed, that Afghanistan was just the start—was "very hard." For most American, it required "a leap of faith," alien to their worldview.

In much of the world, no such leap was required. From Western Europe to Asia, antiwar protests were larger than in the United States. Early into the bombing of Afghanistan, global publics turned against the war. This was true especially in the Middle East, where any goodwill toward America was always fragile.

Claims of a US victory were grossly premature. By late December, the US military feared that bin Laden had fled to Pakistan. Operation Anaconda, begun in March 2002, meant to mop up al-Qaeda and Taliban holdouts in a matter of days. Yet it failed to destroy an enemy more determined than the US military had expected.[29] Despite its battlefield losses, the Taliban were never defeated. Instead, they backed off to fight another day.

Unknown to the United States at the time, in December Taliban leaders held a "war council" in Peshawar, Pakistan, under the watchful eye of Pakistan's Inter-Services Intelligence (ISI).[30] The ISI had largely co-opted the Taliban, supporting its fleeting rule. Just as the Taliban was negotiating its surrender to the United States, the ISI counseled that it prepare for guerrilla war. Continued instability in Afghanistan served Pakistan's interests, even as Pakistan posed as a US ally against terrorism. The Taliban were soon back to wage a tenacious insurgency. Never able to define its mission in Afghanistan, the United States shifted its target. The same day that bin Laden escaped the country, Defense Secretary Donald Rumsfeld attended a Pentagon briefing on plans for war with Iraq.

Public interest in Afghanistan largely moved on. Antiwar groups like ANSWER changed focus, treating Afghanistan as a prelude to the next war. It fell to others to others to break through the media wall and public attitudes toward Afghanistan with a message of compassion and peace.

"I AM BEGGING YOU FOR THE SAKE OF HUMANITY"

On September 11, Kathy Kelly was thirty-seven days into a forty-day fast in Manhattan protesting sanctions against Iraq. Many of those days she spent on a milk crate across from the US Mission to the United Nations. The fast drew attention to civilian suffering Kelly had seen firsthand in Iraq. She was sometimes joined by Denis Halliday, the Irish former UN Humanitarian Coordinator of the Oil-for-Food program into which the sanctions had morphed. In 1998 he quit his post in protest, denouncing the sanctions as "genocide."[31]

During the 1991 Gulf War, Kelly had been part of an international peace team in Iraq. With others, she founded in 1995 Voices in the Wilderness, whose mission was to defy the UN-imposed sanctions by bringing aid into the country. A motto of sorts guided her efforts to help the victims of US violence: "If you smell burning flesh, you better get to where the fire is."[32] After 9/11, she joined American victims of terrorism in efforts to prevent more suffering.

Raised Irish Catholic in Chicago, Kelly came to her courage only gradually. Among early memories was her father saying that Martin Luther King Jr. "got what he deserved" when assaulted during a march in the city. She bristled at this view, but "could not imagine being somebody who spoke up beyond the dinner table." The Holocaust documentary *Night and Fog* had a big impact on Kelly. It convinced her to "never be the person who sits and watches" evil unfold, doing nothing to stop it.

Local organizers pushed Kelly toward work in Chicago's poor neighborhoods, where she felt most at home. She also fell in with the city's Catholic Worker community, which drew her toward activism and a new understanding of her faith.

Founded in 1933 in New York City by Dorothy Day, the Catholic Worker movement saw action in service of justice as the heart of Christ's teachings.[33] Catholic Workers houses formed nationwide to provide direct service to the poor. They also served as bases for organizing against militarism and war. The movement established a long legacy of nonviolent resistance, pronounced in the civil rights and antiwar struggles of the 1960s. Brothers Daniel and Philip Berrigan, famously arrested in 1968 for protests at a Maryland draft board office, became the great lodestars of that tradition. In the early 1980s, they and others began high-risk protests of nuclear weapons known as "plowshares actions," often drawing long sentences in federal prison.[34] Catholic Workers were also deeply involved in solidarity work in Central America, where churches largely backed the struggles of the poor.

In Chicago, Catholic Workers returning from the region described the effects of US violence. Kelly herself made trips to Nicaragua, where US-backed Contra armies sought to overthrow the elected socialist government. In Nicaragua, she learned to manage fears for her physical safety and bring comfort to civilian populations suffering war. In 1988–89 she spent a year in prison for breaching a restricted area and planting corn atop a nuclear missile silo.

When Western armies threated war with Iraq in 1991, she leaped at the chance to go.

After 9/11, Kelly and fellow Voices in the Wilderness members called off the UN protests, finishing their fast at a nearby church. The group committed to literal silence, as they "had no words" adequate to the tragedy. After three days they decided, "Our work is to prevent the next war," and began speaking out. Learning that the bombing of Afghanistan had begun, Kelly "wept and wept." "This war is not gonna end," she thought.

Voices was moved by the antiwar statements from the families of 9/11 victims, posting them to its website. Kelly and trusted ally Danny Muller came up with a plan to bring the statements from the Pentagon to New York City. Their idea was a "Walk for Healing and Peace" between the two locations, ideally joined by 9/11 families.

Around the same time, 9/11 peace families were finding one another. Among them was David Potorti, a marketing consultant in North Carolina who had lost his brother in the World Trade Center. In early October, he published a widely read piece on *Alternet*. Its refrain repeated the answer a Beltway journalist gave when asked whether anyone in Congress opposed the bombing of Afghanistan.[35] Her reply, "None that matter," cynically described for Potorti the lives destroyed by US policies: Iraqi children killed by sanctions, Afghan civilians, and even victims like his brother, who would have wanted no part of vengeance.

Potorti found Voices and offered to recruit victims' families for the peace walk, starting with the Amundsons.[36] Craig's wife, Amber Amundson, and brother Ryan decided to join. Ryan was motivated by his disgust with the official one-month memorial of 9/11. Bush and Rumsfeld "talked more about eliminating the evil doers" than they did the victims.[37]

For the journey, Voices converted a bus it had used to protest US policy in Iraq. The tours were named after Omran Harbi Jawait, an Iraqi boy killed in a US air strike. Colorfully painted with antiwar slogans and a giant dove, the "rainbow bus" was fitting for the post-9/11 trip. US aggression had jumped from Iraq to Afghanistan.

The trip began on October 25 with a visit to Arlington National

Amber Amundson, draped in the American flag, and David Potorti (to her left) on the Walk for Healing and Peace in New York City on December 1, 2002. Amber's husband, Craig Amundson, was in the Pentagon on 9/11. David's eldest brother, Jim Potorti, died in the World Trade Center. The two would soon help found September 11 Families for Peaceful Tomorrows. Photographer unknown; photograph from the September 11th Families for Peaceful Tomorrows Records, Swarthmore College Peace Collection.

Cemetery, where Craig Amundson was buried. Amber then personally delivered a letter to the White House. Addressed to Bush, it asked, "Could you please exclude Craig Scott Amundson from your list of victims used to justify further attacks? I do not want my children to grow up thinking that the reason so many people died following the September 11 attacks was because of their father's death. . . . I am begging you for the sake of humanity and my children to stop killing."[38] The same day, US troops in Afghanistan received a huge American flag sent to them from Ground Zero.

Voices and the 9/11 families drove north, parading for peace in Baltimore, Philadelphia, and Jersey City. Members of Veterans for Peace and Pax Christi joined them. The families carried "Not in Our Name" signs, along with tributes to their loved ones. "For the family members," Potorti wrote, "who had never really participated in public demonstrations, it was a whole new world."[39] Onlookers were variously supportive, bemused, and only rarely hostile. The last stop was in New York City. It included an emotional walk through Ground Zero, a service at the church where Voices had ended its fast after 9/11, and a press conference at Union Square.

The 9/11 families were grateful to Voices for organizing the journey and nurturing their dissent. A Voices member returned the appreciation. "I have had the privilege to stand in the presence of forgiveness in situations of incalculable loss and have been awed by its transformative power.... They, along with other families of victims of 9/11, have become a moral compass to the nation."[40]

On the trip, the families talked about forming an organization. One discussion took place at Baltimore's Jonah House, home to the Berrigans. The fledgling group was rapidly joining the American pacifist tradition. In New York City, they were met by Colleen Kelly, who had lost her brother on 9/11. At the storied White Horse Tavern they discussed how best to combine energies, drafting a statement on napkins. Read at the press conference, it asserted their "right to reject revenge" and to "bond with other innocent victims of terrorism and tragedy all over the world without being labeled unpatriotic."[41]

Colleen Kelly felt "a profound sense of gratitude at finding these people." Born in 1962, she was raised in a large, loving Irish Catholic family in Pennsylvania. Moving to New York City, she worked as a nurse during the HIV/AIDS crisis, participating in struggles for dignity and health care. She also connected with the city's Catholic left. Daniel Berrigan, who gave sermons at the shelters she served, baptized her son.

With three young children, Kelly tried to experience her brother's death as privately as possible.[42] The TV "went into a closet." She had little sense of the push for war and knew nothing of the antiwar statements of victims' families. "I can't believe that we're doing this to another country," she thought when the bombing of Afghanistan began. "It wasn't enough to mourn the loss of my brother. I had to act."

Kelly sent a letter to Detroit's pacifist bishop Thomas Gumbleton, asking that he read it at a conference of bishops. In it, she begged the church to "begin a discussion of the other way, Christ's way," which was the way of nonviolence. "I'm going to be very Catholic here," she said of her position. "Do not kill" is the commandment. "There's no exception." Her new calling was to be a messenger for peace. It was "a very powerful thing inside me."[43]

Unknown to most Americans, the peace families had profound meaning for the War on Terror. More than any other group, they challenged its very foundations. They insisted, above all, that their loved ones not be used to justify war. "Not in Our Name," communicated directly to the nation's leaders, was the rejection of war as just retribution, anchored in their personal loss.

In many cases, they were honoring the wishes of the dead, certain that they would have opposed war. But this confidence was not required. "I have no idea what my brother would want," Kelly confessed. "No one ever asked him, 'if you were murdered in the World Trade Center and there's war . . . '"[44] Kelly's parents were adamant that family members should be free "to honor Bill in their own way." (Inspired by his death, a son-in-law reenlisted in the Marines.) They could speak on behalf of their own values too.

The families' loss gave them a special status within both national discourse and the peace community. News organization barely covering antiwar protest published their letters and ran profiles on them. "He has earned the right to be heard," a reporter said about Orlando Rodriguez, the first family member to publicly oppose war.[45] In October, White House press secretary Ari Fleischer was asked what Bush thought of the peace families. He repeated Bush's belief that "the actions he has taken help save lives."[46] Though evasive, Fleischer had at least to say *something*.

The families' ultimate message was that they did not want others to suffer in the same way they had. Losing her husband, Judy Keane feared that war will "create more widows, more homeless, fatherless children."[47] This concern for civilian casualties turned the War on Terror on its head. The Bush administration argued that *because of the 9/11 deaths, there must be war.* The peace families answered that *because of those deaths, there must not be war.* "If you want to fight," Colleen Kelly said, "go to a big field and whoever wants to be a part of it, be a part of it, but leave civilians alone."[48]

"WARS ARE POOR CHISELS FOR CARVING OUT PEACEFUL TOMORROWS"

The families would soon see firsthand the suffering they had sought to prevent. In January 2002, a small group went to Afghanistan to connect with the civilian victims of US bombings. Once again they had a patron, Medea Benjamin. Intrepid like Kathy Kelly, Benjamin had cofounded Global Exchange in 1988, traveling the globe to promote human rights and economic justice. A savvy campaigner, Benjamin had a vision of what the Afghanistan trip could accomplish.

Born in 1952, Benjamin was a natural rebel, who chafed against her middle-class Jewish upbringing in Long Island.[49] In high school, she organized her classmates against the Vietnam War. One day her sister received from her boyfriend in Vietnam the dried ear of an enemy soldier, taken as a souvenir. Benjamin wondered about the life of the Vietnamese man and other victims of US violence. After a semester at Tufts University, Benjamin dropped out. "I wasn't gonna pay anybody to teach me. I was gonna travel around the world and learn." To celebrate her new freedom, she changed her name from Susan to Medea, a powerful figure in Greek mythology.

Benjamin saw up close the damage of US policies. She got a degree in public health, taking jobs with the UN and other global outfits. In Mozambique, she protested the pushing of baby formula, linked to health risks, by companies like Nestlé. She later disrupted a nutrition conference in Brazil, charging that "Nestlé kills babies." Brazilian authorities expelled her from the country.

The campaign succeeded, showing Benjamin the power of movements to create change. She next took on Nike, bringing Indonesian factory workers to Nike's flagship store, where they could not afford the products they made. Broadcast on national TV, the protest helped force Nike to end its worst labor practices. Most people, Benjamin learned, "are totally clueless about how little it sometimes takes to have an influence."

When 9/11 hit, Benjamin feared that "the U.S. response is going to be worse" than the terrorist attacks. "Transfixed" by news reports of "brilliant smart bombs" that "hit the right people," she knew that this image of the US air assault "was wrong." Benjamin's suspicions were well founded. Early in the bombing campaign, a correspondent for a major American newspaper wrote a story on the leveling of the village of Kama Ado, which claimed civilian lives. "By morning," she reports, "my story wasn't the same. Instead of leading with the news of the crushed village, the top of the story had Pentagon officials denying reports of the bombing."[50]

Intent to see for herself, Benjamin traveled with three other women to Afghanistan just weeks into the bombing. Unable to enter the country, they stayed in Peshawar, Pakistan, flooded by Afghan refugees. One stood out to her: a thirteen-year-old girl—the same age as her daughter, also on the trip—whose mother had been killed by a US bomb. The father had not talked for days, leaving the teenager to care for her siblings.

Among the Americans was the Bay Area's Marla Ruzicka, who had interned with Global Exchange. Just twenty-four years old, she had already traveled to Cuba, Palestine, and parts of Africa. Like Medea, she was a natural rebel. In middle school, she led her classmates in a walkout to protest the 1991 Gulf War. With Global Exchange, she passionately confronted corporate executives about their companies' misdeeds.

Ruzicka was deeply affected by the Afghan girl they met in Pakistan. When the other Americans left, she stayed behind, hitchhiking with journalists into Afghanistan. She quickly fell in love with the country and its people, devoting herself to understanding their experience of the war and helping to ease their loss.

When back in the United States, Benjamin held a press conference at the National Press Club in Washington, DC, to report on the trip. Only foreign press attended. "We are not the right spokespeople," she concluded, to tell the stories of Afghan victims. "I realized that there is one group of people that the U.S. press would listen to": families of the 9/11 dead.

While Benjamin was planning a second trip, another American was making her way to Afghanistan. Born in Kandahar in 1978, Masuda Sultan had moved to the United States at age five and settled in New York City. In July 2001 she went to her birthplace, for the first time since leaving, to connect with her roots.

After the US bombing began, Sultan decided to return to Afghanistan. With the award-winning filmmaker Jon Alpert she would make a documentary film to "bear witness" to unfolding events.[51] Traveling in late December, she found members of her family living as refugees in Pakistan. Her cousin and others told her the story of how their village near Kandahar, Chowkat-Karez, had been bombed by the Americans on the night of October 22. Terrified children ran from their homes, only to be gunned down by helicopter gunships. A third of the village's population was killed. Among them were nineteen members of Sultan's extended family. None had supported al-Qaeda or the Taliban.

Democracy Now! broadcast an interview via satellite phone with Sultan, still shaken, the day after she learned the horrifying story.[52] "It breaks your heart," she said, "to know that this is the collateral damage of war." Everyone in America "needs to know" what the Afghans have "gone through."

Reaching out to the 9/11 families, Benjamin at first got "'Are you crazy?' kinds of responses." "I'm dealing with the loss of my husband and you expect me to go to Afghanistan?" She then talked to Rita Lasar, whose brother died on 9/11. Age seventy, Lasar was a Jewish, secular, tough-minded New Yorker with a raspy voice to match. She agreed to make the daring trip. Encouraged by a horoscope referencing a significant journey, she recruited others.

The trip got an added boost when *Democracy Now!* host Amy Goodman invited both Lasar and Masuda Sultan, freshly returned from Afghanistan, into the studio just as Lasar was set to leave.[53] The two women shared their stories of loss and their sympathy for one another. Lasar's great hope was to get more media interest in the plight of Afghan civilians.

Global Exchange handled the logistics and presswork for the trip, with Marla Ruzicka lining up meetings with aggrieved Afghans. Youthful, energetic, and free of self-importance, Ruzicka both charmed and confounded the foreign correspondents and humanitarian workers in the country.[54] Lacking the resources they had, she cajoled them for rides, money, and contacts. Helping Afghanistan's civilian victims became her consuming passion. She spent hours interviewing bereaved mothers, who shared tender memories of their slain children, and visited their destroyed homes. "Just being antiwar," she felt, "wasn't enough."[55]

The delegation left for Afghanistan on January 15, 2002. Joining Lasar and Benjamin were Derrill Bodley (father to the slain Deora), his stepdaughter Eva Rupp, and Colleen Campbell. As their plane landed, Benjamin saw a throng of journalists on the tarmac. At first she thought they were there to cover the historic visit of Secretary of State Colin Powell. The press was there for the families, rushing to the plane as it stopped.

On the drive into Kabul, Lasar saw a mosque destroyed by US bombs. Its twisted metal eerily evoked the remains of the World Trade Center tower where her brother had died. That image sealed her sense of purpose: "I was to be a witness to the sorrow, horror, and suffering of the innocent people who were being made to pay for the September 11 attacks."[56]

The Americans visited schools, orphanages, and hospitals, sharing their compassion and whatever encouragement they could muster. The Afghans they met were grateful for the removal of the Taliban but stung by the US assault. Parents who had lost their children tearfully greeted the visitors. Campbell felt "relief" in meeting people "who didn't look at you with the kind of scared, blank stare" she got in the United States.[57] The Afghans "knew what it felt like." "The children's eyes," Laser observed, "are big and brown and almond shaped and sad in a way that nobody in America can imagine."[58] "Every day we cried," recalls Benjamin.[59]

The trip gave rise to a specific goal: the creation of a fund for civilian victims of the US assault. The idea came from the despera-

Eva Rupp (left) from Washington, DC, and Derrill Bodley from Stockton, CA, both relatives of victims from the 9/11 terrorist attack, sing "You Are My Sunshine" on January 18, 2002, at an orphanage in Kabul, Afghanistan. Global Exchange's development associate Marla Ruzicka and cofounder Medea Benjamin join in the singing. Photo by Paula Bronstein / Getty Images.

tion of an Afghan mother whom Ruzicka had befriended. Harafa Ahmad's husband and several of her children had been killed by US bombs. Dressed in her burqa, she took a letter explaining her loss to the newly reopened US embassy. The guards told her that they "don't deal with beggars."[60]

Learning of the incident, Lasar was incensed. In response, the US delegation organized a march to the embassy. Lasar, Ahmad, and other Afghan victims were at the lead. The international press was invited, reporting on the tense encounter at the embassy gate. "I demand to meet with somebody!," Lasar said to the guards. "I'm a 9/11 family member, an American citizen!" Within days, Benjamin handed twelve civilian claims to the embassy's commanding Marine officer, who pledged to pass them on to higher-ups.[61]

Major Western media filed reports on the Americans' trip. "This was a unique story, one that went against the grain of conventional wisdom," explained David Potorti.[62] The press highlighted the emotional plight of the 9/11 families, while muting their antiwar stance. It also paid unprecedented attention to what concerned them most: Afghanistan's civilian victims.

The Americans returned from Afghanistan with a new sense of mission. Colleen Kelly drove the exhausted travelers from the New York City airport straight to Washington, DC, to lobby Congress for a victims fund.[63] Both Democrats and Republicans were receptive to the idea, which Hamid Karzai also supported.[64] Masuda Sultan helped lead the campaign. So too did Ruzicka.

In Afghanistan, Ruzicka assembled a team of Afghan researchers to conduct the first thorough survey of civilian losses. Starting in March 2002, the team toured hospitals and bombing sites and conducted interviews with families, humanitarian workers, and local political and religious leaders. They also compiled detailed information on the victims, their dependents, and their surviving family members' needs.

Humanizing the Afghans was key to the push for compensation. "You'd read those stories" about the 9/11 victims, Benjamin explained, "and you'd cry." "We thought we'd have to do the same thing for the people in Afghanistan. . . . What was their favorite food and music, what did their parents and relatives have to say about them?"[65]

Ruzicka also established in Kabul a small NGO called Civilian Innocent Victims in Conflict (CIVIC). Its creed, as Ruzicka saw it, was that "it doesn't matter if you are for against the war. Innocent civilians should not be harmed in conflict. And when they are you must investigate the case, and you must help them reconstruct their lives."[66] Some of her most important work was in Washington, where she pressed Congress for a victims fund. The Vermont Democratic Senator Patrick Leahy—a longtime advocate for civilian assistance in war zones—became her main ally. "It's not like this woman was fixed on saving the world," he said of Ruzicka. "She was fixed on saving individuals. There's a big difference."[67]

Through Leahy's staff, Ruzicka worked with both the State Department and military to develop a comprehensive assistance program for Afghanistan's civilians, distinct from ad hoc "condolence payments." It would include prosthetic limbs, other medical care, home reconstruction, and help to maintain or establish businesses. By the end of 2002, Congress had appropriated $10 million for the program—the first of its kind in the history of US wars.[68]

Following the Afghanistan trip, the next step for the 9/11 families was to form an organization: September 11th Families for Peaceful Tomorrows. The name came from Martin Luther King Jr.'s statement that "wars are poor chisels for carving out peaceful tomorrows." King used the line in a 1967 address, just after his famous speech at Riverside Church denouncing the Vietnam War.[69]

On Valentine's Day 2002, chosen for its theme of love, Peaceful Tomorrows announced its existence at a press conference.[70] The core group was now a dozen or so. The speakers described the group's mission, told their stories, promoted the victims fund, and displayed a letter to President Bush, pasted into a giant heart.

"It was the name of the group that immediately attracted me," recalls Anne Mulderry, who lost her son on 9/11.[71] "There isn't a word" in the press statement, "with which I don't agree." The group's website soon included a long list of media spots and speaking engagements with religious, university, and peace groups. The demand was enormous. Frank Brodhead attended the press conference to scout speakers for a local peace group, Concerned Families of Westchester.[72] He landed Lasar, who mesmerized the Westchester gathering with accounts of the Afghanistan trip. A movement was growing around the peace families, eager for their voice.

"WE WILL RESIST THE MACHINERY OF WAR"

Forming just weeks after Peaceful Tomorrows, Not in Our Name tapped into the unease and even anger many Americans felt as the War on Terror intensified. Its Pledge of Resistance anchored public demonstrations, while its Statement of Conscience rallied both public figures and everyday people.

On September 19, NION published a message in *The New York Times* that had been mostly absent from its pages. The full-page ad, designed by a Yale art professor and costing around $40,000, placed hundreds of signatures over the words "Not in Our Name." At the bottom, its statement read:

> Let it not be said that people in the United States did nothing when their government declared a war without limit and instituted stark new measures of repression. . . .
>
> The government now openly prepares to wage all-out war on Iraq—a country which has no connection to the horror of September 11. . . .
>
> Let us not allow the watching world today to despair of our silence and our failure to act. Instead, let the world hear our pledge: we will resist the machinery of war.[73]

The VIP signers were impressive. From entertainment: Laurie Anderson, Mos Def, Steve Earle, Jane Fonda, Danny Glover, and Tom Morello. From academia: Judith Butler, Noam Chomsky, Kimberley Crenshaw, bell hooks, Robin Kelly, and Howard Zinn. From the arts: Barbara Ehrenreich, Eve Ensler, Tony Kushner, Gore Vidal, and Alice Walker. From activism: Angela Davis, Ramsey Clark, Tom Hayden, and Medea Benjamin. Thousands of others, famous and not, endorsed the statement.[74]

Not in Our Name gave Americans a way to refuse being made ideological conscripts in the War on Terror. To back the pledge was to reject the idea that "you can't challenge the grief" of 9/11.[75] "Suddenly, the clarion bell of dissent was ringing again," declared a story on the protest ad.[76] "People were waiting for this," said an NION organizer.

Not in Our Name was mostly the creation of the Revolutionary Communist Party (RCP). It began with a March invitation in New York City to potential collaborators. The proposed launch would be "a day when an amazing breadth of people come out in a few key cities, including NYC, under the theme 'Not in Our Name.'"[77] Many liberals embraced the project, often unaware of its communist origins. Among those in the know, some saw duplicity. Others praised the group's inclusive message.

NION's success was both more and less remarkable given its

RCP origins. The RCP was a tiny organization, at the fringes of the left. Yet it had deeply committed organizers, with ties to communities of color, the labor movement, and the academic and entertainment worlds.

The RCP's own roots lay in the radicalism of the 1960s, when many young activists declared themselves Marxist revolutionaries. "Marxism-Leninism," Max Elbaum observed, "provided a worldview unmatched in scope, depth and revolutionary lineage. It revealed the structural roots of (and connections between) war, discrimination, [and] violence."[78] Yet bitter faction fights erupted over how to apply Marxism to the current world and unify a fractured left. Founded in 1975 from this scrum, the RCP reached a peak membership of a thousand or so. Following the conservatism of the Reagan years, the collapse of the Soviet Union was a further blow to American communism. The RCP survived, maintaining connections with noncommunist forces.

Debra Sweet, with the RCP since the 1970s, served as NION's national coordinator.[79] Born in 1951, she experienced—like Kathy Kelly and Benjamin—the civil rights movement and Vietnam War mostly as an adolescent. All had been independent-minded young women who embraced activism as a total commitment. Drawing on decades of experience, they became leaders in the post-9/11 antiwar movement.

Sweet was raised outside of Madison, Wisconsin. Though not political, her mother was dedicated to her church and shaped by the liberal culture of the nearby university. At age thirteen, Sweet saw Fannie Lou Hamer on television blasting the Democratic Party for locking the Mississippi freedom movement out of the presidential nominating convention. Soon after, she and her mother saw Hamer speak in Madison, inviting her home for the evening. Hamer grew close to the Sweet family, staying with them when touring the Midwest. Sweet was moved by Hamer's stories of oppression and resilience, which included surviving savage beatings for her voting-rights work. Instead of feeling "angry at the system," Hamer sought its redemption. As Sweet grew more radical, she felt "much less American" than Hamer.

A second moment of seeming destiny involved President Richard Nixon. In high school, Sweet organized a walk of three thousand students to raise money for global aid projects, winning the praise of the State Department. "No fucking way" was her reaction when invited by the White House, a month after the massacre of students at Kent State, to receive a Young American Medal. Convinced by her parents to attend, she was met at the White House by FBI head J. Edgar Hoover and hordes of media.

As Nixon approached Sweet with her medal, she softly said to him, "I find it hard to believe in your sincerity in giving the awards until you get us out of Vietnam." The encounter made the front page of *The New York Times*.[80] Friends heaped praise on her, while left-wing groups battled to recruit the young provocateur. Sweet dropped out of college to pursue politics full time. Her odyssey took her into inner-city organizing, factory work, battles for abortion rights, and support for liberation struggles worldwide.

"A juggernaut of war and repression is coming," Sweet thought on 9/11.[81] The detention of Arab and South Asian immigrants was an early sign. As to the war in Afghanistan, the RCP felt that part of the "ruling class" never forgave the US defeat in Vietnam and loss of Iran to revolution in 1979. Worse, the United States failed to assert itself as the world's sole superpower after the Soviet Union's collapse. The "neocons," as the country came to know Bush's war cabinet, were "chomping at the bit to carry out" a new bid for global power. 9/11 was the trigger for a push to control the oil-rich Middle East. After Afghanistan, Iraq was the next domino to fall, with Iran as the ultimate goal.

To succeed as a mass campaign, NION needed a broadly resonant message. For the Statement of Conscience, it enlisted Hollywood screenplay writer Jeremy Pikser. The pledge was drafted by spoken word artist Saul Williams. Both authors stressed Americans' *personal* responsibility to resist the War on Terror, which made victims of foreign peoples. "You had to go in on the moral question," explained Sweet.[82] Deeply internationalist, the materials stressed basic rights of sovereignty and the danger of unchecked US power. NION's logo was a picture of the globe.

Not in Our Name might appeal even to Americans who at first supported the war in Afghanistan but had grown troubled by US conduct. Civilian casualties continued to mount, with misguided bombs hitting large gatherings like weddings. On January 11, 2002, the first detainees were brought from Afghanistan to a newly erected prison camp at the US naval base in Guantánamo Bay, Cuba. The military released photos of caged men dressed in orange jumpsuits, hoods, and blackened goggles.[83]

In secret memoranda, the Bush administration asserted that the Geneva Conventions did not apply to these captives.[84] Rather than treating them as prisoners of war, the government designated them "enemy combatants"—an invented category meant to strip them of human rights and legal protections. In February, Center for Constitutional Rights president Michael Ratner and other attorneys filed habeas corpus petitions on behalf of three prisoners—two British and one Australian—challenging their detention.[85] These filings began grueling litigation that stepwise revealed the gross mistreatment of captives and Bush administration efforts to evade, or mangle, the law. "The dark side" of the War on Terror was becoming visible.

On the domestic front, worry grew over the USA PATRIOT Act, passed just six weeks after 9/11. The House voted 357–66 in favor. Only one senator, Wisconsin Democrat Russ Feingold, opposed the bill. Few legislators knew what was in the massive law, which greatly expanded the government's surveillance powers and authorized the indefinite detention of immigrants, even absent proof of any national security violation.[86] Critics warned that it gave law enforcement unprecedented access to private phone, banking, and internet data, inviting abuse.

NION's pledge and the statement steadily gathered signatures. Describing the War on Terror as also a "war of ideas," Sweet stressed the importance of support from "the intellectuals."[87] VIP signatures were both solicited and appeared unannounced.

Leslie Cagan, a veteran activist with Communist Party ties of her own, marveled at how quickly RCP-inspired groups gained prominent backers for their statements. Cagan considered the RCP among the most "narrow-thinking leftist organizations."[88] The first to sign were typically revered figures like Noam Chomsky and Howard Zinn, who freely supported countless petitions. "Other people say, okay, this is good, this is legitimate, and before you know it you've got 500 names. . . . People don't know that Not in Our Name is not really an organization. It's a project of the RCP."

Whatever its origins, NION brought together diverse communities. The big breakout was "ArtSpeaks! A Concert Against the War" put on by the NION-affiliated Artists Network of Refuse and Resist.[89] Held on May 12 in Hollywood, the sold-out event featured artists from the hip-hop, spoken word, Latin music, and jazz worlds. Among them were Boots Riley, Ozomatli, the Pan Afrikan People's Arkestra, and Dred Scott.[90]

Korean artist Ji Sung Kim rejected the death of her cousin on 9/11 as a justification for war. Saul Williams's masterful reading of the Pledge of Resistance was another highlight.[91] Broadcast by *Democracy Now!*, it gave NION a national profile.[92] The Palestinian American poet Suheir Hammad performed a piece written just after 9/11. Having a brother in the US Navy, the poem describes, did little to shield her from hateful taunts. "Laying out a personal perspective with passion and grace," the *Los Angeles Times* wrote, "the piece concludes with a statement worth ritualizing: 'You are either with life or against it. Affirm life.'"[93] The arts community had spoken, and the media took notice. The antiwar movement was inching into the mainstream.

It was also spreading, powered by local organizers. Ward Reilly was active with Veterans for Peace (VFP) in his hometown of Baton Rouge, Louisiana. He had served as a volunteer infantryman between 1971 and 1974.[94] Stationed in Germany, he joined his fellow soldiers in open revolt against the Vietnam War and the military itself. He became after his (honorable) discharge a fierce, public critic of US militarism. Away from home on 9/11, he wrote on hotel stationary by nightfall, "Today both World Trade Centers in N.Y. were destroyed. . . . An act of war that will give the military establishment the green light to go crazy."[95]

War with Iraq was just the kind of "crazy" he feared. As Bush's threats escalated, he worked with a newly formed group, the Coalition Against War in Iraq. It was made up of students and faculty from Louisiana State University (LSU), some VFP members, and plenty of citizen activists. From the spring of 2002 on, the group rallied every Friday at the federal building in Baton Rouge and on the LSU campus. Reilly worked as well with "Conscience, Concern, and Commitment," a New Orleans–based group that also held frequent protests.

On June 6, NION held "kick off" events for its campaign. Dozens took place, in large cities like Los Angeles and Atlanta but also in small communities in Florida and Wisconsin.[96] Most recited the pledge, described by a local activist as "a useful simplification that gets to the heart of what unites us."

The main event was in New York's Washington Square Park. Churches participated, as did Muslim groups, including the Council on American-Islamic Relations. Philip Berrigan gave a moving endorsement. Suffering cancer, he had been released from prison before finishing a thirty-month sentence for his last arrest action: hammering on A-10 Warthog planes, which used munitions with depleted uranium during the Gulf War.[97] Berrigan's statement urged, "Let us make this splendid pledge with all of our hearts. But let us also back our words with our bodies."

Speakers included Jeremy Glick, who had lost his father on 9/11; Syed Ali, a securities trader jailed for 105 days after being falsely accused of terrorist ties; and Lynne Stewart, the attorney recently indicted for improper communications with her client Omar Abdel-Rahman, convicted for the 1993 World Trade Center bombing. Not in Our Name got another boost when the British daily *Guardian* printed the full Statement of Conscience in a story about dissent in the United States.[98] The world too was learning that not all Americans supported the War on Terror.

"OUR WAR AGAINST TERROR IS ONLY BEGINNING"

The surge of antiwar protest was fueled, above all, by threats against Iraq. In his January 2002 State of the Union address, Bush named North Korea, Iran, and Iraq as an axis of evil, "arming to threaten the peace of the world."⁹⁹ Aiming his remarks squarely at Iraq, Bush announced: "We will work closely with our coalition to deny terrorists and their state sponsors the materials, technology, and expertise to make and deliver weapons of mass destruction. . . . [We] will not permit the world's most dangerous regimes to threaten us with the world's most destructive weapons." "Our war against terror," he declared, "is only beginning."

Reports of serious preparation for war first appeared in April. A *New York Times* headline bluntly ran "US Envisions Blueprint on Iraq Including Big Invasion Next Year."¹⁰⁰ Talk of Iraq heated up in the spring and reached a boil in late summer. On September 12, Bush made the case for war before the United Nations. Next was the push for congressional authorization, with a vote planned the week of October 7.

The central charge was that Iraq possessed, or had the means to develop, weapons of mass destruction (WMD). New in the public vocabulary, WMD could be biotoxins, chemical weapons for battlefield use, a radioactive "dirty bomb," or even a full-fledged nuclear device. A second accusation held that Iraq had ties to al-Qaeda, whom it allegedly trained in the use of WMD. Officials also suggested that Iraq had a role in 9/11 itself. The Bush administration claimed the right to attack Iraq *before* it could further develop or deploy WMD. This was the doctrine of "preemptive war," upending longstanding ideas about when a nation can lawfully act in self-defense.

Allegations came as statements of fact, delivered with steely confidence. Vice President Cheney told CNN in March 2002 that Hussein "is actively pursuing nuclear weapons."¹⁰¹ In August, he declared, "there is no doubt that Saddam Hussein now has weapons of mass destruction" and is "amassing them to use" against the United States.¹⁰² One storyline held that Iraq had tried to obtain uranium-laden "yellowcake" to create a dirty bomb. Cheney also repeated the false claim that 9/11 hijacker Mohammed Atta had met with an Iraqi intelligence officer prior to 9/11.¹⁰³

Iraq denied all the charges against it. Some US experts—notably Scott Ritter, a former UN weapons inspector in Iraq—said that Iraq no longer had WMD or the ability to produce them. Others, like Ritter's former boss David Kay, supported the administration's charges. An anxious public labored to follow the back-and-forth, with no sure means to judge who was right.

A credulous media reported administration claims, rarely performing research that might call them into question. Sometimes, the press directly fed government efforts to hype the threat. *The New York Times* ran a blockbuster story on September 8. It cited anonymous US officials insisting that Iraq had sought aluminum tubes "specially designed" to enrich uranium in mobile labs.[104] The officials warned that "the first sign of a 'smoking gun' may be a mushroom cloud." (The chilling phrase, it was later revealed, was a "carefully constructed piece of rhetoric" drafted by a White House speechwriter.)[105] That same day Cheney told *Meet the Press* that he had "absolute certainty" that Saddam "is using his procurement system" to "build nuclear weapons."[106] As evidence, Cheney cited the *Times*'s reporting.[107] Judith Miller, coauthor of the aluminum tube story, was a main conduit far false information about the Iraqi threat.

Few media stories asserted direct links between Iraq and 9/11. Yet the press ran countless pieces in which al-Qaeda, 9/11, terrorism, Iraq, and WMD swirled together, suggesting Iraq's central place in a shape-shifting threat.[108] Long after the Bush administration retracted the charge, a majority of Americans still believed that Iraq was involved in 9/11.[109]

Hostility between the United States and Iraq ran deep. Some in the foreign policy establishment regretted that the United States had not taken out Saddam during the 1991 Gulf War. Instead, it opted for "containment," achieved through economic sanctions and weapons inspections. Machinations on all sides caused this fragile arrangement to erode. For hotly disputed reasons, weapons inspectors were withdrawn from Iraq in 1998. The official US policy became "regime change," though little was done to pursue it.

Some in the Bush administration made removing Saddam a priority, with their voices growing after 9/11.[110] On September 11 itself, key officials suspected that Iraq had a major role in the attacks, despite all signs pointing to al-Qaeda. On September 12, President

Bush ordered counterterrorism personnel to search for "any shred" of evidence of Iraqi involvement.[111] No evidence was found, but powerful figures in the administration still wanted to go after Iraq. Bush made the decision to deal first with Afghanistan and leave Iraq for later. By December 2002, the Pentagon was secretly drafting plans to attack Iraq.

To back war with Iraq, the American people would need a compelling justification. To build support, the Bush administration wove Iraq into the War on Terror on the basis of the Iraqi regime's prior actions, which included the use of WMD against Iran and Iraqi Kurds. The thuggish Saddam was "evil," like bin Laden. The administration also cultivated intelligence sources to generate or verify its accusations. These included "Curveball," an Iraqi defector known by intelligence services to spread falsehoods. Another source was al-Qaeda's Ibn al-Shaykh al-Libi, captured in November 2001. Curveball invented stories about Iraqi WMD programs.[112] The Americans turned al-Libi over to Egyptian officials for torture. After his abuse, he falsely reported that Iraq had trained al-Qaeda in the use of chemical weapons.[113]

The administration also suppressed internal doubts about its allegations. Department of Energy experts strongly questioned whether Iraq's aluminum tubes were being used to create weapons. Yet Bush officials repeatedly cited the tubes as proof of Iraq's nuclear intentions.[114] In early 2002, former ambassador Joseph Wilson was tasked to investigate rumors of Iraq's efforts to purchase yellowcake uranium in Africa. The rumors, he determined, were false. Undeterred, Bush said in a major speech in October: "Facing clear evidence, we cannot wait for the final proof—the smoking gun—that could come in the form of a mushroom cloud."[115]

Believed by many Americans, the administration's claims were doubted by many others. War skeptics resented being bullied by a calculated politics of fear. There were the ominous statements playing to the ultimate worry of a nuclear explosion. There was also the "terror alert system," introduced by the Department of Homeland Security in early 2002, that issued color-coded threat levels based on unspecified criteria. Some also questioned the Bush administration's urgency in dealing with Iraq. If Iraq's WMD capability was the main issue, why not restart weapons inspections and see what they find?

NOT IN OUR NAME

NION's fall gatherings were part of a season of protest. More than a thousand peace actions took place in September alone.[116] By then, the Iraq Pledge of Resistance had thousands of signers. Organized by the American Friends Service Committee and the Fellowship of Reconciliation, it directed them, should the United States invade Iraq, "to engage in nonviolent civil disobedience."[117] To protest Bush's September 12 speech at the United Nations, activists floated helium balloons over the East River with a huge banner reading "Earth to Bush: No Iraq War!" A week later, Medea Benjamin and Diane Wilson disrupted Secretary Rumsfeld as he made the case for war to the House Armed Services Committee.

Benjamin had just returned from Iraq, touring without government minders. "How am I going to protect my children?" mothers asked her, fearing a US attack.[118] "When you have those kinds of connections," she reports, "you can be ferocious."

Benjamin had no idea until then that congressional hearings were even open to the public. "How many civilians will we kill? How many servicemen will we kill?" she thundered at Rumsfeld, with cameras rolling. She and Wilson yelled, "Inspections not war!" for a full minute before police removed them.[119] The disruption was a major story in US and world media.

Weeks earlier Benjamin had been arrested for confronting Bush during a California speech.[120] She also led early morning "Wake Up Call" protests outside the DC home of the Democratic minority leader Tom Daschle. The *SF Gate* called her the "Zelig of political protest," seemingly everywhere.[121]

The first anniversary of the 9/11 attacks brought both official remembrances and peace actions. Peaceful Tomorrows' Derrill Bodley attended the service in Shanksville, Pennsylvania, where his daughter had died. President Bush personally greeted the grieving families. Clasping his hand, Bodley begged Bush not to "go down the path of war" in Iraq.[122]

Colleen Kelley organized with local groups the Vigil for Peaceful Tomorrows in New York City's Washington Square Park.[123] The event spanned September 10 and 11, closing at 8:35 a.m., when the first plane had struck a year before. Speakers included Martin Luther King III, Kathy Kelly, Debbie Almontaser of the Muslim American Society, and Masuda Sultan. Talat Hamani, a Pakistani American new to Peaceful Tomorrows, also spoke. Though her son, a police cadet, died trying to save others, he was at first accused by the government of involvement in the attacks. The evening of September 11, thousands gathered on Brooklyn's scenic promenade for an interfaith vigil blending Muslim, Christian, and Jewish calls for peace.[124]

Soon after, Peaceful Tomorrows members toured the country promoting *Afghan Portraits of Grief: The Civilian/Innocent Victims of U.S. Bombing in Afghanistan*.[125] The sixteen-page report was based on the investigation into civilian casualties by Marla Ruzicka, Ahmad Hashimi, and Baz Mohammed. Sultan wrote the introduction. Global Exchange and Peaceful Tomorrows funded it.

The report contained a detailed breakdown of civilian casualties by province and recommendations for the US government, chiefly the creation of a victims fund. It also included profiles of fourteen Afghan victims, four of whom were under age ten. Complete with pictures and loving remembrances, these mirrored the feature "Portraits of Grief" that *The New York Times* published for the 9/11 dead. The hope was to stir similar sympathies for the Afghans. Peace groups and some church communities embraced the report. The US media largely ignored it, disappointing its creators.

Congress was a frequent focus as its vote on Iraq neared. Working with Representative Dennis Kucinich (D-OH), Peaceful Tomorrows held a press conference on Capitol Hill in late September, staying on for legislative visits.[126] On October 3, sixteen demonstrators were arrested in the Philadelphia office of Republican senator Rick Santorum.[127] Democrats, whether the ultraliberal Paul Wellstone (D-MN) or the hawkish Richard Gephardt (D-MO), were also hit with sit-ins. Bush administration officials still drew the biggest crowds, with three thousand rallying at Dick Cheney's DC-area home.

In advance of its October protests, NION ran the Statement of Conscience in more newspapers, distributed talking points for use nationwide, and posted additional endorsements. Writing on behalf of the newly formed Ground Zero for Peace, EMT Megan Bartlett announced:

> We, a group of 9/11 Ground Zero rescue workers,
> Take this pledge of nonviolent resistance—
> Because we feel we have a responsibility to those we could not save
> And to those who calls us heroes
> To do everything in our power to make sure that no one, ever again,
> Experiences such horror, here or abroad[128]

The protests on Sunday and Monday, October 6–7, were impressive for their size, breadth, and spirit.[129] San Francisco, Seattle, Los Angeles and Portland each turned out six to ten thousand people, with four thousand rallying in Chicago. In Seattle, "Mennonites mixed with anarchists" to oppose "a brewing war" in Iraq.[130] Representative James McDermott (D-WA), just returned from Iraq, was given a hero's welcome. While in Iraq, he had suggested that Bush might mislead Americans about the need for war, which had earned him condemnations back home.[131]

In San Francisco's Union Square, the veteran activist Starhawk led the mass recitation of the pledge. Musicians Bonnie Raitt and Boots Riley performed. A banner declaring "Our Grief Is Not a Cry for War" hung from the iconic Macy's sign atop the plaza. In Los Angeles, the Arab American radio legend Casey Kassem and actor Ed Asner lead the reading of the pledge. One thousand people rallied in smaller cities like Minneapolis and Santa Fe. Brattleboro, Vermont, nearly matched that. From Ames, Iowa, to Buffalo, New York, the demonstrations got local print and television coverage.

In New York City on October 6, up to twenty thousand people

gathered at Central Park's sloping East Meadow.[132] Speakers blasted the War on Terror and its threatened expansion to Iraq. A woman whose husband was imprisoned for nine months and then deported shared her harrowing story. A civil rights attorney angrily threw a copy of the PATRIOT ACT into the crowd, which promptly shredded it. 9/11 families spoke, as did Representative Cynthia McKinney (D-GA). Actor Martin Sheen, president on the television drama "The West Wing," performed Dr. King's "I Have a Dream" speech. Actors Susan Sarandon and Tim Robbins brought additional star power.[133] "Do we the people really want to be a new Rome that imposes its rule by the use of overwhelming force?" Sarandon asked.[134] The recitation of the pledge in fading sunlight was the moving capstone to the day.

Debra Sweet spent the afternoon pinned to the media station by teeming reporters.[135] Coverage was plentiful and positive. "Thousands Rally to Protest an Iraq War," ran the *New York Times* headline.[136] It quoted one activist delighted with how big the protest was compared with early rallies against the Vietnam War. It ended with another expressing disappointment that the protest had not been bigger. "Maybe something has to start before it can be stopped," she said.

The *San Francisco Chronicle* described the nationwide protests as a "rising rumble."[137] "Voices that were never mute became full throated, amplified by anger and apprehension over saber rattling against Saddam Hussein." Media stories also mentioned antiwar protest elsewhere: the passage of antiwar resolutions in Santa Cruz, California, and Ithaca, New York; the National Day of Student Action on October 7, turning out thousands; and the hundreds of thousands demonstrating in the United Kingdom, Italy, and Greece.

"The lively and youthful demonstration" in Central Park, wrote Featherstone, "was a beautiful sight."[138] It included people like herself who had been "ambivalent about, or supported, war in Afghanistan." She did not mention the RCP, instead praising NION as an alternative to ANSWER. Others were less reassured. *Salon*'s Michelle Goldberg warned of the "peace kooks" in the movement—the "extremist" IAC and now the RCP.[139] Yet her alarm was triggered by

NION's very success at reaching the mainstream. She described the pledge as a "beautifully written declaration of conscience whose sentiments would be shared by a great many liberals." The protest attracted "middle-class families, Muslim women from Brooklyn and Queens in headscarves and sneakers, wry upper West Side yuppies, downtown hipsters, rabbis and angry grandmothers."

Goldberg's worries revealed a great irony. Pacifists and Marxists were among the first to demonstrate against the War on Terror. The pacifists led with a moral critique of war, aware of the economic motives often driving it. The Marxists decried war as an instrument of empire, while attuned to its human cost. At first, their positions conflicted sharply with public sentiment. Their antiwar message gained broad appeal at precisely the point that the War on Terror wildly veered—just as they had predicted—beyond retribution for 9/11 and the defense against proven threats. The convictions of radicals helped shape the concerns of the mainstream.

"We took that pledge together," said one protester, "and we want that to have meaning."[140] For now, the pledge *was the resistance*. It also carried a vow of greater commitment, should the moment call for it. NION had helped carry a revived movement to new heights. Other forces, determined to bring it to far greater size and power, rose to meet the coming conflict.

CHAPTER 5

UNITING FOR PEACE AND JUSTICE

L. A. Kauffman spent the first anniversary of 9/11 at a writing retreat to finish a book about the history of direct-action protest. Sickened by the push for war in Iraq, she made the "very painful decision" to set aside the manuscript, perhaps forever, and "organize against the war instead." Kauffman soon took a key role with the newly formed United for Peace and Justice. It quickly became the country's leading antiwar coalition, pledging to hold a mammoth demonstration in February 2003 as part of a global day of protest. Kauffman worked tirelessly to make it happen.

Kauffman's commitment tracked with the growing intensity of the movement. From fall 2002 on, seasoned activists made life-altering decisions to oppose the war full time. Groups devoted to other causes joined the antiwar effort. New organizations formed, rallying women against war. The calendar filled with protests big and small, while Western delegations made trips to Iraq to plead for peace.

This was the most spirited and even important phase in the entire history of the anti–Iraq War movement, coming *before the war started*. Critics warned that a US invasion would be a political and moral disaster. The only true victory would be to prevent the war from happening at all. The burning question was how.

Part of the work was to make the case for peace. For months, whether the United States should attack Iraq seemed up for literal debate. Opponents flooded the public square with their arguments, clinging to faith in the power of persuasion. The work was institutional as well, with disappointment quickly coming. Despite intense lobbying, in early October Congress voted by a strong majority— 296–133 in the House and 77–23 in the Senate—to back the war. Its resolution authorized the president to use military force to "defend the national security of the United States against the continuing threat posed by Iraq" and enforce "relevant" UN resolutions.[1] The Democratic leaders of both chambers supported the resolution, as did key senators like Hillary Clinton, John Kerry, and Joe Biden. With Congress's vote sewn up, the movement mostly took its message to the Bush administration and the American people.

The challenge was also organizational. To become a major political force, the movement had to grow as big as possible, as quickly as possible. This required capable leaders, a compelling message, a big tent, and the resources of know-how and money. Competition stirred among rivals. The result was a major rift among national antiwar organizations, which struggled to maintain an uneasy alliance.

The presence of the past was profound. The country's historic conflict with Iraq propelled the new drive for war. It also created legacies of protest on which the antiwar movement could draw, and conflicts that the movement would repeat. All sides grappled with memories of the Vietnam War, so important to Americans' views of war and peace

"WE'VE KICKED THE VIETNAM SYNDROME ONCE AND FOR ALL"

The Bush administration presented war with Iraq as a necessary response to an urgent threat and a central part of its War on Terror. This was a doubtful frame. Direct retaliation for 9/11 did not apply. The claim of self-defense was based on unproven allegations about Iraq's capabilities and intent. 9/11, critics suspected, was the pretext for military action in Iraq, not its cause.

A rather old conflict, the 1991 Gulf War, was the foundation for the new one. Saddam Hussein had been a nemesis of George H. W. Bush, allegedly plotting to assassinate him in 1993. "This is the guy who tried to kill my dad," said the younger Bush in 2002, suggesting a filial motive for war.[2] More pressing were the geopolitical ambitions left unfulfilled by the Gulf War.

The trouble began when, on August 2, 1990, Iraq invaded Kuwait, citing a dispute over oil revenue. (Deeply in debt from its war with Iran, Iraq accused Kuwait of "slant drilling" into its territory to steal its oil.) The United States and Great Britain immediately condemned the invasion as an intolerable breach of the international order. The United Nations demanded that Iraq withdraw, imposing sanctions to force its hand. Over the next months, the United States sent more than half a million troops to Saudi Arabia, both to defend the oil kingdom and to prepare for an attack on Iraq. It also assembled a coalition of nearly forty countries, with European and Arab members committing troops of their own.

Saddam made for an easy target. He was caricature of a strongman, who wielded a rifle as he railed against Western enemies. His repression of fellow Iraqis, use of chemical weapons against Iran and Iraqi Kurds, and nuclear ambitions—loudly trumpeted by Bush Sr. as reasons for war—added a sinister edge to this image. Following the invasion, his regime took hundreds of Americans and other foreign nationals hostage in Kuwait and Iraq. To Saddam, they were bargaining chips. To Americans, they confirmed his villainy. The US government also alleged that Iraqi soldiers committed atrocities in Kuwait, like tearing babies from hospital incubators. (The story was a fabrication, promoted by the Kuwaiti government.)[3] Saddam, for his part, relished defying the West, which played well on the Arab street.

US-Iraqi relations were more complicated than this shared hostility suggests. Despite its official neutrality, the United States had backed Iraq in its war with Iran, doing nothing to prevent Iraq's use of chemical weapons. Donald Rumsfeld, while an envoy in the Reagan administration, repeatedly met with Saddam. Iraq served US interests as a bulwark against Iran, eager to assert its power in the region. Closer to the 1990 crisis, there was the communication to Saddam by US Ambassador April Glaspie just days before the invasion. She told him that the United States has "no opinion on your

Arab-Arab conflicts, such as your dispute with Kuwait." Publicized at the time, her words appeared to green-light Iraq's invasion.

This history begged the question of why the United States was now so determined to confront Iraq. One obvious answer was oil. Iraq's invasion of Kuwait threatened access to the vital commodity. The rapid decline of the Soviet Union—soon to collapse altogether—made US military action newly possible. With it came the chance to exorcise the demons of the Vietnam War. Among its legacies was the "Vietnam syndrome," which discouraged the country from full-scale military interventions.[4]

The Gulf crisis presented the United States with the opportunity to fight and win a popular war. The benefits went beyond repair to the national psyche and success at particular policy goals. "At stake," asserted Max Elbaum, "was Bush's fundamental strategy of relying on military power to secure U.S. hegemony in the 'New World Order.' It's not possible to be the world's policeman . . . if the ability to employ massive violence is checked by domestic political considerations. So this country's 20-year-old Vietnam syndrome had to be crushed as thoroughly as Saddam Hussein."[5]

The Vietnam War also shaped how a new war would be waged. Guiding the Iraq campaign was the Powell Doctrine, named after Colin Powell, then Chairman of the Joint Chiefs of Staff and a veteran of the Vietnam War. The doctrine laid out how major, post-Vietnam conflicts could avoid past mistakes. The key was to have a clear objective, domestic and international support, and an exit strategy.[6] The war itself was to use overwhelming force to annihilate the enemy and limit American casualties, so important to the public's response.

George H. W. Bush followed the Powell Doctrine with methodical efficiency. The official war aim was limited to restoring Kuwait's sovereignty. A November 1990 UN Security Council resolution set a January 15 deadline for Iraq's withdrawal, after which force was authorized by the global body. This timetable permitted the United States to assemble in Saudi Arabia the largest fighting force in human history. It also gave the administration months to condition the American people to the near-inevitability of war.

Domestic support was a sticking point. Much of the public, as well as some in Congress, questioned whether a distant quarrel between oil states was worth American sacrifice. An antiwar movement snapped into being. It included peace groups, military veterans and some active-duty personnel, organized labor, major churches, students, and community organizations, with strong representation of people of color. Its core charge was that Bush's public stand against Iraq's aggression masked the true, economic motive for war. "No Blood for Oil" was the movement's rallying cry, echoed by antiwar publics worldwide. Concern for civilian casualties, the diversion of resources from domestic needs, and the racial and class inequities in the volunteer army filled out the antiwar message.

The Vietnam syndrome weighed heavily on the antiwar movement as well. During Ronald Reagan's presidency (1980–1988), the United States largely used covert operations and proxy forces to wage its battles, in Latin America especially. But domestic pressure, playing to fears of "another Vietnam," held the line against a major military conflict. A generation of North American activists did often dangerous solidarity work in war-ravaged countries, defending socialist states and popular movements against US attack. War with Iraq would be a blow to years of antiwar efforts.

Within days of Iraq's invasion, the National Coalition to Stop U.S. Intervention in the Middle East formed. Founding it were many of the same people in the International Action Center who later formed ANSWER. It refused to openly condemn either Saddam or his invasion of Kuwait, keeping its focus on US policy. A second coalition quickly formed, the National Campaign for Peace in the Middle East. Led by traditional peace advocates, it was the forerunner to United for Peace and Justice. Condemning the invasion and Saddam's brutality, the Campaign sought broad appeal, including within the Democratic Party.

In October 1990, the two groups joined for a day of protest in scattered cities. But negotiations broke down over holding a joint demonstration in Washington, DC. From the split emerged separate rallies: one held by the Coalition on January 19, 1991, and another, a week later, held by the Campaign. "Bitter accusations flew back and forth," reports Elbaum, "along with widespread criticisms of both formations."[7] Much local organizing was unaffected by the conflict, and many activists attended both protests. But the split badly weakened the movement at a key phase in the US-Iraq crisis.

The conflict went to issues of ideology and approach. The Campaign condemned the invasion of Kuwait both on principle and as a way to gain credibility on the national stage. It also endorsed sanctions as an alternative to war. The Coalition took a hard line. The United States, in its view, had not just green-lighted but baited Iraq's invasion. To denounce Saddam was to excuse America's role in the orchestrated crisis. The truly pivotal issue, it felt, was sanctions. "Sanctions are war," it insisted, when they "deprive a country" of the means "to sustain civilian life."[8] Publicly opposing Iraqi's wrongdoing was a slippery slope, leaving no option but to endorse US coercion—including sanctions—as a just response.

The Coalition's position translated poorly in the public debate and rankled others in the movement. The Campaign accused the Coalition of coddling a repellant dictator, while offering no real alternative to war. Elbaum was long familiar with the view on the left that "anyone who's opposed to US imperialism, you say nothing bad about them." "But it was a big mistake," he felt, "to not tell the truth" about Iraq.[9] The Coalition, in turn, accused the Campaign of allying with the liberal wing of American empire.

Some protested the coming war with nonviolent direct action. In late December, eleven activists were arrested after jumping the White House fence.[10] Called the "Leap of Faith," the protest was the doing of Catholic pacifists, with some pouring their own blood or red dye into a White House fountain. Yet high-risk protests like this were rare. Overwhelmingly, the movement sought to shape public opinion through conventional displays of its size and strength.

The divisions within the movement turned out to be largely moot. On January 12, Congress authorized war by a narrow margin, with the planned demonstrations too late to directly influence the vote. On January 16, one day past the UN deadline, the United States began bombing Iraq. In response, Bay Area activists blockaded the Golden Gate Bridge, resulting in more than a thousand arrests.

Drawing tens of thousands, the Coalition's January 19 rally seethed with outrage. The crowd was notably diverse, with a strong presence of Arab Americans. Drawing perhaps a quarter million, the Campaign's protest stressed the patriotism of responsible dissent. "Conducted amid a blizzard of American flags," wrote *The New York Times*, it "seemed intent on conveying a mainstream message that Americans can best support their troops by stopping a war that is not in the nation's interest."[11] Even modest pleas for peace appeared futile. Once the war began, its popularity soared.

Behind the prowar surge lay a tension in the national memory of the Vietnam War. After the US defeat, the perception grew that the military had been sold out. Many on the right wrongly believed that antiwar protesters commonly demonized US soldiers. Some also held that the government, bowing to antiwar pressure, forced the military to fight "with one hand tied behind its back" by denying it the firepower to win. An opposite view—made by antiwar activists at the time and bolstered as damaged vets came home—was that "the individual soldier" was a "tragic figure," sacrificed in an immoral, unwinnable war.[12]

All sides in the debate over the Gulf War recognized the need to "support the troops." To the war's backers, that meant equipping the military for victory, while casting the opposition as anti-troop and anti-American. Symbols were important too. Yellow ribbons—displayed both in sympathy with the hostages in Iraq and to back the troops—were everywhere. The war's opponents argued that the troops were being set up for another betrayal. Truly supporting them meant bringing them home before a war started. When the bombs started falling, and US soldiers risked dying, the prowar position easily prevailed. Many in Congress turned on a dime. A leading Democrat declared, "The debate is behind us; the battle is upon us, and victory is before us."[13]

Weeks of bombing crushed Iraq. The ground war roared through Kuwait and into Iraq, lasting just a hundred hours.[14] Likely tens of thousands of Iraqi soldiers were killed, including in defenseless massacres while fleeing the battlefield. Perhaps a hundred thousand civilians died as a direct result of the American assault. US bombs hit roads, bridges, railroads, ports, power stations, medical facilities, water treatment plants, and industrial sites. More than four hundred Iraqis—including scores of women and children—were killed when US planes bombed Baghdad's Amariyah air-raid shelter. The US military claimed that it had credible grounds to believe that the facility housed military functions. Others allege a deliberate civilian massacre.

The attack on civilian infrastructure brought Iraqi society to heel, while inviting credible charges of war crimes. US combat deaths were minuscule at 148.[15] "The narrative of Desert Storm as Vietnam-done-right," declared a military historian "became all but irresistible."[16] President Bush announced, "By God, we've kicked the Vietnam syndrome once and for all."[17] In early June, crowds packed the Washington Mall for the National Victory Celebration, the country's biggest military parade since World War II. Saudi Arabia helped foot the bill. Two days later, US troops received a ticker-tape celebration in New York City's Canyon of Heroes. "Manhattan's gray financial district," *The New York Times* observed, "suddenly boomed into a dazzling holiday of music, marching, balloons and deliriously roaring crowds."[18]

The Gulf War had powerful lessons for the US state and antiwar forces alike. The Bush administration was well served by the Powell Doctrine. Patient diplomacy and congressional approval helped legitimize the war, while the lopsided victory assured its popularity. Yet the doctrine was far from binding. Unknown at the time, Bush told advisers that he would launch the war *even if* Congress voted against it.[19] The bid for support was, in part, for show.

The war also revealed the ease with which public opinion could be managed. The Pentagon asserted unprecedented control over a flag-waving media, requiring journalists to embed with the US military. It also touted its use of precision-guided "smart bombs," which purportedly spared Iraqi civilians. (The vast majority of ordnance dropped on Iraq was still by means of conventional "dumb bombs," though this garnered scant attention.) Americans ultimately needed little coaxing. The war tapped into a national hunger to feel again martial pride, organized around support for the troops.

For the antiwar movement, the lessons were bitter. Surging patriotism, often freighted with anti-Arab prejudice, proved an unstoppable force. The nation's near-exclusive focus on the risk to Americans made Iraqi suffering nearly irrelevant. Swift victory stymied both the movement's radical and moderate wings. With neither vindicated, they persisted side-by-side, to clash again as a new war loomed.

If the military victory was decisive, the war's geopolitical outcome was not. As the conflict was ending, Bush Sr. encouraged an uprising of Iraq's Shias and Kurds, assisted by the CIA. Yet the United States permitted Saddam to retain the use of helicopter gunships. These helped to crush the rebellion, claiming thousands of lives and destroying the rebels' trust in the Americans.[20]

The United States itself could have toppled Saddam but did not, partly at the urging of the Saudis. They were loath to see a fellow Sunni regime topple at the hand of a Saudi ally. The Americans had their own fears. "To occupy Iraq," Bush Sr. believed, "would shatter our coalition, turning the whole Arab world against us. . . . It would have taken us way beyond the imprimatur of international law . . . condemning [US soldiers] to fight in what would be an unwinnable urban guerrilla war."[21] The same words could have been said years later as a warning to his son.

US restraint also concealed an uncomfortable reality: that Saddam continued to serve US interests, especially with respect to Iran. Here the nature of the war was crucial to its aftermath. The deliberate crippling of Iraq's infrastructure made the country dependent on the West for its basic functioning. Highly restrictive sanctions—which regulated incoming resources like food, medicine, and machinery—were a means of geopolitical control. They were also a source of great suffering for Iraqis. Even vital civilian technologies were banned based on their alleged, dual use for military purposes, affecting everything from health care to sanitation.[22]

The establishment of no-fly zones for Iraq's air force, officially meant to protect vulnerable populations like Iraq's Kurds, gave the United States air supremacy over huge parts of the country. Bombing sorties, often hitting civilians, were a routine part of this arrangement. Infiltrated by US intelligence agencies, the UN-mandated weapons inspections were another source of control. Saddam was for America the "devil they knew," containable through a mix of soft and hard power.

Another legacy was the Gulf War Syndrome—a debilitating illness affecting hundreds of thousands of US veterans. Its possible origins include anti-chemical weapons agents meant to protect the soldiers, the depleted uranium in US weapons, chemical agents possessed by Iraq, and environmental hazards unleashed by the war. With no known cause or cure, the illness seemed a metaphor for the murky origins and perilous irresolution of the war itself.

Throughout the 1990s, small groups of Americans defied the sanctions. The International Action Center (IAC) and Voices in the Wilderness took the lead, organizing trips to Iraq to deliver medicine and other goods. These were the citizen experts, desperate to limit the suffering of Iraqis and draw attention to their plight. Aware of Saddam's role in his own people's misery, they faulted the US government for using civilian harm as leverage against him.

The Iraqi American Kadouri al-Kaysi had served as the interpreter on Ramsey Clark's trip to Iraq during the Gulf War. Back many times since on humanitarian missions, he described at a January 2002 press briefing how Iraq's system of free health care and education had been decimated by sanctions and bombings. Malnourished students with "no pencil, no textbook" worked on the streets to support their parents.[23] Visiting hospitals, Brian Becker reported, "was like walking into a nightmare," where mothers clung to "literally dying babies."[24] Bishop Thomas Gumbelton, himself a visitor to Iraq, described the sanctions as a "moral evil of immeasurable proportion."[25] Shortly after 9/11, Kathy Kelly toured the West Coast to report on the sanctions' toll, calling it "the best-kept secret in America."[26]

Art Laffin embodies the long arc of protest against US policy in Iraq. Arrested in the 1990 Leap of Faith, he participated in antisanctions demonstrations after the war's end.[27] In 1997, he and Kelly confronted Madeleine Albright during her confirmation hearing for secretary of state. The two demanded that she retract a statement she had made on *60 Minutes*, while she was the US ambassador to the United Nations, that the deaths of half a million Iraqi children from the sanctions were "worth it" to achieve US policy goals.[28] In 1998 Laffin went with Voices to Iraq, where he delivered a message of peace and repentance at the Amariyah shelter.[29] He spoke at the first ANSWER rally in September 2001 and became a fixture at protests against a new war with Iraq.

"Sanctions are war," declared an IAC broadside from the mid-1990s.[30] Many Iraqis agreed, believing that America's war against their country, started in 1991, had never ended. Another invasion would simply be its next chapter.

"THERE IS NO JUSTIFICATION FOR GOING TO WAR"

Millions of Americans, mostly unaware of this complex history, viscerally felt that a second invasion of Iraq would be unnecessary, risky, and wrong. As with the Gulf War, the Bush administration sought to secure domestic and international support for military action, while at least appearing to exhaust alternatives. This lengthy buildup also gave antiwar forces time to make their case.

Starting in mid-2002, antiwar pundits, intellectuals, and activists feverishly developed their positions. Global Exchange issued in summer its "Top Ten Reasons Not to Invade Iraq." Among them were:

- There is no justification for going to war
- Iraq does not pose a clear and present danger
- When it comes to invading Iraq, the U.S. has few allies
- An attack on Iraq would make us less safe
- Invading Iraq would be difficult—and without a clear victory
- A war would kill thousands of people
- We should not wage a war for oil
- Other options besides war are available[31]

The full statement noted that Iraq had no proven connection to 9/11, no verified WMD capability, and no seeming desire to initiate suicidal hostilities with the United States.

Richard Falk saw the looming conflict as a fateful expansion of the War on Terror. The Bush administration seemed "recklessly determined to wage a preemptive war against Iraq that is contrary to international law and morality."[32] Why, *The Nation*'s editors asked, should the United States abandon containment to take on the risk of mass casualties and a new quagmire. "Are we willing to deploy 100,000 or more American soldiers for ten or twenty years (at a cost of tens of billions of dollars a year) to defend a US-imposed government?"[33] As Congress's vote neared, they warned also of "a monster of unbalanced and unaccountable" executive power.[34]

The Bush administration, Jonathan Schell charged, "has claimed nothing less than a right and a duty of the United States to assert military dominance—a Pax Americana—over the entire earth."[35] His alarm was shared beyond the antiwar left. From the Senate floor, Senator Robert Byrd (D-WV) asked whether America was to be "a bully that is ready to go out at high noon with both guns blazing [and] wipe out other nations with a preemptive strike."[36]

The Middle East expert Stephen Zunes warned, "In addition to possible ongoing guerrilla action by Saddam Hussein's supporters, American occupation forces would likely be faced with competing armed factions among the Sunni Arab population, not to mention Kurdish and Shiite rebel groups seeking greater autonomy. This could lead the United States into a bloody counterinsurgency war. Without the support of other countries or the UN, a US invasion could leave American forces effectively alone attempting to enforce a peace amid the chaos of a post-Saddam Iraq."[37]

Tensions existed within the antiwar position. Some critics warned that a war would go badly. As in Vietnam, America's imperial ambitions would run aground, with death and destruction consuming all sides. To forestall war with Iraq was to prevent another episode of tragic folly.

Other critics feared that the United States might succeed in imposing its will. The danger was not so much another Vietnam as another Gulf War, this time toppling Saddam. By this forecast, the purpose of the antiwar movement was to defend Iraq and other nations from a new era of predatory American power. No sharp line divided these diverging perspectives. They might appear in separate speeches at the same rally or even in the same antiwar treatise. At the heart of the tension lay uncertainty as to just how powerful American power was.

Opponents of the war faced another, more complicated adversary in the "liberal hawks." Appearing everywhere in the media, these intellectuals accepted that America was an empire, echoing the left. But they reimagined the United States as an *empire of virtue* using force to spread freedom and democracy.

By now, Hitchens was a pro-Bush belligerent. More typical of the liberal hawks was Paul Berman, once a leading progressive journalist. During the Gulf War he was little moved by America's defense of international borders. Most important to him was the chance to slay a "totalitarian menace."[38] A second Iraq war might realize the thwarted potential of the first to liberate the Iraqi people from Saddam's tyranny. Writing in *The New York Times*, Michael Ignatieff also urged that the United States assume the full burdens of liberal empire and fight to free Iraq, not just disarm it.[39]

Journalist George Packer argued that there could be no *principled, liberal opposition* to war with Iraq because its essential aims were liberal; there could only be doubts about its chance of success.[40] He painted the war's opponents as naive "moralists," willing to condemn Iraqis to lifetimes of oppression.[41] War critics rejected these views as themselves dangerously naive. By idealizing America's motives, they felt, the liberal hawks offered moral cover to a military gambit driven by reckless ambition, not the desire to be liberators.

The ultimate prize in debates about war was Americans' hearts and minds. From late summer 2002 into the new year, between 57 and 68 percent of Americans favored "military action to force Saddam Hussein from power."[42] This support was highly conditional. It steadily dropped as pollsters increased the projections of US casualties.[43] Though most Americans believed Iraq had WMD, they wanted more evidence of the need for military action and greater efforts at diplomacy. They also favored international backing for war. In September, nearly 80 percent approved of a US attack if other countries joined the fight and the United Nations endorsed it.[44] Without such support, six in ten Americans opposed military action. In December 2002, with Congress's prowar vote in hand, a majority still insisted on international participation (52 percent) and UN authorization (58 percent).[45]

Given this mix of views, the case the Bush administration made for war mattered. In September, Cheney proclaimed that US soldiers would be "greeted as liberators," all but assuring the war's success.[46] The administration also doggedly sought UN authorization. The antiwar movement had an opportunity as well. Its repeated warnings of grave risk might spook a nervous public and even some politicians. The movement might also affect the attitudes of global institutions, so important to domestic opinion.

How much power the movement had to shape the actions of government remained uncertain. By the end of 2002, 87 percent of Americans—up from 71 percent in August—thought the country was "headed for war," regardless of what conditions were met. This sense of inevitability indicates widespread doubt as to whether, beyond a certain point, the looming conflict was even subject to genuine public deliberation. "If as fundamental a policy decision as whether to go to war," Zunes wrote, "cannot be influenced by the active input of an informed citizenry, what also may be at stake is nothing less than American democracy."[47]

CODE PINK

Exquisitely blending hope and desperation was Code Pink: Women for Peace. Its start came on November 17, 2002, when a few dozen activists began a vigil in Lafayette Park, across from the White House.[48] Called the Preemptive Strike for Peace, the vigil would last through the biting winter. It ended with a mass protest on March 8, International Women's Day. For four months, thousands of mostly women protesters took part. Media flocked to see the pink-clad vigil, especially when joined by antiwar celebrities. One protester, Diane Wilson, fasted for a grueling forty days.[49] "Determined to stop the Iraq War," said cofounder Medea Benjamin, "we threw our hearts and souls into the effort."[50]

Prominent groups like the National Organization of Women and Greenpeace joined the vigil. Visitors started chapters in their hometowns, as did women learning about the group online. They held vigils, fasts, and protests of touring Bush administration officials. Code Pink became a major force in an antiwar movement powerfully shaped by women.

The inspiration for Code Pink came in May 2002 when a small group of environmentalists calling themselves Unreasonable Women for the Earth met in California to discuss the climate crisis. "A reasonable woman conforms to the world, and unreasonable women lead the world forward" was their motto.[51] Over lunch, they ridiculed the government's terror threat warnings, marked as "code yellow," "code red," and so on. Talk turned to war with Iraq and how women might promote peace and a healthy planet.

The activist-astrologist Carolyn Casey proposed declaring a "code hot pink to save the Earth." The idea lay dormant until September when Jodie Evans, part of the May gathering and on a recent trip to Iraq with Benjamin, grew enraged at growing calls for war. She teamed up with Benjamin and Wilson, fresh from their disruption of Rumsfeld's testimony, for more protests in Washington. Learning that "code hot pink" was taken by a porn website, they shortened the title for their campaign to Code Pink.

On October 3, the women crashed the White House ceremony where Bush and congressional leaders were presenting language for the war resolution. When Wilson climbed atop a White House pole, throngs of media came from the Rose Garden. At the Capitol, they paraded shirtless with "Read My Tits. No War With Iraq" painted on their midriffs, again drawing press. ("Read my lips" was a Bush Sr. catchphrase.) That night, Evans "dreamed of thousands of women creating a beautiful camp of pink tents of music, dancing, knitting circles, joy, and laughter across the street from those beating the drums of war."[52] The idea for the vigil was born.

Evans had no thought when she came to Washington of starting an organization. But the idea of Code Pink clearly had power. When it became a group, its founders saw it as a one-off effort to prevent war with Iraq. Code Pink would endure for decades, addressing a broad range foreign and domestic policies. At its foundation was a view of the War on Terror as a massive, bipartisan project supported by a permanent war economy and a popular culture glorifying combat. It developed campaigns protesting the prison at Guantánamo, domestic repression, drone warfare, Israel's treatment of Palestinians, and the United States' close alliance with autocratic regimes like that in Saudi Arabia. Its telegenic disruptions were among the most recognizable scenes within post-9/11 protest.

Behind Code Pink's rapid rise and staying power were core principles reflecting the experiences of its founders. Jodie Evans's first great jolt of politics came in 1970 at age sixteen, when she worked as a maid in a Las Vegas hotel. The maids successfully fought for a living wage, proving that everyday people could win struggles for dignity and justice. "In that process, I found my power."[53] She became a lifelong activist, serving on the staff of the liberal California Governor Jerry Brown.

Gael Murphy was another Code Pink founder. She had, like Benjamin, a background in global health, fighting the overseas effects of US policies. Wilson had worked on shrimp boats in Texas.[54] Taking on polluting companies, she became a crusader for environmental justice, leading successful David-versus-Goliath campaigns. Starhawk, a celebrated author of spiritual works, brought an ecofeminist sensibility to the group. She also had extensive experience in nonviolent direct action as part of antinuclear and global justice struggles. Possessed of a can-do spirit, the founders were veterans of serious political work. Yet they insisted that Code Pink not be professional. A creature of the NGO world, Benjamin craved a "volunteer experience," with people motivated by their deepest values, not career goals.

The group sought direct connections with those most vulnerable to US violence. It repeatedly sent delegations to Afghanistan, Iraq, and other conflict zones. With women hosts especially, they shared their common humanity and wishes for peace. These bonds shaped Code Pink's advocacy and inspired its daring. During her famous disruptions of government officials, Benjamin often holds in mind a specific person she has met relevant to her protest. At the same time, Code Pink is careful not to confuse standing up for others with speaking for them. "It's my anger at what our government has done to them," Benjamin insists. "I'm giving my voice."[55] Code Pink also brought the victims of US policies to the United States to speak for themselves.

Seeking the biggest impact with the resources at hand was another of Code Pink's hallmarks. Oftentimes success simply meant attracting attention to their cause. Here the spectacle of disruption was key. So often, activists stage protests and invite the press to attend, with disappointing results. Far better, Code Pink discovered, was to go where the media is already present, such as government functions. The group's pink garb, clever signs, and mix of whimsy and defiance added to the power of its protests.

Code Pink, while open to men, harnessed the power of women in a gendered critique of war. Building on decades of women's antiwar organizing, its founding statement called on "mothers, grandmothers, sisters, and daughters, on workers, students, teachers, healers, artists, writers, singers, poets and every ordinary, outraged woman ready to be outrageous for peace. Women have been the guardians of life—not because we are more moral or purer or more innately nurturing than men, but because the men have busied themselves making war." Written by Starhawk, the statement was powerfully inclusive. It avoided defining women by any fixed nature, while promoting them as bearers of peace.

Benjamin has downplayed the group's feminism. "We'd never have created Code Pink," she suspects, if that first meeting had not been women. "It wasn't so much that we were these hardcore feminists that felt like women" needed to be "in the forefront." Instead, "male testosterone" was "going wild" at the time, making the "feminine voice important." "Women like hanging out with other women," she gleefully added, to explain the group's tight bond.

There was more to Code Pink's women-centered culture and political vision than that. The group built connections among women, while empowering them to be bold in their protest. It combined campy, gendered performances with the fierceness of its activism, striking a chord in the larger culture. "Code Pink," recalls one member, became "*the* tongue-in-cheek response" to the politics of fear promoted by the mostly male national security establishment.[56]

The group also provided a political home to a great variety of people: old-line feminists, seasoned in women's-based activism; older women, politically active in the 1960s but limited by the era's male-dominated protest culture; queer and gender-nonconforming people, who felt affirmed in the group; and more mainstream women, steeped in traditions of volunteerism and civic action. Soon, military wives and mothers, as well as female veterans, were drawn to the group.

Code Pink saw women as the predominant civilian voice, with a special stake in opposing war. This attitude tracked with the evolution of armed conflict. It increasingly killed fewer (mostly male) soldiers, while bringing greater harm to women and children. Just as Code Pink was forming, international women launched in Geneva the Global Peace Initiative, which explored gendered aspects of war.[57] Code Pink's wager was that women themselves, with robust and even unruly institutions, could meaningfully counter war.

Liza Featherstone described Code Pink as less an organization than a "phenomenon," atop a "rising tide of creative and memorable feminist antiwar activism."[58] That activism ranged from the Raging Grannies to the Missile Dick Chicks. The former were elderly women who, in fussy Victorian garb, scolded the male war makers. The latter were youthful artists dressed in red-white-and-blue outfits, with giant missiles attached to the groin. Adopting the personae of Texas debutantes and women of leisure, they performed as a sardonic, antiwar chorus line.[59] Closer to the mainstream were Women Against War from New York's Capital Region. Forming in fall 2002, they organized a months-long rolling fast and protests at the state house, attracting members new to activism.[60] Liberal and radical alike, women were energizing—and leading—the antiwar movement.

"A DEMONSTRATION OF SOMETHING BIG"

After 9/11, ANSWER organized the mass demonstrations that gave the antiwar opposition its greatest visibility. ANSWER's early vision of a national movement and skill at staging protests enabled it to draw large crowds. So too did Americans' growing antiwar feeling. Claire Bayard, back in California, where ANSWER was strong, saw its success as "less a sign of, oh, they're doing some great organizing, and more, wow, if ANSWER can be the vehicle through which tens of thousands of people are starting to come out, that means we have something brilliant."[61]

Mass demonstrations have a storied place within American dissent, including antiwar protest. Yet even during the anti–Vietnam War protests, many participants began to question their worth, given the redundancy of the "stop the war" message and the government's seeming indifference to them. In the decades since, the media and some activists have seen large protests as drab civic rituals, worthy of special attention only when turning out huge numbers. Still, ANSWER remained committed to them. "All the instruments of political control are firmly in the hands of the ruling political forces," explained Becker.[62] "The only way the opposition advertises its own capacity . . . is by a demonstration of something big."

Mass protests also served as touchstones for divisions among activists. The anti–Gulf War movement further divided over plans for a large-scale protest. The protests planned for April 2002 were a new flashpoint. The National Youth and Student Peace Coalition called for a demonstration in Washington, DC. The student group was aided by veteran organizers outside the ANSWER camp. ANSWER made its own call for a separate date in April, prompted in part by Israel's new, deadly incursion into Palestinian territories. "Free Palestine, No War on Iraq" was the protest's billing.

Palestine had long been both an important and vexing issue for the American left.[63] Going back to the Vietnam War, some activists argued that solidarity with Palestine must be a part of any comprehensive challenge to US foreign policy and to imperialism more broadly. Especially following the 1967 Arab-Israeli War, Black radicals in the United States strongly backed the Palestinian cause, in step with revolutionaries worldwide and a growing Arab American left. Others in the US antiwar movement and larger left insisted that Israel was not a conventional imperial oppressor and itself faced gross abuse on the world stage. Too much attention to the issue, they felt, diluted opposition to the Vietnam War and risked turning off American Jews, within and beyond the movement. In the decades since, virtually every US movement addressing foreign policy has grappled with the Arab-Israeli conflict.

For ANSWER, a just resolution to the conflict was both a moral imperative and a way to relieve the anger in the Arab world that helped fuel 9/11. "The issue now really is Palestine," Brian Becker felt, knowing how controversial it remained.[64] Peace groups had shunned ANSWER, he insisted, "because they said we were going to alienate the Democrats. Now they really didn't want to work with us!" Themselves pro-Palestine, many in those groups saw things differently. They felt that war with Iraq, threatened by the US government, should be the strong focus of the Washington protest. The compromise was to have separate demonstrations on the same day, April 20, followed by a joint march and rally.

ANSWER toured DC-area mosques and met with Arab and Muslim groups to build support for its protest. Israel's assault on the Palestinian city of Jenin in early April created a new, global wave of sympathy for the Palestinian cause. Attracting tens of thousands, the ANSWER demonstration was the largest pro-Palestinian gathering in US history. Featherstone recorded touching scenes of "women in headscarves, strollers in tow" marching "alongside pink-haired, pierced 19-year-olds."[65] "Today is a beautiful day," remarked a Palestinian American military veteran. The student-led protest, backed by the Muslim Student Association and the Black Radical Congress, had its own powerful diversity.

Tensions flared between the two camps. ANSWER members, Featherstone alleged, tried to bully a student organizer to greatly exaggerate the turnout to the press. She called ANSWER a "gang of liars" up to its usual tricks, even as she acknowledged its skill at "calling a rally on the right issue at the right time." ANSWER took great satisfaction that its Palestine-themed protest outdrew the more conventional antiwar demonstration. For the moment, a fragile peace within the movement still held.

In late June, ANSWER called for nationally coordinated, local protests on October 26. The focus would be Iraq. The pressure of events caused ANSWER in mid-September to change its plan to another mass demonstration in Washington. The Bush administration was giving increasing signals that the target date for war was sometime in late 2002 or early 2003. On September 7, the White House chief of staff was asked why the president had waited until fall to press for war with Iraq. "From a marketing point of view," he replied, "you don't introduce new products in August."[66]

ANSWER also got a firsthand sense of how close war was. In late August, Clark and Becker again went to Iraq. They learned of America's stepped-up bombing, conducted as a likely prelude to a massive assault. The Iraqis were wholly unprepared. Clark and Becker met with senior Iraqi officials, who insisted that Israel and "the Jews" are behind America's threats. "Look, the US is going to go to war against you guys," Becker shot back. "Half the antiwar movement is Jewish" anyhow.[67] "You should say you're an independent country" and "this is an unnecessary war." "If you have these ridiculous explanations [about Jews], that's just going to make you sound pitiful." Becker and Clark returned with a new sense of urgency.

Drawing up to a hundred thousand people, ANSWER's October 26, 2002, demonstration was a milestone for the movement. The anti–Vietnam War movement took until 1967, two years into major US military involvement, to turn out that many in a single protest.[68] The 2002 rally bore the hallmarks of ANSWER, starting with its militant antiwar stand and critique of US empire. Speakers pledged support for Palestine and the imprisoned Black radical Mumia Abu-Jamal.[69] "No Blood for Oil" was the main theme.

The demonstration also included more mainstream figures like Jesse Jackson, Representative Cynthia McKinney (D-GA), and Ben Cohen of Ben & Jerry's ice cream. "George Bush has put the interests of big business," Al Sharpton declared in his show-stopping speech, "over the interests of human life." The War on Terror had descended into a "bogeyman politics" that used contrived enemies to distract from pressing issues like health care and stagnant wages. Medea Benjamin led the crowd in chants of "Regime change begins at home!" The antiwar movement was rapidly becoming anti-Bush and anticorporate, allied with a progressive agenda.

"No Blood for Oil," Becker privately felt, "was a useful slogan because it showed people that there was a predatory imperial element" to US policy.[70] He doubted, however, that the threatened war was fundamentally about oil. Instead, the Bush administration—knowing precisely how weak Iraq was—went after Saddam "because it could." The Middle East still had nominally anticolonial regimes in resource-rich nation-states like Iraq, whose survival had been guaranteed by the Soviet Union. The priority for the neocons running Bush's foreign policy was now to "take out" the offending regimes and show, with the Soviet Union gone, that "America is boss." Rallying to Iraq's defense, ANSWER sought to limit US power.

With the October 26 demonstration, ANSWER pulled off a large-scale event that had both reasonable ideological breadth and a leading left-wing message. The show of unity went only so far. Prior to the demonstration, ANSWER had convened a meeting with major peace groups and congressional opponents of war. Only Representative McKinney, among the many invited legislators, showed up at the protest. "Gutless wonders" was Becker's view of the Democratic Party, including progressive leaders like Barbara Lee and Bernie Sanders.

Some in the liberal-left intelligentsia grew panicked, fearful that ANSWER's leadership would badly hurt the antiwar cause. "The moment," insisted Todd Gitlin, "cries out for a smart, extensive, inclusive popular movement."[71] Bundled with his concern were positions out of step with many in the movement. Gitlin blasted ANSWER's opposition to sanctions, ignoring their well-documented harm. The liberal journalist David Corn revealed that ANSWER speakers were often *really* Workers World Party members, duping fellow protesters in age-old communist fashion.[72] These attacks prompted Alexander

Perms for Permawar contingent at the October 26, 2002, antiwar protest in Washington, DC. L. A. Kauffman is the last figure in a wig on the right. Ben Shepard is holding the Bush "Obey" sign. Photographer unknown; photograph courtesy of L. A. Kauffman.

Cockburn, *The Nation*'s salty British socialist, to label Gitlin, Corn, and other liberals the "anti-anti-war movement."[73]

Still, many activists desperately sought an alternative to ANSWER. After 9/11, L. A. Kauffman had vowed never again "to go to an event sponsored by the Workers World Party" or its offshoots.[74] She still attended the October 26 protest because, "so many of us felt like we had to." Kauffman came with "Perms for Permawar," dressed in festive gowns and brightly colored beehive wigs. "Trying to hold ironic distance from ANSWER while standing up against the war" was "a tough dance." David McReynolds, head of the War Resisters League, said outright, "ANSWER's monopoly has to be broken, and it will be."[75]

Some in Washington were planning to do just that. Becker had approached peace movement stalwarts to help build for the October

26 protest but got "no takers."[76] "Big street demonstrations," they told him, are "passé." They preferred, he assumed, to lobby Congress. Instead, they were forming an antiwar coalition of their own.

UNITED FOR PEACE

The night before the October 26 demonstration, another important gathering took place in the nation's capital. Representatives of more than seventy organizations met in the offices of the Institute for Policy Studies (IPS).[77] There by invitation, the groups were intent to build a new organization with the power to stop a war with Iraq. "Nobody needed to have it explained to them," recalls a participant, "why we should have a broad and effective antiwar movement."[78]

These were the heavy hitters of the institutional left. Chairing the meeting were Bill Fletcher Jr., director of the TransAfrica Forum, and veteran organizer Leslie Cagan. Present also were leaders of the American Friends Service Committee (AFSC), Black Voices for Peace, the Central American Resource Center-LA (CARECEN), the Fellowship of Reconciliation, Global Exchange, MoveOn.org, the National Council of Churches, Peace Action, RootsAction, Women's Action for New Directions (WAND), and the United Methodists. New to this level of organizing, a representative from the National Student and Youth Peace Coalition was there too.

The meeting was interrupted by the devastating news that Minnesota Senator Paul Wellstone, beloved by progressives and staunchly antiwar, had died in a plane crash, along with his wife and daughter. Pushing through the emotion, the group established itself as a formal organization. It chose as its name United for Peace (UFP), taken from a website donated to it by Global Exchange. That evening, the group phoned ANSWER with word of its creation.[79]

UFP's formation seemed inevitable. But someone had to have the idea and work to pull it off. Holding its first conference call on September 2, the core group started with Fletcher, David Cortright, CARECEN's Angela Sanbrano, and Van Gosse.[80] It soon brought in Cagan, Darcy Scott Martin of WAND, Andrea Buffa of Global Exchange, Kevin Martin of Peace Action, and, from IPS, Phyllis Bennis and John Cavanaugh. Meeting at TransAfrica's offices on October 11, this cohort invited other groups to the larger meeting on October 25. Each new partner would bring "troops, money, smarts, and credibility."

Working as a coalition was all but a required for the rapid mobilization UFP sought. Full-on wars in the West had for years been rare, limiting the presence of standing peace organizations. The once-strong antinuclear movement had withered with the end of the Cold War. The country also lacked left-wing electoral political parties that could organize against war. More so than in other nations, antiwar mobilizations in the United States had to draw on the "resources from other movements typically not involved in peace politics."[81] True to this model, the bulk of groups forming UFP did not have peace as their main focus.

The seeds for UFP had been planted earlier still in conversations between longtime colleagues David Cortright and Van Gosse.[82] Cortright had led the antinuclear group SANE/Freeze, while Gosse had worked in its successor organization, Peace Action. Meeting by chance at the April 2002 demonstration in Washington, they were impressed with its energy but convinced that something bigger was needed to stave off war with Iraq.

Gosse proposed a "moratorium" modeled on the anti–Vietnam War Moratorium. A months-long effort of hundreds of organizations, it culminated in a single day of protest in October 1969. Up to three million Americans attended demonstrations nationwide. Gosse envisioned a similar campaign, cresting with peace actions in all fifty states.[83] Cortright favored a top-down approach in which ex-diplomats, foreign officials, religious figures, and everyday citizens would press US leaders for "sensible non-military alternatives" to war with Iraq.[84] Committed to the grassroots approach, Gosse reached out to trusted allies, like Bill Fletcher Jr.

The vision for UFP very much reflected the background and perspective of its main instigators. Born in 1957, Gosse had been shaped at a young age by the movements of the 1960s.[85] Splitting his youth between New York City and Lewisburg, Pennsylvania, he saw the broad reach of antiwar protest. In May 1975, he was among thousands celebrating in Central Park the final end to the war. "The Vietnamese people won," he marveled, proving that US power could be challenged. The American people, as the antiwar movement had shown, could challenge that power too.

In New York City, Gosse got involved in the campaigns of radical City Council members and national figures who challenged the Democratic Party from the left. His big leap into organizing was with the Committee in Support of the People of El Salvador (CISPES). Founded in 1980, and teaming with 1960s-era radicals, its main mission was to prevent a US war in El Salvador against leftist rebels. Its goals were practical, pursued by door-knocking, walkathons, demonstrations, civil disobedience, and lobbying. CISPES got millions of Americans to care about the tiny country and Congress to limit US aggression there, paving the way for a 1992 peace accord.

Bill Fletcher Jr. was a movement intellectual long involved in labor and antiracist organizing. He was instrumental in the formation of the Black Radical Congress (BRC) in June 1998. Made up of organizers, academics, community leaders, and youth activists, it sought to rally a "united front of the Black Left."[86] At first focused on domestic issues like mass incarceration, the BRC took an early stand against the War on Terror. Many BRC organizers worked with Black Voices for Peace. Fletcher was also the head of the TransAfrica Forum, a Washington-based research and advocacy organization representing the foreign policy interests of peoples of both Africa and the African diaspora. In the 1980s it played—as a prominent, Black-led organization—a singular role in the US movement to end South African apartheid. During Fletcher's tenure, it continued to promote international solidarity, while pushing US policies toward greater concern for human rights, equity, and justice. For Gosse and Fletcher—each with victories to claim—no sharp distinction existed between working within and against the system.

United For Peace was built on its founders' belief that it could stop the United States from waging war with Iraq.[87] Success required building a movement that reached into the mainstream. "As people in the US," Gosse explained, "we have an absolute obligation to the people of the world to restrain what our government does to them." That meant trying "to influence people in power, Democrats, Republicans, the media, Congress, possibly corporate leaders, military, Hollywood, popular culture."

This approach distinguished UFP from its movement rival. "ANSWER will never do that," Gosse insisted. He also saw ANSWER as a coalition in name only, whose member groups were mostly "extensions" of the Workers World Party.[88] ANSWER had a very different take on what separated the two groups. Their core positions on Iraq, Becker noted, were "actually the same: stop the war before it starts. [Our] slogan wasn't 'Long live the proletarian dictatorship!'"[89] He saw UFP's resistance to collaboration as a "response from organizations that felt they we were too left-wing."

To some progressives, even UFP was too far left. The evening of UFP's founding meeting, David Cortright and a handful of powerful groups like MoveOn privately met at a Washington restaurant to lay the groundwork for yet another coalition. In December, it announced itself as "Keep America Safe: Win Without War." "We are patriotic Americans," its founding statement declared, "who share the belief that Saddam Hussein cannot be allowed to possess weapons of mass destruction. We support rigorous UN weapons inspections to assure Iraq's effective disarmament. We believe that a preemptive military invasion of Iraq will harm American national interests [and] make us less, not more, secure."[90]

With religious and business organizations as its key members, Win Without War sought mainstream appeal and institutional clout. Its discreet origins and acceptance of Iraq as a national enemy irked some in UFP. "What the fuck are you trying to win?" was Cagan's view.[91] Even so, some organizations joined both coalitions and encouraged their cooperation. Multiple antiwar lanes had opened, creating friction but also robust options for opponents of war.

"A GROWING WAVE OF POPULAR DISSENT"

United for Peace saw an opportunity in the public's ambivalence toward a new war and even Congress's prowar vote. The majority of House Democrats and many senators had voted no. Ex-military and government officials cautioned against "another Vietnam." Antiwar Americans were speaking out. Properly shaped, antiwar dissent could become a potent force.

UFP's earliest work was internal. The founding body established an interim leadership group, with Fletcher, Cagan, and Buffa as co-chairs. Other members were balanced in terms of gender, geography, and issue focus. People of color, as a core commitment of the group, were strongly represented.[92] Among this inner circle were leaders from AFSC and the United Methodist Church, Bob Wing from *War Times*, and Reverend Graylan Hagler, a fixture in DC-area activism. Kai Newkirk, known for his organizing at Hampshire College, was the main student voice.

United for Peace also affirmed the decision to be a true coalition. By late November, around two hundred groups had signed on. The eclectic mix included established human rights, environmental, pacifist, religious, student, and antiracist organizations. Arab, Muslim, and Jewish groups were among them. New antiwar groups, like Peaceful Tomorrows, Not in Our Name, and Code Pink, also joined.[93]

UFP's first public-facing plan was for regional and local actions on December 10, International Human Rights Day. It also backed events in Washington, hosted by Black Voices for Peace, for Martin Luther King Jr. Day and peace gatherings in New York City.[94] The plan worked.

On December 10, more than 130 cities and towns held antiwar actions.[95] In Chicago, protesters picketed the Federal Building, with twenty arrested in the lobby. In New York City, nearly a hundred interfaith clergy were arrested for blocking an entrance to the United Nations. In Goshen, Indiana, Mennonites assembled relief packages for Iraq's poor, while Michigan college students lined a campus walkway with tombstones to represent civilian victims of war. Various gatherings offered words of tribute to Philip Berrigan, who had died of cancer on December 6.

Some protesters honored Berrigan with the kind of bold action he favored. On December 30, three members of the Catholic

Worker community—Steve Baggarly and Bill Streit from Norfolk, Virginia, and Steve Woolford from Raleigh, North Carolina—spilled human blood on pillars of the Pentagon. Their act was to protest the buildup of US troops in the Middle East. "War is a bloody business," Baggarly explained, "and an invasion of Iraq would be a bloodbath." "This is for you, Phil," they said as they threw the blood.[96] The three men, professing deep religious motivations, were convicted on misdemeanor charges and sentenced to six months in federal detention, all of which they served. Harsh by any standard, it was by far the longest sentence for any War on Terror protest to that point.

The major press acknowledged, as never before, a "growing wave of popular dissent."[97] *The Washington Post*, admitting that antiwar groups "operate largely without the attention of the media," printed a tender piece about Mothers Against War.[98] The group was the brainchild of Daphne Reed in Amherst, Massachusetts, worried for her grandson in the Coast Guard. *Time* magazine ran profiles of exemplary protesters like "the Debater," "the Convert," and "the Veteran," each with their own reasons for opposing war.

The media also noted growing institutional opposition to war. The AFL-CIO, the National Council of Churches, and the National Catholic Conference of Bishops, with combined memberships in the millions, all came out against an assault on Iraq. "Union people are the most patriotic of Americans," a labor organizer explained. "Yet you can't find all-out aggressive support for a Bush war" because "it's our sons and daughters who could die."[99] MoveOn launched a "Let the Inspections Work" petition, garnering two hundred thousand online signatures and donations for antiwar ads.

Press accounts of the December 10 actions gave UFP its due, prominently quoting UFP leaders Andrea Buffa and Damu Smith. In *The Nation*, Fletcher stressed the importance to UFP of bringing the "urban racial justice movement" into antiwar work, while tapping the "deep pockets of antiwar sentiment among African-Americans, Muslims and Latinos."[100]

United for Peace was on the map, poised for bigger things. In early January, more than one hundred activists gathered at New York City's famous Judson Church. At the meeting, the coalition changed its name to United for Peace and Justice. Lisa Fithian argued hard for the shift, which was "a struggle." "We can't build a new peace movement," she insisted, "if we don't talk about justice," both abroad and at home.[101]

The coalition also sealed its participation in a global day of action on February 15, agreeing to anchor the protest in the United States.[102] Hired as UFPJ's first staffer, Leslie Cagan would lead the organizing. At the Judson meeting, L. A. Kauffman approached Cagan with the offer of help. Within minutes, she became the second hire. Alone in UFPJ's vast office—a floor of a midtown office building donated by a labor union—the two women started planning a demonstration to stop a war.

CHAPTER 6

"THE WORLD SAYS NO TO WAR"

A Day of Global Protest

Describing preparations for the February 15, 2003, protests, L. A. Kauffman and Leslie Cagan expressed the same regret: They wished they had documented in photos the transformation of the UFPJ workspace. The first image would have shown them huddled in mid-January over the sole workstation in the huge, empty office. Soon after, the space was buzzing, with staff and volunteers spilling into hallways. They conducted outreach, fielded media queries, culled speakers, and coordinated the distribution of posters and flyers. From her corner cubicle, Cagan directed the entire operation. Word of new cities joining the protest sent ripples of excitement through the room.

Responding to a global call, far-flung cities united under the slogan "The World Says No to War." As the day of protest neared, scenes of frenzied organizing played out across the world. Hopes soared at achieving something extraordinary.

On or around February 15, antiwar protests took place in 789 cities in seventy-two countries, spanning all seven continents.[1] Drawing five hundred thousand people, the New York City demonstration was the largest in the United States.[2] Protests in Seattle, San Francisco, and Los Angeles combined for another half million. One and a half million more people attended nine hundred or so smaller protests across the country.

The most massive numbers were in Europe. Rome alone drew more than three million protesters. Madrid, Barcelona, and Seville combined for three million more—a staggering 6.7 percent of Spain's population. London turned out a million and a half or more. Paris and Berlin together yielded nearly a million, while Australian cities reached half that. Thousands turned out in cities throughout Asia, Africa, and Latin America. Under the watchful eye of security services, handfuls of protesters braved the streets of Cairo. In Israel, Jews and Arabs rallied for peace.

In total, between fifteen and thirty million people demonstrated worldwide. "February 15," marveled UFPJ cofounder Phyllis Bennis, "was the single largest mobilization of people in the history of humanity." Jesse Jackson called it "the biggest demonstration, coordinated, in the history of the whole earth."[3]

Everywhere, the protests were the day's big story. As if in a science fiction movie reporting on alien landings, television stories featured world maps lit up with participating cities. In *The New York Times* on February 17, Patrick Tyler gave the protests their iconic description. "The huge demonstrations around the world are reminders that there may still be two superpowers on the planet: the United States and world public opinion."[4]

February 15 was the zenith of efforts to prevent the Iraq war—the one day when antiwar forces had both the headlines and momentum. The global justice movement had created robust institutions and networks. These were tapped to rally the world to a shared message and common action, allowing "world public opinion" to speak.

Opposition to the war was profoundly global, shaping the War on Terror. After 9/11, the United States had the sympathy of most of the world and broad support for its war in Afghanistan, meant to deal with a global threat. As the Bush administration threatened Iraq, the feeling grew that America was now pursuing its self-interest in a new bid for conquest. Rather than leading the world, the United States grew isolated from it.

In America itself, the protests were the antiwar movement's great breakthrough, raising the stakes of Bush's decision. To go ahead with the war would be to go against the will of a huge vocal part of the public. It could only be fought without the consent of many of the governed, adding to the danger of an already risky war. For their participants, the protests stirred grand hope. Surely the voices of the world, rising in a vast chorus on a single day, might prevail.

"WE CAN STOP THIS WAR"

Before a crowd of thousands in a disused railway station in Florence, Italy, a leader of the first-ever European Social Forum (ESF) closed the November 2002 gathering with a bold appeal. "All citizens of Europe" were to organize antiwar demonstrations "in every capital on February 15. We can stop this war!"[5] The delegates erupted in songs of solidarity. The address sprang from a formal call adopted by the ESF at the meeting. "This war, whether it has UN backing or not, will be a catastrophe for the people of Iraq," the statement declared. "It should be opposed by everyone who believes in democratic, political solutions to political conflicts."[6]

Part of the global justice movement, the ESF brought together diverse forces for dialogue about political economy, human rights, and the environment. But the looming war with Iraq dominated the Florence gathering. A planning meeting in Barcelona had proposed opposition to the war as a main theme for the forum itself and an accompanying demonstration. This focus, some feared, might "alienate sectors of the movement." It would also "antagonize the authorities"—chiefly Italy's right-wing Berlusconi government, still angered by the protests at the G-8 summit in Genoa in 2001.[7] The antiwar message energized the ESF, boosting attendance to sixty thousand. "An attack on Iraq was the priority for those at the headquarters of neo-liberalism in Washington," explained a British delegate, "and by a simple law of symmetry it had to be ours."[8] Colleen Kelly from Peaceful Tomorrows was there too, addressing the biggest audience of her life.

Between five hundred thousand and one million people attended the November 9 antiwar protest, welcomed by Florentines with open arms. The first mass European action against war with Iraq, it boded well for February 15. A follow-up meeting in Copenhagen in December brought together peace activists from ten European nations.[9] Americans from UFPJ attended as well, beginning the group's key role in the protests. The plan quickly billowed from Europe-wide demonstrations to a truly global day of action. "I don't know what we were thinking," recalls the UK's John Rees. "It was a completely left field idea even for us, and we'd had a few."[10]

The plan was next endorsed at an antiwar conference in Cairo, attended mostly by Arab activists. Eager to forge global connections, ANSWER's Brian Becker made the trip to Egypt. (Religious activists and secular socialists from the region sharply clashed, and the organizers were arrested by Hosni Mubarak's government at the conference's end.)[11] The gathering set January 18 as a day of international actions in select cities, building toward February.

The demonstrations got additional backing from the World Social Forum, meeting in Porto Alegre, Brazil in early January. Attended by 150,000 people from countless nations, the gathering included a special session on February 15. The leading lights of the global peace movement were there. Meeting face-to-face helped supercharge activist networks and make a day of worldwide protest seem within reach. "The sense from this group was tremendous," reports Media Benjamin, part of a US delegation. It brought the idea to the forum as a whole for quick ratification. "People were coming up to us," recalls the UK's Chris Nineham, "and saying, 'Yes, Guatemala will have a demonstration!,' 'Yes, Canada will have a demonstration!'" An evening event with Noam Chomksy and Arundhati Roy ended with a twenty-thousand-person arena chanting "Don't attack Iraq!" in Portuguese.[12]

Outside the United States, the global justice and antiwar movements worked hand in hand. The Social Forums served as "the main, driving force of the transnational coordination and mobilization" behind February 15.[13] But what most propelled the protests was the intensity of antiwar feeling, in Europe especially.

Europe's antiwar passions ran deep. As early as the post–World War II reconstruction, many Europeans opposed America's aggressive foreign policy. Nations like Germany were all but encouraged in their pacifism, and the whole continent was now leery of armed conflict. Leftists saw America's alleged defense of European democracy against communism as part of a project of American domination. With its war in Vietnam and other military interventions, the United States had taken over the colonial mantle from faded European empires. To confront US power was to reckon with a broader imperial legacy. In the 1960s, European intellectuals, rebel youth, and even some politicians rejected America's claim of leading the "free world." In the 1980s, millions protested Ronald Reagan's escalation of the Cold War, with Europe on its frontlines.

The left in Europe, compared with the United States, was strong. Multiparty parliamentary systems allowed for left ideologies—from social democrat, to Green, to communist—to enjoy formal representation. Skewing left, Europe's trade unions remained powerful. Many European countries, in addition, had far larger Muslim populations than the United States. They often shared with Muslims in the Middle East intense criticisms of US policy, especially its support for Israel. As the result of all this, views derided as "anti-American" in the United States were commonplace in Europe.

9/11 blunted European suspicions of US power. Popular sympathies initially lay with the United States as the victim of a terrible attack. Though the leader of the center-left Labour Party, UK Prime Minister Tony Blair was George Bush's main ideological and military ally. With greater eloquence than Bush, he promoted the War on Terror as the defense of civilization against al-Qaeda's revanchist barbarism. Other nations directly aided the US-led effort. When major US military operations ended in Afghanistan, the International Security Assistance Force took over. Its soldiers were drawn from leading NATO powers in Western Europe, including Germany, and east European nations new to the alliance. Even Denmark, best known for humanitarian aid, joined in.

Support for Bush's policies was far from universal. In European capitals, antiwar movements quickly formed. Just after September 11, a normally routine London meeting of the Trotskyist Socialist Workers Party (SWP) was packed, pulsing with worry over the US response. From it came plans for a larger meeting to start organizing against war. On September 21, thousands jammed the Friends Meeting House, an iconic Quaker hall in London, where the Stop the War Coalition (StWC) was born.[14]

The name was taken from a flyer drafted for the gathering by the SWP's John Rees. The flyer already named Iraq as a likely US target. The SWP spearheaded the organizing, though StWC leaders included key figures from the Labour Party. Muslims were involved from the start, creating Just Peace to represent Muslim interests. In the first months after 9/11, the StWC held demonstrations that drew tens of thousands against the war in Afghanistan, as did leftists and pacifists elsewhere in Europe. Together, they were a vocal antiwar minority.

Escalating threats of war against Iraq dramatically shifted the views of the European mainstream.[15] Only in the United Kingdom, whose government echoed false US claims of Iraqi WMD, was the public more or less split over the war. Most Spaniards and Italians opposed the conflict, despite their leaders' support for it. All other populations in Western Europe were antiwar, with some adamantly so. In January 2003, nearly 65 percent of Germans and three-quarters of all Greeks opposed war with Iraq. Eastern Europeans, on the whole, were even more antiwar. Europe's media intensely covered the brewing conflict. Much more so than in the United States, it presented reasons for *not* going to war.

Europeans largely rejected the war as unjust, not simply unwise. Absent from the European Social Forum's call was any mention of the risk to American blood and treasure. Instead, it stressed the danger America posed to Iraq and the larger world order. A huge majority of Europeans, whether for the war or not, felt that oil was America's "main motivation" for attacking Iraq.[16]

Into the fall of 2002, antiwar momentum built. In the United Kingdom, a potent alliance formed between the Stop the War Coalition, the Cold War–era Campaign for Nuclear Disarmament, and the Muslim Association of Britain (MAB). Led by young activists, the MAB helped to make Islamophobia and Palestine major issues in the movement. A hallmark of the British movement was unprecedented interaction between Muslims and non-Muslims and a new respect for Muslim concerns in public life. Tensions sometimes arose between socially conservative Muslims and antiwar progressives. (Whether to play music at rallies could be a sticking point.)

But the collaboration was mostly strong. MAB organizers were stunned when on September 30—just days after Blair released an intelligence dossier hyping the Iraqi threat—several hundred thousand protesters jammed London for a rally against war with Iraq and in solidarity with Palestine.

Outside the United States, the antiwar movement in the UK had the greatest potential impact on US policy. Blair's support for Bush made Americans more inclined to support war with Iraq. To antiwar Brits, this was galling. They derided Blair as "Bush's poodle," seeking to restore military glory to a lapsed empire by piggybacking off an American war. By weakening Blair at home, the British movement might fracture Britain's alliance with Bush and derail US war plans.

Establishment figures were vocal in opposing war. Labour Party leader Jeremy Corbyn was an early convener of the StWC, touring the United Kingdom to build antiwar energy. The StWC's president was the retired Labour Party figure Tony Benn. A long-serving member of Parliament and former cabinet minister, Benn was widely admired in Britain. His main role was to make the public case against war. A strong minority party, the Liberal Democrats widely criticized Blair's justifications for attacking Iraq.

The United Kingdom had as well an established peace community, reaching into popular culture. Damon Albon, the lead singer of Blur, came from two generations of conscientious objectors. He gave star power, publicity, and money to the antiwar cause. Joining him were celebrity artists like the filmmakers Ken Loach and Alex Cox and musician Robert del Naja.

Voices in the Wilderness had a UK chapter, which made sanctions-busting trips to Iraq. Milan Rai, a longtime antinuclear activist, first went in 1998. On September 11, 2002, he published in the United Kingdom and the United States *War Plan Iraq: Ten Reasons Against War in Iraq*.[17] Intended to expose "the realities behind official and media distortion and lies," the book begins and ends with essays by members of Peaceful Tomorrows. The rest features detailed policy histories and antiwar polemics, as well as statements from former diplomats, retired generals, and political officials opposing war.

People in the Global South, long critical of US foreign policy, quickly soured on the War on Terror. South Africa's president, Nelson Mandela, led the way. After 9/11, Mandela offered full-throated support for America's right of self-defense. In January 2002, he softened that position, pointing to needless deaths in Afghanistan.[18] In September, Mandela declared America a "threat to world peace" for threatening Iraq.[19] "All Bush wants is Iraqi oil," he insisted in January 2003. War with Iraq "must be condemned without reservation."[20] Mandela even suggested that Bush was so hostile to the United Nations because it was led by a Black African, Kofi Annan. In all corners of the world, people came to similar conclusions. In Pakistan and Turkey, Muslim-majority countries near Iraq, fully 90 percent opposed a US attack.

Lifted by a rising antiwar tide, the February 15 protests also had the benefit of timing. In November 2002 the United Nations had passed Resolution 1441. It declared Iraq in breach of various agreements dating back to the Gulf War, demanded the return of weapons inspectors, and threatened "serious consequences" for further noncompliance. It stopped short, however, of authorizing war. At Blair's pleading, in early 2003 the Bush administration sought to rally the Security Council for an explicitly prowar resolution, despite Iraq's acceptance of new inspections.

Above all, a UN resolution would give legitimacy to military action. The legality of the war was at stake as well. This was of special concern in the United Kingdom, a signatory—unlike the United States—to the International Criminal Court. In principle, the court could hold British soldiers liable for their conduct in an unlawful conflict. In a memo delivered to Blair on January 30, 2003, the UK's attorney general, Lord Peter Goldsmith, concluded that a war would *only be lawful* with a new UN resolution. Senior officials pressured Goldsmith to revise his view, which Blair nonetheless disregarded.[21]

On January 31, Bush declared in a private meeting with Blair his intent to engage in military action, even without a UN war resolution or evidence of Iraqi WMD. Blair pledged his support. Both men agreed to mislead their nations in believing that no decision for war had been made.[22] That same day the leaders of the two countries' trade union movements—John Sweeny of America's AFL-CIO and John Monks of Britain's Trade Union Congress—sent a joint message to Bush and Blair appealing for peace.[23]

In much of the world, UN endorsement of a possible war with Iraq figured heavily in public opinion. In late January 2003 between 57 and 87 percent of Europeans "rejected war without UN backing."[24] In the United Kingdom, the absence of the United Nations' endorsement drove support for war down to 15 percent. This importance of the United Nations raised the stakes of the February 15 protests. David Cortright described the "creative dialectic" between the United Nations and "global civil society." "Public opposition to war hinged on the lack of UN authorization; the objection of the United Nations in turn depended on the strength of anti-war opposition. . . . The stronger the objections at the United Nations the greater the legitimacy and impact of the antiwar movement."[25] A massive showing in streets, especially in countries with votes in the United Nations' Security Council, might discourage a prowar resolution. The absence of such a resolution, in turn, would boost antiwar feeling. Eager to say their piece, the protesters were poised to make a difference.

"ONE LAST POWERFUL MESSAGE TO THE BUSH ADMINISTRATION"

Joining the global day of action only in January, New York City was at the center of the entire effort. Its protest would appeal directly to the US government. The city was also host to the United Nations, the second great target, and the main site of the 9/11 attacks. For New Yorkers to say "Not in Our Name" would undercut with unique power the case for war and inspire people all over the world.

UFPJ quickly contributed to the global effort. UFPJ activists coined "The World Says No to War" as its tagline. "We didn't call people in England or Italy," recalls Cagan, to ask, "'What do you

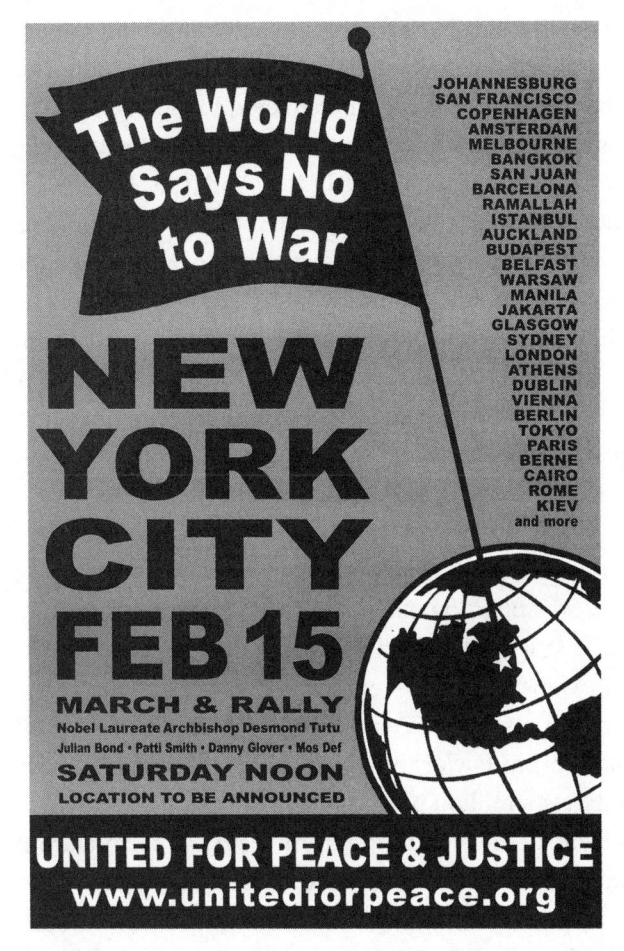

United for Peace and Justice poster for the February 15, 2003, "The World Says No to War" protest in New York City. The location of the rally is not given, due to legal wrangling over permits. Image from the author's collection.

think about the slogan?' We just put it out."[26] The phrase was instantly adopted worldwide.

Next came the creation of a graphic for the event, which fell to L. A. Kauffman. Simple but effective, her logo was "born of the moment, without an entire steering committee involved in trying to frame the message."[27] The core image is a globe in the lower right corner, set against a bright blue background. Rising from New York City is a flagpole with a banner that reads "The World Says No to

War." Down the side runs a list of participating cities, among them Barcelona, Cape Town, Ramallah, Istanbul, and London. The image was used throughout the world, adapted to include local information. Kauffman had it translated into eight languages and produced numerous versions just for use in New York City.

Practically overnight, UFPJ turned into a mobilization machine. Its goal was not to persuade Americans to oppose the war. Instead, it was to get word of the protest out and motivate people to come. The initial outreach to boost organizing efforts was "minimal." "It was the in-reach," joked Cagan.[28] "People just flooded us." Full-time students and workers spent every spare minute helping out. Volunteers from a "whirlwind of organizations" did "old-fashioned" leafleting at subway stops and city landmarks.[29]

Posters and flyers drove turnout efforts. Kauffman oversaw the distribution of two million pieces of printed material. She sensed that buzz was building when she saw teenagers hawking T-shirts with the bootlegged protest graphic. Her work grew to managing the UFPJ website, with resources for the media and out-of-town protesters. It also served as the main clearinghouse for information about protests worldwide. In the days before February 15, it had well over a million page views.[30]

Much of the heavy lifting—from securing permits, to renting equipment, to dealing with authorities—fell to Cagan. Years of experience prepared her to organize such a massive event. A *New York Times* profile called Cagan "one of the *grande dames* of the country's progressive movement."[31] In 1982, she was the lead organizer of the June 12 march for nuclear disarmament in New York City. Drawing more than a million people, it was the largest single protest in US history. A key figure in gay liberation, Cagan helped organize the landmark LGBTQ demonstration in Washington in 1987. Cagan was also a leader of the National Campaign for Peace in the Middle East, instrumental in its mass, anti–Gulf War protest.

Born in 1947 to a leftist Jewish family in the Bronx, Cagan was a quintessential red diaper baby. More than any ideology, her parents imbued in her "a set of values" and the willingness "to jump in when you see a problem."[32] While a student at New York University, she threw herself into anti–Vietnam War activism. She also developed a talent for organizing, rising (as one of few women) in the student antiwar hierarchy.

From the Vietnamese's struggle and Cuba's revolution, she developed a long view of social change, avoiding both the burnout and revolutionary fantasies of others in her late-1960s cohort. In the 1970s, she joined a progressive faction in the Communist Party, seeking radical change from within the structures of US democracy. Instead of a conventional career, she became a full-time organizer, always bringing to her work a commonsense decency and a desire to see people resist and thrive in the face of oppression.

Through the decades, she remained a strong believer in mass demonstrations. "Fundamental, systemic change," she explained, "is secured when massive numbers of people are involved."[33] The labor, women's, civil rights, and anti–Vietnam War movements had proved that premise. Mass protests were a way to involve large numbers of individuals in protest and put "people power" on display. "You come to a big gathering and you feel you are part of something bigger than yourself. [Bringing] people together in the public square is an important part of a vibrant democracy."[34]

Following the 9/11 attacks, Cagan helped with protests against the Afghanistan war. As war with Iraq loomed, she was called to do more. "It's crazy, but I felt like I needed to do it," she said of organizing the February protest. "I had the experience and the skills." Cagan also brought contacts who could help finance the demonstration. Van Gosse led the fundraising, appealing to "deep pockets" like the legendary left-wing activist and donor Cora Weiss. "UFPJ has a chance—a bare chance but a real one—to send one last powerful message to the Bush administration," the pitch letter ran. Cagan, it stressed, believed that February 15 could see "the largest demonstrations for peace and justice in world history."[35] "There are times when numbers do matter," Cagan reflected. "This was one."[36]

Organizers insisted that the day of action could prevent war with Iraq. But did they believe it? "In my heart of hearts," Cagan confessed, "I hoped it would. In my head, I thought it wouldn't. I bounced back and forth, because what was different was the massive mobilization, not just in New York and not just in the US, but the global effort."[37] Gosse remembers no one in UFPJ's inner circle publicly doubting the aim of stopping war. Kauffman sensed that UFPJ was "operating on two levels of reality," in which preventing the war both was and wasn't possible.[38] Kai Newkirk, who had experienced the world-changing impact of the WTO protests, believed victory could be had. So did Medea Benjamin, who spent weeks working her contacts to build demonstrations worldwide. They would make February 15 "so resounding" that Bush and his allies could not "resist" the call for peace.[39]

Not everyone close to her was so hopeful. Like a daughter to Benjamin, Marla Ruzicka had done much to secure compensation from the US government for Afghanistan's civilian victims. Spending time in Washington to lobby for aid, Ruzicka grew convinced that war with Iraq was "inevitable," making protest pointless.[40] She already began planning compensation efforts for Iraqi civilians. "I was heartbroken," Benjamin recalls, of the "falling out" with her friend and ally. "I thought, until the moment war starts, you have to act like it's not going to happen and do everything you can to prevent it."

The success of February 15 depended on the enthusiasm of UFPJ's member groups. Organizations could join UFPJ on its website, entitling them to materials and logistical support. By early February, hundreds had signed on. Members included both established organizations and ad hoc groups opposing war with Iraq. They did their own mobilizing for February 15, whether to bring people to the major New York City and West Coast protests or to their own smaller events. In much of the country, this local work was the lifeblood of the movement. In activist strongholds, UFPJ's presence was especially welcome. "Local groups," recalls Cagan, were "so relieved to not have to work with ANSWER."[41]

Some groups brought a wealth of experience to UFPJ, helping define the coalition as a whole. Brooklyn Parents for Peace (BPfP) was a key member, again showing the role of veteran organizers in the new antiwar movement.[42] BPfP was founded by 1960s-era activists who had been pulled away from politics by the demands of family and career. Early in Ronald Reagan's presidency they reconnected with their activist roots, forming a kind of left-wing neighborhood association. Over the years, they protested nuclear weapons, US policy in Latin America, the Gulf War, and sanctions against Iraq.

The group included academics, nonprofit managers, media professionals, and a Middle East expert native to the region. Their activism was informed by an understanding of how political power works, especially at the legislative level. Their elected representatives were literally their peers, subject to the pressure of savvy constituents like themselves.

Brooklyn Parents for Peace responded to 9/11 with its "Brooklyn Says No" campaign. On posters throughout the borough, it urged alternatives to war, while avoiding the shrill tone of some on the left. Working with the Arab-American Family Support Center, BPfP also protested the detention of New York City–area Muslims. For months members attended vigils, sometimes with their children, at a federal facility in Brooklyn holding the beleaguered captives.

When talk of Iraq escalated, the group put out its own "10 Reasons Not to Go to War" and a sign-on statement opposing a US attack.[43] Among signers were legislators from New York State and City Council members. With less success, the group pressed Senators Schumer and Clinton to oppose the war, holding angry demonstrations at their homes and offices. BPfP threw itself into organizing for February 15.

The Nashville Peace and Justice Center was another UFPJ member. It had organized antiwar rallies on October 26 and for Martin Luther King Jr. Day in January, sponsored forums with antiwar veterans, and worked with local groups, like Artists and Musicians for Peace. Just before the February 15 protest, it demonstrated at Bush's Nashville appearance at the Religious Broadcasters' Convention, where he made a pitch for war. It helped organize a Concert for Peace with the acclaimed musicians Bela Fleck and Tim O'Brien. Garnering local, statewide, and national media, it showed how a peace community distant from the nation's power centers could make itself heard. Like other groups nationwide, it sent buses to New York City for the big national protest.

UFPJ's main poster had a glaring omission: where the protesters were to gather.[44] Organizers were adamant in wanting both a stationary rally and a march past the United Nations. City officials pushed back. Into February, the matter was litigated in court, leaving organizers in limbo. The highly public conflict was a test case for the exercise of protest rights in post-9/11 New York City and another sign of how important the United Nations was in debates about the war.

On January 24, UFPJ submitted a permit request for a rally of fifty to a hundred thousand people at Dag Hammarskjöld Plaza, just across from the United Nations. It also sought a short march south past the UN complex, turning west to end in Central Park.[45] Citing security concerns, the city accepted only the rally, informing UFPJ organizers on February 4. The organizers immediately sought an injunction to lift the ban on marching, naming the city; its Republican mayor, Michael Bloomberg; and its police chief as defendants. The New York Civil Liberties Union did the legal work, free of charge.[46] Following a hearing on February 7, for which Leslie Cagan and NYPD Chief Michael Esposito filed depositions, the case was heard in US district court. In the packed courtroom were two lawyers from the Justice Department.[47] Protesters picketed outside.

The battle over the permit came at a crucial moment. On February 5, the Bush administration sent Secretary of State Powell to the UN Security Council to make the case for a war resolution. Powell was well regarded by most Americans, who saw him as a voice of probity and restraint. Any private doubts he had about war were absent from his address. With the world watching, Powell solemnly repeated the administration's core charges—from Iraq's production of WMD to its training of al-Qaeda—rooted in shaky, disputed, and fraudulent intelligence. As proof, he displayed satellite photos allegedly showing mobile weapons labs.

The international community was not swayed. Nothing suggested that Powell had influenced any Security Council votes. Domestically, Powell's performance played well. Most Americans found it persuasive, pushing support for war to nearly 70 percent. Still, millions were unconvinced. As tensions mounted, Congress had little to say. A week after Powell's UN visit, Senator Byrd accused Bush of edging the country toward "the most horrible human experience." Yet the Senate remained "ominously, dreadfully silent," manipulated by a "reckless and arrogant administration."[48]

In court, UFPJ argued that the denial of its march violated its First Amendment rights. It pointed to the city's proud tradition of protest and its granting in 2002 of permits for large cultural parades, like on St. Patrick's Day. A march "would allow people to actively participate by walking, carrying signs, chanting and singing."[49] Privately, Cagan feared that remaining stationary, especially on a cold day, would lead to "frustrations" among the protesters and invite violence by police.

The permit had been denied, the complaint alleged, based on the march's political goals. (During the depositions, Chief Esposito admitted that since the fall of 2002 the NYPD had turned down every single permit application for a protest march.)[50] UFPJ "places great significance on passing 'within direct view of the United Nations,'" read the court ruling, quoting Cagan's testimony.[51] "Just as Colin Powell took his message in favor of war with Iraq to the United Nations," UFPJ sought to "bring its message of 'mass opposition'" to the UN as well.[52]

The city argued that it could not provide adequate security for *any* large march on such short notice, especially at a sensitive site like the United Nations.[53] Recognizing the city's "legitimate security concerns," the judge found no political bias in the treatment of the permit request. On February 10, he denied the march.[54] A rally blocks north of the United Nations would have to do.

United for Peace and Justice fought back, holding a press conference hours after the ruling. City Council member Bill Perkins charged, "The Bush administration does not like political dissent and has influenced the Bloomberg administration to stop it."[55] A leading First Amendment attorney and former counsel for the city called the ruling "a low moment in New York's history." The following day, Harlem's powerful Congressman Charles Rangel denounced it as a blow to basic liberties. In a separate statement, twelve members of the city's Democratic congressional delegation added their voices to the "crescendo of demands that Mayor Bloomberg reconsider his decision." Principles aside, the conflict played into UFPJ's hands. "Having a big public fight over a permit," Cagan admitted, "got us probably millions of dollars worth of free publicity."[56]

The protest got a final boost on February 14 when the UN inspectors in Iraq—led by Hans Blix, a Swedish diplomat and former head of the International Atomic Energy Agency (IAEA)—briefed the UN Security Council. Blix reported that his team had so far found no Iraqi WMD and that Iraq was basically complying—despite ongoing defiance on some matters—with its demands for documents and access. If the inspections were strengthened and refined, Blix believed, they could work. The IAEA, assessing Iraq's nuclear intentions, reported satisfactory progress in its dealings with Iraqi officials. The meeting was chaired by Germany, deeply opposed to war. Days earlier, Donald Rumsfeld had blasted Europe's war skeptics in a conference on international security. Joschka Fischer, Germany's leftist foreign minister, shot back in English, "Excuse me, I am not convinced."[57]

Following Blix's presentation, France's minister of foreign affairs, Dominique de Villepin, delivered the main antiwar address. He repeated that France would consider a war resolution only if the inspectors found violations or were barred by Iraq from doing their work. "What is at stake is our credibility."[58] Other major Security Council countries like China felt that the inspections should continue, making a prowar vote even less likely.[59] One day later, antiwar forces would make their case in the streets.

THE WORLD SAYS NO TO WAR

With the rise of the sun over the spinning globe, protests against war with Iraq circled the world on February 15. Starting in Australia, cities of shared longitudes passed the wave of protest to those further west. The antiwar message swelled to at last crash at the steps of the United Nations, in the country pushing hardest for war.

In near-incantatory language, David Cortright captured the demonstrations' vast size and reach:

In London, the crowd set off from two assembly sites, pouring into and filling much of Hyde Park. More than one million people overflowed the city centre. Tens of thousands also marched in Glasgow, Dublin and Belfast. Rivaling the demonstration in London was a massive protest of perhaps 1 million people in Rome. The historic heart of the city, between the Coliseum and Piazza San Giovani, was packed for hours by slow-moving processions of protestors. Half a million people assembled in Madrid, and the crowd in Barcelona was estimated at one million. Smaller protests occurred in Valencia, Seville, Los Palmas and Cadiz. Half a million marched in Berlin, and crowds of 100,000 or more gathered in Brussels, Paris and Athens, with smaller protests in more than 100 European cities. Over 100,000 demonstrated in Montreal, Toronto, Vancouver and other Canadian cities. Tens of thousands turned out in Mexico City, Rio de Janeiro, Montevideo, and Buenos Aires. Several hundred thousand gathered in Sydney and Melbourne. In New Zealand, protests took place in Auckland, Wellington, and more than a dozen cities. Thousands marched in Tokyo, Seoul, Bangkok. Manila, Kuala Lumpur, Jakarta (the week before), Lahore, New Delhi, Calcutta and other Asian cities. Approximately 20,000 people marched in Johannesburg, Cape Town and Durban. In Damascus, some 200,000 demonstrated at the People's Assembly. Tens of thousands rallied in Beirut and Amman.[60]

In city after city, similar scenes played out: larger-than-expected crowds marched in giant columns, sometimes growing too massive to move. From stages, key organizers, religious figures, labor leaders, artists and some politicians demanded that Bush and Blair not attack Iraq. With rare exception was there any violence or major trouble with police.

Some protests were distinguished by their daring and pluck. On Ross Island in Antarctica, the research staff at the US government–run McMurdo Center braved the cold and censure from their employer. In the lead-up to February 15, *Nation* columnist Alexander Cockburn announced that the protests would reach Antarctica. "We can't let down the great Alexander Cockburn!" thought McMurdo computer tech Robbie Liben, an avid *Nation* reader. "So we're gonna have to do something." On the fifteenth, seventy residents at the station held antiwar placards and formed a peace sign with their bodies on the snow. Liben and others were fired but claim no regrets.

The protests' last great stop before jumping the Atlantic Ocean was London. The UK capital had pride of place among European cities holding demonstrations, given Blair's support for war. Government officials urged major media to downplay the significance of the London protest. Blair privately worried that a large showing might hinder the planned war.

Organizers had reason to be hopeful. For weeks, StWC leaders traveled throughout the United Kingdom to drum up support for the protest. Local organizers rallied their communities. Sleepless activists distributed millions of leaflets and sweated logistics as they chipped up estimates of the likely crowd. "The phones went bonkers," recalls the StWC's Ghada Razuki. "It was twenty hours a day."[61]

The main embarkation point for the march was the picturesque Embankment lining the River Thames. A second meeting place was set up near the city's main transit hub to accommodate out-of-towners. The media relentlessly covered organizing efforts. Itself antiwar, *The Mirror* printed thirty thousand placards for the occasion, complete with the paper's logo.[62]

The protest was further boosted, as in New York City, by a clash with authorities. The culture secretary at first denied use of London's sprawling Hyde Park for the rally. The decision threatened public safety, given the crowd's likely size, and invited charges of suppressing dissent. Bowing to pressure, the government reversed its decision.

On February 15, trainloads of protesters and caravans of rented buses from hundreds of cities and towns converged on London. By late morning, the Embankment was its own waterway of people. From all points in the city, protesters joined in Piccadilly Circus for the three-and-half-mile march to Hyde Park. "The whole of London," observed an organizer, "was moving from East to West." The march included a bloc of several thousand Liberal Democrats—the largest-ever gathering of party members at one time. In biblical tones, a party official observed: "They came from Scotland, they came from Guernsey, they came from Wales, they came pregnant, they came invalided, they came with sticks, they came ancient, they came young, they came with babies [to say] 'This is where we stand.'"

Near Piccadilly, *The Observer* reported, "the ground shook" underneath "a perfect storm of people," decorated with a "bobbing cherry blossom of banners."[63] It counted nuns, barristers, a woman's choir, hairdressers, poulterers, and poets among the crowd. "I've never been on a march," confessed a Black Londoner. She and her friends there knew "there something going wrong in this country," including increased racism, bringing them into the streets.

In Hyde Park, the massive protest was on full display. Cheers erupted when the StWC's Anas Altikriti announced that the crowd, recorded on a digital counter on stage, had reached one and a half million people. Even city authorities estimated a staggering 750,000.[64] Whatever the true number, the protest was the largest the United Kingdom had even seen. The immense turnout was the main message to Blair. "You can't ignore this many people," thought Salma Yaqoob, chair of the Birmingham StWC. "This is going to do it," felt John Rees. "This is going to stop the war."[65]

The keynote speech was delivered by Jesse Jackson, invited by an StWC member while at an antiwar protest in Washington, DC, weeks earlier. Off stage, organizers debated whether Tim Robbins, there with Jackson but not on the program, should speak. The idea was rejected, though Robbins, clenched fist aloft, flanked Jackson during his address. Elected officials from throughout the United Kingdom spoke as well. Cultural voices, like the rapper Ms. Dynamite, stole the show. "She was fucking awesome," exulted the StWC's Chris Nineham, normally a serious-minded politico.[66] The entire protest, marveled Damon Albon, was "off the hook."[67]

Among the protesters was a key group: residents and citizens of Iraqi origin, well represented in the United Kingdom. Altikriti, an StWC leader, was born in Iraq and brought to his advocacy deep concern for his relatives there. The war's backers stressed, above all, the need to disarm Iraqi. They also tarred the opposition as enemies of freedom, who would condemn Iraqis to continued misery under Saddam. The morning of the fifteenth, Blair was in Glasgow, Scotland, addressing a Labour Party meeting. Responding to the protest, he instructed: "As you watch your TV pictures of the march, ponder this: if there are 500,000 on that march, that is still less than the number of people whose deaths Saddam has been responsible for. . . . Ridding the world of Saddam would be an act of humanity. It is leaving him there that is in truth inhumane."[68]

Some within the UK Iraqi community puzzled over why anyone would reject a war that promised to end Saddam's loathsome rule. Many more opposed an invasion. Months earlier, one hundred or so UK Iraqis published an open letter. It stated: "As professionals, writers, teachers and other responsible and concerned citizens, many of whom have personally experienced the persecution of the dictatorship, we say 'No to war; not in our name, not in the name of the suffering Iraqi people.'"[69] At the London protest, an exiled Iraqi family held a placard with "Iraqis say no to war" on one side. The other side read, "No to Saddam's dictatorship." An emotional moment came for organizer Carol Naughton when she was called from the stage area by an Iraqi man. He had been phoning family and friends in Iraq. "They know you are doing this," he told Naughton, "and they say thank you."

"A MOMENT THAT IS CHANGING THE WORLD"

The protest in New York City was many events in one, separated by who and where one was. The official program at Forty-Ninth Street near the United Nations anchored the whole affair. Those speaking, performing, or managing the presenters were an inner circle, responsible for core messaging and press statements. A second rung of perhaps thirty thousand was close enough to the stage to be a proper audience, amplifying the speeches' emotion and filling out the protest tableau. By far the largest group was everybody else, blocks from the rally site.

The denial of a march, along with the bitter cold, raised the pressure on the rally to inspire and entertain. Organizers broadcast the program on jumbotrons, donated by the labor union SEIU 1199. It also encouraged attendees to listen on portable radios to the independent station WBAI. Dubbed "the people's sound system," it carried the rally in full. But the great masses of people would have to generate the protest mostly on their own. The wildcard was the police, which for weeks had taken a hard line. Even portable bathrooms were forbidden, allegedly for security reasons.

The prestige of the occasion, as well as UFPJ's clout, yielded a star-studded lineup. South Africa's Nobel laureate Archbishop Desmond Tutu was the headliner. Key to the defeat of apartheid, he was a voice of near-singular moral authority, beloved worldwide. "President Bush, listen to the voice of the people," he implored, "because many times [it] is the voice of God."[70] "What does the world say to war?" Tutu called out. "No!" the crowd thundered.

Marquee speakers were drawn from America's Black freedom movement. These included Martin Luther King III, Al Sharpton, Angela Davis, and NAACP head Julian Bond.[71] The Reverend Graylan Hagler was co-MC. They and others made the connection between war, racism, inequality, and the neglect of domestic needs. Labor leaders, Arab Americans, the heads of women's groups, UFPJ's Phyllis Bennis, Eli Pariser of MoveOn, an Israeli draft resister, and Derrill Bodly from Peaceful Tomorrows also spoke. Entertainers ranged from the folk legend Pete Seeger to musicians Richie Havens and Patti Smith to the spoken word artists The Welfare Poets and Saul Williams

The seventy-six-year-old Harry Belafonte gave the crowning oration. "The world has sat by with tremendous anxiety," he said to the sea of protesters, "that we did not exist."[72] Unlike the nation's leaders, he said, "we stand for peace" and the true "heart of the American people." "Were my friend, Dr. King, alive today," Belafonte concluded, "he would smile, because we will make a difference!" The most stirring moment was delivered by actor-activist Danny Glover. He led the crowd in slow, rhythmic chants of "Not in Our Name." They crept blocks up First Avenue to rise as a mighty roar. "I will never again have an opportunity like this," Bennis thought during heart-stopping scene, "to be present at a moment that is changing the world."[73]

Bennis was involved in another of the day's highlights. That morning, she, Belafonte, and Archbishop Tutu had met with UN Secretary General Kofi Annan to ask that he "stand with the global peace movement" and publicly denounce the threatened war. (Though personally opposed to the war, Annan refused.) During the rally, the Associated Press reported that the United States and the United Kingdom would no longer push for a new Security Council resolution on Iraq. The protest, Bennis felt, should know about this "huge victory." Pushed onto the stage, she said, "For all you who think that protests like this don't matter, listen up!" She then read, to wild applause, the two-line AP story.[74]

Behind the grand spectacle were littler dramas. Originally slated to be an MC, Leslie Cagan grew ill from working twenty-hour days.[75] The morning of the protest, she could barely get out of bed. Arriving late via cab, she listened to the speeches on the radio, tuned by chance to WBAI. When a speaker expressed regrets that she could not come, Cagan, her partner, and the cabbie exploded with delight. She was rushed to the stage to give an unscripted speech.

However powerful, the program was missed by the great majority of protesters. The problem was not their enormous numbers. City officials could have allowed access to a large gathering spot and a march past the United Nations. Instead, police routed people north on parallel avenues—sometimes blocks above the UN plaza—and prevented them from crossing east to reach the rally site. Confusing or contradictory police instructions further stymied the crowd. The scene was like the arms of an octopus struggling to attach to its head.

The denial of a mass march prompted up to sixty feeder marches from all over the city, meant to converge near the United Nations. For many demonstrators, these marches *were the protest*. Engulfing whole avenues, they experienced the élan of chanting, clapping, and screaming no to war. Most came to dead halts far from the stage. By midafternoon, large parts of the gridlocked city seemed under occupation by a peace protest.

Naeem Mohaiemen, a New York City–based artist, met up for a feeder march with a South Asian contingent at Bryant Park, not

"The World Says No to War" protest in New York City on February 15, 2003. Metal stanchions, erected by the New York Police Department, hem in parts of the crowd. Photograph by Garth Liebhaber, Chicago Indymedia.

far from the rally. For a newspaper in his native Bangladesh, he recounted the scene.[76] Setting off from the park, his group was thrilled to bring Second Avenue's traffic to a stop. "We get our march after all!" exclaimed one protester when the crowd was routed all the way to Seventy-Second Street. Lustily they chanted, "George Bush, corporate whore, we don't want your evil war." "We don't need no Hateration. Registration. Deportation. War on Nations," ran another. "Oh my God!" a demonstrator with a radio yelled. "They're saying London had two million people!" Others pressed her for the numbers in Rome. Mohaiemen's crew made it close enough to the

Street-level shot of "The World Says No to War" protest in New York City on February 15, 2003. Photograph by Garth Liebhaber, Chicago Indymedia.

rally to faintly hear some speeches, before breaking for warm food. Interrupting their meal were phone calls from panicked friends reporting trouble with police.

Many came to the protest already feeling that their rights, given the ban on marching, had been abused. Police tactics added to their anger. Starhawk blasted the "heavy-handed and sometimes brutal police presence that penned the official rally behind barricades and prevented thousands from even getting there."[77] Only the resolve of protesters to stay nonviolent, she felt, prevented bloody mayhem.

Field-tested at the World Economic Forum in Manhattan two

weeks earlier, the "pens" were metal stanchions used to wall in demonstrators. On February 15 they kept huge crowds crammed on sidewalks. Confined "against their will," reported policing expert Alex Vitale, protesters "feared for their safety."[78] Some were pepper-sprayed to move them away from the barricades. When overflow crowds spilled into streets, they met mounted police. Accounts of police horses charging at protesters, unprovoked arrests, and beatings by police popped up across the city. Some demonstrators were hospitalized for treatment of their injuries. Legal observers from the People's Law Collective, anchored by the National Lawyers Guild (NLG), tracked the abuses. In a handful of instances, irate protesters broke through police barricades, leading to small scuffles.

"Appalled and disappointed beyond measure" was the reaction of Virginia's Ellen Fitzrider, expressed in a complaint to police commissioner Raymond Kelly.[79] She too had come to a standstill far from the stage, with mounted police patrolling the crowd. "Suddenly, the horses drove forward, without warning, scattering people in their wake." She feared that her two-year-old daughter, carried on her back, would be crushed. Even for rally speakers, the pens were a problem. Much of the Peaceful Tomorrows delegation, meant to accompany Derrill Bodly on stage, was stuck in a pen as his turn to speak came. Only by pleading with police and climbing over metal fencing did some make it to the podium.[80]

All told, about 350 people were arrested, with six accused of felonies. Most were released within twenty-four hours, though two were freed on February 17 only after the NLG filed habeas petitions on their behalf.[81] A group of arrestees wrote an open letter describing their "inhumane treatment."[82] Some were packed into dark, unheated police vans for hours, with the injured smearing blood from their wounds on the windows.[83] One group, handcuffed and chained together, was made to stand outside a precinct for more than an hour in the freezing cold.[84] City Council member Gale Brewer wrote her own angry letter to Commissioner Kelly, citing numerous reports of "excessive force" and "rude and vulgar comments" by police.[85] Nearly two hundred complaints of mistreatment were filed with the New York Civil Liberties Union.

On February 18, UFPJ held a press conference to condemn the police's conduct, showing amateur footage of police abuse.[86] Cagan called for Commissioner Kelly to resign. Police officials, who put the massive crowd at just a hundred thousand, praised NYPD officers for the absence of greater turmoil. "The real intention of the city in refusing people the right to march," the NLG concluded, remained "unclear." "But they clearly knew the chaos and danger their refusal could produce."[87] Cagan placed ultimate blame with the Bush administration. "An order had come from 'higher up' to make things difficult for the protesters."[88] Others were more philosophical. The arrestees' letter measured the financial cost in bogus prosecutions and protesters' lawsuits. The greater price was "the loss to every American of constitutional rights."[89]

Starhawk warned that the more a small elite "resorts to brute force to keep control, the more it loses legitimacy" and that "every person denied access to a legal rally, every person shoved or bullied lost a bit of that belief" in the American system. "In the face of injustice and enormous provocation, people responded with restraint, with passion and joy, and discovered our collective power," she concluded. "And that's what happened in New York."[90]

"IT SEEMED THAT THE WORLD HAD SAID NO TO WAR"

"Congratulations, everyone!" posted UPFJ to its website on the evening of February 15. The group reported that ten million people turned out worldwide, including five hundred thousand in New York City. UFPJ's short note belies the enormity of the day. The tally of participating cities and people quickly grew, as fuller accounts came in. The protests made global headlines, demanding a response from world leaders. Among activists, they were the stuff of instant legend, later memorialized in works of history and film. Anniversary retrospectives have treated February 15 as a stand-in for the antiwar movement as whole, whose impact could be measured by what the demonstrations did, or did not, accomplish.

Hopes at first ran high. "I felt elated," recalls Benjamin. "There's no leader that could go ahead with a war when they see a global movement saying no!"[91] For Cagan, the ultimate success would be the policymakers realizing, "Oh, you're right, we're wrong," and calling off the war.[92] This was always "a long shot, but I thought, oh my God, maybe this time it will be different. Maybe we could actually stop this war."

The Bush administration shot down that hope. Denying that the White House was "rattled" by the large crowds, National Security Advisor Condoleezza Rice affirmed that "people have a right to protest." But "they're not saying what they think in Baghdad, because that's a regime that cuts out people's tongues" if they do.[93] "Democracy is a beautiful thing," Bush said, only to condemn Iraq's tyranny. He and Rice turned the protests on their heads: The outpouring of antiwar dissent underscored why Saddam, as an enemy of democracy, had to be removed. Bush continued: "You know, size of protests, it's like deciding, 'Well, I'm going to decide policy based on a focus group.'"[94] Bush tried to claim the mantle of a statesman, guided by principle, not popularity. Yet his glib comment, which infuriated protesters, likened millions in the streets to a mere "focus group."

Even without a change in policy, US organizers had reason to be satisfied. One triumph was who showed up. The crowd in New York City, Cagan observed, went well beyond "the predictable people" at protests. Starhawk noted the diversity with respect to race, age, and class. She delighted in seeing "young students and gray-haired veterans of the peace marches of the sixties, punks and hippies and ordinary citizens." Countless media stories stressed the great variety of people in the streets.

Cagan counted the "tremendous" press coverage as a great success.[95] Media stories featured notable signs and slogans, as well as quotes from speechmakers and marchers alike. They also made mention of the protests' global reach and the powerful message that sent. "Today, tens of millions of people view America as an arrogant bully," wrote a US reporter. "They distrust Bush's unilateralist policies, dislike his cowboy swagger, suspect he seeks to control Iraq's oil reserves and reject the leadership of an American government that views international treaties and law with disdain."[96] "The demonstrations," concluded scholars of protest, received coverage "of which most organizers can only dream."[97] "It seemed," in the media's telling, "that the world had said no to war."

Politically momentous, February 15 was also a golden opportunity for researchers. They might illuminate what drove the record-setting day, beyond what the media reported and even organizers at the time understood. To that end, a crack team of scholars surveyed demonstrators in countries with uncommonly large protests and parsed the responses.[98] The surveys were conducted in the United States and the United Kingdom, as the main belligerents; in nations with prowar governments and antiwar publics, like Spain and Italy; and in countries whose leaders and citizens opposed war, like Germany.

Organizers and the media alike claimed that the protesters, coming from "all walks of life," reflected their societies as a whole.[99] Broad-based opposition to war, in this view, drove the protests' massive size. But was it true? In their answer, the researchers addressed the question of who, in key parts of the world, spoke out against war with Iraq.

"In all countries," the topline conclusion ran, the protests "attracted people from all pockets of society."[100] Still, significant differences separated the protesters from the surrounding population, and national protests from one another. Women made up the majority of demonstrators in most locales. In the United States, they were fully 63 percent.[101] In many places, the protesters also skewed young. Yet in America, just 11 percent were below age 24. The largest US age group was those 45–64 (43 percent), greatly exceeding their proportion in the general population. The high number of the middle-aged is telling. They were the Vietnam War generation, socialized during the Cold War into concern with US war-making. They, and not the youth, drove the new American antiwar movement, though youth voices were hardly absent.

The protesters were also highly educated. In the United States, more than 90 percent of those surveyed had at least some secondary education. Most were professionals or independently employed in fields like education and health care. Just 6 percent were manual workers. Other countries tilted much more toward students and clerical workers, often connected to antiwar trade unions. These social factors encouraged public dissent. The young and those with basic means have the time to protest, while education gives the educated a sense of the "right to be heard."

Overwhelmingly, the demonstrators came from the left end ideological spectrum. More than 90 percent reported left-wing sympathies, with the "most committed hard core" made up of "staunch leftists."[102] Protesters typically expressed grievances with their national governments beyond issues of war and peace. The US and UK demonstrators were strongly anti-Bush and anti-Blair, with a dim view of their nations' democracies.[103] The greatest political diversity was in countries like Germany, where antiwar views spanned rival parties, including among elected officials.

The demonstrators also showed high levels of political engagement. Nine in ten adult protesters in the United States had voted in the last election. Nearly all had been involved in political advocacy, such as supporting electoral campaigns. About a third of demonstrators were participating in their first protest in years, with many new to protest altogether. Half of those in London were first-timers. Yet in most places a strong majority had recent protest experience. In Europe, the global justice movement was "the main reservoir of committed activists."[104] US demonstrators were involved in causes from women's rights to the environment to antiracism. A small minority on the far left, in Italy most of all, had engaged in disruptive or even violent protest.

The researchers concluded that the protesters "were not representative of the populations of their countries."[105] This was scarcely surprising, as "social movements defend certain interests and are rooted in corresponding population segments." By skewing female, educated, middle-class, left-wing, and, in most places, young, the protesters matched the profile of participants in current movements like environmentalism and global justice. "Movements that are able to mobilize true cross-sections of the population," the researchers quipped, "have yet to be invented."

The implications for the antiwar movement were profound.

Much as it claimed to represent the popular will, the movement had so far mostly turned out people already inclined to oppose war. Its greater power depended on mobilizing broader parts of the public. At the same time, antiwar feeling surely exceeded those who actively protested. The movement had work to do to draw in more people—especially among the working class and the poor—who shared its position.

The research also surveyed the reasons protesters opposed war with Iraq.[106] In continental Europe, many rejected all war as wrong. Some in the United States and the United Kingdom shared this view. Many more focused on the weakness of Bush and Blair's case for attacking Iraq and the risks war carried. Protesters everywhere were adamant that seizing Iraqi oil was a major American goal. Sizable numbers also thought the war was "racist" or part of a "crusade against Islam." Many conceded that Saddam was a tyrant but rejected this as grounds for war.

A related question was what drove people to engage in protest. The reasons were often personal and heartfelt, ranging from concern for Iraqi civilians and one's own children, to belief in the ability to make a difference, to the sense that war was inevitable but that one must still speak out.

Published in 2008, the study had the perspective of hindsight. A central claim was that the protests were not the product of either long-standing or sustained peace movements. Instead, they were the peak of a fast-forming "protest wave" that "quickly declined after the war broke out, with only a few protests in most countries just one month later."[107] "Something new in the history of contentious politics" in its scale and reach, February 15 was a "one-shot action."[108]

This verdict both hit and missed the mark. A global day of protest did not a global antiwar movement make. February 15, Bennis conceded, "could not, by itself, translate" into "a coordinated international mobilization" with the ability "to successfully challenge Bush's Iraq war."[109] Going forward, "strategic political ties" across borders were "sporadic, almost accidental." The sharper judgment that the protests simply came and went as a unique event was outright wrong. Long past February 15, intense antiwar activism continued in the United States, the United Kingdom, and, to a lesser degree, Spain and Italy.

February 15 had qualities of what Mark Engler, challenging traditional social-movement models, calls "momentum-driven mass mobilizations."[110] Unpredictable but far from rare, these often take the form of spectacular protests that shift public conversations. Doing so, they seem to accomplish overnight what movement organizations may strive, often in vain, for years to achieve. Their spontaneity is always, in part, an illusion. Behind February 15 was the foundational work of the World Social Forum. United for Peace and Justice drew on the experience of movement veterans atop well-established organizations, harnessing antiwar energy at the grassroots.

The key challenge for organizers, in Engler's model, is to seize momentum. The energy behind February 15 was enormous: ominous claims of an Iraqi threat; widespread skepticism about those claims and fears of war; a sense that war was just weeks away; and snowballing antiwar activity. United for Peace and Justice and overseas groups were the catalysts for global protests, not their cause. The demonstrations met the demand for them.

"THIS WAR WAS COMING"

The American antiwar movement had made a bold statement on February 15. The protests were, Cagan felt, "a message to people around the world, and particularly the people in Iraq, that there was opposition here in this country to what our government was doing." The demonstrations were also "a message to policymakers that there was a strong sentiment in the country against the war and that we couldn't go away. We will keep fighting you on this."[111]

Yet however massive, the protests confirmed what the Bush administration already knew: that large numbers of people, including in the United States, opposed war with Iraq. The vocal expression of that view changed neither the balance of public opinion nor the administration's sense of what level of criticism it could endure.

If global public opinion were indeed a second superpower, it was a weak one, with no means to impose its will. The United Nations lacked the authority to veto Washington's war. Even US allies like France and Germany were dismissed by Donald Rumsfeld as "old Europe," unwilling to embrace a new era of American leadership. Objections in the Global South were at most an irritant, even when complicating—as in case of Turkey refusing the use of its airspace for war—the Pentagon's plans. The world might say no to war, but nothing required the US government to listen or to care.

"The authorities don't fear much the mere expression of dissent," Starhawk concluded. "What finally may constrain the warmongers is the possibility that the people will become ungovernable if the government continues to disregard its will."[112] Doing so could "unleash the kind of social unrest that makes governments fall." This was unlikely prophecy. America in the late 1960s approached that level of unrest, with the Vietnam War as a major cause. So much else unique to the era—generational revolt, Black Power protest, violent repression, assassinations, and the revolutionary fervor of the times—threatened social stability. Even then, the US government did not fall, nor did it end the Vietnam War to quell dissent.

L. A. Kauffman came to UFPJ with the militant outlook of the global justice movement. What if, she wondered, protesters had pushed past police lines to make it to the UN building? More than a symbolic victory, this defiance would put the Bush administration on notice that the movement could exert real force, ratcheted up should the war begin.

This too was wishful thinking, given UFPJ's emphasis on mass turnout in traditional demonstrations. The pressing issue was what came next. "For seven weeks we were so focused" on February 15, recalled Cagan. "We clearly needed to keep this going, and this war was coming. What were we going to do?"[113]

CHAPTER 7

"TO BOMB THIS SITE WOULD BE A WAR CRIME"

From "Stop the War" to Shock and Awe

Fate had smiled on the antiwar movement. A day after the February 15 protests, New York City was blanketed with two feet of snow. "We got lucky," admitted Cagan.[1] But the blizzard, as it seemed to wipe the city clean of the massive event, also suggested a troubling image for antiwar protest.

Whether anything was different in the political landscape remained unclear. The Bush administration continued to signal that war was coming soon. For weeks, the military and the media had hyped the threatened attack as "Shock and Awe," with bombs to rain down on Baghdad in a great TV spectacle.[2] In preparation, MSNBC fired Phil Donahue, the celebrated host of a popular program that sometimes had antiwar guests. He would be, executives feared, a "difficult public face for NBC in a time of war," when "our competitors are waving the flag."[3] February 15 "was the most people out in the streets" in history, complained one activist, "and we're not seeing any change."[4]

Since 9/11, the work of the antiwar movement work had the quality of a race. First with Afghanistan and then Iraq, could it mobilize quickly enough to overtake and turn back the dogs of war? As war with Iraq drew nearer, a new metaphor from sport grew more apt. The weeks following February 15 saw countless antiwar actions across the country and the world. It was like the trailing team throwing everything at its opponent in hopes of a late-game miracle. But the political scenario had a twist. Protesters battled on without knowing whether the outcome was settled in advance—whether there was *anything* they could do to win peace.

One month after February 15, hundreds of thousands again rallied in Milan, Madrid, and Barcelona. Other major protests dotted the globe. Great throngs marched in San Francisco under banners reading "Fight the Rich—Not Their War," "Blonds Against Dumb War," and, simply, "Truth."[5] Thousands of students in the United Kingdom walked out of class. Montreal protesters, piqued by American anger at antiwar France, bested their numbers on February 15.

In the United States, three coalitions—ANSWER, UFPJ, and Win Without War—rallied the grassroots. Women stayed at the lead, holding gender-themed demonstrations. The arts world sponsored viral protests all their own. Dissent spread to the US Foreign Service. It also touched the armed services community, as military families organized against war. Pressure persisted at the United Nations and in Congress. In Iraq itself, Americans and other internationals continued their humanitarian work, pleading for peace from within America's gunsights. The world, and Americans, kept saying no to war.

"THE DREAM OF ORDINARY, COMMON PEOPLE EVERYWHERE"

On March 3, opponents of a future war spoke in an ancient voice. The means was performances of the 2,400-year-old play *Lysistrata*, sponsored by the Lysistrata Project. From its modest origins came a mighty antiwar statement that echoed the internationalism of February 15.[6]

The mass performances came on the heels of another protest by artists. First Lady Laura Bush had invited Sam Hamill, a major figure in American letters, to lead a poetry symposium at the White House on February 12. Disturbed by the looming war, Hamill asked "a few fellow poet-friends" to send original verses speaking "for the conscience of our country" that he could share at the gathering.[7] Learning of the plan, the White House canceled the symposium. As word of the cancelation spread, submissions soared, with a website set up to manage the deluge. Within weeks, eleven thousand American and global authors had submitted thirteen thousand poems. "Poets," Hamill concluded, "will not be silenced."

A week after the canceled symposium, Poets Against the War sponsored more than two hundred live readings of antiwar poetry. Days later, New York City's Lincoln Center hosted "Poems Not Fit for the White House."[8] Held by Not in Our Name, the event featured tables of communist agitprop in the posh concourse, while a packed hall listened to recitals by Galway Kinnell, Sapphire, Odetta, Saul Williams, and Arthur Miller. "Never before in recorded history," Hamill gushed, "have so many poets spoken in a single chorus."[9]

The poems expressed anger and foreboding, often contrasting the tranquil beauty of nature with the violence planned for distant lands. Some celebrated artistic resistance, while others lamented its weak power. Francisco X. Alarcón's entry asked:

What do we gain
writing
the saddest
lines
tonight
using ink
so bitter
it makes tissue
out of paper
when they
scoff and
jeer at us
their arms
covered with blood.[10]

The poem sought, against its own hard wisdom, to stop the bloodshed.

What the Lysistrata Project's founders lacked in pedigree and connections they made up for in pluck.[11] Kathryn Blume, a New York City actor, had been working on a modern adaptation of Aristophanes' antiwar classic. In the play, the women of warring states withhold sex from their warrior men, forcing their leaders to make peace. Blume's initial thought was to read selections at a protest held by the actor-led Theaters Against War. With Sharron Bower, a bigger idea emerged: to spawn numerous performances of *Lysistrata* on a single day. The play, as they imagined the protest, could be rendered in any setting, manner, length or language.

Bower and Blum were an odd couple in terms of political background. Bower came from a conservative Southern family, with a mother active in right-wing causes. Blume was proudly from a "classic lefty-pinko, Jewish intellectual, union-organizing family." They presented the project as a bold expression of cherished, if beleaguered, American freedoms.

It got a big boost when National Public Radio ran a spot with the two women. Within days, they were overwhelmed with queries as to how one could join in. The website, managed by Bower's partner, became the main vehicle for their "viral democratic effort." It featured the play itself, performance tips, and links to antiwar groups.[12]

The idea quickly snowballed, scooping up enthusiasm as it bounded the globe. Readings were scheduled in all fifty US states. Participation climbed to hundreds of sites in dozens of countries. Among locations were the Acropolis in Greece, Karachi, Pakistan, and northern Iraq, where the international press corps planned a reading. The play also made it to conflict zones, like in the Philippines, where its antiwar message was local as well. Major American networks, local press, and college newspapers ran stories in advance of the performances.

On March 3, 1,026 readings of *Lysistrata* took place in fifty-nine countries, becoming the largest theatrical event in human history. In New York City, theater troupes held performances at famous landmarks. Screen and stage stars like Mercedes Ruehl, Kevin Bacon, and F. Murray Abraham participated in promotion and performance, closing the day with a reading at the Brooklyn Academy of Music. In London, professional actors performed a guerrilla version outside Parliament and then a major, evening show. All proceeds went to antiwar groups.

The great majority of performances were nonprofessional. Amateur actors, high school and college drama departments, community theaters, and activist groups tried their hands at the play. An especially moving rendition took place in a refugee camp in Patras, Greece, housing Iraqi Kurds. When the electricity cut out in the crowded tent, the play was finished by candlelight.

The Lysistrata Project showed how eager people were to *do something* to stop the war, beyond conventional protest. The project promoted community and creativity as an answer to violence. The performances also celebrated the ingenuity of women. Merging feminist hijinks and antiwar feeling, some versions accentuated the play's bawdiness, with penis props and thickened innuendo.

The play had a deep universality as well, based in the exclusion of women from political power in both ancient Greece and much of the modern world. "The fundamentally comic premise was that women, these non-entities, could take on all the governments of Greece and stop the war," explained a British director. "That's the dream of ordinary, common people everywhere—that I can make a difference." That dream—here bearing the timeless message that "love is good, war is bad"—drove the global antiwar movement at its vast grassroots.

For the second time in three weeks, antiwar voices had risen up with great volume, vigor, and breadth. There was no peace treaty, unlike in *Lysistrata*. But just after the mass performance, the United States' and United Kingdom's on-again, off-again bid for a prowar Security Council resolution hit a final wall.

France remained steadfast in opposing war. In late February, fifty-two African countries, including three on the Security Council, came out in support of the French position.[13] Only Spain and Bulgaria, among Security Council members, backed the US-UK resolution. This pushback was remarkable given America's ability to make nations fall in line with its policies. An Institute for Policy Studies report suggested that the "coalition of the willing" the United States sought as war allies was in truth the "coalition of coerced."[14] American leverage ranged from development aid to security pacts. (Bulgaria's desire to join NATO best explained its support for a prowar resolution.) Yet little of it worked.

The prowar coalition included just thirty-four countries representing 10 percent of the world's population, with some publics deeply opposed to their governments' stance.[15] Former President Jimmy Carter concluded, "The heartfelt sympathy and friendship offered to America after the 9/11 attacks, even from formerly antagonistic regimes, has been largely dissipated: increasingly unilateral and domineering policies have brought international trust in our country to the lowest levels in memory."[16]

On March 5, France, Germany, and Russia reconfirmed their opposition to a use-of-force resolution. As thanks, Medea Benjamin and Gael Murphy greeted French Foreign Minister Dominique de Villepin with kisses outside the United Nations The prowar crowd reacted with florid anger. Two Republican congressmen ordered cafeterias in the Capitol Hill complex to rename french fries "freedom fries." Irate Americans, with TV cameras rolling, poured French wine into gutters.[17]

That same day, students protested by the tens of thousands under the banner "Books Not Bombs." Up to four hundred high schools, colleges, and universities participated in the protests, organized by the National Student and Youth Peace Coalition (NSYPC). Students staged walkouts, held teach-ins, and marched to federal buildings and town squares. It was the largest day of student peace actions since the Vietnam War.

Iraq was top of mind. A student speaker in Cincinnati lauded France, Germany, and Russia for "making it even more difficult for us to get involved in an idiotic war."[18] "Every building we bomb in Baghdad will be another September 11," said NSYPC organizer Amanda Crater. "Innocent people will be dying in them."[19] The protesters also leaned into the economic message, stressing how war drains resources from education and health care.

Dissent was on campuses everywhere: at progressive mainstays like the University of California, Berkeley, but also at state schools and small, private colleges in Shippensburg, Pennsylvania, Greensborough, North Carolina, and San Antonio, Texas. In Madison, Wisconsin, five thousand students descended on the state capitol. Fifteen hundred rallied at Penn State University.

Even younger Americans made their voices heard. One thousand students walked out of their public high school in Evanston, Illinois. Erica Evans attended the Madison rally without her father's permission. "I'm 15 years old and I can't vote," she said. "But that doesn't mean I can't have an opinion."[20] The demonstrations were also global, with students protesting in France, the United Kingdom, Canada, Spain, and Australia.

Once again, the Bush administration doused hopes for peace. The next day, March 6, Bush repeated unfounded allegations of Iraq's hostile intentions and America's readiness to meet them with force.[21] He also called for the United Nations to consider a new resolution declaring Iraq *already in breach* of Resolution 1441. Security Council nations rejected this backdoor way to green-light war.

Protest shifted with the geopolitical winds back to the domestic scene. On March 8, International Women's Day, Code Pink held actions in more than fifty cities, including Anchorage and Honolulu. The main demonstration was in Washington, DC, where Code Pink's lengthy vigil concluded with a mass rally at the White House.

International Women's Day had its origins in the 1908 march of women in New York City in support of shorter working hours, better pay, and the right to vote. Formally established in Europe in 1911, it took up the cause of peace during and after World War I. In 1975 the United Nations recognized the day, celebrated mostly in the Global South. With war nearing, the 2003 edition made international solidarity a major theme.

In Washington, ten thousand mostly women protesters rallied before marching to the White House. The action showed how quickly Code Pink had grown. At a mass demonstration in January, its contingent was just twenty-five people, with few wearing pink. Two months later, it created "a sea of pink" signs and outfits in a mass protest all its own.[22] Allies went pink for the day: Grandmothers for Peace, Black Voices for Peace, D.C. Asians for Peace and Justice, and the Takoma Park Kids for Peace, from the famous peace enclave in Maryland.[23]

The Code Pink protest continued traditions of women-centered "performance activism," echoing the first Women's Pentagon Action in 1980.[24] Giant puppets, observed a sympathetic scholar, towered over the crowd. Each was "the personification of an ideal: war, freedom, growth, and justice." At the rally's close, they were surrounded by people dancing and throwing yarn, "creating a joyous, throttling multi-colored 'web of life.'"[25] The yarn had come from the war puppet, lying on the ground after being hacked at by the crowd. "War was destroyed," the symbolism ran, "through bravery, protest and women's determination."

Ahead of the large march, two dozen women slipped through a police line to hold vigil in front of the White House.[26] Among them were Reverend Patricia Ackerman of the Fellowship of Reconciliation; Alice Walker, Maxine Hong Kingston, and Susan Griffin, literary giants who had flown in from California; and Starhawk, Evans, and Benjamin. As night fell, they sang "Peace, Salaam, Shalom" in mesmerizing repetition before being arrested. Covering the protest for *Democracy Now!*, Amy Goodman and her camera operator were detained as well. Kingston described her arrest as "the least I could do" given what Iraqi women and children faced.

Activists reveled in the "creativity and the passion and bright pinkness" of the protest. It was, according to the group's future national director, the "spark moment that helped Code Pink take off like wildfire."[27] The message was, "You want to be Code Pink? Throw on a pink T-shirt, take action, organize where you are." Throughout the country, and even overseas, women did.

The day before women protested the Republican-led, male-dominated war machine at the White House, demonstrators in New York City targeted the office of the country's leading female politician and professed feminist, Senator Hillary Clinton. Brooklyn Parents for Peace (BPfP) was the main sponsor of the protest. Its billing, "Code Pink Alert: It Takes a U.S. Bomber to Raze a Village," played off the title of Clinton's bestseller *It Takes a Village*, which tenderly addressed the lives of children.[28] Amid pink boas and hats, it blasted Clinton for supporting a war likely "to lead to the wholesale slaughter of Iraqi children."

The demonstration brought welcome exuberance to its serious message. Writer Nancy Kricorian, new to Code Pink, enjoyed the "carnivalesque" and "super kid-friendly" atmosphere. Performing were the Missile Dick Chicks and campy Church Ladies. "And the speeches were good," not "too long" or "sectarian."[29] Kricorian soon became the head of Code Pink's New York City chapter, relishing the group's "heart-driven" and "joyful" spirit.

Rusti Eisenberg, a cofounder of BPfP, used her speech to condemn what she viewed as Clinton's hypocrisy. A contemporary of Clinton's, Eisenberg had developed an "abiding hatred" of the senator.[30] Clinton famously moved from the moderate edge of 1960s protest into the liberal establishment. Eisenberg was a committed New Leftist. While in college in Chicago, she participated in civil rights protests, enduring the "horrifying" violence directed at fair housing marches. As a graduate student, she helped lead the 1968 student uprising at Columbia University protesting racism and the Vietnam War. Her path was into academia, where she became an expert-critic of US foreign policy.

Brooklyn Parents for Peace had tried in vain to engage Clinton on the detention of Muslims and war with Iraq. So Eisenberg sought Clinton out at a panel discussion about woman and war. She went "batshit" listening to Clinton's "spiel" about how "if women were running the country, there wouldn't be war," and how citizens do too little to influence elected officials. After the event, Eisenberg had to be pried away from Clinton as she demanded to know why the senator had blown off the very citizen outreach she encouraged.

At the rally, Eisenberg railed at Clinton's "betrayal of her constituents and her own expressed principles."[31] Noting that "the hour is late," the protesters pledged to "do all that is humanly possible to stop this terrible war." That meant urging Clinton to back the proposal of Senators Kennedy and Byrd that Congress reconsider its war authorization.

Days later, another group of women had their say about the looming war. On March 10, the Dixie Chicks—an all-female country trio from Texas—played a concert in London. The band was riding high, earning Grammys, crushing the country charts, and winning pop fans. During the concert, singer Natalie Maines told the audience, "We're on the good side with y'all. We do not want this war, this violence, and we're ashamed that the President of the United States is from Texas."³²

A firestorm erupted. Major rock and folk artists had long spoken out about political issues, criticizing presidents and policies alike. Things were different in the country world, where fidelity to God, country, and the nation's leaders was assumed. "Literally overnight," reports the head of the Dixie Chicks' record label, the band was besieged with "venom" and "hatred."³³ Countless fans saw Maines's comments as a betrayal of heartland values and even the military service of their loved ones. Radio stations pulled their songs, while former fans destroyed their CDs. Band members, record executives, and radio program directors received violent threats. People around the Dixie Chicks suspected that a coordinated political campaign was behind much of the outrage.

The intense backlash became a major story. It showed how viscerally many Americans embraced the prowar cause, seeing even mild dissent as disloyalty. The dissent itself was also significant. Leading artists in a conservative culture were willing to risk their reputations by taking an antiwar stand. Antiwar feeling was mainstream too.

Political considerations, not cultural tussles, would ultimately decide the US policy toward Iraq. Antiwar forces saw threats against the country as a whole-of-government problem spanning institutions and partisan divides. They organized accordingly, making use of new digital resources. In early December 2002 MoveOn started an online campaign titled "Let the Inspections Work," aimed at all of Congress and the White House. Within days, it got 175,000 signatures and massive donations for national antiwar ads.³⁴

"Virtual organizing became the métier" of Win Without War, reports its cofounder David Cortright.³⁵ On February 26, it held a "virtual march" on Washington, in which antiwar Americans flooded congressional offices with phone calls, faxes, and emails. Sending more than one million messages, it was "the largest lobbying day in US political history." Physical gatherings had their place as well. On March 15–16, the group helped organize six thousand candlelight vigils in more than a hundred countries.³⁶

Local activists delivered pointed messages about the threat of war to civilians. In December, members of the Catholic Worker community in Duluth, Minnesota, were arrested for placing rubble and photos of Iraqi civilians outside a military recruiting center.[37] Michele Naar-Obed and Joel Kilgour insisted on going to trial for the minor offense. Prior to the proceeding, Naar-Obed had visited Iraq with international peace teams. Near Basra, she collected actual rubble from a site where US bombs had killed eight people, bringing it back to the United States. At trial, the judge permitted her to use the debris to show the damage she sought to prevent in Iraq.

Just two days back from the February 15 protest in New York City, the Nashville Coalition for Peace and Justice staged "The Faces of Collateral Damage" at the city's War Memorial Plaza.[38] For five days, protesters slept in the park, eating only small rations of rice and lentils to evoke the meager diet of countless Iraqis under the UN sanctions. Pictures of "regular Iraqi folk," potential "collateral damage," adorned the encampment. "War is a matter of life and death, and I think we forget that," said one organizer.

"CIVIL SERVANTS SHOULD BE PREPARED TO RESIGN"

As the Bush administration sped toward war, cracks appeared within the US government. Dissent came from State Department employees resigning over Iraq policy. Theirs was not the conscientious objection of foot soldiers refusing to be cannon fodder or the daring of whistleblowers, risking prison to expose damning secrets. These were foreign service officers sacrificing their careers for the sake of principle. Their patriotism and expertise made their positions credible, potentially reaching Americans unmoved by conventional protest.

The first to resign was John Brady Kiesling, a twenty-year foreign service veteran. Having served in Athens on 9/11, he had pushed for military action in support of Bosnia's Muslims. Bush's saber-rattling speech before the United Nations in September 2002 permanently offended Kiesling's Greek hosts. "My faith in my country," his February 27 resignation letter read, "was the most powerful weapon in my diplomatic arsenal."[39] The threatened war with Iraq, based in the "manipulation" of both intelligence and public opinion not seen since the Vietnam War, had broken that faith.

"I guess I grew up with this notion," Kiesling told the press, that "civil servants should be prepared to resign on principle."[40] Sounding like an antiwar radical, he lamented that "September 11th did not do so much damage to the fabric of American society as we seem determined to do to ourselves." Next was John Brown, who had served in Eastern Europe.[41] His breaking point was Bush's March 6 speech pressing for war, despite UN pushback. East European dissidents, who had risked far more resisting communism, were an inspiration for him.

Ann Wright, an Army colonel turned diplomat, waited to the bitter end. Wright had specialized in civilian reconstruction following war and the legal aspects of armed conflict. After the invasion of Afghanistan, she helped reestablish the US embassy in Kabul and personally saw Hamid Karzai off to attend Bush's 2002 State of the Union address, where he hoped to secure more aid. In his speech, Bush inveighed against the "axis of evil." No sooner had the mission in Afghanistan started, she feared, than it was being abandoned for war with Iraq.

Restationed in Mongolia, Ann Wright struggled to convince other nations' diplomats of the wisdom of Bush's stance.[42] She had disagreed before with policies she had to represent, but this was different. Attacking Iraq "would be a war of aggression, a war crime."[43] Wright spent chilly mornings drafting her resignation letter. With her were Buddhist texts instructing that individuals are "ultimately accountable for their actions."[44] Wright's faith in her boss Colin Powell—whose lies before the UN had not yet been exposed—prolonged her hope that diplomacy might prevail.

On March 17 Bush delivered his "ultimatum speech" giving Saddam and his sons forty-eight hours to relinquish power or face invasion. Wright cabled her resignation directly to Powell. Scores of colleagues privately reached out to her to praise her courage.[45]

Small in number, these foreign service officers made a big statement. Their dissent lent still greater urgency to the case against war. "It was my patriotic duty," explained Kiesling, "to transmute my own misery into a wake-up call."[46] Kiesling was "instantly adopted by the Internet-driven [antiwar] movement," while Wright soon joined its grassroots. Their protest, in turn, emboldened others working for the American state to speak out, including the military.

There was much to discourage dissent within the armed forces, in the post-9/11 era especially. The Afghanistan campaign was prompted by a terrible attack on the country and at first claimed few US casualties. The military, in any case, prohibits personnel from publicly questioning policies set by civilian leaders. For decades it had been all volunteer, unlike in the first years of the Vietnam War. In principle, the enlisted were enthusiastic about their service, or at least accepted the requirement of loyalty to the mission, regardless of their private views. Unlike draftees, many volunteer soldiers sought, or had, careers in the military. Being disciplined or discharged for dissent meant putting one's family at risk.

The potential for dissent existed as well. Many enlisted for economic reasons and might chafe at blind obedience to all commands. Like other Americans, those in the military might see great differences between war in Afghanistan and in Iraq. And retired and even active-duty military leaders loudly questioned both the justification and plans for an Iraq war. These ranged from General Wesley Clark, commander of NATO's Kosovo campaign; to Brent Scowcroft, Air Force veteran and former National Security Advisor; to General Eric Shinseki, who publicly quarreled with Rumsfeld over the troop levels necessary in Iraq. Their doubts could trickle down the ranks.

Groups like the 1960s-era Vietnam Veterans Against the War and the 1980s Veterans for Peace (VFP) set a powerful precedent for military resistance. Through VFP, the Quakers, and others, a peace infrastructure existed to support dissenting soldiers, revving up as war neared. Antiwar veterans circulated a "Call to Conscience to Active Duty Troops and Reservists" urging them to refuse service in Iraq.[47] Addressed to the individual soldier, it warned, "You will be part of an occupying army. Do you know what it is like to look into the eyes of people who hate you to your core?" It also insisted that in an "unjust war" when "an errant bomb kills a mother and her child it is not 'collateral damage,' it is murder."

The first within the military community to protest were family members of current soldiers, forming as Military Families Speak Out (MFSO). The inspiration for the group first came when union activist Charley Richardson heard people at a shop counter arguing about whether to go to war.[48] He wished he could show them a picture of his son Joe, a marine likely bound for Iraq, so that they would consider the human dimension of war. Richardson and stepmother Nancy Lessin, also with experience in union organizing, began sending letters to other military families in which they shared their concerns. A sympathetic father responded with the wish that they start an organization.

Lessin made it happen, with the help of members of the Gulf War–era Military Families Support Network. The breakthrough was a January 2003 press event in Washington, prompting dozens of families to reach out to the fledgling group. "Thank goodness I found you," was the common message. "I thought I was the only one."[49]

Military Families Speak Out attracted both peace parents who had protested the Vietnam War and patriotic members of generations-long military families. Above all, they were united in their agonizing worry for their children in a conflict they questioned. The group's unique voice was quickly given prime billing by antiwar organizers. Those in uniform "are not George Bush's nameless, faceless military," explained Lessin at Code Pink's March 9 rally. "They are David and John [and] Alejandro and Nichole. We worry about them, and we worry about the beautiful children of Iraq."[50]

Concern for the troops raised issues of class and race as well. The volunteer army, like the one drafted for Vietnam, had disproportionate numbers of the poor and people of color. Reverend Grayson Hagler, the only male speaking at the Code Pink's protest, noted that "Black people are always locked out of the debate in this country. . . . We have always been involved in the military, as a hope for jobs and for benefits to go to school, and then we are used as cannon fodder."[51] Taking the antiwar movement to the military meant fighting on several fronts.

"THESE PEOPLE ARE NO DIFFERENT FROM MY NEIGHBORS"

While the debate over war with Iraq was playing itself out in parliaments, embassies, the media, and the world's streets, a quieter drama was growing in intensity and danger: the humanitarian efforts of foreign nationals in Iraq. Since the 1991 Gulf War, there had been a near-continuous presence of Westerners in the country working to limit the effects of the sanctions and prevent a new large-scale war. Joining America's International Center and Voices in the Wilderness were groups like Italy's Un Ponto Per (Bridges to Baghdad). Together, they were in the 1990s an anti–Iraq war movement unto themselves. Long predating 9/11, this activism was largely unknown even among Americans opposing Bush's threatened war.

The recent precedent was the Central American solidarity campaigns of the 1980s. North Americans went south to assist with civilian infrastructure, education, and health care, sometimes protecting vulnerable communities from state or insurgent violence. They often felt great affinity with the socialism of their Latin American partners. The Catholic Church, deeply influenced in the region by liberation theology, was the social base for much of this work. Many of those called to Iraq were Catholic veterans of the solidarity movement.

Work in Iraq was generally more difficult. The distance was far greater. Few of the Western visitors spoke Arabic. NGOs were sparse, and Christian churches had a small presence. US activists faced reprisals from their own government. They felt no kinship with Saddam's regime, which oppressed its own people and strictly monitored foreign visitors. And they were working, sometimes under US bombardment, with a traumatized, mostly poor population.

This new solidarity movement had its roots in the Gulf Peace Team. Entering Iraq just before the war's start in January 1991, the team was made up of seventy-seven people from eighteen countries, including twenty-five from the United States. The idea, as Peace Team member Kathy Kelly embraced it, was "to stand between the warring parties and negotiate a dialogue."[52] To most media, these were Saddam's willing dupes, used as "human shields" to prevent US bombing.

A motley crew by Kelly's admission, the group at first struggled with the daunting environment. Not "people of consequence" to the Iraqi government, they were hardly poised to broker peace. Still, the regime sought to control their impressions. "If you hear the same line in several [places]," Kelly learned, "you know it's not really what people think." The official message to Americans like her was: "We know that you are not your government, and your people would never do this to us." Talking to doctors dealing with the wounds of war was more revealing.

The most important lessons came in moments of vulnerability with everyday people. Crowding in bomb shelters during US air assaults and visiting squalid refugee camps, Kelly recognized "that these people are no different from my neighbors." Asked whether she felt like an interloper, Kelly answered, "It depends on where you take your evaluation from." In Iraq, she was invited into people's homes and into communities of women coping with terrified children and their own fears. These encounters came with an obligation "to do everything you possibly can to give voice to what you have seen." They also alienated her from many Americans, including her mother, who echoed the military's crude boasts of a battlefield rout.

With the Gulf War quickly over, the Peace Team shifted to bringing in humanitarian aid. The team had mostly exited Iraq by spring of 1991, with Kelly and a handful of others staying into late summer. This tight-knit group, which included a Belgian, Indian, Hollander, Australian, and several Americans, pledged to work together if crisis again called.[53] True to their pledge, some regathered in Peace Teams in the war-ravaged Balkans. Kelly largely moved on from Iraq, while staying in touch with fellow Gulf Peace Team member and Catholic Worker Ann Montgomery, who had continued to make trips to the country.

Voices in the Wilderness was born of both conviction and chance. As Christmas of 1995 neared, the famed scholar of nonviolence George Lakey led a workshop in Chicago, where Kelly lived. An exercise challenged participants to develop a pitch around some difficult campaign. Kelly's group chose resisting the sanctions on Iraq. Yet Catholic Worker Chuck Quilty accused the group of merely "play acting what you *would do* if you *did do* something about Iraq."

Within days, he, Kelly, and the others delivered a letter to the US Treasury Department declaring their intention to bring banned supplies into Iraq. The government warned the three hundred signers of penalties of twelve years in prison and million-dollar fines should they do so. The group, now smaller, answered, "We can't be governed by unjust laws that punish children to death."

In the spring of 1996, Kelly and a small team went to Iraq to set up an aid operation. Ramsey Clark assisted with the visas. With the help of Father Jirbail Kassab of Basra's Sacred Heart Parish, they met with Iraqi officials to explain their plan. The officials gave the green light.

The result was Voices in the Wilderness: A Campaign to End the US Sanctions Against the People of Iraq. Over the next seven years, the Chicago-based group sponsored dozens of delegations. Visitors observed the dismal conditions—hospitals with no anesthetic, pharmacies with no drugs, dying children—and delivered what aid they could. They also formed intense "brotherhood-sisterhood links" with mostly poor Iraqis.

In the United States, Voices ran a speakers bureau, exhibited photo essays of their trips, and sponsored lengthy peace walks and fasts. The Arab American community, Iraqis among them, sponsored frequent presentations by the group. Repeatedly brought into court, Voices was hit with five-figure fines. "Put it on our tab" was its defiant attitude.

Voices' summertime fasts outside the United Nations bore unexpected fruit. The fasters may have "meant nothing to anybody on First Avenue" or the mainstream press, remembers Kelly. Yet Denis Halliday, anguished in his role as humanitarian coordinator of the sanctions program, took note of them. So too did Iraq's

Voices in the Wilderness cofounder Kathy Kelly in Baghdad in 1999 at the Dijla Secondary School for Girls. She and Sister Suzanne (Order of Preachers) lead students in singing verses in Arabic to "We Shall Overcome." Photograph by Alan Pogue.

representative to the UN mission, briefing Deputy Prime Minister Tariq Aziz. Aziz and Voices soon connected.

Voices members were in Bagdad during the US-UK's December 1998 bombing campaign Operation Desert Fox, meant to punish Iraq for alleged breaches of UN resolutions. Months earlier, Halliday had quit his post, denouncing the sanctions. Making international waves, his resignation boosted grassroots, antisanctions work. In early 1999, he teamed up with IPS's Phyllis Bennis for a twenty-two-city speaking tour in the United States. Their hosts were universities, Muslim associations, peace groups, and churches.[54] Halliday was "the hero of the day," able to draw both crowds and media.[55] Each community was required by the speakers to hold a public rally and reach out to both local press and politicians.

Relentless campaigning helped shift global perceptions of the sanctions. The United States' hard line was the main barrier to real relief. In August 1999, Voices helped organize a delegation to Iraq, led by Bennis, with the staff of five members of Congress. It was a fight to get even these allies to commit to the trip.

In Iraq, the Americans met with Halliday's successor, the German diplomat Hans von Sponeck. He detailed the devastating effects of the sanctions, calling them a "serious attack" on Iraq's "social fabric."[56] Five months later, he too quit in disgust. The day he resigned, eighty-six people protesting the sanctions were arrested at the US mission to the United Nations.[57] More and more, major US peace organizations like Peace Action and the American Friends Service Committee sent delegations to Iraq.

When 9/11 hit, Voices immediately knew that it spelled trouble for Iraq. The night that the December 2001 Walk for Healing and Peace concluded, Kelley rushed to the airport for a preplanned trip to the country. By August 2002, Voices began assembling the Iraq Peace Team (IPT), distinct from its usual delegations. Its mission was to "live among the Iraqi people" and "prevent an escalation of the current war against Iraq."[58] Voices recruited seasoned activists, ideally with experience in conflict zones. "We oppose any form of armed aggression," the IPT call explained, and "know that a new war against Iraq will take its greatest toll" on civilians. No side in the conflict, it said, was "blameless." The first IPT group arrived in September, establishing a base at Baghdad's Al-Fanar Hotel.

Partnering with Voices was the Christian Peacemaker Teams (CPT). Its first, thirteen-person delegation arrived in late October. Leading it was Peggy Faw Gish, age 63, from Athens, Ohio.[59] Among the group were teachers and pastors, with the oldest age 77. Only Ann Montgomery had been to Iraq before. Into winter, more CPT members arrived, as others left.

A member of the pacifist Church of the Brethren, Gish had a long history of antiwar and civil rights activism. In 1963, she and her husband attended the famous March on Washington. As war with Iraq loomed, she did her best to stop it. With Athens's People for Justice and Peace, she protested at the local courthouse, lobbied her representatives, and joined the Iraq Pledge of Resistance. Moved by her faith and eager to do more, she made the difficult decision to go to Iraq.

The idea for the CPT came in 1984 when the American Mennonite Ron Sider challenged Christian pacifists to go into conflict zones.[60] Pacifists, he insisted, had to take risks for peace equal to what soldiers faced in war. The CPT soon formed, with its base in North America and members from diverse denominations throughout the world.

In the early 1990s it sent its first official delegations into Iraq, Haiti, and Palestine. Future teams worked in Colombia, Mexico, and even US cities ravaged by violence. The core of CPT's work, as its motto holds, is "getting in the way." By that it means both standing between conflicting parties and following the path of a peace-loving Christ, dedicated to humanity's downtrodden.[61] Drawing on its reputation for piety and Western origins, the group was often able to prevent human rights abuses.

Ed Kinane felt called to Iraq, arriving with the IPT in early 2003.[62] Though a child of the 1960s, he was not much for organized protest, and at first led a "hobo" existence of frequent travel. His big awakening came in 1969 in Guatemala. In its lush countryside he saw the lives of the poor, whose "arduous and penurious" labor fed the profits of US corporations. Graduate study at New York's radical New School gave him a scholarly perspective on the conditions he observed. Deciding that "the world needs activists more than it needs academics," he left university to begin decades of work with the poor and oppressed. Some of it was with the Peace Brigades International in Latin America and Sri Lanka, whose work mirrored that of the CPT.

Mike Ferner, a Veterans for Peace leader from Toledo, Ohio, was another IPT volunteer. Toledo, like Gish's hometown, had a robust antiwar movement. Gripped by "rising anger, frustration, and resolve," Ferner was drawn to Iraq.[63] "I need to do something more than carry a sign," he wrote, "commensurate with the horrors about to unfold."[64] Local TV covered the start to his journey, with one station asking if he was a "traitor."

In Iraq, the peacemakers kept busy. They visited hospitals, schools, churches, and mosques; assisted at a Baghdad orphanage; met with UN agencies; organized press events; and prayed for resolve. "Who am I," wondered Gish, "to think that a small group of us could make any difference"?[65] "The readiness that comes with the gospel of peace" drove her on.[66] In early January, tragedy struck when seventy-three-year-old George Weber from Ontario, Canada, was killed in a highway accident. The shipment of his body to Canada was delayed, as it required clearance from the UN sanctions committee.[67] He would not be the last CPT member to die in Iraq.

The Westerners tried to size up the threat to Iraq while agonizing over whether to stay through the start of a war. Aware of the global protests and confident that weapons inspectors would find no violations, Kathy Kelly was hopeful that war might be avoided. It took an NBC correspondent expert in the region to shake that sense: "They're gonna come," she told Kelly in late December. "Chaos will follow."[68] Ferner, the IPT press contact, was ominously told by Arab journalists: "Your media covers the rockets taking off. We report from where they land."[69]

As desperation grew, Voices and the CPT hung banners reading "To Bomb This Site Is a Violation of the Geneva Conventions Article 94" on a Baghdad school, hospital, electric facility, and water treatment plant.[70] They even went in February to the Kuwait border near Basra to put themselves between Coalition and Iraqi forces. A press statement implored, "Peace can still be preserved. Devastation can be avoided. But you must go beyond what you think you can do."[71] "Our dream" with the prayerful trip, Kinane reports, "was to get in the way" of war.[72]

For four days, a dozen or so Westerners fasted in an impromptu peace encampment, bearing pictures of Iraq civilians. Among the group was Vietnam War veteran Charlie Liteky, who had received the Congressional Medal of Honor for saving the lives of wounded soldiers.[73] In protest of US policy in Latin America, he had become in 1985 the only awardee to return the medal. The group gave UN patrols an antiwar statement, hopeful they would share it with US soldiers in Kuwait. Liteky later thundered into the void, soapbox style, the group's fury at war. Judging the risk too great, the Iraqi government ordered the protesters away from the border. No US media covered the peace action.

The IPT also surveyed Iraqis' attitudes. Some conveyed in whispers that they welcomed a US invasion if it toppled Saddam. Others expressed great fear. A University of Baghdad professor told Voices'

Members of the Iraq Peace Team and Christian Peacemaker Teams at a days-long peace vigil at the Iraq-Kuwait border near Basra, Iraq, in February 2003.

Cathy Breen that while the Gulf War was "terrible," this "time will be the end. I have no doubt that we will all be killed."[74]

The peacemakers learned more about Iraq than much of the media. The major US press, like the US government, was enthralled with exiles like Ahmed Chalabi and his Iraqi National Congress. Chalabi pressed for an invasion, feeding false tales of Iraqi WMD to US intelligence and the media. The Iraqi people, he was certain, were eager for a US attack. Mostly confined to Baghdad's Palestine Hotel, American journalists did little to verify this view. Instead, they focused on the war of words between the US and Iraqi governments and military preparations on both sides.

Voices had a strained relationship with the Western press corps. The media resented that the group could enter and leave the country with relative ease, paying only modest bribes. Voices was also less encumbered inside Iraq, adding to the irritation. Yet Voices helped get journalists out of detention when they ran afoul of the Iraqis' rules, and major news outlets sometimes sent dispatches out of the country on Voices' behalf.

Most of all, the media questioned Voices' purpose in Iraq. The only major piece about the group was written by the British correspondent John Burns for *The New York Times* in October 2002. Under the stinging title "12 Americans Stage Protest Hussein Is Happy to Allow," it described an antiwar demonstration at a small UN office in Baghdad.[75] Burns noted the absence of Iraqi state media, suggesting that the regime did not want to encourage free speech among Iraqis. Around that time, Saddam released thousands of common prisoners in an apparent bid for greater public loyalty. "I wish people in our country would be willing to show the same spirit of forgiveness," he quoted Kelly saying, "to the two million people in our prisons." Burns seized on this as proof that the group was shills for Saddam.

Voices exercised political rights denied to Iraqis and was careful about what it said publicly. So too, Iraqis were limited in what they could share with the group, chiefly their hatred of Saddam. Kinane quickly learned "not to ask certain kinds of questions."[76] Kelly later confessed an "inherent flaw" in Voices, stirring feelings of guilt.[77] When in Iraq, the group did not speak as they would back home, because the danger to themselves and Iraqis was too great. "Had we waited to act perfectly," Kelly also worried, the group "might not have done anything" at all. Whether Voices conceded too much is debatable. But the group, far from shills, plainly reflected on the dilemmas it faced.

One media voice stood out for its curiosity and candor: *The Washington Post*'s Anthony Shadid. Well-read in Iraq's history, Shadid was the only Arab American journalist with Arabic-language skills prominent in the US press. Given leeway by his minder, Shadid sampled the attitudes of ordinary Iraqis. Just the threat of invasion had changed things. "The combustible ambiguities of Iraq—the ancient pride, the desire for justice, the resilience—were emerging beneath the fear, conformity, and silence."[78]

This cautious hope did not mean that most Iraqis welcomed a US attack. "I worry about the bridges, the homes, the beautiful buildings," a Baghdad artist told Shadid. "They're going to burn the forest to kill the fox." Suspicion of US motives ran high. The threatened "invasion has nothing to do with democracy," insisted an Iraqi academic. "It is basically an angry response to the events of September 11 [and] the survival of Saddam Hussein, and it has something to do with oil interests." Above all, Shadid saw that in Iraq either-or choices—like being pro- or anti-American, for or against invasion—hardly captured a complex political and emotional reality.

One of Kelly's encounters conveyed the mood in Iraq and the spirit of her work.[79] In 2002, she visited an Iraqi boy who had endured surgery without anesthetic. Learning the next day of his death, Kelley told her hosts, "You have to show me healthy children." Even she had reached a limit.

She visited the Baghdad School of Folk Music and Ballet, whose director, Hisham al-Shirab, she knew well. Alone with the school's young students, she saw artwork they had made. One piece showed planes smashing into the World Trade Center. "What were you thinking when you made this?" Kelly asked its creator. Mistakenly flattered, he explained in English: "Allah wanted this to happen to people in Am-ri-ca, so Am-ri-cans understand what happens to other people when Am-ri-ca hits them." When a teacher entered, the boy quickly added "and Iraqi people love Am-ri-can people."

Kelly's response to his troubling words was to break down their bitter logic. In America, she explained, music is often played at funerals. One such song, featured in some funerals for the 9/11 dead, is "Finlandia"—a century-old Finnish hymn sung by peace communities. The children asked to learn the song. So Kelly, her minder, their driver, and the school director gathered at a piano to compose a translated version. The song announces:

> This is my song, oh God of all the nations
> A song of peace, for lands afar and mine
> This is my home, the country where my heart is
> Here are my hopes, my dreams, my holy shrine
> But other hearts in other lands are beating
> With hopes and dreams as true and high as mine . . .

Within days, the students had learned "Finlandia" in Arabic and English. Its message seemed intended for the American people as well.

"IRAQ WAS A PLACE I COULDN'T NOT GO TO"

Voices' stepped-up efforts were part of a small surge of Westerners traveling to Iraq. By January 2003, the Iraq Peace Team had 75 members in-country. A month later, more than 150 foreign peace nationals were in Iraq.[80] Their journeys show the depth of antiwar feeling and the meager faith some had in conventional protest. The trips also reveal the challenges to effective solidarity posed by Saddam's regime. They point, finally, to long-standing questions among peacemakers over the purpose and value of their work.

In early February, thirteen women from Code Pink made another trip to Iraq. Among them was the Dallas-based Iraqi American Amira Matsuda, who helped the group connect with everyday Iraqis. It held antiwar protests with children and oil workers, gave blood, pressured aid organizations to publicly oppose war, and met with women civil society leaders.[81] Despite thickets of media following them, few stories made it into the Western press.

Hollywood also got into the act. In October, actor Sean Penn spent $50,000 to publish a statement in *The Washington Post* condemning Bush for a "simplistic and inflammatory view of good and evil" that threatened his presidency with "a legacy of shame."[82] In mid-December, he visited Iraq. "I didn't come here to criticize any government," Penn announced. He met with senior Iraqi officials to discuss how Iraq might avoid war. Back home, Americans tarred him as disloyal. Even the liberal George Packer suggested that Penn had been "taken in by the Baathist propaganda machine."[83] Citizen efforts to avoid war, in the super-heated American environment, went only so far.

The most dramatic trip was by ordinary citizens from many nations. On February 1, three buses departed from Shaftsbury, England, stopped in London, and set off for Iraq. Two were iconic red double-deckers buses owned by Joe Letts. A cameraman in Iraq after the Gulf War, the fifty-two-year-old Letts was haunted by the suffering he saw there. The precise intent of the fifty or so travelers was to serve as "human shields." "We want to make it impossible," explained Letts, "to drop bombs on the Iraqi people because we will

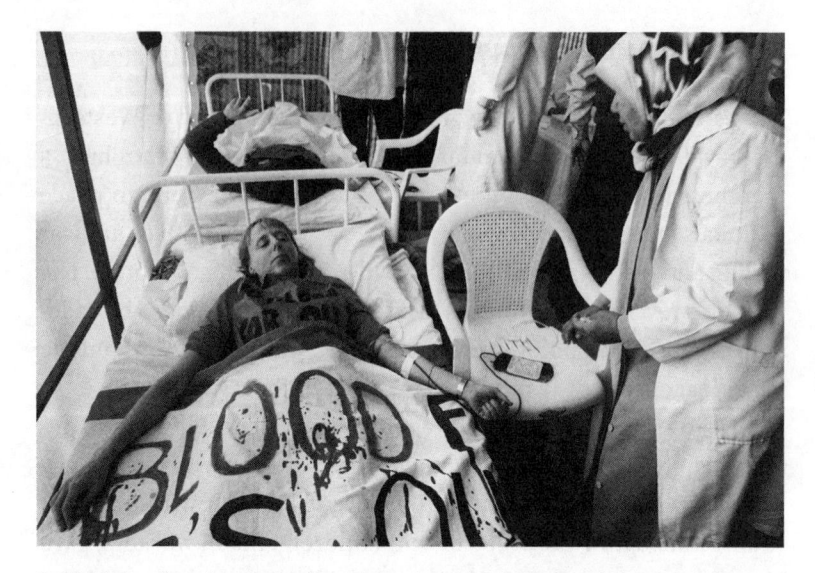

Code Pink cofounder Medea Benjamin gives blood after participating in a peace vigil at the al-Doura oil refinery on February 5, 2003, in Baghdad, Iraq. The banner draping her reads "No Blood for Iraq's Oil." Code Pink had brought a delegation of women to Iraq to protest the threatened US war. Photograph by Oleg Nikishin / Stringer via Getty Images.

be in the way."[84] Emblazoned on one bus was "Not in Our Name," bringing the vaunted slogan directly to Baghdad.[85]

The trip's main instigator was the thirty-four-year-old ex-marine and Gulf War veteran Ken O'Keefe. After leaving the military, O'Keefe became a left-wing radical. In 1999, he renounced his citizenship out of disgust with US violence, including in Iraq. "I would rather die in defense of justice and peace," O'Keefe explained in *The Guardian*, "than 'prosper' in complicity with mass murder and war."[86] O'Keefe's premise was that street protests would fail. But a "mass migration" of thousands of internationals to Iraq might deter an attack.

The fellow travelers included a former British colonial administrator, an Australian architect, a Palestinian hairdresser from London, and the American beatnik poet John Ross, who had been imprisoned decades ago for resisting the Vietnam War–era draft. The buses picked up allies throughout Europe and in Turkey, cheered on by their fellow citizens.

Much like the Gulf Peace Team a decade before, the convoy represented a ragtag internationalism—earnest, intrepid, and out of its depth. Letts and others took issue with the charismatic but domineering O'Keefe, who broke off from the trip to arrive in Iraq on his own.[87] Among debates was how much to stress global goodwill versus "in your face" criticism of the United States.

The steepest challenges were inside Iraq. When the buses arrived in Baghdad on February 15, timed for the global protests, crowds broke into pro-Saddam songs. The government asserted immediate control over the visitors. It took them on orchestrated tours of hospitals and to alleged civil society gatherings, like a "student peace conference." Largely absent of students, and replete with staged chants and a military band, it seemed the stuff of a tin-pot dictatorship.[88]

Convoy members had wanted to shield classic civilian sites like hospitals. Instead, the regime placed them at water treatment plants and power stations. The breaking point came when the shields were stationed near military encampments. After insisting that they first vet all locations, the visitors were expelled by the Iraqi government, just three weeks since arriving.

The trip was a hard lesson in the hazards of citizen diplomacy in a dictatorship mostly hated by its own people. One American denounced Bush to a cab driver, only to hear the cabbie call Saddam evil.[89] "Cold fear," confessed an elderly "church-and-queen Tory" on the trip, caused many of the Westerners to leave. Still, many felt no regrets, believing that they had helped to "humanize" the conflict to people in their home countries.

The original bearers of the Not in Our Name message also traveled to Iraq. On January 5, 2003, Colleen Kelly, Terry Rockefeller, Christina Olsen, and Kathleen Tinley of Peaceful Tomorrows arrived with a small delegation in Bagdad. Voices arranged the trip.

Their goal, explained Colleen Kelly, was to "put a human face on the suffering of the Iraqi people" and "express our hope that there would be no war."[90] In no way did they "support the government" of Iraq. Even so, they knew the trip would be far more controversial than the group's visit to Afghanistan in early 2002. There, the hope was that the United States would compensate civilian victims, which even the war's backers could support. This time, they were visiting a country ruled by America's nemesis to oppose a war sold as vital to Americans' safety.

The group had long received disparaging messages, often accusing it of naivete. "How can you call me naive?" Kelly fumed at this charge. "My brother was just murdered." She most admired "the courage of people who speak out before" a war starts. "That's why I felt so strongly in the lead-up to the Iraq War, because it felt like this is the time."[91] Terry Rockefeller, who lost her sister, first learned about the peace families from their Afghanistan trip. "Iraq was a place I couldn't not go to."[92] "Traveling to Iraq as a witness for peace" seemed to Christina Olsen "the most meaningful way I can honor the memory of my sister," who died on a hijacked plane.[93]

Though spearheading the trip, Kelly had a hard time convincing her family to let her go. Fearful of losing another child, her father volunteered to come along for added safety. He relented, in part, by learning that Bishop Thomas Gumbelton was part of the delegation. The trip was now "God's work," protected by a holy paternalism.

In Iraq, the group made emotional visits to schools, hospitals, and Iraqis' homes. "You can eat our food, we can speak your language," observed one host. So "why should we fight each other?"[94] When accompanied by minders, the travelers could not quite tell what was staged. Kelly, a nurse, sensed that "things didn't exactly match" medical protocol in the hospital she visited. But she also sensed that the Iraqis' suffering was very real, as was their pride. "If war is imposed on us," one Iraqi insisted, "we will never obey the U.S. demand or orders."[95]

Among the foreign visitors to Iraq, Peaceful Tomorrows was a uniquely compelling media story. That did not mean that coverage was favorable. Major media tended to affirm them when speaking to the pain of loss and downplay or belittle their antiwar convictions. In 2002, CNN's Wolf Blitzer had pushed Kelly Campbell to state whether the group rejected "war under any circumstances," in which case its position would not be "serious."[96] Colleen Kelly had been trailed by a TV crew for the NBC special "The Road to Baghdad," hosted by Tom Brokaw. Aired while she was in Iraq, the program surrounded her antiwar message with profiles of a US soldier, an Israeli citizen, and an Iraqi exile, all favoring war.[97]

Upon returning from Iraq, Olsen, Rockefeller, and Tinley were interviewed by CNN's Connie Chung. She suggested, with her combative questioning, that they had been pawns of Saddam.[98] Private messages to the peace families were outright hostile. The worst called them "Fucking Traitors!" who "should be ashamed to call themselves American."[99]

The purpose of Peaceful Tomorrows was not to win over these detractors or even a skeptical media. Speaking out against war was only one part of its activism. David Potorti reflected on both the frustrations and rewards of the group's efforts. He identified "the power of gestures" as "an answer to a question I frequently ask myself about the group's work: Does it matter? Does an act of solidarity with a Muslim group, a gesture of kindness to a kid in Afghanistan . . . really mean anything? Who benefits from those connections? And what changes? The answer, in most cases, is *me*. I change. And in doing so, I begin to achieve the change I want to see. . . . And those moments of peace, when strung together, will create a peaceful world."[100]

Much like Voices and the Christian Peacemaker Teams, Peaceful Tomorrows practiced a politics of connection. Potorti suggests a value to compassion that escapes conventional political measures. That value may have been most deeply felt by antiwar groups like his own, which met with the victims of war. But the belief in the innate reward to the exercise of conscience—the importance of doing the right thing, for its own sake—was broadly shared by antiwar activists. They also formed deep relationships with one another, helping to sustain them through hard and uncertain times.

SHOCK AND AWE

By mid-March, the run-up to "one of the most choreographed and longest-planned wars in history," as Ken O'Keefe described it, was palpably drawing to a close.[101] UFPJ organizers gathered in Washington to launch the Emergency Campaign to Reclaim Democracy & Stop the War Now! For it, they partnered with the Iraq Pledge of Resistance and NSYPC. "Despite the massive showings of opposition to this unnecessary war, Bush still won't turn back," explained Kai Newkirk in a press statement. "We have no choice but to raise the bar of our resistance."[102]

On March 13, the Campaign announced five days of civil disobedience, spread across eight cities. Speakers at the press event included Representative Jim McDermott (D-WA), MFSO's Nancy Lessin, UFPJ's Bob Wing, and an Iraqi American family. Later that day, Lessin, Wing, Kelly Campbell, and NSYPC's Molly McGrath were arrested at the Capitol.[103] The following day, seventy people were arrested in San Francisco's financial district. Among them was Warren Langley, a retired Air Force lieutenant colonel and former head of the Pacific Stock Exchange.[104]

Two days later, Lisa Fithian and Nadine Bloch led a nonviolence training for another arrest action in Washington. Each person shared a word to describe how they felt as war approached. "Stop," "Peace," "Anguish," "Scared" were the staccato replies.[105] On March 17, just hours before Bush's gave his ultimatum, fifty or so people were again arrested at the Capitol. Among them were four members of Peaceful Tomorrows, including seventy-one-year-old Rita Lasar. New to arrests, the peace families took an enormous step. Forty people were arrested at the United Nations, and another thirty in San Francisco, making it the largest day of civil disobedience so far.[106]

Backing arrest actions did not come easily for some in UFPJ. The Emergency Campaign was largely the initiative of Newkirk, the youthful member of the UFPJ's leadership committee. In the global justice movement he had seen the transformative power of nonviolent civil resistance. He now sought to harness that power to stop a war. "We have to escalate" on a massive scale, he thought.[107] Though approved by UFPJ, the Campaign lacked the active support of key players within it, who felt uncomfortable with extralegal protest and a strategy based in high-risk, nonviolent force. Newkirk saw the Campaign as a "meaningful escalation," but "far from what I had hoped." The antiwar movement had, for now, hit its limit.

The day Bush's ultimatum expired, Code Pink marched with caskets to Donald Rumsfeld's Washington home and toured the halls of congress with desperate pleas to halt the threatened war. Usually festive, its members came as "collateral damage," smeared in ash and red paint. A world away, two intrepid protesters delivered the same basic message. On the morning of March 18, Australia's Dave Burgess and British national Will Saunders painted in giant red letters "No War" atop Sydney's famous opera house.[108] The duo were mild-mannered research scientists intent on making a bold statement as their countries pushed for war. Fearful but determined, they free-climbed sixty-seven meters up the edge of the building's main sail and quickly did their work, before a stunned audience below.

Since the first hint of a US war with Iraq, Americans and peoples of the world rose in protest. They editorialized and argued and drafted "top ten reasons" not to go to war. They petitioned, lobbied, called, and emailed their political leaders. They fasted and held vigils. They made placards and puppets and formed peace signs with their bodies. They dropped banners and painted buildings. In record-smashing numbers, they marched the world's streets, recited poems, and performed theater. They resigned and got fired. They sat in, blockaded, and went to jail. They were attacked by police horses and violently arrested. And some went to Iraq to put themselves in harm's way.

A question hovered over all of it: Would it stop the war?

Just before dawn in Iraq on March 19, the United States launched a "decapitation" attack targeting Saddam, mistakenly thought to be on a farm at Baghdad's edge. Fighter jets dropped four massive bombs, followed by forty cruise missiles. One bomb missed its target, killing an Iraqi civilian.[109] "American and coalition forces," Bush announced hours later, "are in the early stages of military operations to disarm Iraq, to free its people and to defend the world from grave danger."[110]

Shock and Awe followed. Developed in the 1990s, its idea was to so overwhelm the enemy that they quickly conclude, in the words of its architect, "This is hopeless. We quit."[111] At 9 p.m. on March 20, Baghdad and its night sky were lit up by flares, tracers, anti-aircraft

Code Pink members, dressed as "collateral damage," visit congressional offices on Capitol Hill in Washington, DC, on March 19, 2003. That evening President Bush announced the start of the US assault on Iraq. Photograph by Stefan Zaklin / Stringer via Getty Images.

fire, and explosions. The world's media captured the attack from cameras atop their hotels. For hours, US networks broadcast live footage, with military experts and correspondents guessing at the kind, size, and target of the blasts. More than thirteen hundred missiles and bombs were delivered in this opening air assault.

Even seasoned journalists were spellbound. Virtually alone on American television, CNN's Peter Arnett had rigorously covered the Gulf War, away from Pentagon censors. Now with NBC, he shared with Tom Brokaw what he saw: bombs "blowing apart the prized presidential compound of Saddam Hussein. Many of his major administrative buildings going up in smoke and fire, Tom. Again, another. Another, just disintegrating. Bigger than the Gulf War. . . . This is Shock and Awe, Tom."[112]

"The overture is over," agreed Brokaw. "This is the main piece of Shock and Awe."

The dogs of war, for now, had won.

CHAPTER 8

"ARE WE PROTESTING THE WAR OR THE OCCUPATION?"

The US War in Iraq

Shock and Awe, wrote *War Times*, was "a moment of global pain," with "grief and anger spread[ing] as the casualties mounted."[1] Mohammed Elbaradei, head of the International Atomic Energy Agency, called the invasion "the saddest day of my life," because he was sure that the Americans would find no WMD.[2]

"A lot of us screamed in fury that these demons had started this war," said UFPJ leader Bill Fletcher Jr.[3] After February 15, Phyllis Bennis observed, "so many people were saying, 'They can't go to war now with this kind of protest all across the country and the world.' And then, what a surprise, they can, and they do, saying 'Fuck you' to everybody."[4] Bill Streit was in a Virginia jail serving time for spilling blood on the Pentagon three months earlier to protest the looming war. When he learned that it had started, he went to his cell and wept.[5]

Demonstrations followed all over the world, roughly mirroring the protest map of February 15. Groups in the United States had called for "day after" protests to meet the war's start. Organizers recorded more than five hundred antiwar actions on March 20 alone.[6] Through the weekend, cities and towns in all fifty states saw demonstrations rivaling their largest so far. UFPJ had already planned a protest in New York City on March 22. Authorities this time permitted a march. Hundreds of thousands came, moving down Broadway in a giant column of bitter resolve.

In Seattle, protesters blocked major traffic arteries. In Chicago,

Protestors in Chicago, Illinois, occupy Lake Shore Drive on March 20, 2003, just after the start of the US assault on Iraq. Photograph by Garth Liebhaber, Chicago Indymedia.

they shut down Lake Shore Drive. Nearly forty cities, from Wichita, Kansas, to Wilmington, Delaware, held smaller civil disobedience actions as part of the Iraq Pledge of Resistance. Close to two hundred colleges and universities staged walkouts. More than a thousand students exited Harvard classrooms, with five thousand walking out in Berkeley.[7]

The Bay Area alone witnessed mass disruptions. Going back to the 1960s, it had been home to a radicalism virtually unthinkable anywhere else in the country. Forming in late 2002, Direct Action to Stop the War (DASW) spent months devising its response to the war's anticipated start. Its plan was to bring business to a halt in San Francisco's financial district. Now a DASW organizer, Claire Bayard recalls the desire to go beyond mere symbolism by hitting corporate profits and unsettling public routines.[8]

The group spanned leftist worldviews and cultures. One wing came out of the global justice movement and sought to use the tactics so successful in Seattle in 1999. Another saw the war in Iraq mainly as a form of imperialism in keeping with historic assaults on the Global South. It attracted young people of color but also older sectarian Marxists, whose hard-line politics rankled the antiauthoritarian set. Managing these differences, DASW drew the praise of one activist for "facilitating perhaps the best, most sustained, affinity-group-based, hundred-plus-person spokescouncil-meeting, coordinated, consensus-process-using collection of autonomous actions ever."[9]

At 7 a.m. on March 20, protesters began assembling at predesignated actions sites, like key intersections and the offices of companies profiting from war.[10] Thousands came in established affinity groups, with thousands more arriving unannounced. As blockades, they made human chains, often handcuffing themselves to one another underneath rock-hard PVC pipe. Some even linked to other protesters with high-tech bicycle chains around their necks. "Downtown and all over was a sea of angry, tearful people," observed one demonstrator.[11]

Police laboriously cut protesters apart with saws, hauled them away, and scuffled with roving militants. Radio operators like Bayard tracked the bedlam, raising the spirits of locked-down protesters with word of other, successful blockades. So overwhelmed were police that firefighters with drawn axes stood in as riot cops. "What are you going to do?" Bayard asked them. "Behead us?" Lasting long past midnight, the protests yielded over fourteen hundred arrests, with hundreds more in the following days.

"It is impossible," gushed one protester, "to fully convey the magnitude" of the day. "This time we actually cost them something," declared another, who had disrupted the work of Bechtel, poised for reconstruction work in Iraq. Activists dubbed the protest, in heroic tones, "The Battle of San Francisco." Yet some saw little cause for celebration. "It wasn't glorious," Bayard said, mindful of the unfolding tragedy in Iraq.[12] "We knew this wasn't going to stop [the war]. We had already lost what was about to happen."

The tumult in San Francisco was mostly a local story. National media were strongly prowar, with TV anchors weaving jingoistic commentary into ceaseless coverage of bombardments and Pentagon briefings. Coverage of protest was sparse and fleeting, leaving the impression that public dissent barely existed.

That bubble was pierced at the Academy Awards, broadcast on March 23. Earning the award for Best Documentary was the biting, anti-gun violence film *Bowling for Columbine* by the left-wing auteur Michael Moore. With no prepared speech, Moore agonized over whether to use his platform—33 million Americans watched that night—to denounce the war.[13] Mustering the courage, he explained: "We live in fictitious times [with] fictitious election results that elect a fictitious president . . . sending us to war for fictitious reasons." Boos rose from the glitzy theater, spurring Moore on. "We are against this war, Mr. Bush! Shame on you!" he exclaimed. "And any time you've got the Pope and the Dixie Chicks against you, your time is up." The band was ordered to cut him off.[14] Fearful for his safety, security escorted Moore from the theater. He returned to Michigan to find his house vandalized and for years received physical threats. A national story in both news and entertainment media, Moore's speech was likely the most visible act of antiwar protest to that point.

"MISSION ACCOMPLISHED"

Spirited demonstrations continued into early April, sometimes meeting great force. On April 7 in Oakland, antiwar activists teamed up with dockworkers to protest the shipping of war matériel to Iraq. Police, citing baseless fears of "terrorist" activity, shot at defenseless protesters with wooden dowels, causing severe wounds. The city of Oakland later paid more than $2 million to dozens of the injured.[15] That same day, riot police arrested without warning ninety-four protesters peacefully lining a Manhattan Street. They were there to protest the Carlyle Group, an investment firm with extensive holdings in the military sector and ties to the Bush family. New York City paid a massive settlement for the illegal arrests.[16]

This first wave of protests soon waned. Antiwar leaders warned of "a sense of futility and hopelessness" while offering reasons to "keep fighting for peace."[17] The movement was left to wonder what power it had to shape the actions of the war makers.

Going forward, the politics of the war massively depended on the war itself. For months, the public had been schooled in the reasons for the invasion and expectations for it. Americans were also versed, if to a lesser degree, in the case against the war. Events on the ground would determine which position was right.

The early phases of the war favored the prowar camp, though not without setbacks. US forces and their allies found neither WMD stockpiles nor programs. The war's opponents accused the Bush administration of willful deceit. Some media outlets now probed how and why they had misrepresented the Iraqi threat. The administration claimed that it was misled by the world's leading intelligence agencies, including America's own. Regardless, Bush presented the removal of Saddam as a great gift to both global security and the Iraqi people. The US campaign was named Operation Iraqi Freedom.

The military picture had its own complexity. Shock and Awe may have been more branding than the actual battle plan, which included substantial ground forces. Expectations of a quick knockout punch were so high that pundits expressed surprise when combat dragged on. On March 31, Peter Arnett declared on Iraqi state television that the first US "war plan has failed because of Iraqi resistance."[18] Going too far, he was fired by NBC.

The failure was short-lived. Much of the Iraqi army melted away without a fight. Superior American firepower quickly subdued units that did resist. On April 7, the US military took control of the main presidential palace in Baghdad, finding it empty of regime leaders. That same day came a deadly coda to the "decapitation" strike preceding Shock and Awe. A B-1 bomber dropped four massive bombs on Baghdad's affluent neighborhood of Mansur, where the military thought Saddam and his sons were hiding.[19] The attack killed a dozen civilians.

In another show of force, a US tank fired into the Palestine Hotel, which housed many Western media. The strike killed a journalist with a Spanish outlet and a Ukrainian cameraman working for Reuters. Eyewitnesses disputed the military's claim of sniper fire from the roof, suggesting a deliberate US attack. Elsewhere in Baghdad, US bombs hit the office of the Qatar-based Al Jazeera network, denounced by Bush officials as anti-American. A Jordanian journalist was killed.

In a last bizarre act as Iraq's ruler, Saddam toured a Baghdad neighborhood before going into deeper hiding. On April 14, the United States declared victory in the capital city. More than two dozen coalition soldiers and perhaps two thousand Iraqi fighters were killed in its taking. US forces also captured the northern city of Kirkuk. In the south, the British took Basra, dominated by Shia Iraqis.

The Bush administration and the media cast the military victory as a grand liberation. This frame received its signature imagery when, on April 9, TV cameras broadcast live the toppling of a giant statue of Saddam in Baghdad's Firdus Square.[20] Echoing scenes of communism's collapse, an Iraqi man beat the statue's marble plinth with a sledgehammer. US infantry then dislodged the sculpture, while a small crowd cheered on. Before the statue came down, a Marine draped an American flag over Saddam's face. Noting Iraqi complaints and the terrible optics, US forces quickly replaced it with an Iraqi flag.[21]

Most Americans embraced the war when it was underway. For months, a prowar majority had held steady at between 52 and 59 percent.[22] Opposition ranged from 35 to 43 percent, with a majority of Blacks, Democrats, and the highly educated against the war. Even before Shock and Awe, support for war had inched up. The last preinvasion Gallup poll showed nearly two-thirds of Americans in favor, even without UN support.

The war's start brought support to more than 70 percent, where it stayed through the first weeks of combat. The absence of WMD had little immediate impact on public opinion. In early April, nearly 60 percent thought that the war was justified even without the rumored weapons. Just 31 percent felt that the Bush administration had "deliberately misled" the public.[23] Americans rallied around the flag. More precisely, a "movable middle" ambivalent toward the war moved in its favor. The outbreak of deadly combat evoked a visceral patriotism and concern for the troops, best kept safe by decisive victory.

On May 1, Bush declared "Mission Accomplished." It was a scene worthy of Hollywood. With the president riding shotgun, a Navy fighter-bomber roared onto the USS *Abraham Lincoln*.[24] The carrier, freshly returned from the Persian Gulf, was now just off the San Diego coast. Emerging from the cockpit in full aviator dress, Bush gave a thumbs-up to the five thousand sailors, standing in uniform-white rows. After changing into a suit, he took the podium in front of a massive, red, white, and blue banner with the triumphant slogan. Bush announced that "major combat operations in Iraq have ended" in a victory "for the cause of liberty" and "the peace of the world."[25] Troops from more than a dozen countries, dubbed "the coalition," would soon join security operations.

The victory was big with trouble. The world had seen on television the chaos of Baghdad's collapse. Looters sacked government palaces and ministries but also schools and hospitals. From the National Museum of Iraq, they took Mesopotamian antiquities and treasures of the Islamic world. Asked about the turmoil, Rumsfeld replied that "freedom's untidy" and that "stuff happens."[26]

The US assault caused enormous resentment among Iraqis. Those in Baghdad endured sleepless nights followed by scorching days without electricity. Between 3,000 and 5,500 Iraqi civilians were killed in the war's first month.[27] "What kind of liberation is this," pleaded a wounded Iraqi teenager to the CPT's Peggy Gish. "If this is democracy, we don't want it."[28] "This is freedom?" a Baghdad doctor asked a *Washington Post* reporter, amid the smears of blood in his hospital. Seeing lifeless children pulled from the rubble in Mansur, an Iraqi shouted, "Fuck all Americans."[29] "Popular disdain for Saddam," explained another, did not mean "Come America, we'll throw flowers at you."[30]

Powerful players emerged, like Muqtada al-Sadr and his Mahdi Army. Al-Sadr was the son of a prominent Shia cleric murdered by the Iraqi regime. He now led dispossessed Shia in Baghdad's Sadr City (renamed from "Saddam City"). Thousands strong, his armed followers could turn on US forces at any time. Iraqis "will reject any government brought by America," al-Sadr warned.[31] Other tribal and religious leaders consolidated local power and built militias. Tensions sharpened between Shia and Sunni Iraqis that had for years been managed by Saddam. This divide threatened any bid for national unity or peaceable political arrangement.

Decisions made by the US government added to the peril. It declared as Iraq's sovereign power the Coalition Provisional Authority (CPA), housed in one of Saddam's palaces. Leading the CPA was Paul Bremer, a Republican ex-diplomat with little experience to guide his task. Its first edict dissolved the Ba'ath party and forbade anyone in its higher levels from serving in government. Affecting thirty thousand Iraqis, this disqualified vital technocrats, police, and even teachers from helping to build a new state. The second order disbanded the Iraqi military, leaving three hundred thousand Iraqis unemployed, embittered, and ripe for resistance.[32]

These "drastic actions," observed a military historian, "undercut ongoing plans to involve more Iraqis in shaping and securing their own future."[33] Ideology was one reason for the CPA's hard line. The US officials driving the war saw it through the lens of freedom and tyranny, punishing anyone on tyranny's apparent side. This stance failed to appreciate that for many Iraqis Ba'ath party membership or military service was compulsory and signaled no loyalty to Saddam. Other CPA measures opened Iraq's economy to Western investments and profit, including by selling off state-owned companies.

The CPA's diktats and America's pomp in victory raised profound questions about the war, symbolized by the shifting flags over the toppled Saddam statue. Was the invasion an act of conquest, as the American flag suggested and the antiwar movement charged? Or was it an act of liberation, as the Iraqi flag suggested and the Bush administration claimed? The fate of the entire campaign hinged on which was truer, in Iraqi perceptions most of all.

The choice between American hypocrisy or benevolence was potentially deceptive. After 9/11, Bush repeatedly described liberty as the "gift of the almighty," not held by America alone. He also claimed for the country a special obligation to bring liberty to the world. This liberal universalism gave the war its lofty purpose.

And yet, as geographer Neil Smith has argued, US military interventions, no matter how self-serving, are always wrapped in professed virtue.[34] Within an inherently expansionist idealism, the American language of freedom and force are one and the same. By these terms, the war makers could remain credible believers in their own good intentions—even as the United States invaded a foreign nation, killed its people, rewrote its laws, and threw it into chaos. "Few things are more dangerous," said the legendary British historian Eric Hobsbawm near the war's start, "than empires pursuing their own interests in the belief that they are doing humanity a favor."[35]

The Bush administration played a risky game of manufactured narratives. The absence of WMD enflamed the war's critics. "We see dead young Americans," seethed Sean Penn in a May advertisement in *The New York Times*. "We see no WMDs. We see dead Iraqi civilians. We see no WMDs."[36] If initially excused by many Americans, the false claim undermined trust in the administration's word and judgment. Should the costs of the war rise, Americans might ask why it was being fought at all.

Reports soon emerged that the US military, and not Iraqis, had begun the destruction of the Saddam statue. The homecoming of the *Lincoln's* sailors, after a grueling ten months at sea, was delayed for the sake of Bush's photo op. The ship was angled to avoid sight of the California coast and suggest that Bush was somewhere near Iraq.

In West Virginia's Private Jessica Lynch, the war got an early hero. In late March, her convoy was ambushed, killing eleven US personnel. Lynch was knocked unconscious and captured. US Special Forces soon rescued her from an Iraqi hospital. Yet initial Pentagon reports claimed that Lynch had resisted her attackers in a daring firefight. Publicly correcting government and media falsehoods, the photogenic Lynch grew to resent her image as "little girl Rambo," perfect for selling the war.[37]

Most audacious was the claim of Mission Accomplished. It declared the end of a conflict that was really just beginning. Nowhere was this truer than in Fallujah. Fallujah was a pious, fiercely independent city of three hundred thousand in the Sunni heartland.

Spared ground combat, it was entered by US troops only in late April, after Saddam's fall. It had already built new governing bodies, which prevented the looting that plagued other cities. Local leaders also showed some willingness to work with the Americans.

The Americans proved reckless invaders. Residents were offended by the military's aggressive surveillance and use of a school as an operating base. On April 28, US forces shot into a small, likely unarmed crowd protesting the school's takeover, killing seventeen civilians. Two days later—and just hours before Bush's triumphant speech—US troops fired on another unarmed crowd protesting the initial shootings. Three more civilians were killed. The city turned on the Americans, soon to become the epicenter of the Iraqi resistance.

"ARE WE PROTESTING THE WAR OR THE OCCUPATION?"

The first months of the Iraq campaign had the antiwar movement on its heels. Its predictions of drastic overreach or regional conflict had yet to come true. The United Nations joined reconstruction efforts, establishing in August its assistance mission in Iraq. However cynical, the Bush administration's imagecraft appeared effective. Most Americans seemed content to believe that the US triumph was near total and that the Iraqis were now happy.

Shortly after Baghdad's fall, an activist asked the War Resisters League, "Are we protesting the war or the occupation?"[38] David McReynolds replied that the war appeared over. The pressing task was to contain the Bush administration's "permanent attack mode," evident in a "ghoulish casting call for the next war's enemy," like Iran. Brooklyn Parents for Peace issued a statement opposing the occupation. It called for the transfer of authority in Iraq from the CPA to the UN General Assembly, the restoration of Iraqi sovereignty, the withdrawal of invading armies, and the presence of international peacekeepers, if requested by an Iraqi government. Such was the antiwar position, post–Mission Accomplished: an earnest yet unenforceable internationalism asking weak global bodies to manage the fallout of an invasion they had opposed.

In July, the scholar-activist Barbara Epstein gave a public assessment of the antiwar movement, speaking of it already in the past tense. She praised its embrace of the concept of imperialism, which many opponents of the Vietnam War had avoided for its far-left associations. Its current use, she felt, "reflects a widespread understanding" that "the attack on Iraq was one component of a larger agenda of world domination."[39] This outlook "gives reason to hope" that antiwar dissent might outlast "the U.S. victory" in Iraq.

Activists pursued a number of approaches. The first was to maintain visibility through ongoing protests, which might again grow if circumstances in Iraq changed. Antiwar vigils and rallies remained part of the national landscape. More ambitious was to build for the long haul by strengthening the movement's base, scope, and organizational capacity. *War Times* declared the need to "link the peace movement to the social justice movement" and, with an eye to the next election, "place regime change on the U.S. political agenda in 2004."[40] A small number of activists opposed the occupation from inside Iraq. They became heralds of disturbing information that falsified the triumphant picture of the war presented by the US government and media.

United for Peace and Justice, like the larger movement, faced a crossroads. Looking back, UFPJ leaders recall no letup on Iraq or belief that the war was remotely over. Yet the invasion, organizers conceded at the time, left many in the movement "demoralized," while costing it "wavering supporters."[41] Traffic on the UFPJ website had fallen 90 percent from the war's start.[42] "Our movement is going to get smaller before it gets bigger," conceded Win Without War co-chair Bob Edgar.[43] Less than a year old, his organization even debated closing up shop.

To remain a force, the antiwar movement had to evolve quickly. On May 31, UFPJ held a teach-in in Washington, DC, on "Iraq, Preemptive War, and Democracy" drawing a thousand people. Edward Said, Howard Zinn, and Arundhati Roy, among others, put the invasion into larger contexts and warned of the war's expansion.[44] "The same thing is going to happen to other countries," a sixteen-year-old Yemeni American told a *Washington Post* reporter at the event.[45] The future of the movement, it seemed, lay in opposing future wars.

Days later, UFPJ held its first National Strategy and Planning Conference in Chicago. More than five hundred people from thirty-eight states attended, representing dozens of groups.[46] They ranged from the Peoria Area Peace Network to Black Voices for Peace to antiwar mainstays like the American Friends Service Committee. The participants ratified a "unity statement," adopted a structure for the group, and set a strategic vision for the coming year.

It was a "watershed event," said the UFPJ's main press contact, "bringing the U.S. antiwar movement to a new level of strength." Leslie Cagan echoed that sense of triumph. Months into the invasion, she and others wondered whether UFPJ and the broader antiwar movement had true staying power. "Were we real, or would we be fifteen people from the hardcore left talking to each other? The response was terrific," with the Chicago hotel unable to accommodate everyone who came.[47] "We weren't about building an organization called United for Peace and Justice," she said of the conference. "This really was a movement-building moment."

"The war on Iraq," the conference unity statement declared, "was the leading edge of a relentless drive for U.S. empire."[48] Attendees were adamant that UFPJ reject "single focus" politics and instead address a nexus of interrelated issues.[49] The convention pledged to protest the occupations in Iraq, Afghanistan, and Palestinian territories; new bids for "preemptive" war; assaults on civil liberties and immigrant communities; and ongoing corporate globalization. Approved action plans included protests at an upcoming trade summit and mobilizations at the Republican and Democratic national conventions in 2004. Opposing the occupation of Iraq was just one of seven organizing areas identified by the meeting.

Developing a structure for UFPJ, now with 650 member groups, was no small feat. The main work fell to Lisa Fithian and Van Gosse. The structure, they insisted, "actually has to be functional," while honoring the democratic spirit of the members.[50] Ideal for the task, Fithian was a skilled "in-betweener," successful at bringing together various forces on the left. As coordinator of the Washington Peace

Center, she had helped "internal processes grow."[51] She also pushed the traditionally white center toward antiracist work, making it both a catalyst and a resource for diverse communities and political struggles. The key challenge for UFPJ was to be a "mass democratic organization" that enables "lots of people" in a large country "to do collective work."

The proposed structure called for a steering committee led by co-chairs, answerable to a larger "assembly." An array of working groups would address specific issues. It was especially important that "everyone can see themselves somewhere in the leadership." By rule, the steering committee was to be at least half people of color and women, with queer folks and youth each making up 15 percent. The conference ratified the structure and elected to the committee thirty-five people representing a broad spectrum of the US left.

UFPJ's efforts to promote diversity had their limits. Nationally, people of color were least supportive of the Iraq War. They were integral to UFPJ's founding, active in the conference planning, and prominent in the workshops. But only between 10 and 15 percent of conference participants were from communities of color. Arabs, South Asians, and Latinos were especially few in number. Only a small minority of attendees were under thirty.[52] UFPJ organizers conceded their targeted outreach for the conference was "too little, too late." Despite its strong critique of racism, the organized antiwar movement remained largely white, sustaining the historical reputation of so much peace work.

UFPJ opposed the Iraq occupation as part of a comprehensive campaign against empire, war, and domestic inequality. This approach encouraged the linking of issues and the collaboration among coalition groups on UFPJ projects. Most ambitiously, it promised to make UFPJ a potent, progressive force in US politics, able to address a broad range of policies. This model had its risks, beyond spreading resources thin. It might align the antiwar movement with causes unpopular among many Americans, including in its own ranks. In late August, a prominent member organization privately complained of "UFPJ's seeming inability to focus" on

Iraq.[53] It questioned the relevance of global justice protest to the occupation, while doubting that opponents of the war widely shared anticapitalist views. Critical of ANSWER's radicalism and mission creep, UFPJ itself contended with how sharp and broad its message should be.

"JUST YOU TAKE IT BACK TO YOUR COUNTRY"

In Iraq itself, any sense that the conflict was over was plainly a mirage. Americans at all familiar with the country knew that its people were unlikely to embrace the occupation. Brian Becker, who had been to Iraq several times, certainly felt that way. "Not only are they imperialists, they're fools," he said of the Bush administration. "The whole national psychology [is that] 'We are a proud people. We're not going to be humiliated.' . . . So the idea that you're going to go in with American, Western, non-Muslim troops and destroy their country, and take it over, and create some little passive puppet government in Baghdad, it's so absurd."[54]

Becker's impressions squared well with Anthony Shadid's studied perspective. "Perhaps more than any other Arab citizens," Shadid observed, "Iraqis are instilled with traditions of pride, honor, and dignity."[55] To many Iraqis, "it was not Saddam under attack, but Iraq," preventing "them from putting their destiny in the hands of another country."[56]

The invasion itself was a great wound. Peace activists like Voices saw this firsthand, assisted by the Iraqi government. Since their first meeting in 1996, Kathleen Kelly and Tariq Aziz had drawn somewhat close. Aziz was one of Saddam's henchmen, at his side during Saddam's murderous purge of Ba'ath Party members in 1979. Other sins followed as part of Iraq's leadership circle. Admitting that "Aziz has blood on his hands," Kelly was adamant that Voices not be Saddam's "silent servants."[57]

At the same time, she felt that Aziz "earnestly wanted to see something different" for his country. He helped Voices reach Iraqis "in the poorest areas, in the hottest temperatures." He also worked with the United Nations to secure food baskets with staples like lentils and cooking oil as a major part of its relief program, adopted elsewhere in the world.

It was an "odd choreography," Kelly admitted, between Voices and Aziz. She openly challenged his brazen anti-Semitism, which seemed to bolster his respect for her. As thanks for Voices' efforts, Aziz sent flowers to Kelly on her birthdays. Her subtle gift to him was to encourage his atonement. A Christian, Aziz spent February 15, 2003—the great day of global protest—in the Italian city of Assisi, home to the medieval priest St. Francis. A day earlier, he had met with Pope John Paul II, outspoken in his opposition to war.[58]

For his trip, Kelly had given Aziz a book about an epic cross-cultural encounter. It chronicled Francis's willing capture and appearance before Malek al-Kamil, the sultan of Egypt, during the Crusades. The sultan was so impressed by Francis's piety, bravery, and message of peace that he spared his enemies' lives and negotiated with the Crusaders for an end to war. Aziz, Kelly learned, read the book and spent his night in Assisi prostrate in prayer. Whether he felt "repentance," she could not say.

Aziz enabled the Iraq Peace Teams to remain in Iraq through Shock and Awe. "Nowhere" in Baghdad, Kelly reports, "was really safe." By night, the Al-Fanar Hotel took local families into its crude bomb shelter, left dark by the absence of electricity. Kelly tended to the daughters of a frightened mother. The youngest acted out a pantomime of death, shooting Kelly's flashlight like a gun at her family. On the worst nights, the adults struggled to stay calm as "earsplitting, gut-wrenching, huge, rip-it-apart bombs" exploded nearby.

Kelly stayed in touch with Hisham al-Shirab, the music school director whose students had learned "Finlandia." When the looting started, he begged her to "go to your military and just get one jeep" to protect the school. The military's response was "zero," and looters ravaged it. "This is what I have left," al-Shirab later said to Kelly, showing her a compact disc with the students singing "Finlandia." "Do you think you'll ever teach this song to kids again?" she asked. "It is too much, this that you ask, Kathy," he replied. "Just you take it back to your country." In Baghdad Kelly later organized what amounted to a "birthday party in defiance of war" for the daughter of a widowed mother. During the party, a massive US bomb hit nearby, turning the mother's face to "pure contempt" for the United States.

The chaos of war also strained the goodwill of the Iraq government toward the Iraq Peace Team. A week into the invasion, a huge explosion rocked a telecommunications building near the Al Dar Hotel housing some IPT members. Straying from their minders, Peggy Gish and others took unauthorized video and photographs of the building, which they thought had been hit by a US bomb. An Iraqi weapon was the culprit. Wishing to conceal this fact, police arrested the small group of Westerners. Gish and others were deported.[59] It felt, she said, like "being thrust out of a tornado" (though she would soon return). Those remaining faced painful orders from Iraqi officials to further winnow their ranks.

The US press, to be sure, reported on civilian casualties. When US strikes hit Baghdad neighborhoods, correspondents described the carnage, interviewed witnesses, and surveyed hospitals for casualty counts. Occasionally they profiled the victims and their families. They also reported the official denials of the US military. These typically claimed that the bombs were seeking valid targets, while offering rote language about the regrettable loss of civilian life in any armed conflict.

This reporting was faint in the din of war. Human Rights Watch issued in mid-June detailed findings from its investigation into the killings in Fallujah by US troops.[60] It found scant evidence to back the military's claim that US soldiers had responded to hostile fire. (Rocks had been thrown at them.) The report's release, like the killings it discussed, was at best a passing story.

"Collateral damage"—a term burned during the war into the American psyche—rationalized the cost to civilians of an invasion that the Iraqi people *should* want. It was, US leaders claimed, the unavoidable price that Iraqis paid for their own freedom. From the American public, collateral damage demanded little more than generic pity. The far splashier story was the military's release in early April of "most wanted" card decks. These profiled Saddam, his sons, and other regime officials as the invasion's prized targets, whose fate the media vigilantly tracked.

Voices and the IPT worked to broadcast what they observed. When in Iraq, they issued press releases, did radio interviews, and published accounts of their witness in peace newsletters and religious publications. (The key tools of citizen-journalism, the camera phone and social media, had not yet been invented.) When back in the United States, they held public events and were occasionally profiled by the hometown press. Most of this was confined to antiwar media and communities, rarely reaching the broader public. The IPT efforts may have strengthened the convictions of the war's opponents but did little to sway its backers.

The mainstream US press in Iraq, with mild exception, kept Voices at arm's length. One journalist had told Kelly, "As soon as the war starts, you don't exist, you are a ghost," useless in her antiwar stance.[61] Shared danger softened attitudes. During a US bombing raid, John Burns—the *New York Times* columnist who had skewered Voices—was caught in a stairwell with Kelly and other media. Terrified, he tugged at her and declared to his colleagues, "This is the heart and soul of the humanitarian witness. If you want to hear about that, talk to her." "Well, they didn't want to hear about that," Kelly reports, though she appreciated the kind words.

The Western peacemakers sometimes showed a gumption that the major media lacked. Ed Kinane attended a Pentagon briefing in Baghdad's "Green Zone," the fortified seat of the occupation. He asked General Ricardo Sanchez, the top commander in Iraq, "When the US military commits abuses, what kind of follow-up is there?"[62] For his question, which the press at the time "wouldn't dare ask," Kinane was briefly detained by US soldiers.

The Iraq Peace Team could also see increasing tensions among Iraqis. Another canned line fed to Kelly in Saddam's Iraq ran: "We are Sunni and Shia, there is nothing between us, we are all brothers and sisters." Yet in Basra she saw the "seething resentment" of many Shia and "knew there was going to be chaos" if the US invaded. After the invasion, "kids in Sadr City" formed into teams of armed

US soldiers, shortly after the invasion of Iraq, outside Baghdad's Al-Fanar Hotel, where the Iraq Peace Team was based. Hung by the group, the main banner reads "Courage for Peace . . . Not for War." Photograph by Thorne Anderson.

looters. In another ominous sign, she crossed into post-invasion Iraq with a duffle bag full of sheet music for the forlorn music director. No one checked its contents. Weapons were flooding through the border to various militias. "Desperation," shared by the "very poor," those "who just wanted out," and those who now sought "the upper hand," all made for a "brew" of "deterioration."

As Baghdad fell, US troops massed near the Al-Fanar Hotel. From its balconies, Voices held banners reading, "Courage for Peace, Not for War" and "War Is Terror." Echoing the hospitality Iraqis had shown them, Voices offered water and dates to the parched soldiers, baffled as to who these Americans were. Over several days, young soldiers who never dreamed of being in Iraq confessed remorse for violence they had already committed against defenseless Iraqis. One soldier asked to pray with the Voices team.

Peace activists also observed the ignorance and callousness of the American occupiers. Voices reached out to the Office for Reconstruction and Humanitarian Assistance, the precursor to the CPA. At Iraqis' urging, they pleaded with US officials to protect a Baghdad warehouse stocked with food and blankets badly needed for winter. Voices was told that they "have no business here." They also alerted the US military to a cholera outbreak in Halla. Even higher-ups had no idea that Halla was a large city—some mistook it for a Baghdad street—and ignored the request for help.

A month into invasion, the Christian Peacemaker Teams implored the US military to guard open weapons depots and unexploded bombs, which killed or maimed children playing with them. (UNICEF estimated one thousand of these casualties.)[63] The military refused. Overseas friends answered the CPT's desperate pleas for brightly colored tape to at least mark where the weapons were. "Either they couldn't or wouldn't pay attention to reality," was Kelly's sense of the occupiers. Eventually, US soldiers posted at their base a "stay out" message to Voices: a cardboard sign with its logo and seven silver bullets taped around it.

Code Pink made another foray into Iraq shortly after Shock and Awe. In Baghdad, they worked with the Organization for Women's Freedom in Iraq, run by Yanar Mohammed. Together, they held a protest of the US occupation, as was becoming common. Iraqis' complaints included the absence of water, electricity, and security, as well as the violence of the invasion itself. The women gathered at Firdus Square, where the Saddam statue had fallen. The US military, recalls Benjamin, "screeches up and says, 'What the fuck are you doing? Who's in charge?'" "The Iraqis," replied the diminutive Yanar, setting the "massive men with all their paraphernalia" against her. One tells her, "To do anything like this you need a permit." "She looks up at him and says, 'You've got to be kidding me. Where's your permit to be in my country?'"

Where the occupation failed Iraq's civilians, the Western peacemakers tried to step in. Part of the work was documenting Iraqis' grievances and unmet needs. In May and June, CPT surveyed seven hundred or so Baghdad residents. Nearly half of respondents felt unsafe in their neighborhood and kept their children home from school as a result. Massive majorities reported a lack of sufficient income and access to health care and medicine. To publicize their findings, the CPTs held their own demonstration in Firdus Square. Their signs asked, "Is this Freedom?" and listed common Iraqi hardships.[64]

Another American was trying to help Iraq's civilians: Marla Ruzicka.[65] Ruzicka had spent much of the last year in Afghanistan building the NGO she founded, CIVIC. It continued to survey civilian victims and win support for them from the US government through the Afghanistan Civilian Assistance Program. Hoping to do the same in Iraq, she arrived in Baghdad not long after the invasion, bringing CIVIC's mission with her.

Ruzicka immediately began working with journalists, aid workers, CPA officials, and US military personnel, first to learn about Iraq's victims and then to find a way to get them aid. Complicating her efforts, the US military insisted that it kept no records on the number or identity of the civilians it harmed. Civilians could make claims but were entitled to compensation only for injuries or deaths that occurred outside of combat operations. This was almost never the case, given how the US military defined the rules of engagement. An innocent family shot at a US checkpoint or in a firefight would not be eligible for compensation.

Ruzicka and her Iraqi colleague Faiz Ali Salim began traveling throughout the country to document civilian losses, as she had done in Afghanistan. In Iraq, the losses were vastly greater. She eventually found allies in the US military willing to help. The main one was Judge Adjutant General Jonathan Tracy, with the Army's First Armored Division in Baghdad. Assisting civilian victims, she told him and others, was both the right thing to do and a way to win Iraqis' "heart and minds." With Ruzick's help, Tracy had established by September an ad hoc "Condolence Payment Program" that made modest payments to Iraqis for injuries, deaths, and property loss.[66] CIVIC teams often found the victims, investigated their cases, and brokered the payments. The program remained imperfect, serving only a fraction of the Iraqis who needed it. But it was something, leading to more robust efforts at civilian assistance.

Once firmly antiwar, Ruzicka now sought to limit war's damage by working with those responsible for it. Her famous dedication, despite her own mental health struggles, enabled her and CIVIC to achieve what established human rights organizations and humanitarian agencies could not.

"OUR FRAGILE SENSE OF WHO WE ARE AS A PEOPLE"

Western peace activists in Iraq saw great challenges for the occupation. The situation was even more volatile than they could tell. An Iraqi perspective, attuned to the nation's history and mindset, elaborated Iraqis' anguished rage.

Mustafa Muhsin's family was one of distinction.[67] It included patriots of Iraq's first independent state, established in 1932, and leaders of its modernist culture. From the 1958 coup on, he lamented, Iraq was ruled by tyrants and thugs—worst of all, Saddam. Incorruptible, his father worked in Iraq's foreign service and was personally protected by Tariq Aziz from state reprisals. His father's wish was for Iraq to be a credible nation, respected on the world's stage.

Raised mostly in diplomatic posts overseas, Muhsin earned an engineering degree in Iraq, doing contract work with the government in the 1990s. He later fled Iraq for a better future, paying exorbitant bribes. In his adoptive American home he cursed Saddam, while protesting the post–Gulf War sanctions. His disappointment ran in all directions, including with the US left. Saddam, he felt, "almost wanted people to starve to have a better story." Ramsey Clark, whom he met in Iraq, "came across as angry and a crank." With his acerbic manner and extreme positions, Clark did a "disservice" to the very Iraqis he sought to help. The religious wing of the antisanctions movement seemed to Muhsin both the most principled and pragmatic.

After 9/11, Muhsin demonstrated against the threatened war. Few antiwar Iraqis in the United States joined public protests. They feared Saddam's overseas agents, who might see them at an antiwar rally in the company of an alleged communist, who was also a Jew, with relatives in Israel, and therefore suspect. Even one's family members in Iraq could be put at risk. Guilt and punishment by such flimsy association happened "all the time."

Undeterred, Muhsin was in the streets of New York City on February 15. As preparations for war dragged on, he grew resigned that it "was inevitable," while hoping that "something good comes of it." Iraqis, he felt, would greet the invasion with some measure of "joy" if it brought the end of Saddam's rule and a path to true Iraqi sovereignty. The Bush administration's vision, however, that "the wall comes down and everybody sings Kumbaya" was fantasy. Iraqi resentment of the United States, responsible for years of brutal sanctions, ran deep.

The day Shock and Awe began FBI agents visited Muhsin's New Jersey home. Aware of work he had done on Iraq's sanitation system, they pressed him for details, presumably to assist in the postwar administration. They also asked if he "knew of anyone who wanted to harm the United States." Dumbfounded, he answered, "bin Laden." The true purpose of the interview, he felt, was "intimidation." Other Iraqis he knew in America were paid similar visits.

Those Muhsin knew in Iraq experienced the invasion as "sheer terror." His grandparents' house was in the Mansur neighborhood, hit by the April 7 air strike. It shattered the windows and blew the solid oak door blocks from the house while his grandmother was inside. The civilian casualties were wrenching for him to see on television. Yet for Muhsin and other Iraqis, the initial violence of the invasion did not fully eclipse the promise of a better future for Iraq or even discredit the occupation. So much depended, going forward, on *how* the Americans treated the Iraqi people.

"The Americans made a mess of things," Muhsin quickly concluded. CPA head Paul Bremer "invariably, almost on purpose, made the wrong decision." Behind his de-Ba'athification measures lay extraordinary ignorance. The Ba'ath party, in the first instance, was not an actual governing entity, with a coherent ideology and a party apparatus. Instead, it was a means of control, based on submission to its rule ruthlessly enforced by Saddam and his operatives. Bremer's edicts "disenfranchised" everyday Iraqis in a great variety of professions, leaving them "suddenly unemployed and angry."

De-Ba'athification also played a poisonous role in fomenting sectarianism. Saddam, Muhsin insisted, was not at heart a sectarian.

(His leadership circle, like the Ba'ath Party as a whole, had Iraqis of all sects and ethnicities.) Far from religious hostility, he oppressed the Shia chiefly because some resisted his rule based on a Shia identity. After the invasion, opportunistic Shia—chief among them Ahmed Chalabi—convinced the Americans that the Ba'ath Party was a Sunni institution. They manipulated the purge process to target Sunnis and empower themselves. Sunnis pushed back.

In July 2003 the CPA appointed Iraqis to an Iraqi Governing Council (IGC). It used a quota system for the distribution of Shia, Sunnis, Kurds, and others within the body. Outrageous to many Iraqis, this reinforced sectarian divisions and reeked of a "divide and conquer" strategy. It was the reason that Muhsin's father, designated as a "Sunni" for the council, refused the offer to join. One by one, IGC members were assassinated, whether for alleged collaboration with the occupiers or in various power plays.

Sectarianism at an institutional level trickled down, transforming Iraqi culture. For years, Iraqi Sunnis, Shia, Kurds, and Christians had freely commingled. Post-invasion, one was increasingly thought to have a Sunni name, or live in a Shia neighborhood, or work in a Sunni ministry, with natural rivals among one's compatriots.

The deeper blow of the occupation, Muhsin felt, was to a spirit of Iraqi sovereignty. Cursed with "arrogance," the Americans "underestimated people's sense of their own being." Iraqi companies were blithely shut down or sold off, with US contractors like Halliburton handling most everything. "The sense of Iraqiness or being in control" gave way to "Excuse me, we took over your country, sit here, behave." Iraqis both felt, and were, sidelined in their own destiny.

But the "one thing every Iraqi screamed about" was the looting of the Iraqi National Museum. "Where do the tanks stop?'" Muhsin asked. "Ministry of Oil. Ministry of Defense. Why didn't they try to protect the museum?" To explain what the museum meant to Iraqis, he first said that "Iraq is the cradle of civilization." He then asked with rhythmic precision, "Where was writing invented? Iraq. Agriculture? Iraq. Mathematics? Iraq. Schools? Iraq. Government? Iraq. Hierarchy? Iraq. Constitution? Iraq." The loss of the museum far transcended the looted objects, which quickly found their way onto the global market, and even the history they represented. "It's an affront to our identity," Muhsin explained. "We're poor. We've been killed. We've been starved by the sanctions. This is all we have left. Our fragile sense of who we are as a people."

For those on the ground, the anger was boiling over. In June, ex-members of Iraq's disbanded military held a demonstration. One protester explained, "We are all very well-trained soldiers and we are armed. We will start ambushes, bombings and even suicide bombings. We will not let the Americans rule us in such a humiliating way."[68] US forces fired into the crowd, killing two.

Broken by outsiders, Iraq was about to further break from within. The US military and government, the media, the antiwar movement, and the American people would soon discover how badly, reshaping the politics of the war.

CHAPTER 9

FROM "BRING 'EM ON" TO "BRING THEM HOME"

The Unraveling of the Iraq War

The Bush administration stuck to its line of Mission Accomplished. Deputy Defense Secretary Paul Wolfowitz described anti-US violence as the "last remnants of a dying cause."[1] Only in late June, with up to twenty attacks a day on US forces, did a leading general concede that, "It's war, however you describe it."[2] Pressed about insurgent strikes, Bush replied on July 2, "Bring 'em on." It was a stunningly glib way to welcome a fight claiming American lives.

Instantly incorporated into antiwar messaging, Bush's words spurred some to action. On August 13, Military Families Speak Out and Veterans for Peace launched in Washington, DC, the "Bring Them Home Now!" campaign as a direct response to Bush's provocation.[3] It demanded the immediate withdrawal of US troops from Iraq. MFSO's Nancy Lessin opened the press event by excoriating Bush for his "words of false bravado," which "taunted those shooting at our loved ones." "From proud liberators," she said, "our troops have become oppressors and occupiers in a hostile nation." Stan Goff, an outspoken antiwar veteran with a son serving in Iraq, called the administration "rich men in very expensive suits conducting statecraft like gangsters."

The campaign came at a vulnerable point in the war. Victory had already been declared, leading soldiers and their families alike to wonder why US troops were still there. Charges of Iraqi WMD were quickly evaporating. Some soldiers had returned from their first deployments, candidly describing to loved ones the conditions they faced. Others would never come back, begging the question of what their sacrifice was for.

At the event was Fernando Suárez del Solar, whose marine son Lance Corporal Jesus Suárez del Solar was killed a week into the invasion by a US cluster bomb. (The family was initially told that he died at enemy hands.) The *Los Angeles Times* profiled the foreign-born Jesus and his family, stressing their dual ties to the United States and Mexico.[4] At first the distraught father sought to get the military to pay for a proper Mexican funeral. He soon turned against the war, becoming among the first Gold Star parents to publicly condemn it.

"Mr. Bush, enough of this, enough deceit," he said in Spanish. "You are destroying the American people." His wife, Rosa, also present, began loudly sobbing. The soldiers still in Iraq, other parents stressed, were like canaries in the coal mine, though little able to warn the country of the growing peril. The military, they charged, was concealing the numbers of attacks on US forces, as well as the number of injured soldiers, who often lacked proper armor.

The US military was poorly prepared for the war it now faced. Despite its experience in Vietnam, counterinsurgency was not part of its current doctrine. Much about the Iraq occupation worked against counterinsurgency, which required winning the trust of occupied peoples. The seat of US power was Baghdad's Green Zone, a vast, heavily fortified complex closed off from the city. In it, US personnel enjoyed plentiful food, multiple bars, a lavish gym, and the internet. Iraqis coped with shortages of water, electricity, and basic security.

Supplying the Green Zone required massive convoys from Kuwait, which were vulnerable to attack. The soldiers and contractors defending them were prone to fire with little provocation, often hitting civilians. The use of artillery against alleged insurgents also punished common Iraqis. Apparent battlefield victories, as in Vietnam, might prove political and even military setbacks.

The US military had little sense of who the insurgents were. Among them were shadowy "foreign fighters," intent to sow mayhem in a country already upended by invasion. In late August, the

Fernando Suárez del Solar, whose son Marine Lance Corporal Jesus Suárez del Solar was killed in Iraq on March 27, 2003, sits among boots symbolizing the US war dead near at a protest of the Republican National Convention in New York City on September 2, 2004. Photograph by Lee Celano, WireImage via Getty Images.

United Nations assistance mission in Iraq was hit by a suicide truck bomb. The blast killed twenty-two people, including its Brazilian director, Sérgio Viera de Mello. The Jordanian-born Abu Musab al-Zarqawi, who formed an al-Qaeda affiliate in Iraq after the invasion, claimed responsibility. A second strike on UN offices all but ended the UN's reconstruction efforts.

The US military turned to "cordon-and-sweep" operations to suppress attacks. Soldiers rounded up thousands of Iraqi males, who were often held, zip-tied and hooded, for hours in public view. Among them were family members of alleged insurgents, held as hostages to coerce surrender. Most harrowing were the nighttime raids, in which the Americans might ransack households; seize money, jewelry, and personal documents; terrorize women and children; and haul fathers and sons away. The raids violated family honor, touching deep nerves in Iraqi society.[5] The US military increasingly became, just as MFSO had said, an isolated, clumsy, and brutal occupier.

The Bush administration scuttled its plans to dramatically draw down US forces while doing little to promote Iraqi sovereignty. There was no political figure like Afghanistan's president, Hamid Karzai, to serve as a unifying force. Long in exile, Ahmed Chalabi had pressed for an invasion in hopes of being anointed Iraq's leader. US officials turned on him, allegedly for sharing intelligence with Iran. The US media tracked the small but steady drip of American casualties, challenging Bush's upbeat picture of the war. Even so, the major press—mostly confined to the Green Zone and fortressed hotels—was slow to grasp the extent of the peril.

For the antiwar movement, this landscape was both daunting and grimly auspicious. There was no heroic protagonist among resistance leaders in Iraq. Many opponents of the Vietnam War had praised North Vietnam's Ho Chi Minh as a patriot, leading his country in a bid for independence, much like the United States' founders. He and other leftists, like Che Guevara, emerged as near-messianic heralds of an emancipated future.

Saddam, by contrast, had mercilessly repressed the Iraqi left. Largely organized on tribal, local, and religious lines, the resistance was little versed in a language of national liberation. No one in the antiwar movement was cheering on the insurgency, whose extremes were distinguished by their cruelty. (Al-Zarqawi personally beheaded Western journalists and aid workers and slaughtered fellow Muslims.) The Iraqi commoner—presented as the essential victim of war—became a main focus of the movement's sympathy. But this was a figure with little standing in the American imagination.

At the same time, the war discredited itself. Each day further pried open the gap between promises of victory and the violence and chaos on the ground. The antiwar movement might best succeed by pointing to that chasm while highlighting the war's deceitful origins and growing costs. Information, within this effort, was a vital front in the antiwar struggle.

Changing perceptions was a tall order. It depended on the American people receiving news and forming opinions undistorted by prejudice, partisanship, blinding patriotism, media bias, and the manipulated narratives of the government. Months of propaganda had taken a toll. In the spring of 2003 a third of Americans wrongly believed that the US military *had found* WMD in Iraq.[6] The myth of an Iraq-9/11 connection also lived on.

US casualties were among the conflict's mounting costs. Antiwar groups lifted up bereaved and anxious military families. To end the occupation, as mass rallies demanded, was to bring the troops home. The coming year brought steep challenges for the war and efforts to maintain support for it. Combat intensified, while the press exposed the horrific abuse of Iraqi prisoners. Vindicated as never before, the antiwar movement had a new chance to make a difference.

"EVERY MAN WILL BECOME A BOMB"

In July 2003, Global Exchange established the International Occupation Watch Center in Iraq, registering it as an NGO with US authorities. Its advisory board included Middle East experts, Iraqi academics and civil society leaders, journalists, and human rights professionals. Its mission was to monitor "coalition military forces and foreign corporations, provide the international community with reliable, independent information . . . support local efforts to improve the lives of the Iraqi people and move toward Iraqi self-rule."[7] Funding came, in part, through UFPJ, as ratified at its first convention.

Run largely by Iraqi women, the group issued damning reports on the occupation. Topics ranged from US crackdowns on the independent press, to mass unemployment, to Iraqis' skepticism toward the US-appointed Iraqi Governing Council. The center also documented civilian deaths at Coalition hands.[8]

Obvious to Iraqis, the dismal state of the occupation was little known to most Americans. Occupation Watch sought to change that by bringing Iraqis to America. The Fellowship of Reconciliation, Code Pink, and other peace groups sponsored in late 2003 a "Women of Iraq Tour." It hosted Amal al-Khedairy and Nermin al-Mufti—professional Iraqi women who had endured the Gulf War, sanctions, and now invasion—to address policymakers, university communities and peace groups.[9] "Everything was destroyed," Al-Mufti said of the occupation's first months.[10]

Iraqi voices spoke only so loudly, and mostly to small, antiwar audiences. A bigger megaphone was needed to reach the American people. Dahr Jamail became an unlikely beacon of journalistic truth in Iraq.

Lebanese American, Jamail grew up in Texas, giving little thought to politics.[11] That changed in his twenties, when he worked in Alaska assisting Duane French, a quadriplegic man key in the passage of the Americans with Disabilities Act. French challenged Jamail's "apathy," recommending works by Noam Chomsky and Howard Zinn. Jamail also studied the post–Gulf War sanctions, developing "a deep caring" for Iraq and its people.

Prior to 9/11, Jamail wrote for an Anchorage newspaper. One of his stories profiled the Taliban, whom he had encountered on a mountaineering trip in Pakistan's Himalayas. When the paper ran pieces explaining America's prior support for mujahideen fighters like bin Laden, the editor was fired. Jamail quit in response. "This is the censorship Chomksy writes about, and I was experiencing it directly."

Jamail found "intolerable" the US media's "cheerleading for war" in the run-up to the Iraq invasion.[12] On the icy slopes of Mount Denali, he had the burning sense that he could watch the war in "frustration and impotence" or do something about it, beyond standard protest. That something was to go to Iraq to deliver the truth to the "horribly misled population of my own country."

Jamail "knew nothing" of the Iraq Peace Team, which might have helped with his journey.[13] He arrived in Jordan in November 2003, alone but on a mission. He set up shop in a Baghdad hotel as one of a handful of independent Western journalists, untethered from the US military or even an established news organization. His first posts were mainly read by his friends, and then on electroniciraq.net. By his second trip in April 2004, major foreign press ran his stories. For American antiwar outlets like *Democracy Now!*, he became a vital source for reliable news from Iraq. Though not a traditional part of antiwar movements, this kind of reporting was essential to the antiwar cause.

In Iraq, Jamail saw that the situation was far worse than the US government claimed. Baghdad was lashed with the physical scars of war, untouched by reconstruction efforts. Residents in cities deemed insurgent strongholds, like Ramadi, insisted that the Americans withheld basic services as collective punishment. Stories of abuse in US detention facilities abounded.

In early December, the US military claimed it killed fifty-four insurgents in Samarra after a convoy was ambushed. Yet the locals Jamail interviewed reported that US soldiers, engaging two insurgents, killed eight civilians and wounded fifty others. Near Ramadi, he uncovered the massacre, in a farmhouse raid gone wrong, of the males of an innocent family. He later met a father of nine who was beaten nearly to death while in US custody. Months later, the US military returned him in a comatose state to his family.

Jamail discovered that the US military was routinely lying about its conduct. Official statements contradicted eyewitness testimony and physical evidence. Pro-occupation rallies were transparently staged by the US military. The "corporate" US media, as Jamail came to disdain it, was complicit in the deception. When embedded with US combat troops, journalists were restricted in what they could cover. They felt natural sympathy for the young American soldiers, who were also their protectors. The press might first report the Pentagon's version of apparent firefights as uncontested truth. Any pushback was typically a minor story, with the truth left hazy in competing claims. No news organization responded to Jamail's 150 emails pleading that they report on the comatose man.[14]

A major effect of government propaganda and media quiescence was to misrepresent the nature of the Iraqi resistance and the war as a whole. The Bush administration cast the enemy as "criminals" and "terrorists" thwarting a free Iraq. Most US media assumed that they were bad actors: Saddam loyalists, religious fanatics, foreign fighters, local potentates, bloodthirsty militiamen, and witless belligerents. Prestige media like *The New Yorker* or PBS's *Front Line* offered more nuanced portraits of the resistance. But their audience was small, dominated by the antiwar choir. To the average American media consumer, the conflict might seem an inscrutable mess, with Iraqis squandering the gift of freedom.

Jamail saw something very different. US conduct plainly fomented the insurgency. "If the occupation power continues to hurt and humiliate the people here," insisted a sheik in Samarra, "every man will become a bomb."[15] Iraqis of every age and affiliation responded to US aggression with a version of this prediction. From 9/11 on, antiwar voices cautioned that US violence would beget more violence from *newly created* enemies. Exactly this scenario was coming to pass.

Common Iraqis were victims of the US war and also the backbone of their nation's fight. The resistance, which Jamail likened to what would happen if a foreign power occupied the United States, was not so inscrutable after all. The insurgents, he concluded, were "only defending their freedom, their cities, their families, and their holy places."[16] His great hope was that his reporting would rile more Americans to oppose the war and hasten its end.

The fall and winter of 2003–4 saw only modest protest focused directly on the Iraq war. The second anniversary of 9/11 brought demonstrations addressing the totality of the US response. On September 10, Peaceful Tomorrows led eight thousand people in a candlelight march to Ground Zero, ringing it in a "Circle of Hope." The Bush administration had claimed Ground Zero as the symbolic center of the War on Terror, elevating the first responders as its first heroes. That image of visceral, hypermasculine patriotism transferred to the construction workers, who draped American flags and military insignia from worksite scaffolds. The peace marchers challenged that presentation.

Peaceful Tomorrows had come fully into its own, lending its unique voice to antiwar protest and the plight of civilian victims of armed conflict. In August 2003, four members went to the Hiroshima and Nagasaki commemorations in Japan. The group also brought atomic bomb survivors, known as Hibakusha, to lower Manhattan.

The presence of these aged Japanese proved controversial. In

April 2002, the first Hibakusha had come to the United States to pay respects to the 9/11 dead. Colleen Kelly sought to host them at the Family Center, controlled by the Lower Manhattan Development Corporation (LMDC), overlooking the impact site. Yet the LMDC, fearing a "political statement," denied them access, even though other families had brought guests. The double standard "exploded in front of me," recalls Kelly.[17] The 2003 return of the Hibakusha was a triumph.

The next big event on the antiwar calendar was a mass rally in Washington, DC, on October 25. ANSWER led the action, with the cautious backing of UFPJ. Large-scale protests came with challenges. For organizers, it was the same exhausting logistics of permits, sound, stage, program, and presswork. For those attending, it was the same slog to the nation's capital to deliver a familiar antiwar message. February 15 had upped the ante. "You want to demonstrate your strength," explained Phyllis Bennis.[18] Declining numbers, inevitable after February 15, risked showing weakness.

Even so, mass demonstrations remained a movement staple, with each important in its moment. Drawing up to a hundred thousand, the October protest showed, according to Leslie Cagan, "that there still is a very viable and dynamic anti-war movement."[19] The protest also had a powerful twist: the presence of a thousand military veterans and family members, marching with the "Bring Them Home Now" contingent near the front.

The war's first six weeks claimed just over a hundred US personnel by hostile fire.[20] The post-Saddam phase saw several dozen combat deaths per month, peaking at forty-three in October. If tiny in battlefield terms, even these small numbers threatened public support for the war. Conscious of this, the US military banned images of coffins entering the United States and limited coverage of the American wounded.

With some controversy, *Democracy Now!* ran graphic footage of the carnage, mostly provided by foreign outlets. Host Amy Goodman railed against press restrictions, whether from the US government or self-censorship.[21] For the families of the dead, each loss was the ultimate nightmare. "George Bush," Suárez told the

Washington protesters, "doesn't own our children's lives."[22] "The only way to 'support the troops' is to end the war," added a Veterans for Peace speaker.[23]

A continent away, a makeshift memorial echoed the rally's message. One Sunday in November, on a picturesque beach, members of Santa Barbara's Veterans for Peace (VFP) chapter planted crosses for each US soldier killed in Iraq.[24] VFP volunteers repeated the solemn ritual every week, setting up the crosses at sunrise and removing then at sundown. A "Wall of the Fallen" was soon added—expanding as casualties mounted—with a chronological list of the dead, like the famous Vietnam Veterans Memorial in Washington, DC. The display became known as Arlington West.

Some crosses were given dog tags with the names of individual soldiers. From all over the country, grieving families visited the crosses as substitute graves, mixing tears with the ocean mist. Volunteers built, stored, and repaired the elaborate materials. Thousands of local residents and tourists saw the weekly display. They often engaged VFP members, took antiwar literature, left notes of appreciation, and discussed the war. Brought to other beaches, like Los Angeles' Santa Monica pier, and replicated in other cities, Arlington West was among the most haunting protest actions of the entire war.

The movement also sought to show how the war was connected to other issues. At its summer convention, UFPJ pledged to support the annual protest in Georgia of the School of the Americas, which trained foreign security forces in repression, and a bus tour promoting migrant rights. It also voted to back demonstrations at the Free Trade Agreement of the Americas (FTAA) in Miami in late November.

Fearing drift from Iraq, some members asked that UFPJ leaders at least explain how war and corporate globalization were related. L. A. Kaufmann, Lisa Fithian, and others responded in UFPJ's broadside for the fall, "Resist the Empire!" In their telling, war and globalization served the same drive "to control resources and expand corporate profit-making." Poverty, forced migration, and religious and ethnic hostilities—all worsened by "free trade" policies—were terrorism's deep roots.[25] Economic justice meant greater peace.

These arguments continued the work of the antiwar critics to put 9/11 and the US response in broader context. But if the Iraq War was a bid for oil profits, as many claimed, it was an early bust. Security troubles badly hurt oil production. America's Iraqi partners insisted that oil remain a state industry, mostly free from private plunder. Unpopular worldwide, the war hardly helped most US-based multinational corporations or the American "brand," challenging the view that the war's motive was economic.

Movement intellectual Mark Engler shed light on this puzzle by distinguishing between the state-driven globalization behind the war and corporate globalization, which prefers relative, profit-friendly peace.[26] The Iraq War had sharpened tensions within the US elite, divided over how best to advance its interests. Protesting the FTAA with an antiwar message was a way to address both poles of US power.

United for Peace and Justice was a major, if mostly stealth, backer of the FTAA mobilization, funding the convergence center and helping with bail payments. Activists set to protest the World Bank/IMF meeting in 2001 came to Miami, hoping to revive the global justice movement. Yet the hallmark of Miami was the crackdown. David Graeber condemned the police "raids and preemptive attacks on protesters, employing the full arsenal of old and newly developed 'non-lethal' weaponry," like tasers and rubber bullets.[27] This force, protesters charged, was deployed based on calculated lies about their alleged, malicious intent and penchant for violence, framed as "terrorism." Tom Hayden, the famous 1960s student leader, had brought to the protests his Harvard politics class, which got caught in the fray. Once again, dissent was suppressed in the name of "national security."

Supporting the FTAA protests, UFPJ made good on its ambition to address war, empire, and global economy in their interlocking dimensions. The police thwarted efforts to revive a global justice agenda. More broadly, the War on Terror proved so consuming that global justice forces remained largely dormant, unable to command sustained attention even within the antiwar movement. Culture and ethos played a role as well. Global justice activism, explained Kauffman, had been highly "fluid," based more in local affinity groups than established, national or regional organizations.[28] In UFPJ's coalition model, the "only way to participate was through organizations." There was in the end, she felt, "no way" for global justice work "to be formally represented" in the antiwar movement "commensurate" to its role in recent history.

"DAD, THESE GUYS DON'T WANT US HERE"

"Ladies and gentlemen, we got him," crowed Coalition Provisional Authority head Paul Bremer to announce the capture of Saddam Hussein on December 13, 2003. Hiding near his hometown of Tikrit, Saddam was met exiting a concrete bunker by an Iraqi translator for US forces, whose Shia family had been persecuted by Saddam's regime.[29] The military claimed that its intelligence efforts had located the dictator. The US media trumpeted the operation as the invasion's finest hour. *60 Minutes* ran a segment from the capture site, aglow with praise for Army Colonel James Hickey, who had led the hunt.[30] Public support for the war ticked up.

Celebrations erupted across Iraq, especially its Kurdish regions. Yet Saddam's capture was no sure sign of better days. It was an open secret, reported Jamail and some in the foreign press, that Saddam had been led to US forces by a Kurdish militia, tipped off by a man whose family had been aggrieved by Saddam's son.[31] Jamail described the staged capture as a "publicity stunt," most useful to US and British leaders.[32] Some Iraqis, whether for national or tribal loyalties, responded to Saddam's capture with rage.[33]

Attacks on US forces declined only modestly. Asked if the "mission" was now "accomplished," even Colonel Hickey would not say. The pyrrhic quality of Saddam's defeat was later verified by his first interrogator, the CIA's John Dixon. Dixon had initially backed the invasion, trusting that Iraq had WMD. The war, its aftermath, and his many hours with the deposed leader changed his mind. "The thought of having Saddam Hussein in power," he wrote, "seems almost comforting in comparison to the awful events and wasted efforts of America's brave young men and women."[34]

Once again, it fell to antiwar forces to alert Americans to the extent of the danger in Iraq. December saw a new wave of travelers to the country. One was Sean Penn, reprising his visit a year earlier with a weeklong trip, recounted for the *San Francisco Chronicle*.[35] Penn sought to learn whether his criticisms of the war were justified. His verdict was mixed. The US soldiers he met showed "dignity and grace" toward Iraqis. Visits to the Free Prisoners Association, which aided victims of Saddam's regime, made its tyranny vivid. Iraqis were now able to speak their minds, and they quarreled freely.

Those whom Penn met insisted that "there is no freedom in occupation" and warned of big trouble should America fail to meet its promises. They also demanded national elections, not the regional appointments favored by the CPA. Penn's most frightening encounter was being detained by armed men from DynCorp—a private military corporation of a sort barely known to the US public. As the country would later learn, the US war drew on thousands of military contractors, who provided security services and aided combat efforts.

In Iraq, Penn met more important American visitors: a nine-person delegation, organized by Global Exchange and led by Medea Benjamin. The group was made up of Vietnam War veterans with Veterans for Peace and the parents of children deployed to Iraq, including Suárez del Solar. Bremer himself agreed to meet with this special group of Americans.

The delegation's purpose, a press event in Washington explained, was "to find out for ourselves what is happening on the ground" and to help bring the troops home.[36] Veteran John Gant worried that the United States had again attacked a country it knew little about. The CPA was an "unreal bubble of America-Washington consciousness." Most soldiers were cut off from the Iraqi people. This was, as in Vietnam, "a recipe for disaster."

Most chilling was the testimony of the parents, who knew that their children's fate was tied to conditions in Iraqi. Michael Loperci, a Phoenix businessman at first supporting the war, noted the "decimated" infrastructure, wrecked economy, long gas lines, and lack of basic services. Should the hardship continue, US forces would take the heat. The delegation also heard firsthand accounts of terrible abuses in US detention facilities.

"Dad, these guys don't want us here," reported Loperci's son on a surprise visit to his base. "They hate us." Before the war's start, antiwar veterans had predicted exactly this reception in their "Call to Conscience" to US soldiers. In Iraq, Suárez put a crucifix where his son died and took some of the sand home. He used it to plant a white rose representing peace. Only by relieving the suffering of Iraqi children, he felt, could his son's death be redeemed.

On its return, the delegation met with US officials at the United Nations and with congressional staff. The antiwar movement was newly breaking through, however faintly. Broadcast by C-SPAN, the press event was hardly packed. The reporters' questions suggested that these were peacenik parents, projecting their own views onto the soldiers. Suárez corrected them. "I don't want to kill women and children," a Latino soldier confided to him. "I want to be home." Once divided over the war, the delegation was now united in the wish that it end. Some favored an immediate US withdrawal. Others pleaded that the military at least end its noxious deadly patrols and retreat to bases outside of major cities.

The war took another blow when, in January 2004, the Iraq Study Group shared its findings. Headed by David Kay, who long backed charges of Iraqi WMD, it concluded that Iraq had in fact destroyed its stockpiles in the 1990s.[37]

That same month came a new effort to mark the war's cost. The American Friends Service Committee (AFSC) debuted its exhibit "Eyes Wide Open."[38] Conceived by Michael McConnell, it placed 504 combat boots—one for each US soldier killed in Iraq to that point—in Chicago's Federal Plaza. Future displays had individual names on the boots and regular shoes, often in children's sizes, to symbolize Iraq's civilian dead. In March 2004, AFSC took "Eyes Wide Open" on the road, exhibiting it by 2006 in more than a hundred cities. Some displays featured the recitation of names, echoing the annual remembrances in New York City of those killed on 9/11. Like Arlington West, it became a pilgrimage site for families of the dead and military veterans.

The war's first anniversary in March 2004 was occasion for all sides to take stock of the conflict. *The Nation* blasted the "5 Lies" behind the invasion: a nonexistent Iraq–al-Qaeda connection, the threat posed by Iraq's lapsed WMD programs, and the promise of swift victory, turning Iraq into a beacon of democracy.[39] Iraq represented instead, Jonathan Schell concluded, the "folly of imperial rule."[40] Even Senator Ted Kennedy (D-MA), the standard bearer of American liberalism, joined *The Nation*'s pages. The Bush administration, he wrote, had "broken faith with the American people" and must be replaced.[41]

For the anniversary, Bush addressed the representatives of eighty-three nations, including skittish Coalition partners. Admitting no error, he used the same grandiose language as after 9/11. "There is no neutral ground . . . in the fight between civilization and terror, because there is no neutral ground between good and evil, freedom and slavery and life and death."[42] It was stunning rhetoric, which again sought to present Iraq as a central front in the War on Terror. Global terror attacks persisted. On March 11, just days before Spain's national elections, al-Qaeda-style cells bombed Madrid's subways, killing 183 people. Among their aims was to punish Spain for its involvement in Iraq. The Iraq War was now a *cause* of terrorism. Spaniards responded, in a sudden shift from the polling, by ousting Prime Minister José María Aznar, who had taken Spain to war. Aznar's successor ordered the rapid withdrawal of Spain's fourteen hundred troops from Iraq.[43]

The fighting in Iraq further muddied the picture. Nationalist at its core, the resistance had operational likeness to "terrorism." It was carried out by nonstate actors, sometimes hit nonmilitary targets, and was meant to coerce political change. But this had long been true of guerrilla insurgencies seeking to kick out occupiers. The invasion had also attracted foreign al-Qaeda-inspired fighters to Iraq, where they had not been before. Only by semantic confusion could the Bush administration claim that the war sought mainly to stamp out terrorism.

Pressed for a "report" on a war already claiming 571 service members, the US military hedged. Any illusion of returning calm was smashed by lethal insurgent strikes against Baghdad and Basra hotels frequented by Westerners. Assuring reporters that "we are winning," Major General Dempsey clarified what that meant.[44] The defeat of Saddam loyalists was nearly total, completing the war for which the United States had prepared. But it now faced a murkier enemy that "uses the tools of terror." Privately, military officials said that the conflict could last years.

As conditions in Iraq worsened, public support for the war declined. One year into the invasion, 55 percent of American believed it was the "right decision," with 39 percent judging it "wrong."[45] Support was sharply down from the 70-plus percent backing the war at its start. Just 44 percent now approved of "the way Bush is handling the situation in Iraq," with 55 percent disapproving. (Ten months earlier, 69 percent had approved.)[46] Antiwar dissent had a new opening.

Protests to mark the Iraq war's first year circled the globe. Millions took part, in hundreds of cities, in dozens of countries.[47] In Global South hotspots, like cities in Pakistan and the Philippines, the protests were militantly anti-American. Massive crowds gathered in Spain, cheering the promised withdrawal of Spanish troops. Activists in London climbed the Big Ben clock tower with a banner reading "Time for Truth." Drawing one million people, Rome's protest was the day's largest, swelled by opposition to Bush ally Premier Silvio Berlusconi. In Australia, opposition to the prowar John Howard government galvanized protest. The wife of David Hicks, a (white) Australian Muslim detained in Guantánamo and a cause célèbre, addressed the Sydney demonstration. The stance of individual governments on Iraq, as well as domestic political dynamics, continued to shape antiwar protest.

The United States saw local actions nationwide, anchored by large protests in San Francisco, Chicago, and New York City. United for Peace and Justice counted demonstrations in more than 260 cities.[48] One thousand people protested in Fayetteville, North Carolina, home to the Fort Bragg military base. It was the city's largest demonstration since the Vietnam War. "There are a lot of vets and military family members who think this war is wrong," said Lou Plummer, an MFSO and North Carolina Peace Action organizer.[49] The dead and wounded were "victims of a government that does not care about them." Protesters also gathered near Bush's ranch in Crawford, Texas, where Navy veteran Don Marshburn minced no words: "I hate George Bush and everything he stands for and this war of vanity."[50] In Montpelier, Vermont, protesters laid boots representing military casualties on the steps of the state capitol.

The largest protest was in New York City. Police again planned to use metal barricades to confine demonstrators. Arrestees from February 15, 2003, issued a statement blasting the physical danger posed by the "protest pens."[51] In a separate brief, a policing expert described the pens a form of "intimidation" that illegally restricted expressive aspects of protest.[52] Even City Council members pleaded against use of the barricades.[53] The police response was to modestly ease access to the rally site. Mayor Michael Bloomberg monitored the protest with law enforcement, partly as a dress rehearsal for the summer's Republican National Convention, hosted by the city.[54] The protest stayed calm, with only a handful of arrests. Its most stinging message for Bush came from New Jersey's Sue Sapir-Niederer. She held a sign reading, "You Killed My Son," who had died weeks earlier in Iraq.[55]

Part of the day's drama was growing tension between UFPJ and ANSWER, cosponsors of the New York City protest. Each organization, an elaborate agreement held, would produce its own publicity and run half of the program. Both groups had people of color as emcees, demanded an immediate end to the war, promoted greater resources for domestic programs, and denounced the abuse of Muslim and Arab communities. UFPJ's tagline ran, "One Year Later—The World Still Says No to War." ANSWER's was, "Bring the Troops Home Now! End Colonial Occupation from Iraq to Palestine to Everywhere."[56]

The group's differences were most apparent in the speakers.

UFPJ's program featured local and state politicians, the British former member of Parliament Tony Benn, Peaceful Tomorrows and MFSO members, and movement heavies like Medea Benjamin. ANSWER's roster was strong on attention to Palestine, while also addressing Venezuela and Cuba as historic targets of US imperialism. Here were the two, national faces of the antiwar movement, representing a loose divide between the progressive and radical left.

The public unity between UFPJ and ANSWER barely concealed their hostility. "Many activists," noted one observer, "are bored by the endless internecine rivalries," of little concern in much of the country.[57] But the conflict was based in important differences affecting the character, image, and impact of the movement.

Each organization had accused the other of unilaterally calling for the anniversary protest in an effort to dominate it. The biggest political disagreement, as in past collaborations, was over the place of Palestine in the protest. Several dozen Arab American and Muslim organizations allied with ANSWER issued an open letter to the movement, whose thinly veiled target was UFPJ. "The struggle for Palestine," it held, must be "central to any peace and justice mobilization."[58] The protest, they felt, should link the occupations of Palestine and Iraq and endorse the "right of return" of Palestinian refugees. Elias Rashmawi of the Free Palestine Alliance later accused UFPJ of sidelining, in "racist" and "neo-orientalist" fashion, Arab peoples and their concerns."[59]

UFPJ's Leslie Cagan, trying to calm the waters, explained that the March 20 date was chosen as the anniversary of the Iraq War, where the emphasis should remain.[60] The United States, while backing Israel, was not occupying Palestine. The linkage desired by ANSWER would "confuse people" and weaken the protest. Working with ANSWER, which many in UFPJ opposed, was "not a great situation," but still better than holding separate rallies.

UFPJ's Lisa Fithian objected less to ANSWER's politics than its behavior, like its sanctimonious public attacks.[61] The accusations of racism hurt. By the same token, she conceded, ANSWER was able to mobilize Arab voices and young activists of color in ways the more traditional peace movement was not. Bennis had long championed the Palestinian cause and was impressed by the passion of the pro-Palestinian groups that ANSWER rallied. But she sometimes doubted their appreciation of the broader antiwar cause.[62] All these tensions, mostly behind the scenes, came to a head backstage. A UFPJ member alleged that ANSWER's Brian Becker, during a "contentious disagreement" over allotted stage time, "struck me."[63]

Despite its divisions, the US antiwar movement had shown its salience and staying power during the Iraq War's first year. Its charge of the war's specious origins and troubled course had been borne out. It could still turn out massive numbers, in concert with protests worldwide. Intrepid journalists and NGOs worked to reveal the worsening reality in Iraq. Military families gained new prominence, while public support for the war started to decline.

With sustained strengths also came familiar limits. Large demonstrations now earned only fleeting headlines. Little had been done to create a global protest infrastructure to coordinate actions, as in February 2003. And no matter how badly the war seemed to unravel, it still had stubborn support among much of the US public. The impact of the antiwar movement remained tethered to the war itself and its ability to reach the public and political class in a new way.

"IT HAS ALL BEEN LIES"

April 2004 was the cruelest month in the Iraq War so far. Its second week saw six hundred attacks on US forces, including in Shia strongholds.[64] On April 4, California's Casey Sheehan with the First Cavalry Division was killed in a Baghdad ambush. His mother Cindy, at first reacting with private sorrow, soon became the leading face of military families protesting the war. Weeks later Pat Tillman, who had left NFL stardom to become an Army Ranger, was killed in Afghanistan, after first deploying to Iraq. The military lauded the handsome Tillman as a hero, while concealing that he had been killed by friendly fire. His family began a years-long saga to reveal the truth of his death and his misgivings about the Iraq War.

The same day as Sheehan's death, Major Antonio Taguba submitted to General Ricardo Sanchez his investigation into the mistreatment of Iraqi detainees in the US-run Abu Ghraib prison. At month's end, the US media exposed the abuse, causing global outrage. For much of April, US forces waged the First Battle of Fallujah, plainly showing that a true war raged on.

On March 30 in Fallujah, insurgents ambushed four Americans working with Blackwater, a private security contractor. Their bodies were burned and dragged through the streets, with two hung from a bridge. Broadcast worldwide, the gruesome image triggered American memories of similar carnage in Somalia a decade earlier.

The episode was the first strong indication to Americans of the heavy reliance in Iraq on contractors—typically ex-military and law enforcement—with private security companies. Their presence came with problems. Not subject to US military justice, they were nearly impossible to punish for potential misdeeds. As private soldiers, they kept official deployments artificially low. And they were paid vastly better than regular military, bloating the war's cost and causing resentment among regular military. Regardless, the deaths were sure to meet a stern response.

The military cordoned off Fallujah and told noncombatants to shelter or leave. Marines would rid it of insurgents by means of grinding urban warfare. The US media largely portrayed young Americans risking their lives to liberate everyday Iraqis. Once again, this image of US benevolence—whatever the soldiers' acts of individual bravery—was deceptive. Iraqi military units, reluctant to attack other Arabs, refused the fight.[65]

Dahr Jamail had returned in January from Iraq to Alaska, where he felt "tremors" of PTSD. "Infuriated" by the poor coverage of the war, he went back to Iraq in April and rushed to cover the assault on Fallujah.[66] Despite US promises, he learned, humanitarian convoys were barred access to the city or attacked. Makeshift clinics treated scores of civilians wounded by US bombs and sniper fire, including during a ceasefire. "I believed in American democracy," fumed a clinic director, with no medicine to offer. "Now I see that it has all been lies."[67]

Despite the danger, Jamail felt obliged to "bear witness" to the unfolding "atrocities" and help the victims as best he could. He teamed with the Italian group Un Ponto Per and Rahul Mahajan, an American author and UFPJ leader touring Iraq. Together, they delivered aid to desperate Fallujahns.

Sunni and Shia Iraqis, including Baghdad's Mahdi army, brought food, weapons, and fighters into the besieged city. Civilian harm grew so severe that America's Iraqi partners convinced the Americans to suspend the assault. Far from suppressing the insurgency, the siege helped to rally Iraqi support for Fallujah as an "island of proud resistance."[68]

The war's next great shock went to its moral heart, further spiking Iraqis' anger. For months, Iraqi families contended with their loved ones' disappearance into a sprawling US detention system. Hundreds gathered every day outside Abu Ghraib—a notorious Saddam-era prison near Baghdad now run by the Americans. At its peak, nearly four thousand Iraqis were held there by US forces. Most were detained without charge or notice of when they might leave. Anticipating swift victory over Saddam's armies, the US military had no plans for mass detentions.[69] The result was indiscriminate roundups, unmanageable numbers of detainees, inadequate staffing, and a malice born of panic and policies encouraging abuse.

Word of ghastly treatment in US facilities reached Western critics of the war, whether journalists like Jamail or the Global Exchange delegation. In October 2003, the American Civil Liberties Union filed a Freedom of Information Act request for "all documents concerning the treatment and interrogation of detainees" in US-run facilities, including Abu Ghraib.[70] The Christian Peacemaker Teams built a database to help Iraqi families track missing loved ones. As prisoners were released, they "heard stories of physical and mental abuse during their arrest, interrogation, and imprisonment."[71]

In December, CPT submitted a report documenting the abuse of seventy-two prisoners to Bremer, General Sanchez, and officials in the United States. By its estimate, 80 percent of those detained had no involvement in violence against Coalition or Iraqi forces. (A US military investigation found that up to 90 percent of Abu Ghraib prisoners had "no intelligence value.")[72] Working with Iraqi human rights groups, CPT developed an "adopt a detainee" campaign, in which people around the world circulated stories about individual prisoners and advocated for their release. A smattering of foreign press cautiously reported allegations of mistreatment.

Late to the story, major US press blew open the abuse. On April 28, CBS's *60 Minutes II* reported that seventeen US soldiers had been relieved of their duties for the alleged mistreatment of detainees at Abu Ghraib.[73] The greater revelation was what *60 Minutes* showed: photos of the abuse. The lead image was of a hooded man with wires attached to his hands, standing on a box. (Should he fall, he was told, he would be electrocuted.) Others showed naked, hooded men stacked in pyramids or positioned to mimic sexual acts. Smiling US guards, including female soldiers, appeared in some of the scenes.

The pictures that CBS aired were a tiny sample of the hundreds that had triggered an internal investigation, begun in January 2004, into the abuse. Two days after the CBS piece, Seymour Hersh published his own story in *The New Yorker*, quoting from the leaked Taguba report.[74] The report documented what it described as numerous "sadistic, blatant, and certain criminal abuses." These included chemical attacks, sodomy and threats of rape, severe beatings, mock executions, and the menacing use of military dogs. The sexual humiliation was especially offensive within Iraqi culture.

The Abu Ghraib pictures sparked worldwide furor, beyond prior critics of the war. The US government at once denounced and minimized the abuse. On the CBS program, a high-ranking officer described it as the "actions of a few" who "let their fellow soldiers down."[75] Bush insisted that the misconduct did not represent America and praised the investigations as proof of US adherence to the rule of law.[76] Grilled before Congress, Defense Secretary Donald Rumsfeld did the same. Obvious violations of human dignity and rights were occasion for US leaders to boast about America's commitment to these ideals.

The Arab world rejected Bush's apologies, denouncing the abuse as part and parcel of an illegitimate war that dehumanized Arab

Iraqi artist Salah Edine Sallat finishes a wall painting in May 2004 in Baghdad's Sadr City based a widely published photograph of a detainee abused by US forces at the Abu Ghraib prison. Photograph by Ramzi Haidar, AFP via Getty Images.

and Muslim peoples. Muslims in America felt special pain. Phyllis Bennis was disturbed but not shocked by the abuse, which followed historic patterns of military occupation.[77] The antiwar movement instantly adopted the Abu Ghraib images as protest icons, carried at rallies and vigils. To many throughout the world, Abu Ghraib became synonymous with the Iraq War.

In Iraq, Abu Ghraib was devastating for the occupation. In May, Islamic militants beheaded American Nick Berg, a private communications worker in Iraq. The grisly act, his assassins declared, was payback for Abu Ghraib. By June, attacks on US forces stood at fifty a day.[78] A CPA poll, conducted weeks into the scandal, showed that 55 percent of Iraqis would feel safer if the Americans left. A majority also believed that "all Americans behave like the [prison] guards." The CPA's "confidence rating" stood at 11 percent, down from 47 percent in November.[79]

Abu Ghraib also pointed—as journalists, attorneys, academic researchers, human rights organizations, and congressional investigators would expose—to the brutality running through the War on

Terror. Far from the rogue acts of a few "bad apples," the abuses extended policies and practices set in motion after 9/11. US authorities quickly concluded that the best way to foil terrorist plots was to interrogate potential conspirators. Early on, the CIA sought to use methods beyond what the law permitted.[80] Seeking legal cover, it turned to the Department of Justice (DOJ). Starting in August 2002, DOJ's Office of Legal Counsel issued secret memoranda, later dubbed the "torture memos." These briefs used outlandish legal theories to argue that the Geneva Conventions, other treaties, and domestic laws did not prohibit interrogation methods they plainly sought to ban.

The CIA identified for use euphemistically named "Enhanced Interrogation Techniques" (EITs), derived from Cold War–era methods developed by communist China for extracting false confessions from prisoners of war. Approved by Secretary Rumsfeld, these included agonizing stress positions; extended isolation; hooding; controlled beatings; forced nudity; sleep deprivation; the exploitation of phobias and aggressive use of dogs; the manipulation of heat, cold, and sound; and forced drowning called "waterboarding." The EITs were intended to leave no physical wounds as evidence of mistreatment.

The EITs were first administered in "black sites" in Afghanistan, Guantánamo Bay, and countries in Eastern Europe and East Asia. The EIT program was intended for the 120 or so "high-value detainees" thought to be directly involved in global terror operations. Perhaps hundreds more—often held without credible suspicion of wrongdoing—were also subject to its methods.

Abu Ghraib revealed that "enhanced interrogations" had bled into military operations. To thwart shadowy insurgents, US forces now turned to torture methods. This was no aberration. The military sought to punish low-ranking guards for the Abu Ghraib abuse. Their defense was that they were responding to the request of intelligence personnel to "break" detainees prior to interrogations, where more rough treatment followed.[81]

Just prior to the worst abuses, Major General Geoffrey Miller visited Iraq from Guantánamo, where he had implemented "enhanced interrogations." Seeking to "Gitmo-ize" detentions in Iraq, he secured authorization for brutal methods there as well.[82] Improvised by regular soldiers, abusive interrogations filtered also into scattered field detentions.[83] With good reason, human rights attorneys titled a massive volume of government documents about interrogation policies, *The Torture Papers: The Road to Abu Ghraib*.[84] Popular culture played a role as well. Jack Bauer, the CIA hero of Fox's hit TV series *24*, routinely tortured bad guys, thwarting devilish plots with information extracted from torture. This fanciful imagery, grounded in no reliable military protocol, falsely suggested to US personnel that torture methods worked and piqued their interest in trying them out.

Abu Ghraib had a knock-on effect for antiwar efforts. The photographs lent new credence to claims of abuse elsewhere in the US detention system. They also enhanced concern with detainee mistreatment as a major troubling dimension of the War on Terror. In June, Center for Constitutional Rights President Michael Ratner and muckraking journalist Ellen Ray published a short book titled *Guantánamo: What the World Should Know*.[85] At the time, even attorneys and human rights campaigners knew relatively little about the island prison. Tales of prisoner abuse mostly came from the International Committee of the Red Cross, private statements to lawyers, and a handful of public letters from detainees. Some of the worst treatment was in US prisons in Afghanistan, about which even less was known. A lawsuit claiming that the Guantánamo prisoners had rights in US federal courts was just making its way to the Supreme Court.

As Ratner and Ray were preparing the text, the Abu Ghraib scandal broke. "Allegations," Ray explained, "became facts," prompting the authors to remove qualifiers like "claims" of torture and "alleged" beatings.[86] This violence, and the legal regime behind it, led Ratner to conclude that "Guantánamo represents everything that is wrong with the U.S. war on terrorism." The Bush administration had thrown the United States "back to a pre-Medieval system" of "executive fiat, where the king—or in this case the president—simply decides . . . I am going to throw you into prison." The War on Terror was "a descent into barbarism."

The Abu Ghraib scandal cast a damning verdict on the Iraq War and larger War on Terror, confirming the fears of critics all along. Just after 9/11, Representative Barbara Lee pleaded that the United States not "become the evil we deplore." In Iraq, a war of supposed self-defense and liberation had turned into one of sickening abuse.

In a May 2004 commencement speech at Barnard College, author Barbara Ehrenreich declared that the "last moral justification" for the Iraq War—"that we had removed an evil dictator who tortured his own people"—"died with those photos."[87] A feminist, Ehrenreich also cursed the involvement of women in the torture. The nation's enemies, Bush repeatedly said, resented America's freedoms. "But here in these photos," she observed, "you have every Islamic fundamentalist stereotype of Western culture": "imperial arrogance, sexual depravity," and even, "gender equality." The worst of America was on literal display, making a mockery of Bush's words.

Jamail quoted an Iraqi doctor asking, "Did America not become barbarians from killing Indians, Vietnamese, Central Americans, Afghanis, and bombing us and our young children, who now have psychological scars? If these did not reveal the true barbarian nature of America, then Abu Ghraib certainly did."[88] Here was the burning anger of an occupied people, who saw their suffering as part of a global legacy of American violence. It was this legacy, left-wing critics charged after 9/11, that partly led to the terror attacks. By not confronting its own violence, they warned, the United States risked repeating the abuse of foreign peoples and continuing cycles of retribution.

The terrible events of spring 2004 gave the antiwar movement new hope that the country might turn decisively against the war. In April, General Anthony Zinni uttered about Iraq the dreaded words in US politics: "I have seen this movie, it was called Vietnam."[89] In May, disapproval of Bush's handling of the war reached a new peak at 58 percent.[90] A month later, a majority of Americans felt, for the first time ever, that sending troops to Iraq had been a "mistake."[91]

The airing of abuse at Abu Ghraib was itself a tribute to conscientious objection. The photos had been turned over to military investigators by Specialist Joseph Darby, publicly named by both Hersh and Rumsfeld. (Rumsfeld, many suspected, sought to out Darby for reprisals, not to honor him.) Darby had asked a member of his unit for scenic pictures of Iraq and was mistakenly given CDs with the offending images. "I've always had a moral sense of right and wrong," he said of his decision, sure to anger his tight-knit unit. "Friends or not, [the abuse] has to stop."[92] Senator Ted Kennedy and Ethel Kennedy honored Darby with the family's Profile in Courage award.[93] Soon, the US electorate would have the chance to say whether it too had seen enough of the war.

CHAPTER 10

"SORRY EVERYBODY, WE TRIED"

The Antiwar Movement and the Reelection of George W. Bush

The chaos in Iraq proved no fatal blow to Americans' support for the war. Approval of the conflict dropped but did not plummet. In a sign of fitful progress, in late June 2004 the Iraqi Governing Council appointed an interim prime minister, formally establishing Iraq's sovereignty and dissolving the Coalition Provisional Authority.

The Bush administration continued to pin Abu Ghraib on the actions of a few, while the military punished only the prison's low-ranking guards.[1] Radio host Rush Limbaugh likened the abuse to a college hazing.[2] Reservist Darby was seen as a traitor in his small Maryland hometown. Veterans there held a vigil *for the accused soldiers in his unit*, not the Iraqi victims. When returned to military bases in the United States, he needed around-the-clock protection from physical attack.[3]

The first of the torture memos was leaked to the press in June, adding to the outcry over Abu Ghraib. Bush officials reasserted the lawfulness and military necessity of the harsh treatment of "enemy combatants," deemed outside the protections of the Geneva Conventions. Their arguments built on years of demonizing alleged terrorists, deserving of rough handling, not legal rights. Many Americans were aghast at US conduct. Many others were not. The country, and the electorate, were badly divided.

Elections never hinge on a single issue, and 2004 was no exception. Bush and his Democratic challengers held very different views on taxes, health care, abortion, and the environment. Yet Bush's tenure was defined overwhelmingly by the War on Terror. The election would be, perhaps above all else, a referendum on Bush's most controversial choice within it: to go to war in Iraq. Bush campaigned on the unwavering promise of victory. More broadly, he ran as the "9/11 president," touting his national security record and painting the Democrats as "soft on terror."

In March, a campaign ad praising Bush's leadership featured a montage of Ground Zero. In response, Peaceful Tomorrows and some firefighters urged that "all parties pledge not to use Sept. 11 images for political campaigns."[4] A shared tragedy, they felt, should not be fodder for partisan gain. Peaceful Tomorrows also asked that Bush refrain from holding campaign events at Ground Zero. Conservative media denounced the group as shills for the left, triggering vicious personal attacks on its members.[5]

For the antiwar movement, continued support for Bush deepened a maddening dynamic in which no apparent failure—the security lapses leading to 9/11, the absence of WMD, the fallacy of Mission Accomplished, and now a torture scandal—could sink the president and his war. Held in liberal New York City, August's Republican National Convention was occasion for the movement to confront Bush and his party. The demonstrations promised to be the largest since February 15, 2003, repeating the standoff with city authorities and police over the right to protest in post-9/11 America.

The election would show whether a breaking point on the war had at last been reached. A Bush defeat would prove the antiwar movement's impact, while advancing many of its goals. A victory would show the depths of the county's embrace of the War on Terror, the administration's ability to shape perceptions, and the limits to the politics of truth driving the antiwar movement.

"THE BIGGEST NOTHING IN HISTORY"

Campaigning began even before the war's start, when the first Democrats declared their intent to run. The field was rocked by the early momentum of Vermont Governor Howard Dean. Dean ran as an unapologetic progressive, promoting universal health care and the renegotiation of trade deals that hurt US workers. His big opening was on Iraq. Much of the party establishment voted for the 2002 war authorization. For left-wing Democrats, the vote "marked a tipping point," in which "resentment turned to fury."[6]

"What I want to know," Dean asked at a major party gathering in February 2003, "is why in the world the Democratic Party leadership is supporting the president's unilateral attack on Iraq."[7] Such talk made Dean "the antiwar candidate."[8] At the time, just 52 percent of Democrats supported military action.[9] By October, a majority opposed the war, with 56 percent wanting US forces brought home as soon as possible. Anti-Republican partisanship "helped to fuel the growth of the antiwar movement," and Dean rode that wave.[10]

Saddam's capture in December 2003 earned bipartisan praise. Even after that, Dean insisted that Bush "launched the war in the wrong way, at the wrong time, with inadequate planning, insufficient help and at extraordinary costs."[11] Also mounting an antiwar candidacy was Ohio Representative Dennis Kucinich. In 2002, he decried a potential attack on Iraq as "unjustified, unwarranted and illegal." Among primary candidates, he alone had voted against the war authorization.[12] More so than Dean, Kucinich won the hearts of the war's staunch opponents.

Dean's campaign stalled out by early 2004, owing in part to concerns about electability.[13] Kucinich never moved beyond the margins, where he sought to be the party's conscience. Pulled to the left on the war, the Democratic field was open to more viable candidates, including the eventual nominee, Senator John Kerry, and his running mate Senator John Edwards.

Kerry had a remarkable antiwar pedigree, defining his candidacy in varied ways. Born of means and Yale-educated, he could have easily avoided the draft for the Vietnam War. Yet in 1966 he enlisted in the Naval Reserve, volunteering for deployment. In Vietnam, he served on river-patrol Swift Boats, earning medals for valor and two Purple Hearts. Like so many soldiers, Kerry turned bitterly against the conflict. When back home, he joined Vietnam Veterans Against the War. In early 1971 he attended its "Winter Soldier" hearings, in which veterans described war crimes they had witnessed or even committed.

Months later, Kerry testified before the Senate Foreign Relations Committee. Striking in his combat jacket and sweep of long hair, he annihilated the war with mesmerizing eloquence. The war's central myth was that America faced a genuine communist threat. Most Vietnamese simply wanted to live in peace, free from foreign aggression. US soldiers risked dying "for the biggest nothing in history," leaving them with "a sense of betrayal which no one has yet grasped."[14] "How do you ask a man to be the last man to die for a mistake?" he asked. Kerry became an instant hero to antiwar vets, who felt that he spoke for them as well.

Kerry then built a political career in Massachusetts, being elected senator in 1984. Some voters saw his opposition to the Vietnam War as an asset. Others viewed it as its own betrayal. The 2004 election, now with Iraq at its center, reactivated conflicts over the Vietnam War, Kerry's connection to it, and what true patriotism meant.

Kerry's dovish past was little evident following 9/11. He voted for the Iraq War authorization, while stressing that military force should be a last resort in response to proven threats.[15] After the war began, Kerry became a critic of it. He argued that the Bush administration had exaggerated the danger Iraq posed and badly failed to win the peace. Ambiguity about his position lingered, clouding his campaign.

In fall 2003 Kerry had supported an early version of a massive appropriations bill that would fund the wars in Afghanistan and Iraq by rescinding Bush's tax cuts. Yet he voted no on its final, GOP-backed version, which left the tax cuts in place. Exhausted at a campaign event, he remarked, "I actually did vote for the 87 billion dollars, before I voted against it."[16] Absent context, his shifting position appeared a classic flip-flop. The Bush campaign hammered Kerry for his maladroit line and apparent inconsistencies on the war.

Also damning were efforts to question Kerry's heroism in the Vietnam War and cast his opposition to it as disqualifying. Leading the charge was Swift Boat Veterans for Truth (SBVT). In coordinated media attacks, they accused Kerry of distorting both his service and the conduct of his fellow soldiers. Kerry contended as well with a doctored photograph falsely showing him at a 1970s protest with actress Jane Fonda, who incensed the war's backers. Though its allegations were discredited, SBVT damaged Kerry's campaign.

Kerry had hoped that his twin status as a Vietnam War hero *and* protester would make him a broadly credible critic of the Iraq War. He frequently said that his combat experience gave him a special understanding of the human stakes of policy choices. George Bush, as his critics howled, had avoided service in Vietnam by volunteering for the "Champagne Unit" of the Texas Air National Guard, known for shielding privileged young men from war. Regardless, crude appeals to patriotism held power, even against a decorated combat veteran.

To many opponents of the war, Kerry was far from ideal. There was his 2002 vote and continued support for the US mission in Afghanistan. He now described the Iraq campaign as a geopolitical error—not, like the Vietnam War, as a moral abomination revealing American malice in world affairs. And it was unclear whether a Kerry presidency could truly end the war.

Kerry's plan was to more deeply "internationalize" the conflict by transferring security and reconstruction efforts to US allies and the United Nations. The US military would retain a reduced presence to conduct counterterrorism operations, while quickly training Iraq's military. This plan begged the question of why nations and institutions the Bush administration had berated over the war would now bail the United States out. It remained doubtful whether any occupying force could pacify Iraq, especially if US troops remained there. Bush's policies might prove irremediable.

The antiwar movement grappled with the available choices. United for Peace and Justice had a policy of not endorsing candidates. Many member groups were nonprofits, legally barred from electoral work. Picking among contenders would stir fierce debate and even, some feared, "tear the coalition apart."[17] Most of all, UFPJ sought to keep the focus on ending the war and advancing a justice agenda. The election was a means to that end. The defeat of Bush—and, hence, a Kerry victory—was paramount.

Hard-left groups like ANSWER saw Democrats and Republicans as co-stewards of an imperialist system. They rejected calls for the internationalization of the occupation, regardless of who the occupiers were. A Kerry presidency might temper the worst of the War on Terror while leaving the imperialist system intact. ANSWER accused UFPJ of being a wing of the Democratic Party, compromising its antiwar position.

Such arguments went only so far, even in the movement's left wing. The bitterness over the 2000 election, decided only when the Supreme Court stopped Florida's recount, loomed large. A Gore presidency could have spared the world the Iraq War, Guantánamo, and even the 9/11 attacks. Ralph Nader's Green Party candidacy, election data showed, had helped Bush win by taking votes from Gore. With the stakes so high, any challenge to the Democratic nominee was an extraordinary risk. Staying in the race long after the nomination was settled, Kucinich chose not to mount a third-party bid. For the vast majority of the movement, the passion to end the war became a crusade to defeat Bush.

This stance did not spare Kerry and the Democrats from protest. Antiwar groups, including UFPJ, held demonstrations at the Democratic National Convention (DNC) in Boston in late July. Modest in size, they were confined behind fences to "free-speech zones" some distance from the convention site, infuriating demonstrators. The protests both condemned the Democrats for their complicity in the war and urged them to be a genuine opposition.

Antiwar veterans sharply expressed this mix of sentiments. Veterans for Peace (VFP) deliberately chose Boston for its 2004 annual convention, ending just as the DNC started. Attended by four hundred or so, the convention would permit the group to address Kerry, the Democratic establishment, and any media interested in its message.

Founded in 1985, VFP was open to former service members from any era or military branch. A core group were past or current members of Vietnam Veterans Against the War (VVAW), itself still in existence. In its first years, VFP sponsored relief and reconciliation missions in Vietnam, did solidarity work in Latin America, protested the Gulf War, and even helped restore a Baghdad water treatment plant damaged in the conflict. After 9/11, its relevance and energy grew. Around seven hundred in 2001, its membership soared into the thousands.

VFP members went to Iraq with the Iraq Peace Team, attended antiwar rallies, joined antiwar coalitions, and spoke from personal experience against the country's new wars. Just before the invasion of Iraq, VFP member Ward Reilly represented the antiwar position in a debate before a thousand people at Louisiana State University, steeped in Southern military tradition. (The antiwar panelists, he recalls, won over most of the audience.)[18] The group also mentored members of the military community, like those forming Military Families Speak Out, in dissent.

At its Boston gathering, VFP called for the immediate withdrawal of US troops from Iraq, appealing directly to Kerry and his antiwar past. Much connected VFP to the Democratic nominee. Like Kerry, VFP leader David Cline earned medals for injury and valor in Vietnam. Permanently disabled, he lived after his discharge near Fort Hood in Texas, organizing GI resistance with VVAW. Pennsylvania's William Perry, also a Vietnam War combat veteran, personally knew Kerry from past organizing. During the DNC, he displayed a huge banner in a convention hotel reading, "How do you ask a soldier to be the last person to die for a lie?" (The banner replaced "mistake" with "lie," and "man" with "soldier" in Kerry's famous line.) "I want Kerry to come home to his roots," he told the press, "to the true passionate feeling he had" when condemning the Vietnam War.[19]

Privately, VFP had its doubts. "By 2003," Reilly reports, Kerry was "widely disliked by most antiwar veterans, because he had become a typical sellout politician."[20] Still, they were excited by the chance to "have our voices heard in the White House." Three VFP members served as delegates at the DNC, while Reilly and others did some work for the Kerry campaign.

The VFP convention produced its own drama, linking generations of dissident soldiers. On its opening day, it held a press event for six veterans of the Iraq War at Boston's City Hall, where "Eyes Wide Open" was being exhibited.[21] The lineup included the Marines' Michael Hoffman, Jim Massey, and Alex Rybov; Army Chaplain Ivan Medina; the Air Force's Tim Goodrich; and Diana Morrison, with the military police. All participated in the 2003 invasion and now condemned a war in which they had fought.

With VFP's blessing, the group also held the following day a workshop called "Iraq Vets Sound Off," attended by 150 conventioneers. Their presentations criticized the war for its false pretenses, brutality, and danger to those fighting it. "Some had never spoken publicly before," noted one observer, "but made eloquent by the rawness and urgency of their message, they had stunned their listeners."[22]

That evening, VFP gathered in storied Faneuil Hall, where the Sons of Liberty had declared their opposition to the British crown. Speeches by Howard Zinn and VFP member Daniel Ellsberg stirred the crowd. Hoffman, Massey, Ryabov, Goodrich, and MP Kelly Dougherty took stage, where they announced to "thunderous applause" the formation of Iraq Veterans Against the War (IVAW).[23] Taking the Vietnam War–era group as its namesake, it sought to end another disastrous conflict.

The group originated in conversations going back months. Hoffman started speaking out as early as November 2003, when first home from Iraq.[24] At the time, he recalls, the only active-duty soldiers publicly denouncing the war were himself, Massy, and Steven Funk. A Marine Reservist, Funk went AWOL when mobilized and declared himself a conscientious objector. The military rejected his claim. After his court-martial, Funk spent six months in prison. More soldiers would protest the war, Hoffman predicted, when they returned from their tours. True to his prediction, Hoffman met Tim Goodrich at a demonstration at Dover Air Force Base on the war's first anniversary in March 2004. The two began discussing plans for a new antiwar group. Through VFP and MFSO networks, more antiwar soldiers found one another.[25]

Veterans for Peace offered crucial support to IVAW when it was little more than a daring idea. The VFP convention served as the stage for IVAW's public birth. Kelly Dougherty had been invited to the Boston gathering by her father—a Vietnam veteran and new VFP member who had gone to Iraq with American military families in December 2003. (Her father in fact volunteered her for the Iraq Vets Sound Off forum.) VFP also served as IVAW's fiscal sponsor, lending office space and staff. Most of all, it helped the new generation of soldiers navigate—both politically and emotionally—their public antiwar stand.

FOUR MORE WARS!

"Who would want to give up their child?" asked Michael Moore at the close of his award-winning documentary *Fahrenheit 9/11*.[26] "Would you?" The film had just shown Lila Lipscomb sobbing in grief and anger at the White House gate. Her son, Sargeant Michael Pederson, had been killed in Iraq in June 2003. Furious with Bush, his last letter home complained that "they got us out here for nothing." It was a chilling echo of Kerry's testimony about Vietnam.

Released in June 2004, the film quickly became the highest-grossing documentary to date. It screened as well in Europe and much of the Middle East and was even shown at a CPA facility in Baghdad. Its reach was well beyond what any demonstration could achieve, making the filmmaker a hero to the antiwar movement.

Though not endorsing Kerry, Moore explicitly hoped that *Fahrenheit 9/11* might help unseat Bush. The film cast the president as the dim-witted scion of an American oligarchy, beholden to weapons manufacturers and the Saudi oil interests interpenetrating his family. Moore's vignettes of the war are unsparing: US forces, amped on heavy-metal music, wreaking havoc; grief-stricken Iraqis cursing the Americans; young soldiers in agony from gruesome wounds.

The military and their families occupy the film's moral heart. For Moore, the soldiers are victims of a grossly unequal society that lures those most vulnerable into the armed services, where they fight to protect the very system that disenfranchises them. Hope lies in service members seeing through the ruse. Moore interviews Corporal Abdul Henderson, willing to risk jail if ordered to return to return to Iraq. "I will not let anyone send me back over there," he announces, "to kill poor people, especially when they pose no threat to me or my country." For families like Lila Lipscomb's, it was too late for any life-saving protest.

Controversy added to the film's buzz. Disney prevented its original distributor from releasing it. Prowar groups urged theaters not to show it. Critics denounced it as emotionally manipulative and factually suspect. Christopher Hitchens dismissed Moore as a propagandist, though without the talent of Nazi booster Leni Riefenstahl.[27] Unfazed, Moore defended his research and his loathing of Bush.

The success of *Fahrenheit 9/11* pointed to something bigger: the 2004 election as the catalyst for a broad-based movement *culture*, with antiwar protest at its center. Antiwar media had evolved rapidly. *Democracy Now!* was the niche staple for critical coverage of the conflict and news about the movement itself. Host Keith Olbermann brought his antiwar jeremiads to MSNBC's *Countdown*, establishing the rebranded network as a liberal powerhouse. Popular with the young, Jon Stewart's *The Daily Show* satirized the perfidy of Bush and his administration. Air America emerged as a progressive answer to right-wing radio, reaching sizable audiences. Jeremy Scahill of *The Nation* did hard-hitting exposés about the war, including its reliance on private military contractors. Indymedia outlets covered antiwar protest at its grassroots. *War Times*, sold in bundles to antiwar groups, achieved national distribution.

All manner of progressive groups—whether focused on health care, housing, economic and racial justice, immigrant rights, or feminist concerns—mobilized against Bush, stressing how war impacted their cause. Union locals and academic associations passed resolutions condemning the president and the war. Leading artists from the worlds of rock, hip-hop, Hollywood, and Broadway came out against Bush, with some doing benefit performances for Kerry. Playful protests blossomed. Code Pink chapters bird-dogged the campaign appearances of Bush and his political allies, issuing "pink slips"—whether mock termination notices or pink lingerie slips—to have them fired. In New York City especially, protests might be crashed by the media sensation of the election season, the Billionaires for Bush.

Billionaires for Bush was largely the brainchild of Andrew Boyd, a gifted activist and humorist deeply attuned, like the Yippies of yore, to media frames. It first formed in 2000 as Billionaires for Bush or Gore, reflecting left-wing discontent with both candidates as proud champions of American capitalism. Three years of Bush changed its tune. The new premise was that the GOP—far more than the Democrats—was bought and paid for by the super-rich, whose priority was profit-friendly policies.[28] Yet through contrived populist appeals, Republicans hoodwinked Americans into voting against their economic interests and for pliable figures like Bush. To expose the deception, the Billionaires adopted Monopoly-style personae bearing clever names like Phil T. Rich, Meg A. Bucks, Fillmore Barrels, and Merchant F. Arms. Dressed in top hats and tiaras, the Billionaires could be seen at left-wing rallies condescending to the "little people" and turning protest slogans on their head with chants of "This is what plutocracy looks like!" and "Whose street? Wall Street!"

Boasting professional actors and media producers, the group rejected the aesthetic of the earnest left, prone to making a spectacle of its righteous anger. Instead, it used satire and glamour to playfully deliver a serious message about inequality. (Aware of Kerry's vast wealth through marriage, the Billionaires dubbed him a "class traitor" for his modestly progressive policies.) The group also skewered the War on Terror, stressing how it made for handsome defense industry profits. The media was charmed. *The New York Times* and cable news ran features on the group. Chapters formed nationwide and showed up at swing-state events, where they rallied Bush crowds to chants of "Four more wars!" By late summer the Billionaires would descend, like much of the antiwar movement, on the streets of New York City.

In January 2003, the Republican National Committee (RNC) chose, for the first time ever, to host its nominating convention in

New York City, where Democrats outnumbered Republicans five to one. Party officials cited the city's symbolic importance in the War on Terror.[29] At the heady start of the Iraq War, they likely saw the choice as a brilliant "coup de théâtre" promising a "fabulous blow" to the opposition.[30] By the summer of 2004, it was a risky move.

Mayor Michael Bloomberg had lobbied hard to host the convention, set for late August 2004. The Department of Homeland Security designated it a National Security Special Event, vulnerable to terrorist attack. The Secret Service coordinated security, buttressed by dozens of federal agencies, mazes of barricades, and high-tech surveillance. The true intent behind "Fortress Manhattan," charged blogger Nick Turse, was to "dishearten, frighten, and intimidate prospective protesters."[31] Adding to the outrage, many convention events were held on cruise ships on the city's rivers, shielding delegates from the opinions of New Yorkers.

Planned for months, dozens of events held by myriad groups would make for a days-long carnival of dissent before and during the RNC, recalling the elaborate "convergences" of the global justice movement. A glossy, trifold brochure mimicking New York City's famous subway map featured a calendar of protest actions, the location of delegate hotels, and legal information in case of arrest.[32] Antiwar activities included the display of "Eyes Wide Open" at multiple city locations, an Iraq War Crimes Tribunal organized by the International Action Center, a Women Against War concert at Riverside Church, and civil disobedience targeting the convention site. The centerpiece was a mass demonstration on August 29, the day before the convention's start. Organized by UFPJ, its tagline was "The World Says No to the Bush Agenda: No to War, Lies, Greed, & Hate."

UFPJ applied more than a year earlier for a permit to use Central Park's Great Lawn for a rally of 250,000 people. In December, it held a press briefing, demanding from the city a "commitment in advance that our constitutional rights will be honored."[33] In April, the city denied the permit. It argued that the crowds would destroy, at great financial cost, the park's grass.

The NYPD offered for the rally Flushing Meadow Park in Queens— miles from Madison Square Garden, where the RNC was held.

After UFPJ rejected the laughable offer, the NYPD approved a stretch of the West Side Highway in lower Manhattan for the rally and a protest march past Madison Square Garden. UFPJ again cried foul, noting the highway's remoteness and the danger posed by its asphalt in the August heat.

For months, the struggle over the park was a story all its own, with big political stakes. "The effectiveness of the protests," explained an internal UFPJ memo, "depends on legitimizing them in the public sphere. If non-activists view the demonstrations in a context of fear about terrorism and the overarching need for security, then the police and media will be able to suppress and distort our message."[34] The group sought, as the defender of "cherished freedoms," to "create a broad outcry" over the permit issue. Its approach worked. Local politicians, the public, turf experts, and even conservative media chastised the city's position. The city did not budge.

In late July, UFPJ grudgingly accepted the highway location. Coalition groups now threatened to stay away from the approved protest. A city poll, released just after UFPJ's decision, showed that 75 percent of New Yorkers felt that the rally should be in Central Park. UFPJ quickly reversed itself, filing a lawsuit challenging the permit denial, which New York State's Supreme Court rejected.[35] Refusing the approved location, UFPJ negotiated with police to hold an outdoor press event near midtown, followed by a march.

The battle over the Great Lawn was a proxy conflict over the war itself. Unable to directly confront the war machine, the movement could take a stand against a local target doing its bidding. Not in Our Name pleaded with UFPJ not to capitulate. "There is a profound immorality," it insisted, "to acquiescing as our government terrorizes and destroys whole peoples."[36] The controversy also revealed strategic and ideological divides within the movement. At a mass meeting in early August, UFPJ leaders urged that they stick with the city's offer and get on with the organizing.[37] More militant voices favored pushback, with a flyer instructing Bloomberg to "Take your filthy Nazi fantasy and go to hell."[38]

The fight was also over civil liberties in the post-9/11 era. "The city has literally pushed us to the edge of Manhattan," Cagan complained to the press. "We don't want to be marginalized."[39] More deeply, the controversy spoke to the essence of the War on Terror and what it meant to protect. Harlem City Council member Bill Perkins decried the permit denial as "un-American."[40] "We cannot allow" al-Qaeda, he charged, "to think that their attacks have forced the people of America's greatest city to abandon America's greatest law—The First Amendment."

"THEY ALL LIED"

On the morning of August 26, a banner appeared on the facade of the famous Plaza Hotel, marking the start of the RNC protests. Sixty feet across, it had the word "TRUTH" inside an arrow pointing to the right. Below it, an arrow labeled "BUSH" pointed left. The daring action, which required rappelling down the building, was the doing of four young activists working as "Operation Sybil." The group, its press statement explained, was named after the Greek oracle Sybil, "whose role was to expose truth to humankind."[41]

The anti-Bush slogan quoted an iconic banner from the 1999 Seattle protests with "WTO" (World Trade Organization) and "DEMOCRACY" in the opposing arrows. The Sybil members themselves embodied legacies of protest. Born in 1978, Terra Lawson-Remer was the daughter of activists who had met while organizing against the Vietnam War. In high school, she protested California's restrictions on immigrants' rights. She soon joined the global justice movement, getting arrested in Seattle and working with STARC. Now studying law, Lawson-Remer was joined by architect Cesar Maxit, seminary student Rebecca Johnson, and David Murphy, a trapeze teacher. "We love our country, but Bush and Cheney are taking us in the wrong direction," Lawson-Remer said about the protest.[42] The four were charged with felony assault for the injury an officer sustained while climbing the roof to arrest them. Mayor Bloomberg called the protest an "outrage."[43] Law enforcement too had set a tone.

The same day, a dozen members of ACT UP Philadelphia were arrested for blocking midtown traffic, with some stripping entirely naked. "Drop the Debt" and "Stop AIDS" were stenciled on their bodies, used to expose the "naked truth" of Bush's policies. It was a captivating image of vulnerability and resolve. (Legendary photographer Richard Avedon featured the group, along with the Billionaires for Bush and other notables from the campaign season, in a photo essay for *The New Yorker*.) The following evening, police detained more than two hundred and sixty people participating with Critical Mass in a thousands-strong bike ride through the city.

The arrests appeared arbitrary. Some people were held for a night or more in a newly created detention center at Pier 57 on the Hudson River. A cavernous decommissioned bus depot housed the makeshift jail. "The conditions were terrible" in the oil-slicked facility, reported an arrestee, with "tall fence cages with barbed wire at the top" serving as jail cells.[44] The seeming plan, according to another, was to leave the protesters "physically dirty" and "mentally broken."

What promised to be a grueling day of mass protest on August 29 got off to an elegant start. The Billionaires for Bush broadcast that in "behind the scenes negotiations [we] convinced the NYPD to bar hundreds of thousands of anti-Bush protesters from Central Park's Great Lawn, so that our members could honor a previously scheduled game of croquet."[45] At 10 a.m. on the Great Lawn, a few dozen Billionaires, croquet mallets in hand, met many dozens of reporters from around the world to boast how they kept the antiwar riffraff out of their beloved park and to pay homage to Bush. "Never has one man," exclaimed a Billionaire, "done so much, for so few, at the expense of so many."[46] It was the group's own coup de théatre, using a clever stunt and an eager media as the force multiplier for its message. Later in the day, the group gathered at the Plaza Hotel for its "Million Billionaire March" joining, like feeder marches from all over the city, the UFPJ protest.

The press briefing for the march, held on two-foot risers on Eighth Avenue, demanded "a government that will end the disastrous occupation of Iraq, cancel the obscene war contracts to war profiteers like Halliburton, and give the Iraqi people the financial resources they need to rebuild their own country."[47] It also highlighted key communities among the marchers: Arab and Muslim Americans, "unfairly rounded up, detained, and labeled as terrorists"; immigrants, who have been "profiled, scapegoated, and deported"; and "people of all colors who have given our lifeblood to build this country," despite historic abuse. Speakers included Michael Moore, Arundhati Roy, ex–State Department official Ann Wright, IVAW's Kelly Dougherty, and Bhairavi Desai of the New York Taxi Worker Alliance, dominated by South Asian members.[48]

The march slowly moved in a horseshoe, filing north past Madison Square Garden and turning south to end in Union Square, where the city's first organized protests against the War on Terror had begun. Hundreds of thousands took part. (In 2007, an NYPD Commissioner put the crowd at a staggering 800,000; the original police tally was 120,000.)[49] Progressive blogger Tom Engelhardt detected an angrier mood than in protests past.[50] One sign had a blunt label for Bush: "War Monger, War Criminal." A New Jersey protester, who had worked to elect Bush in 2000, turned against his administration, "because of the terrible lies. The WMD lies. They all lied. . . . We lost all those wonderful young [soldiers] for those rotten lies." To symbolize the military dead, clergy and veterans carried a thousand flag-draped coffins in the hours-long procession. Marching near the front was New York City's first post-Bloomberg mayor, Democratic City Council member Bill de Blasio. As to the national election, a cheeky sign captured a common sentiment: "Kerry-Edwards, They Suck Less."

The police presence, which included dogs, thick rows of officers, and surveillance helicopters, was intense. The protesters, observed Engelhardt, "felt that their presence was a statement in favor of the very existence of civil liberties." The torching of a paper mâché dragon as marchers moved past Madison Square Garden was the only major security incident. Many protesters ended their day, as UFPJ had urged, in Central Park. Yet nightfall brought more arrests of peaceful demonstrations, including people heckling GOP delegates as they attended Broadway shows.

Demonstrations on August 30, when the convention opened, focused mostly on domestic issues. Community groups and poor

Filmmaker Michael Moore (left), United for Peace and Justice cochair Leslie Cagan, Rev. Jesse Jackson, and actor Danny Glover outside New York City's Madison Square Garden with the lead banner for the massive antiwar march on the eve of the Republican National Convention on August 29, 2004. Lee Celano, WireImage via Getty Images.

people's advocates held large rallies and marches, demanding that resources be spent at home, not on foreign wars. The main RNC protests concluded with a second crescendo the following day, reserved for direct action. Police made more than a thousand new arrests. Quickly dubbed "Guantánamo on the Hudson," Pier 57 was clogged with protesters and luckless passersby. It was the high-water mark of militancy within the antiwar movement, rivaling Saturday's mass demonstration as the main storyline of the week's dissent.

Protests dotted the city. Code Pink held a "Fox News Shut-Up-a-Thon" outside its midtown headquarters. At multiple locations, The Naming Project recited the names of all those killed by US military action since 9/11. Veterans for Peace, IVAW, and others teamed up for a Veterans Vigil for the Fallen at Union Square. Through tears, parents paid tribute to their slain children. With a bagpipe playing, protesters drifted through a tight maze of boots, crosses, and coffins. It was a chilling coda to the weeks after 9/11, when memorials to the dead were everywhere.⁵¹ The War Resisters League (WRL) sought, in somber tones, to bring its message directly to the convention. The police's conduct, and the protesters' resolve, made for the day's greatest drama.

Frida Berrigan was a lead organizer of the WRL protest. Cut of activist cloth, she brought years of perspective to the tangle with both war politics and law enforcement. Born in 1974, Frida grew up in Jonah House, an "intentional community focused on nonviolent resistance to war-making" in a low-income Baltimore neighborhood.⁵² Her parents and uncle Daniel were "luminaries" in the Catholic left, famous for their high-risk protests and time in federal prison. A "rotating cast" of activists were part of the house's "intense, austere" life.

In that culture, going to jail or prison was considered "the fullest expression of one's commitment to making a change in the world." At the same time, the Catholic stress on the spiritual power of sacrifice, regardless of its outcomes, "freed people from thinking" narrowly about the "efficacy" of their arrest actions. Frida's first arrest was at age nine, with more than a dozen following. Among the only white children in a poor Black school, she learned that incarceration was part of other kids' lives too. Yet their elders so often lacked the resources and support her parents enjoyed, while suffering "stigma and shame" alien to those locked up for protest.

Frida charted her own path, working after college as an analyst of US militarism. Her arrest at a White House protest of the Afghanistan war further challenged her esteem for civil disobedience. Unexpectedly going to trial, and calculating the costs in time and money, she concluded that "we're not ending the war more by sitting on a courtroom bench for eight hours waiting to dazzle a tired old judge with our brilliance." The movement needed both a "bigger toolbox" and a more "strategic approach." She found both in the War Resisters League.

For weeks, WRL designed a protest alongside other groups in RNC Not Welcome—an ad hoc, anarchist-tinged coalition that coordinated much of the week's direct action. The WRL plan was to gather at the edge of Ground Zero wearing white as a color of mourning; carry pictures of US military dead and civilian victims in Afghanistan and Iraq; and "die-in" on the floor of the convention. Aware that it would not reach its target, the group drew on the power of its intention. The action got a surprise boost when *The New York Times* advertised the protest in its convention coverage. The couple of hundred people organizers expected grew to more than a thousand. Most were unprepared for arrest.

Frida's excitement turned to panic when she learned that those at the front were surrounded by police just minutes into the march. The group—which at first included media and even RNC delegates walking the block—was pinned for hours to a long fence by police bikes and plastic "kettle tape" fencing. More than two hundred people were arrested, including most of the leadership. Frida had to make the protest happen with whomever was left.

Allowed a new route, the remaining group of 150 or so was stopped just blocks from Madison Square Garden. After deep breaths, Frida joined hands with Megan Bartlett from 9/11 First Responders Against War. The two women lay down, sobbing, in a busy intersection. When the light turned green and traffic was stopped, a "terrific noise" rose from the crowd. Dozens more joined them, "dying-in" for more than an hour before their arrest.

Their next stop was Pier 57. By now it held hundreds of protesters, some still in handcuffs, in giant cages. A "huge cheer" from the first batch of WRL arrestees met their arrival. For hours, a "nonstop" flow of buses deposited more people rounded up at protests throughout the city, including its famous public library. Pushing through chaos and nerves, Frida was elated at having pulled off a "very readable antiwar die-in that centered the victims of US militarism." She and others—some in visible distress—coped with scarce water and food, the grime of auto grease, and hostile guards. A young African American man, swept up while shopping near MSG, blasted the "criminalization of blackness."

Early morning brought Frida to the notorious jail called "the Tombs," with whole sections emptied out to house protesters. Also on the police bus were Starhawk and Lisa Fithian, arrested at other protests. At the Tombs, Frida was put off by the rampant complaints about the food and lack of access to phone calls, which smacked to her of "entitlement." She disdained, in addition, "the idea that we need anything" from the jailers. A guard confided that they had cleaned the jail before the protesters' arrival, signaling what "normal" inmates endured. "Guantánamo on the Hudson" seemed to Frida a wholly inappropriate moniker, distorting a sense of the War on Terror's truest violence and victims.

The mass arrests unfolded as a real-time scandal. In a holding cell below Manhattan's main courthouse, a diabetic man denied access to his medication called 911 from a payphone, prompting an ambulance to come. The WRL's Matt Daloisio used the phones to conduct an on-air interview with *Democracy Now!*, which tracked the fate of the arrestees. Frida was released after twenty-three and a half hours—thirty minutes before prisoners became eligible for eventual payouts for excessively long detention. Others were held for two days or more, often released without arraignments by judges alert to the violation. The protesters insisted that the city, favoring GOP optics over their civil rights, meant to clear them from the streets for the length of the convention.

Much of the fallout from the RNC protests concerned the eighteen hundred or so arrests and lengthy lockups. Organizations, individual protesters, and local politicians bitterly complained, while the City Council held hearings to unpack what happened. Attorneys filed lawsuits on behalf of hundreds of plaintiffs alleging wrongful arrests and the denial of their civil rights. Nine in ten arrestees had their charges dismissed, while the handful of trials often ended in acquittal. In one of them, video evidence revealed that an NYPD officer had openly lied in court about the conduct of Dennis Kyne, a Gulf War veteran fraudulently prosecuted for resisting arrest.[53] In 2006, the FBI opened a criminal investigation into the NYPD's actions during the RNC.

Six year later, a federal judge ruled that the first arrests at the WRL protest were unconstitutional. A mass arrest near Union Square was also deemed illegal, as were detentions longer than twenty-four hours. In January 2014, the New York Civil Liberties Union won an $18 million settlement from the city. Among recipients of the payouts were protesters, journalists, legal observers, and bystanders.[54] Refusing the settlement, four people took their claims to trial, together winning $185,000.[55] The courts were clear: The city broke the law on a massive scale in response to nonviolent dissent.

Protest organizers had worried about police surveillance, making planning more difficult. Police activity was far greater than they had feared. In spring 2007, *The New York Times* revealed that a year or more before the RNC, the NYPD conducted extensive surveillance on potential convention protesters.[56] Undercover agents were also active in at least fifteen places outside of New York, including in Canada and Europe. They attended meetings, befriended participants, and filed nightly intelligence reports. Other investigators scoured websites and chat groups.

Coordinating the effort was the ominously named "RNC Intelligence Squad." Its roots lay in the months after 9/11, when the NYPD argued the need to conduct its own intelligence operations. In early 2003, a federal judge granted the city new powers to "investigate political, social, and religious groups," setting the stage for the RNC spying.[57] Most of it was directed at people with "no apparent intention of breaking the law." These included environmentalists, bicycle advocates, members of church and community groups, antiwar organizations, theater companies, music collectives, and even the Billionaires for Bush. New lawsuits after the *Times*'s exposé challenged the legality of the surveillance, which appeared to skirt requirements for probable cause.

Some groups, like the WRL, openly planned for arrests and were not surprised by the infiltration. Others were bemused. The Billionaires reported suspicion that an undercover cop was in their midst when "he kept asking for stock tips."[58] The fate of hapless protesters showed the dubious lengths of Intelligence Squad efforts. Joshua Kinberg was investigated based on his design of a bicycle—dubbed by police a "quick vehicle of escape"—that could use chalk to draw anti-RNC slogans on the pavement. He was arrested at the protests while being interviewed on MSNBC, with his equipment held for a year.[59] The NYPD also went after alleged ringleaders. Months after the RNC, Frida Berrigan and other WRL principals were served with subpoenas demanding notes, emails, and other information for an apparent investigation into the planning of their nonviolent protest. A whole legal fight was required to quash the investigation into a demonstration *subject to police misconduct*.

Most immediately, movement forces assessed the RNC protests in political terms. UFPJ's Hany Khalil judged the main antiwar mobilization a success. "Incredibly uplifting" to its participants, the march dominated news coverage on the convention's first day.[60] Equally important, UFPJ built a "broad-based demonstration" in alliance with "Latino community-based organizations, Islamic centers, labor unions, South Asian immigrant rights groups, African American church leaders [and] youth groups." Even so, police threats likely scared away many immigrants and people of color.

Some organizers were less impressed with the efforts at coalition building. Monami Malik was the cofounder of Desis Rising Up & Moving, representing working-class immigrants in New York. For the RNC, it joined with Still We Rise, Racial Justice 9/11, and other community groups to address both local needs and the War on Terror. Underwhelmed by the solidarity shown them, Malik complained of the familiar "divide between community-led movements of poor people of color and mainly white direct action or 'mass mobilization' activists." Other activists repeated the criticisms of February 2003 that UFPJ was too timid in its focus on a peaceful march, missing an opportunity for mass, disruptive action.[61] Some protesters, finally, felt that too much attention was being paid by the movement and the media to their arrests, distracting from concern with the victims of Bush's wars.[62]

Next for the movement was a two-month dash to the election, in which antiwar protest and efforts to unseat Bush were nearly one and the same. Kerry made the work hard. In early August, he stated that he still would have authorized Bush to attack Iraq, even knowing that it had no WMD.[63] The president, he felt, should have that authority but had used it unwisely. "It's just too important to important to get rid of Bush," said IVAW cofounder Mike Hoffman, explaining why he was sticking with Kerry.[64]

Some in the movement assisted with the Kerry campaign or

helped to elect down-ballot Democrats. Kai Newkirk, who left UFPJ's Steering Committee as he finished college, took a strategic approach. Kerry, for all his flaws, was the only "vehicle for the things I cared about, including the war."[65] Still hopeful of one day taking part in a "nonviolent revolution," he took a job as a field organizer for the Democrats in West Virginia. Working for Kerry, Ward Reilly had a faint wish of influence. On the campaign trail, he twice met Kerry, "looked him dead in the eye, and said 'You have to end these criminal occupations.'" Kerry answered, "I know."

Others in the movement worked to register and energize voters. California's Rae Abileah had turned eighteen on election day in 2000.[66] While in New York City's Barnard College on scholarship, she went to antiwar actions and organized for the mental health of fellow students. As the Iraq invasion approached, she found it "devastating" to "see in slow motion what you know is going to result in massive death." Her time at Barnard ended with Barbara Ehrenreich's commencement speech about Abu Ghraib.

Just after the RNC protests, Abileah got a rideshare back to California with Code Pink's Van Joi, a dynamic, older woman. The two slowly made their way west in Joi's truck, painted with antiwar slogans and updated totals of the civilians and US soldiers killed in Iraq. Everywhere they went, they did two things: set up an ironing board in a parking lot to register voters and hold an antiwar vigil. Returning east, Abileah did get-out-the-vote work in Wisconsin and Pennsylvania, before arriving in Washington to work for Code Pink.

Campaign media put a face to the country's loss. In October, MoveOn ran a television ad in swing states featuring Cindy Sheehan.[67] Captioned as "a message to George W. Bush," the ad shows Sheehan fighting through tears as she describes her sense of betrayal at the death of her son Casey in Iraq. "You haven't been honest with us," she tells the president, while asking him to imagine how it feels to lose your child to a lie. In Washington, DC, to promote the ad, she marched with military families from Arlington National Cemetery to the White House to share their anger at the war. At the protest were Lila Lipscomb, featured in *Fahrenheit 9/11*, and Michael Berg, father of the murdered Nicholas.

"SORRY EVERYBODY, WE TRIED"

For all the tumult on the streets during the RNC, most alarming from an antiwar standpoint was the sentiment inside the convention. Tom Engelhardt talked with GOP delegates, whose emotion-laden "belief system" appeared to him impervious to rational argument. No one was troubled by the administration's empty claims about WMD or thought that the Iraq War was a mistake. "Saddam himself," they claimed, "was a Weapon of Mass Destruction." Above all, they had the sense that "we" were attacked by an amorphous, freedom-destroying "them," which included bin Laden, Saddam Hussein, and other interchangeable enemies. US firepower made the world safer and better. Millions of other Americans believed that too.

George Bush was reelected, narrowly winning the Electoral College by 286–251. He took the entire South and nearly all of the Midwest. This time, he won the popular vote, by a margin of 50.7 to 48.3 percent.

For opponents of the war, the election was a crushing defeat. "This is shattering," wrote UFPJ's Rahul Mahajan. "It will be interpreted, rightly, by the world and by many in this country as a ratification of Bush's imperialistic, dictatorial, dishonest, and unbelievably destructive policies."[68] "These are grim times," Dennis Loy Johnson wrote in early December to preface essays by progressives reacting to the election.[69] Their grand theme was that democracy itself was broken, with the Iraq War its most glaring wreckage. "People are not upset, they are distraught." Three days after the election a young, well-adjusted man "in despair" over the result drove from Georgia to Manhattan, climbed into the "gaping pit" at Ground Zero, and shot himself.

Just after Kerry's concession, a California college student posted a photo of himself with a handwritten message to the world: "Sorry Everybody, We Tried."[70] The post went viral, attracting thousands of similar signs. They were displayed on a website receiving tens of millions of hits.

Various theories sought to explain Bush's victory: the image of

Kerry as a "coastal elite," lacking Bush's heartland authenticity; his fickleness on the Iraq War and doubts about his patriotism; GOP efforts to stir up culture-war issues and turn out evangelicals; deepening partisanship, resistant to electoral swings; and the majority view, as revealed by exit polls, that Bush would best keep the country safe. Transcending these explanations was, perhaps, something else, with stinging implications for the antiwar movement.

Just before the election, a *New York Times* reporter recounted his conversation with a Bush staffer.

> The aide said that guys like me were "in what we call the reality based community," which he defined as people who "believe that solutions emerge from your judicious study of discernable reality." I nodded and murmured something about enlightenment principles and empiricism. He cut me off. "That's not the way the world really works anymore," he continued. "We're an empire now, and when we act, we create reality. And while you are studying that reality—judiciously, as you will—we'll act again creating other new realities [. . .] You, all of you, will be left to just study what we do."[71]

The comment suggests a robust propaganda mechanism that manipulates perceptions as a means to political ends. "Power," concluded one pundit from the exchange, "can shape truth [and] determine reality, or at least the reality of what most people believe—a critical point" for an administration "singularly effective in its recognition that what is most politically important is not what the *New York Times* believes, but what most Americans are willing to believe."[72] But more than that, the aide expresses a vision of a pure imperialism or will to power. Its aim—beyond territory, or resources, or geopolitical control—is to dominate reality itself, enabling all other conquests.

In either guise, the aide's assertion posed an enormous challenge to the politics of truth at the antiwar movement's heart. Decades before, author Paul Goodman wrote, "We assume that most Americans don't 'really' will the Vietnam War but are morally asleep and brainwashed . . . and that an awakened populace can throw it off."[73]

Echoing this view, so much Iraq War protest sought to expose the truth in the precise hope of awakening the public to the wrongfulness of the war. "If you only knew the number of Iraqi civilians who were dying," protesters thundered to fellow Americans, "then clearly you would change your mind!"[74]

Activists and independent journalists went to combat zones to bear direct witness to US violence, engage its victims, and broadcast what they saw. The movement had, in 9/11 family members and the parents of military dead, seemingly unimpeachable messengers. The convention protests—from Operation Sybil to naked bodies to coffins marking the costs of war—were awash in appeals to truth.

And yet, Bush won. Some voters remained beholden to falsehoods, like the existence of Iraqi WMD, or bothered to learn little about the war. Others, like those Engelhardt interviewed, acknowledged the mistruths and still backed Bush, as if captive to a "belief system" and a concocted "reality" in which truth did not matter. People's "perceived need for protection," speculated one activist, prevented them "even from seeing the violence" the United States inflicted on other peoples.[75] The power of revelation, against this closed system, was neutralized, calling into question so much antiwar activism.

Bush and his aides hardly had the last word. Iraqis and other actors in the conflict had a say as well. Could the administration, in the face of a growing insurgency and US misdeeds, sustain its fantastical vision of inevitable victory in a just cause? Might a noncompliant reality prove more powerful than imperial conceit? And could the antiwar movement aid the war's undoing by making truth speak in new ways?

CHAPTER 11

"REAL SUPPORT FOR THE TROOPS"

The Antiwar Movement and Military Dissent

After Bush's reelection, both the war in Iraq and the movement to stop it faced highly uncertain futures. Bush continued to wrap his policies in world-saving benevolence. "Our military has brought justice to the enemy and honor to America," he said in his acceptance speech, "and served the freedom of all mankind."[1] "All who live in tyranny," his inauguration speech proclaimed, "can know that the United States will not ignore your oppression."[2]

Iraq now had a path to meaningful sovereignty. In January 2005, Iraqis voted in a National Assembly, tasked with writing a constitution. The world's governments and media celebrated the milestone. Future elections would seat the first post-Saddam parliament. At long last, the promise of Iraqi independence was coming into view. But much stood in the way.

The resistance raged on. "The great, liberating march upcountry of 2003," concluded a retired US general, "had degenerated into the heat, squalor, and blood of Iraqi resentment, prisoner abuse, and baby-killing."[3] Millions of Iraqis saw the Americans as the oppressors and wanted them gone. 2004, the last year of Bush's first term, saw twenty-six thousand attacks on coalition forces.[4]

Bush's election was followed by a second assault on Fallujah. It was pitched as the defining battle of what had become, long past Mission Accomplished, the *real* war in Iraq. Fallujah would repeat the false promise of victory. US forces, in the short term, achieved their military objectives. But the attack was devastating for civilians, deepening Iraqis' anger. In 2005, insurgent attacks rose to thirty-four thousand.[5]

Iraqi politics remained combustible. The large Shia population, oppressed under Saddam, welcomed majority rule. Even so, some Shia groups continued to fight the Americans, while jockeying for position in a new government. The Sunni minority, long favored by Saddam (himself a Sunni), faced the further loss of its status and power. Many Sunnis refused to participate in the political process, while foreign fighters pushed for civil war. Sectarian division, crudely depicted in the United States as an all-encompassing battle between Shia and Sunni, was only one basis upon which Iraqis clashed. Ideology, local ties, and the raw pursuit of wealth and power played roles as well.

US policy became a high-wire act. It sought to find pro-American Shia partners in forming a new state, to train an Iraqi army that would fight the insurgency, and to separate Iraqi Sunnis from foreign "extremists." How, or if, the war might end on terms favorable to the Bush administration was unclear. In early 2005, 150,000 mostly American coalition troops were in Iraq. Their continued presence invited Vietnam War–tinged charges of "quagmire," with light forever beyond the tunnel's bend. The cost to the United States was $5 billion a month.[6]

The chaos in Iraq meant no immediate advantage for the antiwar movement. The chance to vote the war out of its current existence had come and gone. Republicans increased their majority in Congress, further thwarting legislative action against the war. Sunken spirits added to the challenge.

Ever hopeful, Medea Benjamin laid out a postelection program for the movement. The policy goals were the get to US government to pledge to withdraw its forces by end of 2005 and to have UN peacekeepers enter Iraq when US forces leave. "How do we build a peace movement," she asked, "that can put forward these demands in an effective way?"[7]

Benjamin's answer was to press harder on the politics of truth by redoubling efforts to make "real the human cost of the war." The core problem, she felt, was that the US public was being given a "sanitized version" of the conflict. "If [Americans] were to see the gory reality of this war—the children without limbs, the wailing mothers, the shivering refugees, the US soldiers coming home in body bags or incapacitated for life—support would plummet and the war would end." Leslie Cagan knew well the power of this imagery. "One of the great lessons that the US government learned from Vietnam was don't show it on the nightly news. Don't show all those bodies. Don't show the dead babies, which they did in Vietnam day in and day out."[8] The media itself, Benjamin suggested, must become a target of protest.

This program may have made good moral and logical sense. It was also a long shot. Nothing suggested that the US media would dramatically change its coverage of a long-gruesome conflict. Even disturbing images, like the Abu Ghraib photos, could be spun as an aberration or the excusable hell of war. Eyewitnesses from Iraq, who came to the United States in tiny trickles, scarcely reached the mainstream. New messengers would have to carry the antiwar message. Benjamin named who they might be, calling on activists to "support military families who are speaking out against the war, and soldiers who are speaking out and refusing to fight."[9]

For those in the military community, the wounds were deeply personal, scarcely soothed by talk of progress in Iraq. Bush's victory left Cindy Sheehan feeling "betrayed by the American people."[10] Two days after the election, she wrote an open letter to Bush vowing to hold him accountable for the deaths of US soldiers. In late summer, she and other bereaved families set up a protest camp near Bush's Texas ranch. Like no other protest, it captured the hearts of Americans and the attention of the media.

Joining Sheehan in Texas were relative newcomers to the antiwar scene: veterans of the Iraq War, denouncing the conflict in which they had fought. Resistance in the military existed from the start. Some service members had refused deployment. As soldiers returned from Iraq, military protest grew bigger, louder, and more organized. It described the reality of US conduct, rejected the muddled mission, and modeled opposition to war as service to both the country and its troops. The turning of some in the military could not, in itself, turn the country against the war and force its end. But it further undermined the war's legitimacy, energized the antiwar movement, and challenged the nation's conscience.

"THEY CAME IN TYRANNY"

The Bush administration's political ambitions for Iraq depended on containing the military resistance inside the country. This meant, above all, pacifying Fallujah as the insurgency's heart. A second attack, named Operation Phantom Fury, came just days after Bush's reelection. "The enemy has got a face," declared a US commander. "He's called Satan. He's in Fallujah, and we're going to destroy him."[11]

More than 13,000 US and British forces massed outside the city, supported by Iraqi units. The target was Fallujah's 3,000 or so insurgents. The city's 300,000 civilians were told to leave. The evacuation order hardly spared them. For weeks before the ground attack, US bombs flattened homes and killed and wounded civilians, trapping them in the city. Others lacked the means to leave. Tens of thousands remained in Fallujah when the main offensive began. Evacuees huddled in tents at the city's edge or slept in fields, sickened by the lack of clean water. Little of this was admitted by the military or reported by the major US press. It largely fell to antiwar forces to broadcast the destruction to the American people.

Led by the Marines, the battle was days of block-by-block combat, followed by dangerous mop-up work. By its end in mid-December, ninety-five Americans had died, with more than six hundred wounded. The Bush administration trumpeted Phantom Fury as a great victory, opening the "liberated" city to congressional and media tours. "Fallujah—Graveyard of the Americans," had been painted on "Blackwater Bridge." On it, Marines put new words: "This is for the Americans of Blackwater murdered here in 2004. Semper Fidelis."[12]

Phantom Fury far from did the job. Many insurgents fled before the main fight began. The destruction of the city, home to historic mosques, further enflamed the resistance. To the war's opponents, Fallujah repeated the core folly of the War on Terror: violent retribution, in the name of American dead, that punished innocents and caused more violence.

Like most other journalists, Dahr Jamail was kept by the violence outside the city. In Baghdad, he heard "horrific stories" from Iraqis fleeing Fallujah, publishing their accounts in the online NewStandard.[13] Iraqi males over fourteen were barred from leaving the city. An Iraqi journalist saw US forces kill family members in private homes because they did not understand English-language commands. Escapees claim to have seen US troops shooting civilians bearing white flags and tanks rolling over the dead and dying. US soldiers, some recounted, dumped bodies in the Euphrates River, while snipers shot people trying to swim across it to safety. Jamail and other journalists also reported on the battlefield use of white phosphorous munitions, banned as combat weapons.

The Red Cross estimated eight hundred civilian casualties, though the total may have been several times that.[14] Thousands of structures were destroyed, including the majority of Fallujah's homes and dozens of schools and mosques. Possible war crimes were at once concealed by the military and shrugged off. NBC aired Kevin Sites's footage of US soldiers executing a wounded combatant. The incident "was most noteworthy," observed a veteran journalist, "because it caused such a small, short-lived stir."[15] Exposés on digital news sites and *Democracy Now!* reached only so far. What informed protesters saw as among the war's darkest episodes likely appeared to many Americans as just another distant fight against bad guys.

In late December, Global Exchange organized a trip to Jordan to deliver more than $600,000 in aid to Fallujah's refugees. Billed as "Families for Peace," the delegation included Adele Welty from Peaceful Tomorrows, whose firefighter son died on 9/11; Amalia Avila, Nadia McCaffrey, and Rosa and Fernando Suárez del Solar, who lost their sons in Iraq; Benjamin and Jodie Evans from Code Pink; and UFPJ's Hany Khalil.[16] The Americans met with Iraqis who had lost loved ones to US attacks, in some cases just days before. The tense meetings ended with the tearful hugs of parents united by loss.[17] "The first step to peace," Welty said, is "up to us," not any government.

Documenting the trip was Mark Manning. After 9/11, Manning left a successful career working on offshore oil rigs. Learning film, he toured the country asking Americans what they thought of the terror attacks. Manning also spent time with Vietnam's famous Buddhist monk Thich Nhat Hanh, drawing him to the ways of peace.

In Lebanon with the peace delegation, Manning met a remarkable Iraqi journalist, Rona al-Aioby. At the height of battle, she had gone into Fallujah to deliver aid. When the US delegation left, Manning and al-Aioby entered Fallujah and its environs, filming in secret. They captured the misery of the refugees and a city in ruins. The Americans "came to rid us of tyranny," said a woman in the rubble of her home. "But they came in tyranny."[18] The Iraqis desperately wanted their stories told to the American people. When back home, Manning presented his footage to peace groups and approached members of Congress, asking them what the United States would do for Fallujah's civilians. Most shooed him away, declining answer.

The Second Battle of Fallujah was a source of ongoing humanitarian work. The Justice for Fallujah Project brought together activists, academics, journalists, health experts, and US veterans troubled by their role in the siege. For years, it documented the city's destruction and long-term health crisis, including increases in cancer and birth defects.[19]

The project continued long-standing efforts to bring attention to Iraqis' suffering, which focus on American losses could obscure. Nancy Kricorian, head of Code Pink's New York City chapter, became "obsessed" with Iraqbodycount.org.[20] Run by British and American volunteers, the website listed the names and ages of the dead, drawn from public records. Entries for children disturbed her the most.

Kricorian and others created "Walk in Their Shoes," partly as a complement to "Eyes Wide Open." Debuting at Hillary Clinton's Senate office in New York City, it displayed everyday shoes, many in children's sizes. At first thinking the shoes were for sale, people reacted in shock and sadness when learning their meaning. "Eyes Wide Open" itself grew to feature civilian shoes, while Arlington

West put up signs showing the vast stretch of beach needed to memorialize Iraqi losses. For the antiwar movement, Iraqi and American casualties were indelibly connected. Each had a role in ending the war.

Sometimes the violence in Iraq made unique victims. On April 16, 2005, Marla Ruzicka, the American aid worker, was killed by an insurgent bomb on Baghdad's perilous "airport road." The blast also killed her Iraqi research partner, Faiz Al Salim. After establishing CIVIC in Iraq and helping to build a civilian assistance fund, Ruzicka had returned to the United States, partly to tend to her failing health. Away from Iraq, she found evidence to confirm suspicions that the US military, despite its denials, in fact keep records on the civilians it harmed. She returned to Baghdad to find out more.

From a US brigadier general, Ruzicka confirmed the existence of military data on civilian casualties. This revelation blew open new possibilities for aid work, as potential recipients could be more easily identified. Before she could act on her discovery, she was killed.

Ruzicka's death was mourned by the many journalists, aid workers, activists, and civilian victims whose lives she had touched. Memorial services were held in Baghdad, Kabul, San Francisco, Washington, DC, and her California hometown. Senator Patrick Leahy eulogized her from the Senate floor. She was, he said, "as close to a living saint as they come."[21] The assistance program she helped set up with the State Department was renamed the Marla Ruzicka Iraqi War Victims Fund. The work of CIVIC continued in Afghanistan and Iraq, later expanding to other conflict zones.

"REAL SUPPORT FOR THE TROOPS"

After Phantom Fury, the family of Jerry Zovko, one of the Blackwater contractors killed in Fallujah in 2004, insisted that he "wouldn't want innocent children to die" as a result of his terrible death. Another Blackwater parent explained that she did not "have any space in my heart or soul for vindictiveness."[22] More and more, military families were saying "Not in our name."

One grieving parent, Cindy Sheehan, would soon stand out in the force of her anger, ability to lead, and the attention she and her antiwar message gained. Her rise to prominence was nurtured by the solidarity of others struck with sorrow and layers of organized support.

Seeing the Army's "Angels of Death" in her Fairfield, California, living room, Sheehan collapsed in screams. On April 4, 2004, her son Casey was killed in Sadr City. Her loss was sadly unexceptional in a war that had claimed by that point 650 American lives. But Sheehan was no usual Gold Star parent, privately bearing her grief. Neither was Jane Bright, who had shared her opposition to the war with her son Evan Ashcroft, killed in Iraq in July 2003. "This anguish is unspeakable," she told the *Los Angeles Times*. "We're not speaking enough about the losses."[23]

After Casey's death, Sheehan "felt like a piece of rotted meat surrounded by flies and ugliness," and fought thoughts of suicide.[24] She and other grieving parents were invited to meet with President Bush in Fort Lewis, Washington. The meeting, she sensed, was designed to show his concern for them, useful to his reelection campaign. She found him hollow and insincere, uninterested even in pictures of her fallen son.

Sheehan had sensed from the start that the administration was lying about Iraq. But she never protested the war. "I ultimately allowed [Bush]," she told herself, "to kill my child." A poem written by her daughter brought her out of her stupor and into protest. In this transition, Casey's death gave "spiritual birth" to his "real mom," who would "try to stop others from being killed." In a frequent pattern of post-9/11 dissent, violent death spurred efforts to protect life.

In the summer of 2004, Sheehan discovered Military Families Speak Out, bonding with parents like Jane Bright. Joining them were Sheehaan's sister, Dede Miller, and Bill Mitchell, whose son was killed with Casey. Sheehan first spoke publicly against the war in California on July 4, 2004. That same day, "Eyes Wide Open" was displayed outside of Philadelphia's Independence Hall, seen by twenty thousand people.

After Bush's reelection, this small group and several others formed Gold Star Families for Peace (GSFP). Its first mission was to go to the Pentagon the day before Bush's inauguration to demand a meeting with Donald Rumsfeld. "Frozen stiff and miserable," the parents met only police and military guards.[25] Interviewed by major national media for their inauguration coverage, Sheehan was thrust into an awkward fame. She was—as a white, middle-class mom from a small California city—a compelling, "all-American" messenger. Her heart-on-the-sleeve, say-what-you-think manner also made her a thorn in the war's side. To the bromide that her son died doing what he loved, Sheehan shot back that he did not want to be killed "thousands of miles from home, fighting a people who only wanted him out of their country."[26] Gold Star Families for Peace would take this attitude to the nation.

As more military families and veterans protested the war, peace organizations made the most of their presence. For the war's second anniversary, UFPJ declined to hold a demonstration in Washington, DC, as might be expected. Instead, it backed three days of protest activity on March 18–20 in Fayetteville, North Carolina, home to Fort Bragg military base.

Now one thousand groups strong, UFPJ held in February its Second National Assembly in St. Louis, Missouri. The coalition's main goal, its new "strategic framework" announced, was to "force an end to the war in Iraq and bring the troops home" by attacking "points of vulnerability" in the war effort.[27] Another priority was to oppose the recruitment of the poor, so often youth of color, into the armed services.

The assembly also took up plans for Fayetteville. The focus on the military town was a moral choice, given the burdens borne by the armed services. It was also a strategic one. Going back to the Gulf War, peace activists contended with the myth that anti-Vietnam War protesters commonly disparaged US troops. They responded with "extensive positive references to soldiers" in efforts to "shift the role of betrayer from the peace movement to the government."[28] In this spirit, opponents of the Iraq War argued that the troops lacked proper training and armor, received poor medical care both in Iraq and back home, and were sacrificed to the false claims of the war makers.

Bryan Profitt, a North Carolina activist with Hip Hop Against Racist War, led efforts in UFPJ to back the Fayetteville protests.[29] It was important, he stressed, to support antiwar work in the South, falsely seen as a citadel of unquestioned nationalism. Fayetteville had traditions of both military service and an "oppositional consciousness," evident in civil rights and anti–Vietnam War protest. In 1970 its Quaker House, which aided military resisters, was burned to the ground. The Quakers remained a force in the community, forming after 9/11 Fayetteville Peace with Justice. Profitt's pitch worked. UFPJ endorsed the Fayetteville demonstration, sent buses from New York City, and gave it prime billing on its website, among the 750 anniversary peace actions nationwide.[30]

The main work was done by local antiwar groups and national veterans' organizations, like Veterans for Peace. It played a key role in encouraging the leadership of new veterans. VFP's Ward Reilly and Bill Perry had first suggested to Michael Hoffman, IVAW's president, that he bring the fledgling group to the demonstration. "Nobody knows the truth about a war," Reilly insisted, "better than the people that were just there."[31] Reilly also understood the power of vets reaching out to other vets. "These guys are coming home shell-shocked [after] being the bad guy, when they thought they were going to go be the good guy. It's soul-crushing. So for them to find a bunch of old veterans who knew exactly where they were coming from" was tremendous. Reilly made a point of connecting with the younger generation. "First comes the big hug, and then the eye-to-eye contact. Trust has to be established, and most veterans trust other veterans. If you haven't been in the military, you simply can't understand."[32] The recent veterans, in turn, respected elders like Reilly for their resistance when inside the military and years of opposition to foreign wars claiming new generations.

The Fayetteville demonstration drew four thousand people. More than half were local. Military families and veterans led the march behind a banner reading "REAL Support for the Troops, BRING THEM HOME," while rousing the crowd with "sound-off"–

style chants. Among them were two dozen members of IVAW. The group also held its own press event, again announcing its existence. Michael Hoffman explained that in Iraq he saw, "a lot of American casualties and a lot of Iraqi civilians and military laying dead on the side of the road. I saw towns destroyed. I helped do that, and it disturbed me deeply."[33] The rally speakers, who included Sheehan, kept the focus the Iraq War and its impact on the military. US casualties, they somberly noted, had surpassed fifteen hundred. National media ran stories on the protest, rivaling coverage of major rallies in San Francisco and London.

The weekend ended with separate meetings of southern organizers, MFSO, and IVAW, holding its first annual conference. At the conference, IVAW took a big leap as an organization, adopting a structure and defined roles. It pledged itself to three main goals: the "immediate, unconditional withdrawal of all occupying forces from Iraq;" improved "health care and other benefits for all veterans and servicemembers"; and "reparations to the Iraqi people."[34] It was open to all those in the US military since 9/11, regardless of branch or where one had served. It also actively welcomed "military resisters" who had refused to deploy. By the Fayetteville protest, it had 150 or so members.

As the War on Terror expanded, so too did military dissent. It began with veterans of past conflicts, like Veterans for Peace. It soon touched military families, organized as Military Families Speak Out. When parents lost their children in Iraq, Gold Star Families for Peace was born. Completing the evolution were veterans of current wars, speaking out with Iraq Veterans Against the War. Its early members, wrote IVAW's first executive director Kelly Dougherty, "implicitly understood the value of veterans and service members' voices in discussions about Iraq and foreign policy."[35] The same was broadly true of all members of the antiwar military community.

Together, they made up the Military Peace Movement (MPM), as described by activist-scholar Lisa Leitz. (In the early '00s, Leitz was an antiwar graduate student in California and Florida, married to a naval aviator. In 2004, she did events with the Kerry-Edwards "Moms for Peace" tour. After the election, she joined MPM grassroots protests.)[36] Its core groups had overlapping memberships, teamed up on campaigns, and spoke at the same events. More than that, their members were bonded by military culture and shared experiences of war. The support was also personal, often to deal with severe emotional trauma.[37] All this gave the movement an intense "family-like structure," enhanced by its mix of generations.[38] Longtime veterans saw the post-9/11 soldiers as their beloved children. They, in turn, saw "peace moms" like Sheehan and Bright as the movement's mothers.

The Military Peace Movement was both a part of the antiwar movement and distinct within it. For its members, their military identity was fundamental to their activism. They often wore military dress at protests, used cadence-style chants, and marched as a bloc. Most of all, they invoked their military experiences in their opposition to war.

Soldiers' reasons for resisting the Iraq War varied. Some, like Marine Steven Funk, came to their antiwar beliefs after enlisting. In February 2003, Funk refused to mobilize, went AWOL, and then turned himself in. "I object to war," he said, "because I believe it is impossible to achieve peace through violence."[39] Sentenced to six months in a military brig, Funk joined an America tradition of pacifist resistance to armed service.

A striking number of soldiers opposed war with Iraq before it even began. They accepted orders to deploy because they felt they had no other choice. Born in Nicaragua, Camilo Mejia was part of Florida's Army National Guard.[40] He enlisted, like so many others, to help fund college, and was mobilized during his last semester. Going AWOL while on leave in 2004, he became the first soldier to refuse redeployment. Mejia was court-martialed and served nine months in a military prison. A gifted speaker, he became a cause célèbre in antiwar circles, designated by Amnesty International as a "prisoner of conscience." Freed in February 2005, Mejia joined IVAW, becoming one of its most visible members.

Mejia opposed the Iraq War for reasons anyone might have. "There were no weapons of mass destruction," he observed, and "no link between Saddam Hussein and al-Qaeda. We weren't helping the Iraqi people, and the Iraqi people did not want us there."[41] Yet for him and other soldiers, these were not distant observations. *They* were the ones sacrificed to the war, raising the stakes of their dissent.

Time in Iraq deepened their desire to speak out. Stationed near Abu Ghraib, Mejia participated in the occupation's brutality, including the abuse of prisoners at battlefield detention centers. Other soldiers, at first supporting the war, turned against it based on what they saw and did. They chose loyalty to their beliefs over orders to fight in what they felt was an unjust war. "Behind these bars," Mejia wrote from prison, "I sit a free man because I listened to a higher power, the voice of my own conscience."[42]

The means of resistance varied. Starting in 2003, tens of thousands of soldiers went AWOL or deserted, dwarfing normal totals. Some surely sought to avoid being sent to Iraq. Among those openly dissenting, a small number were granted conscientious objector status, exempting them from combat service based on religious or ethical objections to *all* wars. Many others, rejecting the Iraq War in particular, had their conscientious objector applications slow-walked or denied. To avoid deployment, they had to go AWOL or desert. This meant time on the run, put at risk by public statements against the war.

Already in 2004, Mejia and fellow resisters Pablo Parades and Kevin Benderman thought of founding a group tailored to the high-risk dissent of those on active duty. In 2005, they and others formed Courage to Resist.[43] Though rarely discussed, resistance also existed in Iraq itself. Uncounted numbers of troops—whether for reasons of principle or survival—pushed back at combat. They might run "search and avoid" missions that steered clear of hostilities, volunteer for noncombat support, or refuse to participate in treacherous operations, inviting charges of mutiny.[44] Courage to Resist told fellow soldiers was that there was a way out of complicity and harm in a corrupt war.

Fayetteville's Louis Plummer was both a military veteran and a local antiwar leader.[45] His son Andrew was in the Navy. While on leave before the invasion, Andrew told the press that he opposed war with Iraq. Reprisals followed. Wanting out of the military, he twice went AWOL. Captured in South Carolina, he served nine days in a local jail, before military confinement in Illinois. He arrived home the day the 2005 Fayetteville protests started, joining the antiwar vets. Others endured more than a year on the run. Two hundred or so fled for refuge to Canada, as many more had done during the Vietnam War.

In 2006 Lieutenant Ehren Watada became the first commissioned officer to refuse deployment to Iraq. Resisting soldiers, he instructed, "must be aware that they are being used for ill-gain. They must hold themselves responsible for individual action. They must remember duty to the constitution and the people supersedes the ideologies of their leadership. The soldiers must be willing to face ostracism from their peers, worry over the survival of their families, and of course the loss of their freedom."[46] Watada addressed people like himself who faced prison for refusing orders. But a maze of punishments—whether reductions in rank or discharge status, the taking away of benefits, or prosecution for antiwar speech—threatened all resisters, including those leaving the military.

Antiwar protest was difficult. Recounting the violence in Iraq could be traumatizing. Civilian allies might ask ham-fisted questions. Veterans also guarded against being used as "window dressing" at protests.[47] Dissident soldiers, above all, had to reconcile their connection to the military and opposition to war. They did so by opposing the Iraq War in the name of the US Constitution; core American values like democracy; the health of the military, damaged by unnecessary conflicts; and even martial values like honor and courage. Fighting for peace, they believed, was a form of patriotism.

Some prowar Americans rejected this possibility. Disapproval was especially strong in the military, dominated by hawkish views. In Fayetteville, counterprotesters denounced the antiwar soldiers as pawns of the radical left. The VFP's Ellen Barfield sensed "a fair amount of local discomfort" with the protest, whether from "blind patriots" or people economically dependent on the military.[48] IVAW members were occasionally taunted as "traitors."[49] Even potential allies could lash out. A prominent nonpartisan veterans group blasted the Fayetteville protest for "blam[ing] the warriors for the war."[50]

Most in the antiwar movement vocally supported the antiwar soldiers, though some questioned whether warriors could be true messengers of peace. Efi Nwangaza, a civil rights activist going back to the 1960s, complained of "too much deference to the military" at the Fayetteville rally, and too little recognition of "the humanity of the Iraqi people."[51] "It's a little tricky for me," confessed Leslie Cagan, who remembered intense debates about the moral responsibility of US soldiers during the Vietnam War. At an anti–Iraq War panel she attended, a new veteran told "this horrendous story of massacring children, and then he gets to the other side of it, comes out of it and becomes an antiwar activist." The audience was "wildly applauding him, and I'm thinking, yeah, but what about those kids he murdered?"[52]

With the challenges facing MPM members also came a great opportunity: to use their military identities to reach the American public and political class in a new way. Those identities gave them a baseline respect from most Americans, greater interest from the media, and audiences with people inclined to dismiss antiwar protest as un-American. Even police hostile to street protesters often treated antiwar veterans differently.

All this goodwill was needed, given the message of military resisters. "The only way [the Iraq] war is going to end," said Dougherty, "is if the American people truly understand what we have done in their name."[53] IVAW existed to share difficult truths.

"THIS IS THE SIDE I'M ON?"

The core truth was the death and destruction visited on the Iraqi people. That story was partly known through coverage of Abu Ghraib and fleeting media reports on civilian harm. But it was now coming from US soldiers, speaking from experience.

There was no great moment of revelation in which Americans confronted the war through antiwar veterans' eyes. Instead, IVAW members' stories came out in bits and pieces—in media interviews, speeches to peace groups and at rallies, and on the IVAW website and military blogs. Documentary filmmakers and scholars like Leitz also took interest, making soldiers' dissent the best-recorded aspect of the entire antiwar movement.

Some antiwar soldiers, like Tina Garnanez, at first shared little. "I was in Iraq and it was bad," was her message.[54] She soon went to "dark scary places," understanding the value of greater candor. She and her colleagues, as they found their voice, gave a damning portrait of the war, the political and military leaders directing it, and the institution of the military itself.

The greatest offense was to the Iraqi people. Accounting for civilian harm, IVAW members pointed to the vague and shifting "rules of engagement." These were most stringent at the invasion's start, when the enemy was uniformed soldiers. Already by the push to Baghdad, some units "reduced" the standard to "non-existence."[55] Some commanding officers instructed that *anyone* in hostile zones was a combatant. As a result, Iraqis were killed "for simply walking down the street."[56] "When the insurgency took off," recalled sniper Garett Reppenhagen, "everyone was a target."

"You don't go to war with a country," observed the Navy medic Charlie Anderson, "and not go to war with its people."[57] This was especially true in Iraq, where "the enemy could be anyone." "The mission," confessed another IVAW member, "was to get this crap over with and come home." This encouraged a "kill or be killed" mentality. Survival favored killing, often in split-second, friend-or-foe judgments. Checkpoints were especially dangerous, with innocent Iraqis shot for driving too fast or failing to stop in time.

Marine Jeff Huse explained the deadly logic to firefights: "There are fifty fucking people there. It's one guy shooting at us. We can't find the one guy [so it's] kill everything. . . . You don't think, 'there's a lady in a pink dress, let's take her out.' . . . No, blanket the fucking area. It works. It's effective. You don't take fire from that area anymore." IVAW members also witnessed utterly gratuitous violence, like the trashing of Iraqis' cars, bicycles and homes, the killing of farm animals, and the beating of terrified captives.

A condition for much of the violence was the dehumanization of

Iraqis. US soldiers commonly used derogatory and racist epithets for them. This attitude began in basic training, where perverse sound-off drills celebrated the murder of children.[58] Trainees were told that all Iraqis, or all Muslims, were terrorists, wiping out any distinction between civilians and combatants. By the time he deployed, one soldier believed that "the only possible solution" to terrorism "was to kill as many Iraqis as possible."[59] The military, IVAW felt, had trained them to be heartless killers. Their hearts rebelled.

Army sergeant Ricky Clousing saw an innocent teenager, shot at a checkpoint, die before his eyes. "This is the side I'm on?" he wondered.[60] In multiple incidents, James Massey's Marine unit killed innocent Iraqis. In one of these an Iraqi man, whose brother had just died in his arms, confronted Massey. "Why did you kill my brother?" he pleaded. "We're not terrorists." "What are we doing here?" Massey silently asked. Devastated, he was told by his superior that it was a "good day" *because* they had killed civilians.[61]

Reppenhagen gained chilling insight into conflict's heart. After a car sped toward a checkpoint, he pulled the driver out of the window, threw him to the ground, and zip-tied him. "His wife and kids were staring at me" with "this angry look of 'I do not like you. I don't like Americans.'" "The crime," he realized, "was that I was there."[62] The insurgents, observed another IVAW member, were mostly "normal people," tired of US forces "breaking down their doors [and] beating up their dads."[63] Soldiers sometimes reported excessive violence to superiors. The commanding officer typically excused it as self-defense or sought to cover it up, including by planting AK-47 rifles on dead civilians.[64]

"There was no honor in what we did," Army Ranger Chad Reiber concluded.[65] Reppenhagen accepted that the average American soldier is "the victimizer. And I think he feels like a criminal. . . . He comes back to America, and it's 'thank you for your service.' But we're like, 'you have no idea what you are thanking me for. You don't know what I did.'"[66] As "the killing of civilians started to pile up," Mejia found it "really difficult for me morally." He repeatedly apologized to the Iraqi people for the harm he caused. His "cowardice," he felt, lay in not opposing the war earlier. "If Americans actually listened to the veterans that they claimed to respect," said Army reservist Aidan Delgado, "so much would change."

US soldiers suffered "moral injury" on account of their actions. "We all become casualties of war," lamented Huse.[67] Marine Lance Corporal Jeff Lucy told his sister when back home that, "your brother is a murderer." Days later, he hanged himself in his family home. His life, declared his MFSO mother, was "destroyed by the hidden pain" of the war.

Other veterans endured that pain as PTSD, in addiction, violent episodes, broken relationships, and great difficulty living both among civilians and with their own consciences. A major part of IVAW activism, pursued also by other veterans groups, sought to secure better medical care, especially to treat psychological harm. The military and Veterans Administration were slow to diagnose or properly treat PTSD. They little understood, infuriating IVAW members, the role that guilt could play in psychological distress.

The antiwar veterans were left with a terrible dilemma. They were pawns in a war not of their choosing. They had followed commands not easy to resist. At the same time, some committed violence they saw as immoral or even criminal. Excusing their own conduct neither felt right, nor seemed possible. One response was to plead for forgiveness while accepting responsibility for one's unjust acts. Another was to use the inescapable pain as motivation to prevent future suffering. "That guilt fuels my fire," confessed Huse, to oppose the war. "Maybe I *shouldn't* let myself off the hook." But the consciousness of guilt, focused on the antiwar cause, might pull attention away from one's own private ordeal, with personal costs.

Iraq Veterans Against War also condemned what they felt was the predatory nature of military recruiting. As many of their own stories bear out, the military targeted vulnerable youth dealing with economic and family hardship. Many enlisted in order to afford college, or after college and other life plans stalled out, usually for lack of money. The recruitment system, Massey concluded, is "designed to manipulate and lie" by stressing social mobility and the promise of adventure.[68] Those joining the National Guard and Reserve units were told prior to 9/11 that they would never see combat. Most of all, recruiters downplayed the central role of killing in the military enterprise. In response, IVAW and other antiwar groups developed "counterrecruitment" programs that educated young people about the reality of war and alternatives to the military.

Every soldier's experience was unique, and military resisters drew strength from this diversity. There were also common dimensions to their grievances. Joshua Key lived so much of what seemed to IVAW as so wrong.

Key was raised desperately poor in a broken home in Guthrie, Oklahoma. Starting in high school, he was targeted by military recruiters, who promised him a way out of a dead-end future of minimum wage jobs. With a wife, a growing family, and mounting bills, Key enlisted in 2002 at age twenty-four. He considered it "an honor to serve my country."[69] Key's one condition was that he would never deploy overseas. Recruiters assured him he would not. Two weeks after Shock and Awe, Key was sent to Iraqi.

First stationed first in Ramadi, Key was disturbed by the nighttime raids. They terrorized Iraqi families but turned up no insurgents. Sent to an alleged firefight, he saw the bodies of four Iraqi civilians, whose heads had been sliced off by American fire. "Two soldiers," he observed, "were laughing and kicking the[ir] heads." Key was "horrified." And haunted. "Sometimes in my dreams, disembodied heads plagued me with accusations. They told me what I was slowly realizing: that the American military had betrayed the values of my country. We had become a force for evil." His complaints to his superiors went nowhere. "I am not this man," he realized. "I cannot do this any longer."

When home on leave, Key decided he not would return to Iraq. After hiding out for fourteen months, he took his family to Canada, arriving in March 2005. He worked with the Toronto-based War Resisters Support Campaign, touring Canada to speak out against the war, and sought treatment for his PTSD. "When we prosecute an unjust war," he concluded, "or commit immoral acts in any war at all, the first victims are the people unfortunate enough to fall into our hands. The second victims are ourselves." Key found a way to reach

Americans through press interviews and the publication in 2007 of his memoir, *The Deserter's Tale*.

Even as they grew, the ranks of IVAW and other military resisters were tiny relative to the US fighting force. The 10,000–15,000 members of the military community publicly opposing the war were a small fraction of the millions of active-duty soldiers, military veterans, and their families who backed the conflict or opposed it only in private.[70] But the contribution of the Military Peace Movement was still immense. It offered credible and often heartrending opposition to war, based in the conviction that no American solider or family should experience what its members had.

Less than a month after the 2005 Fayetteville protests, Tommy Franks—the newly retired four-star general, who had overseen operations in Iraq—spoke to an elementary school in a Los Angeles neighborhood home to immigrant families ripe for military recruitment. Meeting him there were GSFP's Bill Mitchell and IVAW cofounder Tim Goodrich, along with local protesters. "My son died in Iraq because of that man!" Mitchell yelled at the hulking SUV carrying Franks.[71] Shouts of "murderer," "shame," and "leave our children alone" also greeted the general. Goodrich, wearing a khaki combat jacket, tried to stop the vehicle, which nearly ran him over. Heartache and anger were boiling over, soon to meet a new moment.

CAMP CASEY

The anniversary demonstrations were followed by what Lou Plummer deemed a "lull" in the antiwar movement. Little of its protests in the following months commanded sustained, national attention. UFPJ and ANSWER could not in themselves set an agenda for the movement as a whole. Powered by the grassroots, it functioned as a series of initiatives and campaigns, each vying to galvanize protest energy and public interest. External events, whether in Iraq or the domestic political scene, often dictated the next actions.

A Democrat-led congressional investigation reported in March 2005 that the US "Intelligence Community was dead wrong in almost all of its pre-war judgments about Iraq's weapons of mass destruction."[72] On May 1, *The Sunday Times* published the "Downing Street Memo," just before elections in the United Kingdom. Dated July 23, 2002, the leaked document contained minutes of a secret meeting of leading British officials discussing Iraq, seven months before the invasion. Their comments were based partly on recent meetings in Washington between British intelligence and senior Bush administration figures. "Military action," the notes reported, "was now seen [by Washington] as inevitable. Bush wanted to remove Saddam, through military action, justified by the conjunction of terrorism and WMD. But the facts were being fixed around the policy."[73] The United States, the memo added, had little interest in working with the United Nations save to "help with the legal justification for the use of force."

Progressive media and antiwar forces seized on the memo as smoking-gun proof that the Iraq War was both predetermined and waged on contrived grounds. The months-long drama over Iraqi WMD had been a charade. At first, the memo gained scant coverage in major US media, slow to press Bush for a response. When asked, both he and Blair denied its contents and defended the war.

To antiwar families of the dead and wounded, the brazenness of the deceit was unconscionable. The memo also provided potential evidence of constitutional crimes. On May 26, After Downing Street formed to press the case. The group, as cofounder John Bonifaz described it, was a "coalition of veterans groups, peace groups, public interest organizations or ordinary citizens calling for a formal congressional investigation into whether the president of the United States has committed impeachable offenses."[74] Gold Star Families for Peace was among the first to join. Movement-wide, calls for Bush's removal spiked. A California VFP chapter created a red, white, and blue "Impeachment Tour" bus to travel the country. It was named the White Rose after the famous Munich resistance group, whose mostly young members were executed for denouncing the Nazi regime.

Dozens of Democrats signed a letter demanding a formal inquiry into the administration's apparent deceit. On July 23, the memo's fifth anniversary, three hundred events were held nationwide to demand the same. Representative Maxine Waters led the Los Angeles gathering, which featured MFSO and IVAW speakers, NAACP leader Reverend James Lawson, and youth activists.[75] To thunderous applause, she announced the formation of a congressional Out of Iraq Caucus, already with sixty-four members.

The centerpiece of After Downing Street's efforts had come weeks earlier in testimony to Congress.[76] Convened by Representative John Conyers (D-MI), the hearing featured Joe Wilson, the diplomat who had exposed the ruse that Iraq sought uranium in Africa; retired CIA analyst Ray McGovern, recounting intelligence community doubts about WMD claims; Cindy Sheehan, representing GSFP; and Bonifaz, a young, constitutional lawyer making the legal case for impeachment. At the hearing, Sheehan described the pain of learning anew that her son was "betrayed" into "an early grave." She delivered, for the record, the testimony of nine other antiwar families.

The activism surrounding the Downing Street revelation put the movement squarely back within a politics of truth. Hopes rekindled that support for the war might at last crack, with the war makers held to account. New disappointment was a possibility too. Disappointment won. The Republican majority refused a proper hearing in the Capitol's august chambers. Instead, the testimony was given in a basement room, attended mostly by activists and a few dozen Democrats. Figures on the right lambasted the witnesses.

There would be no impeachment inquiry or mass rejection of the war. In the United Kingdom, where the memo caused far greater controversy, Blair won reelection. Sheehan had permitted herself to believe that Downing Street would cause "millions of Americans" to "rise up" to demand that the troops come home. She was left even more "depressed" than after Bush's 2004 victory.[77] Something different was needed.

That something was Camp Casey, named for Sheehan's soldier son. Set up in Crawford, Texas, it became the signature protest since the war's start, stirring the sympathy of countless Americans. The camp brought together individuals, groups, symbols, practices, and arguments that had long defined the antiwar movement. Deeply meaningful to its participants, it developed a culture and mythology all its own.

On August 3 Sheehan saw on TV that fourteen marines were killed in a single incident in Iraq.[78] Beside herself, she began an email to antiwar contacts. Hearing Bush assure the soldiers' families that they "died for a noble cause," her fingers typed that she would go that weekend to Crawford, where Bush was spending the month at his vacation ranch. She would ask him "for what noble cause did Casey die?" Sheehan volunteered her sister Dede for the trip and brought in another GSFP parent, Amy Branham. Hundreds of emails flooded in supporting the idea. One came from Hadi Jawad of the Crawford Peace House, pledging its help.

Sheehan was already slated to talk at the VFP's annual convention in Dallas, two hundred miles from Crawford. News of her plan electrified the gathering (though some feared that it would wreck the convention agenda). The first night, a small team did basic planning. It included Sheehan, Miller, Jawad and his partner, VFP's new executive director Michael McPherson, and Lisa Fithian, a native Texan based in Austin. As excitement soared, Sheehan grew "terrified to expose myself and my grief" on such a grand scale.

Media outreach was part of the plan. Ward Reilly knew Sheehan from the early days of GSFP. He stayed behind in Louisiana, ready to rush to Crawford on day one. On Friday, August 5, he wrote a piece for the *Baltimore Chronicle*, which had long opposed the war. "If the free press won't come to the truth," it began, "then the truth is going to have to go to the free press."[79] The article invited the nation's media, in Crawford to cover the president, to report on the embodied "truth" represented by Sheehan and the Iraq War veterans who would be with her.

On August 6, the VFP's Impeachment Tour bus set off for Crawford carrying Sheehan and IVAW and VFP members. Among them were Camillo Mejia and Daniel Ellsberg, of *Pentagon Papers* fame. Twenty cars followed, including a Code Pink contingent, with twenty more joining in Crawford. The travelers were stopped by police at a triangle intersection near the ranch, where the media were also waiting. Sheehan told them that she would stay until Bush met with her.

About seventy-five protesters continued on foot, confined to a roadside ditch. Sheehan and other Gold Star parents were at the lead. They carried a "Peace Is Patriotic" banner, while Sheehan clutched a picture of Casey at seven months old. It was a far cry from common images of antiwar protest. The group was middle-aged moms in T-shirts and cargo shorts, young soldiers freshly returned from war, and graying veterans, walking the Texan plain.

When the group crossed on to the pavement, police threatened to arrest them. Here Sheehan took her stand, firing her reputation as "the Rosa Parks of the antiwar movement." "I'm not gonna move," she said, until she met Bush. Chants of "Dubya [slang for Bush] killed her son!" rained down on police. Sheehan and a small group retreated to the "triangle," making it their campsite, while others left for the day. When Mejia suggested "Camp Casey" as its name, Sheehan wept. They dedicated the site to all the fallen service members and to peace.

Later in the evening, Steven Hadley, a senior adviser to Bush, met with the protesters, who rejected his defenses of the war. Seven people, including Code Pink's Diane Wilson, spent the first night under the Texas stars. Driving straight from Louisiana, Ward Reilly and other VFP members arrived by sunrise and set up an IVAW banner. By evening, the camp had grown to two dozen people. Sheehan called it "a miracle."

Over the next three and a half weeks, Camp Casey became the most significant antiwar protest since the February 2003 demonstrations. The work was tough. Moved by police back to the ditch, the protesters had to clear out fire ants and rattlesnakes. Veterans like Reilly used their military sense of order to "keep it from becoming a clusterfuck," overrun by police and local people who "hated us." Under the blazing sun, the camp held press events, ran teach-ins, and memorialized the dead, setting up Arlington West–style crosses by the road. Sheehan had visited the original Santa Barbara memorial one month after Casey's death.

The protesters documented Camp Casey in real time, writing

A banner with an image of Army Specialist Casey Sheehan, son of Cindy Sheehan, billows in the wind on August 20, 2005, at the new Camp Casey protest site near President George W. Bush's ranch in Crawford, Texas. The small banner demands that President Bush "Meet with Cindy." Photograph by Mandel Ngan, AFP via Getty Images.

daily blogs for progressive websites like *Daily Kos*. It became an instant beacon for the war's opponents. Within a week, hundreds were visiting every day, from Texas and beyond. "A lot of people came with a similar story," reports Fithian. "I was driving down the highway, I heard about this [on the radio], and I knew I had to come." A couple drove from Wisconsin just to give Sheehan a hug before returning home. Even active-duty soldiers at nearby Fort Hood visited. More GFSP, MFSO, and IVAW members arrived, with each given a chance to address the camp.

The media response was overwhelming. Nearly a hundred outlets ran stories on Camp Casey in its first week. "We were jumping for joy," Reilly recalls. Sheehan gave hundreds of interviews, including to local radio, major global outlets, CNN's Anderson Cooper, and even Oprah Winfrey. She patiently answered the same questions with the same thoughtful replies, always returning to Casey, her demand to meet with Bush, and the need to end the war. Organizers made a point to arrange media spots with other Gold Star families and IVAW members as well.

Camp Casey also attracted the war's supporters. Rancher Larry Mattlage shot his rifle near the site. Prowar Americans held their own vigils across from the protest. The morning of August 16, a Waco man ran over dozens of the memorial crosses and was arrested. Protesters were also arrested, mostly for alleged violations of zoning rules. Trips to the local courthouse were part of the protest routine. The roadside camp was bursting at the seams, while taking on the divided passions over the war.

A national story, Camp Casey caused ripples of protest. On August 17, tens of thousands attended more than fourteen hundred solidarity vigils nationwide, organized by MoveOn.[80] Five hundred people gathered at the White House, with some wearing nametags like "mother" and "aunt" to mark their relationship to the war dead. Early on, congressional Democrats urged Bush to meet with Sheehan. Representatives Waters, Barbara Lee, Texas's Sheila Jackson Lee, and Dennis Kucinich visited the camp. Forced to respond, Bush affirmed Sheehan's right to protest, stated that he would not meet with her, and spoke of his wish to "keep a balanced life," including with outdoor exercise.[81]

On August 15, Fred Mattage—himself a veteran and a relative of Larry—offered two acres of his nearby land for use by the protesters. They quickly set up a much larger site, Camp Casey II, while maintaining a small presence at the original location. The new camp had a circus tent, generators, a stage, sound system, infirmary, portable bathrooms, and a kitchen. Food Not Bombs collectives from as far as Tucson, Arizona helped feed people at both sites.[82] Local businesses contributed food and other supplies, while peace groups and individuals made donations. Powered by volunteer labor, the camp became a community all its own.

With growth came challenges. Meeting each morning, designated conveners managed camp life. The ex-diplomat and retired Colonel Ann Wright oversaw logistics. After resigning from the State Department in 2003, she connected with VFP, attending its conventions, the March 2005 Fayetteville protest, and the Downing Street hearings in Congress. She had come on the VFP bus to Crawford, pitching her tent on the second night. Wright brought great discipline to the work, while adjusting to a protest culture not used to taking firm orders. The conveners also worked out a daily schedule. "We have to keep things moving," was their attitude, with plenty to stir the "emotions" and "spirit" of the daily visitors.[83]

Activities included interfaith services, rallies, a daily sunset vigil at the memorial crosses, and an evening program featuring speeches, music, and testimonials from veterans and military families. (At the vigils, ex-marine Jeff Key, who had been wounded in Iraq, played taps; a gay man, he came out against the war and about his sexuality on CNN in 2004.)[84] The IVAW "speak outs," Leitz felt, were "some of the more poignant moments" of camp life.[85] The young soldiers shared painful memories, while experiencing the healing power of solidarity. They would often "stand together holding hands" in a "pile-on of love." Campfire sing-alongs and the sharing of poetry also helped the veterans persevere.

Also a convener, Fithian facilitated the endless deliberations over program, messaging, media, and the display of signs. Occasional conflicts led to "hurt feelings," handled by her and others with great sensitivity. The camp's core, Wright noted, was bereaved parents, worried military families, and recent soldiers, all dealing with trauma. Serving in many conflict zones, she called her time at the camp "some of the most intense days [of] my life."

Code Pink's Jodie Evans became a fixture as well, nursing Sheehan through the media attention and other stresses. Evans also helped bring VIPs like Jesse Jackson, Al Sharpton, Margot Kidder, Viggo Mortensen, Martin Sheen, and Joan Baez. Native American activists Russell Means and Dennis Banks, as well as Iraqi Texans, came too. Baez stayed for days, inspiring the camp with her music and stories.

As many as twelve thousand people passed through Camp Casey. Millions more identified with its message. For years, the antiwar movement has spoken truth to power, often in mass demonstra-

Susan House, Melanie House, and baby James House stand with Cindy Sheehan, ex–marine reservist Jeff Key, and singer Joan Baez during a prayer vigil on August 24, 2005, at the Arlington West–style field of crosses at Camp Casey. Navy Hospital Corpsman John House (son of Susan, husband of Melanie, and father of James) was killed in Iraq, along with thirty marines, on January 26, 2005. Photograph by Joe Raedle, Getty Images.

tions targeting the centers or symbols of institutional power. Camp Casey had a personal resonance those protests mostly lacked. Its central image was a lone mother seeking to meet with the man ultimately responsible for her son's death. Sheehan became a stand-in for all parents grieving their fallen soldiers, or any young victim of war. For her to ask why Casey died was to question why the war was fought at all. "That story," remarked Fithian, "got into people's hearts." Bush's indifference added to its pathos. So did its namesake. Casey, through the relentless tributes of his mother and the protest he inspired, became a living presence, summoned to protect life. "The child," observed a minister, "is leading the mother, and the mother is leading the nation."

The intense focus on Sheehan had its downsides. Discrediting her, as right-wing figures tried to do, was a way to dismiss the entire protest. Personal setbacks, like public word of her divorce, became fodder for critics. The "Cindy Doesn't Speak for Me" tour brought counterprotesters from the military community, merging support for the war with the rejection of the strong-willed Sheehan.

The focus on her also drew attention away from many worthy others. Inside the movement, Sheehan's prominence and even celebrity caused resentment. Some GSFP and MFSO members, she claims, tried to wrest control of the camp away from her and even change its name. Others disagreed with her political positions beyond the Iraq War and felt uncomfortable with her leadership. Gold Star Families Speak Out, an alternative to GSFP, grew out of this dissatisfaction. "That's the danger when we create charismatic leaders," observed Fithian. When "the media starts flowing, it all comes apart."[86]

Despite the stresses, Camp Casey's achievements were remarkable. For the first time, opposition to the war commanded headlines for days on end. Those directly impacted, whether veterans or military families, drove this change, educating the country about the reality of the conflict. Bush looked weak, or even cowardly, compared with the mother he took pains to avoid. "People in this country are fed up," Sheehan insisted, "and want the war to stop." Public polling bore her out. As Camp Casey formed, just 44 percent of Americans supported the war, with 57 percent saying it made the country "less safe." Another poll showed just 38percent approving of Bush's handling of the conflict.[87] Weeks into the camp, 53 percent judged the entire war "a mistake" (only 43 percent thought it was "the right decision.")[88] Those numbers would never reverse.

Sheehan had vowed to stay in Crawford until Bush returned to Washington. Both his vacation, and Camp Casey, came to an abrupt end. On August 28, Hurricane Katrina hit the Gulf Coast, ravaging parts of several states. The flood-control system protecting New Orleans failed catastrophically, flooding much of the city. Its poor, mostly Black Lower Ninth Ward, suffered the worst. Many residents pleaded for help from their rooftops or drowned in their homes.

The nation watched with horror the flood damage, human toll, and disastrous response of federal, state, and local government. Deployed in Iraq, the Louisiana and Alabama National Guards were not available for relief efforts. Bush went back to Washington only on August 31, after twenty-nine days at his ranch. A photograph showed him peering out the window of Air Force One as it passed over the Gulf Coast. An instant scandal, it pictured a president detached from human suffering and the avoidable chaos on his watch.

With a contingent from the Gulf States, Camp Casey also closely followed the storm. When it hit, much of the camp quickly demobilized to begin the next phase of protest, now combined with disaster relief. Three buses took separate routes to hold events as part of the Bring Them Home Now Tour. Sheehan left on the VFP Impeachment Tour bus, attending a mass rally in Austin. The bus then headed for New Orleans, bringing water, food, tents, a generator, and other supplies from Camp Casey.[89]

Veterans for Peace set up a base in nearby Convington, Louisiana, also badly flooded. Working with local partners and even the Red Cross, it ran a satellite communication system, provided direct assistance to the community, and raised money for relief. When Michael Moore put an appeal on his website, it was overwhelmed with donations of money and goods. Ward Reilly's home outside of Baton Rouge served as a second base of operations, and a landing spot for relief supplies. The VFP distribution effort received packages from every state in the nation, including Alaska and Hawai'i.[90] Once again, antiwar veterans "walked the walk," showing the good that investments in human needs—not war—could do. Local antiwar organizers, among them former Black Panther Malik Rahim, founded Common Ground. It provided extensive community care, including food distribution, reconstruction help, and medical and legal services. Operating for weeks, Covington's "Camp Casey III" responded to institutional failure, at home and abroad.

The bus routes went into the Midwest, the Northeast, and the South to hold antiwar events. "Hundreds of people in small places turned out," recalls Fithian. "Everybody had a cathartic experience" listening to IVAW members and military families. The southern trip was especially intense. Part of it was a days-long journey, much of it on foot, from Mobile, Alabama, to New Orleans. The insistent message, reports VFP's Ellen Barfield, was that "local needs are being massively neglected" due to the "diversion" of resources to the Iraq War.[91] Conservative parts of the country, feeling the war's consequences at home, were newly open to antiwar protest. Camp Casey had become a mini-movement all its own. "Every ounce of your soul," reports Ann Wright, "was involved to keep [it] going."[92]

The buses were set to reunite in Washington, DC, for a mass protest in late September. Sheehan and others would set up another Camp Casey, again bringing the war to Bush's doorstep.

CHAPTER 12

"FERVENT CALLS FOR PEACE"

The Turning of the Iraq War

"The beginning of the end of the occupation of Iraq," Cindy Sheehan wrote on her first night at Camp Casey, "was on August 6, 2005, in, of all places, Crawford, Texas."[1] Her statement was wishful thinking. The worst of the war was yet to come. In November, US forces in Haditha killed twenty-four noncombatants, including women and children. In March 2006, fourteen-year-old Abeer Qassim al-Jabani was raped and killed by US soldiers, who also killed her parents. In October 2007, Blackwater contractors shot dead seventeen civilians in Baghdad's Nisour Square. All these killings were prosecuted as murder.

In 2006, more than 140,000 US troops remained in Iraq. American losses that year were barely lower than in 2005. In 2007, they hit a peak of 908.[2] Civilian casualties ramped up in late 2005, reaching 16,000 for the year. 2006 was the deadliest year for Iraqis. By July, up to several thousand were dying each month, mostly in a raging civil war. Civilian losses hit nearly 30,000, dropping only slightly in 2007.[3] The major drawdown of US forces began in 2009, and took until the end of 2011 to complete. By that point, US casualties topped 4,500—more than double than when Sheehan first made her stand. "Not one more mother's child" had been her motto.

Yet Sheehan's words were also prophecy. Without activists quite knowing it, the movement's most important work, by the fall and winter of 2005–6, was mostly done. It had built durable national organizations that turned out hundreds of thousands in mass demonstrations. With global antiwar forces, it had isolated Bush and his allies on the world stage. Local groups held near-constant protests. Independent media, humanitarian workers, and returning soldiers described the realities of the war. The antiwar ranks included pacifists, leftists, progressives, families of the 9/11 dead, the kin of active-duty soldiers, veterans, faith communities, and everyday Americans of all stripes. They were now the majority.

In September 2006, the liberal journalists David Corn and Michael Isikoff published *Hubris: The Inside Story of Spin, Scandal, and the Selling of the Iraq War*. Long alleged by antiwar forces, the war's deceitful origins were now laid bare in a bestseller. A month earlier, Thomas Ricks, a military reporter for *The Washington Post*, published *Fiasco: The American Military Adventure in Iraq*. It was instantly touted as the definitive account of a war gone badly wrong. The conflict, concluded a *New York Times* reviewer, was a "misguided exercise in hubris, incompetence, and folly."[4] Even Senator John McCain, firmly prowar, called the book an "accurate" depiction of "serious mistakes." The pressing debate was over *how*, and not if, the war should end, on terms far short of a US victory.

The movement's challenge was to convert antiwar opinion into policy change. Here lay its toughest task. The movement mostly practiced moral suasion, rooted in charges of the war's false cause, disastrous course, and terrible cost. The major new ingredient was growing congressional opposition, encouraged by movement pressure. Antiwar bills gained traction. Though they stood no chance of passing in a Republican Congress, they gave activists a strategic focus and establishment allies. They also signaled that Congress, if the political winds further changed, *could* set limits on the conflict.

The most significant congressional action was the formation in March 2006 of the Iraq Study Group (ISG), made up of senior Republican and Democratic ex-officials. It promised a frank assessment of the war and recommendations for a new direction. Its report concluded what had long been obvious: that "the situation in Iraq was grave and deteriorating," with current US policy "doomed to fail."[5] The ISG called for the phased withdrawal of US forces.

Yet opponents of the war had no means to *force* its end. Antiwar protest was not a catalyst for the kind of social upheavals that had, during the Vietnam War, threatened the stability of American society and worried leaders about its fate. Neither was resistance in the military enough to significantly weaken the fight. The ISG's recommendations could be ignored, as could resolutions calling for troop withdrawals. Even a strongly antiwar Congress would likely struggle to end the war. Until legislators withdrew its funding, the Bush administration could continue waging it.

Doing so, all signs suggested, would only delay the inevitable: the withdrawal of the US military and the defeat of America's political designs for Iraq. The war itself, more than any political pressure, was its undoing. The movement was there to welcome—and hasten—its end.

"WHAT WILL HISTORY SAY?"

"Donald Rumsfeld encouraged the Pentagon press corps," wrote UFPJ's Rusti Eisenberg in September 2005, to ask, "What history will say?" about the Iraq War, instead of reporting its day-to-day setbacks.[6] A professional historian, she answered: "History will say that a reckless President and a coterie of cynical advisers tricked a frightened nation into an unnecessary war." They "multiplied the 3,000 deaths" on 9/11 "into tens of thousands of Iraqi deaths" and sent soldiers to die "in a place they had no right to be." When it mattered most, "the cowardly Democrats" backed the conflict. But Eisenberg saw a way out. "History might say that in 2005" the American people "found their voice," replacing "the President's message of war with fervent calls for peace."

Those calls reached a new peak, making fall 2005 the very turning Eisenberg sought. The movement held the most ambitious protests in its entire history in Washington, DC, from September 24 to 26.[7] Actions included a rally and march, a peace encampment, civil disobedience, and lobbying.

UFPJ and ANSWER cosponsored the main rally. Once again, they struggled to collaborate. Maximum turnout, UFPJ concluded, was worth the ideological quarrels and organizing headaches. Dividing the rally program, the two groups hashed out what slogans would be on stage, what the lead banner would say ("Stop the War on Iraq! Bring the Troops Home Now!—Justice for Hurricane Survivors"), who would hold it, and how disputes would be settled.[8] "NO attacks on each other" until after the protest, their agreement also held.

Representatives John Lewis, Nancy Pelosi, John Conyers, Charles Rangel, and Maxine Waters, and Senator Richard Durbin addressed the crowd, estimated at three hundred thousand. Julian Bond, Jesse Jackson, Joseph Lowery, Harry Belafonte, and Al Sharpton took the stage as well.[9] Union heads, including the AFL-CIO's John Sweeny, also spoke. Willie Nelson and Roberta Flack performed.

Hurricane Katrina was a major theme. The organizers had wondered whether it even made sense to go through with the protest, given the hardship on the Gulf Coast.[10] Forging ahead, demonstrators argued that resources desperately needed at home were being squandered on a pointless war. The hurricane's main victims were poor people of color—populations badly hurt by the war. "Bush doesn't care about Americans," Sheehan concluded, "whether they are in Iraq or America."[11]

Katrina exposed the Bush administration's twin failures on the foreign and domestic fronts. Bush long insisted that relief efforts were going great. But Americans affected by the storm, or watching their televisions, could see otherwise. This split-screen image mirrored Bush's delusions about Iraq. If he was willfully blind to conditions on the Gulf Coast, even his supporters might ask, was same true for the war? His response to Katrina was the irreversible decline of his presidency.[12] It helped to achieve what the movement's politics of truth, alone, could not.

The antiwar march ended with a sea of people and signs descending on the White House. Holding the lead banner was a who's who of the movement: Sheehan, Barbara Lee, Jesse Jackson, and leaders in MFSO, IVAW, and Code Pink. A feeder march of the Mobilization for Global Justice, protesting the World Bank/IMF meetings also taking place, joined the procession. The antiwar movement had come full circle since the first national demonstration in September 2001.

The Peace and Justice Festival, held at the foot of the Washington Monument, had organizational tents and elaborate displays. Military Peace Movement groups set up Camp Casey IV, with a field of crosses. Code Pink erected a giant Plexiglas box, in which demonstrators placed shoes in a "monument to lives lost in occupation."[13] Clergy and Laity Concerned About Iraq held an Interfaith Tent Revival. Hearkening back to a Vietnam War–era group, it had formed in March, with the youthful Reverend Osagyefo Uhuru Sekou as it its National Coordinator. Titled "Remember and Resist," the event closed with a sermon by the scholar-preacher Cornel West.

Clergy and Laity Concerned also conducted training for a mass arrest on September 26. Waves of protesters, led by GSFP, approached the White House gate with the names of US and Iraqi dead and the request that US forces withdraw.[14] When rebuffed, they held their ground. Cindy Sheehan, flanked by sister Dede, was the first to be arrested, dominating press reports.[15] More than 370 arrests followed. The solemn action was in the great tradition of "moral witness," made more powerful by its sheer size. It was also a poignant coda to the civil disobedience of Peaceful Tomorrows members just before the 2003 invasion. Their hope too had been that no other family lose a loved one to war.

While some activists were getting arrested, hundreds more visited 263 House and Senate offices, both Democrat and Republican. It was the biggest, in-person lobbying since the war's start. Sue Udry, the head of UFPJ's legislative working group, praised participants for "making history." Two members of Congress, as a result of the visits, joined the Out of Iraq Caucus. Others signed on to antiwar bills.

UFPJ's legislative working group formed in May 2005. A measure of its importance, Udry was hired as paid staff, with Eisenberg also playing a leading role. The Friends Council on National Legislation, Progressive Democrats of America, Institute for Policy Studies, Peace Action, and Brooklyn Parents for Peace—all with congressional experience—aided its work. Its main tasks were to assess antiwar bills, work with their sponsors, educate UFPJ members about their contents, and coordinate lobbying. The great pleasure of her job, Udry reports, was working with spirited peace communities all over the country pressing their representatives for support.[16]

Prior to summer 2005, lobbying had been sporadic, concentrated mostly around a small handful of bills. MoveOn and Win Without War did much of the work, largely through call-in and email campaigns. The uneven effort reflected meek congressional opposition to the War on Terror and skepticism within the movement toward Congress. Despite its constitutional authority to declare war, Congress had for decades exercised little control over military action led by the executive branch. The near-unanimous AUMF gave Bush sweeping powers to attack alleged terrorists and their allies. The Iraq War authorization passed by a strong margin. Unsurprisingly, the 107th Congress, seated from 2001 to 2003, proposed almost no antiwar legislation.[17]

Sentiment changed somewhat in the next Congress, as the Iraq War bogged down and public support dipped. The main bills sought to establish a Department of Peace, compel information about detention operations, and forbid the funding of permanent US military bases in Iraq.[18] Their backers were generally the most liberal members of Congress, with women and African American legislators strongly represented. Most antiwar legislation failed even to have a committee hearing, let alone a floor vote.

The one arena for successful legislation concerned US captives. Sparked by abuses at Abu Ghraib and in Guantánamo, Congress worked toward passage of the Detainee Treatment Act. Senator McCain, himself a survivor of torture in a North Vietnamese prison, led the effort. The bill codified US commitments to the humane handling of captives, consistent with military protocols. Yet it left in place loopholes permitting de facto torture. It barred Guantánamo prisoners from challenging their detentions in federal court. And it immunized US personnel from prosecution for using interrogation techniques that "were officially authorized and determined to be lawful at the time they were conducted."[19]

By summer 2005, Congress had an antiwar bloc, organized in the Out of Iraq Caucus. Gaining more than 120 supporters, an amendment by cofounder Lynn Woolsey (D-CA) called on the president to develop a plan for the withdrawal of US forces. Other bills sought to investigate misrepresentations of the Iraqi threat or even censure senior Bush administration officials for their apparent deceit. In late June, Senate Democrats held high-profile hearings on the vast overcharging by private military contractors like Halliburton for work in Iraq.[20]

Camp Casey sparked congressional interest, with some legislators supporting the protest. Gold Star Families for Peace launched a "Meet with the Moms" tour of congressional offices. Those refusing to receive them, like former Senate Majority Leader Tom DeLay (R-TX), made the "Hall of Shame." Those embracing the peace families, like California senator Barbara Boxer, earned great esteem. ("Our beloved Mrs. Boxer could be declared Queen of California," Sheehan gushed.)[21] Legislators trying to rationalize their 2002 pro-war vote, like Senator Diane Feinstein (D-CA), were met with caution.

By the September lobby day, antiwar groups rallied around another House bill, introduced by Hawai'i Democrat Neil Abercrombie and North Carolina Republican Walter Jones. It called on Bush to announce by the end of 2005 a plan for the withdrawal of US forces from Iraq, to begin in fall 2006. Jones had been strongly pro-war, leading the effort to serve "Freedom Fries" on Capitol Hill. Seeing the war's toll on military families, he turned sharply against it. (Johnson personally wrote notes of condolence and apology to more than twelve thousand family members of Americans killed in post-9/11 armed conflicts.)[22] With the libertarian Ron Paul (R-TX), he was one of a small handful of Republicans working with ultra-liberals like Dennis Kucinich on antiwar bills.

Activists went into their legislative visits with fact sheets detailing the war's casualties and financial costs and FAQ-style talking points.[23] These mostly addressed fears that an immediate US withdrawal would invite more violence in Iraq. Activists answered that the occupation, rejected by most Iraqis, was itself a source of violence. The very debate over when to end the war signaled the progress the movement had made.

Weeks later, the antiwar cause gained its most important congressional ally, Pennsylvania Democrat John Murtha. Murtha was a decorated Vietnam War veteran and famous war hawk. On November 17, he stunned Washington by announcing his support for the immediate "redeployment" of US forces from Iraq. Murtha blasted the war as "a flawed policy wrapped in illusion."[24] "The American public" was "way ahead" of Congress in wanting the troops home now. His visits to military hospitals, where he saw badly wounded soldiers, and the "overwhelming calls" to his office demanding withdrawal helped sway him. Even military commanders in Iraq, he reported, wanted out of Iraq. So did US troops. In late February, a poll of nearly a thousand soldiers in Iraq showed that 72 percent wanted US forces to withdraw within a year, with a third of those favoring an immediate pullout.[25]

Congressional efforts were boosted with the formation of the Iraq Coordinating Committee, which brought together congressional offices, NGOs, and movement groups. Its purpose was to build "maximum public and congressional pressure" to "bring our troops home and rebuild Iraq."[26] Members included some of Congress's biggest antiwar voices. The Senate side had John Kerry, growing more antiwar as he heard from Iraq War veterans. Among prominent NGOs were FCNL, Peace Action, Win Without War and, as its sole right-wing member, the libertarian Cato Institute. At the grassroots were UFPJ, MFSO, IVAW, and Code Pink. At a December retreat, the group celebrated the shift in Congress against the war. It also shared frustrations with the confusing mix of antiwar bills and lack of a thorough legislative strategy. It pledged, as its main task, to turn the 2006 elections into "a referendum on Iraq."

"THE GUN IS STILL IN CHARGE"

"It's not often that you can pinpoint exactly when a massive undertaking fails," wrote retired US Army General Daniel Bolger in his history of the war. "For the U.S. in Iraq, though, the moment was obvious."[27] It was the February 22, 2006, bombing by al-Qaeda of the al-Askiri mosque, a millennium-old shrine in Samarra revered throughout the Shia world. Shia Iraqis struck back, attacking Sunni mosques and killing hundreds, including imams. Sunni reprisals followed. Observing the mayhem, Bolger echoed in military terms Sheehan's declaration of the beginning of the end of the Iraq War.

Losing the political battle at home, the Bush administration was rapidly losing all control over the war itself. Long before the al-Askiri bombing, Sunni extremists bombed other mosques, Shia crowds, and Shia sectors of the government. The Iraqi special forces, Shia-dominated national police, and private Shia militias all persecuted Sunnis. After al-Askiri, this violence escalated dramatically. By summer, dozens or even hundreds of Iraqis were dying each day, often discovered by US patrols. Thousands of kidnappings yielded millions in ransom. In the war's first year, most civilian deaths were at the hands of US and allied forces. By its fifth year, insurgent and sectarian forces claimed the greatest number.[28] Iraq had become ungovernable, to occupation and Iraqi forces alike.

Sectarian hostility was neither the unleashing of age-old rivalries kept in check under Saddam nor the pure invention or consequence of the occupation. Rather, the violence was a struggle over institutional power, social standing, wealth, resources, local control, and theological influence.[29] For many Iraqis, it was also an existential contest between vulnerable identities enduring a security crisis. Each had historic grievances against the other, memories or fears of oppression, and an image of Iraq as a Shia or Sunni nation. Dueling slogans, sermons, poetry, and militia anthems demonized the adversary as enemies of the true Iraq—whether "Wahhabis," imposing an extremist Sunni Islam, or apostate bullies and collaborators with the Americans.

The challenges for the Americans were immense. The main adversary remained the Sunni insurgency. Cleared from Fallujah, it regrouped in cities like Ramadi and Samarra. Country-wide, the lack of basic security, curfews, and travel restrictions deepened resentment of the occupation.

The United States had enabled a Shia government now using lawless violence against fellow Iraqis. The US abuse of prisoners was largely replaced by Iraqi abuse. Government buildings became torture chambers. To stabilize the country, the Americans needed to rein in their main partner in Iraq. Back home, the drip of US casualty reports was overwhelmed by the flood of stories of Iraqi deaths. When these peaked in July, American support for the war hit a new low.

Iraq's implosion brought no solace to the movement, even as it encouraged a US withdrawal. Mostly, it added to the outrage that the war continued. Not in Our Name (NION) re-formed in September 2005 as The World Can't Wait (WCW). Organizers felt that NION had run its course, demanding a revamped message. The new group held that it was too long until the 2008 election to oust Bush and end the war. The president and his senior advisers had to be impeached, charged with war crimes, or otherwise held to account. WCW addressed a hard-hitting statement to the American people. "Your government," it ran, "is waging a murderous and utterly illegitimate war in Iraq," "openly torturing people" and "enforc[ing] a culture of greed, bigotry, intolerance and ignorance."[30] Major figures in academia, activism, and the arts endorsed the statement. "Arrest Bush" actions met the president any time he left Washington.

The strife in Iraq was most apparent to peace activists inside the country. It claimed Occupation Watch, sponsored by Global Exchange. Sunni and Shia staff members suspected one another of pushing sectarian agendas. Accusations that colleagues were spies for the CIA or various Iraqi factions riled the organization. When the divisions became untenable, it collapsed.[31]

No Western group felt the strain more than the Christian Peacemaker Teams. On November 26, 2005, Sunni militants kidnapped four of its members. Their main prize was America's Tom Fox, a CPT mainstay in Iraq.[32] The others, arriving just days earlier, were Canadians Jim Loney and Harmeet Soodon, and the seventy-four-year-old UK citizen Norman Kember. Kember had marched in London in 2003 to prevent an invasion. Demanding more of himself, he went to Iraq to see what the war had wrought.

The kidnapping was rich in irony and moral confusion, reflecting the morass that Iraq had become. The CPT had mostly assisted Iraqi families in locating relatives in the US detention system and publicized their mistreatment. Increasingly, they documented abuses in Iraqi facilities. Now, CPT members were prisoners of a group demanding what they also wanted: that the US military leave Iraq.

The CPT held true to their Christian principles, which required love of one's enemies. They resisted media efforts to demonize their captors, earning the scorn of right-wing pundits. They refused to pay ransom, which might fund more violence. And they instructed Western governments *not* to engage in military rescues, which might kill the hostages, their captors, and innocent Iraqis. Still, their governments plotted rescue operations.

The CPT flooded Arabic media with information about their humanitarian work, profiles of the hostages, and pleas for their freedom. Muslim groups, in Iraq and beyond, called for their release, stressing the CPTs' solidarity with the Iraqi and Palestinian people. CPT members and their supporters held vigils worldwide, including in Baghdad.

Early on, the captors announced that the hostages would be killed unless the United States and the United Kingdom released all Iraqis in their custody and withdrew their militaries from the country. Videos showed the captives, in Guantánamo-style jumpsuits, supporting these demands. When the deadline passed, grueling boredom and deeper fear set in. For months, the hostages were handcuffed together, even when they slept.

For the captors, anger at the occupation made distinctions of friend and foe irrelevant. (In 2004 an Irish citizen, Margaret Hassan, who for years had helped poor Iraqis with CARE International, was kidnapped and killed.) One young captor explained that his parents, sister, and best friend had been killed by US bombs in Fallujah. He and the others saw themselves, in Loney's description, as "warriors of God enacting a sacred duty to protect their homes and their families from an invading army."[33]

Through the crisis, the CPT continued their work, aided by new volunteers. In response to sectarian violence, they helped bring together Sunni and Shia groups for dialogue and public shows of unity. They also assisted Iraq's Palestinians, displaced by the 1948 and 1967 wars. Confined to ghetto-like "camps" in major cities, they now suffered purges. The CPT helped some win safety in Syria and Jordan.

On March 9, 2006, the body of Tom Fox, shot multiple times in the back, was found by US soldiers on a Baghdad road. Days later, US, UK, and Canadian special forces freed the others. No one was harmed. Intelligence services had worked diligently to locate the hostages, using nighttime raids and interrogations to gather information.

Controversy stirred when media falsely accused the CPT captives of being ungrateful for their liberation. Months later, when the alleged kidnappers were apprehended, the former hostages refused to identify them to prosecutors. The penalty for kidnapping was death. The last thing Iraq needed, they felt, was more death. "We unconditionally forgive our captors," Loney announced. "Some men with guns" freed us, he reflected. "Some men with bigger guns came and took them. But the gun is still in charge."[34]

WITNESS AGAINST TORTURE

While the kidnapping saga was playing itself out in Iraq, another group of religious activists journeyed to a key site of the War on Terror: Guantánamo Bay, Cuba. "As I soaked in the beauty of the Caribbean," Matt Daloisio recalled of the flight south, "I found myself imagining what it must have been like to fly these same skies . . . feet and hands bound, tied to the floor of a windowless cargo plane, destined to be held in an unknown place for an unknown period of time."[35] Daloisio, age twenty-nine, and twenty-four others calling themselves Witness Against Torture (WAT) arrived in Santiago, Cuba, in early December 2005. Their goal was to trek seventy miles to the US naval base housing the notorious prison and visit its five hundred or so detainees. There, they would fast, pray, and protest, hopeful that US authorities and the media might take notice.

The trip to Guantánamo reflected the dynamism of the antiwar movement. The Iraq War was its focus, but tributaries formed to address other outrages, like torture. Torture was the dark heart of the sprawling US system of detentions and interrogations. At first, challenging that system was mostly the work of legal collectives like the Center for Constitutional Rights (CCR) and human rights organizations like Amnesty International. With Witness Against Torture, this effort spread to the grassroots.

Though still murky, a clearer picture of the abuse at Guantánamo

Members of Witness Against Torture on their December 2005 march from Santiago to Guantánamo, Cuba, to visit the US detention center. Bill Streit, imprisoned for a 2004 protest at the Pentagon, is holding the right edge of the banner. Frida Berrigan, wearing a bandanna, is the central figure behind the banner. Art Laffin and Matt Daloisio (bearded, with baseball cap) are above her left shoulder. Photograph by Scott Langley.

had emerged. It included severe beatings, sexual assaults, sensory deprivation, the desecration of Qur'ans, and threats of rape, the murder of detainees' family members, and transfer to Jordan or Egypt for still worse mistreatment. Throughout, Bush insisted that "we do not torture."[36] As with Abu Ghraib, many Americans were horrified.

The first inkling of the trip came when, in May 2005, a small group gathered in the New York City apartment of their recently deceased friend Elmer Maas—a legend within the Catholic left. The group asked what they could do about Guantánamo, especially if they removed the fear of legal consequences from consideration. In monthly meetings, the idea of going to Cuba—in violation of a US travel ban, punishable by fines and imprisonment—was born. Bush's own words were incentive. "If you've got questions about Guantánamo," he said on June 20, "I seriously suggest you go down there and take a look."[37] WAT accepted the invitation.

WAT members were drawn from Catholic Worker communities in New York City, Ithaca, Baltimore, Hartford, New Haven, and Raleigh. Among them were Daloisio and Frida Berrigan, rising figures in the War Resisters League; Ann Montgomery and Art Laffin, long involved in protesting US policy toward Iraq; and Steve Kelly, a Catholic priest and frequent civil disobedient. About a third of the group had been arrested at the WRL protest at the RNC in 2004.

The group came with the explicit goal of performing works of mercy. "Jesus commands that we visit the prisoner and comfort the afflicted," Frida Berrigan elaborated.[38] Engaging in a march—indeed "a pilgrimage" to Guantánamo —was important to the marchers as a ritual of repentance. The atonement was for the sins of the US government and their own complicity as citizens.[39] Jackie Allen, from a family of military veterans, explained that "torture is a terrorist act. To engage in it to fight terrorism means that we have allowed terrorism to penetrate our hearts."[40] "In response," Susan Crane said, "we try to do what is good and faithful" and "walk as our conscience leads us."

Reports in early July of a new mass hunger strike at Guantánamo added urgency to the trip. Virtually from the start, some detainees had refused food to protest conditions at the prison and their very detention. In December, prison staff began using brutal forced feedings to break the protest. This physical suffering bolstered WAT's resolve to make a statement with the presence of their own fasting bodies.

The activists also arrived with something rare in their experience: genuine hope that their actions might make a difference. Fighting vast systems of power, they often put the integrity of their convictions over practical goals. But closing Guantánamo felt like the "low-hanging fruit" of antiwar protest, far easier than ending the war in Iraq. Torture and indefinite detention, Daloisio believed, were far "outside the bounds of even mainstream American thought," sure to stir a broad outcry if properly exposed.[41]

The trip was a rollercoaster of frustration and grace. At first, the Cuban government put a stop to WAT's plans. Their protest, WAT speculated, might further imperil Cuba's fragile relationship with the United States. WAT members soon convinced Cuban officials of the importance of their actions, no matter the risk. Allowed to march over five days to Guantánamo, they set up camp at a Cuban military checkpoint near the American base. Now US officials insisted that they go no further. For the next four days, the group held prayerful vigil, each day calling the US base to ask to visit the prison.

Coverage of the trip by Western outlets was meager, and US personnel refused WAT's request. The group's main triumph was its presence. So much of the War on Terror was meant to be invisible, beyond literal witness, moral scrutiny, and the law. To go to Guantánamo, in religious sympathy with doomed men, was to defy that logic. Daniel Berrigan memorialized the journey. "An unmerry Christmas," he wrote, "at the barbed, hydra headed, land-mined verge of the world: Guantánamo. The twenty-five stood there, knelt there, prayed there, a muted alleluia. Gave thanks to be there—even for that."[42]

The coup de grâce came weeks later with a message conveyed to WAT by attorney Tom Wilner. Wilner had been in Guantánamo in January seeing his client Fayez al-Kandari. Kandari was aware of WAT's vigil and wished to extend thanks to the visitors. They proved, he said, "that there were good people in America who believed in justice."[43]

Witness Against Torture returned to the United States ready to build a campaign focused on Guantánamo.[44] Its work was aided by the publication in February 2006 of blockbuster research. A team at Seton Hall University's law school headed by Mark Denbeaux compiled startling data from Department of Defense sources. It showed that 55 percent of the Guantánamo prisoners were not even accused of hostile acts toward the United States or its allies. Just 8 percent were thought to be connected to al-Qaeda. The majority of detainees had not been captured by US forces. Instead, they were turned over by Afghanistan's Northern Alliance or by Pakistan, often in return for massive bounties.[45] The Seton Hall figures became catechism for activists, used to blast the false claim that Guantánamo housed only "the worst of the worst."[46]

Once again, information was vital to antiwar work. Though not classic social-movement actors, human rights attorneys and researchers were on the front lines of struggles against the War on Terror's most serious abuses. Their work also enabled activists to wage the public fight for human rights and the rule of law. Going forward, WAT closely worked with CCR and other Guantánamo attorneys.[47] The lawyers were the main conduits of information about the detainees, whose images, stories, statements, and poems WAT shared. The lawyers also informed their clients of protests on their behalf, which meant the world to them. The detainees, in turn, conveyed their thanks through lawyers. Through this feedback loop, the separation of Guantánamo from the world was partly overcome.

When back at home, WAT reached out to dozens of peace, human rights, and religious groups to join its campaign. On Ash Wednesday (March 1), it held a "detainee procession" through Washington, with protesters dressed in orange jumpsuits and black hoods. Used in countless protests thereafter, this figure became a globally recognized symbol of US human rights abuses. WAT also held protests at the US Mission to the United Nations. In one of these, twenty-five people—including Daniel Berrigan, age 85—were arrested for blocking the mission's entrance.

A coalition of anti-torture advocates took root. It included WAT, CCR, September 11 Families for Peaceful Tomorrows, Amnesty International, Code Pink, the Council on Islamic-Americans Relations, World Can't Wait, and the interfaith National Religious Campaign Against Torture, founded in 2006. Abusing innocent men at Guantánamo, Peaceful Tomorrows insisted, had nothing to do with justice for their loved ones.[48] Kathy Kelly, Medea Benjamin, and Deb Sweet were stalwart participants in anti-torture actions, as were a rotating cast of Guantánamo attorneys.

The coalition held demonstrations and educational events, lobbied Congress, made art, and staged dramatic arrest actions. A similar grouping came together in the United Kingdom, led by independent journalist Andy Worthington. Anti-torture work was now a small but luminous force in the global antiwar constellation.

"MY ONE SLIVER OF HOPE"

The whole of 2006 saw sustained antiwar activity. Much of it drew from the movement's own playbook, reprising past actions with modest variation. The goals were also familiar: to educate Americans about the war, to shape the national conversation, and to press for an immediate US withdrawal.

The war's March anniversary again brought large demonstrations in US and global cities. In late April, another mass protest followed in New York City, drawing perhaps hundreds of thousands. For it, WAT organized the first-ever "anti-torture bloc." The protest's chief backers—UFPJ, the National Organization for Women, the Rainbow/PUSH Coalition, and labor and student groups—reflected the movement's growing mainstream cast. ANSWER was not part of the organizing. UFPJ complained that it had violated the agreement for the September 2005 rally when its speakers greatly exceeded their allotted time. This infraction stood atop years of bitter conflicts over ideology, messaging, strategy, and organizing styles. It proved the final straw, ending the groups' collaboration.

Even rallygoers sensed that large demonstrations had lost their political punch. The protesters, according to Tom Engelhardt, had "no illusion that the White House was paying the slightest bit of attention to them."[49] Some complained that the Democrats had done too little to stop the war. Major press coverage was minimal. Asked why he was there, one protester said, "I'm doing it out of habit. But it's a good habit."[50] The movement feared settling again into a holding pattern.

The more compelling actions were local or addressed specific issues, often with a creative spark. The military community built off its efforts just after Camp Casey by organizing "Walkin' to New Orleans: Veterans and Survivors March for Peace and Justice." The idea was hatched by David Cline and Ward Reilly in the veterans tent at the September demonstrations in Washington. Stan Goff worked tirelessly on fundraising and logistics.

Beginning on March 14 in Mobile, Alabama, between 150 and 300 veterans, military families, and area residents trekked 140 miles to

Iraq Veterans Against the War members on the Veterans and Survivors March for Peace and Justice in Gulfport, Mississippi, on March 17, 2006. Holding the banner, from left to right, are Jody B. Casey, Michael Blake, Camilo Mejia, and Joshua Dawson. Photograph by Ward Reilly.

the famous port city. "Every Bomb Dropped on Iraq," their main slogan ran, "Explodes Along the Gulf Coast." ("The bombs in Vietnam explode at home," Martin Luther King Jr. had said, destroying "possibilities for a decent America.") "Let's Stop the War and Rebuild Our Own Nation *Now*" was the more positive message.[51] Two dozen IVAW members participated in the march, leading it in desert fatigues.

Throughout the taxing trip, the marchers held events with speeches, music, poetry, and testimonials, including from hurricane evacuees and relief workers. One veteran expressed shock at the physical destruction. "Right here in Biloxi, Mississippi it's the same fucking shit that I saw in that [Iraqi] border town. Absolutely, 100 percent annihilated."[52] Local media ran front-page stories and TV spots on the march. The journey ended on March 19 with a rally and dancing in New Orleans' Congo Square, three years since the war's start. The marchers bonded deeply with one another, again showing the power of the movement to create community. The close connection between the mostly white veterans and mostly Black Gulf Coast residents was another achievement.

On the West Coast, Fernando Suárez del Solar led the Latino

Iraq Veterans Against the War member Garett Reppenhagen with damage from Hurricane Katrina in Biloxi, Mississippi, on March 16, 2006. Photograph by Ward Reilly.

Peace Pilgrimage in a trek from Tijuana, Mexico, to San Francisco, timed with the Iraq War anniversary. Modeled on Gandhi's 1930 Salt March, which challenged British colonial rule, the march highlighted both the historic service of Latinos to the US miliary and their betrayal in misbegotten wars. "I know that I have to do something, not just sit and cry," Suárez told reporters in Spanish.[53] With the marchers was Arizona's Annabelle Valencia, who had both a son and daughter in Iraq. Visiting Iraq in 2003, she had seen "the horrors of war," including "children without legs."[54]

The year 2006 witnessed the further growth of the Military Peace Movement, and of IVAW especially. Headquartered in Philadelphia, it established nearly a dozen chapters. One in Toronto served soldiers who had fled north. Membership rose from around 275 at the time of the Gulf Coast march to more than 1,000.[55]

In May 2006, IVAW held a protest in Washington, DC, called "Silence of the Dead, Voices of the Living" featuring a haunting, silent march. In August, it helped set up a new Camp Casey in a vacant lot near Bush's ranch, purchased by Sheehan. Army Specialist Mark Wilkerson, AWOL for eighteen months to avoid redeploying to Iraq, held a press event there announcing that he would turn himself in at nearby Fort Hood.[56] "I am not willing to kill or be killed," he said, "or do anything else I consider morally wrong."

That same month Ricky Clousing, also AWOL after serving in Iraq, declared at VFP's annual convention in Seattle that he too would surrender in resistance to the war. Antiwar veterans also rallied in support of Army Specialist Suzanne Swift, who refused to return to Iraq after being sexually assaulted in her unit. VFP members created "Camp Suzanne" outside Fort Lewis, where she was detained. They demanded an honorable discharge for her, no prosecution, and greater attention to sexual violence in the military.

Lieutenant Ehren Watada also spoke at the convention. He faced a potential court-martial for refusing in June to deploy to Iraq. Days later at a hearing in Fort Lewis, he called expert witnesses, including Colonel Ann Wright, to testify that the war in Iraq was illegal, justifying his conduct. For the first time, military resisters put the war on trial. Watada's wish was greater still. His "radical idea," as his speech laid out, was "that to stop an illegal and unjust war, the soldiers and service members can choose to stop fighting it." Military prosecutors cited this line in explaining why he was so dangerous.[57]

Months later, active-duty soldiers organized an "Appeal of Redress from the War in Iraq." It stated: "As a patriotic American proud to serve the nation in uniform, I respectfully urge my political leaders in Congress to support the prompt withdrawal of all American military forces" from Iraq.[58] Navy Seaman Jonathan Hutto and Marine Sargeant Liam Madden, both of whom served in Iraq, led the effort. The appeal drew on the little-used Military Whistleblower Protection Act, which permitted active-duty soldiers to lawfully communicate dissent to Congress. In late October, Madden presented the appeal to members of Congress, signed by a hundred or so soldiers.[59]

Lieutenant Watada's defense was not ultimately allowed at his court-martial. Iraq Veterans Against the War came nowhere close to hobbling the actual war by encouraging soldiers to refuse to fight. And the Appeal for Redress was just getting started. But these rising ambitions showed a new resolve from Americans who knew best what the war truly meant.

Washington State, home to many young radicals, witnessed another escalation. In May, the Port Militarization Resistance tried to stop the shipment of Army Stryker vehicles and munitions from the port of Olympia to Iraq. The physical blockade of roads leading to the port led to dozens of arrests. The May protest inspired similar actions in Tacoma and Aberdeen, Washington, and in Oakland, California. Grueling trials followed. Some defendants argued the "moral necessity" of stopping weapons for use in an illegal conflict. Among those moved by the protests was Lieutenant Watada, who cited them in his own decision to refuse the war.[60]

The resistance found new ways of expressing itself. Laurie Arbeiter was a New York City–based painter and activist, long involved in HIV/AIDS and queer politics.[61] For years, she struggled to reconcile her art and her political work, unsure whether she could do both at the same time. The two would come together in one of the iconic protest campaigns of the War on Terror.

The wars in Afghanistan and Iraq, and the Abu Ghraib photos especially, pushed Arbeiter toward politics. The photos, which for her recalled images of the Holocaust, "couldn't get more egregious." The "mandate" to do something was "for everyone."

Setting her painting aside, Arbeiter began working with Artists Against War, boasting artists of great talent and reputation. It made tens of thousands of rainbow flags, stenciled with the words "No Allegiance to Bush," for use in the 2004 RNC protests. With a smaller group, Critical Voice, Arbeiter made a new design: an American flag with an insert reading, "No Allegiance to War, Torture, and Lies." For the Iraq War's third anniversary in March 2006, Critical Voice would display the flag at Ground Zero, the United Nations, Wall Street, and the military recruiting center at Times Square. It was the group's first action, followed by the distribution of thousands of postcards with images of occupied Iraq, the coffins of US soldiers, and War on Terror detainees.

Shortly before the anniversary protest, Arbeiter saw a film about

Founding members of Critical Voice Ann Messner (left) and Caroline Parker, holding a banner at Times Square in New York City on March 20, 2006, the third anniversary of the US invasion of Iraq. Cofounders Laurie Arbeiter, Carole Ashley, and Susan Kingsland were also at the protest. The "We Will Not Be Silent" T-shirts made their debut at the demonstration. Photograph by Carole Ashley.

the White Rose resistance group, whose student leaders were executed for distributing anti-Nazi materials. One of its flyers read: "We will not be silent, we are your guilty conscience." Drawn to the defiant language, the group printed "We Will Not Be Silent" in white letters on black T-shirts, wearing them to its March 20, 2006, actions. Soon, it created an Arabic-language version, captioned in English. "If they're going to criminalize the Arab and Muslim community, then we're going to stand in solidarity" with them by wearing the shirt.

Weeks later, Arbeiter gave a shirt with the Arabic text to Raed Jarrar, a Palestinian Iraqi antiwar activist living in the United States. Wearing it on a return flight from Jordan, Jarrar was instructed by Homeland Security and JetBlue employees to cover the offending slogan. Jarrar informed Arbeiter of the incident. She and others, wearing the shirt, immediately flew on JetBlue to Washington. Doing so, they challenged authorities to repeat the censorship on white Americans, or reveal that they had racially profiled Jarrar. The story of Jarrar's treatment broke, first on *Democracy Now!* and then on CNN. We Will Not Be Silent was born.

Requests for T-shirts flooded in. Over the next year, Arbeiter and fellow artists distributed tens of thousands worldwide, including to US soldiers against the Iraq War. The shirts became a kind of community-based performance art, whose wearers were asked what was behind the slogan. Conversations about the Iraq War, torture, and protest followed.

For years, all manner of antiwar demonstrations had blocs of protesters bearing "We Will Not Be Silent" on their clothing or on signs. Arbeiter's collective came up with new slogans—"Arrest Bush" was its first—to vary the antiwar message. "I was compelled," Arbeiter reflected, to fuse politics, morality, and art in this resonant way. "I feel like I did my work in the world," captured in countless photos of the era's protest.

Helping Iraqis to speak out remained vital to the movement, as it continued to attack myths about the war. In March and April, Code Pink brought seven Iraqi women to the United States to describe life under occupation.[62] Among them were doctors, engineers, and human rights professionals. The visas of two other women, whose families were killed by US forces, were denied. Officials explained that they now had no compelling reason to return to Iraq and could not be trusted to leave the United States.

The speakers fanned out across the country, holding talks at universities, high schools, churches, and private homes. Code Pink's Rae Abileah traveled with pharmacist Entisar Mohammad Ariabi. She recounted treating the wounded in a collapsing health care system. US bombs hit hospitals, where overflow corpses were tucked into corners. Having no medicine made her feel like an angel of death. Other speakers described the damage to Iraqi culture and institutions. Everyday life, they painfully admitted, had been better under Saddam. "My one sliver of hope" for ending the war, Entisar told audiences, "lies with the American people."[63] "There are those brief moments," Abileah recalled of her time with Entisar, "when someone runs into your heart, unexpectedly ripping open chambers you did not know existed, expanding your capacity to love and empathize with people around the world."[64]

Code Pink followed the tour with another invitation to empathy. On Mother's Day, the group held a vigil outside the White House celebrating the holiday's pacifist origins. Protesters sought to create the world's longest scarf, bearing the original Mother's Day proclamation of abolitionist Julia Ward Howe: "We women of one country will be too tender of those of another country to allow our sons to be trained to injure theirs." Code Pink put out a call for knitted squares for use in the scarf. Its Washington headquarters was soon overwhelmed with deliveries of swatches. "People were so eager to do something, anything," reports Abileah, "besides calling Congress."[65]

"IRAQ, IRAQ, IRAQ"

Calling elected officials likely excited few hardcore activists. But Congress, with a change in president still years away, was a key arena for antiwar politics. The November 2006 elections were a chance for Americans to express disapproval of the conflict and push for its end. That required, above all, electing antiwar Democrats.

From before its start, war with Iraq was far more popular with Republicans than with Democrats.[66] In January 2003, more than 80 percent of Republicans, but fewer than half of Democrats, backed an invasion. As the war bogged down, the partisan divide sharpened. Republican support fell only slightly into the low 70s. Democratic support cratered, from a peak of 55 percent at Mission Accomplished in spring 2003 to less than 20 percent by the summer of 2005. Independents also turned against the war, with fewer than 40 percent supporting it from mid-2005 on.

Partisan disdain for Bush, owing massively to the Iraq War, was also intense. In May of 2006, just 4 percent of Democrats approved of Bush's overall performance. (On the eve of his resignation, President Nixon was more popular among Democrats.) Echoing their constituents, liberal Democrats led antiwar efforts in Congress.

Democratic officeholders, on the whole, remained split, but trended antiwar. New Democratic candidates for Congress opposed the conflict, even if resisting a timetable for withdrawal.

Protest was partisan as well. Researchers Michael Heaney and Fabio Rojas polled thousands of demonstrators at major national demonstrations between 2004 and 2006. Forty percent described themselves as Democrats. Thirty-nine percent had no party affiliation, 20 percent backed third parties, and fewer than 2 percent were Republicans.[67]

Individual groups mobilized partisan constituencies. The outreach conducted by ANSWER and UFPJ attracted equal percentages of Democrats to their protests, despite the groups' ideological differences. Organizations like MFSO, whose networks mostly lay outside the activist world, overwhelmingly reached Democrats. Appealing to older Americans, groups like Veterans for Peace did too. Most of the mass lobbying in March 2006 was done by Democrats, comfortable with mainstream civic action, and targeted Democratic officials. Small numbers of Republicans were open to an antiwar position. But most of the party still supported Bush and his war. In this landscape, the antiwar movement's "moral and political struggles [were] with or against the Democratic Party."[68]

Activists' ambivalence toward Democrats persisted. Some "rejected the party as a potential avenue of change" based on its complicity in the War on Terror and position within the nation's elite.[69] They might regret supporting Kerry in 2004 and see the party's recent shift on the war as "opportunistic," threatening to co-opt the movement. Others rallied around outspoken antiwar Democrats, like Maxine Waters and Dennis Kucinich. They hoped that the party's "leadership can be pressured" to back the movement's demands.

Party leaders, Democratic organizations, and individual candidates framed the November midterms as a referendum on the war.[70] Nancy Pelosi bluntly declared, "This election is about three things: Iraq, Iraq, Iraq." Antiwar forces agreed. "We want to ensure that peace is the defining issue," said the UFPJ's Hany Khalil.[71]

Powered by antiwar groups, Voters for Peace collected millions of signatures of Americans pledging to support antiwar campaigns.

Countless activists backed individual candidates with money and labor. One was Ned Lamont, who defeated prowar Senator Joseph Lieberman in Connecticut's Democratic primary. (Staunchly prowar, Lieberman ran as an independent in the general election and won.) Another was Virginia Senate candidate James Webb, an ex-Marine with a son serving in Iraq. While campaigning, Webb wore his son's combat boots as a reminder of the soldiers' sacrifice.

The elections were a rout. Democrats picked up 31 seats in the House, yielding a 232–202 majority. They won six Senate seats from Republican incumbents, giving them a majority in that body too.[72] Dissatisfaction with the Iraq War was the leading reason for the Democrats' success. Voters approached their choice through the lens of national politics. Many sought to punish Bush, his party, and his war. Among the small number of antiwar Republicans, more than half voted for Democrats. Winning candidates pledged to end the conflict and reinvest in America.

The day after the election, Defense Secretary Donald Rumsfeld announced his resignation. Activists saw him as an archvillain of the entire War on Terror. He had authored disastrous strategies and personally approved torture techniques, while arrogantly dismissing all criticism. His resignation felt like a victory.

In early December, the Iraq Study Group (ISG) issued its report, nearly a year in the making.[73] Led by former Secretary of State James Baker and senior Democratic ex-lawmaker Lee Hamilton, the group offered a nonpartisan perspective on the war. It included interviews with US military and Iraqi officials, senior Bush administration officials, and even UK Prime Minister Tony Blair. The report was sold in bookstores and downloaded nearly two million times. Well covered in the press, its release was a major political event.

The ISG painted a dismal picture of unrelenting violence, deep schisms, profound corruption, and growing despair in Iraq. The solutions to the mess, if any existed at all, were political and diplomatic, not military. The Bush administration could no longer be trusted with the war. It had to end.

The report recommended that the United States pressure the Shia-led government to pursue "national reconciliation." This meant demobilizing its militias, ending extrajudicial violence, easing restrictions on ex-Ba'athists, fairly sharing oil revenue, and modifying the constitution to enhance minority rights. Sunnis, the ISG counseled, should be encouraged to quit the insurgency and fight foreign extremists. A "diplomatic offensive" involving regional powers like Egypt and Turkey could constrain Iran and Syria from meddling in Iraq. With progress on all these fronts, the United States could begin drawing down its troops.

Intended as a new approach, the report mostly appeared a monument to past mistakes and, likely, future failure. Its plan required that actors with sharply different agendas align with what the United States wanted, based on America's judgment of what was in their best interest. Little suggested, as the ISG admitted, that Iraq's government was committed to unifying the nation. The report also asked groups benefiting from flawed US policies, like de-Ba'athification, to undo them. The entire war had shown the *limits* of America's ability to bend foreign peoples to its will. Now was no different.

The ISG also recommended that the United States restart negotiations between Israel and the Palestinians. The US goal, reflecting decades-long policy, was an independent Palestinian state in exchange for peace with Israel. This recommendation, and the report as a whole, was steeped in irony. From 9/11 on, critics of the War on Terror pleaded that the United States lead with diplomacy and the rule of law, not military might. For the sake of both security and justice, it should also address the conflicts and grievances giving rise to terrorism. The ISG was now calling for the same, after a disastrous war that enraged the Arab world and undermined America's role as a broker of any peace.

The year 2006 ended with another grisly milestone: the execution of Saddam Hussein. Long in Iraqi custody, he had been convicted by the Iraqi Special Tribunal for the 1982 massacre of nearly 150 Iraqi Shias. The sentence was death. On December 30, Saddam was hanged in the joint US-Iraqi military base Camp Justice. Before his execution, he and the Shia guards exchanged insults. Grainy footage of the hanging, which lacked both dignity and ceremony, was leaked to the media. Even President Bush remarked that the execution "looked like it was kind of a revenge killing."[74] In Iraq, the execution both ended an era and added fuel to burning civil conflicts.

"CREATION OR DESTRUCTION, LIFE OR DEATH"

The antiwar movement largely rejected the ISG's call for a phased drawdown of US forces. Activist Anthony Arnove soon published his own timely study, *Iraq: The Logic of Withdrawal*.[75] Its inspiration was Howard Zinn's 1967 book calling for the immediate, unconditional withdrawal of the US military from Vietnam. Arnove made the same case for Iraq.

While the nation mulled the ISG report, the Bush administration worked on plans of its own. On January 10, Bush declared on national television that "the situation in Iraq is unacceptable to the American people."[76] "Where mistakes have been made," he tepidly added, "the responsibility rests with me." He then announced that he would send more than twenty thousand additional troops to Iraq and extend the deployment of those already there. His administration had considered a phased withdrawal. The risk, it felt, "of the collapse of the Iraqi government" and "mass killings on an unimaginable scale" was too great. US forces, beefed up by the so-called surge, would at last stabilize Iraq. Once stability was achieved, US troops could begin to leave.

Despite Bush's bold move, his administration remained on the defensive, well beyond its Iraq policy. The day after his address was five years since the first detainee was brought to Guantánamo. In response, activists held an "International Day of Action to Shut Down Guantánamo." The burning legal issue—still tangled between the executive, Congress and the courts—was whether the prisoners could challenge their detention through habeas petitions.[77]

On January 11, hundreds of protesters, many in jumpsuits and hoods, descended on the federal district court in Washington, DC. Their aim was to deliver mock habeas filings on behalf of the detainees, most of whom had never been charged with crimes. Eighty-eight people were arrested inside the courthouse. Smaller demonstrations took place throughout the United States, in the United Kingdom, and in Australia. In Cuba, the mother and wife of detainee Omar Deghayes held a vigil at the same checkpoint where WAT had gathered a year before.

Bush's announcement of the Iraq surge reignited fury over the war. Its opponents also brimmed with a new confidence. On January 17, soldiers with the Appeal for Redress again came to Capitol Hill. This time, their statement had nearly two thousand signers and a host of congressional backers. Days later, UFPJ held another mass protest in Washington.[78] Its wish, rejected by Capitol Police, was to have the vast crowd literally encircle the Capitol building.[79] The main protest slogan ran, "The Voters Want Peace. Tell the NEW CONGRESS: ACT *NOW* TO END THE WAR!" The speakers, many members of Congress among them, called out the names of antiwar bills and urged support for them. More lobbying followed the protest.

The once radical "antiwar position," observed Heaney and Rojas, had "become mainstream as prominent members of Congress lined up to denounce the war."[80] Nancy Pelosi, the new House Speaker, proposed John Murtha for a leadership post, where he could rally colleagues for a US withdrawal.[81] Some in Congress, long opposed to the conflict, were interested in immediate results, not antiwar posturing or drawn-out legislative battles. Representative Kucinich issued a public strategy brief aimed at fellow Democrats. It insisted that the only way to end the war was for Congress to cut off its funding.

Through 2006, when the Iraq War fully imploded, appropriations bills still passed with large, bipartisan majorities. Members of Congress, even when soured on the war, were loath to do anything that might be seen as undermining troops still in the fight or abandoning Iraqi partners. This was little surprise to studied observers of war and peace. "An antiwar Congress pressured by an antiwar public," Vietnam War historian Melvin Small flatly noted, "always has the option of refusing to fund the war. But both during the Vietnam War and the Iraq War, most legislators feared being denounced as unpatriotic for withdrawing support for their brave boys and girls who would be left defenseless against a ruthless enemy."[82]

The time for fear and equivocation, Kucinich felt, had passed. His plan called for the United Nations to take over most of the United States' authority in Iraq and deploy a peacekeeping force, funded by the United States. US troops, he proposed, could be home in ninety days, should the political will exist.

Such will did not. Kucinich voiced more an aspiration than a real, legislative possibility. He also named the stakes. "Either we sink deeper into the abyss of violence," he wrote, "with rising casualties and costs. Or we can reunite with the world community in the cause of peace. . . . We must choose between human unity or hegemony, peace or war, creation or destruction, life or death."[83]

The Bush administration chose more death and destruction, until it was expelled from an abyss of its own making. Even its Iraqi allies wanted the United States gone. The US war was not yet over. But its end had begun.

CHAPTER 13

"THE END OF AN ERROR" AND ENDLESS WAR

America's exit from Iraq was long and bloody. The year 2007 was dominated by the surge of more troops, now commanded by counterinsurgency guru General David Petraeus.[1] The goal was greater security, best achieved by protecting civilians. That meant putting US forces in small outposts, increasing checkpoints, and cordoning off Sunni and Shia enclaves, often after they had been violently "cleansed" by their rivals. Revised tactics sought to consolidate battlefield gains by holding territory cleared of the enemy.

At first, US casualties increased. In May, they reached a post-2004 monthly high of 126. Soon after, they fell dramatically. In December, just thirteen US service members were killed. Violence among Iraqis declined as well.

The key to the strategy was the Sunni Awakening, in which Iraqi Sunnis agreed to fight extremist, al-Qaeda elements—not US forces or the national government. The Americans made allies of militias that had once attacked them. Massive cash payouts helped shift insurgents' loyalties.

The surge did little to encourage long-term stability in Iraq. The Shia-dominated government remained uninterested in national reconciliation and still abused Sunnis. It also worried that the US strategy left intact Sunni militias, which might again turn on the national army and police. "We've bought some time," remarked a US commander, "but for what?"[2] The Americans were now a *moderat-*

ing force, trusted more by warring Iraqis than each other. But the Americans could not stay forever.

Domestically, the surge blunted the momentum of the war's opponents, in Congress especially. In September 2007, Petraeus came to Washington for two days of testimony. MoveOn greeted him with a full-page ad in *The New York Times*. It labeled him "General Betray Us" and accused him of "cooking the books for the Whites House" by manipulating battlefield data. The ad, whose own facts many questioned, caused an uproar.

Petraeus described the progress he saw, parrying the criticisms of Congress's heavy antiwar hitters. Who were they to doubt the general, giving Americans the first good news about Iraq in years? Maybe US strategy was finally working, and the risk of withdrawal was still too great. The Democrats' dilemma, as Petraeus's team understood, was "how to end a war without being blamed for how it ended."[3]

The Democrats' difficulties ran deep. Pledging to end the conflict, congressional Democrats remained divided over how, and how hard, to push. Dozens of antiwar bills were proposed throughout the 110th Congress. The most ambitious sought to stymie the surge or set a date for a US withdrawal. Just sixteen bills were discussed in committee. Five were voted on in the House, with four passing. None passed the Senate, where a supermajority was required, to become law.[4]

The surge went only so far in pacifying Iraq or placating Americans. In April 2008, Petraeus was back before Congress facing new, tough questions. Iraq remained badly divided, with violence still routine. Even Republicans wanted to know why progress had not been greater and when the conflict could finally end. Petraeus had no good answers. As never before, the US war lay in the balance.

"TALKING AND MARCHING WASN'T GETTING THE POINT ACROSS"

All the while, protest continued. Some groups escalated their efforts, hitting new peaks of energy and resolve. "There is a steadily increasing sense" in Veterans for Peace, one member observed, that, "marching in the streets simply isn't enough."[5] In September 2007, 200 VFP members broke off from an ANSWER march to get arrested on the steps of the US Capitol. Days later, VFP and IVAW members were arrested for crashing a small, prowar rally on Capitol Hill featuring Senators John McCain and Joseph Lieberman. Spearheading the civil disobedience was Mike Ferner, who had been in Iraq with the Iraq Peace Team in 2003. "2006 was a year where mobilization turned to resistance," exclaimed another VFP member. "2007 is the year to deepen the resistance!"[6]

Iraq Veterans Against War obliged. In mid-2007, it organized "Operation First Casualty." IVAW members in fatigues conducted mock patrols in US cities. Moving silently through crowds, they violently "took down" alleged insurgents before shocked passersby. The eerie street theater sought to dramatize the brutality of a distant war. "Talking and marching wasn't getting the point across," explained IVAW's Garett Reppenhagen.[7]

Soon came IVAW's most ambitious effort. In March 2008, it held near Washington, DC, four days of hearings titled "Winter Soldier: Iraq & Afghanistan—Eyewitness Accounts of the Occupations."[8] Dozens of veterans offered testimony about the disturbing things they had seen and done at war. Iraqi civilians provided videotaped accounts, while journalists like Dahr Jamail shared their experiences. Panels also addressed racism and sexism in the military and the need for greater veterans' benefits. Amy Goodman and David Zeiger, director of a new film about GI resistance to the Vietnam War, live-streamed the entire event.

The hearings were both difficult and cathartic, for the soldiers especially. At their end, Rage Against the Machine's Tom Morello gave the exhausted organizers a private concert. One of them, Ward Reilly, said of the IVAW members: "they were so happy, some for the first time since the war."[9]

Smaller Winter Soldier events were held in cities nationwide. In May, IVAW members spoke before congressional committees against funding for the war, echoing their prior testimony. With greater visibility came growth. By the end of 2008, IVAW had more than thirteen hundred members and nearly sixty chapters, including chapters for active-duty soldiers on bases in North Carolina and Maryland.[10]

One of the most dramatic protests of the entire war combined grisly imagery with high-risk action. On September 16, 2007, contract soldiers with the North Carolina–based Blackwater USA killed seventeen civilians in a traffic circle at Nisour Square in Baghdad. The incident, captured in press photos, caused a major rift between the US and Iraqi governments. Sickened by Blackwater's actions, and inspired by Jeremy Scahill's exposés of the mercenary company, Catholic Worker communities in Virginia and North Carolina planned a response.[11]

The core group was led by Steve Baggarly from Norfolk and Patrick O'Neill of Raleigh. Both were veterans of antinuclear protests, and no strangers to prison. (Baggarly also served six months for his 2002 Pentagon protest.) Joining them was Beth Brockman of Durham, North Carolina, contemplating for the first time a major arrest action. Brockman had worked with the Peace Corps in Sri Lanka during wartime, sensitizing her to civilian suffering. But she was a "very late bloomer" to activism.[12] Through the first year of the Iraq War, she wore a peace button but went to no protests.

A committed Episcopalian, she discovered the Catholic Worker in 2003 and was drawn to its justice message. Starting in 2005, she quickly amassed a handful of low-level arrests and felt called to do more. Scahill himself got in on the planning, encouraging the group to focus on Nisour Square. The highly publicized incident, Brockman felt, "allowed us to put names and faces" to those killed in Iraq.

On October 20, six activists drove onto Blackwater's seven-thousand-acre headquarters in North Carolina's Great Dismal Swamp. There, they recreated the scene at Nisour Square, complete with a car riddled with simulated bullet holes, a bloodied driver, and lifeless bodies on the ground. Brockman played the role of a wailing, Iraqi mother. Throughout, she imagined what it must be like to realize, "I'm alive, and my child's dead."

Mark Colville, coming from Connecticut for the protest, placed a bloody handprint on a sign with Blackwater's menacing bear paw

Mark Colville putting a bloody handprint on the logo of Blackwater, a private military contractor, at its North Carolina headquarters on October 20, 2007. Colville was protesting the killing by Blackwater employees of seventeen Iraqis at Baghdad's Nisour Square in September 2007. Photograph by Chris Curry, *The Virginia Pilot/TCA*.

logo. Supporters and local residents held a small protest nearby. "It's in our backyard," one said. "I'm ashamed that we haven't spoken sooner."[13] Police arrested the six reenactors and a seventh protester, who had joined them to kneel in prayer.

At first anticipating lengthy prison time, the protesters received only modest punishment.[14] (In 2014, four Blackwater employees were convicted for the Nisour Square killings and sentenced to decades in prison. In 2020, Donald Trump pardoned them.) In their statements at sentencing, they recited the name of each victim, explained how their faith had moved them to act, and noted that they were now convicted, while the Blackwater killers remained free.

Witness Against Torture took bold action of its own, at a pivotal moment in the Guantánamo saga. In early December, the US Supreme Court heard oral arguments in a new case, *Boumédiène v. Bush*. It would decide, once and for all, whether the detainees had habeas rights. On January 11, 2008, the prison's sixth anniversary, protesters weighed in.

Hundreds of people in jumpsuits marched to the Supreme Court.

Dozens more, posing as tourists, were stationed inside.[15] They unfurled banners they had smuggled in, while those outside rushed the building's marble steps. Eighty people were arrested for "unlawful protest" on Supreme Court grounds, meant to be free of politics. Capitol Police closed the entire building—the first time they could remember that happening in response to protest.

Most arrestees gave police the name of a detainee instead of their own.[16] The goal was to symbolically grant the Guantánamo prisoners the day in US court that had been denied them. In this clever gesture, WAT embraced a politics of representation connected to the movement's broader politics of truth. By dressing as detainees, the protesters sought to make visible the hidden suffering of the detained men. The outfit echoed other protest symbols—like shoes to represent the dead—that communicated the truth of the war in emotionally compelling ways. Taking detainee names signaled a deeper identification with the War on Terror's victims.

The resulting trial in late May was an extension of the protest. To a waiting press, the thirty-five defendants arrived outside the courthouse in jumpsuits and hoods bearing the name of the detainee they were representing.[17] "We are keenly aware," explained Matt Daloisio, that "in the five months since our arrest, we have made it further in the criminal justice system" than the Guantánamo prisoners had in years.[18] After removing their hoods, the defendants placed the placards with the prisoners' names before a "Temple of Justice" bearing the words "Rule of Law," "Magna Carta," and "US Constitution." With this act, they completed their evolution from detainees back into citizens, convinced that the fate of their society's professed, bedrock principles lay in whether the hapless prisoners would one day receive true justice.

Just days after the protesters were found guilty, the Supreme Court ruled by a narrow majority that the Guantánamo detainees in fact had habeas rights. Public protest did not force the decision. But years of advocacy, inside the courts and on the streets, set the stage for it.

"THIS WAR ISN'T GOING TO END IMMEDIATELY"

Despite areas of growth and occasional victories, the antiwar movement fell from mid-2007 on into a fitful decline. Gone were demonstrations in the hundreds or even tens of thousands.[19] For the fifth anniversary of the war's start, only a thousand people rallied in Washington, DC. Mass civil resistance never materialized. Major antiwar groups like UFPJ and ANSWER soldiered on, while struggling to sustain the energy of years past.

The media and the country as a whole were moving on from Iraq. After Petraeus's September 2007 testimony, coverage of the war dropped sharply.[20] In 2008, major TV networks devoted 79 percent fewer broadcast minutes to Iraq than the year before.[21] Newspaper coverage fell by half. Domestic issues, like the growing financial crisis, dominated Americans' attention.

All sides on the Iraq War had difficulty mobilizing Americans' passions. Iraq Veterans Against the War developed "Operation First Casualty" partly to remind people the war was happening at all. The conflict in Afghanistan was even further off the radar. Media bias remained a problem as well. The Winter Soldier media team, one member fumed, invited *"every* mainstream media TV outlet, *every* newspaper, and *every* radio station" to the event. None showed up.[22]

Much of 2007–8 was a time for reflection and even soul-searching within the antiwar movement. In mid-2008, the War Resisters League interviewed more than a hundred organizers from diverse groups to assess the movement's accomplishments, limitations, and future direction.[23] The organizers reported, above all else, that they wished that the movement were both bigger and more effective in changing policy, not just public attitudes.

"The left in this country," UFPJ's Judith Leblanc elaborated, "is very small." It becomes vital "only when it's related to the mainstream." Yet too often, activists failed to generate "messages and images that reach beyond the choir." The stress on ideological purity put up barriers to broader participation. It also prevented satisfaction in "small wins," like a member of Congress adopting a moderate antiwar position. Nonviolence as a moral philosophy and political ethic was alien to most Americans. "We create a movement that appeals to those already in [it]," concluded Adrienne Maree Brown of the Ruckus Society, "rather than those who need to come to it."

The movement, many felt, also did a poor job mobilizing natural allies. Eric Tang, a community organizer in the Bronx, noted that the large "national coalitions have tried to find the most expedient way to build a mass movement. This is understandable. But expediency rarely facilitates a deepening connection to the issues and struggles of disenfranchised people." The poor and many people of color "don't view Bush's policies" as part of "their America," making engagement around foreign affairs "a stretch." To invest deeply in the antiwar movement, they needed to see how antiwar politics addressed their lives. If the movement could broaden its base with an inclusive justice agenda, its power would expand.

Much stood in the way. White majority groups often failed to create cultures in which people of color felt fully welcomed, empowered, and trusted with leadership. IVAW members pointed out that the US military is essentially a working-class institution, more integrated than most others in the country. They often had greater success connecting with "ordinary Americans" from diverse backgrounds than established peace groups. The profound inequalities in the United States, activists recognized, showed up in their own organizing.

Many organizers thought the movement lacked a strategic vision. This left it "on the defensive, reacting to events beyond our control." Near-constant protest discouraged careful thinking about how to achieve political goals. "Symbolic direct action," one activist confessed, too easily became a "personal rite of passage," unconnected to the goal of "actually ending the war."

In a separate evaluation, Van Gosse took stock of UFPJ, which he had helped found. For years Hany Khalil, the staff coordinator for Iraq War protest, complained that UFPJ was "a mobilizing coalition, not an organizing body." It had, Gosse charged, "no strategy for building a permanent organizational base or regional infrastructure, no field staff, little fundraising beyond constant email blasts to its tens of thousands of supporters plus a small network of major donors, generating just enough funds to maintain a national office while debts mounted." It lived "from mobilization to mobilization," never developing "innovative strategies for ending the occupation."[24] Though less critical, Leslie Cagan conceded that UFPJ never marshaled the resources or will for the comprehensive outreach it sought, including to young people.[25]

Gosse echoed other activists in wishing for a true "peace movement," not merely an antiwar movement protesting individual wars. Such a movement would have a sustained presence in policy debates, where it could promote diplomacy, conflict resolution, and justice in foreign affairs.

Behind activists' criticisms of the movement lay immense frustration with its inability to stop the war. The tendency was to blame themselves for not building a better movement. How much the Bush administration could be swayed by any popular mobilization was debatable. The key factor now, as Max Elbaum saw it, was that "the policy-making elite" was "divided over Iraq."[26] The movement's challenge was "to work that division to the point where some section" of that elite was "actually prepared to get the hell out."

"Many people see us as in a stalemate," confessed IVAW's Jason Hund. "We've got a president who obviously is not going to do anything to end this war. In Congress they can't muster the votes . . . [so] most people are just riding it out until we get a new president. I've been telling people that even when we do, this war isn't going to end immediately."[27]

"THE END OF AN ERROR"

It took the end of Bush's presidency and Republican defeat in 2008 to decisively shift US policy on Iraq. Illinois Senator Barack Obama ran on the promise to end the war. In the primaries, he defeated front-runner Hillary Clinton, tainted by her support for the 2003 invasion. He then beat Republican John McCain, who clung to hope for grand success in Iraq. Even the Bush administration had abandoned that hope.

Mindful of his successor, after the election Bush endorsed a framework for the end of direct, US military involvement in Iraq. (Had McCain won, he might have decided differently.) On December 14, 2008, President Bush held a press conference with Iraq's prime minister, Nouri al-Maliki, in Baghdad's Green Zone. The leaders announced the final approval of the Status of Forces Agreement between their countries. In it, the United States pledged to withdraw its combat forces from Iraq's cities by June 30, 2009, and from the entire country by December 31, 2011.

Yet the headline from the press conference was something different. As the leaders shook hands, Iraqi journalist Muntazer al-Zaidi rose from the press pool to fling his shoes at Bush. "This is a farewell kiss from the Iraqi people, you dog," he shouted, as he let the first shoe fly. (The act was a special insult in Iraqi culture.) The second shoe was "for the widows and orphans" of Iraq.[28]

Al-Zaidi was detained by Iraqi guards, badly beaten, and imprisoned for nine months. Years later, he described his act as "proof" that "a simple person was capable of saying no to that arrogant man, with all his power, tyranny, arms, media, money, and authority." "You were wrong," was his message. "You killed many people" and "changed the fate [of] the whole region." To his country, al-Zaidi was a hero.

Al-Zaidi's words echoed many Americans' own fury at Bush. The antiwar movement had hoped that its "No" might prevent war, or quickly stop it once started. "We were right!" said Frida Berrigan, reflecting on years of protest.[29] "It's so awful that everything we said [might happen] came to pass, and so many people died, so much got destroyed." Like countless antiwar activists, she was left with an uncomfortable sense of vindication, steeped in anger and sorrow.

In 2002, Secretary of State Collin Powell invoked the "Pottery Barn rule" when urging caution about a US invasion. Powell referenced the (apocryphal) policy of the famous housewares retailer: if you break an item in the store, you have to buy it. The US invasion broke Iraq, just as opponents of the war had predicted. The United States would walk away, never owning what it broke. In its grueling defeat, the antiwar movement claimed a terrible victory.

Antiwar groups greeted the change in presidents with a final

"THE END OF AN ERROR" AND ENDLESS WAR 351

The boots and other memorabilia of Veterans for Peace member Ward Reilly, thrown at the White House on January 19, 2009, President Bush's last day in office. Photograph by Ward Reilly.

message for Bush. On January 19, the eve of Obama's inauguration, VFP, IVAW, World Can't Wait, and others came to Washington. They erected a giant blow-up doll of the president, dressed in his "Mission Accomplished" aviator suit. Prompted by a sign to "Give Bush the Boot!," the protesters and passersby hurled shoes at the effigy. More than a cheeky send-off, the shoe-toss echoed al-Zaidi's angry, desperate act. Later in the day, veterans threw combat boots and children's shoes at the White House. A banner for the somber action read "The End of an Error."

On inauguration day, their message was for Obama. Shunted into a "free-speech zone," protesters held printed signs, prepared by Laurie Arbeiter, reading "Arrest Bush." Their hope, if short of that, was that the new administration would enforce meaningful accountability for the mistakes and even crimes of the prior one. Justice, and the deterrence of future errors, demanded it.

Obama's start was auspicious. His first official act was an executive order directing the closure of the prison at Guantánamo within a year. Another affirmed the illegality of torture methods used under Bush. Obama pledged that the battle against terrorists would now be waged "in a manner that is consistent with our values."[30] The American Civil Liberties Union called his actions a "giant step forward."[31] Defense attorneys at Guantánamo celebrated with a rule-of-law conga line.[32]

In his first foreign visits, Obama admitted the recklessness of past US policies. In October 2009, he was awarded the Nobel Peace Prize for his "extraordinary efforts to strengthen international diplomacy and cooperation between peoples."[33] Based on few tangible accomplishments, the award showed how eager much of the world was to believe again in the United States' moral leadership. Archbishop Desmond Tutu and the Dalai Lama congratulated Obama. Other global figures and past Nobel recipients felt the prize was premature.

Obama proved far from the dovish president that many had wished. His administration would conduct no comprehensive legal or moral reckoning with the War on Terror. In April 2009, Attorney General Eric Holder announced that the Justice Department would not prosecute CIA personnel for their use of interrogation methods approved by the "torture memos." Bush's gerrymander of the law had worked, immunizing Americans from prosecution for likely crimes. Obama declared, "Nothing will be gained by spending our time and energy laying blame for the past."[34]

Like its predecessor, the Obama administration asserted the right to detain terror suspects indefinitely and without charge. It grossly mishandled its efforts to close Guantánamo, cowing to Republicans' false claim that the prison still housed only "the worst of the worst" and distorted claims of ex-detainees "returning to the battlefield." Appellate courts, responding to Justice Department challenges, rendered detainees' habeas rights nearly meaningless.[35] The release of men from Guantánamo slowed dramatically.[36]

Obama's Department of Justice worked to quash the efforts of international courts to prosecute War on Terror policies, from torture to "aggressive war" in Iraq. It invoked "state secrets" and executive privilege arguments to battle domestic lawsuits against prisoner abuse. It even fought lawsuits seeking redress for the detention of Muslim, Arab, and South Asian peoples just after 9/11.

Many of Obama's supporters praised his shift in tone and seeming desire to set a new course for the nation. The groups he mobilized for his campaign, from labor unions to young progressives, threw themselves behind his domestic agenda, chiefly the expansion of health care. But others angrily noted that he defended some of Bush's most controversial War on Terror policies, while holding on to executive powers that Bush had claimed.

Afghanistan was a major challenge. It remained, Obama felt, a seedbed for Al-Qaeda's resurgence and a danger to the United States. Plagued by corruption, the Afghani government had failed to secure its rule outside of Kabul. With US policy focused on Iraq, the Taliban and al-Qaeda had made disturbing gains.

In spring 2009, Obama doubled troop deployments to more than fifty thousand. In December, just after receiving the Nobel Prize, he ordered thirty thousand more US soldiers into Afghanistan. The decision did not come easily. Vice President Joe Biden forcefully argued that the United States should abandon "nation building" in Afghanistan, bring most US troops home, and limit itself to counterterrorism operations.

With more troops came more casualties. Military deaths in Afghanistan jumped from near zero in October 2008 to a monthly high of sixty a year later.[37] That same month in Iraq there were fewer than ten US deaths. 2010 saw a wartime peak of 498 US casualties in Afghanistan. Civilians suffered too. Taliban attacks hit marketplaces, schools, and government offices. Nighttime raids and reckless bombings by US forces also claimed the lives of innocents, further turning Afghans against the Americans.

In his tome *Dirty Wars* and accompanying movie, Jeremy Scahill documented civilian losses in Afghanistan under the new president.[38] He also exposed Obama's stepped-up use of lethal drone strikes in Afghanistan, Pakistan, Yemen, and Somalia. Increasingly, the US government sought to wage war without American boots on the ground. It claimed the right to conduct drone operations in countries without their approval or even knowledge. It also left unclear how it identified alleged insurgents and determined what loss of civilian life was acceptable in their targeting.

The War on Terror was expanding, raising new political, legal, and moral questions. At the same time, it faded more and more into the background of American life.

"THE BAD NEWS FOR THE ANTIWAR MOVEMENT"

None of Obama's policies were met by sustained, large-scale protests. By 2009, the antiwar opposition was no longer a "genuine mass political movement" drawing the participation of millions.[39] Instead, it grew both smaller and more focused on select aspects of the War on Terror.

How and why did such a large and robust movement go into such rapid decline? Burnout was a major reason. Hardcore activists had spent years powering organizations that enabled countless others to engage in protest. Key figures, both local and national, stepped back to tend to long-neglected aspects of their lives. Veterans of the current wars faced special challenges. "After 4–5 intense years of work," observed an ally, many IVAW members had "to find their way back into society, and find regular jobs."[40] The economic crisis also took a toll. Time spent on protest was now devoted to making ends meet. Disenfranchised communities faced the greatest pressure, as they struggled with employment, health care, and housing costs. "Debates about race" in the movement, Phyllis Bennis remarked, "always had to do with class."[41]

Resources were a problem at an institutional level as well. United for Peace and Justice had operated on a paltry budget. The economic collapse, which cratered the stock market, further hurt funding. "Rich people were suddenly not quite as rich," Bennis noted, "and didn't want to give us as much money."

The 2008 election had its costs. Money and labor once going to peace groups instead went to political candidates. David Cortright praised the "massive wave of volunteer and financial support" for Obama from "seasoned activists of the antiwar movement."[42] This support could be seen as an investment in the antiwar cause, given Democrats' opposition to the Iraq War. But it also had, according to Leslie Cagan, "a serious, negative impact on the antiwar movement," whose main advocacy had been protest.[43]

Always a unifying figure in UFPJ, Cagan stepped down from her leadership role in the spring of 2009, saying she "had literally been going night and day for seven and a half years" and "needed to slow down." In the battle for Cagan's successor, different visions for the coalition squared off. One sought to leverage UFPJ's mainstream appeal and penetrate more deeply into institutional politics. Another favored a base-building approach that would mobilize populations underrepresented in the coalition. Neither approach was able to reinvigorate the flagging organization.[44]

Partisanship also played a role in the movement's fate. Scholars Heaney and Rojas observed a great irony: that movement activity, including lobbying, receded "at exactly the time" when it might have had the "greatest political effect," given Democrats' control of the White House and Congress.[45] Why, they asked, would the success of seeming allies "lead to a decline in the movement before those allies had effected the change that they promised?"[46]

Party loyalty, they felt, was the culprit. At first, Democrats "mobilized against the war, turning antiwar protest into a mass movement, as part of their hostility toward Bush." With Obama in office, Democrats' attitudes changed. Many backed or rationalized his War on Terror policies, even when mirroring those of Bush. "When Democrats stopped turning out," protests greatly shrunk in size.[47] "Stopping the wars didn't seem as important" to them anymore, Ward Reilly observed. "It was amazing to see that happen right in front of our eyes."[48] Still calling for Guantánamo's closure outside the White House, protesters faced the rebuke from liberals, "But didn't Obama close it already?"[49]

Congressional action receded as well. Antiwar legislation, overwhelmingly sponsored by Democrats, peaked in Bush's last years. With Obama in the White House, it all but stopped. The 111th Congress (2009–11) proposed fewer than a dozen antiwar bills, with none becoming law.[50] "The partisan alignment between the president and Congress," Heaney and Rojas concluded, "was decisive in ending Democrats' push for peace legislation."[51]

"The bad news for the antiwar movement was that activists were more likely to favor their Democrat identities over their antiwar identities," said Heaney and Rojas.[52] Obama, some of his antiwar critics felt, co-opted or even killed the movement by falsely posing as its true ally and taking antiwar moderates with him. Debra Sweet put it bluntly: "The crowning blow to the mass movement against the wars was that the Bush administration was driven out—by a mass movement created from the top to support a president whose mission was to save the system, restore US credibility internationally, speak the language of multiculturalism, while essentially carrying out the program of empire as commander in chief."[53] "You don't get to be president," Cagan said of Obama, "without being a cheerleader for the US military."[54]

Partisanship, while surely a big factor, goes only so far in explaining the antiwar movement's decline. First, it suggests that great numbers of Americans hated the Iraq War *only because* it was Bush's policy. Many hated Bush (or hated him more) *because* of his Iraq policy. Disdain for the lies about WMD, disgust with Abu Ghraib, and sadness at US and Iraqi losses reflected deep-seated convictions, not simply partisan affinities.

Second, some activists downplayed the role of partisanship in the movement's decline. Those who "believed that Obama was gonna do great," Bennis recalls, "were mostly not in UFPJ."[55] His strategy was to drop US casualties to "almost nothing," taking them "off the front pages. Follow the blood means only American blood. Iraqi blood doesn't count. Afghan blood doesn't count." Convincing to some Americans, Obama's pose as an antiwar president failed to persuade others.

Obama, finally, delivered on what mattered most to the antiwar movement at its peak size and strength: leaving Iraq. Against the objection of some in the military and Congress, he diligently executed the timetable for the US withdrawal. How much was there left to protest about a war scheduled to end, especially as US casualties fell to almost zero?

The rise of the Islamic State in Iraq and Syria (ISIS) in 2013/14 again threw the region into crisis. Obama ordered the US military back in, leading an international coalition to defeat ISIS.[56] US operations consisted mostly of aerial bombardments and arming and directing Iraqi and Kurdish forces. American deployments, as well as casualties, were minimal. So was public protest.

Public support for the war in Afghanistan had decreased over time. By 2008, a strong majority of Democrats felt it was "not worth the cost," though Obama's surge lifted hopes of progress.[57] As US casualties mounted, support again dropped. But the fight in Afghanistan never inspired the same hostility as the war in Iraq, widely seen as both a "war of choice" and a grave injustice.

For much of Bush's terms, Democrats disapproved more of the *way* the Afghanistan war was handled than the war itself. It grew deeply unpopular across party lines when dragging on as "endless war," long outliving its purpose of defeating al-Qaeda. Antiwar protest *as a mass movement* went as far as objections to a raging US war in Iraq would take it, and no further.

"THE GREATEST THREAT TO OURSELVES"

Old and new outrages inspired dissent throughout the Obama years. Much of the heavy lifting was done by main drivers of the Bush-era antiwar movement, from Code Pink to Answer to World Can't Wait. Their ongoing efforts required vigilant focus on legal and policy particulars, and the gumption to oppose a popular, liberal president. Under Bush, they were the leading edges of a massive antiwar movement. Now, they were a small, dedicated minority.

January 11, the Guantánamo anniversary, became occasion for an annual rally of several hundred at the White House, educational events, lobbying, and civil disobedience in federal Washington. Rally speakers, all of whom turned against the prison, have included James Yee, the original Muslim chaplain at Guantánamo; Morris Davis, the former chief prosecutor for the Military Commissions at Guantánamo; US military lawyers representing detainees; and former guards at the prison camp.

A new hunger strike at Guantánamo in 2012/13 prompted some of the most intense protest of the entire War on Terror. Three activists—Andrés Thomas Conteris, Code Pink's Diane Wilson, and Elliott Adams from VFP—engaged in grueling, weeks-long hunger strikes to demand justice for the detainees. "It was," Adams confessed, "one of the hardest things I have done. Not the fasting, but watching the pain in people you love as they watch your risk of death slowly rise."[58]

Conteris submitted to nasogastric feedings, mimicking the force-feedings at Guantánamo, in front of the White House and federal courts.[59] Their efforts, along with new litigation and global solidarity efforts, helped jumpstart the release of more detainees.[60]

In 2014, Witness Against Torture reprised its 2005 trip to Cuba, again holding vigil at the edge of the US base. At first mostly Christian, the group now boasted the leadership of Muslims, chiefly Dr. Maha Hilal, who founded in 2016 the Justice for Muslims Collective. For years, anti-torture protesters sought to make the Guantánamo detainees subjects before the law. More and more, they condemned Guantánamo as an expression of American racism and religious bigotry, punishing brown-skinned Muslim men.

Anti-drone activism became its own crusade. Code Pink members made daring trips into tribal lands in Pakistan to expose drone killings and work with devastated communities.[61] A new wave of civil resistance targeted bases that operated lethal drones. Upstate Drone Action protested the Syracuse-area Hancock Air Base, which directed Reaper drones.[62] Starting in 2011, dozens of protesters were arrested for breaching the base. They used their trials to challenge the legality and morality of drone warfare. Catholic Workers in Iowa and Ithaca, New York, led much of the protest.

In May 2013, President Obama gave a major national security address about anti-ISIS and drone operations, broadcast live by major networks. Medea Benjamin interrupted the president, demanding that he close the Guantánamo prison and end drone strikes.[63] In a response unthinkable under Bush, Obama urged that the audience take seriously Benjamin's points. Obama himself called on Congress to lift restrictions on the release of detainees and acknowledged the controversy surrounding drone killings. Yet little in his policies encouraged Guantánamo's closure or constrained drone warfare.

Activists also rallied around US Army Private Chelsea Manning, imprisoned for leaking classified material to dissident journalists. An intelligence officer in Iraq, in 2010 Manning exposed evidence of the killing of civilians and the glib reaction of US soldiers.[64] Chelsea Manning defense committees formed nationwide, staffed by veterans of antiwar protest. To them, Manning was a classic whistleblower, appealing to conscience to reveal government breaches of morality and the law.

Much of Manning's material was publicized through WikiLeaks—a global media group dedicated to exposing secret government documents related to the War on Terror. WikiLeaks became a cause célèbre, attracting the collaboration of antiwar journalists and the passion of advocates for free speech and a free press. The 2013 revelation by the National Security Agency's Edward Snowden of the secret mass surveillance of Americans after 9/11 also rallied the grassroots. American reporters contacted by Snowden formed *The Intercept*—a left-wing investigative news organization rare in American media.

In Congress, even conservatives asked whether government powers had gone too far. A sustained national conversation on the potential excesses of the War on Terror finally took shape. It concerned injuries to the liberties of everyday Americans, not the direct, foreign victims of US violence. Still, it was something.

Viewed in relative terms, the Obama administration was far

Luke Nephew at a Witness Against Torture protest on January 10, 2013, in Washington, DC. Nephew is sitting on bleachers, near the United States Supreme Court building, that were erected for President Obama's second inauguration on January 21. Photograph by Justin Norman.

better from an antiwar standpoint than that of Bush. Its violence was less extreme, more targeted, and defended through appeals to the law. Judged by absolutes, as the rule of law demanded, US conduct was still wanting.

In 2011, with innocent men still at Guantánamo, Witness Against Torture blockaded the entrance of the Justice Department. Part of the protest, poet Luke Nephew intoned: "We cannot steal years of men's lives, based on lies extracted from torture and bribes, without becoming the greatest threat to ourselves."[65] Never able to face this ruin, US politics ground on. So did protest.

CONCLUSION

On November 12, 2008, just days past Obama's election, commuters in New York and other cities were handed a special edition of *The New York Times*. "Iraq War Ends," ran its screaming headline. US troops, it reported, would withdraw in weeks from Iraq and Afghanistan.[1] "Ex-Secretary Apologizes for W.M.D. Scare" ran another headline. Other stories reported that the prison at Guantánamo would immediately close, that George Bush had been indicted for the crime of treason, and that American evangelicals would take in thousands of Iraqi refugees. The *Times* also issued a mea culpa, confessing that it "played no small part in making the case for war" by using unverified sources to hype the Iraqi threat. Its reporters would now embed with peace groups, not the military.

The paper was, of course, a hoax. Clues abounded. It was dated July 4, 2009, as if to declare the nation's independence from ruinous policies. The *Times*'s famous motto "All the News That's Fit to Print" was changed to "All the News We Hope to Print." Above all, the content was nearly beyond imagining. Still, some readers were fooled. "It's like a dream," one said. "This war needs to end, and here the war is over. . . . I'm trembling."[2] Not everyone was impressed. "I don't understand what statement they are trying to make," complained a *Times* executive. "We set the standard for coverage of the Iraq War."

By evening, the paper's creators were on CNN explaining the ruse to a gushing anchor. The ploy had begun months earlier when distraught friends wondered what more they could do to stop the war.[3] Among them was Andy Bichelbaum from the Yes Men, a group known for its audacious stunts skewering corporate greed. Dozens of authors, including from UFPJ and Code Pink, helped write the text of the fake *Times*, while hundreds of volunteers distributed eighty thousand copies. "It would be lovely one day," the CNN anchor said, "to see a *real* headline that says 'War is over.'"[4]

The paper spoke to a nation weary of war. Decades earlier, John Lennon and Yoko Ono declared, "Merry Christmas, War is Over" in billboards and song. For the Vietnam War to end, they felt, one had first to imagine that it could. The stunt spoke as well to a chronic complaint about protest, often felt by protesters. "We say 'no!' We say what we don't want," explained its main instigator, Steve Lambert. "And we repeat it over and over."[5] The paper offered instead a vision of comprehensive justice. The United States could not undo the damage of the War on Terror. But it could compensate the victims, hold the perpetrators to account, and set a new course.

With its dreamy headlines, the paper also marked the vast chasm between what the antiwar movement had sought and the post-9/11 record of death and destruction. How did antiwar activists assess their own efforts and the difference they made? How might observers, or a broader posterity, measure their protest?

Activists were very rarely asked their views, reflecting the limited place of the movement in public consciousness. Their perspectives have mostly been confined to anniversary retrospectives of key protests and discussions on left-wing blogs. Opinions vary, revealing both the movement's diversity and the ambivalence many activists feel toward an antiwar movement that neither fully succeeded nor failed.

At one extreme, David Cortright boasted that "a vast and unprecedented mobilization" had created the "largest antiwar movement" in history.[6] In a "watershed victory," the US press had presented it as "diverse, legitimate, and representative."[7] Though the movement was "unable to stop the march to war," it "exerted considerable international influence." Chiefly, it isolated the United States and the United Kingdom and made the war harder to fight. The movement eventually won the American "struggle for hearts and minds," reflected in Obama's election. Antiwar opposition moved from the streets to the voting booth to the White House. The system worked.

"Many of us were disappointed by Obama's military escalation in Afghanistan," Cortright conceded, "and are deeply concerned by his extensive drone warfare program. But on the issue that mattered most to us, ending the occupation of Iraq, the commitment to Obama's candidacy proved to be a sound antiwar strategy."[8] When US troops finally left, the White House reached out to Cortright to thank him and other activists for making that possible.

Eric Stoner, the youthful editor of *Waging Nonviolence*, cast a mixed verdict. "The movement," he concluded, "hastened the turning of the tide against the war in Iraq, which likely pushed the US to withdraw its forces on a shorter timeline than it would have otherwise. How many lives were saved can never be known."[9] A more powerful movement might have prevented the war or ended it sooner. Above all, Stoner felt that the US government successfully applied lessons from the Vietnam War. Ending the military draft and limiting US casualties, it blunted protest.

Kai Newkirk also saw both strengths and weaknesses: "How much we were able to cash the check" of supporting Obama and other Democrats "was very limited, but it was not nothing." Able to make huge inroads with the public, he said, the movement lacked the "vision and willingness to do what would have been necessary"—including mass nonviolent direct action—to thwart the government's ability to wage war.[10]

Against claims of qualified success stood the bitter feeling that the antiwar movement counted for far too little. "Why Was the Biggest Protest in World History Ignored?" ran the title of a *Time* magazine piece on the tenth anniversary of the February 15, 2003, demonstrations.[11] On the streets in New York City that day, its author felt when the war began: "We failed." The protests "were brushed aside with blithe nonchalance by the Bush administration and a rubber-stamp Congress that approved the war. The UN's Security Council was bypassed, and the largely feckless, acquiescent American mainstream media did little to muffle Washington's drumbeats of war."

Protesters in the United Kingdom, also home to massive demonstrations in February 2003, felt the same way. *The Guardian* titled its survey of activists' reflections, "We Were Ignored."[12] Some protesters praised the movement for helping to discredit the Iraq War, Prime Minister Blair, and the conservative turn of his Labour Party. Still, many felt "profound disillusionment."

"I felt so joyous, righteous, passionate," recalled a London protester, age seventeen at the time. "But we were utterly ignored and we learned dangerously early, before we could even vote, that politicians don't care what we think." "It was a huge show of anger," Tariq Ali said of the 2003 protests. "But that's about it. It left no lasting legacy.... This is what we are left with—celebrating anniversaries."[13] "It's incredibly sad," Phyllis Bennis agreed, that democracy in the United States and the United Kingdom was "so broken that public opinion just didn't matter" when the state was intent on war.[14]

Colonel Ann Wright gave up her State Department job in protest of the Iraq War. Schooled in geopolitics, she concluded that the antiwar movement failed to make "a bit of difference to the Bush administration. They were hell bent to leather; they didn't give a rat's ass who was opposed to [war]. They were going to do whatever they wanted."[15] Wright would have welcomed evidence showing greater success but saw none.

Protesters also voiced the conviction that "We were right," compounding their upset. "There's no satisfaction," one explained, "in looking back and saying, 'I told you so'—not with the blood that has been spilled." All sides, noted another, appeared to lose. "There's no way to describe [the] outcomes as the products of a happy story," either for the Bush administration or for the peace movement.[16]

The sense of being right was most obvious with respect to the Iraq War. Predicting disaster, masses of humanity begged the United States not to invade. When it did, disaster followed. The rise of the ISIS after the US withdrawal deepened the danger for Iraqis. Many grew to curse the Americans both for invading their country *and* for leaving it.

Even the earliest dissidents—braving protest when the 9/11

wounds were fresh and support for war ran hot—were vindicated. The War on Terror, they feared, would be driven by vengeance and imperial ambition, not the desire for justice or true security. It might begin in Afghanistan but not end there. They also warned that the United States would become, as it waged its fight, "the evil we deplore." "Let us think about a rational response that brings real peace and justice to our world," pleaded bereaved family members just after 9/11.[17]

Some activists cautioned that simple judgments of victory and defeat are too crude a way to view the antiwar movement. Social-movement scholars have in recent years encouraged a broader understanding of the impact of protest, beyond "win and losses" with respect to protest goals. Instead, they stress how movements may affect great swaths of policy, public attitudes, political alignments, culture, and other movements.[18]

The influence of the movement was widely felt, if often indirectly. Most likely, it tempered US enthusiasm for fighting wars. In 2013, President Obama abruptly stopped a planned assault on Syria, asking Congress to authorize the strike. When legislators and their constituents pushed back, Obama nixed the assault.[19] President Bush had named Iran as part of the "axis of evil," suggesting it as America's next target after Iraq. Yet Obama pursued diplomacy to slow Iran's pursuit of nuclear weapons and rebuilt global alliances as the preferred means to greater security.

The 2016 election showed how deeply "hearts and minds" had been won on the Iraq War. Candidates Hillary Clinton and Donald Trump tarred each other as supporters of the conflict and tried to play up their alleged antiwar bona fides. Trump's rejection of "stupid wars" directed by globalist "elites" (including the Bush family) was part of his populist appeal. For all his saber rattling toward Iran and his strongman's love of the military, he never launched a war against the country.

President Biden's full withdrawal of US forces from Afghanistan in August 2021 executed policies that the Trump administration had set in motion. Ending America's longest war was a bipartisan wish.

US support for Ukraine in its war with Russia and for Israeli operations in Gaza—each deeply controversial—has come with a strict condition: no commitment of US combat soldiers.

This dramatic political shift was hardly a direct consequence of the antiwar movement of the early '00s. Instead, it was a national response to failed policies. But the movement had helped the country recognize those failures, take stock of the costs, and seek to avoid repeating past mistakes. Much like "the Vietnam syndrome," a new, invisible limit was set—partly as the result of mass protest—on what kinds of military intervention both the political class and public would endorse. Whether an "Iraq syndrome" will hold in a second presidency of Donald Trump, still seething with martial bluster and nativist hatred, remains to be seen.

The movement's impact extended beyond reticence to war. United for Peace and Justice, according to Bennis, helped define a whole era of progressive politics, which made real gains in domestic policy. Antiwar activism was also a catalyst in the United States for public support for Palestinian independence. Over time, this work gave a new credibility to a pro-Palestinian politics on the American left, among young American Jews, and even at the margins of the political establishment. The loud condemnation of Israel's conduct in the Gaza War by millions of Americans is testament to that shift.

The antiwar movement—and the February 2003 protests especially—also set a new precedent for global dissent. Among beneficiaries was the 2011 Arab Spring, facilitated by internet organizing and the very sense that transnational protest was possible. Arab peoples, on their own terms, rose up against both the despotism of their nations' regimes and the interference of foreign powers in their nations' affairs. It is "incredibly powerful," Bennis marveled, "to realize that the impact of a protest goes way beyond what happens on [a given] day and whether or not you achieve" your "official" goal.

The Arab Spring, in turn, gave rise to the global Occupy movement protesting economic inequality. Countless American Occupy activists had previously participated in antiwar protest, learning valuable organizing skills. The global justice movement, Occupy showed, was not so much dead as in remission. It roared back to life, now with a domestic focus, after years of antiwar protest. Groups that formed to oppose the Iraq War brought their work to new struggles. We Will Not Be Silent developed signs for Occupy ("Greed Kills"), the Movement for Black Lives ("Unarmed Civilian"), environmental activism ("Restore the Earth"), and other campaigns. Code Pink remains a robust direct-action advocacy group addressing an array of issues. Peaceful Tomorrows has a new generation of members, who barely knew their slain parents.

The question of the ends of one's protest further complicates activists' views of the antiwar movement. Deeply humble, Leslie Cagan takes pride in her leading role within it. Her efforts made the movement "just that little bit crisper," "more powerful," "bigger," and "more creative" than it might have been.[20] Other activists, in UFPJ and beyond, contributed that way too.

At the same time, Cagan asserted the importance of protest *regardless of its results*. Elaborating, she invoked the view of the famous pacifist A. J. Muste. During the Vietnam War, a reporter asked him, "Do you really think you are going to change the policies of this country by standing out here alone at night in front of the White House with a candle?" Muste answered, "I don't do this to change the country. I do this so the country won't change me."[21] "Sometimes you just have to do something," Cagan felt, "because it's the right thing to do, even if you're one person." "You have to stand up," agreed Ann Wright, "even if it's only for your own self-worth."

That spirit was shared by Witness Against Torture. Responding to a call from Archbishop Tutu, in the fall of 2005 its founders began fasting every Friday in solidarity with the hunger strikers at the prison. Some pledged to continue doing so until the prison was closed. "Over the years," one member conceded, "participation has waned. In fairness, none of us thought we were making a lifetime commitment."[22] Two decades later, he still fasts every Friday, with no expectation that his "stubborn" act will shutter the prison. Instead, it is "a weekly reminder" of those still at Guantánamo, and "the small victories and ultimate failure in closing that fucking place." In the waning days of the Biden presidency, just fifteen detainees remain.

Dahr Jamail grew philosophical as he weighed the impact of his reporting from Iraq. His early hope was that his stories would rile more decent-hearted Americans to speak out against the war and hasten its end. As the war ground on and domestic support for it held, he fell back on the view of the Israeli journalist Amira Hass, famous for her reporting on the plight of Palestinians: that at least those enabling terrible violence would not be able to claim ignorance as their excuse.[23]

Few Americans, if any, worked so hard as Kathy Kelly to limit US harm to the Iraqi people. Her efforts long predated the 2003 invasion and continued well past the major withdrawal of US forces. Her efforts, she acknowledges, failed both to "lift the vicious and lethally punitive" sanctions and to "stop the war and the devastating civil war it created."[24]

Kelly rued "the general indifference" of so many Americans to the "human suffering" of armed conflict. Yet it did not surprise her. Her own mother, an avid Fox News viewer, supported the Iraq War. Her mother and many other Americans saw in the war the "essentially humanitarian" purpose of giving Iraqis their freedom. That conviction, Kelly speculated, enabled them to excuse the terrible costs of war, experienced also by US soldiers. Though diminishing over time, Americans' belief in the virtue of their nation's mission after 9/11—professed by Bush at every turn—proved a great force.

Knowing the power of that visceral nationalism, Kelly has remained undeterred. The task, no matter the circumstances, is the same: to "reclaim [our] humanity through action." She has done so, like small numbers of other Americans, with ongoing service to Iraqis, Afghans, and other victims of war. "We must persist with the tasks of education and outreach," she reflected, "looking for nonviolent means to take risks commensurate to the crimes being committed. . . . We're supposed to do what everyone is supposed to do: live as full humans, as best we can, in a world whose destiny we can never predict, and whose astonishingly precious inhabitants can never be given enough justice, time, or love."

ACKNOWLEDGMENTS

"It's very dangerous to forget," Iraq's Omar Mohammed told Western interviewers for a 2020 film, "because memory" is all that is "left for us."[1] In 2014, after the withdrawal of US forces from Iraq, the Islamic State of Iraq and the Levant (ISIL) stormed into Mohammed's hometown of Mosul. Its reign of terror included daily public executions. As the risk of death, Mohammed operated the anonymous blog *Mosul Eye*. It beamed to the internet reports of life under ISIL and messages of resistance. In July 2017, after an eight-month assault, Iraqi forces backed by US firepower reclaimed the city.

What Mohammed most wanted to remember was life in his beloved Mosul before the US invasion, the civil war that followed, and ISIL's rule. Children, he tenderly recalled, had played in the streets with "no fear." Mosques, churches, and shrines had intermingled. "You could feel that the sun is shining just because Mosul is there. . . . Unfortunately," he concluded with steely sorrow, "everything I describe has been destroyed." The battle to retake Mosul leveled huge parts of the city and claimed more than ten thousand civilians, including Mohammed's brother.

Memory, as the great enemy of forgetting, makes different tasks for different people. For Iraqis like Mohammed, the main task is to remember a vanished past in order to build a future that carries on something of its customs and spirit. For Americans, it is to recall how their government—well beyond credible measures to prevent another attack like on 9/11—caused untold destruction in Iraq and other countries targeted in the War on Terror.

As a national project, this encounter with memory would in its own way be painful. It would require a comprehensive reckoning, undistorted by self-serving falsehoods and excuse-making, with a new legacy of grave harm to other peoples of the world; US service members too were victims of wrongheaded policies. No such reckoning has remotely taken place. Indeed, there is today virtually no sustained national conversation about any aspect of the War on Terror.

Alongside the crime of forgetting lies the shame of never having known in the first place. Most Americans endured the War on Terror with only a small inkling of what was really going on in Iraq, how badly US forces abused detainees, or what US solders both suffered and wrought. Any true reckoning would also require a basic education in a difficult history.

This book hopes to play a small role in the battle against forgetting and ignorance by exploring the efforts of Americans to oppose the War on Terror. Millions of people engaged in countless acts of protest. Yet the antiwar movement for years struggled to break through in the national consciousness and command the ongoing attention of policymakers. Part of the movement myself, I had, prior to my research, little awareness of the vast majority of antiwar activity.

Recording the words and deeds of the antiwar protesters of the early '00s seems to me vital for three main reasons. First, the perpetration of grave injustices such as those the War on Terror entailed raises the question of who spoke up against them and why. Those protesting the War on Terror, I believe, have a deserving place in the annals of conscientious American dissent, as they sought to create a more peaceable and moral world. Telling their collective story is to honor their commitment, from which future movements may learn.

Second, I seek to guard against any revisionism insisting that the great hazards of what became failed US wars in Afghanistan and Iraq were both unforeseen and unforeseeable. With remarkable clarity, antiwar voices predicted the military, geopolitical, and moral disaster of much of the War on Terror *before* it took place.

Third, knowing this past may help to prevent the next reckless war. Protest against the War on Terror shows that the critical citizen voice—however much ignored or even maligned—can be more thoughtful than the views of political leaders, prominent media figures, and self-anointed experts. Much of the country now rues the path the Bush presidency took after 9/11, especially the invasion of Iraq. A great salve against future regret is to take opposition to war more seriously in its own day. To do so is to honor democracy itself and to respect the humanity of all those put at risk by armed conflict.

Bringing the antiwar movement to life required the generosity of friends and strangers. My broadest gratitude is to the people I interviewed. Some I knew through my past antiwar activism or longtime work with Witness Against Torture. Others came into this research at the suggestion of fellow activists or by chance.

With the interviews, I hardly sought a representative sample of a truly massive, deeply variegated antiwar movement. Instead, I have been drawn to key players in leading organizations whose energy and vision enabled the activism of countless others. This focus in no way diminishes the contributions of the vast antiwar rank and file, or of local organizers far from the centers of national power. Their work, especially when enacted in strongly prowar parts of the country, was often more difficult and more consequential in the lives of their neighbors and local leaders. So many stories, about so many individual and groups, remain to be told.

Several people I interviewed lead lives of public consequence as recognized leaders within peace and justice movements. Among them are Kathy Kelly, Leslie Cagan, Medea Benjamin, Debra Sweet, and Brian Becker. Their tireless activism is hardly motivated by the hope that historians will one day record their efforts, always pursued with larger groups. Even so, they recognized the importance of a thorough account of the post-9/11 antiwar movement and spent real time with me to discuss its inner workings.

Others I interviewed served as more than valued interlocutors.

Van Gosse and Max Elbaum, themselves scholars, supplemented their testimony with documents from their private archives. L. A. Kauffman treated me to posters, buttons, and other antiwar memorabilia, making the movement newly vivid to me. Veterans for Peace stalwart Ward Reilly shared with me hundreds of his photographs of antiwar protests, several of which appear in this book. He also engaged questions of fact and judgment, explained the culture of antiwar veterans, and offered sweet encouragement as I brought this project across the finish line. I am so very grateful.

I extend my thanks to the other photographers who pulled images for the book from old photo libraries. They are Thorne Anderson, Carole Ashley, L. A. Kauffman, Scott Langley, Garth Liebhaber, Justin Norman, and Alan Pogue. Katherine Feil of September Families for Peaceful Tomorrows, Billy Cheng-Yen Wu, and Archivist Vicky Russo at the Swarthmore Peace Collection also helped secure photos. Alex Aleinikoff, dean of the New School for Social Research, kindly subsidized licensing fees, as did my dear friend Ajay Agrawal.

Jeff Berryhill and Aidan Noell jump-started the project with their early research assistance. Michael Koncewicz, a kindred spirit, introduced me to the massive United for Peace and Justice collection at New York University's Robert F. Wagner Labor Archives. James Miller helped with last-minute edits. I thank also Phyllis Greenhill for her transcription work.

Tim Mennel, executive editor at the University of Chicago Press, has been the indispensable patron of this book. He has brought to it his knowledge of history and skill with language. He also solicited manuscript reviews from two superb scholars. Their praise meant the world to me, while their criticisms made for a better book. Senior editorial associate Andrea Blatz consummately handled the production process, holding me to the highest standard while understanding the stresses of authorship. Freelance editor Charles Dibble and then the press's senior production editor Tamara Ghattas did valuable copyediting and other production work. Anthony Arnove—literary impresario to some of the world's finest critical thinkers—was the ideal agent.

I've been blessed with the close company of gifted historians, who helped me set the project's design and scope. Chief among them are Michael S. Foley, a scholar of the Vietnam War; my sister Elizabeth R. Varon; and my brother-in-law William Hitchcock. Several cohorts of students at The New School aided me in discerning the book's key themes. I drew insight and inspiration, finally, from fellow activists, above all my Witness Against Torture family. Their dedication, kindness, and courage have been my lodestars. For many years, we tried to stop the War on Terror's worst abuses. I hope this book puts our efforts in new perspective.

My greatest appreciation goes to my wife, Alice Varon. Herself a veteran of good causes, she reminded me of the value of my undertaking when it seemed most daunting. She also read numerous drafts of this book, lending her editorial talents. Our son Arlo motivated me with his evident pride in his father's passion and hard work. So thank you, Alice and Arlo.

ABBREVIATIONS USED IN THE NOTES

UFPJ: United For Peace and Justice Records at the Tamiment Library and Robert F. Wagner Labor Archives, New York University, TAM 513.
BFP: Brooklyn for Peace Records at the Brooklyn Public Library, Center for Brooklyn History.

NOTES

INTRODUCTION

1. George W. Bush, "Bullhorn Address," September 14, 2001, https://www.americanrhetoric.com/speeches/gwbush911groundzerobullhorn.htm.
2. I use the term "War on Terror" even though critics questioned whether it was truly motivated by opposition to global terrorism. I do so to highlight the way in which US war-making after 9/11 was framed.
3. George W. Bush, "Address to the Nation on the Terrorist Attacks," September 11, 2001, https://millercenter.org/the-presidency/presidential-speeches/september-11-2001-address-nation-terrorist-attacks.
4. Phyllis and Orlando Rodriguez, "Not in Our Son's Name," September 14, 2001. Reprinted in David Potorti, with Peaceful Tomorrows, *September 11th Families for Peaceful Tomorrows: Turning Our Grief into Action* (RDV Books, 2003), 22–23.
5. These numbers, as of winter 2005, are from *Costs of War*, compiled by the Watson Institute at Brown University, https://watson.brown.edu/costsofwar.
6. Patrick E. Tyler, "A New Power in the Streets," *New York Times*, February 17, 2003.
7. Literature on the US antiwar movement is indeed paltry. I reference what work there has been throughout this book.
8. Even works highly critical of the war leave out the antiwar movement or grant it only a bit part. See, for example, Michael MacDonald, *Overreach: Delusions of Regime Change in Iraq* (Harvard University Press, 2014) and Spencer Ackerman, *How the 9/11 Era Destabilized America and Produced Trump* (Penguin Random House, 2012).
9. Melvin Small, "Bring the Boys Home Now! Antiwar Activism and Withdrawal from Vietnam—and Iraq," *Diplomatic History* 34, no. 3 (June 2010): 543.

CHAPTER 1

1. Laura Flanders, "Live Reports from Manhattan: A Web Log," September 11, 2001, *WorkingForChange*. Her first post was at 10:33 a.m. and the second was at noon. All posts are recorded at https://web.archive.org/web/20010918124143/http://www.workingforchange.com:80/article.cfm?ItemID=11899.
2. David McReynolds, "Statement on September 11 Attack," https://www.warresisters.org/resources/wrls-statement-911.
3. George W. Bush, "Address to the Nation on the Terrorist Attacks," September 11, 2001, https://millercenter.org/the-presidency/presidential-speeches/september-11-2001-address-nation-terrorist-attacks.
4. Flanders, "Live Reports from Manhattan," 1:56 p.m., September 12.
5. Flanders, "Live Reports from Manhattan," noon, September 13.
6. Rahul Mahajan, "The War Comes Home," *Common Dreams*, September 12, 2001, https://web.archive.org/web/20010921161600/http://www.commondreams.org/views01/0912-07.htm.
7. Robert Jensen, "Stop the Insanity Here," *Common Dreams*, September 12, 2001, https://web.archive.org/web/20010918051145/http://www.commondreams.org/views01/0912-08.htm.
8. Stephen Zunes, "U.S. Shouldn't Fight Violence with Violence," *Baltimore Sun*, September 12, 2001, https://www.baltimoresun.com/2001/09/12/us-shouldnt-fight-violence-with-violence/.
9. Saskia Sassen, "A Message from the Global South," *Guardian*, September 12, 2001, https://www.theguardian.com/politics/2001/sep/12/september11.uksecurity.
10. Naomi Klein, "War Isn't a Game After All," *Globe and Mail*, September 12, 2001, https://web.archive.org/web/20010918051216/http://www.commondreams.org/views01/0914-07.htm.
11. Noam Chomsky, "A Quick Reaction," September 12, 2001, https://chomsky.info/20010912/.
12. Cheney made the remark on *Meet the Press* on September 16, 2001; video available on YouTube at https://www.youtube.com/watch?v=KQBsCIaxMuM.
13. The September 17 Covert Action Memorandum of Notification is discussed in the Report of the Senate Select Committee on Intelligence—Committee Study of the Central Intelligence Agency's Detention and Interrogation Program, Released on December 9, 2014, 11 (hereafter Senate Torture Report), https://www.intelligence.senate.gov/sites/default/files/publications/CRPT-113srpt288.pdf.
14. The CIA now openly touts its secret foray into Afghanistan. See "Flashback: Sept. 26, 2001—CIA Is 'First in' After September 11th Attacks," https://

www.cia.gov/news-information/featured-story-archive/2013-featured
-story-archive/flashback-sept-26-2001.html.
15 See US Department of Justice, Office of the Inspector General, "The September 11 Detainees: A Review of the Treatment of Aliens Held on Immigration Charges in Connection with the Investigation of the September 11 Attacks," April 2003. The total number of detentions remains unclear. The US government admitted to 1,200 detentions in the first weeks after 9/11. The 2003 Inspector General report documented 762 detentions under the auspices of the Immigration and Naturalization Service. Yet attorneys and others allege that domestic detentions, including under subsequent law enforcement programs, may have exceeded 5,000 by May 2003. See David Cole, *Enemy Aliens: Double Standards and Constitutional Freedoms in the War on Terrorism* (New Press, 2003), 25.
16 Gerda Lerner, "Alternatives to War Will Work Best in Long Run," *Capital Times* (Madison, WI), October 1, 2001, https://web.archive.org/web/20011005194650/http://www.commondreams.org/views01/1002-06.htm.
17 John R. MacArthur, "When the Puritan Citadel Cracked," *Globe and Mail*, September 14, 2001, https://www.theglobeandmail.com/opinion/when-the-puritan-citadel-cracked/article763124/.
18 Martin Amis, "Fear and Loathing," *Guardian*, September 18, 2001, https://www.theguardian.com/world/2001/sep/18/september11.politicsphilosophyandsociety.
19 Klein, "War Isn't a Game After All."
20 Barbara Kingsolver, "A Pure, High Note of Anguish," *Los Angeles Times*, September 23, 2001, https://www.latimes.com/archives/la-xpm-2001-sep-23-op-48850-story.html.
21 Margaret Krome, "How We Grieve Defines Us," *Capital Times* (Madison, WI), September 13, 2001. https://web.archive.org/web/20010918051213/http://www.commondreams.org/views01/0914-05.htm.
22 Slavoj Žižek, "Welcome to the Desert of the Real!" September 17, 2001, https://www.wussu.com/current/zizek.htm. In 2002, Žižek published *Welcome to the Desert of the Real: Five Essays on September 11 and Related Dates* (New York: Verso, 2002), which expands on the short essay he wrote just after 9/11. Subsequent quotes are from the original essay.
23 Arundhati Roy, "The Algebra of Infinite Justice," *Guardian*, September 29, 2001, https://www.theguardian.com/world/2001/sep/29/september11.afghanistan.
24 Ward Churchill, "Some People Push Back: On the Justice of Roosting Chickens," September 12, 2001. The original essay is at https://theanarchistlibrary.org/library/ward-churchill-some-people-push-back-on-the-justice-of-roosting-chickens.
25 George F. Will, "The End of Our Holiday from History," *Washington Post*,

September 12, 2001, https://www.washingtonpost.com/archive/opinions/2001/09/12/the-end-of-our-holiday-from-history/9da607fd-8fdc-4f33-b7c9-e6cda00453bb/.

26 George W. Bush, "Remarks by the President Upon Arrival," September 26, 2001, https://georgewbush-whitehouse.archives.gov/news/releases/2001/09/20010916-2.html. Bush shortened the phrase to "War on Terror" in his September 20 address to Congress.

27 Harold Meyerson, "Life, Liberty and the Obligation to Defend Both," *American Prospect*, September 12, 2001, https://prospect.org/features/life-liberty/.

28 World Islamic Front, "Jihad Against Jews and Crusaders," February 23, 1998, https://fas.org/irp/world/para/docs/980223-fatwa.htm.

29 Samuel P. Huntington, "The Clash of Civilizations?" *Foreign Affairs* 72, no. 3 (1993): 22–49.

30 Francis Fukuyama, "The End of History?" *National Interest* 16 (Summer 1989): 3–18.

31 Huntington, "The Clash of Civilizations?," 3.

32 Huntington, "The Clash of Civilizations?," 9.

33 Huntington grants nominal credibility to some anti-Western grievances but scarcely sees the West as an imperial bully. Prior to 9/11, Edward Said criticized Huntington in "The Myth of the 'Clash of Civilizations,'" https://www.mediaed.org/transcripts/Edward-Said-The-Myth-of-Clash-Civilizations-Transcript.pdf.

34 George W. Bush, "Address to a Joint Session of Congress," September 20, 2001, https://georgewbush-whitehouse.archives.gov/news/releases/2001/09/20010920-8.html. All quotes are from the speech.

35 Joseph Margulies, *What Changed When Everything Changed: 9/11 and the Making of National Identity* (Yale University Press, 2013), 136. Subsequent quotes from pages 40 and 141.

36 Human Rights Watch, "'We Are Not the Enemy': Hate Crimes Against Arabs, Muslims, and Those Perceived to be Arab or Muslim after September 11," *Human Rights Watch—America* 14, no. 6 (November 2002), 3.

37 Human Rights Watch, "'We Are Not the Enemy,'" 18.

38 See Irum Sheikh, Muslims' Stories of Detention and Deportation in American after 9/11 (Palgrave McMillian, 2011).

39 Klein, "War Isn't a Game After All."

40 Mahajan, "The War Comes Home."

41 Roy, "The Algebra of Infinite Justice."

42 Susan Sontag et al., "Tuesday, and After," *New Yorker*, September 24, 2001, https://www.newyorker.com/magazine/2001/09/24/tuesday-and-after-talk-of-the-town.

43 Tariq Ali, "A Political Solution is Required," *The Nation*, September 17, 2001, https://www.thenation.com/article/political-solution-required/.

44 Noam Chomsky, *9-11* (Seven Stories Press, 2001), 11. Subsequent quotes from pages 12, 82, and 80.
45 Chomsky, *9-11*, 17. The phrase "diabolical trap" comes from France's foreign minister. As talk of war with Afghanistan escalated, Fisk warned, "President Bush appears to be heading for the very disaster that Osama bin Laden has laid down for him." Robert Fisk, "Bush Is Walking into a Trap," *The Independent/UK*, September 16, 2001, https://www.the-independent.com/voices/commentators/fisk/robert-fisk-bush-is-walking-into-a-trap-9220337.html.
46 Peter Bergen, *The Rise and Fall of Osama bin Laden* (Simon & Schuster, 2021).
47 Chomsky, *9-11*, 13.
48 Chalmers Johnson, "The Lessons of Blowback," *Los Angeles Times*, September 30, 2001, https://www.latimes.com/archives/la-xpm-2001-sep-30-op-51582-story.html.
49 Sandy Tolan, "Despair Feeds Hatred, Extremism," *USA Today*, September 20, 2001.
50 Edward Said, "The Necessity of Skepticism: Backlash and Backtrack," *Counterpunch*, September 20, 2001.
51 See Lee Nichols, "War of Words," *Austin Chronicle*, September 28, 2001, https://www.austinchronicle.com/news/2001-09-28/83161/.
52 Rod Dreher, "Painful to Live in Stricken N.Y.," *New York Post*, September 20, 2001, https://nypost.com/2001/09/20/painful-to-live-in-stricken-n-y/.
53 Quoted in Susan Faludi, *The Terror Dream: Fear and Fantasy in Post-9/11 America* (Metropolitan Books, 2007), 27.
54 Quoted in Faludi, *The Terror Dream*, 27–28.
55 Quoted in Faludi, *The Terror Dream*, 30.
56 Katha Pollitt, "Put Out No Flags," *The Nation*, September 20, 2001, https://www.thenation.com/article/put-out-no-flags/.
57 Faludi, *The Terror Dream*, 29–30.
58 Said, "The Necessity of Skepticism."
59 Chomsky, *9-11*, 13, 27, 78, 83.
60 David Horowitz, "The Sick Mind of Noam Chomsky," *Salon*, September 26, 2001, https://www.salon.com/2001/09/26/treason_2/.
61 Jeffrey C. Isaac, "Thus Spake Noam," *American Prospect*, October 2001, https://prospect.org/article/thus-spake-noam.
62 Christopher Hitchens, "Against Rationalization," *The Nation*, September 20, 2001, https://www.thenation.com/article/against-rationalization/.
63 Hitchens, "Against Rationalization."
64 Christopher Hitchens, "Of Sin, the Left and Islamic Fascism," *The Nation*, September 24, 2001, https://www.thenation.com/article/sin-left-islamic-fascism/. See also Christopher Hitchens, "Stranger in a Strange Land: The Dismay of an Honorable Man of the Left," *The Atlantic*, December 2001.

65 A view of terrorism as a "weapon of the weak" permeates the literature on it. Martha Crenshaw, a leading scholar of terrorism, wrote in 1981 that "terrorism is a logical choice when oppositions have [political] goals and when the power ratio of government to challenger is high. The observation that terrorism is a weapon of the weak is hackneyed but apt." Martha Crenshaw, "The Causes of Terrorism," *Comparative Politics* 13, no. 4, (1981): 387.

66 In research that predates 9/11, Mark Juergensmeyer develops the idea of "cosmic war" in *Terror in the Mind of God: The Global Rise of Religious Violence* (University of California Press, 2000).

67 Hitchens, "Of Sin, the Left and Islamic Fascism."

68 Chomsky wrote two responses, "Reply to Hitchens" and "Reply to Hitchens's Rejoinder," in *The Nation*'s October 15, 2001, issue, https://www.thenation.com/article/reply-hitchens/ and https://www.thenation.com/article/reply-hitchenss-rejoinder/.

69 Hitchens, "On Sin, the Left and Islamic Fascism."

70 Bush, "Address to Congress."

71 George W. Bush, "President's Remarks at National Day of Prayer and Remembrance," September 14, 2001, https://georgewbush-whitehouse.archives.gov/news/releases/2001/09/20010914-2.html. For a superb account of Bush's use of religious language and themes in framing the War on Terror, see Patrick G. Coy, Gregory M. Maney, and Lynne M. Woehrle, "Blessing War and Blessing Peace: Religious Discourses in the US During Major Conflict Periods, 1990–2005," *Research in Social Movements, Conflicts and Change* 29 (2008): 113–50.

72 Elizabeth Becker, "Renaming an Operation to Fit the Mood," *New York Times*, September 26, 2001, https://www.nytimes.com/2001/09/26/us/a-nation-challenged-renaming-an-operation-to-fit-the-mood.html.

73 Žižek, "Welcome to the Desert of the Real!"

74 Roy, "The Algebra of Infinite Justice."

75 Barbara Kingsolver, "And Our Flag Was Still There," *San Francisco Chronicle*, September 25, 2001, https://web.archive.org/web/20011022035435/http://www.commondreams.org/views01/0925-08.htm.

76 *Post*/ABC Poll: Terrorist Attacks. September 11, 2001, http://www.washingtonpost.com/wp-srv/politics/polls/vault/stories/data091201.htm. The first poll, conducted the evening of September 11, had 608 adult respondents. The figures below are from the same poll.

77 *Post*/ABC Poll: Terrorist Attacks. September 13, 2001, http://www.washingtonpost.com/wp-srv/politics/polls/vault/stories/data091401.htm.

78 Pew Research Group, "American Psyche Reeling from Terror Attacks—September 19, 2001," http://www.people-press.org/2001/09/19/american-psyche-reeling-from-terror-attacks/.

79 *Post*/ABC Poll: Bush Addresses Nation; War on Terrorism, September 20,

2001, http://www.washingtonpost.com/wp-srv/politics/polls/vault/stories/data092001.htm.

CHAPTER 2

1 Rahul Mahajan, "The War Comes Home," *Common Dreams*, September 12, 2001, https://web.archive.org/web/20010921161600/http://www.commondreams.org/views01/0912-07.htm.
2 Jonathan Schell, "A Sense of Proportion," *The Nation*, September 20, 2001, https://www.thenation.com/article/sense-proportion/.
3 *Washington Post* Poll: Attack on Afghanistan, October 8, 2001, http://www.washingtonpost.com/wp-srv/politics/polls/vault/stories/data100801.htm.
4 *Washington Post*-ABC News Poll: America at War, November 7, 2001, http://www.washingtonpost.com/wp-srv/politics/polls/vault/stories/data110701.htm.
5 Gallup, "Overwhelming Support for War Continues," November 29, 2001, https://news.gallup.com/poll/5083/overwhelming-support-war-continues.aspx.
6 *Washington Post*-ABC News Poll: America at War, November 28, 2001, http://www.washingtonpost.com/wp-srv/politics/polls/vault/stories/data112801.htm.
7 The 6 percent figure opposing war is quoted in Chris Good, "When and Why Did Americans Turn Against the War in Afghanistan?" *The Atlantic*, June 22, 2011, https://www.theatlantic.com/politics/archive/2011/06/when-and-why-did-americans-turn-against-the-war-in-afghanistan/240880/.
8 United Nations Security Council, Resolution 1386 (2001), https://documents-dds-ny.un.org/doc/UNDOC/GEN/N01/708/55/PDF/N0170855.pdf?OpenElement.
9 Michael Betzold, "Enough!" *Common Dreams*, September 13, 2001, https://web.archive.org/web/20010918051201/http://www.commondreams.org/views01/0913-08.htm.
10 *The O'Reilly Factor*, September 13, 2001, available on YouTube at https://www.youtube.com/watch?v=GUQSY4C6CwE.
11 Anthony B. Robinson, "Let Response Be Decent, Noble," *Seattle Post-Intelligencer*, September 15, 2001, https://web.archive.org/web/20010918051236/http://www.commondreams.org/views01/0915-09.htm.
12 Robinson, "Let Response Be Decent."
13 William Sloan Coffin, "'God Bless America,'" in Mary Susannah Robbins, *Peace Not Terror: Leaders of the Antiwar Movement Speak Out Against U.S. Foreign Policy Post 9/11* (Lexington Books, 2008), 10.
14 Coffin, "'God Bless America,'" 12.
15 Jim Wallis et al., "Deny Them Their Victory: A Religious Response to Ter-

rorism." *Sojourners*, https://web.archive.org/web/20011008003413/http://www.sojo.net:80/response/.

16 The Dalai Lama, "Letter to President Bush," September 12, 2001, https://www.shambhala.com/snowlion_articles/letter-to-president-bush-from-the-dalai-lama/.

17 Wilson Powell, *Veterans for Peace Comes of Age: A Highlight History*, https://www.veteransforpeace.org/files/4514/8183/6284/VETERANS_FOR_PEACE_-_A_HISTORY.pdf, 79–80.

18 Howard Zinn, "A Just Cause, Not a Just War," *The Progressive*, December 2001, https://progressive.org/magazine/just-cause-just-war-Zinn/.

19 Crispin Sartwell, "If You're Not Killing the Killers, It's Terrorism," *Philadelphia Inquirer*, October 9, 2001, https://web.archive.org/web/20011016033132/http://www.commondreams.org/views01/1009-08.htm.

20 Marion Winik, "A Sorrowful Certainty That the Worst Is Yet to Come," *Philadelphia Inquirer*, October 8, 2001, https://web.archive.org/web/20011130193641/http://www.commondreams.org/views01/1008-05.htm.

21 Marc Herold, "Counting the Dead," *Guardian*, August 7, 2002. In the piece Herold, a professor at the University of New Hampshire, revises his December 2001 figures to 2,650–2,790.

22 In January 2002 the Project on Defense Alternatives published "Operation Enduring Freedom: Why a Higher Rate of Civilian Bombing Casualties," Briefing Report no. 13 (January 18, 2002). It concluded that by January 1, 2002, "it is very likely that the bombing campaign" in Afghanistan "claimed 1000–1300 civilian lives." See Carl Conetta: "Operation Enduring Freedom: Why a Higher Rate of Civilian Bombing Casualties," Project on Defense Alternatives Briefing Report no. 13, January 18, 2022, https://www.comw.org/pda/02010ef.html.

23 David Potorti, with Peaceful Tomorrows, *September 11th Families for Peaceful Tomorrows: Turning Our Grief into Action* (RDV Books, 2003), 21.

24 Phyllis and Orlando Rodriguez, "Not in Our Son's Name," September 14, 2001. Reprinted in David Potorti, with Peaceful Tomorrows, *September 11th Families for Peaceful Tomorrows: Turning Our Grief into Action* (RDV Books, 2003), 22–23.

25 George W. Bush, "Remarks at Prayer Service," September 14, 2001, https://www.washingtonpost.com/wp-srv/nation/specials/attacked/transcripts/bushtext_091401.html.

26 Rita Lasar, "To the Editor," *New York Times*, September 18, 2001, https://www.nytimes.com/2001/09/18/opinion/l-one-week-later-how-to-answer-the-horror-229725.html.

27 Amber Amundson, "An Open Letter to Our Nation's Leaders—September 19, 2001," *Chicago Tribune*, September 25, 2001, http://www.pbs.org/now/transcript/transcript_amberletters2.html.

28 Potorti, *September 11th Families*, 31–32.

29 John Nichols, "A Growing Opposition," *The Nation*, September 27, 3001, https://www.thenation.com/article/growing-opposition/.
30 Ben Fenton, "The Lone Voice Against the 'Spiral of Violence,'" *Daily Telegraph*, September 18, 2001, https://web.archive.org/web/20021220060357/http://www.commondreams.org/headlines01/0918-01.htm.
31 *Counterpunch*, "A Lone Voice of Dissent," Davey D interview with Barbara Lee, *Counterpunch*, September 18, 2001, https://web.archive.org/web/20010925010801/http://www.counterpunch.org/lee.html.
32 Nichols, "A Growing Opposition."
33 "Statement of Representative Barbara Lee (D-CA) in Opposition to S. J. Res. 23, Authorizing the Use of Military Force," http://www.house.gov/lee.
34 Phyllis Bennis, interview with author, June 27, 2022.
35 Nichols, "A Growing Opposition"; *Counterpunch*, "A Lone Voice of Dissent."
36 Nichols, "A Growing Opposition."
37 Institute for Policy Studies, "Justice, Not Vengeance," Sept. 19, 2001, https://ips-dc.org/justice-not-vengeance-read-our-2001-statement-on-the-9-11-attacks/.
38 Arundhati Roy, "'Brutality Smeared in Peanut Butter': Why America Must Stop the War Now," *Guardian*, October 23, 2001, https://www.theguardian.com/world/2001/oct/23/afghanistan.terrorism8.
39 Robert Scheer, "Dry Up the Vast Pools of Discontent," *Los Angeles Times*, October 8, 2001, https://archive.commondreams.org/scriptfiles/views01/1009-06.htm.
40 Arundhati Roy, "The Algebra of Infinite Justice," *Guardian*, September 29, 2001, https://www.theguardian.com/world/2001/sep/29/september11.afghanistan.
41 Tamim Ansary, "War on Afghanistan?," reprinted by *Counterpunch*, September 16, 2001, https://web.archive.org/web/20010924230745/http://www.counterpunch.org/ansary.html.
42 Charles Krauthammer, "To War, Not to Court," *Washington Post*, September 12, 2001, https://www.washingtonpost.com/archive/opinions/2001/09/12/to-war-not-to-court/86d5f7a6-b901-4a70-93be-01e718471169/.
43 Steve Dunleavy, "Simply Kill These Bastards," *New York Post*, September 12, 2001, https://nypost.com/2001/09/12/simply-kill-these-bastards/.
44 James Carroll, "We Need the Rule of Law, Not the Rule of War," *Boston Globe*, September 15, 2001, https://www.commondreams.org/views/2001/09/15/we-need-rule-law-not-rule-war.
45 Kevin Danaher, "Justice, Not War," *Washington Post*, September 29, 2001.
46 David Cortright, "The Right Fight," in Mary Susannah Robbins, *Peace Not Terror: Leaders of the Antiwar Movement Speak Out Against U.S. Foreign Policy Post 9/11* (Lexington Books, 2008), 16.
47 Noam Chomsky, *9-11* (Seven Stories Press, 2001), 26.

48 Chomsky commented on September 19, "The immediate reaction [to 9/11] was shock, horror, anger, fear, a desire for revenge. But public opinion is mixed, and countercurrents did not take long to develop. They are now even being recognized in mainstream commentary." Chomsky, *9-11*, 20.
49 Chomsky, *9/11*, 36.
50 Chomsky mentions the Nicaraguan case four times in the post-9/11 interviews contained in Chomsky, *9-11*. See pp. 25, 42, 56, 85.
51 Bob Wing and Max Elbaum, "The Strategic Implications of Sept. 11 and the War on Terrorism: War & Peace, and Anti-racism as the New Axis of Politics," October 5, 2001, manuscript donated to author by Elbaum.
52 Biographical information about Wing, as well as some of his many writings, are available at https://bobwingracialjustice.org.
53 On STORM's history and post-9/11 activities, see "Reclaiming Revolution: History, Summation, and Lessons from the Work of STORM," 2003, unpublished manuscript.
54 Max Elbaum, interview with author, July 30, 2017. Elbaum also shared private documents about Bay Area organizing just after 9/11.
55 Wing and Elbaum, "The Strategic Implications of Sept. 11."
56 "September 11 Attacks and Civil Liberties," C-SPAN, November 20, 2001, https://www.c-span.org/video/?167419-1/september-11-attacks-civil-liberties. All quotes below are from the forum.
57 Damu Smith died in 2006, at age fifty-three, from colon cancer. Numerous obituaries from the political world celebrated his life and work.
58 On American reactions to 9/11 by race, see Roxanna Harlow and Lauren Dundes, "'United' We Stand: Responses to the September 11 Attacks in Black and White," *Sociological Perspectives* 47, no. 4 (Winter 2004): 439–64.
59 Richard Falk, "Defining a Just War: Ends and Means," *The Nation*, October 11, 2001, https://www.thenation.com/article/defining-just-war/. *The Nation* often posted stories online substantially before they appeared in its print edition. Throughout, I cite the earliest version of the referenced material.
60 Richard Falk, "A Just Response," *The Nation*, September 20, 2001, https://www.thenation.com/article/just-response-0/.
61 Falk, "Defining a Just War." Subsequent quotes are from the same essay.
62 Katha Pollitt, "War and Peace," *The Nation*, October 18, 2001, https://www.thenation.com/article/war-and-peace/.
63 The letters, along with Falk's response, are published in "Richard Falk and Our Readers—Is This Really a 'Just War?," *The Nation*, November 11, 2001, https://www.thenation.com/article/archive/really-just-war/.
64 Falk, "Is This Really a 'Just War'?"
65 Richard Falk, "In Defense of Just War Thinking," *The Nation*, December 7, 2001. https://www.thenation.com/article/defense-just-war-thinking/.
66 Falk, "Is This Really a 'Just War'?"

CHAPTER 3

1. Patrick F. Gillham and Bob Edwards, "Global Justice Protesters Respond to the September 11th Terrorist Attacks: The Impact of an Intentional Disaster on Demonstrations in Washington, D.C," in *Beyond September 11: An Account of Post-Disaster Research*. Institute of Behavioral Science, Natural Hazards Research and Applications Information Center, University of Colorado, Special Publication no. 39 (2003), 484.
2. Russell Mokhiber and Robert Weissman, "September in Washington, D.C.," *Common Dreams*, September 8, 2001, https://www.commondreams.org/views/2001/09/08/september-washington-dc.
3. "Ruckus Society Global Justice Action Camp Cancelled; Condemns Terrorist Attacks; Calls for End to Violence," September 12, 2001, https://web.archive.org/web/20010918181717/http://www.commondreams.org/news2001/0912-04.htm.
4. "Mobilization for Global Justice Cancels Its Call for Street Demonstrations Against World Bank/IMF at End of September," September 16, 2001, https://web.archive.org/web/20010919204939/http://www.commondreams.org/news2001/0916-02.htm.
5. "News Brief: World Bank Group and International Monetary Fund Will Not Hold Annual Meetings," September 17, 2001, https://www.imf.org/en/News/Articles/2015/09/29/18/03/nb0189.
6. L. A. Kauffman, interview with author, February 21, 2018.
7. Kauffman, interview with author.
8. Nadine Bloch, interview with author, February 17, 2022.
9. Lisa Fithian, interview with author, June 29, 2022.
10. Bloch, interview with author.
11. Gillham and Edwards, "Global Justice Protesters Respond," 500. Subsequent material and quotes from the same article.
12. Kauffman, interview with author.
13. Bloch, interview with author.
14. Claire Bayard, interview with author, July 31, 2017.
15. Kauffman, interview with author.
16. Bayard, interview with author.
17. On the MGJ's demise, see Gillham and Edwards, "Global Justice Protesters Respond," 494–550.
18. "Mobilization for Global Justice Cancels Its Call for Street Demonstrations Against World Bank/IMF at End of September."
19. Gillham and Edwards, "Global Justice Protesters Respond," 505.
20. Bloch, interview with author.
21. Bayard, interview with author.
22. "Anti-Capitalist Convergence Issues New Call to Action," September 20,

2001, https://web.archive.org/web/20011009025107/http://www.abolish thebank.org/en/new_call.html.

23 From "Interview Concerning September 28th Protest Against War & Globalization," The Green Mountain Anarchist Collective, *The Black Bloc Papers: An Anthology of Primary Texts from the North American Anarchist Black Bloc 1988–2005* (2006), https://theanarchistlibrary.org/library/the-black-bloc-papers#toc82.

24 Bayard, interview with author.

25 Kauffman, interview with author.

26 Bayard, interview with author.

27 Sarah Noor, interview with author, August 4, 2020.

28 "News and Announcements for the Greater Wesleyan Community," September 14, 2001.

29 Noor, interview with author.

30 Kai Newkirk, interview with author, June 5, 2024.

31 "Call to Action"—A Group of Concerned Wesleyan Students for Peaceful Justice," n.d., https://web.archive.org/web/20010926071514/http://www.peacefuljustice.cjb.net:80/. See also Press Release, September 19, 2001, National Student Day of Action for Peaceful Justice, https://web.archive.org/web/20010918180814/http://www.commondreams.org/views01/0918-08.htm.

32 Andrew Kramer, "1,200 March for Peace in Portland," Associated Press, September 17, 2001, https://web.archive.org/web/20021219074042/http://commondreams.org/headlines01/0917-02.htm.

33 Eric Pianin, "Peace Groups Are Urging Restraint," *Washington Post*, September 20, 2001.

34 On the protests, see Derek Thompson, "Calls for Restraint: Groups Urge Peaceful Alternative to a Military Response," ABCNews.com, September 20, 2001, https://web.archive.org/web/20011009201849/http://www.abcnews.go.com/sections/us/DailyNews/WTC_peacegroups_010920.html; Eric Lords and Marsha Low, "Antiwar Rallies Are Vocal and Peaceful," *Free Press*, September 21, 2001, https://web.archive.org/web/20011007085324/http://www.freep.com/news/nw/terror2001/march21_20010921.htm; Willian Weir, "On College Campuses: A Plea for Peace," *Hartford Courant*, September 21, 2001, https://web.archive.org/web/20021219074402/http://commondreams.org/headlines01/0921-05.htm; "Campus Aftershocks," *Christian Science Monitor*, September 25, 2001, https://www.csmonitor.com/2001/0925/p11s1-leca.html; Bettina Boxall, Richard Colvin, and Rebecca Trounson, "On Campus, Rumblings of Peace," *Los Angeles Times*, September 21, 2001, https://www.latimes.com/archives/la-xpm-2001-sep-21-mn-48172-story.html. Estimates of crowd sizes for the same protests vary somewhat across accounts.

35 "Students Rally for Peace on McDermott Court," MIT News Office, September 20, 2001, https://news.mit.edu/2001/peacerally.
36 Noor, interview with author.
37 Boxall et al., "On Campus, Rumblings of Peace."
38 Zoe Mitchell, "Zoe's Diary #1–#5: at the ACC March," https://web.archive.org/web/20030620225855/http://www.dc.indymedia.org/front.php3?article_id=12971. See also "Thousands Take to the Streets in San Francisco and Washington, D.C. to Call for Peace and Justice," *Democracy Now!*, October 1, 2001, https://www.democracynow.org/2001/10/1/thousands_take_to_the_streets_in.
39 Mitchell, "Zoe's Diary."
40 "Peace Activists Rally," *San Francisco Chronicle*, September 30, 2001, https://web.archive.org/web/20021227144911/http://www.commondreams.org/headlines01/0930-02.htm.
41 "Thousands Take to the Streets."
42 "For Now, a Global Movement Is Stymied," *Boston Globe*, September 30, 2001, https://web.archive.org/web/20021221130136/http://www.commondreams.org/headlines01/0930-03.htm.
43 Walden Bello, "The American Way of War," *Focus on the Global South*, December 2001, https://archives.globalresearch.ca/articles/BEL201A.html.
44 Eddie Yeun, "Prologue," in *The Battle of Seattle: The New Challenge to Capitalist Globalization*, ed. Eddie Yuen, Daniel Burton-Rose, and George Katsiaficas (Soft Skull Press, 2002).
45 Benjamin Shepard, review of *The Battle of Seattle: The New Challenge to Capitalist Globalization*, http://sdonline.org/35/the-battle-of-seattle-the-new-challenge-to-capitalist-globalization/.
46 Benjamin Shepard, "On the Road Again: IMF/World Bank Protests Show a Revived Movement for Global Justice," *Counterpunch*, October 1, 2002.
47 "Interview Concerning September 28th Protest Against War & Globalization."
48 The Black Bloc virtually disappeared, making a modest revival with the new wave of anarchism accompanying the 2011 Occupy movement.
49 "For Now, a Global Movement Is Stymied."
50 The demonstration was broadcast by C-SPAN as "Rally Against War and Racism," September 29, 2001, https://www.c-span.org/video/?166387-1/rally-war-racism. All quotes from rally speakers are from the video.
51 Ion Bogdan Vasi, "The New Anti-war Protests and Miscible Mobilizations," *Social Movement Studies* 5, no. 2 (September 2006): 143. To gather the data, six administrators conducted randomized surveys with 299 respondents. The following quotes are from pp. 142–45.
52 C-SPAN, "Rally Against War and Racism."
53 Brian Becker, interview with author, January 3, 2018.

54 Peter Hart, "Covering the 'Fifth Column': Media Present Pro-war Distortions of Peace Movement's Views," *FAIR*, November 1, 2001, https://fair.org/extra/covering-the-fifth-column/.
55 "Protestors in Washington Urge Peace with Terrorists," *New York Times*, September 30, 2001, https://www.nytimes.com/2001/09/30/us/a-nation-challenged-protesters-in-washington-urge-peace-with-terrorists.html.
56 Matthew Engel, "Mixed and Messy Anti-war Message Blunted," *Guardian*, October 1, 2001.
57 Marc Cooper, "Liberals Stuck in Scold Mold," *Los Angeles Times*, October 14, 2001.
58 Todd Gitlin, "Liberal Activists Finding Themselves Caught Between a Flag and a Hard Place," *San Jose Mercury News*, October 28, 2001, https://archive.commondreams.org/scriptfiles/views01/1031-02.htm.
59 Liza Featherstone, "Operation Enduring Protest," *The Nation*, October 18, 2001, https://www.thenation.com/article/operation-enduring-protest/.
60 The official name was "International A.N.S.W.E.R," commonly shortened to ANSWER.
61 Becker, interview with author, January 3, 2018.
62 *Citizen Clark . . . A Life of Principle*, directed by Joseph C. Stillman (La Paloma Films, 2018).
63 Becker, interview with author, January 3, 2018.
64 Brian Becker, "I Was with Muhammad Ali on His Hostage-Release Trip to Iraq—and the Media Has It All Wrong," June 10, 2016, https://www.answercoalition.org/i_was_with_muhammad_ali_on_his_hostage_release_trip_to_iraq_and_the_media_has_it_all_wrong.
65 Ramsey Clark, *The Fire This Time: U.S. War Crimes in the Gulf* (Thunders Mouth Press, 1992).
66 Becker, interview with author, January 3, 2018.
67 Becker, interview with author, January 3, 2018.
68 On the case and its settlement, see "Partnership for Civil Justice Fund—April 2000 IMF False Arrests," http://www.justiceonline.org/april-2000-imf-mass-false.
69 Becker, interview with author, January 3, 2018.
70 Gillham and Edwards, "Global Justice Protesters Respond," 496.
71 Kauffman, interview with author.
72 Vasi, "The New Anti-war Protests and Miscible Mobilizations," 143, 147. According to his survey, 36 percent of respondents at the protest "definitely," and 21 percent "probably," "planned to participate" in the original World Bank/IMF protests.
73 Joe Garofoli, "'Innovative Strategies' Needed as Peace Rallies Planned in San Francisco, DC," *San Francisco Chronicle*, September 28, 2001, https://web.archive.org/web/20021227143737/http://commondreams.org/headlines01/0928-01.htm.

NOTES TO PAGES 73-77   391

74 "Peace Activists Rally, Thousands Protest in San Francisco, DC," *San Francisco Chronicle*, September 30, 2001, https://www.sfgate.com/bayarea/article/Peace-activists-rally-Thousands-protest-in-S-F-2872942.php.
75 War Resister League Roundup of Antiwar Demos Fall 2001 at https://web.archive.org/web/20011014192703/http://warresisters.org/demos.htm and Nowar Collective event listing at https://web.archive.org/web/20011003205044/http://www.nowarcollective.com:80/.
76 Nowar Collective event.
77 Nowar Collective event.
78 Geov Parrish, "Hawks vs. Doves: The Race Has Begun for the Peace Movement to Catch Up and Overtake the War Momentum," *Common Dreams*, September 19, 2001, https://archive.commondreams.org/views01/0919-06.htm.

CHAPTER 4

1   Matea Gold, "'War Is Not the Answer,' Pacifists Tell Their Fellow Mourners," *Los Angeles Times*, September 16, 2001, https://www.latimes.com/archives/la-xpm-2001-sep-16-mn-46437-story.html.
2   Robert Cohen, Diana Kirk, and Emily Klein, "Debating War and Peace in Washington Square Park," *Social Education* 65, no. 7 (2001): 398–404.
3   Scott recounts the protest's origins in "Our Grief Is Not a Cry for War" Project—September 2001, *Revolution Newspaper* #245, September 11, 2001, http://revcom.us/a/245/grief_not_a_cry_for_war.en.html.
4   "2000 Presidential General Election Results - New York," *US Election Atlas*, https://uselectionatlas.org/RESULTS/state.php?year=2000&fips=36&f=0&off=0&elect=0.
5   Scott, "Our Grief Is Not a Cry for War" Project—September 2001, *Revolution Newspaper* #245.
6   Not in Our Name website, October 12, 2002, https://web.archive.org/web/20011012153235/http://www.nynotinourname.org/other.html.
7   The pledge is available at https://web.archive.org/web/20021202213746/http://www.notinourname.net/
8   Geov Parrish, "The Peace Movement Lives," *Alternet*, Septmber 26, 2002, www.alternet.org/print/story/14189/the_peace_movement_lives.
9   For early suspicion of war crimes, see "UN Reports Mazar-e-Sharif Executions," Associated Press, November 12, 2001, reprinted at http://www.rawa.org/un-maz.htm; and "US Afghan Ally 'Tortured Witnesses to His War Crimes,'" *Guardian*, November 17, 2002, https://www.theguardian.com/world/2002/nov/18/afghanistan.unitednations.
10 David Mendell, "Afghan Activist Decries U.S. Bombing," *Chicago Tribune*, November 9, 2001, https://www.chicagotribune.com/2001/11/09/afghan-activist-decries-us-bombing-2/.

11 Susan Sachs, "US Muslim Groups Urge Bush to Halt Air Strikes," AFP News, October 28, 2001, https://web.archive.org/web/20011029045442/http://www.commondreams.org/headlines01/1028-04.htm.
12 Alessandra Stanley, "Opponents of War Are Scarce on Television," *New York Times*, November 9, 2001.
13 Stanley, "Opponents of War."
14 Ronald Bishop, "The Whole World Is Watching, but So What? A Frame Analysis of Newspaper Coverage of Antiwar Protest," in *Leading to the 2003 Iraq War: The Global Media Debate*, edited by Alexander G. Nikolaev and Ernest A. Hakanen (Palgrave Macmillan, 2006), 39–64.
15 Susan Milligan, "Keeping Quiet So Far, Politicians' Dissent Left Out of the War," *Boston Globe*, December 3, 2001. https://web.archive.org/web/20011214051425/http://commondreams.org/headlines01/1203-03.htm.
16 Maureen O'Hagan, "Shot Just Misses Antiwar Demonstrator," *Washington Post*, December 4, 2001, https://www.washingtonpost.com/archive/local/2001/12/04/shot-just-misses-antiwar-demonstrator/f36ae899-ac35-4d0a-a28c-595d7d38e1ca/.
17 Emily Wax, "The Consequences of Objection," *Washington Post*, December 9, 2001, https://www.washingtonpost.com/archive/local/2001/12/09/the-consequences-of-objection/2ed24b8b-5043-4cee-be9d-6522a53f5aac/.
18 Lynne Cheney et al., Defending Civilization: How Our Universities are Failing America and What Can Be Done About It (ACTA, 2003), 1.
19 Cheney, Defending Civilization, 5, 3, 13, 21.
20 Tim McCarthy, interview with author, January 10, 2019.
21 Jonathan Schell, "Letter from Ground Zero," *The Nation*, November 21, 2001, https://www.thenation.com/article/archive/letter-ground-zero-45/.
22 Liza Featherstone, "Students Wrestle with War," *The Nation*, November 29, 2001, https://www.thenation.com/article/students-wrestle-war/.
23 Kai Newkirk, interview with author, June 5, 2024.
24 "Proposed Statement for All-Community Vote," archived at: https://www.hampshire.edu/chapter-2-september-11-2001-and-anti-war-protests#42c.
25 Cheryl B. Wilson, "Hampshire College Takes Anti-war Stance," *Daily Hampshire Gazette*, December 6, 2001.
26 Carl Campanile, "Kooky College Condemns War," *New York Post*, December 8, 2001, https://nypost.com/2001/12/08/kooky-college-condemns-war/; Newkirk, interview with author.
27 "Statement: NYC Labor Against War," November-December 2001. Unpublished document in author's possession.
28 Brian Becker, interview with author, March 24, 2018.
29 Sean Taylor, "The Lessons of Anaconda," *New York Times*, March 2, 2003.
30 The meeting is recounted in Carlotta Gall, *The Wrong Enemy: America in Afghanistan, 2001–2014* (Houghton Mifflin Harcourt, 2014), 19–21. Gall

thoroughly documents the Taliban's reconsolidation after its formal surrender and Pakistan's role in its revival.
31. "Former UN Official Says Sanctions Against Iraq Amount to 'Genocide,'" *Cornell Chronicle*, October 1, 1999, https://news.cornell.edu/stories/1999/09/former-un-official-says-sanctions-against-iraq-amount-genocide.
32. This quote, and the surrounding material, is drawn from Kathy Kelly, interview with author, November 16, 2018.
33. A leading Catholic Worker gave this definition: "The Catholic Worker movement is made up of people motivated by the teachings of Jesus, especially as they are summarized in the Sermon on the Mount, and the teachings of the Catholic Church . . . to bring about a 'new society within the shell of the old, a society in which it will be easier to be good.' A society in tune with these teachings would have no place for economic exploitation or war, for racial, gender or religious discrimination, but would be marked by a cooperative social order without extremes of wealth and poverty and a nonviolent approach to legitimate defense and conflict resolution." Tom Cornell, "A Brief Introduction to the Catholic Worker Movement," September 11, 2005, https://catholicworker.org/cornell-history-html/.
34. The name comes from the Biblical command in Isaiah to "beat swords into plowshares."
35. David Potorti, "I Lost My Brother on 9-11; Does He Matter?," *AlterNet*, October 10, 2001, https://web.archive.org/web/20020204082217/http://www.alternet.org/story.html?StoryID=11686.
36. This account of the origins of the protest is drawn from David Potorti, with Peaceful Tomorrows, *September 11th Families for Peaceful Tomorrows: Turning Our Grief into Action* (RDV Books, 2003), 34–51; and email correspondence with Kathy Kelly and Colleen Campbell, February 15, 17, 20, 2020.
37. "Family Members of September 11 Victims March from Pentagon to New York City to Call for Peace," *Democracy Now!*, November 26, 2001, https://www.democracynow.org/2001/11/26/family_members_of_september_11_victims.
38. "Family Members of September 11 Victims."
39. Potorti, *September 11th Families*, 43.
40. Mike Mile, "Forgiveness: The Harsh and Dreadful Precursor to Justice," *Common Dreams*, December 20, 2001, https://archive.commondreams.org/views01/1220-04.htm.
41. Potorti, *September 11th Families*, 50–51.
42. Here and elsewhere, I refer to Colleen Kelly as Colleen to avoid confusion with fellow Peaceful Tomorrows member Kelly Campbell and their ally Kathy Kelly.
43. Colleen Kelly, interview with author, February 25, 2020.

44 Colleen Kelly, interview with author.
45 Juan Gonzalez, "Grieving Voice Pleads for Peace," *New York Daily News*, September 19, 2001.
46 Russell Mohikber, "Ari & I," *Common Dreams*, October 26, 2001, https://web.archive.org/web/20020202122249/http://www.commondreams.org/headlines01/1026-07.htm.
47 "Stop the War, Plead Parents of NY Victim," *Observer of London*, October 14, 2001, https://web.archive.org/web/20011110003959/http://commondreams.org/headlines01/1014-02.htm.
48 Colleen Kelly, interview with author.
49 This portrait of is compiled from Medea Benjamin, interview with author, December 5, 2017; "In Depth with Medea Benjamin," C-SPAN, August 2, 2015, https://www.c-span.org/video/?326441-1/depth-medea-benjamin; and "I Was Born a Rebel," *The Real News Network*, February 16, 2014, https://therealnews.com/stories/mbenjamin0207raipt1.
50 Megan K. Stack, *Every Man in This Village Is a Liar: An Education in War* (Anchor Books, 2010), 12.
51 Sultan summarizes her trip in *Afghan Portraits of Grief: The Civilian/Innocent Victims of U.S. Bombings in Afghanistan* (Global Exchange and Peaceful Tomorrows, 2002), 2. She later published a memoir: Masuda Sultan, *My War at Home* (New Atria Books, 2006).
52 "Afghan Journey: En Route to Kandahar," *Democracy Now!*, December 27, 2001, https://www.democracynow.org/2001/12/27/afghan_journey_en_route_to_kandahar.
53 "Shared Grief After 9/11: Sister of WTC Victim Meets Afghan Who Lost 19 Family Members in U.S. Attack," *Democracy Now!*, rebroadcast on September 10, 2021, https://www.democracynow.org/2021/9/10/rita_lasar_and_masuda_sultan_2002.
54 On Ruzicka, see PBS, *Home/Front: Marla's War*, Part I, June 30, and *Home/Front: Marla's List*, Part II, July 9, 2021; and Janet Reitman, "The Girl Who Tried to Save the World," *Rolling Stone*, May 2005, https://www.rollingstone.com/culture/culture-news/the-girl-who-tried-to-save-the-world-62716/.
55 PBS, *Home/Front: Marla's War*, Part I.
56 Lasar, "Afghanistan Memories"; Potorti, *September 11th Families*, 70.
57 Quoted in Potorti, *September 11th Families*, 67.
58 "From One Ground Zero to Another," *Democracy Now!*, January 18, 2002, https://www.democracynow.org/2002/1/18/from_one_ground_zero_to_another.
59 Benjamin, interview with author. Benjamin, Potorti, and several news stories give accounts, differing slightly in some details, of the push to establish the fund.
60 Benjamin, interview with author.

61 Melanie Fonder, "Afghan Victims of US Bombing Demand Compensation," AFP News, January 22, 2002, https://web.archive.org/web/20021008090154/http://www.commondreams.org/headlines02/0122-02.htm.
62 Potorti, *September 11th Families*, 61.
63 Colleen Kelly, interview with author.
64 "Afghan Victims' Families Lobby for Fund," *The Hill*, February 6, 2002, https://web.archive.org/web/20021019175915/http://www.hillnews.com/020602/lobbying.shtm.
65 Reitman, "The Girl Who Tried to Save the World."
66 PBS, *Home/Front: Marla's List*, Part II.
67 Reitman, "The Girl Who Tried to Save the World."
68 For a thorough account of this and other civilian compensation and assistance programs, see "Assistance of Civilian Casualties of War—Hearing before a Subcommittee of the Committee on Appropriation—U.S. Senate," April 1, 2009, https://www.govinfo.gov/content/pkg/CHRG-111shrg49742/html/CHRG-111shrg49742.htm.
69 The speech is available at http://www.aavw.org/special_features/speeches_speech_king02.html.
70 On the group's founding, see Potorti, *September 11th Families*, 52–55, 83–85.
71 Peace Talk Radio, interview transcript, 8/31/2007, http://www.goodradioshows.org/peaceTalksL52.htm.
72 Frank Brodhead, email to author, February 20, 2020.
73 "Not in Our Name," *New York Times*, September 19, 2002, http://66.media.tumblr.com/09f4936c8e5aba2d75ef31e60e8f0fb4/tumblr_odeslyRvcP1qzoglfo1_1280.jpg.
74 Subsequent postings of the Statement new VIPs and reported the current number of total signatures.
75 Debra Sweet, interview with author, July 18, 2017.
76 Frank Rizzo, "Artists, Activists Join 'Not in Our Name' Protest," *Hartford Courant*, September 21, 2002, https://web.archive.org/web/20021204090935/http://www.notinourname.net/news/9-21-02_hartford_courant.html.
77 "History of the *Not in Our Name* Project" from NION website, https://web.archive.org/web/20020803095435/http://www.notinourname.net/history.html.
78 Max Elbaum, *Revolution in the Air: Sixties Radicals Turn to Lenin, Mao and Che* (Verso, 2002), 85–86.
79 The following profile of Sweet, including the quotes, is drawn from Debra Sweet, interview with author, June 23, 2017.
80 "Girl Accepting an Award Asks Nixon to End War," *New York Times*, December 4, 1970, https://www.nytimes.com/1970/12/04/archives/girl-accepting-an-award-asks-nixon-to-end-the-war-a-girl-bids-nixon.html.
81 Sweet, interview with author, June 23, 2017; "Girl Accepting an Award."

82 Sweet, interview with author, June 23, 2017.
83 On the origins of the outfits and War on Terror interrogation methods, see Alfred W. McCoy, *A Question of Torture: CIA Interrogation, from the Cold War to the War on Terror* (Holt, 2006), 21–59.
84 Voluminous, early documents on the legal status of detainees are in Karen J. Greenberg and Joshua L. Dratel, eds., *The Torture Papers: The Road to Abu Ghraib* (Cambridge University Press, 2005). See also Michael Ratner and Ellen Ray, *Guantanamo: What the World Should Know* (Chelsea Green, 2004).
85 "Rasul v. Bush," Center for Constitutional Rights, https://ccrjustice.org/home/what-we-do/our-cases/rasul-v-bush.
86 Paul Blumenthal, "Congress Had No Time to Read the USA PATRIOT ACT," March 2, 2009, https://sunlightfoundation.com/2009/03/02/congress-had-no-time-to-read-the-usa-patriot-act/; ACLU, "How the Anti-terrorism Bill Permits Indefinite Detention of Immigrants," October 23, 2001, https://www.aclu.org/documents/how-anti-terrorism-bill-permits-indefinite-detention-immigrants. For a thorough description and critique of the act, see Susan N. Herman, *Taking Liberties: The War on Terror and the Erosion of Democracy* (Oxford University Press, 2014).
87 Sweet, interview with author, July 18, 2017.
88 Leslie Cagan, interview with author, October 22, 2016.
89 Information and media about the event is available at https://web.archive.org/web/20020601091241/http://www.artistsnetwork.org/news3/news155.html.
90 Michael Slate, "ArtSpeaks 2002: Jammin' Against the War," *Revolutionary Worker*, May 6, 2002, https://web.archive.org/web/20020806220433/http://rwor.org/A/V24/1151-1160/1152/artspeaks.htm.
91 Video of Williams performing the pledge is available on YouTube at https://www.youtube.com/watch?v=oQ_o66odooc.
92 "Not in Our Name Pledge of Resistance Launched Nationwide," Not in Our Name, June 6, 2002, https://web.archive.org/web/20020803095911/http://www.notinourname.net/kickoff.html.
93 The *LA Times* article is archived at https://web.archive.org/web/20020601091241/http://www.artistsnetwork.org/news3/news155.html.
94 Reilly shares his biography in the *Courage to Resist* podcast episode "Intentionally Trying to Disrupt the Machine," June 12, 2019, https://couragetoresist.org/podcast-ward-reilly/.
95 A photograph of the note was shared by Reilly with the author in an email from July 17, 2024.
96 Reports on the June 6 actions are available at https://web.archive.org/web/20020804003529/http://www.notinourname.net/boston.html.
97 In prison on 9/11, he was placed in solitary confinement, allegedly for

his safety. Others jailed for political acts got similar treatment, leading his family to believe that the government was isolating dissidents in the prison system. Frida Berrigan, interview with author, July 14, 2023.
98 "We Won't Deny Our Consciences," *Guardian*, June 14, 2002, https://www.theguardian.com/world/2002/jun/14/usa.internationaleducationnews1.
99 George W. Bush, "State of the Union Address," January 29, 2002, https://www.mtholyoke.edu/acad/intrel/bush/stateoftheunion.htm.
100 Tom Shanker and David E. Sanger, "U.S. Envisions Blueprint on Iraq Including Big Invasion Next Year," *New York Times*, April 28, 2002, https://www.nytimes.com/2002/04/28/world/nation-challenged-military-us-envisions-blueprint-iraq-including-big-invasion.html.
101 "Cheney: Arab leaders worry about Iraq," CNN, March 24, 2002, https://www.cnn.com/2002/WORLD/asiapcf/central/03/24/cheney.iraq/?related.
102 "Full Text: In Cheney's Words," *New York Times*, August 26, 2002, https://www.nytimes.com/2002/08/26/international/middleeast/full-text-in-cheneys-words.html.
103 David Johnson and James Risen, "Officials Say 2 More Planes May Have Been in the Assault," *New York Times*, September 26, 2001; "The Vice President Appears on NBC's Meet the Press," White House news release, December 9, 2001, https://georgewbush-whitehouse.archives.gov/vicepresident/news-speeches/speeches/print/vp20011209.html.
104 "U.S. Says Hussein Intensifies Hunt for A-Bomb Parts," *New York Times*, September 8, 2002, https://www.nytimes.com/2002/09/08/world/threats-responses-iraqis-us-says-hussein-intensifies-quest-for-bomb-parts.html.
105 Michael Isikoff and David Corn, *Hubris: The Inside Story of Spin, Scandal, and the Selling of the Iraq War* (Crown, 2006), 35.
106 Cheney interview: *Meet the Press*, September 8, 2002, https://www.leadingtowar.com/PDFsources_claims_aluminum/2002_09_08_NBC.pdf.
107 "Top Bush Officials Push Case Against Saddam," CNN, September 8, 2002.
108 W. Lucas Robinson and Steven Livingston, "Strange Bedfellows: The Emergence of the Al Qaeda-Baathist New Frame Prior to the 2003 Invasion of Iraq," in *Leading to the 2003 Iraq War: The Global Media Debate*, edited by Alexander G. Nikolaev and Ernest A. Hakanen (Palgrave Macmillan, 2006), 23–37.
109 "U.S. Public Thinks Saddam Had a Role in 9/11," *Guardian*, September 6, 2002, https://www.theguardian.com/world/2003/sep/07/usa.theobserver.
110 No consensus understanding exists about why, precisely, the Bush administration went to war with Iraq. One notable account, at odds with my own, comes from Melvyn P. Leffler, *Confronting Saddam Hussein: George W. Bush and the Invasion of Iraq* (Oxford University Press, 2023).

Based on interviews with all the principals—save President Bush—in the White House, the Pentagon, and the national security establishment, Leffler makes a host of claims. Far from a foregone conclusion, he asserts, the US invasion was the product of a strategy of "coercive diplomacy." In Leffler's account, the escalating threats of attack, and military mobilization for it, were meant to force Saddam to voluntarily step down as Iraq's leader, or comply more for fully with US demands for information about potential WMD, or both. Bush finally decided to go to war only in early 2003 after Saddam's alleged defiance forced Bush to make good on his threats. Leffler also maintains that Bush administration officials operated entirely in good faith; were genuinely motivated by fear of an Iraqi terror attack, not any wish for conquest; had no designs on Iraq prior to 9/11; sincerely believed that Iraq had WMD; and initially sought to avoid war.

Hotly debated by scholars of foreign policy, Leffler's account has a number of problems. First, Leffler accepts at face value the potentially self-serving testimony from ex-officials about their motivations and decisions. Second, he ignores, minimizes, or excuses the outrageous claims of administration officials asserting the certainty that Iraq had both WMD and hostile intent. Third, Leffler excuses these claims too easily, given documented doubts within the intelligence community about their veracity. And fourth, Leffler fails, in my view, to make a credible case that Saddam's alleged defiance or efforts to thwart the new weapons inspectors, installed in late 2002, in any way necessitated a US attack—even as a way to ensure the credibility of US threats. Leffler also downplays the role of neoconservative ideology in and around the Bush administration favoring a new Pax Americana achieved by military means.

Acknowledging the disaster the Iraq War became, Leffler faults primarily bad military and political planning and the "hubris" of government officials who believed too strongly in the global appeal of US-style democracy. Much of the Iraq insurgency, as I show, was driven not by resistance to American ideals or the effects of bad planning but by the brutality—including the killing of civilians and abuse of Iraqi captives—of the US invasion. Violence of this sort plays virtually no role in Leffler's understanding of why Iraq policy failed.

111 The episode was reported by Bush's top counterterrorism official, in testimony and his book. Richard C. Clarke, *Against All Enemies: Inside America's War on Terror* (Free Press, 2004).
112 On Curveball, see Isikoff and Corn, *Hubris*, 129–32, 164–65, 308–9.
113 Douglas Jehl, "Qaeda-Iraq Link U.S. Cited Is Tied to Coercion Claim," *New York Times*, December 9, 2005, https://www.nytimes.com/2005/12/09/politics/qaedairaq-link-us-cited-is-tied-to-coercion-claim.html. See also Isikoff and Corn, *Hubris*, 119–25.

114 Isikoff and Corn, *Hubris*, 33–42.
115 A transcript of the speech is available at https://edition.cnn.com/2002/ALLPOLITICS/10/07/bush.transcript/.
116 Liza Featherstone, "Peace Gets a Chance," *The Nation*, October 10, 2002, https://www.thenation.com/article/archive/peace-gets-chance/.
117 "Join the Pledge of Resistance!," https://web.archive.org/web/20021004040027/http://www.peacepledge.org/resist/default.htm. The pledge is available at https://web.archive.org/web/20021028094116/http://peacepledge.org/pledgecombined.pdf.
118 Benjamin, interview with author.
119 Video of the disruption is available at https://therealnews.com/stories/mbenjamin0207raipt3.
120 Jennifer Pearson Bonnett, "Lodians Flock to Stockton to See President Bush," August 23, 2002, https://www.lodinews.com/article_e0073ad0-14ea-5c9b-be46-11e0e32ecaca.html.
121 Joe Garofoli, "S.F. Woman's Relentless March for Peace," *SF Gate*, October 26, 2002, https://www.sfgate.com/politics/joegarofoli/article/S-F-woman-s-relentless-march-for-peace-Global-2759423.php.
122 Potorti, *September 11th Families*, 170.
123 See Potorti, *September 11th Families*, 155–60, 165–66.
124 Flyer for vigil, BFP, box 30, folder 4.
125 "Afghan Portraits of Grief: The Civilian/Innocent Victims of U.S. Bombing in Afghanistan," Global Exchange and Peaceful Tomorrows, Fall 2002.
126 Potorti, *September 11th Families*, 179–81.
127 Featherstone, "Peace Gets a Chance."
128 Meg Bartlett, "Emergency Medical Worker on 9/11, Ground Zero for Peace," Not in Our Name, https://web.archive.org/web/20021005085259/http://www.notinourname.net/emtforpeace.html.
129 This summary of demonstrations is based on diverse media stories and report-backs posted on NION's website, http://www.notinourname.net/Reports/oct6natl.htm.
130 Jennifer Langhston, "Thousands Walk for Peace," *Seattle Post-Intelligencer*, October 7, 2002, http://www.why-war.com/cgi-bin/fulltext.cgi?id=2382.
131 "McDermott Speaks Out Against War," Associated Press, October 7, 2002.
132 On the New York City protest, see http://www.notinourname.net/Reports/oct6_nyc.htm.
133 "Sarandon, Robbins Join War Protest in NYC," Associated Press. October 7, 2002, http://www.why-war.com/cgi-bin/fulltext.cgi?id=2360.
134 John Tarleton, "20,000 Gather in Central Park to Say No to Endless War," October 7, 2002. http://www.johntarleton.net/centralpark.html.
135 Sweet, interview with author, July 18, 2017.
136 Michael Wilson, "Thousands at Central Park Rally Oppose an Iraq War," *New York Times*, October 7, 2002, https://www.nytimes.com/2002/10

/07/nyregion/thousands-at-central-park-rally-oppose-an-iraq-war
.html.
137 Elizabeth Fernandez, "8,000 in SF Part of Growing Resistance," *San Francisco Chronicle*, October 7, 2002, http://www.why-war.com/cgi-bin/fulltext.cgi?id=2366.
138 Featherstone, "Peace Gets a Chance."
139 Michelle Goldberg, "Peace Kooks," *Salon*, October 17, 2002, https://www.salon.com/2002/10/16/protest_14/.
140 Tarleton, "20,000 Gather in Central Park."

CHAPTER 5

1 House Joint Resolution 114, "Authorization for Use of Military Force Against Iraq Resolution of 2002," https://www.congress.gov/bill/107th-congress/house-joint-resolution/114.
2 John King, "Bush Calls Saddam 'The Guy Who Tried to Kill My Dad,'" CNN, September 27, 2002, https://edition.cnn.com/2002/ALLPOLITICS/09/27/bush.war.talk/.
3 This episode and other Gulf War propaganda are discussed in John R. MacArthur, *Second Front: Censorship and Propaganda in the Gulf War* (Hill and Wang, 1992).
4 On the Vietnam syndrome and its evolving meanings, see Myra Mendible, "Post-Vietnam Syndrome: National Identity, War, and the Politics of Humiliation," Library of Social Science, https://www.libraryofsocialscience.com/essays/mendible-post-vietnam/.
5 Max Elbaum, "The Storm at Home," *Crossroads*, April 1991, 7.
6 These tenets reflect the popular understanding of the doctrine, which had in military discourse additional, technical aspects.
7 Elbaum, "The Storm at Home," 15.
8 Brian Becker, interview with author, January 3, 2018.
9 Max Elbaum, interview with author, July 30, 2017.
10 Art Laffin, "Speaking Truth to Power," *The Little Way*, Spring 1998; Eric Charles May, "19 Arrested Protesting Gulf Action," *Washington Post*, December 31, 1990, https://www.washingtonpost.com/archive/local/1990/12/31/19-arrested-protesting-gulf-action/af8a4623-7db8-481c-b66c-9acc7f40edf4/.
11 Peter Applebome, "Day of Protests Is the Biggest Yet," *New York Times*, January 27, 1991, https://www.nytimes.com/1991/01/27/us/war-in-the-gulf-antiwar-rallies-day-of-protests-is-the-biggest-yet.html.
12 Patrick G. Coy, Lynne M. Woehrle and Gregory M. Many, "Discursive Legacies: The U.S. Peace Movement and 'Support the Troops,'" *Social Problems* 55, no. 2 (2008): 168. My depiction of the Vietnam Syndrome draws heavily on this essay.

13 Steven Komarow, "House Overwhelmingly Approves Gulf Resolution," January 18, 1991, Associated Press, https://apnews.com/c46a546216fe5bf51f5afdfbb8a5f6a4.
14 There is no consensus estimate of the number of Iraqi casualties, and proposed figures differ greatly. On debates over the numbers, see Jack Kelly, "Estimates of Deaths in First War Still in Dispute," *Post-Gazette*, February 16, 2003, https://old.post-gazette.com/nation/20030216casualty0216p5.asp. The figure of a hudred thousand civilian deaths comes from researcher Beth Daponte, though other estimates are lower.
15 "U.S. Service Casualties in Gulf War," Associated Press, April 4, 1991, https://apnews.com/0239d33021c62c008393a02fadfcc7ef.
16 Andrew J. Bacevich, *America's War for the Greater Middle East* (Random House, 2017), 128.
17 E. J. Dionne Jr., "Kicking the 'Vietnam Syndrome," *Washington Post*, March 4, 1991, https://www.washingtonpost.com/archive/politics/1991/03/04/kicking-the-vietnam-syndrome/b6180288-4b9e-4d5f-b303-befa2275524d/.
18 Robert D. McFadden, "In a Ticker-Tape Blizzard, New York Honors the Troops," *New York Times*, June 11, 1991, https://www.nytimes.com/1991/06/11/nyregion/new-york-salutes-in-a-ticker-tape-blizzard-new-york-honors-the-troops.html.
19 Bush told Deputy National Security Advisor Richard Gates, "If I don't get the votes, I'm going to do it anyway. And if I get impeached, so be it." Quoted in John Meachum, "The Hidden Hard Line Side of George H.W. Bush," *Politico*, November 30, 2018, https://www.politico.com/magazine/story/2015/11/jon-meacham-book-george-h-w-bush-213347.
20 Daponte estimates tens of thousands of casualties, which other researchers place higher or lower.
21 Quoted in Hussain al-Qatari and Jon Gambrell, "1991 Gulf War Looms Large over Bush's Mideast Legacy," Associated Press, December 1, 2018, https://apnews.com/5d2c40647d4e43a6adf65c94c534cb86.
22 See Anthony Arnove, ed., *Iraq Under Siege: The Deadly Impact of Sanctions and War* (South End Press, 2000).
23 IAC Press Conference, US-Iraq Relations, January 2, 2002, https://www.c-span.org/video/?168036-1/us-policy-iraq.
24 Becker, interview with author, January 23, 2018.
25 IAC Press Conference.
26 Seth Sandronsky, "Voices for the Voiceless," *Common Dreams*, November 2, 2002.
27 Laffin, "Speaking Truth to Power."
28 Rahul Majahan, "We Think the Price Is Worth It," *FAIR*, November 1, 2001, https://fair.org/extra/we-think-the-price-is-worth-it/.
29 Art Laffin, email to author, February 13, 2015.
30 IAC, "The Sanctions Must be Ended," BFP, box 22, folder 14.

31 Global Exchange, "Top Ten Reasons Not to Invade Iraq," flyer, author's possession.
32 Richard Falk, "A Dangerous Game," *The Nation*, September 19, 2002, https://www.thenation.com/article/archive/dangerous-game/.
33 "Iraq: The Doubters Grow," *The Nation*, August 15, 2002, https://www.thenation.com/article/archive/iraq-doubters-grow/.
34 "An Open Letter to the Members of Congress," *The Nation*, September 25, 2002, https://www.thenation.com/article/archive/open-letter-members-congress/.
35 Jonathan Schell, "Letter from Ground Zero," *The Nation*, September 5, 2002, https://www.thenation.com/article/archive/letter-ground-zero-50/.
36 Robert Byrd, "The War Debate," *Los Angeles Times*, October 9, 2002, http://www.commondreams.org/views02/1009-07.htm.
37 Stephen Zunes, "The Case Against the War," *The Nation*, September 12, 2002. https://www.thenation.com/article/archive/case-against-war/.
38 Paul Berman, *Terror and Liberalism* (W. W. Norton, 2003), 4.
39 Michael Ignatieff, "The American Empire; the Burden," *New York Times Magazine*, January 5, 2003, https://www.nytimes.com/2003/01/05/magazine/the-american-empire-the-burden.html.
40 George Packer, "The Liberal Quandary Over Iraq," *New York Times*, December 8, 2002, https://www.nytimes.com/2002/12/08/magazine/the-liberal-quandary-over-iraq.html.
41 George Packer, *The Assassin's Gate: America in Iraq* (Farrar, Straus & Giroux, 2005), 84–87.
42 *Washington Post-ABC News Poll*, January 21, 2003. The poll released for this date also shows data for prior months. Extensive polling was conducted on attitudes toward an Iraq war by numerous research and media organizations. My summary of public opinion is based on a few exemplary polls.
43 Lydia Saad, "Top Ten Findings About Public Opinion and Iraq," Gallup, October 8, 2002, https://news.gallup.com/poll/6964/top-ten-findings-about-public-opinion-iraq.aspx. With five thousand American dead, 60 percent opposed the conflict, according to a fall 2002 survey.
44 Saad, "Top Ten Findings."
45 *Washington Post-ABC News Poll*, December 18, 2002.
46 Vice President Cheney made the "greeted as liberators" remark on *Meet the Press* on September 14, 2002, http://www.nbcnews.com/id/3080244/ns/meet_the_press/t/transcript-sept/#.Xr7EPC-ZPaY.
47 Zunes, "The Case Against the War."
48 Nancy Trejos, "Antiwar Activists Plan to Stay the Course," *Washington Post*, November 18, 2002.
49 Ann Moline, "'Code Pink' White House Vigil Continues," *We-news*, December 29, 2002, https://womensenews.org/2002/12/code-pink-white-house-vigil-continues/.

50 Medea Benjamin, interview with author, December 5, 2017; Medea Benjamin and Jodie Evans, "Preface," in *Stop the Next War Now: Effective Responses to Violence and Terrorism*, edited by Medea Benjamin and Jodie Evans (New World, 2010), xv.
51 SHE Living TV, "SHE Speaks: Jodie Evans of Code Pink," February 23, 2016, https://www.youtube.com/watch?v=2idHbLmKkTE.
52 Jodie Evans, "A Fierce and Tender Heart," in *Moonrise: The Power of Women Leading from the Heart*, edited by Nina Simons (Perk Street Press, 2010).
53 Interview with Jodie Evans, *The Progressive*, November 30, 2011, https://progressive.org/magazine/interview-jodie-evans/.
54 Wilson was the subject of a documentary, *Texas Gold*, directed by Carolyn M. Scott, 2005.
55 Benjamin, interview with author.
56 Rae Abileah, interview with author, August 12, 2021.
57 Stephen Henderson, "Women Press a Call for Peace," *Seattle Times*, October 8, 2002, https://web.archive.org/web/20030302214103/http://www.commondreams.org/headlines02/1008-01.htm.
58 Liza Featherstone, "Mighty in Pink," *The Nation*, February 13, 2003, https://www.thenation.com/article/archive/mighty-pink/.
59 See Rachel V. Kutz-Flamenbaum, "Code Pink, Raging Grannies, and the Missile Dick Chicks: Feminist Performance Activism in the Contemporary Anti-war Movement," *NWSA Journal* 19, no. 1 (2007): 89–105.
60 Darryl McGrath, "Women in New York State Fast for Peace," *We-news*, December 18, 2002, https://womensenews.org/2002/12/code-pink-white-house-vigil-continues/.
61 Claire Bayard, interview with author, July 31, 2017.
62 Brian Becker, interview with author, March 24, 2018.
63 On this history, see Michael R. Fischbach, *The Movement and the Middle East: How the Arab-Israeli Conflict Divided the American Left* (Stanford University Press, 2019); Michael R. Fischbach, *Black Power and Palestine: Transnational Countries of Color* (Stanford University Press, 2018).
64 Becker, interview with author, March 24, 2018.
65 Liza Featherstone, "Strange Marchfellows," *The Nation*, April 25, 2002, https://www.thenation.com/article/archive/strange-marchfellows/.
66 "Quote of the Day," *New York Times*, September 7, 2002, https://www.nytimes.com/2002/09/07/nyregion/quotation-of-the-day-766518.html.
67 Becker, interview with author, March 24, 2018.
68 Tom Wells, "Two Wars, Two Movements: Iraq in Light of Vietnam," *Fast Capitalism* 1, no. 2 (2005): 39. Wells offers a detailed comparison, as of spring 2005, of the two movements.
69 The full protest was broadcast live on C-SPAN: "Anti-war Rally," October 26, 2002, https://www.c-span.org/video/?173521-1/anti-war-rally. All quotes and descriptions of the protest are taken from the broadcast.

70 Becker, interview with author, March 24, 2018.
71 Todd Gitlin, "Who Will Lead?" *Mother Jones*, October 14, 2002, https://www.motherjones.com/politics/2002/10/who-will-lead/.
72 David Corn, "Behind the Placards," *LA Weekly*, October 30, 2002, https://www.laweekly.com/behind-the-placards/.
73 Alexander Cockburn, "The Antiwar Movement and Its Critics," *The Nation*, November 14, 2002, https://www.thenation.com/article/archive/antiwar-movement-and-its-critics/.
74 L. A. Kauffman, interview with author, February 21, 2018.
75 Esther Kaplan, "A Hundred Peace Movements Bloom," *The Nation*, December 18, 2002, https://www.thenation.com/article/archive/hundred-peace-movements-bloom/.
76 Becker, interview with author, March 24, 2018.
77 My account of the October 25 meeting is drawn from Van Gosse, interview with author, July 22, 2017; Leslie Cagan, interview with author, October 22, 2016; and "The Founding of United for Peace and Justice," n.d., UFPJ, box 5, folder 5.
78 Gosse, interview with author.
79 Becker, interview with author, March 24, 2018.
80 "Plan for Antiwar Appeal" (minutes of 9/2/02 conference call), donated to author by Van Gosse.
81 Michelle Beyeler and Dieter Rucht, "Political Opportunity Structures and Progressive Movement Sectors," in *The World Says No to War: Demonstrations Against the Iraq War*, edited by Stefaan Walgrave and Dieter Rucht (University of Minnesota Press, 2010), 33.
82 Gosse, interview with author.
83 Van Gosse, "Proposal for a National Moratorium Campaign: No War on Iraq," August 2002, unpublished manuscript donated to author.
84 David Cortright, "Emergency Campaign to Prevent War in Iraq," August 6, 2002, unpublished manuscript donated to author.
85 This biographical sketch, and all quotes, are from Gosse, interview with author.
86 Gerald Sanders, "What Next for the Black Radical Congress?" *Slingshot*, December 27, 1998, https://slingshotcollective.org/05686642ffa835a7d3850f444dcbf773/. On the evolution and demise of the BRC, see Bill Fletcher Jr. and Jamala Rogers, "Creating a Viable Black Left," BlackCommentator.com, April 4, 2013, https://blackcommentator.com/511/511_cover_brc_fletcher_rogers_share.html.
87 Gosse, interview with author.
88 Van Gosse, "Antiwar Movements in the New Century," n.d., unpublished manuscript donated to author.
89 Becker, interview with author, March 24, 2018.

90 "Religious, Civic Leaders Form 'Keep America Safe: Win Without War,'" December 11, 2002, http://www.ncccusa.org/news/02news100.html.
91 Cagan, interview with author, October 22, 2016.
92 Deliberations over the composition of the committee are contained in Van Gosse to Leslie Cagan, private note, n.d., circa late October 2002, donated to author.
93 "About United for Peace & Justice," UFPJ, box 3, folder 5.
94 "About United for Peace & Justice"; see also Van Gosse, "Note to UFP members," circa late October 2002; "United for Peace Conference Call," minutes, November 8, 2002, documents donated to author.
95 Gosse, "The Founding of United for Peace and Justice"; Lynette Clemetson, "Protests Held Across the Country to Oppose War in Iraq," New York Times, December 11, 2002, https://www.nytimes.com/2002/12/11/us/threats-responses-dissent-protests-held-across-country-oppose-war-iraq.html; Allan Thompson, "Diverse Groups Gather to Protest War with Iraq," Toronto Star, December 10, 2002, https://web.archive.org/web/20030817094748/http://www.unitedforpeace.org/article.php?id=304.
96 Steve Baggarly, email to author, July 11, 2004. On their conviction, see "Six Months for Holy Innocents Witness," Nuclear Resister, April 24, 2003, 132–33.
97 Clemetson, "Protests Held Across the Country."
98 Evelyn Nieves, "Antiwar Effort Gains Momentum," Washington Post, December 2, 2002, https://www.washingtonpost.com/archive/politics/2002/12/02/antiwar-effort-gains-momentum/7ec4a2e4-9cf0-4174-880e-08323576333b/.
99 Nieves, "Antiwar Effort Gains Momentum."
100 Kaplan, "A Hundred Peace Movements Bloom."
101 Lisa Fithian, interview with author, June 29, 2022.
102 Cagan, interview with author, October 22, 2016.

CHAPTER 6

1 This tally comes from the documentary about the protests *We Are Many*, directed by Amir Amirani (We Are Many Productions, 2014).
2 Estimates of the size of individual protests vary widely. These figures are drawn from essays in Stefaan Walgrave and Dieter Rucht, eds., *The World Says No to War: Demonstrations Against the Iraq War* (University of Minnesota Press, 2010). See especially "February 15: Country, City, Organizers, Turnouts and Mobilization Level," 17–18.
3 *We Are Many*.
4 Patrick E. Tyler, "A New Power in the Streets," *New York Times*, February 17, 2003, https://www.nytimes.com/2003/02/17/world/threats-and-responses-news-analysis-a-new-power-in-the-streets.html.

5 *We Are Many.*
6 Joris Verhulst, "February 15, 2003: The World Says No to War," in Walgrave and Rucht, eds., *The World Says No to War*, 9.
7 Chris Nineham, "The European Social Forum in Florence," *Z-Net*, December 17, 2002, https://zcomm.org/znetarticle/the-european-social-forum-in-florence-by-chris-nineham/.
8 Nineham, "The European Social Forum in Florence."
9 On international organizing for February 15, see Verhulst, "February 15, 2003," 8–13.
10 *We Are Many.*
11 Brian Becker, interview with author, March 24, 2018.
12 Quoted in Ian Sinclair, *The March That Shook Blair: An Oral History of 15 February 2003* (Peace News Press, 2013), 115–16.
13 Verhulst, "February 15, 2003," 12–13.
14 On the StWC's origins, see Sinclair, *The March That Shook Blair*, 52–63.
15 On European attitudes, see Joris Verhulst and Stefan Walgrave "Politics, Public Opinion, and the Media: The Issues and Context Behind the Demonstrations" in Walgrave and Rucht, eds., *The World Says No to War*, 42–60.
16 Verhulst and Walgrave, "Politics, Public Opinion," 56.
17 Milan Rai, *War Plan Iraq: Ten Reasons Against War in Iraq* (Arrow, 2002). Verso, with offices in New York City, also published the text.
18 Dina Kraft, "Mandela Backs Away from Unconditional Support of the War on Terror," Associated Press, January 3, 2001, https://web.archive.org/web/20020911140308/http://www.commondreams.org/headlines02/0103-03.htm.
19 "Mandela: U.S. a Threat to World Peace," UPI, September 10, 2002, https://www.upi.com/Defense-News/2002/09/10/Mandela-US-a-threat-to-world-peace/69631031699916/.
20 "Mandela on War on Its Eve," *The Independent*, January 30, 2003, https://web.archive.org/web/20030217011930/http://www.unitedforpeace.org/article.php?id=756.
21 On Goldsmith, see Ann Wright and Susan Dixon, *Dissent: Government Insiders Speak Out Against the Iraq War* (Koa, 2008), 8–22.
22 Wright and Dixon, *Dissent*, 12–13.
23 "US and UK Unions Pen Anti-war Letter," *Guardian*, January 31, 2003, https://www.theguardian.com/politics/2003/jan/31/tradeunions.uk.
24 Verhulst and Walgrave, "Politics, Public Opinion," 57.
25 David Cortright, "The World Says No: The Global Movement Against the War in Iraq," in *Iraq Crisis and World Order: Structural, Institutional, and Normative Challenges*, edited by Ramesh Thakur and Waheguru Pal Singh Sidhu (United Nations University Press, 2006), 87.
26 Leslie Cagan, interview with author, October 22, 2016.

27 L. A. Kauffman, interview with author, February 21, 2018.
28 Cagan, interview with author, October 22, 2016.
29 Kauffman, interview with author.
30 UFPJ Traffic Dashboard, March 19–August 4, 2003, UFPJ, box 3, folder 5.
31 Chris Hedges, "A Longtime Antiwar Activist, Escalating the Peace," *New York Times*, February 4, 2003, https://www.nytimes.com/2003/02/04/nyregion/public-lives-a-longtime-antiwar-activist-escalating-the-peace.html/
32 CUNY TV, "Eldridge & Co.: Leslie Cagan," May 4, 2011, https://www.youtube.com/watch?v=Py5LlAEMd1Y.
33 Dennis Loy Johnson and Valerie Merians, eds., *What We Do Know* (Melville House, 2004), 81.
34 Cagan, interview with author, October 22, 2016.
35 "UFPJ appeal, letter to groups," early 2003, unpublished manuscript donated to author by Van Gosse.
36 Cagan, interview with author, October 22, 2016.
37 Cagan, interview with author, October 22, 2016.
38 Kauffman, interview with author.
39 Medea Benjamin, interview with author, December 5, 2017.
40 Benjamin, interview with author.
41 Cagan, interview with author, October 22, 2016.
42 This profile of BPfB is based on Rusti Eisenberg, interview with author, June 13, 2019; and work in the group's archives. The group later changed its name to Brooklyn for Peace.
43 BPfP, "10 Reasons Not to Go to War Against Iraq" and "15 Feb NYC—No to War," BFP, box 17, folder 16.
44 Into February, UFPJ posters listed "Location TBD"; on the eve of the protest the Forty-Ninth Street selection was inserted.
45 Opinion—*United for Peace and Justice v. The City of New York; Michael Bloomberg, Mayor of the City of New York; and Raymond Kelly, Commissioner of the New York City Police Department*, February 10, 2003, 1–2 (hereafter *UFPJ v. NYC*), UFPJ, box 2, folder 2. A detailed timeline of negotiations and legal wrangling is also in Christopher Dunn, Arthur Eisenberg, Donna Lieberman, Alan Silver, and Alex Vitale, "Arresting Protest: A Special Report of the New York Civil Liberties Union on New York City's Protest Policies at the February 15, 2003, Antiwar Demonstration in New York City," NYCLU, April 2003, 3–6.
46 Cagan, interview with author, October 22, 2016.
47 Dunn et al., "Arresting Protest," 4.
48 Robert Byrd, Speech on Senate Floor, February 12, 2003, https://web.archive.org/web/20030821073914/http://www.unitedforpeace.org/article.php?id=955.
49 *UFPJ v. NYC*, 4.

50 Dunn et al., "Arresting Protest," 5.
51 *UFPJ v. NYC*, 23.
52 *UFPJ v. NYC*, 23.
53 *UFPJ v. NYC*, 16.
54 *UFPJ v. NYC*, 11–12. To no avail, UFPJ filed an "emergency appeal." Memorandum in Support of Plaintiff's Request for a Preliminary Injunction," NYCLU Foundation, February 11, 2003, UFPJ, box 2, folder 2.
55 Susan Saulny, "Court Bans Peace March in Manhattan," *New York Times*, February 11, 2003, https://www.nytimes.com/2003/02/11/nyregion/court-bans-peace-march-in-manhattan.html.
56 Cagan, interview with author, October 22, 2016.
57 Thomas E. Ricks, "NATO Allies Trade Barbs over Iraq," *Washington Post*, February 9, 2003.
58 "Statement by France to Security Council," *New York Times*, February 14, 2003, https://www.nytimes.com/2003/02/14/international/middleeast/statement-by-france-to-security-council.html.
59 CNN, "U.N. Report Reinforces Security Council Divisions," February 14, 2003, https://www.cnn.com/2003/US/02/14/sprj.irq.un/.
60 Cortright, "The World Says No," 80.
61 Sinclair, *The March that Shook Blair*, 167.
62 Sinclair, *The March that Shook Blair*, 188. Subsequent quotes from pages 180 and 181.
63 Eugene Ferguson, "One Million. And Still they Came," *The Observer*, February 16, 2003, https://web.archive.org/web/20031021120047/http://www.unitedforpeace.org/article.php?id=1074.
64 "'Million' March Against Iraq War," *BBC News*, February 16, 2003, http://news.bbc.co.uk/2/hi/uk_news/2765041.stm.
65 *We Are Many*.
66 Sinclair, *The World Says No to Blair*, 211.
67 *We Are Many*.
68 "Blair Speech—Key Quotes," *BBC News*, February 15, 2003, http://news.bbc.co.uk/2/hi/uk_news/politics/2765763.stm.
69 Sinclair, *The World Says No to Blair*, 190. Subsequent quotes from 191–92, 199.
70 "Cities Jammed in Worldwide Protest of Iraq War," CNN, February 16, 2003, https://www.cnn.com/2003/US/02/15/sprj.irq.protests.main/.
71 The full speakers list as of a February 10 is on the UFPJ website at https://web.archive.org/web/20030513150805/http://www.unitedforpeace.org/article.php?id=799.
72 "Singer Harry Belafonte, Danny Glover, and Activist Angela Davis Speak to Hundreds of Thousands in NYC," *Democracy Now!*, February 17, 2003, https://www.democracynow.org/2003/2/17/singer_harry_belafonte_danny_glover_and.

73 *We Are Many.*
74 Phyllis Bennis, interview with author, June 27, 2022.
75 Cagan, interview with author, October 22, 2016.
76 Naeem Mohaiemen, *Daily Start* (Bangladesh), February 19, 2003, https://web.archive.org/web/20031021121714/http://www.unitedforpeace.org/article.php?id=1179.
77 Starhawk, "What Happened in New York," February 19, 2003, https://web.archive.org/web/20030529052721/http://www.unitedforpeace.org/article.php?id=1174. For a detailed account of the chaotic day and testimony of police abuse, see Dunn et al., "Arresting Protest," 7–22.
78 Alex Vitale, "Analysis of the NYPD's Use of Demonstration Pens," March 2004, UFPJ, box 2, folder 2.
79 "Draft Letter to Mr. Raymond Kelly by Dr. Ellen Fitzrider," March 17, 2003, UFPJ, box 6, folder 33.
80 David Potorti, with Peaceful Tomorrows, *September 11th Families for Peaceful Tomorrows: Turning Our Grief into Action* (RDV Books, 2003), 224–25.
81 Ian Head, "Legal Observers Maker Presence Felt at New York Anti-war Demonstration," *Guild Notes*, Spring 2003, 11–12.
82 "A Statement from Those Arrested at the Peace Demonstrations in New York on February 15, 2003," UFPJ, box 6, folder 33.
83 Marina Sitrin and Mae Scott, "Sing, Shout, Resist," *Guild Notes*, Spring 2003, 13; Dunn et al., "Arresting Protest," 21.
84 Dunn et al., "Arresting Protest," 10.
85 Gale Brewer, Letter to Raymond Kelly, February 21, 2003, UFP, box 2, folder 2.
86 Shaila K. Dewan, "Protesters Say City Police Used Rough Tactics at Rally," *New York Times*, February 19, 2003, https://www.nytimes.com/2003/02/19/nyregion/protesters-say-city-police-used-rough-tactics-at-rally.html.
87 Sitrin and Scott, "Sing, Shout, Resist," 13.
88 Dewan, "Protesters Say City Police Used Rough Tactics at Rally."
89 "A Statement from Those Arrested at the Peace Demonstrations."
90 Starhawk, "What Happened in New York."
91 *We Are Many.*
92 Cagan, interview with author, October 22, 2016.
93 Sinclair, *The March that Shook Blair*, 228.
94 Sinclair, *The March that Shook Blair*, 228.
95 Cagan, interview with author, October 22, 2016.
96 Ruth Rosen, "Global Protest, New World Politics," *San Francisco Chronicle*, February 20, 2003, https://web.archive.org/web/20030506000106/http://www.unitedforpeace.org/article.php?id=1182.
97 Dieter Rucht and Joris Verhulst, "The Framing of Opposition to the War on Iraq," in Walgrave and Rucht, eds., *The World Says No to War*, 255.
98 The research was published in the multiessay volume *The World Says No*

to War, cited above. The methodology of the surveys is explained in Appendix A, 175–284.
99 Stefaan Walgrave and Dieter Rucht, "Introduction," in Walgrave and Rucht, eds., *The World Says No to War*, xiv.
100 Stefaan Walgrave, Dieter Rucht, and Peter van Aelst, "New Activists or Old Leftists? The Demographics of Protestors," in Walgrave and Rucht, eds., *The World Says No to War*, 84–85.
101 Thorough demographic date is arrayed in Walgrave et al., "New Activists or Old Leftists?," 83. The below data is drawn from 82–93.
102 Donata Della Porta, "Paths to February 15 Protest: Social or Political Determinants?," in Walgrave and Rucht, eds., *The World Says No to War*, 131.
103 Walgrave et al., "New Activists or Old Leftists?," 93–94.
104 Della Porta, "Paths to February 15 Protest," 127, 131–32.
105 Walgrave et al., "New Activists or Old Leftists?," 87. Subsequent quotes from the same page.
106 Bert Klandermans, "Peace Demonstrators or Antigovernment marches? The Political Attitudes of Protestors" in Walgrave and Rucht, eds., *The World Says No to War*, 102–3.
107 Walgrave and Rucht, "Introduction," xvi.
108 Sydney Tarrow, "Preface," in Walgrave and Rucht, eds., *The World Says No to War*, xvi; Walgrave and Rucht, "Introduction," xvi.
109 Phyllis Bennis, *Challenging Empire: How People, Governments, and the UN Defy US Power* (Olive Branch Press, 2006), 90.
110 See Michael Bush, "This Is an Uprising: A Conversation with Mark Engler," http://www.warscapes.com/conversations/uprising-conversation-mark-engler.
111 Cagan, interview with author, October 22, 2016.
112 Starhawk, "What Happened in New York."
113 Cagan, interview with author, October 22, 2016.

CHAPTER 7

1 Leslie Cagan, interview with author, October 22, 2016.
2 The intended use of a "shock and awe" strategy was first reported by *CBS News* on January 24, 2003, as communicated by a Pentagon official. The phrase, debatable as a description of the actual assault, was quickly picked up by the media, everywhere appearing in the run-up to the war. See John T. Correll, "What Happened to Shock and Awe?," *Air Force Magazine*, November 1, 2003, https://www.airforcemag.com/article/1103shock/.
3 "Some Critical Media Voices Face Censorship," *FAIR*, April 3, 2003. Donahue was fired on February 23, 2003.
4 Claire Bayard, interview with author, July 31, 2017.

NOTES TO PAGES 172–177   411

5   Footage of the San Francisco protest is available on YouTube at https://www.youtube.com/watch?v=Yvg7uZm4UW8.
6   The theatrical protests were documented in *Operation Lysistrata*, directed by Michael Patrick Kelly (Aquapio Films, 2006).
7   Sam Hamill, ed., *Poets Against the War* (Thunders Mouth Press, 2003), xvii. Subsequent quotes from xviii.
8   *Playbill*, "Poets Not Fit for the White House," donated to author by Matt Daloisio.
9   Hamill, *Poets Against the War*, xvii.
10 Hamill, *Poets Against the War*, 8–9.
11 My description of the project, and the quotes below, are drawn from *Operation Lysistrata*.
12 The website is archived at http://lysistrataprojectarchive.com/lys/.
13 See "The UN's Decline: Timeline," Al Jazeera, March 16, 2004, https://www.aljazeera.com/news/2004/3/16/the-uns-decline-timeline.
14 Sarah Anderson, Phyllis Bennis, and John Cavanagh, "Coalition of the Willing or Coalition of the Coerced?" Institute for Policy Studies, February 26, 2003.
15 Anderson et al., "Coalition of the Willing," 11.
16 David Cortright, "The World Says No: The Global Movement Against the War in Iraq," in *Iraq Crisis and World Order: Structural, Institutional, and Normative Challenges*, edited by Ramesh Thakur and Waheguru Pal Singh Sidhu (United Nations University Press, 2006), 84.
17 Sean Loughlin, "House Cafeterias Change Names for 'French' Fries and 'French' Toast," CNN, March 12, 2003, https://www.cnn.com/2003/ALLPOLITICS/03/11/sprj.irq.fries/.
18 "Students Gather by Hundreds for War Protest," CNN, March 5, 2003, https://www.cnn.com/2003/US/03/05/sprj.irq.rallies/.
19 Brian Long, "Students Pencil in Iraq Protest," CNN, March 5, 2003, http://www.cnn.com/2003/US/03/04/sprj.irq.college.protest/index.html.
20 "Students March to Demand Peace," *Chicago Tribune*, March 6, 2003, https://www.chicagotribune.com/2003/03/06/students-march-to-demand-peace/.
21 "Transcript of Bush news conference on Iraq," CNN, March 6, 2003, https://www.cnn.com/2003/US/03/06/bush.speech.transcript/.
22 Rachel V. Kutz-Flamenbaum, "Code Pink, Raging Grannies, and the Missile Dick Chicks: Feminist Performance Activism in the Contemporary Anti-war Movement," *NWSA Journal* 19, no. 1 (2007): 89–105; quote at 94.
23 Sylvia Moreno and Lena H. Sun, "In Effort to Keep the Peace, Protesters Declare 'Code Pink,'" *Washington Post*, March 9, 2003, https://www.washingtonpost.com/archive/local/2003/03/09/in-effort-to-keep-the-peace-protesters-declare-code-pink/c1e2cf33-1424-46be-9528-307bd0cb1432/.

24 Kutz-Flamenbaum, "Code Pink," 92.
25 Kutz-Flamenbaum, "Code Pink," 94.
26 "Thousands Gather in Washington for Code Pink Peace Demonstration," *Democracy Now!*, March 10, 2003, https://www.democracynow.org/2003/3/10/alice_walker_maxine_hong_kingston_medea.
27 Rae Abileah, interview with author, August 12, 2021.
28 BPfP flyer, Demonstration at Clinton Office, March 8, 2003, BFP, box 17, folder 16.
29 Nancy Kricorian, email to author, August 17, 2021.
30 Rusti Eisenberg, interview with author, June 13, 2019.
31 "Vigil Outside the Office of Senator Hillary Clinton," Brooklyn Parents for Peace, document donated to author by Rusti Eisenberg.
32 Betty Clarke, "Review: The Dixie Chicks," *Guardian*, March 12, 2003. See the documentary *Dixie Chicks: Shut Up and Sing*, directed by Barbara Kopple and Cecilia Peck (Lionsgate Films, 2006); Steve Knopper, "An Oral History of The Chicks' Seismic 2003 Controversy from the Industry Execs Who Lived It," *Billboard*, June 14, 2022, https://www.billboard.com/music/country/chicks-radio-banned-george-bush-oral-history-1235087442/. In 2020, the group dropped "Dixie," renaming itself "The Chicks."
33 Knopper, "An Oral History of The Chicks' Seismic 2003 Controversy."
34 Lynette Clemetson, "Protests Held Across the Country to Oppose War in Iraq," *New York Times*, December 11, 2002, https://www.nytimes.com/2002/12/11/us/threats-responses-dissent-protests-held-across-country-oppose-war-iraq.html.
35 Cortright, "The World Says No," 7–8.
36 Cortright, "The World Says No," 78.
37 Michele Naar-Obed, "Aftermath of a Blockade," *Nonviolent Activist*, May–June 2003, 14.
38 Colleen Creamer, *Nashville City Paper*, February 18, 2003.
39 Kiesling's letter is in Ann Wright and Susan Dixon, *Dissent: Government Insiders Speak Out Against the Iraq War* (Koa, 2008), 27–28.
40 Rone Tempest and Aaron Zitner, "Antiwar Movement Embraces Diplomat Who Quit Over Iraq," *Los Angeles Times*, March 21, 2003, https://www.latimes.com/archives/la-xpm-2003-mar-21-war-kiesling21-story.html.
41 Wright and Dixon, *Dissent*, 30–31.
42 "An Iraq War Dissent—Interview with Ann Wright," Association for Diplomatic Studies and Training, https://adst.org/2014/07/an-iraq-war-dissent/.
43 Wright and Dixon, *Dissent*, xii.
44 Wright and Dixon, *Dissent*, xiii.
45 Wright and Dixon, *Dissent*, 33.
46 Tempest and Zitner, "Antiwar Movement."
47 "Call to Conscience from Veterans to Active Duty Troops and Reservists," December 6, 2002, UFPJ, box 6, folder 33.

48 Jane Collins, *For Love of a Soldier: Interviews with Military Families Taking Action Against War with Iraq* (Lexington, 2008), 1-2.
49 Collins, *For Love of a Soldier*, 2.
50 "Alice Walker, Maxine Hong Kingston, Medea Benjamin & 20 Other Women Arrested Outside the White House," *Democracy Now!*, March 10, 2003, https://www.democracynow.org/2003/3/10/alice_walker_maxine _hong_kingston_medea.
51 Moreno and Sun, "In Effort to Keep the Peace."
52 This account of the Gulf Peace Teams and the formation Voices in the Wilderness, as well as the following quotes, are drawn from Kathy Kelly, interview with author, November 16, 2018.
53 The others were Belgium's Jean Dreze, Bela Bhatia from India, the Dutch American Curtiss Doebbler, Neville Watson from Australia, John Steele from the UK, and the American priest Bob Bossie.
54 On of these talks, organized by the Colorado Muslim Society, is available on YouTube at https://www.youtube.com/watch?v=dgtGEQf9V2Y.
55 Phyllis Bennis, interview with author, June 27, 2022.
56 "Congressional Staffers' Iraq Trip Report, 27 August-6 September 1999," March 21, 2000, https://reliefweb.int/report/iraq/congressional-staffers -iraq-trip-report.
57 "U.N. humanitarian chief for Iraq quits in frustration," CNN, February 14, 2000, http://www.cnn.com/2000/WORLD/meast/02/14/un.von.sponeck /index.html.
58 Voices, "Call for Iraq Peace Team," http://web.archive.org/web/2002080 2063719/http://www.iraqpeaceteam.org:80/pages/announcement.html.
59 On Gish's biography and the CPT's origins, see Peggy Faw Gish, *Iraq: A Journey of Hope and Peace* (Herald Press, 2004), 17-27.
60 On the CPT's founding, philosophy, and activities, see also Tricia Gates Brown, ed., *118 Days: Christian Peacemaker Teams Held Hostage in Iraq* (CPT, 2008); Cassidy Casey, "Unarmed Against the Gunfire," *Nonviolent Activist*, May-June 2000, 4-6; Tricia Gates Brown, ed., *Getting in the Way: Stories from the Christian Peacemaker Teams* (Herald Press, 2005), 11-15.
61 Brown, *118 Days*, 7.
62 This biographical sketch is drawn from Ed Kinane, interview with author, December 12, 2021: Ed Kinane, "Becoming a Counterterrorist," in Steve Breyman, John W. Amidon, Maureen Baillargeon Aumand, eds. *Bending the Arc: Striving for Peace and Justice in the Age of Endless War* (SUNY Press, 2020).
63 Mike Ferner, *Inside the Red Zone: A Veteran for Peace Reports from Iraq* (Praeger, 2006), xiv.
64 Ferner, *Inside the Red Zone*, 7.
65 Gish, *Iraq: A Journey of Hope*, 23.
66 Gish, *Iraq: A Journey of Hope*, 20.

67 Gish, *Iraq: A Journey of Hope*, 87.
68 Kathy Kelly, interview with author. The subsequent quotes from Kelly are from the same.
69 Ferner, *Inside the Red Zone*, 10.
70 Ferner, *Inside the Red Zone*, 9–11.
71 Ferner, *Inside the Red Zone*.
72 Kinane, interview with author.
73 Gish, *Iraq: A Journey of Hope*, 98.
74 Cathy Breen, "A Letter from Baghdad," *Nonviolent Activist*, Jan.–Feb. 2003, 14.
75 John Burns, "12 Americans Stage Protest Hussein Is Happy to Allow," *New York Times*, October 27, 2002, https://www.nytimes.com/2002/10/27/world/threats-and-responses-iraq-12-americans-stage-protest-hussein-is-happy-to-allow.html.
76 Kinane, interview with author.
77 Kathy Kelly, "The View from Missile Street, Iraq," *Nonviolent Activist*, Nov.–Dec. 2003, 4.
78 Anthony Shadid, *Night Draws Near* (Henry Holt, 2005), 5. Subsequent quotes from 17, 47.
79 The story, and all quotes, are drawn from Kathy Kelly, interview with author.
80 Gish, *Iraq: A Journey of Hope*, 92.
81 See Anne-Marie O'Conner, "Women Take a Leading Role in Protesting Against War with Iraq," *Los Angeles Times*, March 15, 2003; and Aaron Rockett, "Iraq: Code Pink," Full Monte Productions, May 28, 2006, https://www.youtube.com/watch?v=0BmnsCfllO4.
82 John Burns, "Actor Follows His Own Script on Iraq and War," *New York Times*, December 16, 2003, https://www.nytimes.com/2002/12/16/world/threats-and-responses-hollywood-actor-follows-his-own-script-on-iraq-and-war.html; "Sean Penn Questions U.S. Policy, Visits Iraq," *ABC News*, January 7, 2002. https://abcnews.go.com/Travel/story?id=118513.
83 George Packer, *The Assassin's Gate: America in Iraq* (Farrar, Straus & Giroux, 2005), 85.
84 Richard Savill, "Bus Peace Convoy Heads for Baghdad," *London Daily Telegraph*, February 2, 2003, https://web.archive.org/web/20030224093521/http://unitedforpeace.org/article.php?id=766.
85 The buses are pictured in the short Australian documentary *Human Shields* (Journeyman Pictures–SBS Australia, 2003), https://www.journeyman.tv/film/1559/human-shields.
86 Ken Nichols O'Keefe, "Back to Iraq as a Human Shield," *Guardian*, December 28, 2002, https://www.theguardian.com/world/2002/dec/29/iraq1.
87 O'Keefe was accused of anti-Semitism, even by movement allies, and consorted with far-right American political figures.
88 These and other travails are depicted in O'Keefe, *Human Shields*.
89 Fawn Vrazo, "Human Shields leave Iraq Disheartened but Not Regretful,"

NOTES TO PAGES 197-201 415

McClatchy, February 2003, https://www.mcclatchydc.com/latest-news/article24435982.html.
90 Colleen Kelly, "Seeking the Human Face of the Iraqi People," *Norwood News*, January 30–February 12, 2003, http://www.bronxmall.com/norwoodnews/opinion/page2.html.
91 Colleen Kelly, interview with author, February 25, 2020.
92 David Potorti, with Peaceful Tomorrows, *September 11th Families for Peaceful Tomorrows: Turning Our Grief into Action* (RDV Books, 2003), 193.
93 Press release, "9/11 Family Members Visit Iraq," January 5, 2003.
94 Potorti, *September 11th Families*, 196.
95 Potorti, *September 11th Families*, 197.
96 Potorti, *September 11th Families*, 182.
97 Colleen Kelly, interview with author.
98 *Connie Chung Tonight*, CNN, January 15, 2003, https://transcripts.cnn.com/show/cct/date/2003-01-15/segment/00.
99 Potorti, *September 11th Families*, 199.
100 Potorti, *September 11th Families*, 142–43.
101 O'Keefe, "Back to Iraq as a Human Shield."
102 Press release, Emergency Campaign to Reclaim Democracy & Stop the War Now!, "Mass Non-violent Civil Disobedience Scheduled for Monday," March 14, 2003, UFPJ, box 6, folder 30.
103 Press release, Emergency Campaign to Reclaim Democracy & Stop the War Now!, "4 Peace Activists Arrested," March 13, 2003, UFPJ, box 6, folder 30.
104 Press Release, Direct Action to Stop the War, "Sit Down Actions in SF," March 14, 2003, UFPJ, box 6, folder 30.
105 Footage of nonviolence training and protest: C-SPAN, "Protesting Against War with Iraq," March 16, 2003, https://www.c-span.org/video/?175562-1/protesting-war-iraq.
106 Press release, Emergency Campaign to Reclaim Democracy & Stop the War Now!, "50+ People Arrested in Washington," March 17, 2003, UFPJ, box 6, folder 30.
107 Kai Newkirk, interview with author, June 5, 2024.
108 Fiona Purcell, "The Faces and Fallout of Australia's Historic Iraq War Protests," *Extraordinary Things*, May 28, 2004, https://www.abc.net.au/news/2024-05-29/dave-burgess-will-saunders-opera-house-no-war-protest/103879226. Arrested just before finishing their graffiti, they received modest, weekend prison terms and, for Will Saunders, expulsion from Australia.
109 "Decapitation Attempt Was Worth a Try, George," *Sydney Morning Herald*, March 22, 2003, https://www.smh.com.au/world/middle-east/decapitation-attempt-was-worth-a-try-george-20030322-gdgh06.html.
110 "U.S. Launches Cruise Missiles at Saddam," CNN, March 20, 2003, https://www.cnn.com/2003/WORLD/meast/03/19/sprj.irq.main/.

111 Correll, "What Happened to Shock and Awe?"
112 NBC News, "Shock and Awe," March 20, 2003, https://www.youtube.com/watch?v=eVqkf3WXGX8.

CHAPTER 8

1 Phyllis Bennis, "Bush Isolated, Launches Terrifying Attack," *War Times* 9 (February–May 2003): 1.
2 Quoted in Thomas E. Ricks, *Fiasco: The American Military Adventure in Iraq* (Penguin, 2006), 407.
3 *We Are Many*, directed by Amir Amirani (We Are Many Productions, 2014).
4 Phyllis Bennis, interview with author, June 27, 2022.
5 Frank Deland, "Peace Activists Paying a Price for Their Convictions," *Free Lance-Star*, April 5, 2003, C1.
6 Andrea Buffa, "The World Still Says No to War," *War Times* 9 (February–May 2003): 3.
7 Buffa, "The World Still Says No to War."
8 Claire Bayard, interview with author, July 31, 2017.
9 Jim Haber, "What the Bay Area Did During the War," *Nonviolent Activist* 20, no. 3 (May–June 2003): 16.
10 For eyewitness accounts, see Michael Steinberg, "Stay Strong, This War Is Long!: The Battle of San Francisco," FoundSF.org, https://www.foundsf.org/index.php?title="STAY_STRONG,_THIS_WAR_IS_LONG!"_THE_BATTLE_OF_SAN_FRANCISCO.
11 Haber, "What the Bay Area Did," 16.
12 Bayard, interview with author.
13 See Michael Moore, "Why I Gave That Infamous Anti-Bush Oscars Speech," *Hollywood Reporter*, February 23, 2017, https://www.hollywoodreporter.com/news/general-news/michael-moores-2003-oscars-speech-filmmaker-reveals-full-story-977566/.
14 Moore's speech is available on YouTube at https://www.youtube.com/watch?v=M7Is43K6lrg.
15 See William Brand, "Protesters Recall 2003 Rally That Turned Violent," *East Bay Times*, April 8, 2007, https://www.eastbaytimes.com/2007/04/08/protesters-recall-2003-rally-that-turned-violent/; and Carolyn Marshall, "Oakland Nears Final Payouts for Protesters Hurt by Police," *New York Times*, March 20, 2006, https://www.nytimes.com/2006/03/20/us/oakland-nears-final-payouts-for-protesters-hurt-by-police.html.
16 Center for Constitutional Rights, "Antiwar Activists Win $2 Million Settlement from New York City in Major Victory for Free Speech Rights," August 19, 2008, https://ccrjustice.org/home/press-center/press-releases/antiwar-activists-win-2-million-settlement-new-york-city-major.

17 Robert Jensen and Rahul Mahajan, "Why Keep Fighting for Peace," *War Times* 9 (April–May 2003): 3.
18 "Just fired, Peter Arnett Hired by British Paper," CNN, April 1, 2003, https://www.cnn.com/2003/WORLD/meast/03/31/sprj.irq.arnett/.
19 On the first days of the war, see Anthony Shadid, *Night Draws Near* (Henry Holt, 2005), 74–116.
20 Footage of the event is available at https://www.theguardian.com/world/video/2013/mar/09/saddam-hussein-statue-toppled-bagdhad-april-2003-video.
21 "Iraqi Who Toppled Saddam Hussein Statue 15 Years Ago Regrets His Action," NPR, April 9, 2018, https://www.npr.org/2018/04/09/600761800/iraqi-who-toppled-saddam-hussein-statue-15-years-ago-regrets-his-action.
22 These figures are drawn from Caroline Smith and James L. Lindsey, "Rally 'Round the Flag: Opinion in the United States During and After the Iraq War," Brookings, June 1, 2003, https://www.brookings.edu/articles/rally-round-the-flag-opinion-in-the-united-states-before-and-after-the-iraq-war/.
23 Extensive polling on the Iraq war is contained at https://www.pollingreport.com/iraq.htm. This figure comes from a CNN/ORC poll from March 15–17, 2003.
24 This account draws on Stephen Duncombe, *Dream: Re-imagining Progressive Politics in an Age of Fantasy* (New Press, 2007), 28.
25 "Text of Bush Speech," *CBS News*, May 1, 2003, https://www.cbsnews.com/news/text-of-bush-speech-01-05-2003/.
26 A transcript of Rumsfeld's April 11, 2003, press conference is available at https://www.huffpost.com/entry/6-years-ago-stuff-happens_b_185691.
27 The Associated Press put the number at 3,240, while Iraq Body Count, an initiative of UK and US academics, estimated more than 5,570.
28 Peggy Faw Gish, *Iraq: A Journey of Hope and Peace* (Herald Press, 2004), 125.
29 Shadid, *Night Draws Near*, 110.
30 Shadid, *Night Draws Near*, 87.
31 Shadid, *Night Draws Near*, 174.
32 Conrad C. Crane, "Military Strategy in Afghanistan and Iraq," in *Understanding the U.S. Wars in Iraq and Afghanistan*, edited by Beth Bailey and Richard H. Immerman (NYU Press, 2015), 133.
33 Crane, "Military Strategy," 132.
34 Neil Smith, *The Endgame of Globalization* (Routledge, 2005), 1–2, 8–12.
35 Quoted in Max Elbaum, "Blatant Lies and Deadly Occupation," *War Times* 11 (July–August 2003): 2.
36 Sean Penn, "Statement on Iraq," *New York Times*, May 30, 2003.
37 Mark Tran, "'Little Girl Rambo' Decries U.S. Propaganda," *Guardian*, April 24, 2007, https://www.theguardian.com/world/2007/apr/24/usa.marktran.

38. "The Peace Movement Between War," *Nonviolent Activist* 20, no. 3 (May–June 2003): 3.
39. Barbara Epstein, "Notes on the Antiwar Movement," *Monthly Review* 55, no. 3, https://monthlyreview.org/2003/07/01/notes-on-the-antiwar-movement/.
40. "Peace Movement at a Crossroads," *War Times* 10 (May–June 2003): 5.
41. UFPJ, "Reportback on Landmark UFPJ Anti-war Strategy and Planning Conference," n.d., UFPJ, box 3, folder 7.
42. "UFPJ Traffic Dashboard, March 19–August 4, 2003," UFPJ, box 3, folder 5.
43. Quoted in Tom Wells, "Two Wars, Two Movements: Iraq in Light of Vietnam," *Fast Capitalism* 1, no. 2 (2005): 37.
44. "Program—National Teach-in on Iraq, Preemptive War & Democracy," UFPJ, box 6, folder 24.
45. Henri E. Cauvin, "Iraq War Critics Gather to Continue Their Fight," *Washington Post*, June 1, 2003, https://www.washingtonpost.com/archive/local/2003/06/01/iraq-war-critics-gather-to-continue-their-fight/ba30ed28-1169-4f10-b859-5ff3928cd309.
46. Press release, "United for Peace and Justice Holds First-Ever National Conference," June 11, 2003, UFPJ, box 3, folder 7.
47. Leslie Cagan, interview with author, December 21, 2016.
48. UFPJ, "UFPJ Unity Statement," UFPJ, box 1, folder 15.
49. UFPJ, "Reportback on Landmark UFPJ Anti-war Strategy."
50. Van Gosse, interview with author, July 22, 2017.
51. Lisa Fithian, interview with author, June 29, 2022.
52. UFPJ, "Reportback on Landmark UFPJ Anti-war Strategy."
53. Email exchange, David Tykulsker, Hany Khalil, et. al, August 25, 2003, BFP, box 30, folder 32.
54. Becker, interview with author, March 24, 2018.
55. Shadid, *Night Draws Near*, 87.
56. Shadid, *Night Draws Near*, 87.
57. Kathy Kelly, interview with author, November 16, 2018.
58. Nicole Winfield, "Iraq's Aziz Joins Peace Prayers in Italy," Associated Press, February 15, 2003, https://apnews.com/article/835ad622937f377ce8ae23fc460f47cf.
59. Gish, *Iraq: A Journey of Hope and Peace*, 133–139; Kathy Kelly, interview with author.
60. Human Rights Watch, "Violent Response: The U.S. Army in Al-Falluja," June 16, 2003, https://www.hrw.org/report/2003/06/16/violent-response/us-army-al-falluja. Its investigators interviewed numerous Iraqi eyewitnesses to the shootings, as well as medical staff and US military personnel of varying ranks. The Iraqis alleged that the protesters were unarmed and that there was no hostile fire at the US soldiers—claims the US mili-

tary denied. Forensic analysts found, however, no compelling evidence to back the Americans' core claims.
61 Kathy Kelly, interview with author.
62 Ed Kinane, interview with author, December 12, 2021.
63 Gish, *Iraq: A Journey of Hope and Peace*, 154.
64 Gish, *Iraq: A Journey of Hope and Peace*, 163–64.
65 On Ruzicka's efforts in Iraq, see Janet Reitman, "The Girl Who Tried to Save the World," *Rolling Stone*, May 2005, https://www.rollingstone.com/culture/culture-news/the-girl-who-tried-to-save-the-world-62716/; and PBS, *Home/Front: Marla's War*, Part I, June 30, and *Home/Front: Marla's List*, Part II, July 9, 2021.
66 Tracy provided extensive testimony about the compensation fund before the US Senate in 2009. See "Assistance of Civilian Casualties of War—Hearing before a Subcommittee of the Committee on Appropriation—U.S. Senate," April 1, 2009, https://www.govinfo.gov/content/pkg/CHRG-111shrg49742/html/CHRG-111shrg49742.htm.
67 The following material is from Mustafa Muhsin, interview with author, September 5, 2021.
68 Ricks, *Fiasco*, 164.

CHAPTER 9

1 Thomas E. Ricks, *Fiasco: The American Military Adventure in Iraq* (Penguin, 2006), 168.
2 Ricks, *Fiasco*, 185.
3 All quotes from "Military Deployments in Iraq," C-SPAN, August 13, 2003, https://www.c-span.org/video/?177784-1/military-deployments-iraq.
4 Mark Arax, Rich Connell, Jennifer Mena, and Amma Gorman, "Green Card Marines: Jesus Suarez del Solar, a Tijuana boy who swore allegiance to the U.S.," *Los Angeles Times*, March 27, 2003, https://www.latimes.com/local/california/la-me-green-card-marines-solar-archives-snap-htmlstory.html.
5 Ricks discusses the detentions in *Fiasco*, 188–89, 253.
6 PIPA/Knowledge Networks Poll, "Misperceptions, the Media and the Iraq War," October 2, 2003, 4.
7 Press release, Corpwatch, "International Occupation Center Launches in Iraq," July 9, 2003, https://www.corpwatch.org/article/international-occupation-watch-center-launches-iraq.
8 Occupation Watch reports are available at https://web.archive.org/web/20040707060125/http://occupationwatch.org/article.php?&list=type&type=24&all=1&nointro=1.
9 Fellowship of Reconciliation, "Amal Al-Khedairy and Nermin Al-Mufti

Speaking Tour in the United States," October 27, 2003, https://web.archive.org/web/20031206083523/http://www.occupationwatch.org/article.php?id=1577.

10 C-SPAN broadcast a presentation of the tour at Georgetown University on November 4, 2003: https://www.c-span.org/video/?178954-1/iraqi-culture.

11 The following portrait is drawn from Dahr Jamail, interview with author, February 21, 2023.

12 Dahr Jamail, *Beyond the Green Zone: Dispatches from an Unembedded Journalist in Occupied Iraq* (Haymarket, 2007), 2.

13 Jamail, interview with author.

14 Jamail, *Beyond the Green Zone*, 80.

15 Jamail, *Beyond the Green Zone*, 25.

16 Jamail, *Beyond the Green Zone*, 26.

17 Colleen Kelly, interview with author, February 25, 2020.

18 Phyllis Bennis, interview with author, June 27, 2022.

19 Hans Bennet, "Resisting War: October 25 and Beyond," *Z Magazine*, January 2004, 17.

20 Defense Casualty Analysis System, https://dcas.dmdc.osd.mil/dcas/app/conflictCasualties/oif/byMonth.

21 Amy Goodman, "War, Peace & the Media," *Nonviolent Activist* 20 (2003): 6, 15.

22 Bennet, "Resisting War," 17.

23 Bennet, "Resisting War," 19.

24 On the history and impact of Arlington West, see Wilson Powell, *Veterans for Peace Comes of Age: A Highlight History*, https://www.veteransforpeace.org/files/4514/8183/6284/VETERANS_FOR_PEACE_-_A_HISTORY.pdf, 303–6.

25 UFPJ, "Resist the Empire: A Fall of Action for Peace and Justice," fall 2003, document in author's possession.

26 Mark Engler, *How to Rule the World: The Coming Battle over the Global Economy* (Nation Books, 2008), introduction, chaps. 1–2.

27 David Graeber, "On the Phenomenology of Giant Puppets: Broken Windows, Imaginary Jars of Urine, and the Cosmological Role of the Police in American Culture," *Anarchist Library*, April 2007, https://theanarchistlibrary.org/library/david-graeber-on-the-phenomenology-of-giant-puppets.

28 L. A. Kauffman, interview with author, February 21, 2018.

29 Maureen Callahan, "The Iraqi Who Captured Saddam," *New York Post*, December 4, 2011, https://nypost.com/2011/12/04/the-iraqi-who-captured-saddam/.

30 *60 Minutes*, "Saddam's Last Stand," December 17, 2003, https://www.youtube.com/watch?v=l1sK0_-2ngs.

31 See, for example, "We Got Him: Kurds Say They Caught Saddam," *Syd-*

ney Morning Herald, December 22, 2003, https://www.smh.com.au/world/middle-east/we-got-him-kurds-say-they-caught-saddam-20031222-gdi11c.html.

32 Jamail, *Beyond the Green Zone*, 56.
33 Jamail, *Beyond the Green Zone*, 58–60.
34 John Nixon, *Debriefing the President: The Interrogation of Saddam Hussein* (Blue Ridge Press, 2016), 1–2.
35 Sean Penn, "A Year Later, Sean Penn Returns to Iraq," *San Francisco Chronicle*, January 14, 2004, https://www.sfgate.com/entertainment/article/COMMENTARY-2nd-act-A-year-later-Sean-Penn-2830141.php.
36 "Military Families Delegation to Iraq," C-SPAN, December 10, 2003, https://www.c-span.org/video/?179507-1/military-families-delegation-iraq. All quotes from the broadcast.
37 Ricks, *Fiasco*, 376–78.
38 American Friends Service Committee, "Bringing the War Home: On the Road with Eyes Wide Open (2006)," October 24, 2012, https://www.youtube.com/watch?v=ujeoKlRFxLI. AFSC; "Frequently Asked Questions," flyer, donated by Matt Daloisio.
39 Robert Scheer, Christopher Scheer, and Lakshmi Chaidry, "Bush's Lies About Iraq," *The Nation*, March 11, 2004, https://www.thenation.com/article/archive/bushs-lies-about-iraq/.
40 Jonathan Schell, "The Empire Backfires," *The Nation*, March 11, 2004, https://www.thenation.com/article/archive/empire-backfires/.
41 Edward Kennedy, "Iraq and US Leadership," *The Nation*, March 11, 2004, https://www.thenation.com/article/archive/iraq-and-us-leadership/.
42 Richard W. Stevenson, "President, Marking Anniversary of War, Urges World to Unite to Combat Terrorism," *New York Times*, March 20, 2004, https://www.nytimes.com/2004/03/20/world/struggle-for-iraq-diplomacy-president-marking-anniversary-war-urges-world-unite.html.
43 "Last Spanish Troops Leave Iraq," *NBC News*, April 27, 2004, https://www.nbcnews.com/id/wbna4845463.
44 John F. Burns, "Hotel Attacks Linked to War Anniversary," *New York Times*, March 19, 2004, https://www.nytimes.com/2004/03/19/world/the-struggle-for-iraq-bombings-hotel-attacks-linked-to-war-anniversary.html.
45 Pew Research Center, "Public Attitudes Toward the War in Iraq: 2003–2008," March 19, 2008, https://www.pewresearch.org/2008/03/19/public-attitudes-toward-the-war-in-iraq-20032008/. *USA Today*/Gallup recorded similar numbers; see https://www.pollingreport.com/iraq4.htm.
46 *Newsweek* Poll, 3/25–6/04, recorded at https://www.pollingreport.com/iraq4.htm.
47 On the global protests, see "Iraq War Anniversary Rallies," *CBS News*, March 20, 2004, https://www.cbsnews.com/pictures/iraq-war-anniversary-rallies/3/; and "Millions Protest Against Iraq War," Al Jazeera, March 20,

2004, https://www.aljazeera.com/news/2004/3/20/millions-protest-against-iraq-war.
48   UFPJ, "March 20, 2004, Global Day of Protest," UFPJ, box 2, bolder 14.
49   Press Release, "Anti-war March in Fayetteville, NC Planned for March 20 Global Day of Action," UFPJ, box 6, folder 21.
50   "Millions Protest Against Iraq War."
51   "A Statement from Those Arrested at the Peace Demonstration in New York on February 15, 2003," UFPJ, box 6, folder 22.
52   Alex S. Vitale, "Analysis of the NYPD's Use of Demonstration Pens," March 2004, UFPJ, box 6, folder 22.
53   Deborah J. Glick, "Letter to Mayor Bloomberg," March 15, 2004, UFPJ, box 6, folder 22.
54   Michael Wilson, "Police Release Ground Rules for Antiwar Demonstration," *New York Times*, March 20, 2004, https://www.nytimes.com/2004/03/20/nyregion/police-release-ground-rules-for-antiwar-demonstration.html.
55   "Iraq War Anniversary Rallies."
56   ANSWER leaflet, "March 20, 2004. Global Day of Action," UFPJ, box 6, folder 21.
57   Bill Weinberg, "Power Play in the Anti-war Movement," *World War Three Report*, UFPJ, box 6, folder 23.
58   "An Open Letter from the Arab-American and Muslim Community to the US Antiwar Movement," UFPJ, box 6, folder 21.
59   Elias Rashmawi, email to Leslie Cagan, January 18, 2004, UFPJ, box 6, folder 21.
60   Weinberg, "Power Play in the Anti-war Movement."
61   Lisa Fithian, interview with author, June 29, 2022.
62   Bennis, interview with author.
63   Virginia Giordana, Letter to Leslie Cagan, March 21, 2004, UFPJ, box 6, folder 22.
64   Ricks, *Fiasco*, 337.
65   Ricks, *Fiasco*, 340.
66   Jamail, *Beyond the Green Zone*, 104.
67   Jamail, *Beyond the Green Zone*, 139.
68   Jamail, *Beyond the Green Zone*, 130.
69   "Detainee Operations in Iraq," in Rand Corporation, *The Battle Beyond the Wire: U.S. Prisoner and Detainee Operations from World War II to Iraq*, 2011, https://www.jstor.org/stable/10.7249/mg9340sd.13, 49.
70   American Civil Liberties Union, "ACLU et al. v. Department of Defense," June 27, 2007, https://www.nyclu.org/en/cases/aclu-et-al-v-department-defense-seeking-access-government-documents-under-foia.
71   Tricia Gates Brown, ed., *118 Days: Christian Peacemaker Teams Held Hostage in Iraq* (CPT, 2008), 20.

72 Ricks, *Fiasco*, 261.
73 CBS, *60 Minutes II*, "Court Martial in Iraq," April 28, 2004, https://www.youtube.com/watch?v=onPH6Xkq2zQ.
74 Seymour M. Hersh, "Torture at Abu Ghraib," *New Yorker*, April 30, 2004, https://www.newyorker.com/magazine/2004/05/10/torture-at-abu-ghraib.
75 CBS, "Court Martial in Iraq."
76 "Arab World Scorns Bush's TV 'Apology,'" *Guardian*, May 4, 2004, https://www.theguardian.com/media/2004/may/06/broadcasting.iraqdossier.
77 Bennis, interview with author.
78 Ricks, *Fiasco*, 329.
79 John Solomon, "Poll of Iraqis Reveals Anger Towards U.S.," Associated Press, June 15, 2004.
80 On the origins and evolution of post-9/11 torture, see Alfred W. McCoy, *A Question of Torture: CIA Interrogation, from the Cold War to the War on Terror* (Macmillan, 2006); and Jane Mayer, *The Dark Side: The Inside Story of How the War on Terror Turned into a War on American Ideals* (Anchor, 2009).
81 This defense appeared in the original *60 Minutes* story and was elaborated in the many trials, reports, and lawsuits Abu Ghraib spawned.
82 Josh White, "General Refuses to Be Interviewed in Abuse Cases," *NBC News*, January 12, 2006, https://www.nbcnews.com/id/wbna10811147. See also Center for Constitutional Rights, "Complaint of Torture—Defendant Dossier: Geoffrey Miller," court filing in Madrid, January 4, 2011.
83 On detainee abuse beyond the EIT program and Abu Ghraib, see Joshua E. S. Phillips, *None of Us Were Like This Before* (Verso, 2010).
84 Karen J. Greenberg and Joshua L. Dratel, eds., *The Torture Papers: The Road to Abu Ghraib* (Cambridge University Press, 2005).
85 Michael Ratner and Ellen Ray, *Guantanamo: What the World Should Know* (Chelsea Green, 2004).
86 Ratner and Ray, *Guantanamo*, xiii. Following quotes from pages 92, 6, and 92.
87 Barbara Ehrenreich, Barnard commencement speech, May 18, 2004, https://www.c-span.org/video/?181991-1/barnard-college-commencement.
88 Jamail, *Beyond the Green Zone*, 195.
89 Ricks, *Fiasco*, 362.
90 ABC News/*Washington Post* poll, October 29–November 1, 2007, https://www.pollingreport.com/iraq3.htm.
91 *USA Today*/Gallup Poll, July 6-8, 2007, https://www.pollingreport.com/iraq4.htm.
92 CBS, *60 Minutes*, "Exposing the Truth of Abu Ghraib," December 7, 2006, https://www.cbsnews.com/news/exposing-the-truth-of-abu-ghraib/.
93 "Joseph Darby," John F. Kennedy Presidential Library and Museum, https://www.jfklibrary.org/events-and-awards/profile-in-courage-award/award-recipients/joseph-darby-2005.

CHAPTER 10

1. "Officers Untouched by Abu Ghraib Prosecutions," National Public Radio, April 6, 2006, https://www.npr.org/2006/04/06/5327137/officers-untouched-by-abu-ghraib-prosecutions.
2. Dick Meyer, "Rush: MPs Just 'Blowing off Steam,'" CBS News, May 6, 2004, https://www.cbsnews.com/news/rush-mps-just-blowing-off-steam/.
3. CBS, *60 Minutes*, "Exposing the Truth of Abu Ghraib," December 7, 2006, https://www.cbsnews.com/news/exposing-the-truth-of-abu-ghraib/.
4. Peaceful Tomorrows, "9/11 Families & Firefighters Call on Bush Campaign to Withdraw Ads Using WTC Imagery," March 4, 2004, https://peacefultomorrows.org/911-families-firefighters-call-on-bush-campaign-to-withdraw-ads-using-wtc-imagery/.
5. Colleen Kelly, interview with author, February 25, 2020.
6. Matt Bai, "Dr. No and the Yes Men," *New York Times Magazine*, June 1, 2003, https://www.nytimes.com/2003/06/01/magazine/dr-no-and-the-yes-men.html.
7. "Howard Dean DNC Winter Meeting Address, Feb. 2003," C-SPAN, https://www.c-span.org/video/?c4456690/user-clip-howard-dean-dnc-winter-meeting-address-feb-2003.
8. Bai, "Dr. No."
9. Pew Research Center, "A Look Back at How Fear and False Beliefs Bolstered U.S. Public Support for War in Iraq," March 14, 2023, https://www.pewresearch.org/politics/2023/03/14/a-look-back-at-how-fear-and-false-beliefs-bolstered-u-s-public-support-for-war-in-iraq/.
10. Michael T. Heaney and Fabio Rojas, *Party in the Street: The Antiwar Movement and the Democratic Party After 9/11* (Cambridge University Press, 2015), 4.
11. Matt Bai, "Dean Does Not Waver on Iraq Criticism," *New York Times*, December 16, 2003.
12. John Frank, "Kucinich Opposed the War Early, but First?" *Politifact*, August 28, 2007, https://www.politifact.com/factchecks/2007/aug/28/dennis-kucinich/kucinich-opposed-the-war-early-but-first/.
13. His campaign was also hurt by the "Dean Scream." After losing the Iowa Caucus, Dean gave an energetic campaign speech punctuated by an awkward scream, further amplified by an uncommonly loud microphone. An object of national ridicule, the episode made him appear "unpresidential," though his candidacy faced tougher challenges.
14. "Transcript: Kerry Testifies Before Senate Panel, 1971," National Public Radio, April 25, 2006, https://www.npr.org/2006/04/25/3875422/transcript-kerry-testifies-before-senate-panel-1971.
15. John Kerry, "We Still Have a Choice on Iraq," *New York Times*, September 6, 2002, https://www.nytimes.com/2002/09/06/opinion/we-still-have

-a-choice-on-iraq.html; "John Kerry's Statement on Iraq Before the War," October 9, 2002, https://web.archive.org/web/20040627090007/http://www.independentsforkerry.org/uploads/media/kerry-iraq.html.
16 "Kerry Discusses $87 Billion Comment," CNN, September 30, 2004.
17 Leslie Cagan, interview with author, December 21, 2016.
18 Ward Reilly, email to author, July 17, 2024. Reilly shared clippings from the local press about the LSU event.
19 "Reporters' Notebook, 7/29/04" and Woody Powell, "The VFP 2004 Convention Summary," in Wilson Powell, *Veterans for Peace Comes of Age: A Highlight History*, https://www.veteransforpeace.org/files/4514/8183/6284/VETERANS_FOR_PEACE_-_A_HISTORY.pdf, 121–26.
20 Reilly, email to author, July 17, 2024.
21 Press release, "Veterans for Peace Press Conference, July 22," in Powell, *Veterans for Peace*, 120–21.
22 Nan Levinson, *War Is Not a Game: The New Antiwar Soldiers and the Movement they Built* (Rutgers University Press, 2014), 5. Drawing on interviews and other accounts, Levinson chronicles the origins of Iraq Veterans Against the War at the Boston VFP conference. She notes that individuals' memories and other accounts differ widely, preventing any certain version of IVAW's origin story. (My own research confirms this confusion.) Which of IVAW's eight or so founders were in Boston remains unclear. Ivan Medina, named in the VFP press release, did not, according to Levinson, show up in Boston. My own brief account is therefore necessarily approximate.
23 "Veterans for Peace Press Conference" and "The VFP Convention Summary" in Powell, *Veterans for Peace*, 120–22.
24 "Breaking Ranks: An Interview with Mike Hoffman," *Mother Jones*, October 11, 2004, https://www.motherjones.com/politics/2004/10/breaking-ranks-interview-mike-hoffman/.
25 For a detailed account of how IVAW congealed, and the assistance of VFP, see Levinson, *War is Not a Game*, 4–23.
26 *Fahrenheit 9/11*, directed by Michael Moore (Lions Gates Films, 2004).
27 Christopher Hitchens, "Unfahrenheit 9/11: The Lies of Michael Moore," *Slate*, June 21, 2004.
28 I was part of the Billionaires, and this synopsis is my own. See also Angelique Hagerud, *No Billionaire Left Behind: Satirical Activism in America* (Stanford University Press, 2013).
29 Adam Nagourney, "Republicans Choose New York for '04 National Convention," *New York Times*, January 6, 2003, https://www.nytimes.com/2003/01/06/politics/republicans-choose-new-york-for-04-national-convention.html.
30 Nick Turse, "Republicans in Green Zone Manhattan," *Tom Disptach*, July 20, 2004, https://tomdispatch.com/nick-turse-on-republicans-in-green-zone-manhattan/.

31 Turse, "Republicans in Green Zone Manhattan."
32 "The People's Guide to the Republican National Convention," brochure in author's possession.
33 UPFJ, "News Advisory—Anti-war Coalition to Republicans: Major Protest Coming," December 15, 2003, UFPJ, box 6, folder 47.
34 UFPJ, "Media Plan in Advance of the RNC—5/19/04," UFPJ, box 6, folder 48.
35 American Civil Liberties Union, "United for Peace and Justice v. Bloomberg," July 16, 2007, https://www.nyclu.org/en/cases/united-peace-and-justice-v-bloomberg-challenging-denial-permit-central-park-protest-rally.
36 NION to UFPJ, "Proposal to Reopen Battle for a Permit," UFPJ, box 6, folder 56.
37 Tom Robbins, "Don't Take Me to the River," *Village Voice*, August 3, 2004, https://www.villagevoice.com/2004/08/03/dont-take-me-to-the-river/.
38 Robbins, "Don't Take Me to the River."
39 "Group Rallies for Central Park Protest," *Newsday*, July 15, 2004.
40 Bill Perkins, "Tuesday Morning Report, August 10, 2004," UFPJ, box 1, folder 4.
41 "Activists Hang 60-Foot Banner on Plaza Hotel," press release, August 26, 2004.
42 "Activists Hang 60-foot Banner on Plaza Hotel."
43 Susan Saulney, "Plaza Climbers Tell of a Grim Night in Jail," *New York Times*, August 28, 2004, https://www.nytimes.com/2004/08/28/nyregion/preparing-for-convention-court-cases-plaza-climbers-tell-grim-night-jail.html.
44 "Critical Mass: Over 260 Arrested in First Major Protest of RNC," *Democracy Now!*, August 31, 2004, http://www.democracynow.org/article.pl?sid=04%2F08%2F30%2F1453256.
45 Michael Froomkin, "Billionaires for Bush to Luxuriate in Publicity," Discourse.net, August 12, 2004, https://www.discourse.net/2004/08/billionaires_for_bush_to_luxuriate_in_publicity/.
46 *NYC Protests the RNC*, directed by Mark Voelpel (MVMEDIA LLC, 2006).
47 UFPJ, "Who We and Why We Are Marching," August 29, 2004, UFPJ, box 6, folder 57.
48 UFPJ, "Press Conference—List of Speakers," August 29, 2004, UFPJ, box 6, folder 57.
49 "Today in History: Mass Arrests in 2004 Republican National Convention Crackdown," *People's World*, August 31, 2015, https://www.peoplesworld.org/article/today-in-history-mass-arrests-in-2004-republican-national-convention-crackdown/.
50 The account of the march, including the quotes below, are from Tom Engelhardt, "Return to Ground Zero (part 1)," *Tom Dispatch*, August 29, 2004, https://tomdispatch.com/return-to-ground-zero-part-1/.

51 This and other actions are depicted in *NYC Protests the RNC*.
52 The portrait of Frida Berrigan and her RNC arrest, including all quotes, is from Frida Berrigan, interview with author, July 14, 2023.
53 "FBI Launches Criminal Civil Rights Investigation of NYPD Over RNC Protests," *Democracy Now!*, May 17, 2006, https://www.democracynow.org/2006/5/17/fbi_launches_criminal_civil_rights_investigation.
54 American Civil Liberties Union, "Victory in Unlawful Mass Arrest During 2004 RNC," January 15, 2014, https://www.nyclu.org/en/press-releases/victory-unlawful-mass-arrest-during-2004-rnc-largest-protest-settlement-history.
55 "4 Protesters Awarded $185K over 2004 RNC Arrests," Associated Press, July 3, 2014, https://www.presstelegram.com/2014/07/03/4-protesters-awarded-185k-over-2004-rnc-arrests/.
56 Jim Dwyer, "City Police Spied Broadly Before G.O.P. Convention," *New York Times*, March 25, 2007, https://www.nytimes.com/2007/03/25/nyregion/25infiltrate.html. The below account is from this lead article. The *NYT* made public countless NYRP intelligence reports, archived at "Police Surveillance at the Republican National Convention," https://archive.nytimes.com/www.nytimes.com/ref/nyregion/RNC_intel_digests.html.
57 Dwyer, "City Police Spied."
58 Michael Froomkin, "Why the Cops Spied on 'Billionaires for Bush,'" Discourse.net, March 27, 2004, https://www.discourse.net/2007/03/why_the_cops_spied_on_billionaires_for_bush/.
59 Dwyer, "City Police Spied."
60 From Max Uhlenbeck, "Reflections on RNC Organizing," *Left Turn*, February 1, 2005, http://leftturn.org/possibilities-movement-reflections-rnc-organizing/.
61 AK Gupta, "Moving Forward: UFPJ and the Anti-war Movement," *Left Turn*, March 1, 2006, http://leftturn.org/moving-forward-ufpj-and-anti-war-movement/.
62 Matt Daloisio, interview with author, October 6, 2022.
63 Jonie Wilgoren, "Kerry Says His Vote on Iraq Would Be the Same Today," *New York Times*, August 10, 2004.
64 "Breaking Ranks: An Interview with Mike Hoffman."
65 Kai Newkirk, interview with author, June 5, 2024.
66 Rae Abileah, interview with author, August 12, 2021.
67 "2004 Bush vs. Kerry," Living Room Candidate, http://www.livingroomcandidate.org/commercials/2004/a-mothers-tears.
68 Rahual Mahajan, "Fallujah—the Geneva Convention is Out the Window," *Empire Notes*, November 13, 2004, http://www.empirenotes.org/november04.html.
69 Dennis Johnson and Valerie Merians, eds., *What We Do Now* (Melville House, 2004), xi.

70 See the book version, *Sorry, Everybody: An Apology to the World for the Re-election of George W. Bush* (Hylas, 2005).
71 Ron Suskind, "Faith, Certainty and the Presidency of George W. Bush," *New York Times Magazine*, October 17, 2004, https://www.nytimes.com/2004/10/17/magazine/faith-certainty-and-the-presidency-of-george-w-bush.html.
72 Mark Danner, "How Bush Really Won," *New York Review of Books*, January 13, 2005, https://www.nybooks.com/articles/2005/01/13/how-bush-really-won/.
73 Quoted in Jeremy Varon, *Bringing the War Home: The Weather Underground, the Red Army Faction, and Revolutionary Violence in the Sixties and Seventies* (University of California Press, 2004), 137.
74 Abileah, interview with author. Abileah uttered the line to criticize it as too simple an approach to antiwar protest.
75 Abileah, interview with author.

CHAPTER 11

1 Politics 101, "George W. Bush 2004 Victory Speech," November 7, 2016, https://www.youtube.com/watch?v=AFvQjRDukV8.
2 "George Bush's Second Inaugural Address," National Public Radio, January 20, 2005, https://www.npr.org/templates/story/story.php?storyId=4460172.
3 Daniel P. Bolger, *Why We Lost: A General's Inside Account of the Iraq and Afghanistan Wars* (Houghton Mifflin Harcourt, 2014), 182.
4 Thomas E. Ricks, *Fiasco: The American Military Adventure in Iraq* (Penguin, 2006), 414.
5 Ricks, *Fiasco*, 414.
6 Ricks, *Fiasco*, 431.
7 Dennis Johnson and Valerie Merians, eds., *What We Do Now* (Melville House, 2004), 174.
8 Leslie Cagan, interview with author, October 22, 2016.
9 Johnson and Merians, *What We Do Now*, 175.
10 Cindy Sheehan, *Peace Mom: A Mother's Journey Through Heartache to Activism* (Atria, 2006), 106.
11 Dahr Jamail, *Beyond the Green Zone: Dispatches from an Unembedded Journalist in Occupied Iraq* (Haymarket, 2007), 222.
12 Bolger, *Why We Lost*, 191.
13 Dahr Jamail, "Fallujah Refugees Tell of Life and Death in the Kill Zone," *New Standard*, December 3, 2004.
14 Mike Marqusee, "A Name that Lives in Infamy," *Guardian*, November 10, 2005, https://www.theguardian.com/world/2005/nov/10/usa.iraq.
15 Ricks, *Fiasco*, 401.

16. Peaceful Tomorrows, Humanitarian Aid to Iraq," December 27, 2004, https://peacefultomorrows.org/stories/press-release-firefighters-mom-delivers-humanitarian-aid-to-iraq/; press release, "Families for Peace," December 24, 2004.
17. *The Road to Fallujah*, directed by Mark Manning (Conception Films, 2006), https://archive.org/details/the-road-to-fallujah-2004-480p-30fps-h-264-128kbit-aac.
18. *The Road to Fallujah*.
19. See the Justice for Fallujah Project at https://www.thefallujahproject.org.
20. Nancy Kricorian, interview with author, August 30, 2021.
21. Quoted in Janet Reitman, "The Girl Who Tried to Save the World," *Rolling Stone*, May 2005, https://www.rollingstone.com/culture/culture-news/the-girl-who-tried-to-save-the-world-62716/.
22. *The Road to Fallujah*.
23. Steve Lopez, "Killed in Iraq—He Isn't Just a Statistic, He's a Mother's Son," *Los Angeles Times*, July 27, 2003.
24. This, and the following quotes, are from Sheehan, *Peace Mom*, 27–85.
25. Sheehan, *Peace Mom*, 109.
26. Sheehan, *Peace Mom*, 72.
27. UFPJ, "Proposed New Strategic Framework," UFPJ, box 3, folder 9.
28. Patrick G. Coy, Lynne M. Woehrle and Gregory M. Many, "Discursive Legacies: The U.S. Peace Movement and 'Support the Troops,'" *Social Problems* 55, no. 2 (2008): 162.
29. My account of the Fayetteville protest is drawn from Michael T. Heaney and Fabio Rojas, "The Place of Framing: Multiple Audiences and Antiwar Protests Near Fort Bragg," *Qual Social* 29 (2006): 485–505; as well as Ward Reilly, interview with author, August 20, 2024; and Ellen Barfield, interview with author, September 29, 2023.
30. UFPJ, "U.S. Cities and Towns Holding March 18–20 Anti-war Events," UFPJ, box 3, folder 15.
31. Reilly, interview with author.
32. Ward Reilly, email to author, August 7, 2004.
33. Dahleen Green, "Army Town Draws Anti-war Protest," *Chicago Tribune*, March 20, 2005, https://www.chicagotribune.com/news/ct-xpm-2005-03-20-0503200526-story.html.
34. IVAW and Aaron Glantz, *Winter Soldier—Iraq and Afghanistan: Eyewitness Accounts of the Occupations* (Haymarket, 2008), 3.
35. IVAW and Glantz, *Winter Soldier*, 3.
36. Lisa Leitz, interview with author, October 13, 2023. My description of the MPM, and the role of identity within it, is drawn primarily from Lisa Leitz, *Fighting for Peace: Veterans and Families in the Anti-Iraq War Movement* (University of Minnesota Press, 2014).
37. Leitz, *Fighting for Peace*, 148–50.

38 Leitz, *Fighting for Peace*, 25.
39 Ann Wright and Susan Dixon, *Dissent: Government Insiders Speak Out Against the Iraq War* (Koa, 2008), 152–53.
40 Camilo Mejia, *Road from Ar Ramadi: The Private Rebellion of Sergeant Camilo Mejia* (New Press, 2007).
41 Wright and Dixon, *Dissent*, 142.
42 Wright and Dixon, *Dissent*, 144.
43 "What We Have Done (2004–2010)," Courage to Resist, https://courageto resist.org/what-we-have-done-2004-2010/.
44 On this in-country resistance, see Dahr Jamail, *The Will to Resist: Soldiers Who Refuse to Fight in Iraq and Afghanistan* (Haymarket, 2009).
45 Interview with Louis Plummer, 2005, *Southern Oral History Project (SOHP): Military Dissenters: Veterans, Military Families, and the Iraq and Afghan Wars*, https://dcr.lib.unc.edu/record/f1426ebb-194e-4e33-b600-1677d3a8cab4. The full interview archive is available at https://dcr.lib.unc.edu/record/211e2f05-61b1-4bed-90a68ca42fffe849.
46 Wright and Dixon, *Dissent*, 162–63.
47 Heaney and Rojas, "The Place of Framing," 497.
48 Barfield, interview with author.
49 Green, "Army Town Draws Anti-war Protest."
50 Ellen Barfield, "Bring Them Home Now—or Not?," *Nonviolent Activist*, July–August 2005.
51 Heaney and Rojas, "The Place of Framing," 498–99.
52 Cagan, interview with author, October 22, 2016.
53 IVAW and Glantz, *Winter Soldier*, back cover.
54 Matthew Gutman and Catherine Lutz, *Breaking Ranks: Iraq Veterans Speak Out Against the War* (University of North Carolina Press, 2010), 170. The book is based on interviews with IVAW members conducted by researchers at the University of North Carolina in 2005–7 as part of *Southern Oral History Project (SOHP): Military Dissenters: Veterans, Military Families, and the Iraq and Afghan Wars*.
55 IVAW and Glantz, *Winter Soldier*, 17–18. The first section of the book, which draws from IVAW testimony, describes the lax rules of engagement.
56 IVAW Glantz, *Winter Soldier*, 22.
57 *The Ground Truth: The Human Cost of War*, directed by Patricia Foulkrod (Plum Pictures, 2006). The following quotes are from the same course.
58 *The Ground Truth*; and IVAW and Glantz, *Winter Soldier*, 58–101.
59 Joushua Key and Lawrence Hill, *The Deserter's Tale: The Story of an Ordinary Solider Who Walked Away from the War in Iraq* (Grove, 2007), 51.
60 Gutman and Lutz, *Breaking Ranks*, 114–15.
61 *The Ground Truth*.
62 Gutman and Lutz, *Breaking Ranks*, 102.
63 Gutman and Lutz, *Breaking Ranks*, 116.

NOTES TO PAGES 296–305   431

64 IVAW and Glantz, *Winter Soldier*, 22.
65 *The Ground Truth*.
66 Gutman and Lutz, *Breaking Ranks*, 145.
67 *The Ground Truth*.
68 *The Ground Truth*. The Lucy material is from the film as well.
69 Key and Hill, *Deserter's Tale*, 3. Subsequent quotes from pages 105, 106, 110, 9, and 213.
70 Leitz, *Fighting for Peace*, 17.
71 A video of the episode is included in "Opposition to War in Iraq Rally," C-SPAN, July 23, 2005, https://www.c-span.org/video/?187909-1/opposition-war-iraq-rally.
72 Lawrence H. Silberman and Charles Robb, "The Commission on the Intelligence Capabilities of the United States Regarding Weapons of Mass Destruction—Report to the President of the United States," March 31, 2004, 1.
73 "Downing Street Memo," https://nsarchive2.gwu.edu/NSAEBB/NSAEBB328/II-Doc14.pdf. For analysis, see "Controversy Continues over 'Downing Street' War Memos," PBS, June 16, 2005, https://www.pbs.org/newshour/show/controversy-continues-over-downing-street-war-memos. Additional memos were released, all considered part of the Downing Street Memos," though I focus mainly on the first leaked documents.
74 "Downing Street Memo and Pre-War Intelligence," C-SPAN, June 16, 2005, https://www.c-span.org/video/?187209-1/downing-street-minutes-pre-war-intelligence.
75 "Opposition to War in Iraq Rally," C-SPAN, July 23, 2005, https://www.c-span.org/program/public-affairs-event/opposition-to-war-in-iraq-rally/145482.
76 "Downing Street Memo."
77 Sheehan, *Peace Mom*, 112.
78 My account of Camp Casey is drawn from many sources, among them, Sheehan, *Peace Mom*, 133–189; Cindy Sheehan, *Not One More Mother's Child* (Koa, 2005), 69–154, which includes daily diary entries from the camo; Michael Moore, "Cindy Sheehan's Historic August 6, 2005 Trip to Crawford, TX," June 25, 2007, https://www.youtube.com/watch?v=a9R8E3Y3kMw; Wilson Powell, *Veterans for Peace Comes of Age: A Highlight History*, https://www.veteransforpeace.org/files/4514/8183/6284/VETERANS_FOR_PEACE_-_A_HISTORY.pdf; Lisa Fithian, interview with author, June 29, 2022; Barfield, interview with author; and Ann Wright, interview with author, October 7, 2023. Except when indicated, all quotes are from these texts.
79 "Truth Gathers in Crawford," *Baltimore Chronicle*, August 5, 2005.
80 Edwin Chin, "Soldier's Mother Inspires Protests Across U.S.," *Los Angeles Times*, August 18, 2005.
81 Jordan Smith, "Sheehan's Field of Dreams," *The Austin Chronicle*, August 19, 2005. https://www.austinchronicle.com/news/2005-08-19/285406/.

82 Keith McHenry, "Food Not Bombs Feeds Camp Casey," Food Not Bombs, http://foodnotbombs.net/fnb_camp_casey.html.
83 Lisa Fithian, interview with author, June 29, 2022.
84 Key also became an accomplished playwright, authoring *The Eyes of Babylon* based on his time in Iraq. See "A Gay Marine's Journey Home," *American Theatre*, July 1, 2010, https://www.americantheatre.org/2010/07/01/a-gay-marines-journey-home/; and "Jeff Key," https://www.warriorwriters.org/artists/jeff.html.
85 Leitz, interview with author.
86 Fithian, interview with author.
87 The polling numbers are included in Smith, "Sheehan's Field of Dreams."
88 AP-IPSOS poll, August 22–24, 2005, https://www.pollingreport.com/iraq3.htm.
89 Pat Tate, "Hurricane Relief Effort," in Powell, *Veterans for Peace*, 139–40.
90 Reilly, interview with author.
91 Barfield, interview with author.
92 Wright, interview with author.

CHAPTER 12

1 Cindy Sheehan, *Not One More Mother's Child* (Koa, 2005), 73.
2 Defense Casualty Analysis System, https://dcas.dmdc.osd.mil/dcas/app/home.
3 Neta C. Crawford, "Civilian Death and Injury in the Iraq War, 2003-2103," *Costs of War*, March 2013, 3.
4 Reviews from the front flap of Thomas E. Ricks, *Fiasco: The American Military Adventure in Iraq* (Penguin, 2006) (2007 edition).
5 *The Iraq Study Group Report* (Vintage, 2006), ix, xiii.
6 Rusti Eisenberg, "What Will History Say?," unpublished document in author's possession. Eisenberg intended to deliver the speech at the September 2005 rally but was unable to do so due to time constraints.
7 Flyers and organizing documents for the protest are in UFPJ, box 6, folder 44.
8 MOU, UFPJ-ANSWER, draft, August 18, 2005, UFPJ, box 2, folder 15.
9 UFPJ, "Speakers and Performers," UFPJ, box 2, folder 10.
10 Leslie Cagan, interview with author, October 22, 2016.
11 Sheehan, *Not One More Mother's Child*, 158.
12 Kenneth Walsh, "The Undoing of George W. Bush," *U.S. News & World Report*, August 28, 2015, https://www.usnews.com/news/the-report/articles/2015/08/28/hurricane-katrina-was-the-beginning-of-the-end-for-george-w-bush.
13 Rae Abileah, interview with author, August 12, 2021.

14 UFPJ, "Remember and Resist: A Call to Action for Fall Civil Resistance," UFPJ, box 2, folder 12.
15 See, for example, "Protest and Arrest," *CBS News*, September 26, 2005, https://www.cbsnews.com/pictures/protest-and-arrest/15/. The Associated Press wrote a story on the arrest, syndicated in many regional news outlets.
16 Sue Udry, interview with author, January 5, 2018.
17 Michael T. Heaney, "The Partisan Politics of Antiwar Legislation in Congress, 2001–2011." *University of Chicago Legal Forum* 2011 (2011): 137.
18 For a summary of antiwar legislation, see Heaney, "Partisan Politics," 161–68.
19 US Congress, "Detainee Treatment Act of 2005," https://www.govinfo.gov/content/pkg/COMPS-489/pdf/COMPS-489.pdf.
20 "Contracting in Iraq," C-SPAN, June 27, 2005, https://www.c-span.org/video/?187363-1/contracting-iraq.
21 Sheehan, *Not One More Mother's Child*, 165.
22 Katherine Q. Seelye, "Walter B. Jones, 76, Dies; Republican Turned Against Iraq War," *New York Times*, February 13, 2019, https://www.nytimes.com/2019/02/13/obituaries/walter-b-jones-dead.html.
23 UFPJ, "Talking Points: 'Stay the Course' or Get Out Now"; "Questions for Congress"; "Local Costs of the Iraq War," FPIP "The Iraq Quagmire," UFPJ, box 2, folder 13.
24 "Murtha Calls for a 'Change in Direction,'" *New York Times*, November 17, 2005, https://www.nytimes.com/2005/11/17/politics/murtha-calls-for-a-change-in-direction.html. See also Melissa Block, "Murtha: Military Supports Call for Iraq Withdrawal," National Public Radio, December 1, 2005, https://www.npr.org/2005/12/01/5035043/murtha-military-supports-call-for-iraq-withdrawal.
25 "Poll of Troops in Iraq Sees 72% Support for Withdrawal Within a Year," *Stars and Stripes*, March 1, 2006, https://www.stripes.com/news/2006-03-01/poll-of-troops-in-iraq-sees-72-support-for-withdrawal-within-a-year-1969573.html1.
26 "Iraq Coordinating Committee Strategy Retreat Summary," UFPJ, box 2, folder 15.
27 Daniel P. Bolger, *Why We Lost: A General's Inside Account of the Iraq and Afghanistan Wars* (Houghton Mifflin Harcourt, 2014), 214.
28 Crawford, "Civilian Death and Injury," 9–12.
29 See Fanar Haddad, *Sectarianism in Iraq: Antagonistic Visions of Unity* (Columbia University Press, 2011).
30 For the statement and other WCW activities, see https://web.archive.org/web/20051013054850/http://www.worldcantwait.org/.
31 Medea Benjamin, interview with author, December 5, 2017.
32 On the kidnapping, see *118 Days: Christian Peacemaker Teams Held Hostage*

in Iraq (CreateSpace, 2008) and the "Captive" episode of the TV program *The Peacemakers, Iraq* (Lightbox Productions), aired December 9, 2016.

33 "Captive."
34 "Captive."
35 Matthew W. Daloisio, "Pilgrimage to Guantanamo," *Catholic Worker*, March–April 2006, 1. My account of the Cuba trip and Witness Against Torture more broadly is drawn from the named edition of *The Catholic Worker*; Chandra Russo, "Witness Against Torture, Guantanamo and Solidarity as Resistance," *Race and Class*, no. 2 (2016): 4–22; and *Witness Against Torture: The Campaign to Shut Down Guantanamo* (Yellow Bike Press, 2008), a self-published book chronicling the group's early history. As a longtime member of the group, I draw also on my own memories and my conversations with its members.
36 This was Bush's consistent mantra, which he repeated while in Panama in November 2005. *Witness Against Torture*, 16.
37 Quoted in Russo, "Witness Against Torture," 9.
38 *Witness Against Torture*, 15.
39 Amanda W. Daloisio, "To Walk & Not Grow Weary," *Catholic Worker*, March–April 2006, 4.
40 Allen and Crane quotes from *Witness Against Torture*, 12, 18.
41 Russo, "Witness Against Torture," 10.
42 Daniel Berrigan, "Pilgrimage to Guantanamo," in *Witness Against Torture*, xiii.
43 *Witness Against Torture*, 27.
44 The US Department of Treasury made clumsy efforts to investigate the Cuba trip but soon dropped the matter.
45 Mark Denbeaux et al., "Report on Guantanamo Detainees: A Profile of 517 Detainees from Department of Defense Data," Seton Hall University, 2006. Figures quoted in *Witness Against Torture*, xx. The data was culled from nonclassified documents related to the so-called Combatant Status Review Tribunals—sham proceedings run by the US military, in lieu of proper evidentiary hearings, to determine whether the prisoners were justly detained.
46 Khalid Sheikh Mohammed (KSM), the likely mastermind of 9/11, and other "high-value detainees" were brought to Guantánamo only in late 2006. Prior to that, KSM was held, and tortured, in incommunicado detention at secret CIA prisons, whose existence the Bush administration never officially admitted. Their transfer to Guantánamo, in part, was meant to ease passage of the Military Commissions Acts, which established special courts to try terror suspects.
47 On the work of the attorneys, see Mark P. Denbeaux and Jonathan Hafetz, eds., *The Guantanamo Lawyers: Inside a Prison Outside the Law* (New York University Press, 2011).

48 Valerie Lucznikowska, Colleen Kelly, and Terry Rockefeller led the involvement of Peaceful Tomorrows in anti-torture work. Periodically, members attended legal hearings in Guantánamo, whether as family members of the 9/11 dead or representative of the group itself. Britain's Andy Worthington, an independent journalist and Guantánamo researcher, was key in the UK's anti-Guantánamo coalition.
49 Tom Engelhardt, "Giving the President a Pink Slip in New York City," *Tom Dispatch*, April 30, 2006, https://tomdispatch.com/giving-the-president-a-pink-slip-in-new-york-city/.
50 Nick Confessore, "Tens of Thousands in New York March Against Iraq War," *New York Times*, April 30, 2006, https://www.nytimes.com/2006/04/30/nyregion/tens-of-thousands-in-new-york-march-against-iraq-war.html.
51 Ward Reilly, "Mobile to New Orleans: Resistance Defined in Epic Action," *The Veteran* 36, no. 1 (2006), https://www.vvaw.org/veteran/article/?id=592.
52 Quoted in Jose N. Vasquez, "Groundswell: The Veterans' and Survivors' March from Mobile to New Orleans," unpublished manuscript, https://kairoscenter.org/wp-content/uploads/2014/11/Groundswell-Vasquez.pdf, 30.
53 Carolyn Quinn, "Anti-war March In-Country," *Ventura County Star*, March 22, 2006, 41.
54 "Tests Stop Marchers from Visiting School," *Ventura County Star*, March 22, 2006, https://www.newspapers.com/article/ventura-county-star-tests-stop-marchers/104707552/.
55 "History," Iraq Veterans Against the War, https://www.ivaw.org/history.
56 "AWOL Colo. Soldier Turns Himself In," *Denver Post*, August 31, 2006, https://www.denverpost.com/2006/08/31/awol-colo-soldier-turns-self-in/.
57 Eli Sanders, "Putting the Iraq War on Trial," *Time*, August 18, 2006, https://time.com/archive/6919855/putting-the-iraq-war-on-trial/.
58 The appeal can be found at https://appealforredress.org.
59 Ann Scott Tyson, "Grass-Roots Group of Troops Petitions Congress for Pullout from Iraq," *Washington Post*, October 25, 2006, https://www.washingtonpost.com/archive/politics/2006/10/25/grass-roots-group-of-troops-petitions-congress-for-pullout-from-iraq/29f824d5-5f7e-4069-8e2b-4a5d61ed0577/.
60 See Peter Bohmer, "10 Days that Shook Olympia," *Z-Net*, November 15, 2007.
61 My account of We Will Not Be Silent is based on Laurie Arbeiter, interview with author, August 18, 2024, from which all quotes are drawn.
62 The tour is documented at https://web.archive.org/web/20060615171043/http://www.womensaynotowar.org/article.php?id=803.
63 Entesar Mohammad Ariabi, "Welcome to Liberated Iraq," March 20,

2006, https://web.archive.org/web/20060614180617/http://www.women saynotowar.org/downloads/WelcometoLiberatedIraq.pdf.
64 Rae Abileah, "Entisar's Tour: NYC and Saying Goodbye," March 28, 2006, https://web.archive.org/web/20060910041440/http://www.womensay notowar.org/article.php?id=921.
65 Abileah, interview with author.
66 This and the voting data below are drawn from Gary C. Jacobson, "The War, the President, and the 2006 Midterm Congressional Elections," a speech delivered a meeting of political scientists in 2007. Heaney and Rojas cite other academic and pundit analyses that attribute the Democrats' midterm success to opposition to the war.
67 Michel T. Heaney and Fabio Rojas, "Partisans, Nonpartisans, and the Antiwar Movement in the United States," *American Politics Research* 35, no. 4 (July 2007): 438–42.
68 Heaney and Rojas, "Partisans, Nonpartisans," 433.
69 Heaney and Rojas, "Partisans, Nonpartisans," 431–33.
70 Heaney and Rojas, "Partisans, Nonpartisans," 454.
71 Andrea Buffa, "Mobilizing the Antiwar Majority," *War Times*, Fall 2006, 5.
72 The Senate was now evenly split, with forty-nine Democrats and forty-nine Republicans. But two Independents caucused with the Democrats, given them the functional majority.
73 *Iraq Study Group Report*.
74 "President Bush Defends Decision to Send Additional Troops to Iraq," *PBS NewsHour*, January 16, 2007, https://web.archive.org/web/20070119195715 /http://www.pbs.org/newshour/bb/white_house/jan-june07/bush_01-16 .html.
75 Anthony Arnove, *Iraq: The Logic of Withdrawal* (Metropolitan, 2007).
76 The speech is available on YouTube at https://www.youtube.com/watch?v =V1upGEPdaBU.
77 In its June 2006 *Hamdan v. Rumsfeld* decision, the Supreme Court affirmed *habeas* rights, which Congress then sought to strip with the Military Commissions Act (MCA), signed into law in October. New litigation, pending in court in 2007, challenged key provisions of the MCA, including its denial of *habeas* rights.
78 Michael T. Heaney and Fabio Rojas, *Party in the Street: The Antiwar Movement and the Democratic Party After 9/11* (Cambridge University Press, 2015), 1–2.
79 Cagan, interview with author, October 22, 2016.
80 Heaney and Rojas, "Partisans, Nonpartisans," 455.
81 Murtha failed to win that position, for reasons unrelated to his antiwar stance.
82 Melvin Small, "Bring the Boys Home Now! Antiwar Activism and With-

drawal from Vietnam—and Iraq," *Diplomatic History* 34, no. 3 (June 2010): 544–45.
83 Dennis Kucinich, "There is Only One Way to End the Iraq War, Part II," *Huffington Post*, December 3, 2006. https://www.huffpost.com/entry/there-is-only-one-way-to_b_35453.

CHAPTER 13

1 My sketch of the surge is drawn mostly from Thomas E. Ricks, *The Gamble: General Petraeus and the American Military Adventure in Iraq* (Penguin, 2009).
2 Ricks, *The Gamble*, 262.
3 Ricks, *The Gamble*, 244.
4 Michael T. Heaney, "The Partisan Politics of Antiwar Legislation in Congress, 2001–2011." *University of Chicago Legal Forum* 2011 (2011): 146, 156.
5 Ken Mayers, "Reports on September 15, 2007," in Wilson Powell, *Veterans for Peace Comes of Age: A Highlight History*, https://www.veteransforpeace.org/files/4514/8183/6284/VETERANS_FOR_PEACE_-_A_HISTORY.pdf, 328.
6 Patrick McCann, "Reports on September 15, 2007," in Powell, *Veterans for Peace*, 327.
7 Steve Duncombe and Stever Lambert, *The Art of Activism* (O/R Books, 2021), 36.
8 See IVAW and Aaron Glantz, *Winter Soldier—Iraq and Afghanistan: Eyewitness Accounts of the Occupations* (Haymarket, 2008), and the IVAW website, https://www.ivaw.org.
9 Ward Reilly, email to author, July 14, 2014.
10 "History," Iraq Veterans Against the War, https://www.ivaw.org/history.
11 My account of the protest is drawn from Beth Brockman, interview with author, December 2, 2017; Steven Baggarly, email to author, July 11, 2024; defense documents donated by Brockman; and newspaper stories, chiefly Bill Sizemore, "A Symbolic Assault on Contractor's HQ," *Virginian-Pilot*, October 21, 2007.
12 Brockman, interview with author. All Brockman quotes from the same.
13 Patrick O'Neill, "Blackwater Neighbors Join Protest Against Security Firm," *National Catholic Reporter*, November 16, 2007, 9.
14 The protesters actually had two trials, as the results of the first were thrown out due to misconduct by the judge, who tried six of the defendants in secret. See John Henderson, "Jury Finds Blackwater Protesters Guilty," *Daily Advance*, January 24, 2008; and Jeremy Scahill, "Pioneering Protesters Given Secret Trial and Criminal Conviction," *AlterNet*, January 30, 2008.

15 On the protest, see *Witness Against Torture: The Campaign to Shut Down Guantanamo* (Yellow Bike Press, 2008), 106–139. I was part of the action, arrested inside the court.
16 WAT had used this tactic on a smaller scale at arrest actions in New York City and at the federal courthouse in Washington a year earlier. This time, it was more emphatic, given the trial that followed.
17 Of the eighty arrestees, some pled guilty and others had their charges dismissed, bringing those standing trial down to thirty-five.
18 The press conference at the trial's opening is available on YouTube at https://www.youtube.com/watch?v=B0Fdymwup9E&t=126s.
19 Heaney and Rojas track the size of major antiwar protests between 2001 and 2012, showing a sharp decline starting in 2007: Michael T. Heaney and Fabio Rojas, *Party in the Street: The Antiwar Movement and the Democratic Party After 9/11* (Cambridge University Press, 2015), 242–56.
20 Ricks, *The Gamble*, 254.
21 Gary C. Jacobson, "A Tale of Two Wars: Public Opinion on the U.S. Interventions in Afghanistan and Iraq," *Presidential Studies Quarterly* 40, no. 4 (December 2010): 587–91.
22 Ward Reilly, email to author, July 14, 2014.
23 All quotes are from "Special Issue: Where to From Here?" *WIN* 25, nos. 2–3 (Spring/Summer 2008).
24 Van Gosse, "Antiwar Movements in the New Century," 2009, document donated to author.
25 Leslie Cagan, interview with author, October 22, 2016.
26 "Where to from Here?"
27 "Where to from Here?"
28 Reuters, "Iraqi Who Threw Shoes at President Bush Still Angry After 15 Years," March 14, 2023, https://www.youtube.com/watch?v=Q4xu3ZeAWlw.
29 Frida Berrigan, interview with author, July 14, 2023.
30 "Obama Signs Order to Close Guantánamo Bay," *Guardian*, January 22, 2009, https://www.theguardian.com/world/2009/jan/22/hillary-clinton-diplomatic-foreign-policy.
31 American Civil Liberties Union, "President Obama Orders Guantánamo Closed and End to Torture," January 22, 2009, https://www.aclu.org/press-releases/president-obama-orders-guantanamo-closed-and-end-torture.
32 The "boisterous conga line" was the night of Obama's inauguration. Conor Friedersdorf, "The Enduring Disgrace of Guantanamo," *Atlantic*, April 25, 2011.
33 Steven Erlanger and Sheryl Gay Stolberg, "Surprise Nobel for Obama Stirs Praise and Doubts," *New York Times*, October 9, 2009, https://www.nytimes.com/2009/10/10/world/10nobel.html.
34 Mark Mazzetti and Scott Shane, "Interrogation Memos Detail Harsh Tactics by the C.I.A.," *New York Times*, April 16, 2009, https://www.nytimes

.com/2009/04/17/us/politics/17detain.html. Holder did open investigations into the abuse of captives that potentially exceed "approved" interrogation methods. These concluded in 2012, with the DOJ declining any prosecutions.

35 Early on, the Obama administration discouraged detainees from seeking through *habeas* challenges to have federal judges order their release. Instead, it promoted its system of internal review, by which defense and intelligence agencies assessed the security risk of transferring individual detainees. Deeply flawed, this nonjudicial system was bogged down. Men worthy of their freedom were never "cleared" for transfer. Detainees who had been cleared languished at the prison with no mechanism to compel their release. Meanwhile, appellate judges revised *habeas* protocols to severely hinder the petitioners' ability to contest the government's allegations against them.

36 Of Guantánamo's 780 detainees, 538 left the prison under the Bush administration. In Obama's first year, just 45 of 242 detainees were released. Those leaving were repatriated, or transferred to "third countries" when they could not safely return home, or, in very small numbers, sent overseas to serve sentences after conviction in US courts.

37 Jacobson, "A Tale of Two Wars," 588.

38 Jeremy Scahill, *Dirty Wars: The World as a Battlefield* (Nation Books, 2013).

39 Heaney and Rojas, *Party in the Street*, 68.

40 Ward Reilly, email to author, July 30, 2024.

41 Phyllis Bennis, interview with author, June 27, 2022.

42 David Cortright, "From the Streets to the Ballot Box: Ending the War in Iraq," *Mobilizing Ideas*, July 2, 2012, https://mobilizingideas.wordpress.com/2012/07/02/from-the-streets-to-the-ballot-box-ending-the-war-in-iraq/.

43 Leslie Cagan, interview with author, December 21, 2016.

44 Perceptions of the conflicts in UFPJ, which ran on multiple lines, differ widely. I offer here only a rough characterization of one axis of disagreement.

45 Heaney and Rojas, *Party in the Street*, 4.

46 Heaney and Rojas, *Party in the Street*, 5.

47 Heaney and Rojas, *Party in the Street*, 114.

48 Reilly, email to author, July 30, 2024.

49 I was one of those protesters and repeatedly heard this question.

50 Michael T. Heaney and Fabio Rojas, "The Partisan Dynamic of Contention: Demobilization of the Antiwar Movement in the United States, 2007–9," *Mobilization* 16, no. 1 (2011): 168.

51 Heaney and Rojas, "The Partisan Dynamic," 157.

52 Heaney and Rojas, *Party in the Street*, 98.

53 Quoted in Ron Jacobs, "A Look at the Movement Against the US War in

Iraq," *Counterpunch*, July 12, 2013, https://www.counterpunch.org/2013/07/12/a-look-at-the-movement-against-the-us-war-in-iraq/.

54 Cagan, interview with author, December 21, 2016.
55 Bennis, interview with author.
56 On Obama's ISIS policy, see "What Drove the War's Snapback in Iraq and Syria?," New America, https://www.newamerica.org/future-security/reports/decision-making-counter-isis-war/what-drove-the-wars-snapback-in-iraq-and-syria/.
57 Jacobson, "A Tale of Two Wars," 15.
58 Elliott Adams, email to author, July 25, 2024.
59 See Jeremy Varon, "We Are America: Guantánamo, The Aamer Appeal, and the Passion of Andrés Thomas Conteris," *Public Seminar*, November 24, 2013, https://publicseminar.org/2013/11/we-are-america-guantanamo-the-aamer-appeal-and-the-passion-of-andres-thomas-conteris/.
60 Chiefly, the Obama administration gave new teeth to the prison's "periodic review boards," which had the power to reclassify longtime detainees as "cleared for transfer." Some were repatriated or released to "third countries" willing to take them in. This "transfer diplomacy" entailed political and monetary gifts to recipient countries, coordinated by a Guantánamo czar and limited by Congress.
61 For the case against drones and a partial recounting of Code Pink's anti-drone activism, see Medea Benjamin, *Drone Warfare: Killing by Remote Control* (Verso, 2013).
62 See "About Upstate Drone Action," https://upstatedroneaction.org/wp/sample-page/.
63 *Democracy Now!*, "Medea Benjamin v. President Obama: CodePink Founder Disrupts Speech, Criticizing Drone, Gitmo Policy," May 23, 2013, https://www.youtube.com/watch?v=3FaIMropdOM.
64 See "Chelsea Manning," Biography.com, May 10, 2021, https://www.biography.com/activists/chelsea-manning. The transgender Chelsea transitioned from the male Bradley Manning during her whistleblower saga. Initially, advocacy efforts were on behalf of "Bradley Manning." In 2013, Manning was sentenced to thirty-five years in prison for unauthorized disclosures. In January 2017, President Obama granted her clemency. In May of the same year, Manning was released from prison.
65 Bill Hughes, "Peace Poet Luke Nephew: 'There's a Man Under That Hood!,'" January 12, 2011, https://www.youtube.com/watch?v=5hVaoqjZzuA.

CONCLUSION

1 Fake *New York Times*, July 4, 2009, in author's possession. headlines and quotes are from the paper.

2 "*New York Times* Special Edition—War Is Over," Open Utopia, https://the openutopia.org/watch/.
3 Steve Lambert, "Steve Lambert on the *New York Times* Special Edition," December 14, 2009, https://vimeo.com/8184647; and Steve Lambert, email to author, January 27, 2024.
4 The CNN spot is posted at https://laughingsquid.com/the-yes-men-distribute-fake-new-york-times-iraq-war-ends/.
5 Lambert, "Steve Lambert on the *New York Times*."
6 David Cortright, "The World Says No: The Global Movement Against the War in Iraq," in *Iraq Crisis and World Order: Structural, Institutional, and Normative Challenges*, edited by Ramesh Thakur and Waheguru Pal Singh Sidhu (United Nations University Press, 2006), 75.
7 Rebecca Solnit, quoted in Cortright, "The World Says No," 76.
8 David Cortright, "Ending a War by Electing a President," July 23, 2012, http://davidcortright.net/2012/07/23/ending-a-war-by-electing-a-president.
9 Eric Stoner, "Learning from Shortcomings and Other Movements," *Mobilizing Ideas*, July 2, 2012, https://mobilizingideas.wordpress.com/2012/07/23/learning-from-shortcomings-and-other-movements/.
10 Kai Newkirk, interview with author, June 5, 2024.
11 Ishaan Tharoor, "Why Was the Biggest Protest in World History Ignored?," *Time*, February 15, 2013, https://world.time.com/2013/02/15/viewpoint-why-was-the-biggest-protest-in-world-history-ignored/.
12 Carmen Fishwick, "'We Were Ignored': Anti-war Protestors Remember the Iraq War Marches," *Guardian*, July 8, 2016, https://www.theguardian.com/uk-news/2016/jul/08/we-were-ignored-anti-war-protestors-remember-the-iraq-war-marches.
13 Patrick Barkham, "Iraq War 10 Years On: Mass Protest That Defined a Generation," *Guardian*, February 15, 2013, https://www.theguardian.com/world/2013/feb/15/iraq-war-mass-protest.
14 Phyllis Bennis, interview with author, June 27, 2022.
15 Ann Wright, interview with author, October 7, 2023.
16 David S. Meyer, "Where's the peace movement?" *Politics Outdoors*, July 2, 2012, https://politicsoutdoors.com/2012/07/02/wheres-the-peace-movement-2/.
17 Phyllis and Orlando Rodriguez, "Not in Our Son's Name." Phyllis and Orlando Rodriguez, "Not in Our Son's Name," September 14, 2001. Reprinted in David Potorti, with Peaceful Tomorrows, *September 11th Families for Peaceful Tomorrows: Turning Our Grief into Action* (RDV Books, 2003).
18 See Edwin Amenta and Michael P. Young, "Making an Impact: Conceptual and Methodological Implications of the Collective Goods Criterion," in *How Social Movements Matter*, edited by Marco Giugni, Doug McAdam, and Charles Tilly (University of Minnesota Press, 1999), 22–41; Edwin

Amenta, Neal Caren, Elizabeth Chiarello, and Yang Su. "The Political Consequences of Social Movements," *Annual Review of Sociology* 36, no. 1 (June 2010): 287–307; and Edwin Amenta and Francesca Polletta, "The Cultural Impacts of Social Movements," *Annual Review of Sociology* 45, no. 1 (July 30, 2019): 279–99.

19 Steve Newton, "Obama Sought Congressional Approval for 2013 Military Intervention in Syria," KVUE, April 7, 2017, https://www.kvue.com/article/news/politics/national-politics/obama-sought-congressional-approval-for-2013-military-intervention-in-syria/269-429573242. Obama ordered military operations in Syria in 2014, but they were mostly limited to fighting ISIS and did little to affect Syria's civil war.

20 Leslie Cagan, interview with author, October 22, 2016.

21 "A.J. Muste Quotable Quote," Goodreads, https://www.goodreads.com/quotes/9340879-once-a-reporter-asked-him-do-you-really-think-you.

22 Matt Daloisio, text message to author, July 29, 2024.

23 Dahr Jamail, interview with author, February 21, 2023.

24 Kathy Kelly, "The Longest War: Overcoming Lies and Indifference," *Mobilizing Ideas*, July 2, 2012, https://mobilizingideas.wordpress.com/2012/07/02/the-longest-war-overcoming-lies-and-indifference/.

ACKNOWLEDGMENTS

1 *Frontline*, season 28, episode 21, "Once Upon a Time in Iraq," directed by James Bluemel (Keo Films, 2020). The Islamic State went, over time, by various names, including the Islamic State in Iraq and the Levant (ISIL).

INDEX

Page numbers in italics refer to figures.

Abdel-Rahman, Omar, 99
Abercrombie, Neil, 317
Abileah, Rae, 276, 333–34, 428nn74–75, 436nn64–65
Abraham, F. Murray, 174
absent without leave (AWOL), 261, 291–93, 329–30, 435n56
Abu Ghraib prison, 246–54, 276, 282, 292–94, 316, 323, 331, 356, 423n74, 423n81, 423n83, 424n3
Abu-Jamal, Mumia, 128
ACC. *See* Anti-Capitalist Convergence (ACC)
Ackerman, Patricia, 178
ACLU. *See* American Civil Liberties Union (ACLU)
Act Now to Stop War and End Racism (ANSWER), 51–52, 65–72, 81, 106, 112, 118, 126–31, 134, 141, 150, 172, 216, 235, 243–45, 259, 299, 313–14, 327, 335, 343, 347, 357; official name, 390n60. *See also* International ANSWER Coalition (IAC)
ACT UP, 52, 267–68
Adams, Elliott, 358, 440n58
Afghan Americans, 40, 73
Afghan Portraits of Grief (report), 104, 394n51, 399n125
Afghan Women's Association International, 73

Afghanistan Civilian Assistance Program, 222
Afghanistan war. *See* war in Afghanistan
AFL-CIO, 56–59, 136, 146, 314
Africa: as antiwar, 139, 145, 155, 175; diaspora, 133; drone strikes in, 2; poor in, 25; travel to, 88; uranium in, 102, 301. *See also* South Africa
African Americans, 38, 44–46, 71, 126–28, 133, 136, 159, 208, 272, 275, 316
AFSC. *See* American Friends Service Committee (AFSC)
aggression: and fear, 2; US, and 9/11, 14, 17, 83, 133, 234
Ahmad, Harafa, 91
Al Jazeera network, 208
al-Aioby, Rona, 285
Alarcón, Francisco Xavier, 173
Albon, Damon, 144, 157
Albright, Madeleine, 118
Ali, Muhammad, 69–71, 390n64
Ali, Syed, 99
Ali, Tariq, 21, 364
al-Jabani, Abeer Qassim, 311
al-Kamil, Malek, 217
al-Kandari, Fayez, 325
al-Kaysi, Kadouri, 117
al-Khedairy, Amal, 231–32

Allen, Jackie, 324
Allende, Salvador, 67
al-Libi, Ibn al-Shaykh, 102
al-Maliki, Nouri, 350
Almontaser, Debbie, 104
al-Mufti, Nermin, 231–32
al-Qaeda, 1–2, 14–26, 46–48, 67, 77, 80–81, 89, 100–102, 142, 152, 229, 241–42, 267, 291–92, 318–19, 325, 341, 353, 357
al-Sadr, Muqtada, 209–10
al-Shirab, Hisham, 194, 217
Alter, Jonathan, 23
Alternet, 83
Altikriti, Anas, 157
al-Zaidi, Muntazer, 350–51
al-Zarqawi, Abu Musab, 229–30
American Civil Liberties Union (ACLU), 247, 352, 422n70, 427n54, 439n31. *See also* New York Civil Liberties Union
American Friends Service Committee (AFSC), 72, 103, 131, 135, 189, 214, 240–41, 421n38
American-Arab Anti-Discrimination Committee, 33
America's International Center, 185
Amirani, Amir, 405n1, 416n3
Amis, Martin, 12, 379n18
Amnesty International, 291, 322, 326
Amundson, Amber, 37, 83–84, *84*, 384n27
Amundson, Craig Scott, 37, 83–84
Amundson, Ryan, 83
anarchism, 14, 35, 51, 54–55, 58–60, 64, 72, 105, 271, 389n48
Anderson, Charlie, 295
Anderson, Laurie, 94
Annan, Kofi, 145, 160
annihilation, 257, 328; politics of, 26
"Another World Is Possible" (antiwar slogan), 52–60, 76
Ansary, Amin, 40
ANSWER. *See* Act Now to Stop War and End Racism (ANSWER)

Antarctica, protests in, 155–56
anti-Americanism, 11, 22, 24–27, 78–79, 114, 142, 194, 208, 242, 267, 364
Anti-Capitalist Convergence (ACC), 57–65, 387n22, 389n38
Anti-Capitalist March Against Hate, Capitalism, and War, 59
"Anti-Capitalists Against War Racism Terrorism Property" (ACC march banner), 63
antiracism, 56, 133, 135, 167, 215. *See also* racism
anti-Semitism, 217, 414n87
antiwar movement: activism, 4–5, 38–39, 50–54, 58, 61–65, 82, 125, 135, 169–71, 189, 199, 203–6, 213, 227, 237, 242–43, 275–76, 279, 282, 294, 301, 311–13, 317, 327, 332, 350, 362, 365–66, 370–71, 377n9, 402n48, 407n31, 416n16, 436n82; as antiglobalization movement, 50–51, 63–64, 72; bad news for, 354–57; bigger toolbox for, 271; birth of, 50–73; building, 214; burnout in, 354; and Bush reelection, 254–79; challenges of, 4, 281, 312; and civil-resistance action, 57; in climate of shock, fear, and anger, 29; coalitions, 43–44, 46, 53, 108, 131, 134, 137, 172, 260, 275; collective power of, 164; collectives, 54, 274, 322; and conservatives, 310; demographics, 410n101; and dissent, 5, 9, 32, 94, 99, 134–37, 170–72, 206, 213, 242, 357–58, 364–65, 366; and diversity, 55; and division, 52; dynamism of, 322; energized, 282–83; first national demonstration, 314; and future wars, 213–14; global, 5, 108, 138–70, 172, 175, 191, 197, 203, 217, 242–43, 245, 312, 326–27, 366, 421n47; grassroots, 53–54, 71, 132, 169, 172, 175, 183, 188, 263, 299, 318, 322, 359; growing intensity of, 108; as intergenerational, 60–61; and Iraqi commoners as

victims, 230; largest in history, 362; literature on, 377nn7–8; as mainstream, 339; mass demonstrations and protests, 4, 50–51, 76, 103–7, 121–22, 126–31, 138–70, 172, 175–77, 203–6, 231, 235–36, 242–43, 255, 265–76, 306–7, 310–12, 327, 339, 366, 441n13; as mass movement, 2, 357; and media, 300; and military dissent, 172, 226, 280–310; mobilization, 4–6, 50–52, 56–57, 71, 132, 139, 149–50, 168, 171, 237, 263, 348–49, 362, 442n24; in national memory, 5; as necessary, 57–60; and 9/11, 5, 7–31, 35–39, 42–52, 65–77, 95, 108, 149, 171–72, 237, 255, 364–65; and party support, 335; polemics, 144–45; and policymaking, 73, 121, 312; and politics of truth, 278–79; and predatory American power, defense against, 120; and progressives, 143, 300; in public consciousness, 5; and radicalism, 52, 95, 107, 204, 216; S30, 51, 55–63, 71–72; slogans and shared language, 2, 73–74, 78–79, 105, 391n3; and social upheavals, 312–13; strategic approach, 271; and support for troops, 286–94; sustained, 327–34; telegenic disruptions, 123; tensions, 119; and truth, 279; and unity, 52; vigils, 44, 62, 180, 213, 270, 276; vindicated, 6, 231; and vulnerability and resolve, 268; women in, 108, 121–25, 172, 175, 177–78, 196, 413n50, 414n81; worldview of, 28–29. *See also* peace: movements
AP. *See* Associated Press (AP)
apartheid, South African, 45, 133, 159
"Appeal of Redress from the War in Iraq," 330–31, 339, 435n58
Arab Americans, 18–19, 57, 76, 105, 114, 127, 159, 187, 193, 244, 268–69
Arab Spring, 366

Arab-American Family Support Center, 151
Arab-Israeli War (1967), 126–27
Arabs: abuse of, 243; acts of hate against, 19; advocacy organizations for, 19; and antiwar movement, 62–63, 76, 127, 135, 139, 215, 244–45; apprehensions of, 10; bigotry against, 18–19; civil liberties for, 47; civilizational loyalties of, 17; as combatants with United States, 20; as criminalized, 332; dehumanized by illegitimate war, 248–49; detention of, 19, 96, 353; as internal enemy, 18; military attacks on, 246; and modernity, 17; 9/11 backlash against, 18–19; as patriotic, 18; and peace rallies in Israel, 139; prejudice against, 19, 116; profiling of, 65; racism against, 43, 65; and resentment, 16; roundups of, 19, 75; safeguards and protections for, 47; sidelined, 244; solidarity with, 332; and terrorist label, 269; as threat to nation, 19; and War on Terror, 17. *See also* American-Arab Anti-Discrimination Committee; Muslims
Arbeiter, Laurie, 331–33, 351, 435n61
Arendt, Hannah, 14
Ariabi, Entisar Mohammad, 333–34, 435n63
Arlington National Cemetery (United States), 83–84, 276
Arlington West (makeshift memorial), 236, 241, 285–86, 303, *307*, 420n24
Arnett, Peter, 202, 207, 417n18
Arnove, Anthony, 338, 372, 436n75
Artists Against War, 331
Artists and Musicians for Peace, 151
Artists Network of Refuse and Resist, 98
Ashcroft, Evan, 287

Ashley, Carole, 332, 372
Asia, 43; and antiwar movement, 139. *See* South Asia
Asner, Ed, 105
assassinations, 109–10, 170, 225, 249
Associated Press (AP), 74, 160, 417n27, 433n15
Athens's People for Justice and Peace, 189
Atta, Mohammed, 100
Attica Prison uprising, 71
AUMF. *See* Authorization for Use of Military Force (AUMF)
Australia, and antiwar movement, 138–39, 154–55, 177, 201, 242, 338–39, 414n85, 415n108
authoritarianism, 22, 28, 66; anti-, 54, 205
Authorization for Use of Military Force (AUMF), 9, 38–39, 257, 316
Avedon, Richard, 268
Avila, Amalia, 284
AWOL. *See* absent without leave (AWOL)
Aziz, Tariq, 187–88, 216–17, 223, 418n58
Aznar, José María, 241

Bacon, Kevin, 174
Baez, Joan, 306–7, *307*
Baggarly, Steven (Steve), 135–36, 344
Baghdad (Iraq), 7, 165, 185, 188–202, 207–12, 216–22, 232–33, 242, 245–49, 260–62, 284–87, 295, 321–22, 344–45, 414n74, 414n84; airport road, 286; Al Dar Hotel, 218; Al-Fanar Hotel, 189, 217, 220, *220*; Amariyah air-raid shelter, 115, 118; bombings of, 171, 176, 191, 201–2, 207–9, 219; collapse and fall of, 209, 212, 220; Firdus Square, 208, 221–22; Green Zone, 219, 228–30, 350, 420n12, 428n11; Mahdi army, 209–10, 247; Mansur neighborhood, 207–9, 224; Nisour Square, 311, 344–45; Palestine Hotel, 192, 207–8; reconstruction, 233; Sadr City, 209–10, 219–20, 249, 287; School of Folk Music and Ballet, 194, 217; UN office in, 193
Baker, James, 336
Balkans, 58, 186
Baltimore Chronicle, 302
Baltimore Sun, 8
Banks, Dennis, 306
Barfield, Ellen, 293, 309–10, 431n78
Barnard College, 252, 276, 423n87
Bartlett, Megan (Meg), 105, 272, 399n128
Baxter, Nathan, 38
Bayard, Claire, 57–60, 126, 204–5
Becker, Brian, 68–72, 80, 117, 126–31, 134, 141, 216, 245, 371
Becker, Richard, 71
Belafonte, Harry, 39, 159–60, 314, 408n72
Bello, Walden, 63, 389n43
Benderman, Kevin, 292
Benjamin, Medea, 73, 87–95, *91*, 103, 122–24, 129, 150, 164–65, 176, 178, *196*, 221, 239, 244, 281–82, 326, 359, 371, 394n49, 394n59, 403n50, 413n50, 440n61, 440n63
Benn, Tony, 144, 244
Bennis, Phyllis, 39, 131–32, 139, 159–60, 168, 188, 203, 235, 245, 249, 354–56, 364, 366
Berg, Michael, 276
Berg, Nicholas (Nick), 249, 276
Bergen, Peter, 22, 381n46
Berlusconi, Silvio, 140, 242
Berman, Paul, 120, 402n38
Berrigan, Daniel, 75–76, 82, 85, 271, 325–26
Berrigan, Frida, 271–75, 323–24, *323*, 350, 397n97, 427n52
Berrigan, Philip, 82, 85, 99, 135–36
Berthold, Richard, 78–79
Betzold, Michael, 33, 383n9
BFP. *See* Brooklyn for Peace (BFP)
Bhatia, Bela, 413n53
Bichelbaum, Andy, 361–62

INDEX

Biden, Joe, 109, 353, 365, 367
Billionaires for Bush, 264, 268, 274, 425n28, 427n58
bin Laden, Osama, 1–2, 7, 13–16, 20–22, 29, 32, 35, 40, 47, 62, 80–81, 102, 224, 232, 277, 381n45
Black Bloc, 54–55, 57, 60, 64, 389n48
Black Power, 46, 70, 170
Black Radical Congress (BRC), 127, 133, 404n86
Black Voices for Peace (BVP), 44–46, 131–35, 177, 214
Blacks. *See* African Americans; people of color
Blackwater (private security contractor), 246, 283, 286, 311, 344–45, 437n14
Blair, Tony, 142–46, 155–58, 167–68, 300–301, 336, 364
Blake, Michael, *328*
Blitzer, Wolf, 198–99
Blix, Hans, 154
Bloch, Nadine, 53–59, 72–73, 200
Bloomberg, Michael, 152–54, 243, 265–67, 269
Bluemel, James, 442n1
Blume, Kathryn, 173–74
Bodley, Deora, 90
Bodley, Derrill, 38, 90–91, *91*, 103–4, 159, 163
Boggs, Grace, 39
Bolger, Daniel, 318–19
Bond, Julian, 159, 314
Bonifaz, John, 300–301
Bossie, Bob, 413n53
Boston Globe, 41, 63
Boumédiène v. Bush, 345
Bower, Sharron, 174
Boxer, Barbara, 317
Boyd, Andrew, 264
BPfP. *See* Brooklyn Parents for Peace (BPfP)
Branham, Amy, 302
BRC. *See* Black Radical Congress (BRC)
Breen, Cathy, 191–92, 414n74
Bremer, Paul, 210, 224, 238–39, 247

Brewer, Gale, 163, 409n85
Bright, Jane, 287, 291
"Bring Them Home Now!" campaign, 227–28, 235, 289–90, 309
Bringing the War Home (Varon), 428n73
Brockman, Beth, 344, 437nn11–12
Brodhead, Frank, 93
Brokaw, Tom, 198–99, 202
Brooklyn for Peace (BFP), 375, 407n42
Brooklyn Parents for Peace (BPfP), 150–51, 178–79, 212, 315–16, 407nn42–43, 412n28, 412n31
Brown, Adrienne Maree, 348
Brown, Jerry, 123
Brown, John, 182
Buddhism, 182, 285
Buffa, Andrea, 131, 135–36
Bulgaria, 175
Burgess, Dave, 201
Burns, John F., 192–93, 219, 414n75, 414n82, 421n44
Bush, George H. W., 109–11, 116; hidden hard line side of, 401n19
Bush, George W., 97, 182–85, 195–97, 359–61; and ACT UP Philadelphia protest, 267–68; anti-, 83, 129, 167, 243, 252–53, 263, 267–68, 279, 334–35, 356, 416n13; and antiwar movement, 36, 129, 139–40, 243, 300, 303, 312, 350–51, 356, 359–60; and antiwar movement following reelection, 252–79; apology by, 423n76; on axis of evil, 28, 99–100; and big business interests, 128–29; billionaires for, 264, 268, 274, 425n28, 427n58; Britain's alliance with, 142–46, 150, 155–58, 160, 167–68, 300–301; bullhorn address, 1–2, 36, 377n1; campaign, 255–57, 263–64, 268, 287; Democratic challengers, 254–59; destructive policies, 279; and fantastical vision of inevitable victory in just cause, 279; global protests against, 146–54;

Bush, George W. (*continued*)
heartland authenticity, 278; and imagecraft, 6, 212; impeachment, calls for, 300–302, 320, 401n19; and imperialism, 277–79; inaugural address, 280, 428n2; and Iraq, US policy on, 349; last day in office, 350–51; manufactured narratives, 211, 230–31; and military dominance, 119; mockery of, 252; and neocons, 96, 129; as 9/11 president, 255; and oligarchy, 262; oppression in last year of first term, 280; in Panama, 434n36; partisan disapproval of, 334–35, 357; peace appeals to, 83, 146, 150, 155; perfidy of, 263; and Phantom Fury, 283–84, 286; photo op, 211; as popular and successful, 4; presidential toughness of, 23; ranch, 5, 243, 282, 302–4, 308–9, 329; reelected, 254–80, 287–88; and religion, 17–18, 34, 45, 151, 382n71; saber-rattling speech, 181; as statesman, 165; support for, 142, 308, 335, 353; tax cuts, 257; tenure, 254–55; and tolerance, 19; and treason, 361; ultimatum speech, 182; and United Nations, 145; view of good and evil, 195; and war of vanity, 243; and War on Terror, 1–7, 9, 15, 27–31, 64, 109–10, 254–55, 353, 355, 382n71; and war resolution, 122; and world-saving benevolence, 280; worldview of, 28–29
Bush, Laura, 172
Butler, Judith, 94
BVP. *See* Black Voices for Peace (BVP)
Byrd, Robert, 119, 153, 179

Cagan, Leslie, 97–98, 131–38, 146–54, 160, 164–66, 169–71, 214, 235, 244, 266–67, *270*, 282, 294, 349, 355–56, 367, 371, 404n77, 405n92

CAIR. *See* Council on American-Islamic Relations (CAIR)
Caldicott, Helen, 39
Camp Casey (Crawford, Texas), 282, 299–311, *304*, *307*, 317, 327–30, 431n78, 432n82
Camp Casey II, 305
Camp Casey III, 309
Camp Casey IV, 315
Camp Justice (joint US-Iraqi military base), 337
Campaign for Nuclear Disarmament, 143
Campbell, Colleen, 90
Campbell, Kelly, 198–200, 393n42
Canada: and antiwar movement, 51, 55, 141, 154–55, 172, 177, 274, 298; refuge in, 293, 298–99
capitalism, 11, 13, 264; anti-, 51, 54, 57–65, 216; and democracy, 16; and racism, 43; and war, 55. *See also* Anti-Capitalist Convergence (ACC)
CARE International, 321
CARECEN. *See* Central American Resource Center (CARECEN)
Carlyle Group, 206
Carroll, James, 41, 385n44
Carter, Jimmy, 176
Casey, Carolyn, 122
Casey, Jody B., *328*
casualties, civilian. *See* civilian casualties
Catholic Church, 185, 271
Catholic Worker movement, 75, 82–83, 135–36, 181, 185–87, 324, 344, 359, 393n33
Cato Institute, 318
Cavanaugh, John, 131–32, 411n14
CCR. *See* Center for Constitutional Rights (CCR)
Center for Constitutional Rights (CCR), 97, 251, 322, 326, 416n16
Central America, 48, 82, 131–32, 185, 252. *See also* Latin America
Central American Resource Center (CARECEN), 131–32

Central Asia, 43
Central Intelligence Agency (CIA), 116; assets, 68; and bin Laden network, 22; interrogations, 9–10, 238–39, 250–51, 352, 378n13, 396n83, 423n80, 423n83, 439n34; prisons, 434n46; on secret foray into Afghanistan, 9–10, 378n14; spies, 320; torture program, 9–10, 251, 352, 378n13; waterboarding, 250
Central Park (New York City), 76, 105–7, 132–33, 152, 265–69
Chalabi, Ahmed, 192, 225, 230
Cheney, Dick, 9–10, 35, 78–79, 100–101, 105, 121, 267, 378n12, 397n106, 402n46
Cheney, Lynne, 78–79, 392nn18–19
Chicago Tribune, 24, 37
Chile, 67
China, 154, 250
Chomsky, Noam, 8–9, 21–27, 42, 79, 94, 97–98, 141, 232, 378n11, 381nn44–45, 381n60, 382n68, 385–86nn47–50
Christian Peacemaker Teams (CPT), 189–92, *192*, 199, 209, 221–22, 247–48, 320–22, 413nn59–60, 433n32
Christianity, 11–12, 18, 34, 44–45, 82, 104, 185, 189–90, 217, 225, 321
Chrome, Margaret, 12–13
Chung, Connie, 199, 415n98
Churchill, Ward, 14–15, 379n24
CIA. *See* Central Intelligence Agency (CIA)
CISPES. *See* Committee in Support of the People of El Salvador (CISPES)
CIVIC. *See* Civilian Innocent Victims in Conflict (CIVIC)
civic action, 5–6, 125–26, 335
civil disobedience, 4, 103, 133, 200, 203–4, 265, 271, 313–15, 324, 343, 358, 415n102
civil liberties, 10, 45–47, 66, 70, 214, 266–69, 386n56. *See also* American Civil Liberties Union (ACLU); New York Civil Liberties Union
civil rights, 70, 82, 95, 106, 149, 179, 189, 273, 289, 294. *See also* human rights
Civil Rights Act, 68–69
civil servants, resignations of, 181–85
Civilian Assistance Program, Afghanistan, 222
civilian casualties, 2–4, 9, 25, 32–36, 39–40, 49, 69, 77–78, 83, 86–92, 97, 103–4, 112, 115–18, 150, 201, 207–9, 212, 218–24, 230, 234, 247, 271–72, 276, 280–81, 284–86, 296, 311–13, 344–45, 353–54, 384n22, 395n68, 398n110, 401n14, 401n20, 419n66
Civilian Innocent Victims in Conflict (CIVIC), 92, 222–23, 286
Clark, Ramsey, 68–70, 94, 117, 128, 187, 223, 390n65
Clark, Tom C., 68–69
Clark, Wesley, 183
Clergy and Laity Concerned About Iraq, 315
Cline, David, 260, 327
Clinton, Bill, 9, 25, 67
Clinton, Hillary, 109, 151, 178–79, 285, 349, 365, 412n31
Clousing, Ricky, 296, 330
CNN, 78, 100, 198–99, 202, 304, 306, 333, 361–62, 417n23, 441n4
Coalition Against War in Iraq, 98–99
Coalition Provisional Authority (CPA), 210–12, 220–25, 238–41, 249, 254, 262
Cockburn, Alexander, 129–30, 155–56, 404n73
Code Pink, 121–25, 135, 177–79, 184–85, 195–96, 201–2, 221, 231–32, 263–64, 270–71, 276, 284–85, 302–3, 306, 314–15, 318, 326, 333–34, 357–59, 362, 367, 411nn22–23, 412n26, 440n61, 440n63

Coffin, William Sloane, 34
Cohen, Ben, 39, 128
Cold War, 4, 11, 15–16, 43, 53, 132, 142–43, 166, 250
collateral damage. *See* civilian casualties
colonialism: anti-, 129; British, 196, 329; European, 21; and global protests, 142; and Iraq War, 243; neo-, 46; racial dimensions of, 46. *See also* imperialism
Colorado Muslim Society, 413n54
ColorLines (magazine), 43, 56
Columbia University, 23, 179
Colville, Mark, 344–45, *345*
Combatant Status Review Tribunals, 434n45
Committee in Support of the People of El Salvador (CISPES), 133
Common Dreams (online platform), 8–9, 401n26
Common Ground, 309
communism, 39, 51, 69–70, 94–98, 129–30, 149, 173, 223; in China, 250; collapse of, 208; and democracy, 141–42; East European, 182; and socialism, 70, 142; as threat, 257. *See also* Revolutionary Communist Party (RCP)
communities of color. *See* people of color
Concerned Families of Westchester, 93
conflict resolution: and cooperative social order, 393n33; and diplomacy, 349; and justice, 349
connection, politics of, 199
Conscience, Concern, and Commitment, 99
conscientious objection, 144, 181, 253, 261, 292
conscripts, 27, 94
constitutional crimes, 300
Conteris, Andrés Thomas, 358, 440n59
Conyers, John, 301, 314
Cooper, Anderson, 304

Cooper, Marc, 67, 390n57
Corbyn, Jeremy, 144
Corn, David, 129, 312
Cortright, David, 41–42, 131–32, 134, 146, 154–55, 180, 355, 362–63, 411n16, 441n6, 441n8
costs of war, 3, 230, 279, 281–82, 368
Costs of War (Watson Institute), 377n5
Council on American-Islamic Relations (CAIR), 99, 326
counterinsurgencies, 21–22, 31, 119, 228, 341. *See also* insurgency
Counterpunch, 381n50, 385n31, 385n35, 385n41, 389n46, 439n53
"Courage for Peace, Not for War" (antiwar slogan), 220, *220*
Courage to Resist, 292
Courage to Resist (podcast), 396n94
court martial, 423n73, 423n75
Covert Action Memorandum of Notification, 378n13
covert actions, 21–22, 378n13
Cox, Alex, 144
CPA. *See* Coalition Provisional Authority (CPA)
CPT. *See* Christian Peacemaker Teams (CPT)
Crane, Susan, 324
Crater, Amanda, 176
Crenshaw, Kimberley, 94
Crenshaw, Martha, 382n65
crimes: against humanity, 41, 44; and terrorism, 9, 30, 44; and violence, 8; and war, 40–41, 368. *See also* constitutional crimes; hate: crimes; war crimes
Critical Voice, 331–32
C-SPAN, 65–66, 240, 389n50, 394n49, 401n23, 403n69, 419n3, 420n10, 421n36, 431n71, 431nn74–75, 433n20
Cuba: as historic target of US imperialism, 244; revolution, 149; travel to, 88, 323–26, 358, 434n35, 434n44; vigil in, 339. *See also* Guantánamo Bay (Cuba)

Daily Kos, 303–4
Dalai Lama, 34, 352, 384n16
Daloisio, Matt, 273, 322–24, *323*, 346
Danaher, Kevin, 41, 61
Daponte, Beth, 401n14, 401n20
Darby, Joseph, 253–54, 423n93
Daschle, Tom, 38, 103
DASW. *See* Direct Action to Stop the War (DASW)
Davis, Angela, 94, 159, 408n72
Davis, Morris, 358
Davis, Ossie, 39
Davis, Russ, 64–65
Dawson, Joshua, *328*
Day, Dorothy, 82
D.C. Asians for Peace and Justice, 177
de Blasio, Bill, 269
Dean, Howard, 255–56, 424n7, 424n13
Dee, Ruby, 39
Def, Mos, 94
Defense Department. *See* Department of Defense (United States)
Deghayes, Omar, 339
del Naja, Robert, 144
DeLay, Tom, 317
Delgado, Aidan, 296–97
Dellums, Ron, 38
demagogy, 67
democracy: and capitalism, 16; and communism, 141–42; and freedom, 14, 41, 120; global appeal of, 398n110; and informed citizenry, 121; and protests, 149; and public opinion, 364; and radical change, 149; and war, 241
Democracy Now! (media program), 63, 89, 98, 178, 232–33, 235–36, 263, 273, 284, 333
Democratic National Convention (DNC), 214, 259–60, 424n7. *See also* Republican National Convention (RNC)
Dempsey, Martin E., 242
Denbeaux, Mark P., 325

Department of Defense (United States), 325, 422n70, 434n45
Department of Homeland Security (United States), 102, 265, 332
Department of Justice (United States), 68, 152, 250, 352–53, 379n15, 439n34; protest at, 360; security measures, 19
Department of Peace (United States), 316
Department of State (United States), 96, 181, 269, 286, 305, 364
Desai, Bhairavi, 269
Desert Storm. *See* Gulf War (1990–1991)
Deserter's Tale, The (Key), 298–99, 430n59, 431n69
Desis Rising Up & Moving, 275
dictatorships, 4, 67, 113, 134, 158, 197, 238, 252, 277
diplomacy: coercive, 398n110; and conflict resolution, 349; and legitimizing war, 115; and rule of law, 337
Direct Action to Stop the War (DASW), 204–5
Dirty Wars (Scahill), 354, 439n38
discrimination: gender, 393n33; racial, 393n33; religious, 393n33; and violence, 95; and war, 95. *See also* American-Arab Anti-Discrimination Committee
dissidents: and communism, 182; East European, 182; and media, 10, 359; in prisons, 397n97; and protests, 364–65; soldiers as, 261, 293; voices of, 46; and War on Terror, 364–65
Dixie Chicks, 179–80, 206, 412nn32–33
Dixon, John, 238–39
DNC. *See* Democratic National Convention (DNC)
Doebbler, Curtiss, 413n53
DOJ. *See* Department of Justice (United States)
Donahue, Phil, 171

Dougherty, Kelly, 261–62, 269, 290, 294
draft. *See* military draft
Dreze, Jean, 413n53
drone strikes, 2, 354, 358–59, 440nn61–62
Durbin, Richard, 314

Earle, Steve, 94
Eastern Michigan University, 62
Edgar, Bob, 213
Edwards, John, 256
Egypt, 102, 139–41, 217, 323, 337
Ehrenreich, Barbara, 39, 94, 252, 276, 423n87
Eisenberg, Rusti, 179, 313, 315, 407n42, 432n6
EITs. *See* enhanced interrogation techniques (EITs)
El Salvador, 133
Elbaradei, Mohammed, 203
Elbaum, Max, 42–44, 95, 111–13, 349, 371–72, 386n54
Ellsberg, Daniel, 261, 302
Emergency Campaign to Reclaim Democracy & Stop the War Now!, 199–200
"End US Policy That Breeds Terror" (antiwar slogan), 73
enemy aliens, detained on immigration charges post-9/11, 379n15
Engelhardt, Tom, 269, 277, 279, 327, 426n50
Engler, Mark, 169, 237, 420n26
enhanced interrogation techniques (EITs), 250–51, 423n83
Ensler, Eve, 94
Epstein, Barbara, 213
ESF. *See* European Social Forum (ESF)
Esposito, Michael, 152–53
ethnicity: and identity, 16, 62; and religion, 16, 62, 77, 79, 225, 236–37
European Social Forum (ESF), 140–43, 406nn7–8
Evans, Benjamin, 284

Evans, Erica, 177–78
Evans, Jodie, 122–23, 284, 306, 403nn50–53
exceptionalism, 11, 29
exploitation, 74, 250; economic, 393n33
extremism, 17–19, 78, 281, 319, 337, 341, 381n49. *See also* fanaticism
"Eye for an Eye Will Leave the Whole World Blind, An" (antiwar slogan), 62
"Eyes Wide Open" exhibit, 240–41, 261, 265, 285–87

Fahrenheit 9/11 (Moore documentary film), 262–63, 276, 425n26
faith, 189; civic, 5–6; and conscience, 324; and culture, 18. *See also* religion
Falk, Richard, 46–49, 67, 119, 386n59
Fallujah (Iraq), 211–12, 218, 246–47, 280–86, 319, 427n68, 428n13, 429nn17–22
fanaticism, 23, 233. *See also* extremism
fascism, 25–28, 70; anti-, 26
FBI. *See* Federal Bureau of Investigation (FBI)
FCNL, 318
fears: and aggression, 2; and equivocation, 340; of oppression, 319; politics of, 102, 125; of terrorism, 39, 206; of war, 169
Featherstone, Liza, 67–68, 79, 106, 125, 127–28
Federal Bureau of Investigation (FBI), 10, 19, 96, 224, 273, 427n53
Feingold, Russ, 97
Feinstein, Diane, 317
Fellowship of Reconciliation, 103, 131, 178, 231, 419n9
feminism, 52, 58, 123–25, 175, 178, 252, 263, 403n59, 411n22
Ferner, Mike, 190–91, 343
Fiasco (Ricks), 312, 419n5, 432n4
"Fight the Rich—Not Their War" (antiwar slogan), 172

"Finlandia" (Finnish hymn), 194, 217
Fire This Time, The (Clark), 69–70, 390n65
First Amendment (US Constitution), 70, 153, 267
Fischer, Joschka, 154
Fisk, Robert, 22, 381n45
Fithian, Lisa, 55, 137, 200, 214–15, 236–37, 244–45, 272–73, 302–9
Fitzrider, Ellen, 163
Flack, Roberta, 314
Flanders, Laura, 7–8
Fleck, Bela, 151
Fleischer, Ari, 86
Fletcher, Bill, Jr., 131–36, 203, 404n86
Fonda, Jane, 94, 258
Food Not Bombs, 58, 305, 432n82
foreign policy, 8, 14–17, 22–23, 45–47, 101, 126–29, 133, 141–42, 145, 179, 290, 383n13, 398n110
Foreign Service (United States), 172
Fort Bragg (Fayetteville, North Carolina), 243, 288, 429n29
Fort Hood (Texas), 260, 304, 329–30
Fort Lewis (Washington), 287, 330
Fox, Tom, 320–22
France, 170; and antiwar movement, 138–39, 154–55, 172, 175–77, 381n45
Francis, Saint, 217
Franks, Tommy, 299
Free Palestine Alliance, 244
Free Trade Area of the Americas (FTAA), 51, 60, 236–38
freedom: and democracy, 14, 41, 120; enemies of, 27–28; and force, 211; and justice, 280; and liberty, 210; and slavery, 241; and tolerance, 2; and tyranny, 53, 210
French, Duane, 232
Friends Council on National Legislation, 315
Friends of the Earth, 56
Frontline (PBS), 233, 442n1

FTAA. *See* Free Trade Area of the Americas (FTAA)
Fukuyama, Francis, 16, 380n30
Funk, Steven, 261, 291

Gall, Carlotta, 392n30
Gallup polls, 208, 383n5, 402n43
Gandhi, 62, 329
Gant, John, 239
Garnanez, Tina, 295
Gates, Richard, 401n19
Geneva Conventions, 97, 191, 250, 254, 427n68
genocide, 46–47, 81, 393n31
Georgetown University, 420n10
Gephardt, Richard, 104–5
Germany, 98; and antiwar movement, 138–39, 141–43, 154–55, 166–67, 170, 176
Gish, Peggy Faw, 189–91, 209, 218, 413n59
Gitlin, Todd, 67, 129–30
Glaspie, April, 110–11
Glick, Jeremy, 99
Global Exchange, 41, 53–54, 61, 73, 87–91, 104, 118–19, 131, 231, 239, 247, 284, 320
Global Peace Initiative, 125
global protests, 5, 108, 137–72, 175, 191, 197, 203, 217, 242, 245, 312, 326, 366, 421n47
Global South, 20, 44, 53–54, 59, 145, 170, 177, 204–5, 242, 378n9, 389n43
globalization, 63–65, 214, 236–37; anti-, 50–51, 63–64, 72. *See also* internationalism
Glover, Danny, 39, 94, 159, *270*, 408n72
Goff, Stan, 227, 327
Gold Star: families, 299–305, 308; parents, 228, 287, 291, 302–4
Gold Star Families for Peace (GSFP), 287–88, 290, 299–305, 308, 315, 317
Gold Star Families Speak Out, 308
Goldberg, Michelle, 106–7, 400n139

Goldsmith, Peter, 145, 406n21
Goodman, Amy, 89, 178, 235, 343, 420n21
Goodman, Paul, 278
Goodrich, Tim, 261, 299
Gore, Al, 74–75, 259, 264
Gosse, Van, 131–34, 149–50, 214, 348–49, 372, 404n77, 404n85, 405n92, 405n95
GPTs. *See* Gulf Peace Teams (GPTs)
Graeber, David, 237, 420n27
Grandmothers for Peace, 177
Greece, 58; and antiwar movement, 106, 143, 154–55, 174–75
Greenpeace, 45, 53, 122
grief: and anger, 37, 73, 203, 262; challenged, 94; denial phase of, 12–13; emblems of, 36; of families for lost service members, 287, 302; amid global pain, 203; of Iraqis, 262; from 9/11, 32, 36–37, 94, 104; not a cry for war, 2, 65, 73–74, 79, 105, 391n3; and solidarity, 36, 287, 305–6
Griffin, Susan, 178
Ground Zero for Peace, 105, 399n128
GSFP. *See* Gold Star Families for Peace (GSFP)
Guantánamo Bay (Cuba), 6, 97, 123, 242, 250–52, 259, 270, 273, 316, 321–26, 338, 345–46, 352–61, 367, 396n84, 434n35, 434nn45–47, 435n48, 438n15, 439nn30–31, 439n36, 440nn59–60
Guardian, 8, 14, 67, 99, 196, 364, 423n76
Guatemala, 190
Guevara, Che, 230
guilt: and psychological distress, 297; and punishment, 223; shared, of wars, 21
Gulf Peace Teams (GPTs), 185–86, 197, 413n52
Gulf War (1990–1991), 69, 81–82, 184–86, 191–92, 195–96, 273; and Bush's Mideast legacy, 401n21;

casualties, 401n15; and Iraq, 101, 145; media coverage, 202; and munitions with depleted uranium, 99; opposition to and protests against, 38, 43–45, 88, 126, 145, 148, 151, 260, 288; as popular war, 111; as safe war, 12; sanctions, 223, 231–32; Syndrome, 109–19; and Vietnam, 109–20
Gumbelton, Thomas, 117, 198

Hadley, Steven, 303
Hagler, Graylan, 45, 66, 135, 159, 184
Haiti, 190
Halliburton, 225, 268, 317
Halliday, Denis, 81, 187–89
Hamdan v. Rumsfeld, 436n77
Hamer, Fannie Lou, 95
Hamill, Sam, 172–73
Hamilton, Lee, 336
Hammad, Suheir, 98
Hampshire College, 61–62, 79–80, 135, 392n25
Harper's Magazine, 11
Hashimi, Ahmad, 104
Hass, Amira, 368
Hassan, Margaret, 321
hate: anti-American, 22, 24–27; crimes, 18–19, 380n36; and prejudice, 19; produces hate, 42–46; self-, of left, 27; and US policies, 47; and violence, 22; and war, 42–47
Havens, Richie, 159
Hayden, Tom, 94, 237
Heaney, Michael T., 335, 339, 355–56, 429n29, 433nn17–18, 436nn66–67, 438n19
hegemony: or human unity, 340; and new world order, 111
Henderson, Abdul, 263
Herold, Marc, 35, 384n21
Hersh, Seymour M., 248, 253, 423n74
Hickey, James, 238
Hicks, David, 242

INDEX 455

Hilal, Maha, 358
Hip Hop Against Racist War, 289
Hitchens, Christopher, 24–27, 120, 263, 381nn62–64, 382nn67–69, 425n27
Ho Chi Minh, 230
Hobsbawm, Eric, 211
Hoffman, Michael, 261, 275, 289–90
Holder, Eric, 352, 439n34
Holmes, Larry, 65–66
Holocaust, 14, 82, 331
Homeland Security Department. *See* Department of Homeland Security (United States)
Honkala, Cheri, 66
hooks, bell, 94
Hoover, J. Edgar, 96
Horowitz, David, 24
House, James, *307*
House, John, 307
House, Melanie, *307*
House, Susan, *307*
House Armed Services Committee (United States), 103
Houston Chronicle, 23
Howard, John, 242
Howe, Julia Ward, 334
Hubris (Corn and Isikoff), 312
human rights, 8, 45, 65, 73–75, 87, 97, 133–35, 140, 190, 222–23, 231, 248–51, 322, 325–26, 333. *See also* civil rights
Human Rights Watch, 18, 218, 380nn36–37, 418n60
Human Shields (documentary), 414nn85–89
human unity, or hegemony, 340
humanitarian aid, 5, 58, 79, 92, 142, 172, 185–87, 220–21, 312, 413n57, 429n16
humanity, 2, 6, 16, 20, 41, 44, 64, 73, 81–87, 123–24, 139, 158, 190, 294, 364, 368, 371
Hund, Jason, 349
Huntington, Samuel P., 16–17, 380n33
Hurricane Katrina, 308, 314, *329*

Huse, Jeff, 295, 297
Hussein, Saddam, 4, 32, 69, 100–102, 106, 109–13, 116–21, 129, 134, 157–58, 165, 168, 182, 185–86, 191–94, 197–202, 207–12, 216–25, 230, 233–35, 238–39, 242, 247, 256, 277, 280–81, 291–92, 300, 319, 333–34, 337–38, 398n107, 398nn109–10, 400n2, 415n110, 417nn20–21, 420nn29–31, 421n34
Husseini, Sam, 33
Hutto, Jonathan, 330

"I Have a Dream" (King speech), 106
IAC. *See* International Action Center (IAC)
IAEA. *See* International Atomic Energy Agency (IAEA)
identity, ethnic and religious, 16, 62
ideology, 16, 25, 29, 73, 80, 94, 97, 113, 129, 142, 148, 210, 224, 266, 281, 293, 313–14, 327, 335, 347, 398n110
IGC. *See* Iraqi Governing Council (IGC)
Ignatieff, Michael, 120, 402n39
IMF. *See* International Monetary Fund (IMF)
immigrants: and civil liberties, 214; detention and deportation of, 64, 96, 269; and enemy aliens, 379n15; and law, 19; and police threats, 275; solidarity with, 64; and violence, 11
Immigration and Naturalization Service (United States), 379n15
imperialism: and Afghanistan War, 43, 80; American, 8, 22, 24, 43–44, 68, 80, 113, 119, 126–27, 129, 142, 244, 259, 277–79; anti-, 44, 68, 70; and Bush, 277–79; destructive policies of, 277; evil of, 24; folly of, 241; and foreign policy, 126–27; historic targets of, 244; and imperviousness, 8; and Iraq War, 113, 204–5, 213, 216, 241,

imperialism (*continued*)
277, 279; political stewardship of, 259; and power, 278; and predatory agenda, 80, 129; and racism, 43; and solidarity, 126; and vengeance, 365; and Vietnam War, 43–44, 119, 213; and war, 8, 43, 213, 241, 244, 252; and War on Terror, 80, 259, 365; Western, 21, 252, 380n33. *See also* colonialism

Indymedia collectives, 54

inequalities, 264; domestic, 159, 215, 348; economic, 4, 64–65, 366; global, 50–52, 57, 64–65; and injustices, 64; and terrorism, 64; in United States, 348. *See also* inequities; injustices

inequities: class, 112; economic, 52–53; racial, 112. *See also* inequalities; injustices

infidels, 25

injustices: collective power against, 164; and inequalities, 64; resisting, 76; and terrorism, 64; and war of choice, 357; and War on Terror, 370. *See also* inequalities; inequities; justice

Institute for Policy Studies (IPS), 39, 131–32, 175, 188, 315–16

insurgency, 81, 228–30, 233–34, 241–42, 246–47, 250, 279, 281–86, 295–96, 319, 337, 341–43, 354, 398n110. *See also* counterinsurgencies

intelligence: British, 300; and defense, 439n35; and Iran, 230; manipulation of, 182; and media, 192; and 9/11, 274; and public opinion, 182. *See also* Central Intelligence Agency (CIA); Inter-Services Intelligence (ISI); Senate Select Committee on Intelligence (United States)

Intercept (news organization), 359

Interfaith Service for Justice and Restoration, 58–59

International Action Center (IAC), 67, 112, 117–18, 265

International A.N.S.W.E.R. *See* Act Now to Stop War and End Racism (ANSWER)

International ANSWER Coalition (IAC), 68, 70–72, 106, 118, 401n23, 401n25, 401n30. *See also* Act Now to Stop War and End Racism (ANSWER)

International Atomic Energy Agency (IAEA), 154, 203

International Commission of Inquiry into US Crimes in Indochina, 69

International Criminal Court, 145

International Human Rights Day, 135

international law: and human rights, 8; and morality, 119; and treaties, 165; and war, 42–43, 46–48, 116, 119

International Monetary Fund (IMF), 50–57, 63–64, 71–72, 237, 314

International Occupation Watch Center (Iraq), 231

International Women's Day, 121–22, 177

internationalism, 96, 172, 197, 212. *See also* globalization; nationalism

interrogations. *See* Central Intelligence Agency (CIA); enhanced interrogation techniques (EITs)

Inter-Services Intelligence (ISI), 81

IPS. *See* Institute for Policy Studies (IPS)

IPTs. *See* Iraq Peace Teams (IPTs)

IRA. *See* Irish Republican Army (IRA)

Iran: in axis of evil, 99–100; and Saddam Hussein, 110; and intelligence, 230; and Iraq, 96, 337; and security, 365; and Trump, 365; and WMD, 102

Iranian Americans, 78

Iraq, 122, 157, 168, 194, 197–98, 253; and 9/11, 189; and American peo-

ple, love of, 194; in axis of evil, 99–100; broken from within and from outside, 226; civil conflicts in, 281, 337–38; civilian assistance fund for, 286; commoners as victims, 230; deep caring for, 232; dehumanization of, 295–96; and diplomatic offensive, 337; and foreign extremists, 281, 337, 341; and foreign policy, 290; government, 186, 191–92, 197, 212, 216, 218, 225, 231, 280, 319–20, 338, 344; hostages in, 110, 114, 321; hostilities with, 101; independence, 280; infrastructure and war, 116; Kurds in, 102, 110, 116–17, 119, 175, 225, 238, 357, 420n31; and national reconciliation, 336–37; occupation of, 116, 203–28, 231, 234, 311, 319, 333, 349; and Palestine, 20, 23, 144, 243–44, 321, 332; politics of, 280–81, 283; and predatory American power, 120, 143; prisoners in, 247; refugees, 361; sanctions against, 70, 81, 113, 117–18, 151, 187–89; sectarianism, 225, 319; self-rule, 231; Shia Muslims in, 116, 119, 208–10, 219–20, 225, 238, 245, 247, 280–81, 318–21, 336–38, 341; solidarity with, 4, 185–86, 195, 321; sovereignty, 210, 212, 230, 254, 280; stability in, 341–42; strife in, 320; Sunni Muslims in, 116, 119, 210–11, 219, 225, 247, 281, 318–21, 337, 341–42; threats against, 76; travel to, 195–99; UN authority in, 340; as ungovernable, 319; US policy shifts, 110–11, 349; and war of words, 192–93; and War on Terror, 369–70; and WMD, 102. *See also* Iraq War (2003–2011)
"Iraq, Preemptive War, and Democracy" (teach-in), 213–14
Iraq Coordinating Committee (US Congress), 318, 433n26

Iraq Peace Teams (IPTs), 189–92, *192*, 195–97, 217–20, 232–33, 260, 343, 413n58
Iraq Study Group (ISG), 240, 312–13, 336–38, 432n5
Iraq: The Logic of Withdrawal (Arnove), 338, 436n75
Iraq Veterans Against the War (IVAW), 261–62, 269–70, 275, 289–306, 309–10, 314, 318, 328–31, *328, 329*, 343–44, 347–51, 354, 425n22, 425n25, 430nn54–55, 437n8. *See also* Vietnam Veterans Against the War (VVAW)
Iraq Vets Sound Off forum and workshop, 261–62
Iraq War (2003–2011): and Afghanistan, 2, 31, 74–107, 183, 257, 271–72, 286, 331, 361, 370–71; as aggressive, 353; anniversary, first, 241–45, 261; anniversary, third, 331; battlefield victories as political and military setbacks, 228; bombing, 2–3; coercive diplomacy, 398n110; consequences at home, 310; as contrived, 300; "cordon-and-sweep" operations, 229; deceitful origins, 230, 312; denounced, 206, 339; discredited, 230; diversion of resources to, 309–10; end of, 216, 280, 288–89, 313, 340, 347–49, 361–62; as endless, 3, 118, 341–60; escalation, 331; as failure, 312, 318–22, 337, 341–60, 398n110; as false, 5–6, 206, 312; as geopolitical error, 258; gory reality, 281–82; as grave injustice, 357; grisly imagery and high-risk action, 344; in history, 5, 313–18; and hubris, 312, 398n110; justification for, 102, 118–21, 252; legality, 145; legislative strategy, 318; legitimacy, 282–83; manipulated and manufactured narratives, 211, 230–31; and military dissent, 280–310, 333; misgivings about, 245–53;

Iraq War (2003–2011) (*continued*)
as misguided, 312; as mission accomplished, 206–12, 227, 255, 280, 334; and 9/11, 2, 31, 100–102, 108, 213, 326; and occupation, 203–26; and oil, 143, 145, 165, 194, 237; as one of most choreographed and longest-planned wars in history, 199–200; opposition to and protests against, 77, 81–82, 103–9, 113–14, 117–22, 127–71, 185, 201–26, *202*, 234, 240, 242–43, 252, 260, 277–79, 312–13, 333, 348, 357, 364, 367, 411n19; Phantom Fury, 283–84, 286; polling about, 29–30, 121, 208, 230–31, 308, 383n5, 402nn42–43, 417nn22–23, 419n6, 421nn45–46, 423n90, 424n9, 432nn87–88; popular histories of, 5; as predetermined, 300; as preemptive, 100, 119, 213–14, 418n44; as quagmire, 281; realities of, 281–82, 312; as risky, 139–40; sanitized version of, 281–82; start of, 2, 81, 99–103, 114–15, 202, 204, 208–9, 417n19; support for, 238; and terrorism, 241; truths about, 245–53, 279, 294; turning of, 311–40; unraveling of, 227–53; as victory, 115–16, 213, 227–28, 255, 279–80; and Vietnam, 109–20, 135, 239, 252, 281, 339, 437n82; as war of choice, 357; as war of vanity, 243; and War on Terror, 2, 4, 99–103, 109–10, 241–42, 265, 370; withdrawal from, 230, 281, 311–42, 349–50, 361–62, 364; and world domination, 213
Iraq War Crimes Tribunal, 69, 265
Iraqi Americans, 117, 200
Iraqi Governing Council (IGC), 225, 231, 254
Irish Republican Army (IRA), 42
Isaac, Jeffrey C., 24, 381n61
ISG. *See* Iraq Study Group (ISG)

ISI. *See* Inter-Services Intelligence (ISI)
Isikoff, Michael, 312
ISIL. *See* Islamic State
ISIS. *See* Islamic State
"Islam Is Not the Enemy" (antiwar slogan), 74
Islamic fundamentalism, 252
Islamic State: bigotry against, 18; defeat of, 2–3; extremism and violence of, 17, 26–27; and fascism, 25–26; in Iraq and Syria (ISIS), 357, 359, 364, 440n56, 442n1, 442n19; of Iraq and the Levant (ISIL), 369, 442n1; militants and beheading, 240; names of, 442n1; in post-invasion Iraq, 2–3; and War on Terror, 17. *See also* Council on American-Islamic Relations (CAIR)
Islamophobia, 143
Israel, 22, 25, 70, 123, 126–28, 139, 142–43, 159, 199, 223, 244, 337, 365–66, 368
Italy, 106, 138–40, 143, 154–55, 166–67, 169, 185, 242
IVAW. *See* Iraq Veterans Against the War (IVAW)

Jackson, Jesse, 128, 139, 157, *270*, 306, 314
Jamail, Dahr, 232–34, 238, 246–47, 252, 284, 343, 368, 420n11, 430n44
Japan, 21, 73; and antiwar movement, 34; Hibakusha, 234–35
Jarrar, Raed, 332–33
Jawad, Hadi, 302
Jawait, Omran Harbi, 83
Jensen, Robert, 8, 23
Jews, 87, 89, 148, 174, 223; and anti-Semitism, 217, 414n87; and antiwar movement, 104, 127–28, 135, 139; killing of, 15–16, 46–47, 380n28; and peace, calls for, 104; and peace rallies in Israel, 139; and pro-Palestinian politics, 366

"Jihad Against Jews and Crusaders" (fatwa), 15–16, 380n28
jingoism, 205–6; and vengeance, 23–24
John Paul II (pope), 217
Johnson, Chalmers, 22–23
Johnson, Dennis Loy, 277
Johnson, Lyndon B., 68–69, 317
Johnson, Rebecca, 267
Joi, Van, 276
Jonah House (Baltimore), 85, 271
Jones, Van, 44
Jones, Walter, 317
Jordan, 33, 208, 229, 232, 284, 321, 323, 332
Jubran, Amer, 66
Juergensmeyer, Mark, 382n66
Just Peace, 143
justice: and antiracism, 56; and antiwar movements, 46, 72, 141, 169, 189; and Christianity, 82; and conflict resolution, 349; and destiny, 368; and deterrence of future errors, 351–52; economic, 53–54, 87, 237; environmental, 123; and equity, 133; in foreign affairs, 349; and freedom, 280; and future wars, 352; global, 4, 41, 50–56, 60–65, 71–72, 123, 139–41, 167, 170, 200, 204–5, 215–16, 237–38, 265–67, 314, 366–67; and humanity, 368; infinite, 28, 35; international, 2, 47–48; and law, 40–41; and morality, 11; and peace, 66, 72–73, 108–37, 147–53, 169, 177, 181, 189, 196, 213–14, 237, 242–44, 258, 270, 315, 327–28, 354–55, 365–66, 371–72; racial, 46, 136, 263, 275; and security, 337; swift, and war, 29. *See also* injustices; Mobilization for Global Justice (MGJ)
"Justice, Not Vengeance" (antiwar slogan), 9, 39, 72, 80
Justice Department. *See* Department of Justice (United States)

Justice for Fallujah Project, 285, 429n19
Justice for Muslims Collective, 358

Karzai, Hamid, 77, 92, 182, 230
Kassab, Jirbail, 187
Kassem, Casey, 105
Kauffman, L. A., 52–53, 57–58, 60, 72, 108, 130, *130*, 137–38, 147–50, 170, 236, 238, 372
Kay, David, 100–101, 240
"Keep America Safe," 134
Kelly, Colleen, 85–87, 92, 104, 140, 197–99, 235, 393n32, 393n42, 435n48
Kelly, Kathy (Kathleen), 81–83, 87, 95, 104, 117–18, 186–88, *188*, 191–94, 216–21, 326, 368, 371, 393n42, 413n52, 414n68, 414n79, 442n24
Kelly, Raymond, 163–64
Kelly, Robin, 94
Kelly, Steve, 324
Kember, Norman, 320
Kennedy, Edward (Ted), 179, 241, 253
Kennedy, Ethel, 253
Kent State, 96
Kerry, John, 109, 256–64, 269, 275–78, 290, 318, 335, 424–25nn14–16
Key, Jeff, 306–7, *307*, 432n84
Key, Joshua, 298–99, 430n59, 431n69
Khalil, Hany, 275, 284, 335, 348
Kidder, Margot, 306
Kiesling, John Brady, 181–83, 412nn39–40
Kilgour, Joel, 181
Kim, Ji Sung, 98
Kinane, Ed, 190–93, 219, 413n62
Kinberg, Joshua, 274
King, Martin Luther, III, 104, 159
King, Martin Luther, Jr., 45–46, 82, 93, 106, 135, 151, 159, 328
Kingsland, Susan, 332
Kingsolver, Barbara, 12, 23–24, 29, 379n20, 382n75

Kingston, Maxine Hong, 178, 412n26, 413n50
Kinnell, Galway, 173
Klein, Naomi, 8, 12, 20, 54, 378n10
Kosovo, 38, 58, 183
Krauthammer, Charles, 41, 385n42
Kricorian, Nancy, 178–79, 285–86
KSM. *See* Mohammed, Khalid Sheikh (KSM)
Kucinich, Dennis, 104, 256, 259, 305, 317, 335, 339–40, 424n12, 437n83
Kurds. *See* Iraq: Kurds in
Kushner, Tony, 94
Kuwait: hostages in, 110; Iraq invasion of, 69, 110–15; peace vigil in, 191–92; sovereignty restored, 111
Kyne, Dennis, 273

labor movement, 95, 133, 149, 327. *See also* AFL-CIO; unions
Laffin, Art, 117–18, *323*, 323–24
Lakey, George, 187
Lamont, Ned, 336
Langley, Scott, 323, 372
Langley, Warren, 200
Lasar, Rita, 37–38, 75–76, 89–91, 93, 200
Latin America, 45, 55, 112, 139, 151, 190–91, 260. *See also* Central America
Latinos, 215; antiwar sentiments among, 136, 240, 275, 328–29
law: evasion of, 97; and justice, 40–41; and morality, 119, 358–59; and war, 40–41. *See also* international law; law enforcement; rule of law
law enforcement: apprehensions by, 10; campaign of, 40–42; as contractors in Iraq, 246; and domestic detentions, 379n15; massive campaign of, 40–42; and media, 59; and politics, 271; and protests, 50–51, 55–59, 243, 267, 271; repression by, 57; security measures, 19; and war, 41, 271. *See also* police

Lawson, James, 301
Lawson-Remer, Terra, 267
Leahy, Patrick, 92–93, 286
"Leap of Faith" (protest), 113, 117–18
Lebanese Americans, 232
Leblanc, Judith, 347
Lee, Barbara, 38–39, 129, 252, 305, 314, 385n31, 385n33
Lee, Sheila Jackson, 305
Leffler, Melvyn P., 397n110
Leitz, Lisa, 290–91, 295, 306, 429–30nn36–38
Lenin, Vladimir, 43, 95, 395n78
Lennon, John, 362
Lerner, Gerda, 10, 379n16
Lessin, Nancy, 184, 200, 227
"Let Us Not Commit the Evil We Deplore" (antiwar slogan), 2, 38, 73, 94, 252, 365
Letts, Joe, 195–97
Levant. *See* Islamic State
Lewis, Bernard, 17
Lewis, John, 314
Liben, Robbie, 155–56
Lieberman, Joseph, 336, 343
Limbaugh, Rush, 254
Lindh, John Walker, 77
Lipscomb, Lila, 262–63, 276
Liteky, Charlie, 191
Loach, Ken, 144
lobbying, 92, 109, 131–35, 150, 180, 313–17, 335, 339, 355, 358
Loney, Jim, 320–22
Loperci, Michael, 240
Los Angeles Times, 12, 23, 67, 98, 228, 287
Lott, Trent, 38
Louisiana State University (LSU), 99, 260
Lowery, Joseph, 314
Lucy, Jeff, 297
Lucznikowska, Valerie, 435n48
Lynch, Jessica, 211
Lysistrata Project, 172–75, 411n6, 411n11

Maas, Elmer, 323
MAB. *See* Muslim Association of Britain (MAB)
MacArthur, John, 11–12
Madden, Liam, 330
Mahajan, Rahul, 8, 20, 247, 277
Maines, Natalie, 179–80
Malik, Monami, 275
Mandela, Nelson, 145, 406nn18–20
Manning, Bradley, 440n64
Manning, Chelsea, 359, 440n64
Manning, Mark, 285, 429n17
March on Washington, 189
Margulies, Joseph, 18, 380n35
Marshburn, Don, 243
Martin, Darcy Scott, 131–32
Martin, Kevin, 131–32
Marxism, 43–44, 95, 107, 205
Massachusetts Institute of Technology (MIT), 62
Massey, James (Jim), 261, 296–98
Matrix, The (film), 13
Mattlage, Larry, 305
Maxit, Cesar, 267
MCA. *See* Military Commissions Acts (MCA)
McCaffrey, Nadia, 284
McCain, John, 312, 316, 343, 349–50
McCarthy, Joseph, 70
McCarthy, Tim, 79
McConnell, Michael, 240
McDermott, James (Jim), 105, 200
McGovern, Ray, 301
McGrath, Molly, 200
McKinney, Cynthia, 106, 128–29
McPherson, Michael, 302
McReynolds, David, 130, 212, 378n2
Means, Russell, 306
media: and antiwar movement, 5, 9, 78, 144, 219, 300; bias of, 230–31; credulous, 4; and dissidents, 10, 359; falsehoods, 144–45, 211, 213, 233–34, 266; on institutional opposition to war, 136; and intelligence, 192; and law enforcement, 59; 9/11 in, 23, 29; and politics, 80, 188; progressive, 300; and propaganda, 233–34; and protests, 54, 62–63, 66–67, 78, 106, 121–22, 148, 156–57, 166, 188, 266, 272, 304–5; and public opinion, 78; and truth, 302; underreporting by, 5; war coverage, 144–45, 201–2, 213, 233–34, 282–83, 300, 347; and War on Terror, 80, 264, 280
Medina, Ivan, 261, 425n22
Meet the Press, 101, 378n12, 397n103, 397n106, 402n46
Mejia, Camilo, 291–92, 296–97, 302–3, *328*, 430n40
Mennonites, 105, 135, 189
Messner, Ann, *332*
Mexico, 190, 228; and antiwar movement, 154–55, 328–29; extraterritorial violence in, 21
MFSO. *See* Military Families Speak Out (MFSO)
MGJ. *See* Mobilization for Global Justice (MGJ)
militarism, 7, 11, 29, 48, 58, 60, 82, 98, 271
Military Commissions Acts (MCA), 434n46, 436n77
military community, 5, 172, 184–85, 231, 240–43, 260, 282–83, 290, 299, 308, 327, 330
military dissent, and antiwar movement, 172, 226, 280–310
military draft, 62, 69–71, 82, 159, 196, 293, 363
Military Families Speak Out (MFSO), 184, 200, 227–29, 243–44, 260–61, 287, 290, 297, 301, 304, 308, 314, 318, 335
military force, 47, 109, 207–8, 257, 400n1. *See also* Authorization for Use of Military Force (AUMF)
Military Peace Movement (MPM), 290–91, 294, 299, 315, 329, 429n36
Military Whistleblower Protection Act, 330
militias, 210, 220, 233–34, 238, 319, 336–37, 341–42

Miller, Arthur, 173
Miller, Dede, 287, 302, 315
Miller, Geoffrey, 250–51
Miller, James, 372
Miller, Judith, 101
Milošević, Slobodan, 67, 70
Mirror, The, 156
Missile Dick Chicks, 125, 179, 403n59
MIT. *See* Massachusetts Institute of Technology (MIT)
Mitchell, Bill, 287, 299
Mobilization for Global Justice (MGJ), 50–53, 57–61, 64–65, 68, 72, 314; demise of, 387n17
Mohaiemen, Naeem, 160–62, 409n76
Mohammed, Baz, 104
Mohammed, Khalid Sheikh (KSM), 434n46
Mohammed, Omar, 369
Mohammed, Yanar, 221
"Moms for Peace" (Kerry-Edwards tour), 5, 290–91
Monks, John, 146
Montgomery, Ann, 186, 189, 324
Moore, Michael, 206, 262–63, 269–70, 270, 309, 416nn13–14, 425nn26–27
morality: and justice, 11; and law, 119, 358–59; and oppression, 120; and politics, 335; and war, 2, 6, 8, 11, 252, 331
Morello, Tom, 94, 343
Morrison, Diana, 261
Mortensen, Viggo, 306
Mothers Against War, 136
Movement for Black Lives, 367
MoveOn, 131, 134, 136, 159, 180, 276, 305, 316, 342
MPM. *See* Military Peace Movement (MPM)
MSNBC, 78, 171, 263, 274
Muhsin, Mustafa, 223–26, 419n67
Mulderry, Anne, 93
Murphy, David, 267

Murphy, Gael, 123, 176
Murtha, John, 317–18, 339, 433n24, 436n81
Muslim American Society, 104
Muslim Americans, 268–69
Muslim Association of Britain (MAB), 143–44
Muslim Student Association, 127
Muslims: abuse of, 243; acts of hate against, 19; advocacy organizations for, 19; and al-Qaeda, 15–16; antiwar sentiments among, 77–78, 99, 104, 107, 127, 135–36, 143–45, 151, 223, 244, 321; apprehensions of, 10; assaults on, 22; associations, 188; bigotry against, 18–19, 358; in Bosnia, support of, 181; civil liberties for, 47; civilizational loyalties of, 17–18; and clash of civilizations, 15–16; concern for, 143; criminalized, 332; dehumanized by illegitimate war, 248–49; deportation of, 19; detention of, 19, 151, 179, 242, 353; as extremist enemy, 18; as internal enemy, 18; justice for, 358; killed, 230; 9/11 backlash against, 18–19; and no-fly lists, 19; as patriotic, 18; and pluralism, 18; prejudice against, 19, 24; profiling of, 19; racism against, 19, 358; registration of as foreign nationals, 19; religion and faith of, 17–19; and religious bigotry, 358; roundups of, 19, 75; safeguards and protections for, 47; slaughter of, 230; as socially conservative, 143–44; solidarity with, 18, 332; subjugation of, 25; as terrorists, 17, 269, 296; as threat to nation, 19; and war, 40; and War on Terror, 17. *See also* Arabs; Colorado Muslim Society; Iraq: Shia Muslims in; Iraq: Sunni Muslims in; Muslim Association of Britain (MAB)
Muste, A. J., 367, 442n21

NAACP. *See* National Association for the Advancement of Colored People (NAACP)
Naar-Obed, Michele, 181, 412n37
Nader, Ralph, 259
Naming Project, The, 270
Nashville Coalition for Peace and Justice, 181
Nashville Peace and Justice Center, 151
Nation (magazine), 9, 21, 23, 25, 27, 39, 46–48, 67, 119, 129–30, 136, 155–56, 241, 263
National Association for the Advancement of Colored People (NAACP), 159, 301
National Campaign for Peace in the Middle East, 112–13, 148
National Catholic Conference of Bishops, 86, 136
National Coalition to Stop U.S. Intervention in the Middle East, 69, 112–14
National Committee for a Sane Nuclear Policy (SANE), 41
National Council of Churches, 131, 136
National Day of Prayer and Remembrance, 37–38, 382n71
National Day of Student Action, 106
National Lawyers Guild (NLG), 163–64
National Organization for Women (NOW), 122, 327
National Press Club, 88–89
National Public Radio (NPR), 174, 424n1, 424n14, 428n2, 433n24
National Religious Campaign Against Torture, 326
national security, 15–16, 32, 42–43, 97, 109, 125, 154, 237, 255, 265, 359, 398n110
National Security Agency (NSA), 359
National Student and Youth Peace Coalition (NSYPC), 62, 126, 131, 176, 200
National Student Day of Action for Peaceful Justice, 60–61, 388n31
nationalism, 29, 41, 75, 241–42, 289, 368. *See also* internationalism
nation-states, 16, 28, 31, 129
NATO. *See* North Atlantic Treaty Organization (NATO)
Naughton, Carol, 158
Nazis, 28, 40, 263, 266, 300, 332
Nees, Greg, 34
Nelson, Willie, 314
Nephew, Luke, 360, *360*, 440n65
New Republic, 23
New York City Labor Against War (NYCLAW), 80
New York Civil Liberties Union, 152, 163, 273–74, 407n45
"New York: Not in Our Name" (antiwar slogan), 75–76
New York Police Department (NYPD), 152–53, 161, 164, 265–66, 268–69, 273–75
New York Post, 23, 41, 80
New York Times, 34, 36–37, 66–67, 78, 93–94, 96, 100–101, 104, 106, 114–15, 120, 139, 148, 192–93, 211, 219, 264, 272, 274, 278, 312, 342, 361–62, 427n56, 440n1
New York University, 148, 372
New Yorker, 20–21, 233, 248, 268
Newkirk, Kai, 61–62, 79–80, 135, 150, 200, 276, 363
Newsweek, 23, 421n46
NGOs. *See* nongovernmental organizations (NGOs)
Nhat Hanh, Thich, 285
Nicaragua, 42, 82, 291, 386n50
Night and Fog (Holocaust documentary), 82
9/11 attacks, 75, 80–85, 101–4, 176, 182, 382n76; as act of evil, 28, 34; alleged perpetrators of, 9; anniversary of, first, 103–4, 108; anniversary of, second, 234; and

9/11 attacks (*continued*)
anti-American hate, 24–27; antiwar movement's response to, 5, 7–31, 35–39, 42–52, 65–77, 95, 108, 149, 171–72, 237, 255, 364–65; as backlash against and blowback of US policy, 22–23, 31, 45, 66; as clash of civilizations, 16–19; as crimes against humanity, 41, 44; as criminal acts, 40–41; as end to America's deceptive separation from world, 15; and enemy aliens, 379n15; as evil, 28, 34; and exceptionalism, 11; and families, 1–2, 5, 35–39, 83–93, 106, 279, 312, 365; FBI investigation into, 10, 19; and global protests, 142–44; and global terrorism, 377n2; Ground Zero, 23, 36, 60, 65, 84–85, 105, 146, 234, 255, 271–72, 277, 331, 426n50; and guilt, collective, 14–15; and intelligence operations, 274; justice for, 40–41; mastermind of, 434n46; in media, 23, 29; and "Operation Infinite Justice"/"Operation Enduring Freedom" (Pentagon), 28, 38; on Pentagon, 1, 14–15, 36–37, 84, 136, 203; perpetrators as freedom fighters, 44; and philosophy, 11; polling about, 382nn76–79; race reactions to, 386n58; Shanksville, Pennsylvania, site, 1, 36, 103–4; and solidarity, 20, 36, 74–75; travel restrictions following, 19, 59; and truths, 11–15; and US aggression, 14; victims, 1–2, 7, 9, 14, 20–21, 35–39, 76, 83–93, 98–99, 241, 270, 435n48; and violence, 11; and war, 40–42, 65, 241, 377n2; as war against United States, 27–28. *See also* World Trade Center (WTC)
9/11 Fayetteville Peace with Justice, 289
9/11 First Responders Against War, 272

Nineham, Chris, 141, 157, 406nn7–8
NION. *See* Not in Our Name Project (NION)
Nixon, Richard, 96
NLG. *See* National Lawyers Guild (NLG)
"No Blood for Oil" (antiwar slogan), 112, 128–29
No Sweat campaign, 54
nongovernmental organizations (NGOs), 53–54, 92, 123, 185, 222, 231, 245, 318
nonviolence, 55, 61–62, 67, 82, 86, 103–5, 113–14, 123, 162, 187, 200, 271, 274–76, 347–48, 363, 368, 393n33, 415n105. *See also* violence
Noor, Sarah, 61–62
Noriega, Manuel, 68
North Atlantic Treaty Organization (NATO), 70, 142, 175, 183, 408n57
North Korea, in axis of evil, 99–100
Northern Alliance, 10, 77, 325
"Not in Our Name" (antiwar slogan), 2, 37, 74–107, 146, 158–59, 196–97, *204*, 286
Not in Our Name Project (NION), 76–77, 93–107, 135, 173, 197, 204, 266, 320, 391n6, 395n77, 399n129, 426n36; Statement of Conscience, 96, 99, 105
NOW. *See* National Organization for Women (NOW)
NPR. *See* National Public Radio (NPR)
NSA. *See* National Security Agency (NSA)
NSYPC. *See* National Student and Youth Peace Coalition (NSYPC)
nuclear weapons. *See* weapons of mass destruction (WMD)
Nwangaza, Efi, 294
NYC Protests the RNC, 426n46, 427n51
NYCLAW. *See* New York City Labor Against War (NYCLAW)
NYRP, 427n56
NYT. See *New York Times*

Obama, Barack, 349–65, 439nn30–33, 439nn35–36, 440n56, 440n60, 440nn63–64, 442n19
Oberlin College, 62
O'Brien, Tim, 151
Observer, 157
Occupation Watch, 231, 320, 419n8
Occupy movement, 366–67, 389n48
Odetta, 173
O'Keefe, Ken Nichols, 196–97, 199–200, 414nn85–89
Olbermann, Keith, 263
Olsen, Christina, 197–99
"Once Upon a Time in Iraq" (Bluemel), 442n1
O'Neill, Patrick, 344, 437n13
Ono, Yoko, 362
Operation Desert Fox, 188
"Operation First Casualty," 343, 347
oppression: by America, 280; fear of, 319; and Iraqis, 120, 280, 319; and morality, 120; and persecution, 8; and resilience, 95; resistance to, 149; of Shia population, 280; and tyranny, 280; and world-saving benevolence of Bush, 280
O'Reilly, Bill, 33, 383n10
Organization for Women's Freedom in Iraq, 221
orientalism, neo-, 244
Orwell, George, 25
"Our Grief Is Not a Cry for War" (antiwar slogan), 2, 65, 73–75, 75, 79, 105, 391n3
Out of Iraq Caucus, congressional, 301, 315–17
Ozomatli, 98

pacifism, 47–48, 68, 75, 85–86, 107, 113, 135, 141–43, 189–90, 312, 334, 367, 391n1
Packer, George, 120, 195
Pakistan, 21, 80–81, 88–89, 104, 232, 325, 392–93n30; and antiwar movement, 145, 174, 242; drone strikes in, 354, 358; travel to, 358

Palestine, 20–23, 33, 45–47, 58, 65–66, 69–71, 88, 123, 126–28, 143–44, 190, 192, 196, 214, 243–45, 321, 332, 337, 366, 368
Palestinian Americans, 98, 127
Panama, 68–69, 434n36
Parades, Pablo, 292
Pariser, Eli, 159
Parker, Caroline, *332*
Parks, Rosa, 39, 303
Parrish, Geov, 73, 391n78
partisanship, 18, 123, 180, 230–31, 255–56, 278, 294, 312, 334–35, 339, 355–57, 365, 433n18, 436n72
Patriot Act. *See* USA PATRIOT Act
patriotism, 10, 18, 29, 35, 37, 63, 67, 114, 134, 257–58; and antiwar movement, 116, 183; and expertise, 181; hypermasculine, 234; and Iraq War, 208–9, 230–31, 278, 293, 330, 339; and labor, 136; and peace, 293, 303; and terrorism, 85; and unions, 136; and Vietnam War, 184, 257, 339; and war, 208–9, 293; and War on Terror, 80
Paul, Ron, 317
Pax Americana, and military dominance, 119, 398n110
Pax Christi, 84
peace: activism, 5, 34–35, 73, 103–4, 132, 140–41, 176, 191, 216, 220–21, 223, 288–89, 320, 389n40, 391n74, 415n103, 416n5; advocates, 40–41, 49, 112; calls for, 32–33, 74, 104, 150, 311, 313; collective voices for, 62; and compassion, 81; encampments, 4, 191, 313; global, 125, 141, 160; gospel of, 190; and human rights, 45; and humanity, 6, 123–24; and justice, 66, 72–73, 108–37, 147–53, 169, 177, 181, 189, 196, 213–14, 237, 242–44, 258, 270, 315, 327–28, 354–55, 365–66, 371–72, 400–405n; -keepers, 212, 281, 340; movements, 4, 55, 59, 75–76, 130–31, 137, 141, 160, 168, 213, 244–45, 281, 288–89, 315, 349, 364,

peace (*continued*)
390n54, 391n8, 400n12, 404n75, 418n38, 418n40, 429n28, 441n16; politics, 44, 132; and power of gestures, 199; and prosperity, 8; and religion, 17–18, 104; religions calling for, 104; and repentance, 118; vigils, 60–62, 74, 78, 121–22, *192*, 196; virtue of, 78–79; walks and pilgrimages, 53, 73, 83–84, 187, 189, 327–29; and war, 87–93, 109, 167, 171–72, 339–40, 364

"Peace, Salaam, Shalom" (song), 178

Peace Action, 131–32, 189, 243, 315, 318

"Peace and Justice, Not War" (rally and march), 72–73

Peace and Justice Festival, 315

Peace Corps, 344

Peaceful Tomorrows, 84, 87–93, 103–4, 135, 140, 144–45, 159, 163, 197–200, 234, 244, 255, 284, 315, 326, 367, 372, 393n36, 393n42, 409n80, 415n92, 424n4, 429n16, 435n48, 441n17; formation and founding of, 93, 395n70

Pearl Harbor, 11, 21, 73

Pederson, Michael, 262

Pelosi, Nancy, 314, 335, 339

Penn, Sean, 195, 211, 239, 414n82, 417n36, 421n35

Pennsylvania State University, 176

Pentagon Papers, 302

PENTTBOMB (FBI investigation into 9/11 attacks), 10, 19

People for Justice and Peace, 189

people of color, 8, 46, 56, 112, 135, 184, 205, 215, 243–45, 275, 314, 348

People's Law Collective, 163

Peoria Area Peace Network, 214

Perkins, Bill, 153, 267, 426n40

Perms for Permawar, 130, *130*

Perry, William (Bill), 260, 289

persecution, and oppression, 8

Persian Gulf War. *See* Gulf War (1990–1991)

Petraeus, David, 341–42, 347

Pew Research Center, 29–30, 382n78, 421n45, 424n9

Philadelphia Inquirer, 35

Philippines: and antiwar movement, 174, 242; extraterritorial violence in, 21

Pikser, Jeremy, 96

Pledge of Resistance, 76, 93–99, 103–7, 189, 200, 204

Plummer, Andrew, 292–93

Plummer, Louis (Lou), 243, 292–93, 299, 430n45

pluralism, and Muslims, 18

Poets Against the War, 173

police: and courts, 41; international, 41–42; national, 319; and protests, 50–51, 55, 60, 63, 66, 161–64, 205–6, 237, 243, 255, 266, 269–75, 294, 303, 345, 409n86; at RNC, 427n56; and uprisings, 71; violence, 201. *See also* law enforcement; New York Police Department (NYPD)

political science, 16, 436n66

politics: of annihilation, 26; antiwar, 5, 45, 54, 59, 109, 144–45, 171, 312, 334–35, 348; and billionaires, 264, 268, 274, 425n28, 427n58; of connection, 199; contentious, 168; conventional, 199; of fear, 102, 125; geo-, 11, 16, 110, 116, 177, 258, 278, 364, 370–71; global, 15–19, 50; hard-left, 52; institutional, 355; international, 42–43; and law enforcement, 271; leftwing, 52, 68, 70; and media, 80, 188; and morality, 335; and nonviolence, 347–48; of overkill in War on Terror, 31; peace, 44, 132; post-truth, 6, 278; and power, 278; and propaganda, 6, 278; and protests, ongoing, 360; and public ritual, 76; of representation, 346; single focus, rejected, 214; of solidarity, 4; of truth, 5, 255, 278–79, 281–82, 301, 314, 346; and

war, 180, 207, 226, 245, 271, 313.
    See also partisanship
Pollitt, Katha, 23–24, 47
popular culture, 123, 134, 144, 251
Port Militarization Resistance (Washington state), 331
"Portraits of Grief" (*New York Times*), 36, 104
post-traumatic stress disorder (PTSD), 246, 297–99
Potorti, David, 36–37, 83–85, *84*, 91–92, 199, 393n36, 394n59, 395n70, 409n80, 415n92, 441n17
Potorti, Jim, 36–37, 83–84
Powell, Colin, 69, 90, 111, 115, 152–53, 182, 350
Powell Doctrine, 111, 115
power: of gestures, 199; global, 96; and imperialism, 278; local, and militias, 210; of nationalism, 368; and oil, 63; and politics, 278; of public opinion, 4, 139, 169–70; and racism, 43; and religion, 210; and resistance, 107; of solidarity, 306; and terrorism, 382n65; and truth, 6, 278; unchecked, 96; and War on Terror, 63; and wealth, 281
Preemptive Strike for Peace vigil, 121–22
preemptive war, against Iraq, 100, 119, 213–14, 418n44
prejudice, 17, 19, 24, 61, 116, 230–31
Profile in Courage award, 253, 423n93
Profitt, Bryan, 289
Progressive Democrats of America, 315
propaganda: Baathist, 195; government, 233–34; Gulf War, 400n3; Iraq War, 230–34; and media, 233–34; and post-truth politics, 6, 278; and power, 278
protests, global. *See* global protests
prowar sentiment, 10, 47–48, 61–63, 78, 114, 121, 134–35, 145–46, 154, 166, 175–76, 180, 205–8, 242, 263, 293–94, 305, 308, 312, 335–36, 343, 371
PTSD. *See* post-traumatic stress disorder (PTSD)
Public Citizen, 56
public opinion: and democracy, 364; global, 139, 169–70; and intelligence, 182; manipulation of, 182; and media, 78; on 9/11, 29–30, 78, 386n48; power of, 4, 139, 169–70; and protests, 139; and vigilance, 46–49; on war, 29–30, 46–49, 115–16, 120–21, 139, 146, 169–70, 182, 208, 230–31, 364, 402nn42–43

Quakers, 58, 142, 183, 289
queer, 215; liberation, 58; politics, 125, 331
Quilty, Chuck, 187

racial justice, 46, 136, 263, 275
Racial Justice 9/11, 275
racism, 184–85, 244, 289, 333; and antiwar movement, 215; and capitalism, 43; and colonialism, 46; and dehumanization, 295–96; environmental, 45; and imperialism, 43; in military, 343; and power, 43; and prison-industrial-complex, 56; protests against, 56, 65, 157, 159, 179, 389n50; and religion, 19, 79, 358; and religious bigotry, 358; and sexism, 343; and war, 20, 43, 46, 65, 168. *See also* Act Now to Stop War and End Racism (ANSWER); anti-racism
Rage Against the Machine, 343
Raging Grannies, 125
Rahim, Malik, 309
Rai, Milan, 144–45, 406n17
Rainbow/PUSH Coalition, 327
Raitt, Bonnie, 105
Rally Against War and Racism, at Freedom Plaza, 65, 389n50, 389n52

Rand Corporation, 422n69
Rangel, Charles, 153, 314
Rashmawi, Elias, 244, 422n59
Raskin, Marcus, 39
Ratner, Michael, 97, 251–52
Ray, Ellen, 251–52
Razuki, Ghada, 156
RCP. *See* Revolutionary Communist Party (RCP)
"Read My Tits. No War With Iraq" (antiwar slogan), 122
Reagan, Ronald, 52, 95, 110–12, 142, 151
reconciliation: national, 341; and relief missions, 260; vs. revenge, 7–30; and war, 46–47. *See also* Fellowship of Reconciliation
Red Cross, 251, 284, 309
Reed, Daphne, 136
Rees, John, 141, 143, 157
Reiber, Chad, 296–97
Reilly, Ward, 98–99, 260, 276, 289, 302–4, 309, 327–29, 343, 351, 355–56, 372, 396–97n97, 396nn94–95, 425n18, 435n51
religion: and bigotry, 18, 358; as cultural affinity of humanity, 16; and ethnicity, 16, 62, 77, 79, 225, 236–37; fanaticism, and evil, 23, 233; and identity, 16, 62; and intelligence operations, 274; and interfaith events, 17–18, 58–59, 104, 306, 315, 326; and militias, 210; and peace, 17–18, 104; and power, 210; and protests, 326; and racism, 19, 79, 358; and repression, 230; and rivalries, 77; and scapegoating, 79; and secular socialism, 141; and state, separation of, 25; and war, 33–34, 41, 45, 69, 236–37, 382n71. *See also* Catholic Worker movement; Christianity; Mennonites; Quakers; United Methodists
Reppenhagen, Garett, 295–96, *329*, 343

repression, 57, 76, 94, 110, 123, 170, 236; and war, 96
Republican National Convention (RNC), 56, 229, 243, 255, 264–79, 324, 331, 426n46, 426n49, 427nn51–54, 427n56, 427n60; Operation Sybil, 267, 279. *See also* Democratic National Convention (DNC)
resilience, and oppression, 95
"Resist the Empire!" (UFPJ broadside), 236–37
resistance, 6, 46, 57, 93–99, 107, 149, 173, 183–84, 200, 207, 212, 230, 234, 243, 280–83, 291–93, 313, 331–32, 343, 347
retaliation, 18, 20–21, 34, 38, 62, 65, 77–81, 109
retribution, 86, 107, 252, 283–84
Reuters, 207, 438n28
Revolutionary Communist Party (RCP), 76, 94–98, 106–7
Rice, Condoleezza, 165
Richardson, Charley, 184
Ricks, Thomas E., 312, 419n5, 432n4, 437n1
Riley, Boots, 98, 105
Ritter, Scott, 100–101
RNC. *See* Republican National Convention (RNC)
Road to Fallujah, The (Manning film), 429n17
Robbins, Tim, 106, 157, 399n133
Robbins, Tom, 426nn37–38
Robinson, Anthony B., 33–34
Rockefeller, Terry, 197–99, 435n48
Rodriguez, Greg, 2, 37, 86, 377n4, 384n24, 441n17
Rodriguez, Phyllis and Orlando, 2, 37, 86, 377n4, 384n24, 441n17
Rojas, Fabio, 335, 339, 355–56, 429n29, 436nn66–67, 438n19
RootsAction, 131
Ross, John, 196
Roy, Arundhati, 14, 20, 29, 40, 141, 213–14, 269

Ruckus Society, 51, 53, 348, 387n3
Ruehl, Mercedes, 174
rule of law, 8, 41–42, 248, 326, 337, 346, 360, 385n44
Rumsfeld, Donald, 81, 83, 103, 110, 122, 154, 170, 183, 201, 209, 248, 250, 253, 288, 313, 336, 417n26, 436n77
Rupp, Eva, 90–91, *91*
Russia, 176, 365–66
Ruzicka, Marla, 88, 90–93, *91*, 104, 150, 222–23, 286, 394n54, 419n65
Rybov, Alex, 261

Said, Edward, 23–24, 213–14, 380n33, 381n50
Salim, Faiz Ali, 222, 286
Sallat, Salah Edine, *249*
Salon, 24, 106
Salt March, 329
San Francisco Chronicle, 38, 73, 106, 239
Sanbrano, Angela, 131
Sanchez, Ricardo, 246–47
Sanders, Bernie, 38, 129
SANE (National Committee for a Sane Nuclear Policy), 41
Santorum, Rick, 104
Sapir-Niederer, Sue, 243
Sapphire, 173
Sarandon, Susan, 106, 399n133
Sartwell, Crispin, 35
Sassen, Saskia, 8, 378n9
Saudi Arabia, 22, 110–11, 115–16, 123
Saunders, Will, 201, 415n108
SBVT. *See* Swift Boat Veterans for Truth (SBVT)
Scahill, Jeremy, 263, 344, 354, 439n38
Schaffer, Ruben, 75–76
Scheer, Robert, 40
Schell, Jonathan, 31, 79, 119, 241
School of the Americas, 236
Schumer, Chuck, 151
Scott, Carolyn M., 403n54
Scott, Dred, 74–75, 98

Scowcroft, Brent, 183
Security Council, UN. *See* United Nations (UN): Security Council
Seeger, Pete, 159
Sekou, Osayefo Uhuru, 315
self-defense and self-interest, 100, 109, 139, 145, 252, 296
Senate Foreign Relations Committee (United States), 257
Senate Select Committee on Intelligence (United States), 378n13
September 11. *See* 9/11 attacks
September Eleventh Families for Peaceful Tomorrows. *See* Peaceful Tomorrows
Serbia, 67, 70
Seton Hall University, 325, 434n5
SF Gate, 103
Shadid, Anthony, 193–94, 216, 417n19
Sharpton, Al, 128–29, 159, 306, 314
Sheehan, Casey A., 245–46, 276, 287, 301–7, *304*
Sheehan, Cindy, 5, 245, 276, 282, 287–88, 291, 301–19, *307*, 329, 429n24, 431n78
Sheen, Martin, 106, 306
Shepard, Benjamin (Ben), 64, *130*, 389nn45–46
Shia Muslims. *See* Iraq: Shia Muslims in
Shinseki, Eric, 183
Shock and Awe, 201–3, 207–8, 217, 221, 224, 298; in media, 171; as strategy, 171–203
Sider, Ron, 189–90
"Silence of the Dead, Voices of the Living" protest, 329–30
60 Minutes, 118, 238, 248, 420n30, 423n73, 423n81, 423n92, 424n3
Small, Melvin, 339, 377n9, 436n82
Smith, Damu, 44–45, 136, 386n57
Smith, Neil, 211, 417n34
Smith, Patti, 159
SNCC. *See* Student Nonviolent Coordinating Committee (SNCC)

Snowden, Edward, 359
social: change, 149; movements, 167, 169, 325–26, 365; stability, 170
socialism: British, 129–30; in Chile, 67; and communism, 70, 142; of Latin America, 185; leftist, 52; in Nicaragua, 82; and peace politics, 44; secular, 141; and solidarity, 112
Socialist Workers Party (SWP), 69–71, 142, 143
solidarity: and antiwar movement, 112, 275; with Arabs, 332; Central American, 48, 82, 185; global, 140; and grief, 36, 287, 305–6; healing power of, 306; with hungers strikes, 367; with immigrants, 64; and imperialism, 126; international, 133, 177; with Iraq, 4, 185–86, 195, 321; in Latin America, 260; movement, 185–86; with Muslims, 18, 332; and 9/11, 20, 36, 74–75; with Palestine, 126, 144, 321; politics of, 4; and power of gestures, 199; and socialism, 112; songs of during protests, 140; and war, 36
Somalia, 246, 354
Sons of Liberty, 261
Sontag, Susan, 20–21, 23, 380n42
Soodon, Harmeet, 320
Sorry, Everybody (Hylas), 428n70
South Africa, 145, 155, 159; apartheid in, 45, 133, 159
South Asia, 215; apprehensions of, 10; bigotry against, 18; detention of, 19, 96, 353; as internal enemy, 18; and protests, 160–61, 269, 275
Spain, 241; and antiwar movement, 138–40, 143, 154–55, 166, 169, 172, 177, 242; and US-UK resolution, 175
Spann, Michael, 32
Special Forces (United States), 211
Sri Lanka, 190, 244, 344
Standing Together to Organize a Revolutionary Movement (STORM), 43–44; history and post-9/11 activities, 386n53
STARC. *See* Students Transforming and Resisting Corporations (STARC)
Starhawk, 105, 123–24, 162, 164–65, 170, 178, 272, 409n77
State Department. *See* Department of State (United States)
Steele, John, 413n53
Stewart, John, 263
Stewart, Lynne, 99
Still We Rise, 275
Stoner, Eric, 363, 441n9
Stop the War Coalition (StWC), 142–44, 156–58; origins, 406n14
STORM. *See* Standing Together to Organize a Revolutionary Movement (STORM)
Streit, Bill, 135–36, 203, *323*
Student Nonviolent Coordinating Committee (SNCC), 46
Student Peace Action, 62
Students for a Peaceful Response, 79
Students Transforming and Resisting Corporations (STARC), 54, 61–62, 267
StWC. *See* Stop the War Coalition (StWC)
Suárez del Solar, Fernando, 228–29, *229*, 235–36, 239–40, 284, 328–29
Suárez del Solar, Jesus, 228–29, 419n4
Suárez del Solar, Rosa, 228, 284
Sudan, bombing of, 9, 25
Sullivan, Andrew, 23–24
Sultan, Masuda, 89, 92, 104, 394n51
Sunday Times, 300
Sunni Muslims. *See* Iraq: Sunni Muslims in
Sweeny, John, 146, 314
Sweet, Debra (Deb), 95–97, 106, 326, 356, 371
Swift, Suzanne, 330
Swift Boat Veterans for Truth (SBVT), 257–58

Swift Boats, 256
SWP. *See* Socialist Workers Party (SWP)
Syria: assaults on, 365; bombing of cities in, 2–3; civil war, 442n19; and Iraq, 337; military intervention and operations in, 442n19; safety in, 321

Taguba, Antonio, 246, 248
Takoma Park Kids for Peace, 177
Taliban, 1–3, 7, 9–10, 25–26, 28, 32–35, 40, 48, 77–81, 89, 232, 353, 393n30
Tang, Eric, 348
terrorism: of 9/11, 82, 377n2; allies against, 81; battle against, 352; conflicts and grievances leading to, 337; as cosmic war, 26–27; counter-, 101–2, 258, 353, 398n11, 413n62; and crime, 9, 30, 44; defeat of, 28, 35; demonization of, 254; economic, 66; and enemies as criminals, 234; as evil, 24; fears of, 39, 206; global, 241, 250, 377n2; government's ability to deal with, 29–30; in hearts, 324; and inequalities, 64; and injustices, 64; Iraq War as cause of, 241; and nationalism, 241; persisting, 20; and power, 382n65; and protests, 206, 237; and revenge, 85; root causes of, 10, 45, 47; state-sponsored, 45; understandings of, 26; by United States, 8, 23, 62; uniting against, 41; as unpardonable, 33–35; and violence, 8, 40, 81–82, 237, 273; and war, 7–8, 20–24, 26–27, 30, 32–35, 39–41, 44, 48, 67, 99–103, 300; as weapon of weak, 26, 382n65. *See also* War on Terror
Texas Gold (Scott documentary), 403n54
Theaters Against War, 174
Tillman, Pat, 245

"Time for Truth" (antiwar slogan), 242
Time (magazine), 136, 363
Times Square (New York City), 331–32, *332*
Tinley, Kathleen, 197, 199
Tolan, Sandy, 23, 381n49
torture, 2, 9, 102, 251–52, 254, 322–27, 352–53, 360, 423n80, 434n46, 435n48
Torture Papers, The, 251, 396n84, 423n84
Tracy, Jonathan, 222, 419n66
trade unions. *See* unions
TransAfrica Forum, 131–33
treason, 78, 361
Trotsky, Leon, 142
Truman Show, The (film), 13
Trump, Donald, 345, 365–66, 377n8
truth, 11–15; and antiwar movement, 279; as antiwar slogan, 172, 242, 267; and media, 302; politics of, 5, 255, 278–79, 281–82, 301, 314, 346; and power, 278; and war, 279
Turkey: airspace, 170; and antiwar movement, 145, 170, 196; and diplomatic offensive, 337
Turse, Nick, 265, 425–26nn30–31
Tutu, Desmond, 159–60, 352, 367
Twain, Mark, 61
24 (TV series), 251
Twin Towers. *See* World Trade Center (WTC)
Tyler, Patrick E., 139, 377n6, 405n4
tyranny, 53, 120, 165, 168, 210, 223, 239, 280, 283–86, 350

Udry, Sue, 315–16, 433n16
UFP. *See* United for Peace (UFP)
UFPJ. *See* United For Peace and Justice (UFPJ)
UN. *See* United Nations (UN)
UNICEF, 221
unilateralism, 47, 165, 176, 244, 256
Union Square (New York City), 68, 74–76, *75*, 85, 269–74

Union Square (San Francisco), 105
unions: labor, 137, 158–59, 275, 353; locals, 80, 263; mobilized, 353; and patriotism, 136; trade, 50, 70, 75, 80, 142, 146, 167. *See also* AFL-CIO; labor movement
United for Peace (UFP), 131–37
United For Peace and Justice (UFPJ), 108, 112, 136–41, 146–54, 159, 163–64, 169–72, 199–200, 203, 213–16, 231, 235–38, 243–47, 258–59, 265–70, 275–77, 284, 288–89, 299, 313–18, 327, 335, 339, 347–49, 354–56, 362, 366–67, 375, 408n54, 408n71, 433n7; conflicts in, 439n44
United Kingdom: and antiwar movement, 106, 138–39, 143–46, 154–58, 160, 167–69, 172, 175–77, 242, 326, 338–39, 362–64; as belligerent, 166; and Iraq War, 145, 300–301, 321; and legality of war, 145
United Methodists, 131, 135
United Nations (UN), 46–47, 64, 100, 103, 110–11, 118–19, 121, 135, 158, 170–72, 175–77, 181–82, 187–89, 191, 200, 216–17, 240, 258, 300, 326; and antiwar movement, 75, 172, 331; assistance mission in Iraq, 212, 228–29; authority in Iraq, postwar, 340; Baghdad office, 193; and Bush, 145; General Assembly, 212; and global civil society, 146; humanitarian chief for Iraq, 413n57; Millennium Development Goals, 55–56; Oil-for-Food program, 81; and Palestine, 46; peacekeeping, 212, 281, 340; reconstruction efforts, 212, 229; Security Council, 32, 111, 145–46, 152–54, 160, 175, 177, 363, 383n8; special court, 41–42; Special Rapporteur on Palestine at, 46; US Mission to, 81, 326
universalism: liberal, 210; and women, 175

University of Baghdad, 191–92
University of California, Berkeley, 62, 176
University of Chicago Legal Forum 2011, 433n17, 437n4
University of New Hampshire, 384n21
University of New Mexico, 78
University of North Carolina, 430n54
University of Texas, 8
University of Wisconsin–Madison, 43, 176
USA PATRIOT Act, 97, 106, 396n86

Valencia, Annabelle, 329
Varon, Jeremy, 428n73, 439n49, 440n59
Venezuela, as historic target of US imperialism, 244
Veterans Administration (United States), 297
Veterans and Survivors March for Peace and Justice (Gulfport, Mississippi), 327–28, *328*
Veterans for Peace (VFP), 34, 84–85, 98–99, 183–84, 190, 227, 236, 239, 259–62, 270–71, 289–90, 293–94, 300–306, 309–10, 330, 335, 342–43, 351, *351*, 358, 372, 425n19, 425nn22–23, 425n25
VFP. *See* Veterans for Peace (VFP)
Vidal, Gore, 94
Viera de Mello, Sérgio, 229
Vietnam syndrome, 109–18, 366, 400n4, 400n12, 401n17
Vietnam Veterans Against the War (VVAW), 183–84, 256–57, 259–60, 435n51. *See also* Iraq Veterans Against the War (IVAW)
Vietnam Veterans Memorial (Washington, DC), 236
Vietnam War (1955–1975): and barbarian nature of America, 252; battlefield victories as political and military setbacks, 228; and colonialism, 142; and counterin-

surgency, 228; as defeat, 96; denounced, 45, 93; and disdain for government, 57–58; draft resisters, 196, 293; and emancipated future, 230, 257; end of, 362; and future wars, 111–12, 119–20, 134, 142, 252; GI resistance to, 343; and Gulf War, 109–20; and heroism, 257–58; as imperialism going to war, 43–44, 119, 213; and Iraq War, 109–20, 135, 239, 252, 281, 339, 437n82; lessons learned from, 49, 55, 282, 363; and manipulation of intelligence and public opinion, 181–82; and media, 282; memories of, 109–18; military resistance to, 98, 183–84; as moral abomination, 258; moral responsibility of US soldiers during, 294; moratorium, 132; opposition to and protests against, 5, 39–48, 55–58, 68–71, 78, 82, 87, 93–98, 106, 109, 126–28, 132, 148–49, 166, 170, 176, 179, 183–85, 191, 196, 213, 230, 243, 252, 256–61, 267, 278–79, 288–89, 312–15, 343, 362, 366–67; and playing field of war, 55; political opposition to, 257–58, 339; and politics of truth, 278–79; prisoners, 316; as quagmire, 281; relief and reconciliation missions in, 260; and social upheavals, 312–13; student peace actions against, 176; think tank opposition to, 39; US defeat in, 96, 132; and US policy, 281; veterans, 41–42, 57–58, 183–85, 191, 236, 239–40, 256–60, 262, 317–18; and Vietnam syndrome, 109–18, 366, 400n4, 400n12, 401n17; withdrawal from, 338–39, 377n9, 436n82

Villepin, Dominique de, 154, 176

violence: and 9/11, 11, 36–37; alternatives to, 7; in barbarian, 13–14; and coercion, 21; and crime, 8; and discrimination, 95; of enemies, 15; extraterritorial, 21; and hate, 22; and immigration, 11; of police, 201; and terrorism, 8, 40, 81–82, 237, 273; by United States, 15, 21, 123–24, 196, 252, 279, 359; and vulnerability, 123–24; and war, 8, 33–41, 95, 230, 234, 398n110. *See also* nonviolence

Vitale, Alex, 163

Voices in the Wilderness, 81–85, 117, 144–45, 185–99, 216–21; formation, 413n52

Voices to Iraq, 118

volunteerism, and civic action, 125

Volunteers for Peace, 61

von Sponeck, Hans, 188–89

Voters for Peace, 335–36

"Voters Want Peace, The. Tell the NEW CONGRESS: ACT *NOW* TO END THE WAR!" (antiwar slogan), 339

Voting Rights Act, 68–69

VVAW. *See* Vietnam Veterans Against the War (VVAW)

Waging Nonviolence, 363

Walk for Healing and Peace (New York City), 83–84, *84*, 189

"Walk in Their Shoes" exhibit, 285

Walker, Alice, 94, 178, 412n26, 413n50

"Walkin' to New Orleans" march, 327–28

Wallis, Jim, 34, 383n15

WAND. *See* Women's Action for New Directions (WAND)

war: acts of, 10, 27–28, 98; as clash of civilizations, 19; cosmic, 26–27, 34, 382n66; as counterproductive and unnecessary, 40; credibility of, 41; dogs of, 171, 202; and empire, 46, 214–15, 236–37; ends justify the means in, 41; guerrilla, 81, 116; and guilt, 21; hell of, 32; hidden pain of, 297; institutional opposition to, 136; just

war (*continued*)
cause for, 46–48, 80, 86, 279, 298, 384n18; justification for, 98, 102, 118–21; legal action as substitute for, 41; legality of, 145; legitimized, 115; limited, 48; as matter of life and death, 181; no justification for, 118–21; opponents of, 28–30; and peace, 87–93, 109, 167, 171–72, 339–40, 364; politics of, 207, 226; rejection of, 2; and social struggles, 44; and terrorism, 20–24, 30, 33–35, 99–103, 300; as unpardonable, 33–35; of vanity, 243; and vengeance, 11; victims of, 368; as virtuous, 35; wrongfulness of, 278–79. *See also* prowar sentiment

war crimes, 35, 69–70, 115, 171–202, 256–57, 265, 284, 320, 368, 391n9

war in Afghanistan: bait for, 22; as challenge, 353; civilian losses, 150, 222, 353–54, 384n22; credibility of, 41; as daunting challenge, 30; drone strikes, 354; as endless, 3, 6, 357; escalation, 353–54, 363; fading into background, 354; for and against, 31–49; as good war, 30; in history, 33; and Iraq, 2, 31, 74–107, 183, 257, 271–72, 286, 331, 361, 370–71; as just war, 46–48, 86; as limited war, 48; as long war, 29, 32, 49, 365–66; and 9/11, 1–3, 6, 9, 31–49, 60, 98, 171, 377n2; and occupation, 214; opposition to and protests against, 28–30, 32–34, 39–40, 48, 77, 80, 97, 143, 149, 357; polling about, 29–30, 32; start of, 1–2, 9, 32, 40, 43, 60, 75–76; success in, 32–33, 49; support for, 32, 48, 139; as victory, 76; as virtuous, 35; withdrawal from, 3, 32, 142, 361, 365–66

"War Is Not the Answer—Don't Kill More Innocent People" (antiwar slogan), 65–68, 73, 80, 391n1

"War Is Terror" (antiwar slogan), 220

War on Terror, 237–38; abuses of, 251–52, 373; and antiwar movement, 3, 33, 139, 275; and axis of evil, 28, 99–100; beginning of, 1–2; as bipartisan project, 123; brutality of, 249–51; as civilization's fight, 27–30, 142; condemnation of, 5; damage of, 362; dark side of, 97; as daunting challenge, 30; and defense industry profits, 254; defense of, 353; detainees, 331; and domestic strife, 3; as emphatic choice, 3; and enemies, 42–43, 97, 129; essence of, 267; expansion of, 119, 290, 354; as good war, 30; in history, 33; human costs of, 3; as inexorable, 9; and inhumanity, 2; and injustices, 370; intensification of, 93; and international courts prosecutions, 353; interrogation methods, 396n83; as invisible, 325; and Iraq, 2, 4, 99–103, 109–10, 241–42, 265, 370; key policies of, 3; and media, 80, 264, 280; and military operations, 3; as military-political project, 2–3; moral rot of, 6; and 9/11, 1–6, 16–17, 44, 86, 139, 241, 377n2; and oil, 63; opposition to and protests against, 64, 66, 79, 96, 99, 106–7, 123, 136, 139, 145, 252, 269, 316, 325–26, 331, 337, 354, 358; and patriotism, 80; personal terms of, 2; politics of overkill in, 31; polling about, 45; potential excesses of, 359; and power, 63; proponents of, 2; protection as essence of, 267; rebuke of, 6; reckoning with, 352; religious language framing, 382n71; secret documents, 359; support for, 25, 27, 355; supported by permanent war economy and popular culture, 123; term usage, 377n2; as threat to

world peace, 5; and torture, 352; unsupported, 99, 105–6; and vengeance, 365; violence and victims of, 273, 346; and violent retribution, 283–84; as virtuous, 28; as war at home, 3; as war of ideas, 94, 97. *See also* terrorism
War Plan Iraq (Rai), 144–45, 406n17
"War Prayer, The" (Twain poem), 61
War Resisters League (WRL), 7, 75, 130, 212, 271–75, 324, 347, 391n75
War Resisters Support Campaign, 298
War Times, 44, 135, 203, 213, 263
Washington Peace Center, 55, 72–73, 214–15
Washington Post, 15, 32, 41, 136, 193, 195, 209, 213–14, 312
Washington Square Park (New York City), 74, 99, 104, 391n2
WAT. *See* Witness Against Torture (WAT)
Watada, Ehren, 293, 330–31
Waters, Maxine, 301, 305, 314, 335
Watson, Neville, 413n53
Watson Institute (Brown University), 377n5
WCW. *See* World Can't Wait (WCW)
We Are Many (Amirani documentary), 405n1, 416n3
"We Shall Overcome" (song), 188
We Will Not Be Silent, 332–33, 367, 435n61
weapons of mass destruction (WMD), 31, 41, 48, 82, 100–103, 110, 119–21, 134, 143–46, 151–54, 192, 203, 207–11, 227–28, 231, 238–41, 255, 269, 275–79, 291–92, 299–301, 356, 361, 365, 398n110, 431n72
Weather Underground, 428n73
Webb, James, 336
Weber, George, 190–91
Weiss, Cora, 149
Welfare Poets, 159
Wellstone, Paul, 104–5, 131
Welty, Adele, 284

Wesleyan University, 61–62
Western Mass Global Action Coalition, 61–62
White Rose resistance group, 300, 331–32
WikiLeaks, 359
Wilkerson, Mark, 329–30
Will, George F., 15, 379n25
Williams, Cecil, 73
Williams, Saul, 96, 98, 159, 173, 396n91
Wilner, Tom, 325
Wilson, Diane, 103, 122–23, 303, 358
Wilson, Joe, 301
Win Without War, 134, 172, 180, 213, 316, 318
Winfrey, Oprah, 304
Wing, Bob, 42–44, 135, 200, 386nn51–52
Winik, Marion, 35, 384n20
"Winter Soldier" hearings, 256–57, 343–44, 347
Witness Against Torture (WAT), 322–27, 339, 345–46, 358–60, *360*, 367, 371–73, 434n35, 438n16
WMD. *See* weapons of mass destruction (WMD)
Wolfowitz, Paul, 227
Women Against War, 125, 265
Women for Peace. *See* Code Pink
"Women of Iraq Tour," 231–32
"Women United for Peace," 73
Women's Action for New Directions (WAND), 131
women's rights, 65–66, 149, 167
Woolford, Steve, 135–36
Woolsey, Lynn, 316–17
Workers World Party (WWP), 67–71, 129–30, 134
World Bank, 50–57, 63–64, 71–72, 237, 314
World Can't Wait (WCW), 320, 326, 351, 357, 433n30
World Economic Forum, 162–63
World Islamic Front, 380n28
"World Says No to the Bush Agenda, The" demonstration, 265

World Says No to War, The, 409n98
"World Says No to War, The" global protest (New York City), 138–70, *147*, *161*, *162*
World Social Forum, 54, 141, 169
World Trade Center (WTC), 1–2, 7, 13–16, 37, 44, 58, 62, 68, 83–86, 90, 98–99, 194. *See also* 9/11 attacks
World Trade Organization (WTO), 50–53, 58, 61–62, 150, 267
World War II: as just war, 46; military parade, 115; reconstruction, 141
Worthington, Andy, 326, 435n48
Wright, Ann, 182–83, 269, 305–6, 310, 330, 364, 367
WRL. *See* War Resisters League (WRL)
WTC. *See* World Trade Center (WTC)
WTO. *See* World Trade Organization (WTO)
WWP. *See* Socialist Workers Party (SWP); Workers World Party (WWP)

Yaqoob, Salma, 157
YAWF. *See* Youth Against War and Fascism (YAWF)
Yee, James, 358
Yemen, drone strikes in, 354
Yemeni Americans, 213–14
Yeun, Eddie, 63–64
Youth Against War and Fascism (YAWF), 70–71
Yugoslavia, 70

Zeiger, David, 343
Zelmanowitz, Abe, 37
Zinn, Howard, 34–35, 47–48, 94, 97–98, 213–14, 232, 261, 338
Zinni, Anthony, 252
Žižek, Slavoj, 13–15, 29, 379n22, 382n73
Zovko, Jerry, 286
Zunes, Stephen, 8, 119, 121